S0-ADC-615

Computer-supported Cooperative
Work and Groupware

Computers and People Series

Edited by

B. R. GAINES and A. MONK

Monographs

Communicating with Microcomputers. An introduction to the technology of man–computer communication, *Ian H. Witten* 1980
The Computer in Experimental Psychology, *R. Bird* 1981
Principles of Computer Speech, *I. H. Witten* 1982
Cognitive Psychology of Planning, *J-M. Hoc* 1988
Formal Methods for Interactive Systems, *A. Dix* 1991

Edited Works

Computing Skills and the User Interface, *M. J. Coombs and J. L. Alty (eds)* 1981
Fuzzy Reasoning and Its Applications, *E. H. Mamdani and B. R. Gaines (eds)* 1981
Intelligent Tutoring Systems, *D. Sleeman and J. S. Brown (eds)* 1982 (1986 paperback)
Designing for Human–Computer Communication, *M. E. Sime and M. J. Coombs (eds)* 1983
The Psychology of Computer Use, *T. R. G. Green, S. J. Payne and G. C. van der Veer (eds)* 1983
Fundamentals of Human–Computer Interaction, *Andrew Monk (ed)* 1984, 1985
Working with Computers: Theory versus Outcome, *G. C. van der Veer, T. R. G. Green, J-M. Hoc and D. Murray (eds)* 1988
Cognitive Engineering in Complex Dynamic Worlds, *E. Hollnagel, G. Mancini and D. D. Woods (eds)* 1988
Computers and Conversation, *P. Luff, N. Gilbert and D. Frohlich (eds)* 1990
Adaptive User Interfaces, *D. Browne, P. Totterdell and M. Norman (eds)* 1990
Human–Computer Interaction and Complex Systems, *G. R. S. Weir and J. L. Alty (eds)* 1991
Computer-supported Cooperative Work and Groupware, *Saul Greenberg (ed)* 1991

Practical Texts

Effective Color Displays: Theory and Practice, *D. Travis* 1991

EACE Publications
(Consulting Editors: *Y. WAERN and J-M. HOC*)

Cognitive Ergonomics, *P. Falzon (ed)* 1990
Psychology of Programming, *J-M. Hoc, T. R. G. Green, R. Samurcay and D. Gilmore (eds)* 1990

Computer-supported Cooperative Work and Groupware

Edited by

SAUL GREENBERG

Department of Computer Science,
University of Calgary, Calgary, Alberta,
Canada T2N 1N4

Harcourt Brace Jovanovich, Publishers
London   San Diego   New York
Boston   Sydney   Tokyo   Toronto

Franz Weckesser

ACADEMIC PRESS LTD
24/28 Oval Road,
London NW1 7DX

United States Edition published by
ACADEMIC PRESS INC.
San Diego, California 92101–4311

Copyright © 1991 by
ACADEMIC PRESS LTD.
except Chapter 18, Pages 359–413 © S. Greenberg 1991

This book is printed on acid-free paper

All Rights Reserved
No part of this book may be reproduced in any form by photostat, microfilm, or any other means
without written permission from the publishers

A catalogue record for this book is available from the British Library

ISBN 0–12–299220–2

Printed in Great Britain at the University Press, Cambridge

Contents

Part 5.   Removing rigidity from groupware

Part 6.   Participatory design

Part 7.   Literature sources for CSCW and groupware

Contributors

GARY BIRCH, Object Designers Ltd, Glebe House, Great Hallingbury, Bishop's Stortford, Herts CM22 7TY, UK.

SARA A. BLY, Xerox PARC, 3333 Coyote Hill Road, Palo Alto, California 94304, USA.

DANIEL G. BOBROW, System Sciences Laboratory, Xerox PARC, 3333 Coyote Hill Road, Palo Alto, California 94304, USA.

SUSANNE BØDKER, Computer Science Department, Aarhus University, Aarhus C, Denmark.

NATHANIEL S. BORENSTEIN, Bellcore, Room MRE 2A274, 445 South Street, Morristown, New Jersey 07960, USA.

ROBERT P. CARASIK, Pacific Bell, 2600 Camino Ramon 3N200W, San Ramon, California 94583, USA.

MICHAEL COHEN, Computer Music, Northwestern University, Evanston, Illinois 60208, USA.

STEVE COOK, Object Designers Ltd, Glebe House, Great Hallingbury, Bishop's Stortford, Herts CM22 7TY, UK.

GEORGE COULOURIS, Queen Mary and Westfield College, London E1 4NS, UK.

ALAN R. DENNIS, Management and Information Systems, Eller Graduate School of Management, University of Arizona, Tucson, Arizona 85721, USA.

ELIZABETH A. DYKSTRA, 109 Minna Suite 105, San Francisco, California 94105, USA.

CLARENCE A. ELLIS, Computer Science Department, University of Colorado, Boulder, Colorado 80309–0345, USA.

GREGG FOSTER, Apple Computer, Inc, 20525 Mariani Av. MS: 46A, Cupertino, CA 95014, USA.

SAUL GREENBERG, Department of Computer Science, University of Calgary, Calgary, Alberta T2N 1N4, Canada.

KAJ GRØNBÆK, Computer Science Department, Aarhus University, Aarhus C, Denmark.

JONATHAN GRUDIN, Computer Science Department, Aarhus University, Ny Munkegade 116 Building 540, DK-8000 Aarhus C, Denmark.

PETER JOHNSON-LENZ, Awakening Technology, 695 Fifth Street, Lake Oswego, Oregon 97034, USA.

TRUDY JOHNSON-LENZ, Awakening Technology, 695 Fifth Street, Lake Oswego, Oregon 97034, USA.

MARTIN LEA, Department of Psychology, University of Manchester, Manchester M13 9PL, UK.

LESTER F. LUDWIG, Bell Communications Research, New Jersey, USA.

JAMES R. MILLER, Human-Computer Interaction Department, Hewlett-Packard Laboratories, 1501 Page Mill Road, Palo Alto, California 94304, USA.

ALAN MURPHY, IBM UK Laboratories Ltd, Hursley Park, Winchester, UK.

BONNIE A. NARDI, Human-Computer Interaction Department, Hewlett-Packard Laboratories, 1501 Page Mill Road, Palo Alto, California 94304, USA.

J. F. NUNAMAKER, Jr, Management and Information Systems, Eller Graduate School of Management, University of Arizona, Tucson, Arizona 85721, USA.

MARGRETHE H. OLSON, Leonard N. Stern School of Business, New York University, New York, New York 10006, USA.

GAIL L. REIN, MCC, 3500 West Balcones Center Drive, Austin, Texas 78759–6509, USA.

RUSSELL SPEARS, Department of Social Psychology, University of Amsterdam, Roetersstraat 15, 1018 WB Amsterdam, The Netherlands.

JOHN C. TANG, Sun Microsystems, Inc, 2550 Garcia Avenue MS/MTV 23–41, Mountain View, CA 94043, USA.

DEBORAH TATAR, Department of Psychology, Building 420, Stanford University, Stanford, California 94305–2130, USA.

HAROLD W. THIMBLEBY, Computing Science, Stirling University, Stirling, Scotland FK9 4LA, UK.

CHRIS A. THYBERG, Hamburg Hall, Room 3017, Carnegie Mellon University, Pittsburgh, Pennsylvania 15213, USA.

JOSEPH S. VALACICH, Decision and Information Systems, Graduate School of Business, Indiana University, Tenth and Fee Lane, Bloomington, Indiana, 47405, USA.

JUDITH WEEDMAN, School of Library and Information Studies, University of California at Berkeley, 102 South Hall, Berkeley, California 94720, USA.

IAN H. WITTEN, Department of Computer Science, University of Calgary, Calgary, Alberta T2N 1N4, Canada.

JOHN WOOLSEY, IBM UK Laboratories Ltd, Hursley Park, Winchester, UK.

1

Computer-supported cooperative work and groupware

SAUL GREENBERG

1. Introduction

Although computers are now familiar tools used by people to pursue their own individual tasks, they generally have not been exploited to assist people working together. Off-the-shelf applications in typical use are, for the most part, "single-user" systems. Word processors, spread sheets, idea outliners, drawing tools, and slide preparation packages (to name a few) are all built to support one person's work, with little regard to the fact that people often work together. Even the scientific study of human–computer interaction has emphasized exploring issues involved when a single user interacts with a computer. It is only recently that attention has turned to multi-user systems, through *computer-supported cooperative work* and *groupware*.

Groupware is software that supports and augments group work. It is a technically-oriented label meant to differentiate "group-oriented" products, explicitly designed to assist groups of people working together, from "single-user" products that help people pursue only their isolated tasks. The more familiar groupware examples include electronic mail, bulletin boards, asynchronous conferencing, group schedulers, group decision support systems, collaborative authoring, screen-sharing software, computer equivalents to whiteboards, video conferencing, and so on (e.g. Johansen, 1988).

In contrast, *computer-supported cooperative work* (CSCW) is the scientific discipline that motivates and validates groupware design. It is the study and theory of how people work together, and how the computer and related technologies affect group behaviour. CSCW is an umbrella collecting researchers from a variety of specializations—computer science, cognitive science, psychology, sociology, anthropology, ethnography, management, management information systems—each contributing a different perspective and methodology for acquiring knowledge of groups and for suggesting how the group's work could be supported.

However, CSCW is not particularly well defined, a consequence of its youth and its multi-disciplinary nature. A visible symptom of this uncertainty is the varying and at times controversial mix of papers accepted at CSCW conferences, with attendees often debating why certain topics were considered relevant by the programming committee. Nor is there consensus on what applications should be considered "groupware". Grudin (1991) lists examples of how people have drawn the line between groupware and its substrate, with some believing it starts at a very low technical level (e.g. a Network File Server), and others stating that it begins somewhere above electronic mail. Even the "computer-supported cooperative work" label has come under fire for a variety of reasons (Bannon & Schmidt, 1989; Grudin, 1991). For example:

- *computer*—technologies other than computers (such as video) are considered within the CSCW domain;
- *supported*—while support may be offered to the group as a whole, activities of particular individuals may be disrupted;
- *cooperative*—the social process can include not only cooperation, but aggression, competition, loose coordination and tight collaboration;
- *work*—casual and social interaction must be supported as well, for they are considered a vital precursor to the work process (e.g. Kraut, Egido & Galegher, 1988).

Essays exploring and arguing the foundations of CSCW have been forwarded by Bannon, Bjorn-Andersen & Due-Thomsen (1988), Bannon and Schmidt (1989), Greif (1988) and Grudin (1991). Rather than split semantic hairs of what CSCW is or should be, Bannon *et al.*'s original pragmatism is adopted here.

> We believe that for the moment the name CSCW simply serves as a useful forum for a variety of researchers with different backgrounds and techniques to discuss their work, and allows for the cross-fertilization of ideas, for the fostering of multidisciplinary perspectives on the field that is essential if we are to produce applications that really are useful (Bannon *et al.*, 1988).

2. Overview of the book

This book is based upon the *International Journal of Man Machine Studies* special editions on computer-supported cooperative work and groupware, published in February and March of 1991. The collection contains 16 original articles[1] selected from over 40 submissions to the journal, and an annotated bibliography to CSCW. As the papers were chosen on individual technical merit, the collection does not introduce all aspects of CSCW and groupware. Still, the new reader should gain some insight into what this field is about, while the active CSCW researcher and groupware implementor will be informed of several exciting new findings and perspectives.

This book loosely categorizes the collected papers into seven parts. In order to establish a sense of context for the reader, this section introduces each part and the papers within them.

2.1. STUDYING GROUPS WITHOUT GROUPWARE

Knowing how people work together without groupware is an essential first step for designing appropriate software. The articles in Part 1 take this approach. Tang analyses key aspects of shared activity around a paper sketchpad by studying video transcripts of small group design sessions. The result is a set of specific recommendations for the design of tools to support shared workspace activity, results which have now been taken up by several prototype video and electronic workspaces (for examples see Bly & Minneman, 1990; Greenberg & Bohnet, 1991; Ishii, 1990; Tang & Minneman, 1990).

Nardi and Miller's study is on spreadsheets, long considered a good example of a well designed "single user" application. Much to their surprise, they observed that spreadsheet co-development was the rule, not the exception. They saw a high degree of cooperation in sharing program expertise, transferring domain knowledge, debugging, training and face to face work in meetings. The general implication is

---

[1] A few articles have appeared in substantially different form elsewhere.

that cooperative work happens all the time, in spite of the inherent limitations of the software.

2.2. STUDYING GROUPS WITH GROUPWARE

When groupware is available, its effect on the group can be evaluated and further implications for design developed. Tatar, Foster and Bobrow, for example, review "Cognoter", a multi-user idea organizer that was part of Xerox PARC's original CoLab suite (Stefik, Foster, Bobrow, Kahn, Lanning & Suchman, 1987). They noticed that its users encountered unexpected communication breakdowns, which they attribute to the Cognoter's incorrect model of conversation implicit in its design. By using a more appropriate model of conversation, they were not only able to pinpoint the previous design decisions that had contributed to the difficulties users had, but they were able to amend the design as well.

"Media Space" is a video, audio and computing network established to support distributed research across two quite distant laboratories. Olson and Bly observed the laboratories' usage evolution of Media Space over two years. The resulting article reports on the requirements for distributed research, and indicates where the technology both succeeded and failed to support various aspects of the collaborations.

Borenstein and Thyberg's article describes the "Messages" user interface to the "Andrew Message System" (AMS), a powerful multi-media mail and bulletin board program. The authors talk the reader through the original design assumptions of Messages and detail its features. What makes Messages interesting is that it is a real system, with several thousand users. The continuous user involvement meant that faults quickly became evident, motivating rapid redesign. As an example, they step us through three iterations of the "Adviser", a Messages subsystem designed to allow experts to provide advice to queries from AMS users.

2.3. COMPUTER-MEDIATED COMMUNICATIONS AND GROUP DECISION SUPPORT SYSTEMS

Computer support for meetings is becoming an increasingly common way to assist the group decision-making process. In face to face settings, we are not only seeing specially-built meeting rooms (e.g. Mantei, 1988), but also cheap LED projectors that can display a computer screen's contents on a large screen. In asynchronous environments, electronic mail and computer conferencing enable on-going discussions between time and distance-separated people.

But what makes good electronic meeting support? Valacich, Dennis and Nunamaker Jr have worked with the University of Arizona's "GroupSystems" face to face meeting room for several years. They highlight the theoretical assumptions behind the system's design and describe GroupSystems' workings. Of particular importance is that GroupSystems has been well-studied; 15 experimental and field studies are summarized and contrasted. The authors then provide recommendations for developers of electronic meeting rooms based upon the lessons learnt.

Technology changes the way in which people within a group behave. Lea and Spears discuss how computer-mediated communication affects de-individuation, the anonymity and loss of identity that occurs when people are submerged in a group. If de-individuation does exist, we would expect the social norms and constraints of people's behaviour to be weakened, which would have serious consequences on how decisions made by the group should be interpreted. The authors question past findings on how electronic communication changes the group's psychological states, and then present their own study and alternative view of the role of de-individuation.

What is computer-mediated communication used for? Some systems are based upon the assumption that communication is related to a specific task or action which can be captured and formalized (e.g. the Coordinator, Winograd, 1988). Weedman noticed that typical, asynchronous computer communication also has a large non-task component used for such things as social exchange, expressing frustrations, and so on. She argues that since variety and vigour of communication is important to successful collaboration, the underlying technology should be flexible enough to support informal as well as formal talk.

2.4. NOVEL AND INNOVATIVE GROUPWARE TECHNOLOGIES

CSCW exhibits the same push and pull between theory and creative technologies that exists in traditional human–computer interaction. The four articles in Part 4 demonstrate innovations that may alter our perspectives of groupware fundamentals.

Recent developments in interactive *virtual environments* have sparked interest in spatially-located three-dimensional sound. Cohen and Ludwig describe an audio management system called *audio windows* that integrates spatial sound, audio emphasis, and gestural input recognition. While this exciting use of computer-controlled sound can be applied to *any* aspect of the human–computer interface, the article suggests new enhancements this technology can bring to tele-conferencing.

A large part of a group process is information sharing. While networked computers usually allow people within an institution to share information across common data files, networks are rarely available for loosely-coupled social groups. Witten, Thimbleby, Coulouris and Greenberg describe "Liveware", a socially productive benign virus used to spread information across intermittently connected people and groups. Unlike conventional wired networks, Liveware is cheap, does not require a technical infrastructure, and is intrinsically intertwined with social conventions of "casual" information sharing by mobile and flexible work groups.

Hypertext developers now recognize that hypertext documents will be used and updated by large groups of people. Rein and Ellis take the next logical step by combining both real-time with asynchronous hypertext manipulation in their "rIBIS" system. An rIBIS session is a distributed meeting where participants can be in a "tightly-coupled" or "loosely-coupled" mode. In the first, tightly-coupled members all see the same thing, and take turns controlling and manipulating the hypertext display. In the second, a person works semi-privately by editing a portion of the hypertext—only large-grained changes are broadcast to other members. The result is a system valuable not only for storing information, but also for allowing people to actively capture and structure critical aspects of a meeting process.

Cook, Birch, Murphy and Woolsey are "strict constructionists", i.e. implementors interested in the underlying architectures and technologies supporting groupware. They create a model of a groupware system, and use it to explore, implement and evaluate a system architecture. The paper reveals what constraints the developers chose to work under, how they actually built the system and how they judged what worked and what did not. The paper also highlights a serious problem currently facing all groupware developers: the lack of an adequate toolkit for constructing applications.

2.5. REMOVING RIGIDITY FROM GROUPWARE

Peter and Trudy Johnson-Lenz suggest that today's approach to groupware is *mechanistic*, i.e. based upon some social theory of human interaction or upon a task-oriented approach that can be modelled by a machine. At the other extreme (also supported by Dykstra and Carasik) is *groupware as context*, based on the social theory that human systems are self-organizing and arise out of the unrestricted interaction of autonomous individuals. Dykstra and Carasik's article pursues this latter view. They argue that while systems should nourish conversation and stimulate interaction amongst group participants, they should not directly regulate the actual meeting process. Instead, the technology should be supple enough to allow the group itself to define its own (perhaps changing) conventions, structures and constraints. Several iterations of the "Amsterdam Conversation Environment", a system supporting groupware as context, are described.

The Johnson-Lenzs' delightful article takes the middle ground. Instead of eschewing system support for process, they describe how the computer can perhaps capture the emergence of the group's process, and then create appropriate forms for supporting it. They consider their approach "post-mechanistic" as the model of group behaviour is not rigidly codified into the system but evolves with the group. Their implementation is particularly intriguing not only for technical reasons, but because the subject domain is "self-help", a far cry from the usual business-oriented applications emphasized by developers.

2.6. PARTICIPATORY DESIGN

Unlike conventional interface design approaches that consider user involvement a sequence of intermittent consultations, *participatory design* has the design team comprised of developers and eventual system users. Both actively and continuously participate in planning and decision making in order to build a system that truly matches what the workers need. Participatory design is now touted as a critical requirement for successful groupware design, on the premise that the resulting product will be more usable by all team members.

While participatory design has generally succeeded for software development targetted to producing systems specific to an in-house organizational context, it has not really been applied to product development organizations that design mass-produced off-the-shelf products. Grudin suggests that in spite of the benefits participatory design may offer for improving a system interface (particularly for groupware systems), there are several serious obstacles to user involvement. Most stem from organizational structures and development practices that arose prior to the current market for interactive systems. Recognizing these obstacles is, of course, the first step to overcoming them.

Given an environment conducive to participatory design, how does one go about it? Bodker and Gronbaek describe one method called *cooperative prototyping*. This involves sessions where users experience the future-use situation, and then participate with designers in modifying the prototypes when usage breakdowns require it. Their article is especially valuable as it provides: a theoretical framework; a practical guide for managing cooperative prototyping sessions, and an example of how cooperative prototyping develops in a real situation.

2.7. ANNOTATED BIBLIOGRAPHY

Computer-supported cooperative work is a new multi-disciplinary field with roots in many disciplines. Due to the youth and diversity of computer-supported cooperative work and groupware, few specialized books or journals are available, and articles are scattered amongst diverse journals, proceedings and technical reports. Building a CSCW reference library is particularly daunting, for it is difficult for the new researcher to discover the relevant documents. To aid this task, I have compiled, listed and annotated much of the current research in computer-supported cooperative work into the bibliography in Part 7. The article also includes an overview of the general sources that publish CSCW works and a list of groupware systems and concepts indexed to the bibliography.

2.8. METHODOLOGY

Traditional experimental methodologies employed to study human–computer interactions are often inadequate for studying group situations. When real group dynamics are awkward to replicate in a laboratory, researchers must resort to observing behaviour in the field. Studies are characterized by many variables and uncontrollable factors, and often require observations over lengthy time spans. New methodologies are essential.

Several of the articles interspersed in this collection serve a purpose beyond their specific research findings, for they also introduce methodologies that may be novel to the reader. Both Lea's and Weedman's articles, for example, illustrate how conventional experimental psychology can still be applied to study fine details of group behaviour. In contrast, Tang's use of "video as data" (Mackay & Tatar, 1989) is an example of a relatively new way of collecting data that helps establish insight into group behaviour under less controlled conditions. His article also provides an example of an ethnographic study, particularly in how complex group activity can be categorized, counted and interpreted. Nardi and Miller also offer an ethnographic study, in this case using extensive interviewing of subjects along with an analysis of the artifacts produced by the group. Tatar, Foster and Bobrow show how even brief usability studies—simple observations of "real" users (not developers) interacting through a system—can highlight serious problems that may be otherwise overlooked. They also demonstrate the value of using models and theories from non computer-based fields (in this case conversational analysis and psycho-linguistics) to explain the group's reaction to the particular groupware system. Olson and Bly reveal how an objective outside observer can be brought in to examine a long-term work process.

Although the methods employed by the above researchers are far from exhaustive, they do give an example of the diverse methodologies involved in CSCW research.

The articles in this book are derived from a cross-referee process, where each of the over 40 original submitters was asked to referee three other articles. In spite of the tight deadline, all referees returned their reports promptly. The selection of articles and the recommended improvements in the revised articles are due to their diligence.

Both the Alberta Research Council and Canada's National Science and Engineering Research Council provided me with the resources and funding required to manage and edit this collection. Special thanks goes to Brian Gaines, who was instrumental in motivating me to take on this task.

References

BANNON, L., BJORN-ANDERSON, N. & DUE-THOMSEN, B. (1988). Computer support for cooperative work: An appraisal and critique. In H. J. BULLINGER, Ed. *Eurinfo '88. Information Systems for Organizational Effectiveness.* Amsterdam: North-Holland.

BANNON, L. J. & SCHMIDT, K. (1989). CSCW: Four characters in search of a context. In *Proceedings of the European Community Conference on Computer Supported Work (EC-CSCW)*, pp. 358–372, London, September.

BLY, S. A. & MINNEMAN, S. L. (1990). Commune: A shared drawing surface. In *Proceedings of the Conference on Office Information Systems*, pp. 184–192, Boston, April 25–27.

GALEGHER, J., KRAUT, R. & EGIDO, C. (Ed.) (1990). *Intellectual Teamwork: Social and Technological Foundations of Group Work.* Hillsdale, NJ: Lawrence Erlbaum Associates.

GIBBS, S. & VERRIJN-STUART (Ed.) (1990). *Proceedings of IFIP WG8.4 Conference on Multi-User Interfaces and Applications (Crete).* Amsterdam: North-Holland.

GREENBERG, S. (1991). *An Annotated Bibliography of Computer Supported Cooperative Work: Revision 2.* Research Report, Department of Computer Science, University of Calgary, Calgary, Alberta, Canada.

GREENBERG, S. & BOHNET, R. (1991). Group Sketch: A multi-user sketchpad for geographically-distributed small groups. In *Proceedings of Graphics Interface '91*, Calgary, Alberta, June 5–7. Also available as Research Report 90/414/38, Department of Computer Science, University of Calgary, Alberta, Canada.

GREIF, I. (Ed.) (1988). *Computer-supported Cooperative Work: A Book of Readings.* San Mateo, CA: Morgan Kaufmann.

GRUDIN, J. (1991). CSCW: The convergence of two disciplines. In *ACM SIGCHI Conference on Human Factors in Computing Systems*, April. New Orleans: ACM Press.

ISHII, H. (1990). Team WorkStation: Towards a seamless shared space. In *Proceedings of the Conference on Computer-Supported Cooperative Work*, pp. 13–26, October 7–10. Los Angeles, CA: ACM Press.

JOHANSEN, R. (1988). *Groupware: Computer Support for Business Teams.* New York: The Free Press, Macmillan Inc.

KRAUT, R., EGIDO, C. & GALEGHER, J. (1988). Patterns of contact and communication in scientific collaboration. In *Proceedings of the Conference on Computer-Supported Cooperative Work*, pp. 1–12, September 26–28. Portland, OR: ACM Press.

MACKAY, W. E. & TATAR, D. G. (1989). Special issue on video as a research and design tool. *SIGCHI Bulletin*, **21**(2), October.

MANTEI, M. (1988). Capturing the Capture concepts: A case study in the design of computer-supported meeting environments. In *Proceedings of the Conference on Computer-Supported Cooperative Work*, pp. 257–270, September 26–28. Portland, OR: ACM Press.

OLSON, M. H. (Ed.) (1989). *Technological Support for Work Group Collaboration.* Hillsdale, NJ: Lawrence Erlbaum Associates.

STEFIK, M., FOSTER, G., BOBROW, D., KAHN, K., LANNING, S. & SUCHMAN, L. (1987). Beyond the chalkboard: Computer support for collaboration and problem solving in meetings. *Communications of the ACM*, **30**, 32–47. Reprinted (1988) in I. GREIF, Ed. *Computer Supported Cooperative Work: A Book of Readings.* San Mateo, CA: Morgan Kaufmann.

TANG, J. C. & MINNEMAN, S. L. (1990). Videodraw: A video interface for collaborative drawing. In *ACM SIGCHI Conference on Human Factors in Computing Systems*, pp. 313–320, April 1–5, Seattle. Washington: ACM Press.

University of Guelph (1987). *The Second Guelph Symposium on Computer Conferencing*, University of Guelph, Guelph, Ontario, Canada, June 1–4.

University of Guelph (1990). *The Third Guelph Symposium on Computer Mediated Communication*, University of Guelph, Continuing Education Division, Guelph, Ontario, Canada, May 15–17.

WINOGRAD, T. (1988). A language/action perspective on the design of cooperative work. *Human–Computer Interaction*, **3**, 3–30.

Part 1

Studying groups without groupware

2

Findings from observational studies of collaborative work

JOHN C. TANG

The work activity of small groups of three to four people was videotaped and analysed in order to understand collaborative work and to guide the development of tools to support it. The analysis focused on the group's shared drawing activity— their listing, drawing, gesturing and talking around a shared drawing surface. This analysis identified specific features of collaborative work activity that raise design implications for collaborative technology: (1) collaborators use hand gestures to uniquely communicate significant information; (2) the process of creating and using drawings conveys much information not contained in the resulting drawings; (3) the drawing space is an important resource for the group in mediating their collabora- tion; (4) there is a fluent mix of activity in the drawing space; and (5) the spatial orientation among the collaborators and the drawing space has a role in structuring their activity. These observations are illustrated with examples from the video data, and the design implications they raise are discussed.

1. Introduction

Building computer tools to support collaborative work requires re-examining the design assumptions that have hitherto been used in building tools for individual use. The needs of a group using a tool collaboratively, are different from those of an individual user, and these differences should be reflected in the design of the technology. The research reported in this paper is premised on the need to observe and understand what people actually do when engaged in an activity in order to guide the design, development and introduction of tools to support that activity. Figure 1 represents how this approach is applied to observing, understanding and supporting collaborative work. This paper reports on findings from studies that observed collaborative work, leading to a better understanding of that activity and raising implications for the design of tools to support it.

This research focuses on studying the collaborative drawing space activity of small teams—the writing, freehand drawing and gesturing activities that occur when three or four people work around whiteboards or large sheets of paper. Much human collaboration involves a shared drawing surface (e.g. paper sheets, chalkboards, computer screens, cocktail napkins), and recent research has been exploring computer support for collaborative drawing activity (Lakin, 1986; Stefik, Foster, Bobrow, Kahn, Lanning & Suchman, 1987). However, collaborative drawing tools should not be based only on what features computer technology offers or how com- puters have been applied to support individual activity. Rather, the design of col- laborative technology needs to be guided by an understanding of how collaborative

11

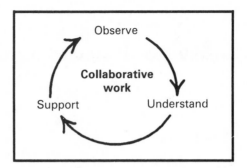

FIGURE 1. Research approach. Actual collaborative work activity is observed in order to understand it and identify opportunities to support it.†

work is accomplished. By understanding what resources the collaborators use and what hindrances they encounter in their work, tools can be designed to augment resources while removing obstacles in collaborative activity.

In this research, video-based interaction analysis methods (Goodwin, 1981; Heath, 1986) are applied to study collaborative drawing activity. This approach involves analysing videotaped samples of collaborative activity to understand how collaboration is accomplished through interactions among the participants and the artifacts in their environment. It emphasizes studying people working on a realistic task in a natural working environment, since that context has a major influence on the work activity. By comparing and contrasting among the many interactions that occur in the data, specific resources that collaborators use and hindrances that they encounter can be identified.

FIGURE 2. Configuration for videotaping collaborative work. Three or four collaborators work around a table on a pad of paper sheets. Their activity is monitored by the experimenter next door and recorded on videotape.

† I would like to acknowledge Scott Minneman (Unpublished data) for initially composing this representation for the relationship of observing, understanding and intervening in an activity.

Eight short sessions (approximately 1–1/2 h) of three to four person teams working on a conceptual design task were videotaped for analysis. Figure 2 shows the typical configuration for videotaping the collaborative activity. Four different design tasks were used in the sessions; all of them emphasized the human–machine interface design for an interactive, computer-controlled system (see sample problem statement in Appendix A). These tasks elicited a substantial amount of group interaction and collaborative drawing activity. For six of the sessions, the groups worked around a conference table sharing a pad of large paper sheets; two groups used a wall-mounted whiteboard. The meetings observed were the first sessions that the participants worked together on the task as a group, thus capturing the earlier, more conceptual stages of the design process. Tang (1989) describes the observational methodology in more detail.

In this paper, an analysis of collaborative drawing space activity is presented. Evidence from the video data is used to illustrate the resources and hindrances in shared drawing activity identified by this analysis. Finally, the design implications for tools to support collaborative work are identified and discussed.

2. Analysis of collaborative drawing space activity

The analysis focused on how the collaborators accomplished their work through their activity in the drawing space. Initial analysis of the data led to a framework (Figure 3) for organizing the study of drawing-space activity. This framework lays out categories of what actions occurred in the drawing space and what functions those actions accomplished. Although this framework is a rather simplified characterization of actual collaborative drawing activity, it has proven to be a useful tool for analysing the activity. Attempting to classify the observed activity into the categories of the framework helped identify resources and hindrances in collaborative drawing activity, as described in Section 3. This section presents the framework, illustrates it with examples from the videotape data, and describes how it was used to identify trends in the data.

2.1. FRAMEWORK FOR STUDYING DRAWING SPACE ACTIVITY

The framework in Figure 3 lays out relationships between *actions* that occur in the drawing space, and *functions* that are accomplished through those actions.

Function \ Action	TALK		
	LIST	DRAW	GESTURE
Store information			
Express ideas			
Mediate interaction			

FIGURE 3. Framework for analysing drawing space activity. A framework for categorizing drawing space activity according to *actions* (how the activity was produced) and *functions* (what the activity accomplished).

The *actions* describe the means for producing the activities:

(1) *List*: actions producing non-spatially located text (alpha-numeric notes);

(2) *Draw*: actions producing graphic artifacts, including textual captions;

(3) *Gesture*: purposeful hand movements which communicate information (e.g. enacting simulations, pointing to objects in the drawing space).

The analysis focused on the list, draw and gesture actions of the group; clearly, their talk was also a substantial part of their activity. While conversation analysis focuses mainly on interaction through conversation (Levinson, 1983), and some research studies drawing activity irrespective of the talk (Lakin, 1986), the research presented here studies collaborative drawing activity in the context of the group's talk. Although their talk was not analysed by classifying it according to various categories, it was used to help interpret and analyse their drawing space activity. By recording the activity on videotape, the context of the complete activity of the session (including the verbal dialog) is available for analysis.

The *functions* in Figure 3 describe the purpose that the activity accomplishes:

(1) *Store information*: preserving information in some form for later reference, typically after attaining group agreement;

(2) *Express ideas*: interactively creating representations of ideas in some tangible form, to enable the group to perceive, react to and build on them;

(3) *Mediate interaction*: facilitating the collaboration of the group (e.g. moderating the turn-taking, directing the group's attention).

While this set of actions and functions does not completely describe all of the activities that occur in the drawing space, it was used as a framework for structuring the analysis.

2.2. ILLUSTRATING THE FRAMEWORK

The categories of the framework are illustrated with examples from a scene in the videotape data, represented in Figure 4. This figure shows a section of transcript of the verbal dialog, annotated with brief descriptions of every drawing space activity that occurred during the section. In order to denote episodes of drawing space activity, an icon is placed in the text of the transcript at approximately the point in the talk where an action begins. That icon is linked to a note describing the drawing space action. The region of the drawing space where the participants are making their marks and sketches is shown on the right side of the figure. The "S" numbers identify which participant is speaking or acting. The line numbers along the left margin will be used throughout this paper to indicate locations in the transcript section. This representation was developed in the NoteCards hypertext environment (Halasz, Moran & Trigg, 1987).

This particular group's design task was to integrate the remote control units of several different entertainment appliances (e.g. television, stereo, videocassette recorder) into one multi-function remote control (see problem statement in Appendix A). This design session took place in 1987, before commercial versions of such a device were common. In this section of the session, the group is discussing new actions for operating the controls on a multi-function remote control.

To summarize what happens in this section, S2 elicits proposals for how to move icons around on a display screen, drawing a news desk icon as an example. S3 gesturally enacts an idea, sliding his finger over the icon to move it around, and

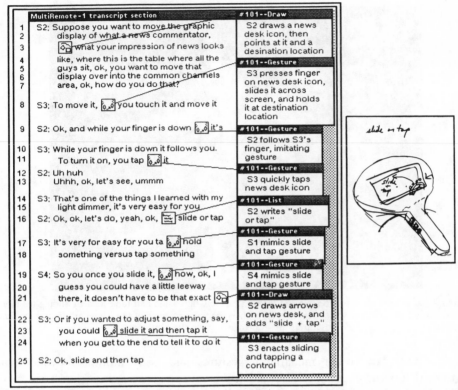

FIGURE 4. Annotated transcript section from a design session. A section of transcript from a design session, annotated with notes describing the episodes of listing, drawing and gesturing that occurred. The marks made in the drawing space during this section are shown at the right.

tapping the icon to activate it. After imitating the gesture, S2 documents this idea as "slide or tap". Meanwhile, the other participants imitate the gesture while S3 continues to elaborate on the idea.

2.2.1. Actions: listing, drawing and gesturing

Listing and drawing are the actions most commonly associated with drawing space activity. List actions result in alpha-numeric text where its spatial location is not of major significance. A simple example of a list action is shown in line 16 of the transcript section in Figure 4, where S2 writes the phrase "slide or tap" at the top of the page. Draw actions result in graphic marks, typically a sketch. A typical draw action is illustrated in line 3 of the transcript, where S2 draws a graphical representation for an icon of a news desk.

Hand gesture actions are more difficult to classify. They are defined as purposeful or intentional hand movements that communicate information. However, for practical reasons, many of the incidental gestures that naturally accompany human dialog (e.g. twiddling a pen, scratching a chin) are not included. The intent is to include hand gestures as a significant drawing-space action without accounting for every hand motion made in the design session. More research is also needed to

FIGURE 5. A gesture example. S3, on the far right, enacts the "slide and tap" idea by sliding his finger across a sketch of a display screen. (Split screen image combines a view of the whole group on top with a closeup of the drawing space on the bottom.)

consider the many other meaningful gestures and body motions beyond hand gestures that occur in collaborative activity.

The hand gesture marked in line 8 of the transcript is shown in Figure 5. This example illustrates how gesture is used to enact or simulate the slide and tap idea. S3 slides his finger over the sketch of the news desk, acting out how he would move the news desk icon across the display screen. Other examples of gesture include pointing at a sketch or signaling towards another group member.

Several of the observed actions displayed characteristics of more than one category (e.g. an activity that involved both listing and drawing). These actions were classified according to what action they primarily constituted. For example, the action noted in line 21 where S2 draws an arrow and writes "slide + tap" is categorized as a draw action, even though the resulting artifact is largely text. It is classified as a draw action because the text is spatially located and integrated with other graphic marks to the extent that the text provides graphic, as well as semantic, information.

2.2.2. Functions: storing information, expressing ideas and mediating interaction

Using the drawing space to store information involves preserving or recording the information to facilitate later reference. This function typically involves chunking the information in some persistent form, such as a textual label or a sketch. There is also some evidence that gestures can help store information, which will be discussed later. An example of using the drawing space to store information is shown on line 16 of the transcript in Figure 4. When S2 perceives that an idea is being proposed, he writes down a label ("slide or tap") at the top of the page.

Using the drawing space to express ideas is a more interactive use of the drawing space to represent and convey ideas to the collaborators. Rather than being intended for later reference, expressing ideas interactively elicits a response or reaction in the present time. For example, in lines 1–7 of the transcript, S2 draws a sketch of a news desk icon as he asks about how to move icons around on the display screen. Other collaborators enact gestures over it (lines 8 and 19) and S2 adds to the sketch (line 21), demonstrating that it is a working drawing rather than a documentary one. Expressing ideas involves using the drawing space as a working scratchpad to represent and interactively construct ideas with others, or to refine one's own thinking.

The drawing space is also used to mediate the interaction of the group, typically by using it to help negotiate the conversational turn-taking or direct the group's focus of attention. As part of the gesture that is marked in line 11 of the transcript, S3's hand moves deliberately toward the sketch, effectively commanding a turn in preparation for his acting out part of the slide and tap idea. Other forms of focusing attention include pointing to a location, or shifting attention from the group drawing to a personal doodle (demonstrating apparent loss of interest in the conversation).

2.3. USING THE FRAMEWORK IN THE ANALYSIS

In order to explore the utility of the framework, portions of the videotaped data were catalogued according to its action and function categories. For one entire one hour and a half design session and a 10 minute section of a second design session (where the group specified a design for one of their ideas), a log of every instance of drawing space activity was made. Each instance was categorized as to what action (listing, drawing, gesturing) and function (store information, express ideas, mediate interaction) it primarily accomplished. This exercise not only led to a deeper familiarity with the data, but also helped focus the analysis on trends that became apparent in the data. For example, it was observed that over one third of the instances of drawing space activity were categorized as a gesture action, suggesting that hand gestures are a prominent part of drawing space activity. Appendix B includes more details about categorizing and counting drawing space activities.

In attempting to catalogue the observed drawing space activity according to the framework it quickly became apparent that the activity is not accurately described by such clean and distinct categories. Rather, actual activity is composed of a fluent mix of listing, drawing and gesturing, and these actions often accomplish more than one function. Although the framework is a simplified characterization of how the activity actually occurs, it has proven to be a useful perspective from which to study collaborative drawing activity.

3. Resources and hindrances in collaborative drawing activity

The analysis of the videotapes led to identifying specific resources used and hindrances encountered by the participants in collaborative drawing activity. The analysis also suggested a grouping for the categories of the framework that illustrates the resources and hindrances identified. As shown in Figure 6, the framework can be grouped into four areas: conventional view, gestural expression, expressing ideas, and mediating interaction. This grouping highlights three aspects

Function \ Action	LIST	DRAW	GESTURE
TALK			
Store information	CONVENTIONAL VIEW		GESTURAL EXPRESSION
Express ideas	EXPRESSING IDEAS		
Mediate interaction	MEDIATING INTERACTION		

FIGURE 6. Beyond the conventional view of drawing space activity. This organization of the framework illustrates three other aspects of drawing space activity beyond storing information through listing and drawing.

of drawing space activity that go beyond the activities that are conventionally considered to be useful in the drawing space.

The "conventional view" of drawing space activity is characterized by its use to record information in text and graphics to document the work that occurred during a session. In the categories of the framework, this activity translates into storing information through listing text and drawing graphics, as indicated in Figure 6. This view is concerned primarily with the resulting text and graphics, and is typically the extent of drawing activity supported by conventional computer tools (e.g. Computer Aided Design tools, graphic editors, fax machines).

However, the video data illustrate that there are other important aspects of drawing space activity. Hand gestures form a substantial proportion of drawing space activity. These gestures accomplish significant work in the collaborative process, and are not incidental to the activity. Furthermore, the drawing space is frequently used to express ideas, not just document them. The drawing space is also a key resource for mediating group interaction. In order to effectively support collaborative drawing, the design of support tools should account for these additional aspects of drawing space activity.

This organization of the framework helped identify several observations on collaborative drawing activity:

- hand gestures are a significant resource for communicating information;
- the process of creating and using drawings conveys important information not found in the resulting drawings;
- the drawing space is a key resource for mediating the group's interaction;
- collaborators fluently intermix among drawing space actions and functions;
- the spatial orientation among the collaborators and the drawing space structures drawing space activity.

Specific resources and hindrances associated with these observations are discussed in this section.

3.1. THE ROLE OF HAND GESTURES

The prevalence of hand gestures in collaborative drawing activity is obvious. Yet a deeper understanding of what gestures accomplish is needed, especially in considering how to design tools to support them. The use of gesture in face-to-face communication is widely discussed and debated in the literature (McNeill, 1985; Kendon, 1986; Feyereisen, 1987). The research presented here focuses on hand gestures in relation to drawing activity and artifacts in the drawing space.

As highlighted in the framework in Figure 6, hand gestures can be used to accomplish any of the three drawing space functions. Although gestures do not leave behind any persistent record in the drawing space, some evidence suggests they can be used to help store information. In the sessions observed, the participants did not experience any problems in remembering hand gestures later in the session or even in later meetings. One aid for remembering gestures is for other collaborators to imitate a hand gesture. In the transcript represented in Figure 4, S3 demonstrates the "slide and tap" gesture in line 8 and that gesture is imitated by three other collaborators (lines 9, 17 and 19). Gestures can also be documented with a label or a sketch, as in line 21 where S2 draws an arrow next to "slide + tap". Through these techniques, the groups observed managed to preserve the information communicated through their gestures.

Hand gestures are commonly used to express ideas, the second function depicted in the framework. The transcript section shows several examples of gestures (lines 8, 9, 11, 23) that express ideas by enacting a simulation of them. Gestures are particularly well-suited to demonstrating a sequence of actions, such as how a person would interact with a proposed machine. Although enacting simulations is a common use of gesture, most current collaboration technology does not support this use of gesture. Hand gestures are also used to mediate the group's interaction. Pointing to locations often directs the group's attention to a common location, and subtle cues from hand gestures (e.g. waving a hand to take a turn of talk) can help the group negotiate the use of a shared drawing space. These mediating gestures are usually unremarkable and typically do not add new information by themselves. Yet, they play an instrumental role in organizing the group's interaction.

In all of these uses of gesture, it would be difficult to accomplish the same effect in any other way. In this sense, hand gestures are a crucial resource for uniquely accomplishing work in collaborative drawing activity. Further analysis of gestural activity identified specific resources or problems associated with gestures.

An important resource in the use of hand gestures is that they are often enacted in relation to objects in the drawing space, such as an existing sketch. The gestures enacting the "slide and tap" idea (lines 8, 9, 11 and 23 in the transcript) are all done in relation to a sketch on the paper sheet. The sketch provides the context needed for interpreting the actions demonstrated by the gestures. Hand gestures are also conducted in relation to the location of the other people in the group, such as pointing to another participant. These observations indicate that it is important to not only see *gestures*, but to see them *in relation to* the sketches and other objects in the drawing space. The spatial relationship between hand gestures and their referents is a resource used in interpreting collaborative drawing activity.

This resource of gesturing in relation to the drawing space is altered in computer-augmented meeting rooms (Cook, Ellis, Graf, Rein & Smith, 1986; Stefik *et al.*, 1987; Mantei, 1988), where each participant has a personal workstation and these workstations are networked together to allow the group to share images. One aspect of gesturing in relation to sketches can be accomplished using a "telepointer" (Stefik, Bobrow, Foster, Lanning & Tatar, 1986), a large cursor that appears on a shared window that any participant can use to point at particular objects in the window. However, telepointing only supports the use of hand gestures to refer to objects in the drawing space. Computer-augmented meeting rooms are unable to support some of the other uses of gesture, such as enacting ideas over a sketch in the drawing space. Participants tend to enact such gestures over their personal workstation screen in front of them, yet the other participants often cannot see these gestures in relation to the referent sketch on the screen.

Another resource in the use of hand gestures is their timing with the accompanying verbal dialog. Hand gestures that express ideas are usually directly accompanied by a verbal explanation of the idea. This direct relationship contrasts with the observation that drawing or listing can be timed to come before, during, after, or without accompanying talk. Since gestures are closely associated with speech, any technology that conveys gestures should avoid disrupting their relationship in time with the accompanying talk.

One problem observed with hand gestures is that sometimes they are not perceived by other group members whose attention is focused elsewhere. Being able to view gestures clearly is often difficult, especially in meetings with many participants. Meetings in computer-augmented rooms that are cluttered with computer equipment, or meetings involving participants in physically remote locations pose greater challenges in sharing gestures. Most current collaborative technology does not adequately convey gestures so that all of the participants can share in viewing them.

3.2. THE IMPORTANCE OF THE PROCESS OF CREATING AND USING DRAWINGS

One of the distinctions that the framework helps reveal is the difference between using the drawing space to store information and using it to express ideas. This contrast between documentary and expressive drawing space activities highlights the relationship between the resulting *artifacts* marked on the drawing space and the *process* of making those artifacts. Typically the goal of storing information is to produce an *artifact* that records information for later recall. The *process* of creating that artifact can be troublesome, since the rest of the group must either wait during that process or can continue working, leaving the documenter behind. However, when expressing ideas, the goal is to enlist the collaboration of the group to develop ideas. Having the group experience and participate in the *process* of creating expressive artifacts is an integral part of expressing ideas.

The importance of experiencing the process of creating and using drawings, especially when expressing ideas, is indicated by the fact that the resulting drawings often do not make sense by themselves. They can only be interpreted in the context of the accompanying dialog or interaction of the participants. This observation is especially apparent with hand gestures, which do not leave behind any persistent artifact, yet do communicate significant information. As can be seen in Figure 4, the resulting marks made in the drawing space do not make much sense without the accompanying dialog and group interaction. It is through the process of seeing how those marks are created and referred to, along with the accompanying verbal explanation, that the group can come to an understanding of what the marks mean. Sharing in the process of creating and using drawings is an important resource that the group uses in order to interpret many of the drawings and gestures produced.

A key resource in the process of creating and using drawings is the timing of activities among the participants. In contrast to storing information, which is often accomplished by a solitary participant, expressing ideas or mediating interaction sometimes involves several people working together in the drawing space. This collaborative process of building on and interactively developing representations in the drawing space often involves fine-grained interactions in time among the participants. Timing a gesture or a drawing with a verbal explanation of it, or timing an activity to coordinate with the activity of other participants, were observed to be important uses of timing. It is in part this familiar sense of timing that enables the group to coordinate the highly engaged, collaborative activity observed in the video data. Timing is a particular concern with computer technology, which can introduce processing and transmission delays that cause the objects appearing on a shared computer screen to fall out of synchrony from the accompanying verbal explanation.

3.3. THE USE OF THE DRAWING SPACE IN MEDIATING INTERACTION

An integral part of collaborative activity is how the group mediates their inter-action—how the collaborators take turns talking or how they negotiate sharing a common drawing space. In face-to-face interaction, one key resource that a group uses to help mediate their interaction is a close physical proximity among the collaborators. This proximity allows a peripheral awareness of the other participants and their actions. Many intricate and coordinated hand motions were observed, such -as avoiding collisions with other hands or working closely together on a sketch. These coordinated actions demonstrate an awareness of the other participants, enabled by being in close proximity with them.

Often, more than one person at a time was observed to be active in the drawing space, indicating the need for concurrent access to the drawing space. Figure 7 shows how the gestures of S3 and S2 (indicated in lines 8 and 9 in the transcript)

FIGURE 7. Multiple people active in the drawing space. S3 (far right) and S2 (middle) enact gestures at the same time in the drawing space.

overlap in time. Sometimes participants even wanted to work in the same area of the drawing space at the same time. Since this was physically impossible, one person would have to wait for the other to vacate the drawing area before being able to mark on the paper. Just as overlapping talk occurs as part of smooth turn taking in conversation (Goodwin & Goodwin, 1987), concurrent activity in the drawing space can be a resource for helping the group smoothly negotiate using it.

By having concurrent access to the drawing space, the collaborators can work in parallel, easing bottlenecks such as the time it takes to store information. It is also a resource for reducing the competition for conversational turn taking, since other people can work in the shared drawing space while one person is talking and holding the audio floor. However, this increased parallelism can be a problem because it makes it harder to keep a shared focus as a group. Thus, concurrent access to the drawing space can at times be a problem as well as a resource.

Another resource available in face-to-face interaction is being able to associate the marks being made with the person who is making them. This resource helps the collaborators interpret the resulting marks and mediate their interaction. Knowing who created the marks often provides additional context for making sense of them. Also, actions in the drawing space are often used to bid for a turn in the conversation. Other group members must be able to associate such actions with the person initiating them in order to yield a turn to him or her. In current computer-augmented meeting rooms, it can be difficult to establish the relationship between the marks appearing on a shared computer screen and who is making them.

3.4. THE FLUENT INTERMIXING AMONG DRAWING SPACE ACTIONS AND FUNCTIONS

One resource observed in collaborative drawing activity does not explicitly appear in the framework in Figure 6, but is a direct result from using the framework to study the activity. As mentioned previously, attempting to categorize drawing space activity according to the framework revealed that the activity does not fit exclusively into separate categories. For example, when S2 draws an arrow and writes "slide + tap" (noted in line 21 of the transcript) it is classified primarily as drawing, even though the action also includes writing text. Likewise, drawing and gesturing mix together when S2 draws a picture of the news desk icon and then points at it (line 3). Rapid alternation between writing and drawing was also observed by Bly (1988) in her studies of a pair of collaborators in various workspace environments. The data show that collaborators naturally and fluently intermix listing with drawing and drawing with gesturing. However, most computer tools (e.g. MacPaint), separate text and graphics into different nodes.

Similarly, some of the activity accomplished more than one function. For example, when S3 enacts tapping the icon to activate it (line 11 in the transcript), his gesture also appears to help him take a turn in the conversation. This observation of accomplishing multiple purposes in human interaction is commonly noted in studies of human activity, especially conversation analysis (Goodwin, 1981). Being able to perform more than one function or action at a time is a resource that the collaborators use to smoothly accomplish their work. Personal computer tools that rigidly separate the activity into the various categories, such as graphic editors that separate text and graphics into different modes, often become a hindrance to the user. Such categorization would be even more problematic in collaborative tools.

Tools to support collaborative drawing activity should not rigidly separate the activity into the actions or functions of the framework. Although these categories are descriptive and useful for analysis, they are not prescriptive suggestions for governing the behavior in the drawing space. Collaborators do not shape their drawing activity according to the actions and functions of the framework, and neither should tools to support shared drawing activity.

3.5. THE ROLE OF SPATIAL ORIENTATION TO THE DRAWING SPACE

Spatial orientation with respect to the drawing space was observed to be both a problem and a resource for the collaborators. It is a problem because people seated around a shared drawing space do not see things at the same orientation (see Figure 7). Instead, objects will appear upside-down or at odd angles to various group members. This situation can make it difficult for the group to share a common physical view of the drawing space and to draw in proper orientation relative to existing sketches. This difficulty is especially noticeable when a group member tries to add text to a drawing that is not oriented to be in front of him or her.

However, orientation was also used as a resource in the group's drawing space activity. Sometimes sketches are drawn in relation to existing drawings or facing a particular group member, so as to establish a context and audience for that sketch. Conversely, marks drawn intentionally small and close to oneself effectively place them within a personal boundary not intended for others to perceive. These observations indicate the utility of providing a common view of the drawing space without losing the ways that orientation is meaningfully used.

4. Design implications

Several design implications are suggested by the resources and hindrances observed in collaborative work. The design of tools to support collaborative drawing activity should consider:

- conveying gestures, maintaining their relationship to the drawing space;
- conveying the process of creating and using drawings, with minimal time delay;
- providing concurrent access to the drawing space;
- allowing intermixing among drawing space actions and functions; and
- enabling all participants to share a common view of the drawing space.

Tools should support gestural expression, since gestures constitute a substantial part of drawing space activity and they communicate much information that can not be readily expressed otherwise. Collaborators should be able to see each others' gestures, and see them in relation to the drawing space and the other participants. Conveying gestures is especially relevant in computer-augmented meeting rooms (where the computer equipment can obstruct a clear view of all the participants) and in remote collaboration (where the participants can not directly see each other). Since gestures are often timed with the accompanying speech, audio must be shared among all participants without introducing any delays in timing.

Collaborators need to see not only the resulting marks, but also the process of creating and using those marks. It is through the interactive process of creating and using marks that the collaborators can come to interpret the marks and smoothly negotiate sharing the drawing space. This process must be conveyed among the collaborators with minimal time delay, to enable coordination with the accompanying talk and other activity. The processing and transmission delays that are inherent in current computer systems can disturb the use of timing as a resource to coordinate group work.

Tools should also provide all group members with concurrent access to the drawing space. Concurrent access should be allowed to the point of being able to work in the same drawing area at the same time. The data show examples where this amount of concurrent access might have been useful. Prototype tools that offer this capability should be constructed and observed in use to determine if the benefits of this capability outweigh the problems that are introduced.

The collaborators should be allowed to fluently intermix among the action and function categories of the framework. Conventional computer tools tend to separate actions into different modes (e.g. text from graphics). However, the naturally occurring activity observed does not exhibit such segregation. Especially in collaborative work, with multiple participants engaged in multiple activities, it is important not to introduce any hindrances in moving fluently from one activity to another.

The tools should also enable all collaborators to have a common view of the shared drawing space, allowing them to see the text and graphics created in the shared space in an upright and proper orientation. Sharing a common view allows each participant to easily perceive and add onto marks made by the other collaborators. Collaborators should still be able to use spatial orientation in the drawing space as a resource, to direct work toward a particular audience or denote space for private work. Providing a common view of the shared space while still allowing these uses of spatial orientation needs to be explored.

Some of these design implications have been embodied in two prototype shared drawing tools: Commune (Minneman & Bly, 1990) and VideoDraw (Tang & Minneman, 1990). Elements of these design implications are also exhibited in other tools that can be applied to shared drawing: VIDEOPLACE (Krueger, 1982), SharedARK (Smith, O'Shea, O'Malley, Scanlon & Taylor, 1989), Freestyle (Francik & Akagi, 1989), and TeamWorkStation (Ishii, 1990). More research is needed to study the use of these and other tools in realistic collaborative situations. Analysing the use of these tools will both suggest specific design improvements for the tools and lead to new perspectives on understanding collaborative work.

5. Discussion

Studying collaborative work activity has led to several observations on how collaborators use a shared drawing space:

- hand gestures, and their relationship to the drawing space, convey significant information;
- the process of creating and using drawings conveys important information not found in the resulting drawings;
- proximity and concurrent access to the drawing space are key resources for mediating the group's interaction;

- collaborators fluently intermix among drawing space actions and functions;
- collaborators need to share a common view of the drawing space, but also use spatial orientation to distinguish regions in the drawing space.

These observations indicate that collaborators rely not only on sharing a view of the drawings and surrounding activity, but also need a sense of awareness of the other participants for effective collaboration. The role of hand gestures, the importance of the process of creating and using drawings, and the use of the drawing space to help mediate interaction are only a few elements that contribute to a shared awareness among the collaborators. Continued research to understand what other resources the collaborators use to maintain this awareness is needed in order to build collaborative tools that enable this sense of awareness. This understanding is especially important in considering tools for remote collaboration or computer supported collaboration, where many of the cues available in face-to-face interaction are absent.

Many of these observations involve resources that the participants use to communicate and to mediate their collaboration. Gestures, the process of making drawings, concurrent access to the drawing space, fluent intermixing of drawing space actions, and the ability to associate the marks with who is making them, all contribute to maintaining effective communication and collaboration. Collaborative drawing tools should support or enhance these resources used to coordinate communication and interaction. Yet, with the current elementary understanding of the collaborative process, tools should not attempt to impose a structure to manage this coordination on behalf of the participants. For example, due to design tradeoffs made in some computer-augmented meeting rooms, such as Capture Lab (Mantei, 1988), only one person at a time can be active in the shared computer screen. However, in the actual collaborative drawing activity studied here, concurrent activity in the shared drawing space was observed to be a resource used by the group to help negotiate their collaboration. This resource would be compromised if access to the shared space is restricted to only one person at a time.

People are generally skilled at coordinating their communication and interaction with each other, and how they accomplish this is not well understood. Consequently, tools to support collaboration should not impose a structure that attempts to manage the interaction of the collaborators for them. Instead, tools should facilitate the participants' own abilities to coordinate their communication and collaboration.

Observing collaborative work has led to a better understanding of that activity and to the design of new tools to support it. In turn, observing how these tools are used not only further refines the design of those tools but also leads to new perspectives in understanding collaborative work. By repeatedly cycling through this process of observing, understanding and supporting collaborative activity (see Figure 1), tools that effectively support the work practice of collaborators can be developed.

I thank Larry Leifer for advising and encouraging me through the graduate research on which this work is based. Lucy Suchman provided consistent guidance and support, and introduced me to a new perspective on studying human activity. My thanks to Sara Bly, Austin Henderson, Scott Minneman and Deborah Tatar for their insights and discussions that they shared in this research. I acknowledge Xerox PARC for funding this research, and the members of the Interaction Analysis Lab there for their help in analysing the videotapes. The Center for Design Research at Stanford University and the System Sciences Laboratory at Xerox PARC provided environments that fostered this research.

References

BLY, S. A. (1988). A use of drawing surfaces in different collaborative settings. In *Proceedings of the Conference on Computer-Supported Cooperative Work,* Portland, Oregon, pp. 250–256.

COOK, P., ELLIS, C., GRAF, M., REIN, G. & SMITH, T. (1986). Project Nick: meetings augmentation and analysis. In *Proceedings of the Conference on Computer-Supported Cooperative Work,* Austin, Texas, pp. 1–6. Reprinted (1987). *ACM Transactions on Office Information Systems,* **5,** 132–146.

FEYEREISEN, P. (1987). Gestures and speech, interactions and separations: a reply to McNeill (1985). *Psychological Review,* **94,** 493–498.

FRANCIK, E. & AKAGI, K. (1989). Designing a computer pencil and tablet for handwriting. In *Proceedings of the Human Factors Society 33rd Annual Meeting* Denver, Colorado, pp. 445–449.

GOODWIN, C. (1981). *Conversational Organization: Interaction Between Speakers and Hearers.* New York: Academic Press.

GOODWIN, C. & GOODWIN, M. J. (1987). Concurrent operations on talk: notes on the interactive organization of assessments. *IPRA Papers in Pragmatics.* **1,** 1–54.

HALASZ, F. G., MORAN, T. P. & TRIGG, R. H. (1987). NoteCards in a nutshell. In *Proceedings of the Conference on Computer–Human Interaction and Graphics Interface,* Toronto, pp. 45–52.

HEATH, C. (1986). *Body Movement and Speech in Medical Interaction.* Cambridge, UK: Cambridge University Press.

ISHII, H. (1990). TeamWorkStation: towards a seamless shared workspace. In *Proceedings of the Conference on Computer-Supported Cooperative Work,* Los Angeles, California, pp. 13–26.

KENDON, A. (1986). Current issues in the study of gesture. In J. L. NESPOULOUS, P. PERRON & A. R. LECOURS, Eds. *The Biological Foundations of Gestures: Motor and Semiotic Aspects,* pp. 23–47. Hillsdale, NJ: Lawrence Erlbaum Associates.

KRUEGER, M. W. (1982). *Artificial Reality.* Reading, MA: Addison-Wesley.

LAKIN, F. (1986). A performing medium for working group graphics. In *Proceedings of the Conference on Computer-Supported Cooperative Work,* Austin, Texas, pp. 255–266. Reprinted (1988) in I. GREIF, Ed. *Computer-Supported Cooperative Work: A Book of Readings,* pp. 367–396. San Mateo, CA: Morgan Kaufmann.

LEVINSON, S. C. (1983). Conversational structure. In *Pragmatics,* pp. 284–370. Cambridge, UK: Cambridge University Press.

MANTEI, M. (1988). Capturing the capture lab concepts: a case study in the design of computer supported meeting environments. In *Proceedings of the Conference on Computer-Supported Cooperative Work,* Portland, Oregon, pp. 257–270.

McNEILL, D. (1985). So you think gestures are nonverbal? *Psychological Review,* **92,** 350–371.

MINNEMAN, S. L. & BLY, S. A. (1990). Experiences in the development of a multi-user drawing tool. In *Proceedings of the Third Guelph Symposium on Computer Mediated Communication,* Guelph, Ontario, pp. 154–167.

SMITH, R. B., O'SHEA, T., O'MALLEY, C., SCANLON, E. & TAYLOR, J. (1989). Preliminary experiments with a distributed, multi-media, problem solving environment. In *Proceedings of the First European Conference on Computer Supported Cooperative Work: EC-CSCW '89,* London, pp. 19–34.

STEFIK, M., BOBROW, D. G., FOSTER, G., LANNING, S. & TATAR, D. (1986). WYSIWIS revised: early experiences with multiuser interfaces. In *Proceedings of the Conference on Computer-Supported Cooperative Work,* Austin, Texas, pp. 276–290. Reprinted (1987). *ACM Transactions on Office Information Systems,* **5,** 147–167.

STEFIK, M., FOSTER, G., BOBROW, D. G., KAHN, K., LANNING, S. & SUCHMAN, L. (1987). Beyond the chalkboard: computer support for collaboration and problem solving in meetings. *Communications of the ACM,* **30,** pp. 32–47. Reprinted (1988) in I. Greif, Ed. *Computer-Supported Cooperative Work: A Book of Readings,* pp. 335–366. San Mateo, CA: Morgan Kaufmann.

TANG, J. C. (1989). *Listing, Drawing and Gesturing in Design: A Study of the Use of Shared Workspaces by Design Teams,* Xerox PARC Technical Report SSL-89-3. Ph.d. thesis, Stanford University.

TANG, J. C. & MINNEMAN, S. L. (1990). VideoDraw: a video interface for collaborative drawing. In *Proceedings of the Conference on Computer–Human Interaction,* Seattle, WA, pp. 313–320.

Appendix A

Assignment statement for the design session:

> You have been hired as designers and human factors experts to make recommendations on the future (two to five year) directions in user-interface design for hand-held remote controllers for home use. In particular, this manufacturer is interested in integrated, multi-purpose remote controllers that might use a video display for feedback; the display could either be integral with the device or superimposed on television.
>
> Become familiar with the controls and features of the following three sets of devices.
> (1) Televisions, Radios, Tape Recorders.
> (2) Analog and Digital Clocks.
> (3) VCR's, Compact Disk Players, Receivers, Tape Decks, Phonographs and Graphic Equalizers.
>
> Prepare at least two typical scenarios that, between them, exercise at least three different devices (from all devices above).
>
> Model—Prepare a 3-D mock-up of the physical parts of your design.
> Story-board—Prepare a story-board that illustrates at least the two scenarios.
> Instructions—Prepare an instruction manual or card that, along with the device makes all of its functions self explanatory.

Appendix B

This appendix presents more details about how the drawing space activity was categorized into the actions and functions of the framework and counted. This exercise of categorizing and counting helped identify some trends in the data that focused the analysis. However, categorizing and counting human activity is an inherently subjective process, and the numbers presented in this appendix should be regarded as indicators, not precise measurements.

The drawing activity was first categorized into discrete units of listing, drawing or gesturing. A unit of activity is described as an act of listing, drawing or gesturing accomplished by one participant to express a thought, idea or piece of information to some level of completion. A unit is not defined strictly by mechanical parameters (e.g. pen touches paper, a duration of time). Rather, the activity was categorized according to semantic units (e.g. documenting a phrase, sketching a remote control shape, enacting a control gesture). Several guidelines were used to help determine

Action / Function	LIST	DRAW	GESTURE	Total
Store information	40	19	1	60 (27%)
Express ideas	2	63	33	98 (43%)
Mediate interaction	0	21	46	67 (30%)
Total	42 (19%)	103 (46%)	80 (35%)	225

FIGURE 8. Distribution of drawing space activities in the framework. Drawing space activities from a 1-1/2 hour design session classified according to the actions and functions of the framework.

the boundaries of units of activity:

- It is specific to a participant (i.e. another participant performing a similar activity is logged as a separate unit);
- it may occur in different spurts over a short period of time (e.g. completing a drawing may be interrupted by pausing to talk but still be counted as one unit);
- it is often indicated by cues from the accompanying talk or mechanical behavior (e.g. shifts in the discussion topic, long pauses, laying down the pen).

Incidental activities that naturally accompany talk (e.g. hand waving, graphic marks that have no apparent intent) are not logged as units of activity.

Each workspace activity was categorized according to what action (listing, drawing, gesturing) and function (storing information, expressing ideas, mediating interaction) it primarily accomplished. Many of the observed workspace activities displayed characteristics of more than one category (e.g. an activity that involved both drawing and gesturing, or that both expressed an idea and directed attention). In some cases, these activities were classified into more than one category, to represent their dual nature. Some insights gained from using this framework emerged from the difficulty in classifying drawing space activities into the categories of the framework and accounting for all of the observed activities.

Figure 8 shows the distribution of drawing space activity units according to the categories in the framework. These statistics were collected from a design session that lasted one hour and a half. The data indicate that a substantial proportion (35%) of the activity involved using gestures. Besides using the drawing space to store information, it was used extensively to express ideas and mediate interaction. Hence, the research focused on the use of hand gestures and the process of creating and using drawings in collaborative activity. Tang (1989) reports on more details from this analysis of units of drawing space activities.

3

Twinkling lights and nested loops: distributed problem solving and spreadsheet development

Bonnie A. Nardi

James R. Miller

In contrast to the common view of spreadsheets as "single-user" programs, we have found that spreadsheets offer surprisingly strong support for cooperative development of a wide variety of applications. Ethnographic interviews with spreadsheet users showed that nearly all of the spreadsheets used in the work environments studied were the result of collaborative work by people with different levels of programming and domain expertise. We describe how spreadsheet users cooperate in developing, debugging and using spreadsheets. We examine the properties of spreadsheet software that enable cooperation, arguing that: (1) the division of the spreadsheet into two distinct programming layers permits effective distribution of computational tasks across users with different levels of programming skill; and (2) the spreadsheet's strong visual format for structuring and presenting data supports sharing of domain knowledge among co-workers.

1. Introduction

People organize themselves and their work so that problems can be solved collectively (Vygotsky, 1979; Bosk, 1980; Lave, 1988; Newman, 1989; Seifert & Hutchins, 1989). We are interested in the artifacts that support and encourage this collective problem solving. A spreadsheet is a "cognitive artifact" (Norman, unpublished manuscript; Chandrasekaran, 1981; Holland & Valsiner, 1988; Norman & Hutchins, 1988) that can be understood and shared by a group of people, providing a point of cognitive contact that mediates cooperative work. In this paper we examine the shared development of spreadsheet applications. We report the results of our ethnographic study of spreadsheet use in which we found that users with different levels of programming skill and domain knowledge collaborate informally to produce spreadsheet applications. In the first part of the paper we present a descriptive, empirical report of collaborative work practices, documenting the kinds of cooperation found among spreadsheet users, and the ways in which problem solving is distributed across users with different skills and interests. In the second part of the paper we describe and analyse the characteristics of spreadsheet software that support cooperative work.

In contrast to studies of computer-supported cooperative work (CSCW) that focus on software systems specifically designed to support cooperative work within an organization (Grudin, 1988), we address how a certain class of traditional personal computer applications—spreadsheets—function as *de facto* cooperative work environments. We describe how spreadsheet users work together, even though spreadsheets lack "designed-in" technological support for cooperative work.

We use the term "cooperative work" in the general sense of "multiple persons working together to produce a product or service" (Bannon & Schmidt, 1989). In this paper we want to draw attention to a form of cooperative computing already well established in office environments. As we will describe, spreadsheets emerge as the product of several people working together, through not in formally designated teams, task forces, or committees. On the contrary, spreadsheet work flows across different users in fluid, informal ways, and cooperation among spreadsheet users has a spontaneous, self-directed character.

Our research highlights two forms of cooperative work that are central to computer-based work and that have received little attention in the CSCW community: the sharing of programming expertise and the sharing of domain knowledge. Because of the CSCW emphasis on computer systems that enhance interpersonal communication (e.g. e-mail, remote conferencing, shared white-boards), the importance of collaboration in programming itself has been over-looked. The current interest in "empowering users" through participatory design methods (Bjerknes, Ehn & Kyng, 1987) and end user programming systems (Panko, 1988) will, we believe, begin to draw attention to collaborative programming practices of the kind we describe in this paper. The sharing of domain knowledge has been only implicitly recognized in CSCW research; studies tend to focus on communication techniques themselves, rather than on what is being communicated. In this paper we discuss the implications of the particular visual representation of the spreadsheet for communicating analyses based on numeric data.

Since 1986 about five million spreadsheet programs have been sold to personal computer users, second in number only to text editors, and far ahead of any other kind of software (Alsop, 1989). Spreadsheets deserve our interest as the only widely used end user programming environment; text editing and drawing packages are used by many, but involve no programming. With spreadsheets, even unsophisti-cated users can write programs in the form of formulas that establish numerical relations between data values. Users who show no particular interest in computers *per se* voluntarily write their own spreadsheet programs, motivated by interests beyond or completely unrelated to job requirements—a claim that cannot be made for any other kind of software that we know of. In large part this is because the spreadsheet's "twinkling lights"†—the automatically updating cell values—prove irresistible. Spreadsheet users experience a real sense of computational power as their modifications to data values and formulas appear instantly and visibly in the spreadsheet.

Despite the prevalence of spreadsheets in the personal computing world, spreadsheets have not been widely studied. Kay (1984), Hutchins, Hollan and Norman (1986), and Lewis and Olson (1987) enumerated some of the benefits of spreadsheets which include a concrete, visible representation of data values, immediate feedback to the user, and the ability to apply formulas to blocks of cells. There are some experimental studies of spreadsheet use that focused on small aspects of the user interface; for example, Olson and Nilsen (1987) contrasted the methods by which subjects entered formulas in two different spreadsheet products. (See also Brown & Gould, 1987; Napier, Lane, Batsell & Guadango, 1989.) In

† We are indebted to Ralph Kimball of Application Design Incorporated of Los Gatos, California for this turn of phrase.

another type of study, Doyle (1990) reported his experiences of teaching students to use Lotus 1-2-3,† though most of his observations could apply to any kind of software (e.g. inconsistencies in file naming conventions). Other researchers have used spreadsheets as a model for various kinds of programming environments (Van Emden, Ohki & Takeuchi, 1985; Piersol, 1986; Lewis & Olson, 1987; Spenke & Beilken, 1989).

Our study began with the traditional "single-user application" perspective. We were (and still are) interested in spreadsheets as computational devices, and wanted to learn more about how spreadsheets users take the basic structure of a spreadsheet and mould it into an application that addresses some specific need. In particular, we were interested in the success *non-programmers* have had in building spreadsheet applications. We saw no reason to dispute Grudin's (1988) comments that spreadsheets are "single-user applications" in which "an individual's success . . . is not likely to be affected by the backgrounds of other group members", and that "motivational and political factors" are unimportant for spreadsheet users. However, as the study progressed, we were struck by two things:

- **Spreadsheet co-development is the rule, not the exception.** In the office environments we studied, most spreadsheets come about through the efforts of more than one person. The feeling of co-development is very strong; people regularly spoke of how "we" built a spreadsheet, and were very aware of the cooperative nature of the development process.
- **Spreadsheets support the sharing of both programming and domain expertise.** Because of our focus on end-user programming, we soon noticed that one reason spreadsheet users are so productive is that they successfully enlist the help of other, more knowledgeable users in constructing their spreadsheets. In the same way, experienced co-workers share domain knowledge with less experienced colleagues, using the spreadsheet as a medium of communication.

We do not mean to suggest that spreadsheets are never developed by individual users working completely independently. But presupposing that spreadsheets are "single-user" applications, blinds us to seeing the cooperative use of spreadsheets of which we found much evidence in our study. We will describe how spreadsheet users:

(1) share programming expertise through exchanges of code;
(2) transfer domain knowledge via spreadsheet templates and the direct editing of spreadsheets;
(3) debug spreadsheets cooperatively;
(4) use spreadsheets for cooperative work in meetings and other group settings; and
(5) train each other in new spreadsheet techniques.

We will elaborate these activities via ethnographic examples from the research.

2. Methods and informants

The ideas presented in this paper are based on our ethnographic research including extensive interviewing of spreadsheet users, and analysis of some of their spread-

† Lotus and 1-2-3 are registered trademarks of Lotus Development Corporation.

sheets which we collected during the course of interviewing. We have chosen to study a small number of people in some depth to learn how they construct, debug and use spreadsheets. We are interested in the kinds of problems for which people use spreadsheets and how they themselves structure the problem solving process— topics that by their very nature cannot be studied under the controlled conditions of the laboratory. We have also examined and worked with several different spreadsheet products including VisiCalc (the original personal computer spread- sheet), Lotus 1-2-3 and Microsoft Excel.†

For the field research we interviewed and tape recorded conversations with spreadsheet users in their offices and homes.‡ Our informants were found through an informal process of referral. We told them that we were interested in software for users with little formal programming education and that we wanted to talk to people actively using spreadsheets. The interviews were conversational in style, intended to capture users' experiences in their own words. A fixed set of open-ended questions was asked of each user (see the appendix for the list of questions), though the questions were asked as they arose naturally in the context of the conversation, not necessarily in the order in which they appear in the appendix. During the interview sessions we viewed users' spreadsheets on-line, and sometimes in paper form, and discussed the uses and construction of the spreadsheets. The material in this paper is based on about 350 pages of transcribed interviews with 11 users, though we focus on a smaller subset here to provide ethnographic detail.

Informants in the study were college-educated people employed in diverse companies, from small start-ups to large corporations of several thousand employees. Informants had varying degrees of computer experience ranging from someone who had only recently learned to use a computer to professional programmers. Most were non-programmers with three to five years experience with spreadsheets. Informant names used here are fictitious. Five sets of spreadsheet users illustrate the cooperative nature of spreadsheet development:

- *Betty and Buzz* run a start-up company with eight employees. Betty is the chief financial officer of the company and Buzz a developer of the product the company produces. Betty does not have a technical background though she has acquired substantial computer knowledge on her own, largely through using spreadsheets. Buzz is a professional programmer. They use spreadsheets for their customer lists, prospective customer lists, product sales, evaluation units, tradeshow activity and accounts receivable.
- *Ray* manages a finance department for a large corporation and has a large staff. He has an engineering degree and an MBA, and some limited programming experience. He uses spreadsheets to plan budget allocations across several different departments, to track departmental expenses and headcounts, and to forecast future budgetary needs.
- *Louis,* in his seventies, is semi-retired and works as an engineering consultant about two hours a day for a large manufacturing corporation. He has been working with Lotus 1-2-3§ for about a year, and has no other computer experience of any kind (he uses Lotus as his word processor). Louis's main application is analysing test data from his engineering simulations of radar designs. He learned Lotus with the help of his son Peter, an architectural engineer.

† Microsoft and Excel are registered trademarks of Microsoft Corporation.

‡ The interviews were conducted by the first author. We use the plural "we" here for expository ease.

§ All those in our study use either Lotus 1-2-3 or Microsoft Excel.

- *Laura and Jeremy* work for a medium size high tech equipment manufacturer. Laura is an accountant, the controller of the company. She directs a staff of eight, all of whom use spreadsheets. Laura is knowledgeable about spreadsheets but has no programming experience. Jeremy, Laura's manager, is the chief financial officer of the company. He is skilled at spreadsheet macro and template development.
- *Jennifer* is an accountant in a rapidly growing telecommunications company. She works closely with the chief financial officer of the company. Jennifer has been working with spreadsheets for about five years. She took a course in BASIC in college but has no other computer science education.

Segments from the interviews will be presented at some length as we feel it is most convincing to let users speak for themselves. The segments are verbatim transcriptions.

3. Cooperative development of spreadsheets

3.1. BRIDGING DIFFERENCES IN PROGRAMMING EXPERTISE

Spreadsheets support cooperative work among people with different levels of programming skill. We have found it useful to break the continuum of skill level into three groups: non-programmers, local developers and programmers. Non-programmers have little or no formal training or experience in programming. Local developers have substantial experience with some applications, and often much more willingness to read manuals. Programmers have a thorough grasp of at least one general programming language and a broad, general understanding of computing. Local developers typically serve as consultants for non-programmers in their work environments. Local developers may in turn seek assistance from programmers.

It is also important to note that the three kinds of users vary along another related dimension: *interest in computing*. In some cases non-programmers may be budding hackers, but many are simply neutral towards computers, regarding them as a means to an end rather than objects of intrinsic interest. A key to understanding non-programmers' interaction with computers is to recognize that they are not simply under-skilled programmers who need assistance learning the complexities of programming. Rather, they are not programmers at all. They are business professionals or scientists or other kinds of domain specialists whose jobs involve computational tasks. In contrast, local developers show a direct interest in computing, though their skills may be limited in comparison to programmers as a result of other demands on their time.

Betty and Buzz's work on spreadsheets for their company's finances offers a good example of cooperation among spreadsheet users with different levels of programming skill. As individuals, Betty and Buzz are quite different. Betty has a strong focus on her work as chief financial officer, and claims few programming skills. She has limited knowledge of the more sophisticated capabilities of the spreadsheet product she uses, knows little about the features of competing spreadsheets, and relies on Buzz and other more experienced users for assistance with difficult programming tasks, training, and consulting. In contrast, Buzz has a clear technical focus and strong programming skills. He is well-informed about the capabilities of the spreadsheet product in use in the company and of other competing products, and provides Betty with the technical expertise she needs.

From this perspective, then, Betty and Buzz seem to be the stereotypical end-user/developer pair, and it is easy to imagine their development of a spreadsheet to be equally stereotypical: Betty specifies what the spreadsheet should do based on her knowledge of the domain, and Buzz implements it. *This is not the case.* Their cooperative spreadsheet development departs from this scenario in two important ways:

(1) Betty constructs her basic spreadsheets *without assistance from Buzz*. She programs the parameters, data values and formulas into her models. In addition, Betty is completely responsible for the design and implementation of the user interface. She makes effective use of color, shading, fonts, outlines, and blank cells to structure and highlight the information in her spreadsheets.

(2) When Buzz helps Betty with a complex part of the spreadsheet such as graphing or a complex formula, his work is expressed in terms of Betty's original work. He adds small, more advanced pieces of code to Betty's basic spreadsheet; Betty is the main developer and he plays an adjunct role as consultant.

This is an important shift in the responsibility of system design and implementation. Non-programmers can be responsible for most of the development of a spreadsheet, implementing large applications that they would not undertake if they had to use conventional programming techniques. Non-programmers may never learn to program recursive functions and nested loops, but they can be extremely productive with spreadsheets. Because less experienced spreadsheet users become engaged and involved with their spreadsheets, they are motivated to reach out to more experienced users when they find themselves approaching the limits of their understanding of, or interest in, more sophisticated programming techniques.

Non-programming spreadsheet users benefit from the knowledge of local developers and programmers in two ways:

(1) Local developers and programmers *contribute code* to the spreadsheets of less experienced users. Their contributions may include: macros; the development of sophisticated graphs and charts; custom presentation formats, such as a new format for displaying cell values; formulas with advanced spreadsheet functions such as date-time operations; and complex formulas, such as a formula with many levels of nested conditionals.

(2) Experienced users *teach less experienced users* about advanced spreadsheet features. This teaching occurs informally, not in training classes. Often a user will see a feature in someone else's spreadsheet that they would like to have, and he or she simply asks how to use it.

As shown in the way Betty and Buzz divide up spreadsheet tasks, the problem solving needed to produce a spreadsheet is distributed across a person who knows the domain well and can build most of the model, and more sophisticated users whose advanced knowledge is used to enhance the spreadsheet model, or to help the less experienced user improve spreadsheet skills. Compare this division of labor with traditional computing which requires the services of a data processing department, or expert system development in which knowledge engineers are necessary. In these cases, the domain specialist has no role as a developer, and domain knowledge must first be filtered through a systems analyst, programmer, or knowledge engineer before it is formulated into a program.

Our interview with Ray offers another example of co-development. Ray is a local developer who makes use of programmers for some aspects of spreadsheet development. As with Betty and Buzz, the chief difference between the spreadsheet environment and traditional programming is that more experienced users develop only specific pieces of the spreadsheet program, working directly off the basic work done by the original user. For example, Ray recently commissioned a set of Lotus macros for custom menus to guide data input for the spreadsheets used by his staff. He prefers to concentrate on using spreadsheets for forecasting future trends and allocating money among the departments he serves—his real work. Ray is not interested in becoming an expert macro writer, even though he has taken an advanced Lotus 1-2-3 class where macros were covered. In the following exchange we are looking at the custom menus:

Interviewer: . . . [these menus] look like they'd be pretty useful. And who developed those for you?
Ray: A programmer down in Customer Support.
Interviewer: Okay, not somebody in your group. You just sent out the work, and . . .
Ray: Yeah, well, essentially, you know, I came at it conceptually, this is what I'd like to see, and they developed it. So [the programmer] made [the menus] interactive, set up the customized use.

Ray has reached the limits of his interest in programming advanced spreadsheet features himself. But he is not limited to spreadsheets without these features; he distributes the work to someone who has more interest in such things. This task distribution is similar to traditional software development in that a user provides a specification to a developer for implementation. The difference, however, is that here the user has constructed the program into which the contributed code fits. In some sense, the roles of user and "chief programmer" (Brooks, 1975) have been merged.

Spreadsheets also support cooperation between users with different programming expertise via tutoring and consulting exchanges. For example, Louis has learned almost everything he knows about Lotus 1-2-3 from his son Peter. He avoids the manual, finding it easier to be tutored by Peter. Louis's spreadsheet use, highlights an important feature of the cooperative development of spreadsheets: because the initial effort to build something really useful is relatively small, less experienced users, having had the reward of actually developing a real application, are motivated to continue to learn more, at least up to a point. Louis is starting to have Peter teach him about controlling the presentation format; for the first several months of use he concentrated only on creating basic models of parameters, data values and formulas. In general, users like Louis successfully engage other, more experienced users in the development of their spreadsheet models. They make use of problem-solving resources—i.e. more experienced users—in a very productive manner, building on their existing knowledge in a self-paced way, as they feel ready to advance.

Distributing tasks across different users and sharing programming expertise are characteristic of many programming environments—programming in Pascal or Lisp or C would almost certainly involve such collaboration. However, with spreadsheets the collaboration is specified quite differently: the end user, usually relegated to "naive user" status in traditional software development, comes center stage, appearing in the role of main developer. Spreadsheets have been successful because they give real computational power to non-programmers. Accountants and biologists and engineers who may never have taken a computer science course build useful, often complex spreadsheet applications (Arganbright, 1986). Spreadsheet users are not "naive users" or "novices"; they command knowledge of both their domain of interest and the programming techniques necessary to analyse problems in their domain. With spreadsheets, problem solving is distributed such that end users do not rely on programmers as the indispensable implementers of a set of specifications; instead end users are *assisted by* programmers who supply them with small pieces of complex code, or with training in advance features, as they build their own applications.

4. Bridging differences in domain expertise

An important aspect of cooperative work is the sharing of domain knowledge. Because spreadsheet users build their own applications, spreadsheets allow the direct transfer of domain expertise between co-workers, obviating the need to include a programmer or other outside specialist in the development cycle. Domain knowledge flows from manager to staff since managers tend to be more experienced than those they supervise, and also from staff to manager, as staff members often have specialized local knowledge needed by managers. This direct transfer of domain expertise provides efficient knowledge sharing and helps co-workers learn from one another. Instead of transferring domain expertise to a programmer or systems analyst or knowledge engineer who may never need it again, less experienced workers directly benefit from the knowledge of co-workers.

Spreadsheets mediate collaborative work by providing a physical medium in which users share domain knowledge. Spreadsheet users distribute domain expertise by directly editing each other's spreadsheets, and by sharing templates. For example, Laura works very closely with Jeremy, her manager, in developing spreadsheets. Jeremy happens to be a skilled spreadsheet user who provides macros and tutoring that Laura and her staff use. However, the more interesting distinction to be drawn here is centered around Jeremy's greater experience with their company, its manufacturing and marketing procedures, and its managerial and budgeting practices. Spreadsheets provide a foundation for thinking about different aspects of the budgeting process and for controlling budgeting activity. In the annual "Budget Estimates" spreadsheet that Laura is responsible for, many critical data values are based on assumptions about product sales, costs of production, headcounts, and other variables that must be estimated accurately for the spreadsheet to produce valid results. Through a series of direct edits to the spreadsheet, Laura and Jeremy fine-tune the structure and data values in "Budget Estimates". Laura describes this process:

Interviewer: Now when you say you and your boss work on this thing [the spreadsheet] together, what does that mean? Does he take piece A and you take piece B—how do you divide up [the work]?
Laura: How did we divide it up? It wasn't quite like that. I think more . . . not so much that we divided things up and said, "OK, you do this page and you do this section of the spreadsheet and I'll do that section," it was more . . . I did the majority of the input and first round of looking at things for reasonableness. Reasonableness means, "What does the bottom line look like?" When you look at the 12 months in the year, do you have some

funny swings that you could smooth out? Because you want it to be a little bit smoother. So what can you do for that? Or, if you do have some funny spikes or troughs, can you explain them? For example, there's one really big trade show that everybody in the industry goes to . . . So our sales that month are typically low and our expenses are high. This trade show is very, very expensive . . .

Interviewer: So there's a spike in your [expenses and a trough in sales] . . .

Laura: Yeah. So as long as you can *explain* it, then that's OK. So what my boss did was, I would do the first round of things and then I would give him the floppy or the print-outs and I'd say, "Well this looks funny to me. I don't know, is that OK, is it normal? Should we try to do something about it?" And so what he did was he took the spreadsheets and then he would just make minor adjustments.

Interviewer: Now was he adjusting formulas or data or . . . ?

Laura: Data.

. . .

Interviewer: . . . So it was a process of fine tuning the basic model that you had developed. And then you of course had to get his changes back, and look at them and understand them.

Laura: Yes. And one thing he did do, was, he added another section to the model, just another higher level of analysis where he compared it to our estimate for this year. He basically just created another page in the model—he added that on.

  In preparing a budget that involves guesswork about critical variables, Laura is able to benefit from her manager's experience. They communicate via the spreadsheet as he literally takes her spreadsheet and makes changes directly to the model. She has laid the groundwork, provided the first line of defense in the "reasonableness" checking; Jeremy then adjusts values to conform to his more experienced view of what a good estimate looks like. Jeremy also made a major structural change to the spreadsheet, adding another level of analysis that he felt would provide a useful comparison. The spreadsheet was cooperatively constructed, though not in a simple division of tasks; instead the model emerged in successive approximations as Laura and Jeremy passed it back and forth for incremental refinement.

  Spreadsheet users often exchange templates as a way of distributing domain expertise. Jeremy, for example, prepares budget templates used by Laura and her staff. They contain formulas and a basic structure for data that he works out because of his greater knowledge of the business. Laura and her staff fill in the templates according to their knowledge of their individual areas. Laura and her staff are doing more than "data entry"; as in the "Budget Estimates" spreadsheet, estimates requiring an understanding of many factors often make up a significant aspect of a spreadsheet, and deriving these estimates demands thought. Users such as Laura may also specialize a template if their particular area requires additional information, such as another budget line item. The use of templates takes advantage of domain expertise at local levels, such as that of Laura and her staff, and higher levels, such as Jeremy's.

  Ray's work with spreadsheets provides another example of how users share spreadsheet templates. Ray prepared "targeting templates" for his staff in order to standardize the process of targeting expenses. Because of his wider perspective looking across several departments, Ray is in the best position to develop a standard. The templates also contain the custom menus that facilitate data input. Each staff member builds the spreadsheet for his or her area on top of the template, insuring that minimum requirements for data collection and analysis are met, and insuring that the best possible information at the local level goes into the spreadsheets. Ray links them together. In these spreadsheets, problem solving is distributed over users who vary in both level of programming skill and domain knowledge: Ray, a local developer with domain expertise, provided the basic template; a programmer created the menus constructed of macros; and Ray's staff members, domain experts in their departments, supply data values for their respective areas.

5. Cooperative use

Many spreadsheets are destined from the start for the boardroom or the boss's desk or the auditor's file. In our study, spreadsheet users were very aware of the importance of presenting their spreadsheets to others—Laura stated, "I usually think in terms of my stuff [her spreadsheets] as being used by somebody else"—and users constructed spreadsheets with effective presentation in mind.

Spreadsheets are a common sight at meetings and in informal exchanges between co-workers—usually in paper copy or slide format. The use of paper copies and slides of spreadsheets is another means by which co-workers share domain knowledge. Some workers work with spreadsheets exclusively in hardcopy form and are not users of the software—for example executives who analyse and modify paper copies of spreadsheet models prepared by their staff members, and who present spreadsheets on slides and handouts at meetings.

In the following exchange we are discussing a budgeting spreadsheet Jennifer created for her company's chief financial officer. She condensed 43 pages of data from a mainframe application (prepared by the MIS department) into one summary page. We begin by looking at the MIS data:

Jennifer: These are the budget numbers. And then it shows the detail of what was purchased against those budget numbers, and when and how much month-to-date and year-to-date against those. And it shows the actual [amount] spent and variance from the budget.
Interviewer: And this really does have a lot of detail—it's down to the fabric on the chains.
Jennifer: Uh huh, ha! . . . everybody wants to know what we spent our money on, and, "How much do we have left?"
Interviewer: Now what do you do with this information?
Jennifer: . . . we have a presentation for the Board of Directors and the CFO [Chief Financial Officer] makes, but I prepare all this information for him. I compile this. I condense it onto a spreadsheet. . . . So I summarize the larger items, say, you know, the H-P 3000 [a Hewlett-Packard computer recently purchased by her company] for example. That's one of the big items that I pull out. . . . The Board of Directors does not want to see [a lot of] detail—they just want something very summarized. . . . So now it's down from 43 pages to one page. So mine shows the year-to-date budget . . . but it's all summarized into large dollar value items within each functional area.
. . .
Interviewer: Now what happens . . . when they go into the meeting and the CFO presents it? Does he explain it to the Board of Directors, or just put it up on a slide, or, what do they do with this?
Jennifer: . . . he hands out a copy to everybody, and then he puts it up on a slide, and he goes through each of the areas where they are going to be over [-budget]. And he was also presenting this so he could get approval for next quarter's budget. . . . he was showing them the . . . Q3 [Third Quarter] forecast column, and saying, "Okay, that is how much we need to approve it." And, "Where are we going from here?" Also, "What are we anticipating?"

The spreadsheet artifact is used by the CFO to organize and stimulate discussion in the Board of Directors meeting. The structures and cell values of the spreadsheet are meaningful to the board members; for example, the CFO points to the "Q3 forecast column" and individual data values such as the number showing "how much we need to approve (the Q3 budget)." Larger issues, e.g. "Where are we going from here?" are also introduced in the context of viewing the spreadsheet in the meeting.

Later in the interview Jennifer describes how the summary spreadsheet was created. The creation of this spreadsheet is an example of cooperative development; we include it here to show how development and use flow together as users collaborate in creating a spreadsheet whose ultimate purpose is a presentation to others. The final spreadsheet presented to the Board was the result of quite a multi-media production: Jennifer created the original spreadsheet in Excel, gave a paper copy to the CFO for his input, made pencil annotations on another paper copy because the CFO's changes came back via voice mail, and finally updated the on-line spreadsheet:

Interviewer: . . . What are your little pencil scribbles on here [a paper copy of the one-page spreadsheet]?
Jennifer: Oh, this is what I gave to the CFO at first, just comparing Q2 year-to-date budget to Q2 year-to-date actuals. And he said, "Well, for the board meeting I want [some other things]". Every time you do this he wants it differently. So I can't anticipate it. I just give him what I think [he wants] and then he says, "Ah, no, well, I want to have projected Q3 and projected Q4, and then total projected, and then have the whole year's plan on there". So that is what I was scribbling on here.
Interviewer: Was this in a meeting with him where he was telling you?
Jennifer: Actually he sent me a voice mail message. So that is why I take notes and go back and listen to the message again and say, "Now did I write this down right?"

Laura also described the use of spreadsheets in meetings. Her comments show that the spreadsheet organizes discussion, as we have seen in the preceding example. She notes the clarifications required to reveal assumptions underlying the spreadsheet models. Making such clarifications is often a part of meetings where spreadsheets are presented. Some spreadsheet users, including Laura, attach memos which list their assumptions (e.g. a budget allocation is based on department revenue not headcount). In the following discussion Laura describes a meeting she attended where executives are poring over spreadsheets and memos:

Laura: . . . So he [the president of the company] is sitting there and he's looking at [the spreadsheets and memos], and you're just kind of sitting there [she mimics slumping over in boredom, waiting for the president to ask a question] and he refers back and forth to various pages, whether he's looking at the budget [a spreadsheet] or whether he's looking at the last year's actuals [a spreadsheet] or he's looking at a list of assumptions.
Interviewer: So he looks at all of them?
Laura: That's right Yeah . . . And occasionally he asks a question and you say, "Oh, okay, that's this here. [She points to an imaginary spot of importance on the spreadsheet.] And you know here's this and this. And *this* was the [she waves her hand indicating a phrase like "such-and-such"] and *that* was because of [another gesture], or, "Oh, I didn't think about that!"

Laura explains how spreadsheets are used in distributed locations:

Laura: . . . And also another thing that's really classic, I mean I've experienced this before [at other jobs], is you do about as much as you can . . . and then he [the executive] gets on the

airplane to go to England [or wherever] and he's on a plane for 10 or 12 hours and he looks at [the spreadsheets] again. And he's totally uninterrupted. . . . And he probably has more space up there than he does in his office! And then . . . they'll get where they are [going] and either phone call or fax.
Interviewer: To ask you a question?
Laura: Yeah. To get an explanation, or more detail, or "What did you say here? What did you assume there?"
. . .
Laura: . . . [Last year my boss and I spent a lot of time on a large spreadsheet that had to be faxed.] . . . We had to make some modifications in the spreadsheet . . . to add more types of expenses, or break things out into more detail. And we sat there together sort of hunched around the screen. We had to fax about 40 [pages of print-out]. No, it was more than that. We faxed a hundred pages to England one night . . . because they had to have it. They needed to have it prior to the meetings.
Interviewer: Wow.
Laura: So they would have an opportunity to digest it and come up with their list of questions.

As the descriptions show, though the spreadsheet provides a great deal of useful data, and is meaningful to the executives and others who use them, it does not fully expose all the assumptions in a model. However, the necessary verbal explanations are quickly produced (as in the faxed spreadsheet followed up by phone calls) because the spreadsheet developers are also the domain experts—there is no need to involve programmers or MIS personnel. While spreadsheets could benefit by better facilities for exposing assumptions, the spreadsheet artifact works as well as it does because users themselves control the process of putting information into spreadsheet models. Problem solving is handled locally, without requiring the intervention of personnel from other work groups—especially valuable, as Laura described, in fighting last minute fires.

A rather emblematic example of the cooperative use of spreadsheets is provided by Louis's meticulous black binder of spreadsheet print-outs that he carries between home (where his computer is) and office (where he has meetings). Although Louis's current spreadsheets contain none of the advanced presentation features provided by spreadsheet products (because he is just learning them), the simple print-outs are a regular feature of Louis's meetings with his colleagues as they discuss new designs for radar. It is a major benefit for Louis, an unsophisticated spreadsheet user, that the development environment and the presentation environment are the same in spreadsheets; once Louis has programmed his model, he has also created an effective presentation for group discussions, with no additional work.

Though users developing spreadsheets sometimes viewed each other's spreadsheets on-line, we found no extended examples of cooperative use of on-line spreadsheets, e.g. for the duration of a meeting. Hardcopies were virtually always used, and seemed to work well since the contents of the spreadsheet were being studied not manipulated. Productive uses of on-line spreadsheets are easily imagined, e.g. organizing a meeting around trying out different what-if scenarios and projecting the spreadsheet views overhead.

6. Cooperative debugging

In an experiment, Brown and Gould (1987) found that almost half of all spreadsheets constructed by experienced spreadsheet users contained errors. Most errors were in the formulas. Formula errors were most commonly caused by inserting erroneous cell references into formulas (pointing to the wrong cell or typing the wrong cell reference); incorrectly copying a formula so that the new formula got erroneous cell references; and putting the wrong item in a column. It is difficult to know how representative these specific types of errors are because the data consisted of only 11 formula errors, out of a total of 17 errors across the nine subjects in the study (each subject committed at least one error in at least one of the three spreadsheets they constructed for the study). It does seem likely that formula errors are more common than data entry errors since much more can go wrong in a formula.

While Brown and Gould's finding seems generally valid, if it were taken out of context—that is, out of the context of the experimenter's laboratory—it could be misinterpreted to suggest that spreadsheets in actual use are full of errors. In our study we found that users devote considerable effort to debugging their spreadsheet models—they are very self-conscious about the probability of error and routinely track down errors before they can do any real harm. Spreadsheet users specifically look for those errors that could have serious consequences. For example, a spreadsheet model with a value for department headcount that is off by one would probably have some budgetary or political implications, whereas being off by one in a forecast of annual budget dollars would not.

Debugging is a task that is distributed across the group—in particular, managers monitor their staffs' spreadsheets. Cooperation is valuable in error correction tasks (in many settings) as errors that become, through over-familiarity, invisible to their authors, are readily apparent when subject to the fresh scrutiny of new viewers.

In the following exchange we are discussing sources of error in the spreadsheets prepared by Ray's staff. Ray checks these spreadsheets himself. He uses "reasonableness checks" (inspecting values to see that they fall within reasonable ranges); footing and cross-footing;† spot checking values with a calculator; and examining formulas, recording the results of the formula checking with pencil and paper:

Interviewer: [Are the staff errors] usually in the data entry of the formulas, or does it vary?
Ray: It's mostly in the formulas. Because I think everybody is careful about making sure they have tie numbers‡ so that you can get the data in. I'm not saying it doesn't happen in data entry, but I think usually it's the formulas that are suspect. Either it's a question of the right kind of formula, or it's a situation where they weren't really careful in terms of . . . what comes first, and link it to what, and that sort of thing, they've got to be careful in that.
Interviewer: [It sounds like] you guys are pretty careful about checking things.
Ray: Yeah, we're pretty careful. Where I think it can get a little difficult is when you have a really large spreadsheet—it's a big model or something—and sometimes it's difficult to check, you know, a pretty extensive spreadsheet.
Interviewer: You mean because of the volume of data, or volume of formulas? What is it about the size that makes it harder?
Ray: You got a tremendous amount of formulas in there that are pointing all kinds of different directions, and you know, it's a pretty big pass to kind of walk back through the whole thing. So you have to be very careful.

† Making sure that the sum of row totals matches the sum of column totals.

‡ A tie number is a known quantity; it provides a sort of anchor within the spreadsheet. If a tie number is incorrect, dependent values are sure to be wrong (unless, by rare chance, incorrect values cancel each other out).

Here Ray noted the difficulty of tracing relations through large spreadsheets ("formulas that are pointing all kinds of different directions"). He finds that while his analysts are generally careful, there is room for error, so he does some checking.

Other informants described similar procedures for catching errors. Laura, for example, described how she verifies cell references in formulas by writing them down and tracing them to their origin in the spreadsheet. Like Ray, she noted that a major source of errors in spreadsheets is complex formulas in large spreadsheets.

Norman (1987) and Seifert and Hutchins (1989) argue that error in the real world is inevitable. Seifert and Hutchins (1989) studied cooperative error correction on board large ships, finding that virtually all navigational errors were "detected and corrected within the navigation team." The errors in spreadsheets could be at least a little less "inevitable" with improvements to spreadsheet software such as views showing cell relations more clearly (perhaps through the use of color, highlighting and filtering), and mechanisms to constrain cell values to allow range and bounds checking. Even with improvements, however, there would still be need for vigilance to eliminate errors, which are, as Norman, Seifert and Hutchins point out, inevitable in the real world. For spreadsheet debugging, as for tasks in other rather different domains (such as navigating large ships), a key part of the error correction solution lies in distributing the work across a group.

7. How spreadsheets support cooperative work practices

We have documented in some detail how spreadsheet users develop, debug and use spreadsheets cooperatively. We now examine the spreadsheet itself, focusing on the support for cooperative work implicit in its design. Though spreadsheets were not deliberately designed to support cooperative work, they nevertheless have two key characteristics that enable collaboration:

(1) Spreadsheet functionality is divided into two distinct programming layers—a *fundamental layer* and an *advanced layer*—that provide a basis for cooperative programming. By cleanly separating basic development tasks from more advanced functionality, the spreadsheet permits a distribution of tasks in which end users accomplish the basic implementation of a spreadsheet model, and those with more sophisticated programming knowledge provide smaller, more advanced contributions in the form of code and training. The notion of "layers" is intended to capture the different aspects of spreadsheet functionality as they relate to the user's tasks of *learning and using spreadsheets*.†

(2) The visual clarity of the spreadsheet *table* exposes the structure and intent of users' models, encouraging the sharing of domain knowledge across users with different levels and kinds of domain knowledge.

7.1. THE SPREADSHEET'S PROGRAMMING LAYERS

How do spreadsheets both meet the needs of the non-programmer and allow for the development of sophisticated applications? The answer lies in the articulation of the two programming layers: the fundamental layer, sufficient for constructing basic

† The layers do not map onto any aspect of the implementation of a spreadsheet product, or a manufacturer's description of a product.

programs, is completely self-contained and independent from the advanced layer of more sophisticated features.

The fundamental layer allows users to build basic spreadsheet models that solve real problems in their domain of interest. Users who know nothing about the advanced layer can create spreadsheets. In our study, Louis was such a user; his work was accomplished entirely within the fundamental layer, and he was just beginning to explore the advanced layer. Once users have grasped the fundamental layer, they learn the advanced layer. The advanced layer is composed of a variety of individual features that can be learned and used separately. Progress in learning advanced spreadsheet features may be very fast or very slow, depending on the user.

Because the features of the fundamental and advanced layers are independent and separately manipulated, the end user can proceed with the main programming of a spreadsheet, leaving more advanced development to local developers or programmers, or learning advanced features when they are needed. We have seen how Ray drew the line at writing macros for data entry, assigning the task to a programmer.

We now look in more detail at the fundamental and advanced layers.

7.1.1. The fundamental layer

To solve a problem with a spreadsheet, the user requires facilities for *computation*, *presentation* and *modeling*. The fundamental layer meets these needs. It is composed of two parts: the *formula language*† which enables computation; and the spreadsheet *table* which provides both a means of structuring data into a model, and a presentation format.

The formula language allows users to compute values in their models by expressing relations among cell values. Each cell value may be a constant or a derived value. A formula is associated with the individual cell whose value it computes. The formula language offers a basic set of arithmetic, financial, statistical and logical functions. To use the formula language, the user must master only two concepts: cells as variables, and functions as relations between variables. The simple algebraic syntax of the formula language is easy to write and understand.

In our study we found that most users normally use fewer than 10 functions in their formulas. Users employ those functions pertinent to their domain (e.g. financial analysis) and do not have need for other functions. Spreadsheet users are productive with a small number of functions because the functions provide *high-level, task-specific operations that do not have to be built up from lower level primitives*. For example, a common spreadsheet operation is to sum the values of a range of cells within a column. The user writes a simple formula that specifies the sum operation and the cells that contain the values to be summed. The cell range is specified compactly by its first and last cell; e.g. SUM(C1:C8) sums cells 1–8 in Column C. In a general programming language, computing this sum would require at least writing a loop iterating through elements of an array, and creating variable names for the loop counter and summation variable. Spreadsheet functions obviate the need to create variable names (cells are named by their position in the grid), and

---

† We refer to "the formula language" because most spreadsheet products have nearly identical languages which differ only in small syntactic details.

the need to create intermediate variables to hold results—non task-related actions that many users find confusing and tiresome (Lewis & Olson, 1987).

Once the user has created some variables and established their relations in formulas, the spreadsheet takes care of the rest. It is responsible for automatically updating dependent values as independent values change. There is no programming effort necessary on the part of the user to make this happen. The spreadsheet user's task is to write a series of small formulas, each associated with an individual cell, rather than the more difficult task of specifying the full control loop of a program as a set of procedures.

The spreadsheet table solves the presentation problems of the basic spreadsheet application. The cells of the table are used to present data values, labels and annotations. In the process of developing the spreadsheet, i.e. entering the data, labels and annotations into the table, the user is at the same time creating the user interface, at no additional development cost. Even a very simple table with no use of color or shading or variable fonts for cell entries is an effective visual format for data presentation (Jarvenpaa & Dickson, 1988; Cameron, 1989; Hoadley, 1990; Nardi & Miller, 1990.

Spreadsheet users must be able to represent the structure of the problem they are trying to solve. The spreadsheet table is a structuring device: the main parameters of a problem are organized into the rows and columns of the spreadsheet, and constants and calculated values are placed in cells. Rows and columns are used to represent the main parameters of a problem. Users know that related things go in rows and columns, and spreadsheet applications take advantage of the simple but powerful semantics provided by the row/column convention. Each cell represents and displays one variable. For calculated values, the spreadsheet associates a visual object, the cell itself, with a small program, the formula. Program code is this distributed over a visual grid, providing a system of compact, comprehensible, easily located program modules (Nardi & Miller, 1990).

What distinguishes the fundamental layer of spreadsheets from the operations a beginner user might learn in a general programming language? First, the high-level facilities for computation, modeling and presentation that we have described shield users from the necessity of working with lower level programming primitives. Users can concentrate more fully on understanding and solving their problems, with much less cognitive overhead devoted to the distraction of coping with the mechanics of the software itself.

Second, because the spreadsheet has so much "built-in" functionality (automatic update, the table as a presentation device), and a high-level language (the formula language), it takes only a few hours for non-programmers to learn to build simple spreadsheet models that solve a real problem in their domain of interest. After a small investment of time, the beginning spreadsheet user has a functioning program of real use (not a toy program or completed exercise), and also an effective visual representation of the application. The spreadsheet user's first efforts yield a complete application, rather than the partial solution that would result from writing the same application in a general programming language. The fast, early success spreadsheet users' experience motivates them to continue to use the software (Nardi & Miller, 1990; Warner, 1990; also Brock, personal communication; Flystra, personal communication).

7.1.2. *The advanced layer*

The advanced layer of the spreadsheet provides functionality that is unnecessary for constructing a basic spreadsheet model. We call its features "advanced" because basic work proceeds without them, not because they are necessarily difficult to learn.

The features of the advanced layer are inessential for basic work, but very useful. They are: conditional and iterative control constructs; macros; advanced functions such as database, date-time, and error trapping functions; graphs and charts; and a user interface toolkit. Each part may be learned and used completely independently of any other part. Some of the advanced capabilities are very easy to learn, such as how to change column width (the first thing Louis was learning), and others are more difficult, such as the use of macros (well-understood by Buzz and Jeremy, used in simple form by Jennifer, understood but avoided by Ray, and not known by Louis, Betty and Laura).

Users learn selected parts of the advanced layer as they need them, and as they feel ready to. Some users in our study could build a spreadsheet and significantly modify the user interface after a day-long training class, and others did nothing but build basic spreadsheets using only the formula language and modeling capabilities of the spreadsheet for several months before learning anything else. Most users do not know all the aspects of the advanced layer.†

The control constructs in the advanced layer of the spreadsheet are simple but useful. They allow users to write IF-THEN-ELSE statements within an individual formula, and to iterate functions over a cell range (a rectangular group of contiguous cells).

The user interface toolkit gives users control over column width, row height, fonts, shading, outlining, color and formatting of cell values (though not all spreadsheet products provide all of these capabilities). Spreadsheets allow users to split the screen so that non-contiguous portions of a spreadsheet may be viewed at once. The graphing and charting capabilities provide graphic views of the individual data values in the cells of the spreadsheet table. Macros allow users to reuse sequences of keystokes. "Advanced" macros provide more general facilities for data and file manipulation, screen control and controlling inter-action with the user during macro execution (e.g. in Lotus 1-2-3, the macro command "GETLABEL" displays a prompt in a control panel, waits for the response to the prompt, and enters the response as a label in a cell). The advanced macros are much like traditional programming functions, but they are stored, loaded, edited and manipulated like other spreadsheet macros.

As we have noted, advanced spreadsheet features often find their way into the spreadsheets of non-programmers as code written by more skilled users. Many users reach the limits of their interest in learning advanced features, at least certain ones such as macros, and do not learn to use them. But spreadsheets also provide a growth path for those interested in continuing to learn. Because the individual features of the advanced layer are independent of one another, users can selectively

---

† We had the fun of stumping Buzz, during an interview, with our knowledge of the IRR—internal rate of return—function in Excel.

learn them when they wish to. Very slow progress in learning features of the advanced layer does not impede the user's ability to do constructive work. Spreadsheets provide a self-paced course of study because the features of the advanced layer are inessential for basic application development and independent of other functionality.

Over time, the distribution of problem solving tasks of an individual user changes; users take on new development tasks as they acquire knowledge of additional spreadsheet functionality. For example, Jeremy described how he "discovered" macro programming. Jeremy is an executive—the chief financial officer of his company—and has never taken a computer science class. He received his MBA from Harvard Business School just prior to the time when quantitative methods (including mandatory instruction in the use of spreadsheets) were introduced into the curriculum. In the following discussion Jeremy explains how he learned about macros from reading the Lotus 1-2-3 manual and talking to programmers. We are examining one of his macros that selects files for printing and sets up printing parameters. The macro utilizes a counter, branching, and binary variables that can have 0 or 1 as values. We have been looking at each line of the macro in detail:

Jeremy: . . . And then [the macro] compares [this variable] with the counter over here.
Interviewer: So this is real programming, basically.
Jeremy: Yes, right! And unfortunately that's what I had to do for me to be able to do this. It is exactly—a program. . . . I found that out later. I didn't realize [that I was programming]. I thought I was being very clever—I was inventing something new!
Interviewer: How did you find out later? Talking to other programmers?
Jeremy: Yeah, well, exactly. I was talking to our programmer, he came over and I showed him, "Look what I've done!" And he looked at me and he says, "Well, any time you want to be a rookie programmer on my staff, you just passed, you just made the grade".
Interviewer: But you were actually able to figure out how to do this by looking at examples in the manual?
Jeremy: That's right. Yeah, because I just mapped out: What is it that I want to do? . . . What I would like to do is to have a series of instructions and have the macro search for those instructions, and based on certain yes/no conditions either perform the operation or go to the next step. That's really all I'm after. And so I kept on looking for [branching mechanisms], and once I found them in the book I found so many different places where I could use them.

There is a gradual tendency for end users to include more complex features in their spreadsheets and to utilize local developers and programmers less. It should be remembered however, that this process may be very gradual, and would not happen at all for many users if they did not have an easy route of entry through the fundamental layer. In contrast, many students resist the frustration and tedium of learning general programming languages and do not become adept at programming in them.

In our study, spreadsheet users most commonly learnt new spreadsheet functionality in collaboration with other users. The non-programmers were extremely resistant to reading manuals (in contrast to local developers like Jeremy who kept searching the manual till he found what he wanted). Non-programmers commented that the manuals often did not explain everything they needed to know to actually use the feature they were trying to learn about. Since this meant that they would have to ask someone to supply the missing information anyway, it seemed easier to ask at the outset.†

Several users in the study, even after learning many aspects of the advanced layer, still relied on more experienced users to show them how to do new things.

7.2. THE SPREADSHEET TABLE

The strong visual representation of an application embedded in the spreadsheet table allows users to directly share domain knowledge through templates and direct edits to the spreadsheets of others, and to collectively use spreadsheets in meetings and other exchanges. Users are able to understand and interpret each other's models with relative ease because the tabular format of the spreadsheet presents such a clear depiction of the parameters and data values in spreadsheet applications.

Spreadsheets have done well at data display by borrowing a commonly used display format—that of the table. Cameron (1989) pointed out that tables have been in use for 5000 years. Inventory tables, multiplication tables and tables of reciprocal values have been found by archaeologists excavating Middle Eastern cultures. Ptolemy, Copernicus, Kepler, Euler, and Gauss used tables. Modern times brought us VisiCalc, in tabular format. VisiCalc was modeled directly on the tabular grid of accountants' columnar paper which contains numbered rows and columns. Today's spreadsheets, while much enhanced in functionality, have not changed the basic VisiCalc format in the smallest detail. A tabular grid in which rows are labeled with numbers and columns are labeled with letters characterizes all commercially available spreadsheets.

Tables excel at showing a large amount of data in a small space and in helping users to identify individual data values (Jarvenpaa & Dickson, 1988; Cameron, 1989)—precisely what is needed for spreadsheet applications because they contain many numeric values, each of which may be important to understanding an application. The perceptual reasons that tables so effectively display discrete data items are not well understood. Cleveland suggests that the notion of "clustering"—the ability to hold a collection of objects in short-term memory and carry out further visual and mental processing—applies to many visual forms (Cleveland, Unpublished data), and it seems relevant to tables. The arrangement of data items in rows and columns appears to permit efficient clustering as users can remember the values in a row or column and then perform other cognitive tasks that involve the values.

The semantics of rows, columns and cells are agreed upon and well understood by spreadsheet users. Because tables are so commonly used to display data of many kinds, most spreadsheet users are already familiar with them. Jarvenpaa and Dickson (1988) noted that many people must be taught to correctly interpret

† Manuals may be confusing at a more fundamental level. Louis gave up completely on manual reading (getting his son Peter to tutor him instead) when he could not figure out the sense in which the word "default" was being used in his Lotus 1-2-3 documentation. (Louis had a rather old copy of the manual, and the newer Lotus 1-2-3 manuals may be less confusing.) The meaning did not jibe with what he understood "default" to mean, nor with the dictionary definition, which, puzzling over the manual, he looked up. During our interview he showed us the definition. Webster's Ninth New Collegiate Dictionary defines default as "failure to do something required by duty or law"; also failure to appear in court, to pay a debt, meet a contract, or agreement, or failure to compete in or finish an appointed contest. Louis' confusion is understandable.

plotted line graphs, but most people are already practised at understanding tables. Users readily comprehend that in a spreadsheet, rows and columns are used to represent the main parameters of a model, and each cell represents and displays one variable. In looking at the spreadsheets of co-workers, the conventions of rows, columns and cells permit users to interpret the intentions of the developer.

Spreadsheets fare less well at clearly exposing the formulas underlying the cell values in the table. As we described in our discussion of debugging, checking a formula from a co-worker's spreadsheet (or from one's own spreadsheet for that matter) involves an awkward pencil and paper procedure of tracking down and verifying cell references in the formulas.† In our study we found that users do follow the pencil and paper procedures to ensure that formulas are correct, but many users cited the necessity of doing this as their main complaint about spreadsheets.

8. Implications for computer supported cooperative work

Our research focused on a single cognitive artifact—the spreadsheet. In the course of examining its structure, following it into meetings, finding out how people use it to solve certain kinds of problems, we learned two things of broad interest to CSCW research:

(1) As users gain more control over computational resources through the use of end user programming systems, cooperative work practices should be anticipated and taken advantage of by designers of such systems. Users will inevitably vary in their skill level, and computational tasks can be distributed over users with different skills through the sharing of code and training.

(2) One of the most fundamental reasons to engage in any kind of cooperative work is to share domain knowledge. Software systems that provide a strong visual format which exposes the structure and data of users' problem-solving models will support and encourage the exchange of domain knowledge.

End user software systems must provide basic development capabilities for non-programmers—what has made spreadsheets so successful is putting computational power into the hands of domain experts. In this distribution of computing tasks, development is shifted away from programmers; they supply limited but technically advanced assistance to developer/domain experts.

The layered design of spreadsheet software seems a good model for other software systems—the ability to build complete, if simple, models with basic, easily learned functionality is the key to getting users off to a quick, rewarding start. The spreadsheet provides for distributed programming by separating the basic functionality of the fundamental layer from the useful but unnecessary features of the advanced layer. End user programming systems should take advantage of the fact that local developers and programmers can reinforce and extend the programs of non-programmers through cooperative work practices—users need not be limited by their lack of programming sophistication.

Non-programmers attain rapid proficiency with the functionality of the fundamental layer because its operations are high-level and task-specific. This implies

---

† Some spreadsheet products provide views of the table in which the formulas are shown instead of cell values. This has its uses, but is not sufficient for formula verification because the cell values are no longer visible, and long formulas are truncated.

that end user programming systems must develop rather domain specific languages and interaction techniques whose operations will make sense to some particular set of users. The requirement that user programming languages be task-specific, contrasts sharply with the commonly advocated proposal to empower end users by helping them acquire competence in using general programming languages (Lewis & Olson, 1987; Maulsby & Witten, 1989; Neal, 1989). In general, we feel that users should be supported at their level of interest, which for many is to perform specific computational tasks within their own specialized domain, not to become computer programmers.

Just as spreadsheets distribute problem solving tasks *across* users differently than traditional computing, there is a different temporal distribution of tasks taken on by an individual user. Some users go on, over time, to learn and use new spreadsheet features (often very slowly)—in contrast to those who completely give up on general programming languages. Once users have successfully developed their own applications, they can begin to add new software techniques to their repertoire as they are ready. Through collaborations with more experienced users, spreadsheet users progress into the advanced layer. It is precisely because users have been supported by a high-level, task-specific software system that allowed them to get their work done and to experience a sense of accomplishment that they can then make progress, if they choose, in learning more general techniques. When spreadsheet users learn macros or the use of conditional and iterative facilities or formatting tricks, they venture into the realm of general programming. Such learning may occur in glacial time from the perspective of an experienced programmer, but perhaps that is appropriate for users whose primary accomplishments lie outside the field of programming.

Spreadsheets succeed because they combine an expressive high level programming language with a powerful visual format to organize and display data. Because the spreadsheet table so clearly exposes the structure and content of spreadsheet applications, co-workers easily and directly exchange domain knowledge. The shared semantics of the table facilitate knowledge transfer between co-workers; the very structure of the rows, columns and cells of the table transmits a great deal of information.

The lesson to be learned from the tabular structure of the spreadsheet is that simple, familiar visual notations form a good backbone for many kinds of scientific, engineering and business applications. Visual notations are based on human visual abilities such as detecting linear patterns or enclosure, that people perform almost effortlessly. Many diagrammatic visual notations such as tables, graphs, plots, panels and maps have been refined over hundreds if not thousands of years (Tufte, 1983; Cameron, 1989). They are capable of showing a large quantity of data in a small space, and of representing semantic information about relations among data. Like the spreadsheet table, these visual notations are simple but expressive, compact but rich in information.

We expect to see computer-based versions of tables, graphs, plots, panels and maps evolve into more sophisticated visual/semantic mechanisms, utilizing knowledge-based representations and interactive editing and browsing techniques such as filtering and fish-eye views (Furnas, 1986; Ciccarelli & Nardi, 1988). Today, visual notations are commonly used for display purposes, but it is less common for users to be able to manipulate their components—to be able to ask about the values behind a point on a plot, for example, or to expand a region on a map to show more detail. It is even less common for these displays and their components to possess any semantic information about their relationships to other displays or components—for example, constraints between specific values, or the mapping from one notation to another.

Visual notations with well-defined semantics for expressing relations will provide useful reusable computational structures. Filling a middle ground between the expressivity of general programming languages and the particular semantics of specific applications, they represent a fairly generic set of semantic relations, applicable across a wide variety of domains. New visual notations are possible and useful as Harel (1988) has shown with his work on statecharts. Statecharts formally describe a collection of sets and the relationships between them. Although Harel's work is quite new, Bear, Coleman and Hayes (1989) have already created an interesting extension to statecharts called object charts, for use in designing object-oriented software systems. Heydon, Maimone, Tygard, Wing and Zaremski (1989) used statecharts to model a language for specifying operation system security configurations.

As we have tried to show in our discussion of cooperative work practices among spreadsheet users, spreadsheets support an informal but effective interchange of programming expertise and domain knowledge. Spreadsheets achieve the distribution of cognitive tasks across different kinds of users in a highly congenial way; sojourners of the twinkling lights mix it up with crafters of nested loops—and all with software for which no explicit design attention was given to "cooperative use".

Many thanks to Lucy Berlin, Susan Brennan, Dave Duis, Danielle Fafchamps, Martin Griss, Jeff Johnson, Nancy Kendzierski, Robin Jeffries, Jasmina Pavlin and Craig Zarmer for helpful discussions and comments on earlier drafts of this paper. Thanks also to our informants, who showed great generosity in taking the time to talk to us, and provided careful explanations of their work with spreadsheets.

References

ALSOP, S. (1989). Q & A: Quindlen and Alsop: Spreadsheet users seem satisfied with what they already have. *InfoWorld*, September 11, 102–103.
ARGANBRIGHT, D. (1986). Mathematical modeling with spreadsheets. *Abacus*, **3**, 18–31.
BANNON, L. & SCHMIDT, K. (1989). CSCW: Four characters in search of a context. *Proceedings of the First European Conference on Computer Supported Cooperative Work EC-CSCW'89*, September 13–15, Gatwick, London, pp. 358–372.
BEAR, S., COLEMAN, D. & HAYES, F. (1989). *Introducing Objectcharts, or How to Use Statecharts in Object-oriented Design*, HPL-Report-ISC-TM-89-167. Bristol, England: Hewlett-Packard Laboratories.
BJERKNES, G., EHN, P. & KYNG, M. (1987). *Computers and Democracy: A Scandinavian Challenge*. Brookfield, Vermont: Gower Publishing Company.
BOSK, C. (1980). Occupational rituals in patient management. *New England Journal of Medicine*, **303**, 71–76.
BROOKS, F. (1975). *The Mythical Man Month: Essays on Software Engineering*. Reading, MA: Addison-Wesley.
BROWN, P. & GOULD, J. D. (1987). How people create spreadsheets. *ACM Transactions on Office Information Systems*, **5**, 258–272.

CHANDRASEKARAN, B. (1981). Natural and social system metaphors for distributed problem solving: Introduction to the issue. *IEEE Transactions on Systems, Man and Cybernetics,* **SMC-11,** 1–5.

CAMERON (1989). *A Cognitive Model for Tabular Editing,* OSO-CISRC Research Report, Ohio State University.

CICCARELLI, E. & NARDI, B. (1988). Browsing schematics: Query-filtered graphs with context nodes. In *Proceedings of the Second Annual Workshop on Space Operations, Automation and Robotics (SOAR'88),* July 20–23, Dayton, Ohio, pp. 193–204.

DOYLE, J. R. (1990). Naive users and the Lotus interface: A field study. *Behavior and Information Technology,* **9,** 81–89.

FURNAS, G. (1986). Generalized fisheye views. *Proceedings of CHI'86, Conference on Human Factors in Computing Systems,* April 13–17, Boston, pp. 16–23.

GRUDIN, J. (1988). Why CSCW applications fail: Problems in the design and evaluation of organizational interfaces. In *CSCW'88: Proceedings of the Conference on Computer Supported Cooperative Work.* September 26–28, 1988, Portland, Oregon, pp. 85–93.

HAREL, D. (1988). On visual formalisms. *Communications of the ACM,* **31,** 514–520.

HEYDON, A., MAIMONE, M., TYGAR, J., WING, J. & ZAREMSKI, A. (1989). Constraining pictures with pictures. In *Proceedings of IFIPS'89,* August, San Francisco, pp. 157–162.

HOADLEY, E. (1990). Investigating the effects of color. *Communications of the ACM,* **33,** 120–125.

HOLLAND, D. & VALSINER, J. (1988). Cognition, symbols and Vygotskty's developmental psychology. *Ethos,* **16,** 247–272.

HUTCHINS, E., HOLLAN, J. & NORMAN, D. (1986). Direct manipulation interfaces. In D. Norman & S. Draper, Eds. *User Centered System Design.* pp. 87–124. Hillsdale, NJ.: Erlbaum Publishers.

JARVENPANA & DICKSON (1988). Graphics and managerial decision making: Research based guidelines. *Communications of the ACM,* **31,** 764–744.

KAY, A. (1984). Computer software. *Scientific American,* **5,** 53–59.

LAVE, J. (1988). *Cognition in Practice: Mind, Mathematics and Culture in Everyday Life.* Cambridge: Cambridge University Press.

LEWIS, G. & OLSON, G. (1987). Can principles of cognition lower the barriers to programming? *Empirical Studies of Programmers: Second Workshop.* pp. 248–263. Norwood, NJ: Ablex Publishing.

MAULSBY, D. & WITTEN, I. (1989). Inducing programs in a direct-manipulation environment. In *Proceedings of CHI'89, Conference on Human Factors in Computing Systems.* April 30–May 4, 1989. Austin, Texas. pp. 57–62.

NAPIER, H., LANE, D., BATSELL, R. & GUADANGO, N. (1989). Impact of a restricted natural language interface on ease of learning and productivity. *Communications of the ACM,* **32,** 1190–1198.

NARDI, B. & MILLER, J. R. (1990). The spreadsheet interface: A basis for end user programming. In *Proceedings of Interact '90,* 27–31 August, Cambridge, UK, pp. 977–983.

NEAL, L. (1989). A system for example-based programming. In *Proceedings of CHI'89, Conference on Human Factors in Computing Systems,* April 30–May 4, Austin, Texas.

NEWMAN, D. (1989). Apprenticeship or tutorial: Models for interaction with an intelligent instructional system. *Proceedings of the Eleventh Annual Conference of the Cognitive Science Society,* August 16–19, Ann Arbor, Michigan, pp. 781–788.

NORMAN, D. (1987). *The Psychology of Everyday Things.* New York: Basic Books.

NORMAN, D. & HUTCHINS, E. (1988). *Computation via Direct Manipulation,* Final Report to Office of Naval Research, Contract No. N00014-85-C-0133. University of California, San Diego.

OLSON, J. & NILSEN, E. (1987). Analysis of the cognition involved in spreadsheet software interaction. *Human–Computer Interaction,* **3,** 309–349.

PANKO, R. (1988). *End User Computing; Management, Applications, and Technology.* New York: John Wiley and Sons.

PIERSOL, K. (1986). Object-oriented spreadsheets: The analytic spreadsheet package. In *Proceedings of OOPSLA'86,* September, pp. 385–390.

SEIFERT, C. & HUTCHINS, E. (1989). Learning from error. In *Proceedings of the Eleventh Annual Conference of the Cognitive Science Society*, August 16–19, Ann Arbor, Michigan, pp. 42–49.

SPENKE, M. & BEILKEN, C. (1989). A spreadsheet interface for logic programming. In *Proceedings of CHI'89 Conference on Human Factors in Computing Systems*, April 30–May 4, Austin, Texas, pp. 75–83.

TUFTE, E. (1983). *The Visual Display of Quantitative Information*. Cheshire, CT: Graphics Press.

VAN EMDEN, M., OHKI, M. & TAKEUCHI, A. (1985). *Spreadsheets with Incremental Queries as a User Interface for Logic Programming*, ICOT Technical Report TR–144.

VYGOTSKY, L. S. (1979). *Thought and Language*. Cambridge, MA: MIT Press.

WARNER, J. (1990). Visual data analysis into the '90s. *Pixel*, **1**, 40–44.

Appendix: Spreadsheet study questions

(1) What do you do here (i.e. what are the tasks of your job)?

(2) What do you do with spreadsheets? (This question involved looking at actual spreadsheets on-line and/or in paper copy. We looked at spreadsheet structure, the use of annotations and labels, formula complexity, how spreadsheets are used during meetings, etc. as part of this question.)

(3) Who else uses this spreadsheet (i.e. of those we talk about in Question 2)?

(4) How did you create this spreadsheet (i.e. of those we talk about in Question 2)? Or alternatively, who created it and who else uses it?

(5) How accurate is your spreadsheet? How do you know?

(6) How do you find errors?

(7) How do you fix errors?

(8) Are there any problems you tried to solve with spreadsheets where the spreadsheet approach didn't work? If so, what are they and what were the problems?

(9) What is your educational background?

(10) What do you like about spreadsheets?

(11) What do you dislike about spreadsheets?

(12) What would make spreadsheets easier to use?

(13) What else would you like spreadsheets to do?

Part 2

Studying groups with groupware

Part 2

4

Design for conversation: lessons from Cognoter

Deborah G. Tatar

Gregg Foster

Daniel G. Bobrow

When studying the use of Cognoter, a multi-user idea organizing tool, we noticed that users encountered unexpected communicative breakdowns. Many of these difficulties stemmed from an incorrect model of conversation implicit in the design of the software. Drawing on recent work in psychology and sociology, we were able to create a more realistic model of the situation our users faced and apply it to the system to understand the breakdowns. We discovered that users encountered difficulties coordinating their conversational actions. They also had difficulty determining that they were talking about the same objects and actions in the workspace. This work led to the redesign of the tool and to the identification of areas for further exploration.

Introduction

The Colab project was an ambitious attempt to provide computational support for group work, particularly for the support of small design teams working together in the same room. The project coordinated several technologies, including networked computers, video network facilities, and a specially designed room. Moreover, Colab had an elaborate and articulated model of the meeting processes it tried to support (Foster, 1986; Foster & Stefik, 1986; Stefik, Foster, Bobrow, Kahn, Lanning & Suchman, 1987a; Stefik, Bobrow, Foster, Lanning & Tatar, 1987b). This approach was exciting and important because it promised to permit significantly more effective ways of working. However, the observation of users working with Cognoter, the most developed Colab tool, showed that there were serious breakdowns in the system.

While trying to understand these breakdowns, it came to our attention that there was a potential conflict between the "interactive" model of communication proposed by recent work in psychology and sociology and the "parcel-post" model implicit in Cognoter. However, the importance of the difference between the two was initially unclear because the interactive model was created to describe situations (two-person, purely verbal communication, often without visual contact) that differed in important respects from the situation we had created in Cognoter. We drew upon sociological work studying the use of traditional representational media such as whiteboards to extrapolate from the interactive model and argue about its significance for our system. This analysis guided the redesign of the system.

This paper starts with an overview of Colab and Cognoter. We then describe some of the difficulties that our users had working with the system. Next, we present elements of the interactive and parcel-post models of conversation. To extend appropriate expectations to the Cognoter situation, we discuss the use of traditional representational media in meetings. This allows us to create a picture of the problems our users faced. Lastly, we talk about the implications of this line of thinking for the redesign of the system, for understanding more about communication, and as embodying techniques which are important for CSCW systems in general.

Colab and Cognoter

The Colab room was designed to enable the use of computers in meetings of two to five people. The room consisted of three specially designed tables arranged in a U-shape facing a large screen at the front of the room (Figure 1). Each table had on it a display, keyboard and mouse. Each display was connected to a separate processor. The processors were connected to one another by an Ethernet network. Additionally, the displays were connected to one another and to the large screen ("Liveboard") by a video network. The video network could be used to project any of the small displays on the Liveboard, as well as allowing any user to project another user's screen on her own display.† When the video network was being used to look at another station's display, the user lost access to the input devices and computational facilities of her own workstation.

Cognoter was software designed for the Colab to aid small work groups in the creation of a plan or outline. Cognoter "implemented" a three-part process of brainstorming, organizing the brainstormed ideas into sequences and groups, and evaluating them. As originally conceived, Cognoter was supposed to be a fairly

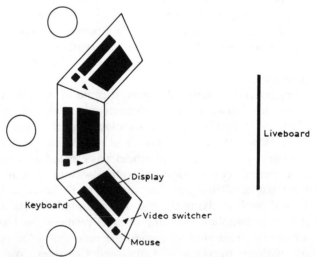

FIGURE 1. A diagram of the Colab room. An Ethernet network connected the computers, and a video network connected the displays and the large display ("Liveboard") at the front of the room.

† This video facility was intended primarily for use with software outside the Colab project.

direct translation of a process that we ourselves used in meetings with the whiteboard and other static representational media.

However, Cognoter took advantage of the Colab setting in several ways. To increase the effectiveness and efficiency of the meeting, the software allowed participants to work on their computers in parallel. They could each use their keyboard and mouse at any time to make contributions. We hoped that this would reduce the "production blocking" (Diehl & Stroebe, 1987) that is an impediment to group idea generation.

The fundamental unit in the Cognoter user interface was the item. Each Cognoter item consisted of an icon made up of a short catchphrase, usually limited to about 20 characters. Additional text could be associated with the item to explain the catchphrase. We thought of this additional text as an annotation to the item icon, although it could also be thought of as the content of an item. A special kind of item, a *group* item, could have other nested items associated with it.

Cognoter had two kinds of windows: *item organization windows,* whiteboard-like spaces used to display and move the icons, and *edit windows,* used to create and change both the catchphrases displayed in the item icons and the annotations associated with the items.

A major innovation of the project over other computerized brainstorming tools was to use the item organization windows to give users *shared workspaces.* The item organization windows appeared on every user's display at the same time. Each user's copy of an item organization window contained the same information and behaved the same way as every other user's copy. This approach and the many possibilities it raises are discussed in Stefik *et al.* (1987*a*).

To create an item, a user opened an edit window. When she completed the entry of the item, the system created an icon to be placed in an item organization window for everyone to see (Figure 2). Once created, the item was equally available to all users. By clicking on the icon, a user could either drag it to a different location or open an edit window and change it. A user could make a group item expand so that its associated group of sub-items appeared in a new item organization window. Icons could be moved within and across item organization windows. Items, nested groups and annotations allowed users to create what may be thought of as an annotated graph of ideas, with items and annotations at the leaves and groups at the nodes (Figure 3). This graph could be useful in its own right as a way of representing a complex problem space, or it could be used to generate a linear outline.

In theory, the computational representational medium seemed to combine the features of several tools in current use (Tang, 1989; 1990). As on a whiteboard, each person shared the same up-down orientation or perspective on the material. As on large sheets of paper (as used by architects and other designers), each person shared a close physical relationship to the representational medium. Lastly, as on a computer, information could be handled flexibly; even if the amount of material was quite large, editing, saving, restoring and printing were all possible and easy.

We believed that Cognoter changed people's patterns of work and even what happened in each person's head: "Cognoter. . . divides the thinking process into smaller and different kinds of steps that are incremental and efficient" (Stefik *et al.,* 1987*a*, p. 35). We also expected it to change the way people relate to one another in meetings. However, initially we considered design trade-offs with regard to meeting

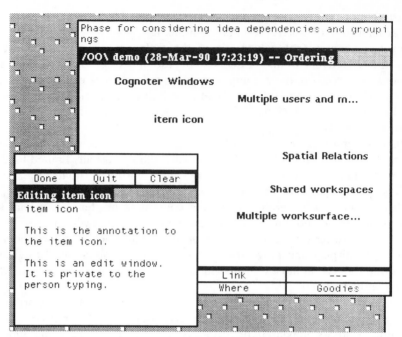

FIGURE 2. Item organization and edit windows. Item organization windows were shared and allowed
users to arrange item icons. Edit windows were used to create and modify items.

processes only as they seemed to fix problems such as overlooked ideas and
inefficiency. We did not consider whether the interventions we proposed manipulated resources at the level of basic human communication.

Experiences working with Cognoter

We had substantial experience using Cognoter in a series of working sessions with
one or more members of the Colab group participating. Reports from these
experiences were mixed, with a number of positive responses, but many unhappy
comments. However, meetings can be good or bad for many reasons not related to
the technology. Although preliminary observations of Cognoter use (Stefik *et al.,*
1987*a*) anticipated the problems detailed here, these observations were hampered
by the impossibility of seeing the details of work between three or four users
working on separate machines. The observations were also, as it turned out,
hampered by the ability of people who were very familiar with the performance
characteristics of the software to compensate for its problems.

To gain an understanding of what happened to "real" people, we asked two
outside groups to work with Cognoter. Each group consisted of three long-term
collaborators who were familiar with the editor, window system, and mouse
conventions Cognoter used. Each group was asked to brainstorm about a subject of
their own choosing that would be useful for their own work. Both groups worked for
two two-hour sessions. To solve the observational problem, we videotaped them at
work and kept a record of all messages sent between the different machines in the
session.

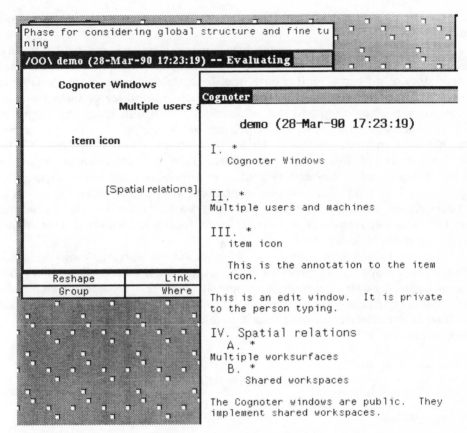

FIGURE 3. Items, annotations, and groups created an annotated graph. The graph could be used to generate a linear outline.

Our trial groups encountered serious problems. In one group, work proceeded in two phases. In the first, each person started an edit window and worked in it. They hardly talked at all and did not look at one another's work. In the second phase, they stopped using the system altogether and resorted to working together with a pad of paper. The other group managed to find a successful way of using the tool by using the video network to look at the screen of whoever was typing, thus employing the shared video workspace instead of the shared computational workspace. This solution worked rather well for them, and they ended up pleased with some aspects of the tool. However, this meant that they lost one of the chief features of the system, the ability to switch typists easily. Far from attaining the expert, fluid trade-off, seen in designers working around a large sheet of paper, they had to spend quite a bit of effort negotiating who would type next.

Both groups bypassed the computational shared workspace either by working privately and then doing the group work on paper, or by giving up on their input devices and using the video connection to create a visually shared workspace. When they tried to use the shared workspace created by the software, they found it so frustrating that they put their heads in their hands, raised their voices, and ultimately threatened to walk out. They expressed astonishment that anyone would build such a system.

There are many reasons why prototype computer systems can be frustrating, especially to novices, but our users were experienced with computers and expected certain kinds of difficulty. Furthermore, the Cognoter developers were available to help them with any problems that arose, and there were three of them to try to figure out difficulties. Bugs and lack of familiarity notwithstanding, the degree of their frustration was surprising. Some sources of frustration were straightforward once observed and led immediately to design solutions, reported by Foster, Tatar and Bobrow (Unpublished data). However, there were two major classes of problems that seemed connected with the worst frustrations and whose implications required more thought. The first kind of problem was that our users felt a need to see things in the workspace that the system would not let them see. The second was that they mistook references in one another's speech or actions and could not resolve the difficulty satisfactorily.

Before the second group found a viable mode of working using the video network, they made five attempts to work in the private editors. Four of the five attempts evoked a complaint from the people who were not typing about what could and could not be "seen." User objections (leaving out the tone of voice, gesture and surrounding detail which are what lead us to think of these as particularly important reactions) included:

- "Why can't I see that?"
- "I don't see what use it is to have a big screen if we can't all contribute to it."
- "Click DONE so I can see it."
- P1: "P2, do you have anything you want to say?" P2: "I won't be able to see it up there, right?"†

These objections are united by participant confusion and difficulty in seeing what they needed to see. Even the second comment, which looks at first glance like a complaint about the distribution of information between the large screen and the individual displays, reflects confusion about what could be seen. (Since the large screen at the front projected one of the individual displays, they could contribute to it simply by contributing to the shared workspace. The fundamental objection concerned what could be seen in the shared workspace and it is particularly telling that they did not immediately recognize that a shared workspace was projected.)

The fifth case, although relatively unproblematic, is still instructive. In this case, one user started to take notes on what the other two were talking about. Subsequently, he read his notes back to them, adding "Well, you can all see this". They could indeed all see it by looking at the large screen at the front of the room which had been set so that it displayed his screen. Yet, even in this unproblematic usage, the user felt he had to read aloud what could have been read by each participant separately, and to comment on the fact that they could have seen it. In other words, he had to take action to bring it back into the conversation.

These objections establish the problem that users could not see things. However, the objections also raise questions. What exactly do the users expect to see? In a meeting involving a whiteboard, one participant might be looking out of the window,

---

† "P" followed by a number is used to denote participants.

or be taking notes, or whispering to someone else, and not see a gesture or drawing as it is put up. Yet this lack of attention does not usually cause extreme frustration or a breakdown of the situation. What was significantly different in the Colab situation?

We also saw a second kind of problem that required explanation. This was a problem with mistaken reference. As Bly (1988) has documented, deictic references, such as pointing to the screen and saying "there", "this", or "that", persist even when such behavior has limited utility, as when we are on the phone. However, any ambiguity raised by this practice is by and large handled without remark. In fact, deictic reference is often ambiguous even in face-to-face conversation. Nonetheless, the ambiguity our users experienced appeared to be more extreme than in these other cases. For example, our users had a problematic breakdown in which they appeared to have quite different interpretations of the word "that". A summary account of what happened follows:

(1) P2 was using the video network to look at P1's machine. There was a general discussion about creating a new item;

(2) P1 hit a mouse button, thereby creating an edit window for entering a new item;

(3) P3 suggested that P2 should type instead of P1;

(4) P2 went to switch her display back to her own machine;

(5) P1 looked at her screen, appeared surprised, typed four characters (the title of the item) and moused the DONE button, thus sending it to the others.

(6) P2 found that her display had gone black (into idle) and was confused, "What! Who did that?" At virtually the same time, the item that P1 had created appeared on P2's and P3's screens.

(7) P3 "P1";

(8) P2 (hitting a space bar which caused the machine to come out of idle) "Oh, it was my fault".

(9) P1 "I did not!"

(10) P3 "P1, Let P2 type!"

(11) P1 "I am!"

(12) P2 "I've forgotten what I was going to type".

P2 said "Who did that?" referring to the fact that her machine had gone into idle. P3 interpreted "that" to mean the thing that had changed in his environment, which was the appearance of a new item. He had not caused this new item to appear, so he replied that P1 had caused it. P3 ended up with the wrong picture of P2's complaint and therefore P1 was unjustly accused of not permitting P2 to type.

In fact, the participants/collaborators moved on without sorting out what had happened, and it was only through careful reconstruction that we as analysts came to understand the sequence. Since both our trial groups consisted of long-term collaborators, the amount of interpersonal damage was probably small, but it did represent a substantial disruption to their work. Furthermore, the incident, combined with the fact that both groups declined to use the computational shared workspace, was telling. It suggested that in this situation people could not rely on familiar mechanisms for coordinating or managing ambiguity. The technology was not increasing their efficiency in this respect.

To proceed, we needed to understand what was causing the difficulties our users experienced. We needed to understand what they needed to see and what factors contributed to the increase in ambiguity. However, since this was not intended as our major line of research, but rather as enabling work for other more central interests, we faced the challenge of trying to work as much as we could with materials already in the literature (rather than constructing a research project to explore this one set of issues). The challenge that we faced is a general one because CSCW systems almost always touch on many different research areas, not all of which can be pursued actively. Designers need approaches that maximize their use of appropriate existing research.

Models of conversation

The fields of conversation analysis (see Goodwin & Heritage, 1990 for an overview of the field) and psycholinguistics (see Clark & Wilkes-Gibbs, 1986; Clark & Schaefer, 1987, 1989; Schober & Clark 1989; for the most relevant aspects) offer a model of conversation which seems highly pertinent to the difficulties our users faced. They present what we may term an "interactive" model of communication. The interactive model emphasizes the notion that conversation is a highly coordinated activity in which meaning is attained and affirmed using a number of mechanisms that have context dependent functions. By contrast, Cognoter implemented and thus supported what we may term a "parcel-post" model in which communication is delivered in parcel-like units.

INTERACTIVE MODEL

The starting point of the interactive model of conversation is the observation that conversation does not consist of one person making a complete utterance while the other person waits passively. Both participants are active even when only one is actually speaking. Thus people nod, complete or reshape one another's phrases, and say "uh-huh" (Duncan, 1973).

A second major point of the interactive model is that the function of an utterance is context dependent. Each conversational move involves not only its own contents but a projection of what the next move will be. For example, one of the resources that people have available in conversation is the *noun phrase*. There are different types of noun phrases (Clark & Wilkes-Gibbs, 1986), the most common being the *elementary* noun phrase, as in "the green cup on the bookshelf" uttered as one tonal sequence. When a person utters "the green cup on the bookshelf", she is projecting that the phrase will be accepted without comment. Other types of noun phrases, e.g. "the whatchamacallit", set up other expectations. If she alters the phrase by the use of a *try-marker* (Sacks & Schegloff, 1979), a tonal, non-lexical request for judgement about its acceptability,† she is indicating that the preferred next move is a listener response indicating whether his meaning is clear. In the case of an unmodified elementary noun phrase, a non-response complies with the projection and asserts that the phrase has been understood. If the phrase is modified with a try-marker, a non-response indicates trouble, perhaps that the other person is no

† A try-marker sounds similar to a question, but it is not a request for agreement on contents, just agreement that the phrase is understood.

longer listening. Furthermore, a response after a pause is not the same as an immediate response. For example, it may set up a question about whether the listener is attending or beginning to signal dissent (Pomerantz, 1984; Pomerantz, 1978; Goodwin, 1980).

Listeners have the ability to make statements explicitly or implicitly which add to, accept, reject, question or modify what the speaker has just said. In the interactive model, this listener response is a crucial part of conversation. In fact, Clark and Schaefer (1987, 1989) have gone so far as to advance the notion that the basic unit of conversation consists of two parts, a *presentation* and an *acceptance* phase. Together the two constitute a *contribution*. Since, as mentioned above, non-response is in fact a statement, the ability to perform the acceptance portion actively is crucial.

The interactive model also draws our attention to the importance of mid-course corrections (Goodwin, 1981; Schegloff, 1981; Clark & Wilkes-Gibbs, 1986). Mid-course corrections happen when speakers or listeners adjust in midstream, either of their own accord or in response to something in the environment. For example, while uttering the phrase "the green cup on the bookshelf", the speaker may note the listener's confused expression and attempt to clarify by adding "in the library". We know that people can succeed in conversing without some elements of this because they succeed in conversing over half-duplex phone lines and with computer TALK systems which may be serial. However, most people find this quite unpleasant and, in face-to-face conversation, mid-course corrections, whether by the speaker or the listener are endemic. According to Clark and Wilkes-Gibbs, mid-course corrections are yet another way that conversationalists obey the general goal of "reducing the collaborative work" of holding the conversation.

In the interactive model, conversation is structured around the work that both participants must do to establish that they are talking about the same things. One aspect of this is establishing what objects they are referring to. To study this problem, Clark and Wilkes-Gibbs (1986) asked pairs of subjects to sort a deck of cards with non-representational pictures on them. The subjects each had their own deck and could not see one another or the other person's deck. The *matcher* was supposed to put the deck in the same order as the *director*. On average, the first references to each card took close to four turns at speech by the director. However, people's ability to refer verbally to particular objects developed through shared experience. As they repeated the task, the references they used to the cards become more compact. They were simplified and/or narrowed to the crucial components. Thus, the second trial took on average two turns and the third averaged at close to one. Furthermore, the number of words per turn at talk declined over time; "the one that looks like a skater with one leg kicked back" turned into "the skater" (Clark & Wilkes-Gibbs, 1986).

Furthermore, in general people preferred to refer to the task items with permanent descriptions rather than temporary views. A permanent reference is one such as describing a drawing as "the rabbit". This contrasts with temporary sorts of references such as "the one we got confused on last time". A reason for this preference may be that permanent descriptions permit successive refinement of the reference.

In the interactive view, conversation is a complex, highly coordinated process in which conversants seek mutual understanding through the coordinated presentation and acceptance of a variety of lexical and non-lexical statements. Projections of the next conversational move and active listener response are crucial for this activity. The abilities to make mid-course corrections and abbreviated references are highly desirable. Time plays a crucial role.

PARCEL-POST MODEL

Although Cognoter permitted people to talk with one another, and thus employ their normal resources, its textual component may be described as embodying a parcel-post model of communication. The qualities of a parcel-post model are that items are packaged and sent by the speaker, and then unpackaged and decoded by the receiver. An additional component of the model is that if the receiver does not open his "mail" right away, he may end up with a bunch of stuff with no particular order.

The differences between these models suggest that one class of problems may occur in coordinating such interactive features as mid-course corrections, projections of the next move, and listener response. A second class of problems may occur in determining that both people are talking about the same thing.

Problems applying the interactive model to Cognoter

The differences between the interactive and parcel-post models suggest that our users had difficulty because they could not accomplish necessary or highly desirable activities described by the interactive model. However, we cannot immediately conclude that this explains our users' problems, because the interactive model arose from studying situations that differed in two important respects from the situation we created in Cognoter: the number of people involved in an interaction, and the type of communication involved. To understand whether and how we would expect the interactive model to generalize to Cognoter, we must understand the impact of these differences.

The first issue arises because most of the work that led to the interactive model studied conversation between only two people. Our Cognoter experiences involved three people. In recent years, there have been some studies of multi-party interaction which extend but do not refute the two-person model (Goodwin & Goodwin, 1990). While these studies provide some assurance of continuity between the situations, they have not concentrated on identifying the differences between the two party and multi-party conversation. They leave open the possibility that, for example, the expectation of response is lessened in the multi-party case. Nonetheless, conversation with three people is, by and large, unlikely to simplify the possibilities or render resources for achieving shared reference less necessary. Although there are unanswered questions, we may safely assume that any factors that seem likely to cause difficulties in the two-person situation will be only more likely to do so in the three.

The second problem originates in the recognition that many forms of communication exist which are not conversational. For example, the parcel-post model works perfectly well for letters. Since people are creating text in Cognoter, we initially assumed that the parcel-post model would suffice. Why should we now attribute their difficulties to conversational impediments?

Clark and Wilkes-Gibbs (1986) propose a highly relevant distinction between conversation and literary communication. They propose that the principle of *mutual responsibility* holds in conversation:

> The participants in a conversation try to establish, roughly by the initiation of each new contribution, the mutual belief that the listeners have understood what the speaker meant in the last utterance to a criterion sufficient for current purposes (Clark & Wilkes-Gibbs, 1986, p. 33).

They contrast this with the principle of *distant responsibility*:

> The speaker or writer tries to make sure, roughly by the initiation of each new contribution, that the addressees should have been able to understand his meaning in the last utterance to a criterion sufficient for current purposes (Clark & Wilkes-Gibbs, 1986, p. 35).

The principle of distant responsibility applies in the many situations—writing a paper, sending e-mail, giving a lecture, broadcasting on TV, dictating a tape to be sent in the mail—that are distinguished from conversation less by the medium carrying the communication (paper, airwaves, Ethernet) as by a relative lack of co-production and therefore of time constraints in the preparation of the communication. In other words, conversation is distinguished from literary forms of communication by the amount of work to ensure understanding that is done *within the time frame* of the actual communication. Cognoter differs from literary communication because Cognoter is not the sole or primary carrier of the communication. Cognoter differs from conversation as we have described it because it involves writing activity. In fact, Cognoter is neither of these, but rather a medium for representation in relationship to the conversation.

A large body of work has been done exploring the relationship between conversation and writing activity in traditional representational media such as whiteboards and large sheets of paper. This work provides evidence that similar constraints apply when working with representational media as with unadorned conversation, and that similar resources are necessary or desirable.

Traditional representational media

Suchman (1988) and Tang (1989, 1990) and Bly (1988) have studied traditional representational media such as whiteboards and large sheets of paper. We can draw on their work to extrapolate from the interactive model to understand how we might expect the parcel-post model of Cognoter to cause users trouble.

Suchman and Tang give evidence that, since writing and drawing activity interacts with conversation, coordination is as important when using these media as it is in conversation without them. Suchman (1988) describes the way in which turns at ". . . the board may be used in taking and holding the floor, or in maintaining some writing activity while passing up a turn as talk. Writing done during another's talk may (a) document the talk and thereby display the writer's understanding, (b) continue the writer's previous turn or (c) project the writer's next turn, providing an object to be introduced in subsequent talk". The writing actions are neither appendages to the verbal conversation nor independent of it. Writing and talking is intricately bound together in a similar fashion to the way a statement and its response are bound together. However, the coordination issues are even more complex because a person can write while talk is occurring. There are therefore more kinds of moves to be made.

The fact that textual items persist makes it tempting to believe that time is less relevant in shared writing and drawing activities than in purely verbal conversation. "Recording information" is usually accounted the chief reason to use a whiteboard and this activity is considered to be independent of the conversation. However, in practice, only a small percentage of the activity in relationship to a whiteboard is recording information (Tang 1989). It is important therefore to look at other functions of work in the shared medium.

Suchman (1988) distinguishes between those actions in reference to the whiteboard that involve the production of textual or graphical objects and those that involve the use. Our construction of this distinction is that whiteboard items hold a dual status as elements *in* the conversation and elements that may be conversed *about*. During production (when they are being created) they are typically, but not always, elements in the conversation and, like verbal conversation, understood according to precise context. Thus, the moment a person starts to write helps determine whether the writing action acknowledges what has already been said (or written) or ignores it, and whether the writing represents agreement, clarification, informed disagreements, a side activity, or an attempt to bring up a new topic. Once created, the textual items are similar to other physical objects such as tables and chairs in the environment and may be conversed about.† As objects in the world, they are not subject to timing considerations. However, participants may have to do work to ensure that they are talking about the same objects in the world, and time is a factor in that work.‡

Recording information for future use is certainly an important function for representational media. However, even while recording information, participants are not free from timing considerations. Tang (1989) reports that the length of time recording information takes, presents a "challenge" for the group. This challenge can be handled in a number of different ways. They may wait for the recorder to finish, occupy the pause with individual work, or move on to another topic. Any of these activities may be accompanied by talk, preceded by it, followed by it, or free of it. Drawing upon the Clark and Wilkes-Gibbs distinction between conversation and literary communication, we may speculate that the challenge arises because the person doing the recording has in an important sense stepped out of the conversation. She is engaged in an essentially literary endeavor in which she must take the time to anticipate what the group or someone else will need to know later on. Meanwhile, the other participants may compensate, e.g. by monitoring the activity (but not always).

A further issue arises when we consider whiteboard items as elements to be referred to, as objects in the world. In everyday conversation and in whiteboard use,

---

† The situation is a bit more complex than this. Since production takes time and items once created may be modified, which is a kind of production, a given item on the whiteboard has the potential to be both an element in the conversation and to be conversed about as an object. People intermix actions in relationship to these different aspects of whiteboard elements smoothly.

‡ Furthermore, we expect that work to be increased over the work people have to do to talk about tables and chairs, because the objects which are in general not familiar, represent other complex ideas, and may not be as easily recognized.

deixis, the ability to point or say "this" or "that" with reference to the objects in the environment, is omnipresent. The success of a deictic reference depends on shared knowledge about the position of an object. This suggests that one reason that whiteboards are so useful is they give a highly salient quality or position to an idea. The salience of position is demonstrated by instances of people referring to the spot on the whiteboard where a particular idea, now erased, once was represented (Suchman, 1988). Clark and Wilkes-Gibbs do not discuss deixis. However, they do note that people prefer permanent qualities to temporary ones. In their study, location was considered a temporary feature. This makes sense because they were talking about stacks of cards that were being continually moved in the course of the task. However, the prevalence of gesture in relation to whiteboard objects and the salience of position, provides evidence that the location of whiteboard objects is regarded as a permanent quality for the purposes of the conversation. Thus, threats to positional information will make object identification more difficult.

The study of traditional representational media contains ample evidence that people use the basic "interactive" conversational paradigm. It is highly structured and dependent on both time and context. While there may be interesting modifications in response to different representational media, we have every reason to believe that the same resources are available for projecting the next move, for making and obtaining listener response, and for mid-course correction. The whiteboard provides increased facilities for determining what objects are being discussed, and the success of this facility appears to be dependent on positional information, as well as on the contents of whatever is written.

Cognoter problems

Cognoter differs from whiteboards and large sheets of paper in important respects: items may be easily rearranged; people work with keyboards; and the participants have not only displays instead of boards, but separate displays. Still, Cognoter is like a whiteboard or large sheet of paper in several important respects: crucially, it allows the visual presentation and inspection of all items by all participants; it allows items to be created and pointed at; and it allows items, though of a limited nature compared with whiteboard elements, to be arranged freely within the available space.

We have drawn a picture of conversation in relationship to a representational medium that emphasizes interactivity and coordination. This picture also contains the notion that an important utility of the representational medium lies in the ability to refer to objects in a succinct way. We have evidence from Cognoter that users could not "see" what they wanted to see, and some evidence about mistaken reference.

To have enough confidence that the differences between the interactive model and the parcel-post model substantially account for the difficulties our users faced, we want to have a picture of how we might expect the interactive processes that the users were engaged in to play out against the system with which they were working. We cannot have a complete model because we don't know all the resources that people have available or their significance at all moments. Nonetheless, demonstrating a severe blockage of the process components that we have identified, both argues for the significance of these processes and highlights specific implementation decisions in the system.

In light of this, eight design decisions which we must consider as possible contributors to the difficulties our users had are as follows:

- Separate screens: We gave each user a separate screen. They were not in fact looking at the same place. This meant that gaze and gesture information was reduced.
- Lack of sequentiality: There was no marked position where the next icon would appear or any way of determining the order of contributions.
- Short labels: Icons could only be short phrases. This meant only a small amount of information per item could be viewed by the group together.
- Anonymity: All changes were anonymous. The results were delivered to others with no indication of who had made them.
- Private editing: Editing of item text was accomplished in private editor windows. The results were delivered to the others wholesale. The catchphrase (and therefore the icon) could be changed entirely. Alternatively, the item could retain the same catchphrase but the annotations which gave it a particular meaning could have changed.
- Unpredictable delay: Changes showed up on other people's screens after an unpredictable delay. Sometimes they showed up as quickly as a third of a second but at times it took as long as 20 seconds.
- Private moving: Moving icons was accomplished privately. On other people's screens, an icon would disappear from one position and appear in another. The object could lose its identifiable position.
- Tailorable windows: Users could tailor their screen individually by moving windows around and by changing their size and shape. Item organization windows could appear in different places in different sizes on each person's screen.

With these design issues in mind, we revisit the Cognoter situation and attempt to describe what we believe the users faced and why these factors contribute to a problem for them. We divide this discussion into two sections: coordination problems and reference problems.

For the purposes of this discussion, the person making the contribution is referred to as "he" and the person responding as "she". The "speaker" is used for the person making the contribution, while "listener", "recipient", and "responder" are used for the person responding.

COORDINATION

Cognoter users are presented with a choice of media; they can choose to communicate: verbally, through text, or by using a combination of the two.† Like all participants in a conversation, they collectively face the need to (1) produce contributions,‡ (2) recognize contributions as such, and (3) make responses. Although by definition making a contribution must be a positive action, response may be made either by positive action or by a non-response. Verbal and writing activities need to be coordinated with one another if made by the same person, and

† For the purposes of this discussion, we treat these as distinct choices. However, people presumably intermix them smoothly.

‡ Although Clark and Schaefer (1987, 1989) have used the term "contribution" to refer to the whole process of saying something and getting a response, we are using the term contribution more colloquially to refer to the spoken or written utterance. They use the term "presentation" for the utterance. "Presentation" is unsatisfactory for our purposes because it sounds as though there is a slice of time in which the listener is purely an "audience".

responses need to be understood in relationship to the contributions that evoked them.

Producing contributions

A person making a contribution in Cognoter has a choice of media. Making a spoken contribution in the Cognoter situation is hardly different from making a spoken contribution in the other situations we have discussed.† However, if the user attempts to include Cognoter in his action, he faces certain difficulties. A purely textual contribution, since it is made privately (private editing), does not in itself contain the elements of a bid for the floor, in the way starting to write at a whiteboard sometimes does.

The speaker may attempt to remedy this by accompanying his writing activity with speech. However, private editing and unpredictable delay mean that the textual and verbal elements of the contribution will be extremely hard to coordinate. On a whiteboard, users can perform different kinds of actions. We've observed that one action, namely recording information, presents a challenge for the other participants, which they handle with a variety of strategies. In Cognoter, even acts which do not involve recording information present a similar challenge insofar as they are invisible. It is as if the person, rather than making a bid for the floor, had simply dropped out of the conversation in the same way they have to when recording information in traditional media.

While the challenge of coordinating talking and writing is similar to the challenge the group faces when handling recording information on traditional media, their resources are not in all cases the same. If the speaker speaks as he starts to type and if his speech succeeds in capturing the attention of the group (i.e. if it is timed carefully enough despite the distraction of typing), then the group faces options similar to the traditional case (although the listeners may be waiting in situations which would not normally require them to wait: recall that our users asked unhappily "Why can't I see it?"). However, if the speaker waits until he has finished typing to speak, he risks losing any projectible connection between the time he initiated the typing and the time the message is received. Furthermore, because of separate screens, unpredictable delay, and lack of sequentiality, there will never be a particular moment at which the speaker knows that his text item has been received by everyone and is being looked at.‡ Lastly, even if the recipients see the item come up, if more than one person was typing, they must figure out who's commentary matched the new (anonymous) item.

This lack of coordination means that the speaker is hampered in several ways. First, he cannot make or obtain mid-course corrections. Even if the speaker does adjust his writing activity in response to something the listener has said or done, this adjustment loses any meaning as acknowledgement or anticipation of listener reaction. The inability to evoke mid-course corrections increases the speaker's burden to complete the work of the phrase by himself, and increases the total work of the group since his extra work could in many cases be avoided.

Second, even once the contribution is complete, he encounters difficulties

† Contributions are not, in general, really made against a clean slate.

‡ As with response, overt work can be done to make everyone look at the item, but this is a far cry from increasing the efficiency of the conversation or the meeting.

projecting a preferred response. Two resources we have identified as important in conversation are try-markers and pauses. These are strictly verbal. The absence of coordination between talk and writing means that try-markers and pauses are ineffective in relation to the computational medium.

Mid-course corrections, try-markers and pauses certainly do not represent the complete set of resources that speakers have available in conversation. However, their absence is quite a significant loss.

Recognizing contributions

We expect from the analysis above that the speaker will have to do more work to make a contribution in relation to Cognoter, than with traditional media or in simple conversation. However, the situation is even worse for the person who attempts to use the system to respond to another's contribution. First, she must know what to respond to and that itself presents difficulties.

The ability to know what to react to and when is reduced. If the speaker is typing and talking, the listener can respond at the appropriate time to either the verbal or the textual component of the turn. Since these are not coordinated, she must choose between them. If she has enough information to respond to the verbal component, then she has the difficulty of timing her response to avoid competing with the typing. If she waits to receive and assess the text, she has the difficulty of spotting it on the screen (lack of sequentiality). If she does spot the item, she must determine that no one else has priority making a response (lack of sequentiality, private editing, unpredictable delay). Furthermore, since people may well occupy their time making their own contributions, even when one contribution is detected, she may have trouble deciding on an order for response.

Additionally, since it is extremely difficult for the speaker to establish a connection between verbal and textual matter, the listener is likely to see the item in the absence of mid-course corrections, try-markers and pauses. This means that the phrase will be seen as "elementary", that is projecting assurance that it can be understood. She will therefore work hard to make sense out of it. This increase in her work is significant because even in everyday conversation, "the heavier burden usually falls on the listener, since she is in the best position to assess her own comprehension" (Clark & Wilkes-Gibbs, 1986, p. 34). Furthermore:

> When the speaker utters I just found the keys, marking the noun phrase as elementary. . . the listener is under strong pressure to accept it. After all, the speaker marked it as elementary; so he must believe it to be adequate for current purposes. If she rejects it, she risks offending him by indicating that it wasn't adequate. She also risks revealing her own incompetence if indeed it should have been adequate. Finally, like the speaker, the listener wants to minimize collaborative effort—to avoid extra steps in the acceptance process—and that too puts pressure on her to accept. All this encourages her to tolerate a certain lack of understanding, even to feign understanding when it is not justified. She may do this trusting that the holes will be filled in later, or that they won't have serious consequences (Clark & Wilkes-Gibbs, 1986, p. 34).

Making a response

Once the listener has identified something she wishes to respond to, she must carry out the response. A non-response becomes extremely ambiguous; it is difficult to distinguish lack of attention from confirmation that all is well from a deliberate snub. If she chooses to make a positive response, she must choose her media. Here she faces the same problems coordinating speech and text that the speaker faced in making the contribution. However, the problems play out a bit differently.

If she responds verbally to a verbal presentation, all is well. If she responds verbally to a textual item, not using the tool at all, she may have to do more work, because she does not know that other people have received the item and consider it an active element in the conversation. She may have to establish what she is talking about, for example, by reading the item aloud.

If a listener responds in text to either a verbal or a textual contribution, then there is a considerable chance for her act or the meaning of her act to be lost. For example, a person could acknowledge agreement by building upon one idea with a related idea or by writing down the idea just mentioned. Alternatively, the same act of beginning to write could signify an attempt to propose a new topic. The lack of coordination between the contribution and the response means neither the fact that one is making a response nor the particular meaning of the response will be fully available to others. In the absence of speech, even if the others notice that the responder has begun to type, there will be nothing to mark her action as a response to a particular contribution. Furthermore, if the recipients are not monitoring exactly the right space on their screen (lack of sequentiality) some unpredictable amount of time after she finishes (unpredictable delay), they may well fail to register that any change was made at all. If the change is made in an annotation, then not only must they each wait for it but they must perform an extra action to find it in the text of the item (short labels). It is quite possible for someone to re-open something that they typed originally and find that the annotations are quite different and no longer make sense to them.†

Just like the speaker, the recipient can also hope to improve on this difficult situation by including both written and verbal components in her response. However, she cannot just say "yes" and begin to write, but must say "yes, I'll write that down" or "yes, even better" to let the other's know the meaning of her beginning to type at that instance. Even if she does this extra work, the others will not necessarily know that what she has written down is consistent with her "yes" until they see it. (She could also tell them what she is writing, but since she is typing, she is in no position to pursue subsequent discussion. This behavior would represent yet more work that had to be done just to manage the logistics of the technology.) By the time she has finished typing, they may well have moved on to other things and the value of the response built on what was said, making a bid for the floor, or in any way guiding the discussion, is lost.

While the burden on the recipient is increased, her ability to respond effectively is curtailed. One way she could handle this increased burden is by inserting some sort of meta-comment, such as a question about why the item looks the way it does, into the text of the item. However, this behavior has strong consequences. For the query to carry enough information for whoever in turn receives it to know how to answer in the absence of sequential order, whatever was typed has to obey the principle of distant responsibility. That means that the responder has to take the time to anticipate what others in the future will need to see to be reminded of the issue. To

---

† Someone may well open an item just to see the annotations and not as a conversational act at all. The mere fact that there is activity does not signify change.

make such a response, the responder might well have to drop out of the conversation. If people drop out of the conversation too much, it is no longer a conversation, and they are no longer working collaboratively. Indeed, we may speculate that something like this is what happened in our first group in which each person worked separately until they turned to pencil and paper for the work they really needed to do together.

Thus, there are difficulties in both making contributions and in making responses. The contribution phase could probably be handled. However, the burden on the listener seems to be too great. Our users complained that they couldn't see enough. Our interpretation of those complaints is that users probably could have waited for the representational content of the items. They did this in the one case that seemed unproblematic for the group, when the text was reintroduced by being read aloud. What they needed to "see" immediately was the written component coordinating the interaction. The absence of coordination between speech and writing led to a highly frustrating experience.

CO-REFERENCE

Clark and Wilkes-Gibbs (1986) point out that shared reference is something that must be achieved. We had hoped that the differences between the displays at Cognoter stations would be transparent to the users or at least be accepted without too much difficulty. However, in fact people were not looking at the same surface (separate screens). This meant that they lost most of the gaze and gesture information and their base-level knowledge of what was being talked about was less than with other representational media. These losses would probably not be crippling since people manage to talk and even work (Bly, 1988) over the phone. Nonetheless, built on top of this basic situation are several discontinuities which combine to make effective co-reference difficult.

Trying to find previously entered items is potentially difficult. By design, windows may be in different places and have different shapes and sizes on different people's screens (tailorable windows). Indexical descriptions such as "It's in the upper left" do not work under these circumstances. To locate an item, you must first determine that you and your colleagues are referring to the same window, then locate the item within the window. Since windows cannot be identified by position or shape, the user must fall back on searching for their titles. Windows may be moved very quickly and invisibly. Therefore, this already time-consuming work may have to be performed repeatedly.

Additionally, trying to keep track of changes to the items presents new difficulties. First, moving or substantially changing items can be done very abruptly. When a user clicks on an item icon to move it, the item greys out on other people's screens, just as it does when an item is being edited. When the user puts the item down elsewhere, it suddenly disappears from its original location on everyone else's screen and reappears somewhere else. Even if one is looking for the flash of its reappearance, it can be hard to find on a busy screen. Furthermore, given the privacy of moving and editing, it is not very interesting to look at the screen while waiting to spot something new. Lastly, unlike with traditional media, an item is not necessarily fully displayed. Therefore, someone may change the text shown in the icon. Subsequently, another person might want to look at the annotations attached to the item and not be able to find the item because the icon has changed.

In the case of other technologies comparable to Cognoter, we have seen that position is treated as a highly salient quality and that compact reference is desirable. In Cognoter the ability to use positional information to achieve compact reference is jeopardized in part by the new facilities we are providing and in part because we provided them in a way that undermines the work that people have to do to be able to refer to positioned items efficiently.

The combination of the eight design decisions mentioned at the beginning of this section with the conversational processes involved in using the tool, made Cognoter items more difficult both to create and to use than whiteboard objects. Our users could not "see" vital portions of the conversation and they could not make sure that each one was seeing the same objects in their representational world. Although people are in general good at compensating, there are limits to their abilities and willingness to do so. Cognoter posed too hard a communicational puzzle for our users in a conversational, time-constrained situation.

Consequences for Cognoter

An important outcome of this work was the development of a second generation tool, Cnoter. The redesign was oriented towards improving the system without giving up those features, such as the ability to move and edit items, that seem to be major benefits of computation for this kind of application. As shown in Table 1, the redesign attempted to fix four out of the eight problems we have discussed.

The major problems we tried to fix were those of private editing, private moving, unpredictable delay, and tailorable windows. We introduced shared editing and moving facilities, a significant speed-up of communication between machines, and consistent positioning of windows across machines. When someone creates a new item in Cnoter, they still open an edit window, but that window opens on everyone else's screen as well. Updates are broadcast every second. Only one person can type in a shared edit window at a time; however, control can be transferred from one person to another by clicking the mouse in the window. Thus, everyone has visual access to items while they are being created, and they can even contribute actively to that creation when appropriate. Likewise, the activity of moving icons is

TABLE 1
Summary of changes motivated by the extended interactive model

Cognoter design issue	Cnoter status
Separate screens	Unchanged
Short labels	Unchanged
Sequentiality	Unchanged
Anonymity	Unchanged
Private editing	Shared editing
Unpredictable delay	Sped up communication
Private moving	Shared moving
Tailorable windows	Windows same on all screens

broadcast several times a second, so that icons no longer disappear from one place and appear suddenly somewhere else.† We not only sped up communication between the machines, but added some more checking to balance out the times at which the text arrived at different machines. We eliminated the occasional very long delay for information to get from machine to machine. Thus, users should not be confused by having a particular text object and not knowing whether or not others can see it. Lastly, we made window position and shape consistent across all machines. This means that people can rely on positional information for resolving the uncertainties of reference.

We have not changed our decisions about short labels, lack of sequentiality and anonymity. With the addition of shared editing and moving, the short labels found in the idea organization windows carry much less communicative weight. They seem to be adequate for the purpose of reminding users of item contents.

The lack of sequentiality interacted poorly with attempts both to coordinate the conversation and to keep track of where items were; however, whiteboards and large sheets of paper function well without maintaining explicit evidence of sequentiality. This suggests that we should distinguish between process and product when considering our design. We had failed to give users sufficient evidence of sequentiality during the process of creating items; however, we did not need to preserve this information after the fact, when the textual contributions became simple objects in the world. The addition of shared editing and moving probably provides enough sequence information, and we do not need to change the basic whiteboard metaphor.

The issue of anonymity is similar to that of sequentiality in that one can have anonymity in the process of creation and anonymity of the eventual product. As we have pointed out, the issue of who has written text on the whiteboard is of primary importance during the process of writing, when it is a component in the conversation. There is not usually a need for a permanent label of authorship. With shared editing, anonymity no longer really exists for groups our size. If people are watching the process of creation, they will see who is doing what. This can be considered a loss, since anonymity in creating an item might permit shy or low status people to make more contributions. However, to implement process anonymity viably, we would need to move away from a basically conversational paradigm.

One of the chief benefits of the forgoing analysis is that it limits what we perceive as the sources of user difficulties. Users had problems that interacted with our decisions about sequentiality and anonymity. However, we came to believe that the designs we had in these areas were not themselves the cause of the problems. This thinking also applies to what is from some perspectives the fundamental problem with Cognoter: that we give users separate screens.

The thought that separate screens are the root of the problem is a very serious one, since they were a premise of the original system and the multiple arrangement is one of the most promising features of Colab. It is extremely flexible and presents the possibility of moving between private and public work. Furthermore, with the multiple screen/multiple keyboard setup, people can type at the same time, which means that, as with a whiteboard, the controls over whether they choose to do so are social and decided upon in response to the situation.

† We believe that this improvement allows perceptual rather than cognitive processing of positional changes, as described in Robertson, Card & MacKinlay (1989).

Although the analysis we have presented is by no means exhaustive, having a rich account of how the users probably came to have the difficulties they did, gives us reason to believe that the difficulties were not inherent in the multiple screen arrangement, but had limited, identifiable causes in what information was displayed on the screens. This means that, rather than giving up on the whole idea, we can try to address the problems in a more local fashion.

The new system has yet to be tested and evaluated. However, preliminary use by non-members of the Colab project suggests that users are much happier. At least one group has been able to work in the system using the computational shared workspace without the distress that we saw in our previous groups.

Other consequences

These changes fix the immediate problem. Since the Colab project's ultimate interest is in higher-level processes such as brainstorming and argumentation built on top of this fundamental conversational level, we needed to fix other difficulties as quickly as possible. Getting conversation right enables us to ask the questions about working with the system that we started with. For example, do the facilities we provide decrease "production blocking" and enable more efficient and effective idea generation and development? Do shy people contribute more or less when given a keyboard? Do people actually have a greater shared understanding of the material due to the less cryptic notes that get taken?

However, in our solutions, we tried not to experiment but simply to provide the facilities to enable successful conversation. The conversational mechanisms themselves provide another interesting source of technological experimentation and possibility. For example, although we now coordinate each participants' window size and shape, and make editor windows as well as item organization windows public, it would be interesting to see what happened if we made this user-tailorable. We might find out under what circumstances it is necessary or desirable for everyone to see the same things in the same way. We might also find out whether there are a class of situations in which it is not necessary for everyone to see the same things in the same way.

Another issue is that we have made Cognoter more conversational, rather than less. However, there is nothing about the Cognoter technology that intrinsically demands that it be used for closely coordinated work. In our studies, we set up a situation in which people would use the technology conversationally. We asked them to bring a task that they wanted or needed to work on together in the course of their own work. Presumably there are reasons why these tasks needed group solution. Our description of the technology revolved around its cooperative nature and its benefits for collaboration. Users were driven by the task, by our set-up, and by their own expectations to attempt to work by minimizing the least collaborative effort and by enjoying the benefits of mid-course correction and listener response. This must always be the case when people are actually working together. However, instead of trying to support activities already done in meetings, we could have tried to make it easier to bring activities normally done in isolation at least partially into a public forum, as when one wanders down the hall and asks a colleague about a word or a paragraph, or the outline of an algorithm, or the arguments to a function without actually involving them in the central work that is being done. The challenge here is to provide easy flow back and forth between the public and the private at the right grain-size. This requires strategies for getting people's attention and agreement about moving from private work to collaboration. These strategies, whether provided through the computer or verbally, must be conversationally viable.

This analysis also has benefits in terms of the study of conversation and interaction. Several questions have been raised: one is how a more complete description of the relationship between talk and action in traditional representational media, might look. What are the mechanisms and resources available to people for incorporating written items into the conversation? Does some more subtle kind of try-marker occur in whiteboard use? Are there certain categories of communications that are never written on whiteboards? Why do we ordinarily not see marks like "????" on whiteboards? Some of these questions have technical implications. For example, would it be helpful to render our notions of certainty about particular items visible in some fashion?

Conclusions

We realize that there were aspects of the original Cognoter system which did not work, and we have given some account of why. We claim that many of the serious problems in Cognoter stem from a culturally prevalent, easy-to-make assumption that communication consists of bits of verbal or textual material passed whole from one person to the next. Under this model, messages could be created, packaged, and sent by one person, unpacked, interpreted, changed, and sent on by others without regard for the exact moments of their creation and distribution. We also believe that we underestimated the problem for users of determining shared reference and therefore allowed too much activity that undermined its reliability. These underlying assumptions permitted a small but crucial number of design decisions in Cognoter that were responsible for much of the difficulty.

While it is possible that given enough time people could, as we did ourselves, learn to work with the system better than our users did, the initial difficulty was too great for a useful tool. Furthermore, whatever efficiency we gained by avoiding "production blocking" through parallel typing, this was certainly lost in the increased amount of work that had to be done to maintain communication.

We had reason to continue work on Cognoter. For one thing, we learned that certain aspects of the system were positively received. Promisingly, the group that used the video network to work around the problems discussed, was quite happy with the system. Although they used only a fraction of its functionality, some felt it could become "addictive", and commented with enthusiasm on the ease of bringing a fourth colleague up to speed on the work they had done in their Cognoter sessions.

Furthermore, we have yet to evaluate the features that we imagine as the most important contributions of the tool. By and large, the qualities we sought to promote in patterns of work are untouched by this analysis. Brainstorming, organizing and evaluating is still an interesting process to support. The ability to use the keyboard, the ability to save, printout, and recall organizations, the ability to rearrange material, and to handle large amounts of material are all important features.

However, we now see that the process we first identified at the whiteboard and later brought to the computer was built on conversational abilities. This affects some of our ideas. For example, we promoted the notion that it would be more efficient to work in parallel. That idea remains; however, it now rests on a deeper notion of what working in parallel means. It does not mean merely working at the same time as someone else, which is after all, what we do when we work alone. Instead, it means giving participants the ability to judge when it is appropriate to overlap, just as they judge the efficacy of other possible moves in a conversation. In other words, to work successfully in parallel, we must have resources for working together.

What happened with Cognoter has significance for CSCW beyond the boundaries of this particular project because Colab was a highly innovative project that encountered serious difficulty because it did not recognize that it had entered a new arena. It slipped up on implicit aspects of the system, places where the system designers didn't realize they were making choices. Although these problems were suspected in preliminary observations, two factors common to CSCW research conspired to make them difficult to pin down convincingly. One is that the problems are at such a fine level of coordination that is not possible to capture and recreate specific incidents of problems without electronic means. The second is that considerable knowledge of the system and its rationale does seem to allow people to function without overt distress, perhaps by causing them to reduce their criteria for understanding what is happening at particular moments.

Human–machine studies are done typically to examine those aspects of systems that are already deemed important for success. In a field that is as new and as complex as computer-supported cooperative work, and equally as liable to fail (Grudin, 1988), highly directed studies need to be augmented by other approaches such as undirected observation. Furthermore, system designers must draw on and reason about social science results such as the interactive model that are not necessarily predictive and which do not necessarily describe the exact situation that they are designing. This is a risky but potentially rewarding strategy.

The ability to use whatever social science insights we have to feed into careful thought about the situation we are trying to create is crucial because, as designers of novel technologies, we must judge whether the technologies we envisage are likely to work. While it is easy to judge failure by the distress expressed by users, it is much harder to judge the success and potential of a system that has encountered difficulty. Although this analysis has focused on problems and addressed potential only incidentally, it also suggests that Cognoter was close to being able to create a multi-user system that people would be able to use with the ease, range of expressive behaviors, and mastery that they employ in conversation. Furthermore, experience suggests that perhaps we can give users much more facility due to the potentially greater expressive power of the computerized representational medium.

Many thanks are due to Sara Bly, Frank Halasz, Steve Harrison, Leigh Klotz, Cathy Marshall, and John Tang for reading early drafts and giving excellent comments. Robert Anderson, Liam Bannon, Marjorie Goodwin, Jonathan Grudin, Susan Newman, Wendy Mackay, Lucy Suchman, and Mark Stefik all contributed through comments and extensive discussion. As usual, Stan Lanning was indispensable in helping us implement the software. Additional thanks to the anonymous reviewers. We were grateful for their suggestions and hope they are pleased with the results.

References

BLY, S. (1988). A use of drawing surfaces in different collaborative settings. In *Proceedings of the Conference on Computer-Supported Cooperative Work,* pp. 250–256, Portland, Oregon, September 26–28.

CLARK, H. H. & SCHAEFER, E. F. (1987). Collaborating on contributions to conversations. *Language and Cognitive Processes,* **2,** 19–41.

CLARK, H. H. & SCHAEFER, E. F. (1989). Contributing to discourse. *Cognitive Science,* **13,** 259–294.

CLARK, H. H. & WILKES-GIBBS, D. (1986). Referring as a collaborative process. *Cognition,* **22,** 1–39.

DIEHL, M. & STROEBE, W. (1987). Productivity loss in brainstorming groups: toward the solution of a riddle. *Journal of Personality and Social Psychology,* **53,** 497–509.

DUNCAN, S. D. (1973). Toward a grammar for dyadic conversation. *Semiotica,* **9,** 29–47.

FOSTER, G. (1986). Collaborative systems and multiuser interfaces. PhD. thesis, University of California, Berkeley.

FOSTER, G. & STEFIK, M. (1986). Cognoter, theory and practice of a Colab-orative tool. In *Proceedings of the Conference on Computer-Supported Cooperative Work,* pp. 7–12. Austin, Texas, December 3–5.

Goodwin, C. (1981). *Conversational Organization: Interaction Between Speakers and Hearers.* New York: Academic Press.

GOODWIN, C. & HERITAGE, J. (1990). Conversation analysis. *Annual Review of Anthropology,* **19,** 283–307.

GOODWIN, C. & GOODWIN, M. H. (1990). Context, activity, and participation. In P. AUER & A. DI LUZO, Eds. *The Contextualization of Language.* Amsterdam: Benjamins.

GOODWIN, M. H. (1980). Processes of mutual monitoring implicated in the production of description sequences. *Sociological Inquiry,* **50,** 303–317.

GRUDIN, J. (1988). Why CSCW system fail. In *Proceedings of the Conference on Computer-Supported Cooperative Work,* pp. 85–93, Portland, Oregon.

POMERANTZ, A. (1978). Compliment responses: notes on the co-operation of multiple constraints. In J. SCHENKEIN, Ed. *Studies in the Organization of Conversational Interaction,* pp. 79–112. New York: Academic Press.

POMERANTZ, A. (1984). Pursuing a response. In J. M. ATKINSON & J. HERITAGE, Eds. *Structures of Social Action,* pp. 152–164. Cambridge, UK: Cambridge University Press.

ROBERTSON, G. G., CARD, S. K. & MacKINLAY, J. (1989). *The Cognitive Co-processor Architecture for the Interactive User Interfaces,* Xerox PARC Technical Report #SSL-89-28.

SACKS, H. & SCHEGLOFF, E. A. (1979). Two preferences in the organization of reference to persons in conversation and their interaction. In G. PSATHAS, Ed. *Everyday Language: Studies in Ethnomethodology.* New York: Irvington.

SCHEGLOFF, E. A. (1981). Discourse as an interactive achievement: some uses of uh-huh and other things that come between sentences. In D. TANNEN, Ed. *Analyzing Discourse: Text and Talk.* Georgetown University Roundtable on Languages and Linguistics 1981, pp. 71–93. Washington, DC: Georgetown University Press.

SCHEGLOFF, E. A. & SACKS, H. (1973). Opening up closings. *Semiotica,* **8,** 289–327.

SCHOBER, M. F. & CLARK, H. H. (1989). Understanding by addressees and overhearers. *Cognitive Psychology,* **21,** 211–232.

STEFIK, M. J., FOSTER, G., BOBROW, D. G., KAHN, K., LANNING, S. & SUCHMAN, L. (1987a). Beyond the Chalkboard. *Communications of the ACM,* **30,** 32–47.

STEFIK, M. J., BOBROW, D. G., FOSTER, G., LANNING, S. M. & TATAR, D. G. (1987b). WYSIWIS revised: early experiences with multiuser interfaces. *ACM Transactions on Office Information Systems,* **5,** 147–167.

SUCHMAN, L. (1988). Representing practice in cognitive science. *Human Studies,* **11,** 305–325.

TANG, J. C. (1989). *Listing, Drawing and Gesturing in Design*: *A Study of the Use of Shared Workspaces by Design Teams,* Xerox PARC Technical Report #SSL-89-3 (Ph.d. thesis Stanford University).

TANG, J. C. (1990). *Observations of the Use of Shared Drawing Spaces.* Videotape, Xerox PARC Technical Memo.

5

The Portland Experience: a report on a distributed research group

MARGRETHE H. OLSON

SARA A. BLY

From 1985 for three years, the System Concepts Laboratory (SCL) of the Xerox Palo Alto Research Center had employees in both Palo Alto, California, and Portland, Oregon. The Portland remote site was intended to be a forcing function for the lab to focus on issues of interpersonal computing in a geographically distributed organization. Interpersonal computing supports people communicating and working together through computers; it includes tools to support interaction separated by time and/or space as well as face-to-face interaction and meetings. A consultant to the laboratory took on the role of outside observer to provide insight into questions about the process of working in a distributed organization and about tools for supporting collaboration in a distributed organization. The primary collaborative work of the lab itself was design. The major tool that developed to support the cross-site environment was Media Space, a network of video, audio and computing technologies. With the Media Space, SCL members were able to make significant progress in supporting their distributed design process. The SCL experience adds to the existing knowledge of collaboration by focusing on intellectual effort where the primary resource is information. The activities of the lab depended on reciprocal interdependence of group members for information. Their work required them to be in touch with one another to share and coordinate information, yet lab members were often not together physically or temporally. The SCL work forced the boundaries of social place to extend beyond the boundaries of physical place.

1. Introduction

In 1984 a new laboratory at the Xerox Palo Alto Research Center (PARC) was formed to expand the vision of personal computing to interpersonal computing. While personal computing supports individuals and involves their interaction with a computer, it is not directed at person-to-person interaction or work group collaboration. The notion of interpersonal computing is that it supports people communicating and working together through computers. Interpersonal computing supports human-to-human interactions whether they be face-to-face or separated by time and/or space. One lab member articulated it this way: "There is a vision of an environment in which it is easy to work with anyone you want to in space and time. That requires the ability to interact, to get in touch, to share resources".

As part of the formation of the System Concepts Laboratory (SCL) in Palo Alto, California, an office was opened in Portland, Oregon, in which all employees were

81

members of SCL. The Portland remote site was intended to force the lab to focus on the issues of interpersonal computing in a geographically distributed organization. This paper summarizes observations of SCL and its "remote work site" experience (to be referred to here as the Portland Experience) from October 1985 until January 1988.

The report is based primarily on the observations of the first author who was a consultant to SCL and who took the role of outside observer to the lab. She made 10 visits between October 1985 and December 1987. Each visit consisted of two full days at each site, interviewing (on an individual basis) as many of the lab members as possible. All interviews were open-ended and unstructured. The lab members discussed a wide range of issues, many of which were not directly related to the Portland Experience. The researcher also spent a considerable amount of time observing activities in the lab, including formal and informal meetings. Through these visits, the researcher was able to learn about the overall social process and culture of the lab as well as about specific projects.

Written records from the interviews and observations provided the basis for this report on the Portland Experience. These records inform the view of the laboratory as research itself as well as describe the research of the laboratory. In January 1988, the Portland site was closed. Thus, this report examines the Portland Experience in light of the fact that it is now complete and the body of knowledge it generated can be summarized.

The central research question addressed as a result of the observations is two-fold: What can be learnt from the Portland Experience in terms of: (1) the process of collaboration in a distributed organization; and (2) the design and implementation of tools to support collaboration in a distributed organization? The report briefly describes the environment, technology and research of the Portland Experience. The research work of the lab during this period is then reviewed and analysed in terms of the researchers' process of collaborating across sites and developing tools to support cross-site collaboration. Finally, the Portland Experience itself is considered in the light of related research on work group collaboration, tool development, socialization and management control.

2. The distributed laboratory environment

The dominant espoused research goal of the SCL distributed organization was to develop tools to support collaboration in a distributed environment. The existence of the Portland site created two types of barriers to the usual communication and collaboration: geographical and cultural. The assumption was that the lab would be forced to develop tools to help overcome these barriers. Thus, a second site geographically closer to PARC, where the barriers could be overcome easily (i.e. by travel between sites), was ruled out.

The Portland site was intended to support up to eight full-time researchers plus one technical and one administrative support person. For most of the two-year period of the evaluation, there were seven full-time researchers, two support people, and occasionally a consultant and a graduate (summer) student. In Palo Alto, there were 12 to 15 full-time researchers, one support person, three visiting scientists and consultants at various times, and one graduate student. The facility in

Portland was to be similar to the one in Palo Alto, with a large Commons area for meetings and informal interaction, individual offices on the periphery of the Commons, and a conference room for more formal or private meetings.

2.1. TECHNOLOGY

Initially, the Portland facility was only able to communicate with the Palo Alto facility by US mail, telephone, electronic mail, and a high-speed data link. As will be described later, a significant portion of SCL's research work was focused on the design process. A design environment, called "Media Space", was built to support the premise that design is a social activity. As conceived, a media space was a system of video, audio and computer technologies to create environments for project teams that span physically and temporally disjoint places (Stults, 1986).

At the time the research reported here began, the notion of the media space had been expanded to connect the lab as a whole across both sites. The key technology providing the link between the two sites was an open communication channel to support (at 56 kb) interactive video and audio at all times. Figure 1 shows a timeline of the technology available for cross-site communication.

The first cross-site use of a media space was to install video (cameras and monitors) and audio equipment in the Commons at each site. This media space was used for informal interaction as well as for group meetings. Figure 2 shows an example of one such small group meeting. Later, experiments were done with moving all or part of the equipment into individual offices for private meetings. By the fall of 1986, a video switch was installed at each site, and the Commons areas, conference rooms, and many individual offices were all equipped with monitors and

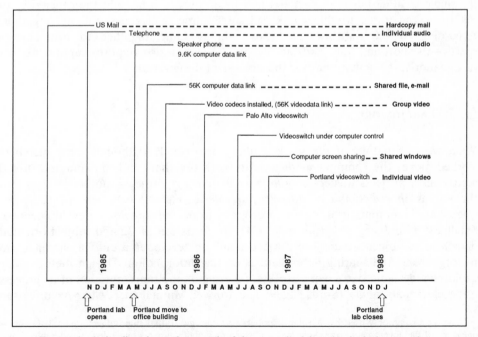

FIGURE 1. A timeline shows the growth of the cross-site lab technological connections.

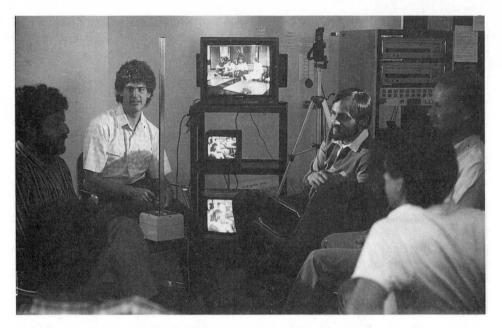

FIGURE 2. Meetings were often conducted cross-site.

cameras. Figure 3 shows a diagram of the link and switches. At each site the video switch was linked to the computing environment, so that a person at a workstation could establish a video connection with another node at the same site, or through the single channel between Portland and Palo Alto, to a node at the other site. In Figure 4, an office-to-office link supports three colleagues talking together. According to one lab member, "two things came together to form media spaces—the Portland link, and the recognition that design requires support for not just goal-oriented activity but for the process of design itself".

2.2. RESEARCH WORK

What was the nature of the work actually performed? Although some members worked alone, the common mode was to work together, and the common thread across many projects was *collaborative development*.† Projects can be grouped into three areas: *shared computing infrastructure, design methodology,* and *media spaces.* The shared computing infrastructure grew from the previous development of Smalltalk (Goldberg & Robson, 1984) to focus on a shared object-oriented database, an object server. The project members developed a unifying architecture for organizing and sharing heterogenous on-line information. Design methodology explored a design group's work process, focusing on the representation of its process using electronic media (Stults, 1989; Harrison & Minneman, 1990). As discussed

---

† The term commonly used by SCL lab members was "design" rather than "development". Design is one stage of the development process, a stage in which many lab members expended considerable effort.

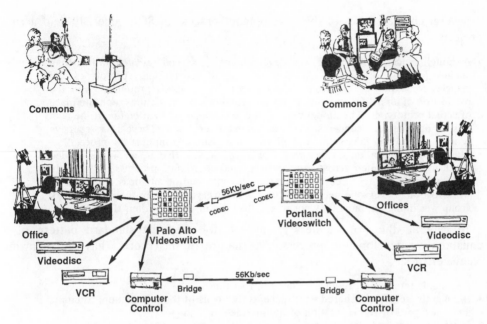

FIGURE 3. A videoswitch formed the basis for Media Space connections.

earlier, to support the design process, the SCL Media Space came into being and expanded to support the work of the entire lab. The resulting media spaces area included the study of the use of the cross-site Media Space (Goodman & Abel, 1986; Abel, 1989), as well as the development of the various software pieces needed to connect and integrate the media space with the computer network.

FIGURE 4. Individuals or small groups could interact in office-to-office connections.

Several characteristics of the development process in SCL generally held across projects:

- Although much of the work was development, it served *research* rather than engineering. The artifacts produced were generally evolutionary prototypes and vehicles for exploring ideas and issues rather than finished products. Even the production of an artifact was not required; occasionally simulations took the place of actual prototypes. The model was more one of *tinkering* than *building*; the goal was to demonstrate concepts. As one lab member said: "There is a recursive process of evolving the system and allowing the system to support the process".
- The mode of operation was *reciprocal interdependence,* that is, resources needed by all were distributed across sites and required coordination across the sites. In SCL, the primary resource to be shared was information or ideas. In order to work together, everyone needed to know what everyone else in the project work group was doing and how they got where they did in terms of their thinking.

In general, the work underway in SCL followed the standard pattern of a collaborative development process. The nature of this process has the following characteristics:

- It is highly interactive, requiring dialog in real time;
- It generally requires a shared workspace as the focus of that interaction, to create a visual record or representation of the interaction;
- It often requires additional reference materials—notes, documents, manuals, etc.;
- It requires some record of past interaction, even though it may be highly informal—memory of work group members (e.g. "Do you remember why we came up with that solution?").

Projects (or project stages) that focused on design were the most numerous, followed by those that focused on programming. Although programming was typically done individually or at a single site, many design activities were done collaboratively and most of these involved both sites. Thus *collaborative design* across the two sites was a predominant activity in the lab over the two-year period.

The dominant output of cross-site collaboration was specifications (the primary output of design). However, it is also worth noting that nearly half of the projects done collaboratively across sites resulted in no tangible output. In comparison, projects done individually or collaboratively at a single site, more often than not did produce tangible output. Having no tangible output does not necessarily mean the project failed. Many of these projects were high-level (abstract) definitions (e.g. early results from the computing infrastructure area) that produced documents reflecting members' thought processes but no operational output in the sense of specifications or code.

3. An interpretation of the research contribution

It is important to understand the research of SCL as a basis for understanding both the process and the tools of collaboration in this particular distributed organization. Their design work was not highly structured and did not benefit from tools to help structure the process. The SCL type of collaborative work depended on the availability of information and the capacity for reciprocal interdependence.

Thus, we consider two dimensions of collaborative design: communication in the design process and the interactions in the design process. We separate communication in real time and communication as records of the process over time. The first is *synchronous* (or supporting real-time interactivity) and the second *asynchronous* (or creating a record). The second dimension deals with focus of the interaction: we shall distinguish *open* process (informal and unstructured) from *focused* process. Using these dimensions as a framework for the contributions of SCL in their design activities, each resulting quadrant may be thought of as a separate design environment for which support tools can be developed.

The activities of the group over the observation period can be classified into understanding and/or building tools for each of the four quadrants. It is important to note that the lab members not only focused on collaboration over a geographical barrier (i.e. remote collaboration), but also on making the design activity more effective even without that constraint. Table 1 illustrates example tools and studies in each quadrant.

Quadrant I: *Open, synchronous activities:* General problem definition takes place in this type of design environment. The primary product of this aspect of design is talk. The forums are frequently open meetings (with many *kibitzers*) for "kicking around ideas", informal spontaneous meetings, and many drop-in conversations. They take up a significant amount of time with the only tangible output being an occasional document of user needs (for example, a scenario paper) or straw proposal. Even the primary purpose of these documents is to provide clarity of ideas for the *writer,* not to inform the reader (although they are generally read). As the design activity becomes more focused, such documents produced along the way become out of date.

One general problem with this aspect of design is maintaining it. According to one member involved with the infrastructure area, "high-level goal issues have not stimulated a lot of interaction. There is a lot of interaction on fairly low-level language issues". According to another lab member, "normally in the lab people

TABLE 1

Projects can be categorized by the process and communication they support

	Synchronous communication	Asynchronous communication
Open process	(I) CONTACT: a workstation tool to make media space connections.	(II) Sense of the Present: written design notes that persist over a short time.
	Media Space Commons link: the default live audio and video connection between sites.	Video notebooks: the ability to capture events that occurred in the Media Space.
Focused process	(III) SharedARK: a shared computational simulation environment.	(IV) CORAL: an early prototype of an object-oriented shared database.
	Office Design Project: a study to observe designers working in a media space environment.	Videodisc access: a workstation tool to allow designers to retrieve and discuss previous work and meetings.

spend 30 seconds thinking about what to do and almost no planning; then they just start coding".

In the lab, tools for "making connections lightweight", which were often labeled as supporting informal interaction, supported this open, synchronous collaboration. The primary tool for this support was the Media Space which permitted both formal and informal interactions to occur. Whenever and wherever there was a live audio/video connection between nodes, spontaneous interactions could occur. As part of the tools for supporting lightweight connections, a software interface called CONTACT was developed specifically to support connection.

Quadrant II: Open, asynchronous activities: This aspect of design deals primarily with capturing the thought processes generated by the high-level design activity in open, synchronous interactions. In informal meetings or spontaneous interaction, a formal record is rarely kept and the primary source of recall for later, more focused design, is human memory. Yet many new research ideas are generated in just such an open, informal interaction. The ability to capture these ideas was viewed as an important research area.

Although the lab did no specific work on capturing informal interaction for later recall, the constant presence of the Media Space in offices and common areas generated a sensitivity to the potential of such a capability. Occasionally lab members would take advantage of the availability of the Media Space to turn on a videotape recorder during a spontaneous, informal discussion that had promise of eliciting good discussion.

In addition to recording spontaneous interactions, some informal discussions took place asyncronously. E-mail was frequently used for sharing thoughts and ideas. An application, called *Sense of the Present,* offered a mechanism for the design area members to store ideas and notes. In keeping with the intention that these notes be lightweight, data disappeared after a few weeks of storage.

Quadrant III: Focused, synchronous activities: A focused design activity resulting in operational design specifications (written, graphic, verbal, etc.) takes place here. Support for this aspect of collaboration requires intensive dialog (audio) support and a shared, focused workspace that includes drawing. Overwhelmingly, regardless of the project, lab members expressed as their greatest need in cross-site design the ability to have a shared workspace. In architectural design it is clear that drawing capability would be essential, but the same need seems to hold true for collaborative systems design. According to one member, "this project pushes some things with respect to ambiguity in collaboration. When people collaborate they need to manipulate the things in their world".

The Office Design Project (Weber & Minneman, 1988), a study in the design methodology area, explicitly examined what happens if the design environment is controlled in such a way that only the focused interaction, without the potential distractions of a more open environment, is available. The study revealed some important insights about the focused design activity. A major theme which emerged was the relationship between working together and privately at the same time. The participants in the study acted as if they were working privately—not taking breaks, not chatting, feeling compelled to work—and they were amazed at the resulting volume of work produced. Yet it was indeed an intense collaboration through shared dialog (as well as live video) and a shared video drawing space. According to one lab member "the tapes show the discovery of moving through the video space. . . . One guy wanted to draw on the other person's screen, and he figured out a way to use tracing paper to essentially do that. It helped that we had very visually oriented people". Another study (Bly, 1988) specifically focused on the use of a shared workspace, comparing face-to-face, video and audio, and telephone only settings. An interesting observation from this study is that "the process of creating drawings may be as important to the design process as the drawings themselves".

These and other studies were pointing the way to rich environments for shared workspaces. Efforts were made to provide capabilities for sharing screen areas on workstations. SharedARK was a particularly sophisticated simulation environment that allowed users on more than one workstation simultaneously (Smith, O'Shea, O'Malley, Scanlon & Taylor, 1989). Because the primary tool developed in the lab supporting all aspects of design was Media Space, many other real-time and focused tools were conceptualized as enhancements to it.

Quadrant IV: Focused, asynchronous activities: Focused design activity frequently takes place over time rather than in a single intensive session. Records of the process are often needed to review assumptions and to bring a new person "up to speed" on a design. One member of the lab articulated the relationship between recording the process over time and supporting the process across space: "We want to say that if you put communication media and ritual into place you can make it easier to participate in the present moment. The present moment has a past. . . up to two weeks. There are fewer interruptions. . . it is about getting rid of overheads that the group demand-driven activity requires".

Early work in the design methodology area demonstrated how a rich record of the design process, primarily based on video recording and selective videodisk access, could be used to bring a new member into a work group in the middle of the design activity. In the Office Design Project mentioned earlier, one of the tools available to the designers was access to videodisc material. The material had been collected earlier from the designers and from the project client. Another major theme of the Office Design study was recording the process so that it could be recreated selectively for the client as well as the designers.

The fundamental notion of needing a repository of "things" for sharing—and thus the shared object database under design—fits into this aspect of collaborative development. A preliminary shared object database, CORAL, gave lab members experience in the development and use of a tool for supporting focused, asynchronous activity (Merrow & Laursen, 1987). In the long term, any applications which were envisioned for the shared object database under design would support focused, asynchronous design.

Experiences in cross-site projects emphasized the need for tools in this area as well. In one such project, there were many complaints about misunderstandings among group members which were generally attributed to the two locations. According to one member, "we have discussions here and they have the same discussions there. Sometimes we make decisions about the same things they do and they conflict". In another case: "There is a small project to develop a database in Palo Alto. Independently I thought it was a good idea and wanted to do it. I didn't know they were already doing it". While it is easy to dismiss these problems as lack of face-to-face interaction, having adequate tools to record the process may have solved most of these kinds of problems.

In general, the group began with a preoccupation with open, synchronous activities

(I), but steadily moved in the direction of supporting more focused collaborative design activities (III and IV). They focused on the task that for them was both the hardest and most rewarding: collaborative design. They did not tackle problems related to other development activities that were less critical to their work, such as programming together. With the Media Space they were making significant progress in supporting focused, synchronous design activities and were moving toward support of asynchronous design. The underlying technology of the shared object database was primarily a critical component for focused, asynchronous activities, but also to some extent for all four categories of activity.

4. The Portland Experience as research

To understand the Portland Experience as research, it is necessary to go beyond the research work done within the lab and examine the lab from outside. For this perspective, it is important to place the lab experience in the context of related work. Four areas will be considered: the nature of the work group collaboration, the approach for development of new tools, the nature of the socialization (i.e. the type of organization in which the lab existed), and the nature of management control.

4.1. THE NATURE OF WORK GROUP COLLABORATION

Recently, computer science and information systems researchers have begun to pay attention to technological support for work group collaboration (Greif, 1988; Olson, 1989). In the academic fields of management as well as social psychology and sociology, there is a considerable body of research on the nature of work groups. While research in social psychology has tended to focus on group process, particularly in decision making (e.g. Kelley & Thibault, 1968), research in sociology has focused more on official work units (i.e. departments) and their interdependence in terms of organizational structure (e.g. Pugh, Hickson & Hinings, 1969; Hage & Aiken, 1979). Research in management theory has focused recently on *teamwork* and participative management (e.g. Tjosvold, 1968). Most of this research has attempted to demonstrate the benefits of teamwork in terms of employee motivation and productivity. Very little research in any field has specifically focused on how work is performed in and managed by groups. Computer scientists interested in building tools to support groups at work have not found a useful framework in any of this research to define how information technology might improve work group process and output.

The type of work group collaboration dealt with in this report is strictly of the *intellectual* variety, as opposed to work groups assigned to assembly, manufacture, or construction of physical artifacts. This type of collaboration has several features:

- There is at least one common goal shared by all group members, although subordinate goals may not be shared by all members or may even be in conflict;
- The primary resource required to carry out the activity is information or ideas, thus there must be some facility for work group members to share information;
- The coordination of effort required to accomplish the task primarily requires knowing what other work group members are thinking and/or doing;
- Work group members are thus interdependent in their work, although for periods of time they may be able to accomplish tasks independently.

The nature of interdependence of collaborative work groups is best defined by Thompson (1967). Thompson defines three types of interdependence of resources in any work process:

- Sequential interdependence, where resources are consumed sequentially, as in an assembly line;
- Pooled interdependence, where the resource to be consumed may be accessed simultaneously by multiple facilities requiring it, as in access to a centralized database for an airline reservations system;
- Reciprocal interdependence, where each of two facilities also has resources required by the other, and coordination of the two is required.

In intellectual work the primary resource utilized is information. Unlike physical resources, information is not consumed when it is used; thus the more information is shared the greater the reciprocal interdependence of the work group and the greater the need for mechanisms to facilitate information sharing. Thus, each facility (in this case, people) needs to know what the other members of the work group are doing and/or thinking. This knowledge must span time (How did they arrive at this solution? What did the group do yesterday when I was out of the office?) and space (What are the other members doing now? Is it necessary for us to meet face to face to resolve this disagreement?).

The lab's experience: It is clear that in terms of the first espoused research goal, to understand and support collaboration in a distributed organization, the lab became preoccupied with collaborative design activities rather than other collaborative activities. In so doing, the model they followed was to build something which they could use in their own work (i.e. collaborative design). A significant number of prototypes were built during the period but few members focused on supporting collaboration in the actual building of these prototypes (although there are some interesting examples). Although at first "programming together" was felt to be necessary and supportable across sites, the needs of the lab over the period did not push them in this direction either.

Dealing with their frustrations in coping with the limitations of the Media Space for design across sites, the group members were able to gain valuable insights related to this particular type of collaborative activity and the tools required to support it. The greatest frustration was expressed for instance, in the computing infrastructure area during design; when they began to implement code, they were able to work effectively with much less communication among group members. One example of the expression of frustration is the following: "Sometimes things were in such a state that the link worked well because we *had* to communicate... We agreed we wouldn't change it any more but it didn't work. There were a lot more changes... It shoved you over the barrier to communications (i.e. the link). The telephone became more important... It was good there was more than one person at each site. It provided local support for sanity testing. For some reason the more bandwidth the easier it is to do perspective shifting".

There are many examples that show the lab members' sensitivity to the design activity and the need to support that activity rather than simply providing more information: "The other labs think of knowledge as a base you can draw on. I think knowledge is also a process... there is knowledge implicit in the process; e.g. knowledge engineering. The design process and knowledge of how different people approach the problem is part of the knowledge base. It is knowledge about process or procedure, not just about content".

"This project has no central management. That is not a problem. The whole group has to come to the revelation of a problem when there is one. It is up to the group to manage itself".

"It is very nice to have them (the other group members) up there in a way. They don't come in and see where I'm at all the time".

The second goal of the research agenda was the design and implementation of tools to support distributed collaboration. The lab made considerable progress toward this goal; the lab had a very clear understanding of the infrastructure required to support collaborative design and was progressing on that infrastructure. In support of specific focused interaction in the design activity, there was also considerable progress with projects related to interaction in the Media Space.

4.2. ALTERNATIVE GOALS FOR DEVELOPMENT OF NEW TOOLS

Different tools have different effects on work group process. Some alternative goals leading to development of different tools are examined here.

(1) To make two separate physical environments *more like* a single environment. This has traditionally been the goal of video teleconferencing: to be as much as possible like a face-to-face meeting.

(2) To improve the *efficiency* of reciprocal interdependence. For a task where reciprocal interdependence is necessary, generally a great deal of time is spent "informing" other members of the work group. Tools that focus on improving the efficiency of this process might reduce the amount of information required to be shared, by increasing specificity or standardization. A common example today is the substitution of electronic mail for the telephone because it eliminates unnecessary "social" conversation. An example of a new tool is an electronic mail system which imposes a structure on the dialog, such as the Coordinator by Action Technologies Corporation.

(3) To increase the *capacity* of reciprocal interdependence by improving the accessibility of shared information. Tools of this type increase the amount of information sharing among work group members, either in order to overcome barriers of space (e.g. interactive video in offices) and time (e.g. videotape recordings) or to make face-to-face interaction more effective (e.g. meeting augmentation, group decision support systems). The shared object service was an example of an infrastructure technology that supports this goal.

The lab's experience: In terms of the three goals of tool development, to which did SCL make a contribution? The group began by focusing on the first, making the two separate environments more like a single one. Many continued with a preoccupation that the link was not as good as face-to-face and thus the split site was a frustrating obstacle. An example was in the process of designing the shared object service, where there were frequent expressions of frustration with the limitations of the media. In this case in particular, the group did not seize on the opportunity to ask "What is the real problem?" and thus articulate a specific need—i.e. a shared work space. In other efforts, such as the Office Design and Shared Drawing studies, the group did take advantage of the opportunity to learn what is different about collaboration in a media space rather than simply measuring it against the metric of face-to-face interaction.

Some members of the group thought (in hindsight) that the direction they expected of the group was in support of the second goal, improving the efficiency of reciprocal interdependence. For instance, they might have developed the next-generation electronic mail system or group authoring system. Instead, much of the ongoing work of the lab focused on the third goal, improving reciprocal interdependence through facilitating accessibility of more information which is needed for collaboration in the design activity. The underlying shared computing infrastructure was in support of this goal, as were aspects of design methodology having to do with creating and accessing a record of the design process. In this work, the SCL group made a contribution which is unique to the computer-supported cooperative work community. It is significantly different from work on meeting augmentation because it opens up many possibilities for interaction across space and time while keeping the interaction at least as effective as, and possibly more effective than, face-to-face interaction with its geographical and timing limitations.

4.3. THE NATURE OF SOCIALIZATION

Another aspect of work group collaboration which has been neglected in research to date is the process by which work group members learn and act out their roles. This has to do with the nature of contracts: who determines who should do what and how is commitment from work group members elicited? There are different models, from highly authoritarian (the manager dictates task assignment and demands commitment) to highly participative (all work group members negotiate together and agree on tasks). Prior to task assignment, understanding of the expertise and knowledge each work group member brings to the project, is particularly important if the work group wants to be cooperative and foster trust among members. For instance, if a person takes on a particular task voluntarily, the other group members should have some *a priori* belief that the person is competent to do the task and can be trusted to deliver as promised.

The primary type of organization of which SCL is a prototypical example is defined by Mintzberg (1979) as an adhocracy. The dominant form of coordination of work in an adhocracy is mutual adjustment, which refers to "coordination of work by the simple process of informal communication". Furthermore, the adhocracy is fairly flat, with few layers of management. Roles and organizational responsibilities are fairly loosely defined and highly ambiguous, with individuals given a considerable amount of leeway to choose how to prioritize their time. The process of adjusting to an organization of this sort involves learning what the appropriate projects to work on are without any explicit direction offered, and establishing and/or demonstrating competence and trustworthiness in order that other work group members seek out the new member for projects.

Many of the phenomena regarding work group process and socialization are, at least traditionally, highly dependent on physical place and physical (i.e. face-to-face) interaction. The considerable body of research on teleconferencing (Short, Williams & Christie, 1976; Johansen, Vallee & Vian, 1979) emphasizes specifically how it is less than face-to-face. For instance, Short and his colleagues operationalize the notion of *social presence* of a media and measure it relative to face-to-face interaction.

In the socialization process, people learn how to act in organizations by watching other people. The *culture* of the organization is reflected in its physical environment (Deal & Kennedy, 1982). Roles and status are reflected in a very formal way in the size of an office, the number of windows, the type of desk (in one organization, the "wooden desk people" are the only ones who make decisions), even the color of the carpet. On a more subtle note, who talks to whom in the elevator, who goes to lunch together, etc. are all cues that are carefully observed by other organization members.

These notions of physical place are challenged by Meyrowitz (1985). Meyrowitz argues that "social place" is becoming a dominant factor in society today. If we examine the role of electronic media (particularly television) in our understanding of the world around us, it is apparent that assuming that physical and social place are equivalent is inadequate. In the case of work groups embedded in an organizational culture, this means that the traditional research and practice assumptions of physical place (epitomized by the face-to-face meeting) are inadequate to understand the impact of electronic media. In essence, electronic media present a new set of roles and meanings that "undermine the traditional relationship between physical setting and social situation".

The lab's experience: As described earlier, socialization is the process by which work group members learn and act out their roles. In SCL, this process was affected by the Portland Experience in dramatic but subtle ways.

Many problems of an adhocracy were exacerbated, if not caused by, the two-site split. This was particularly an issue because so many of the Portland members were new to PARC, and their cues (i.e. what to work on, what is research *vs* play, how much is acceptable, what are acceptable hours, etc.) were mostly provided in Palo Alto. It would be presumptuous to point to any particular personnel problems and attribute their cause to the fact that the person was not in Palo Alto and thus was not properly *socialized*. However, this is a rich area for further investigation.

Meyrowitz (1985) emphasizes the role of television in allowing formerly *private* spheres to become *public*. SCL was experimenting with a social place extended by video and audio that changed the relationship between private and public workplaces. It was not at all unusual for a person's office to be tuned into another office with video as well as audio and for this to be treated as unobtrusive background noise and not regarded as an invasion of the other person's privacy. This type of extension of private workspaces offers whole new possibilities for patterns of socialization which remain unexplored. Some of the experiences with using Media Space are particularly enlightening: "This is more like a window than a workstation or a microphone. It is more like an open office with shared acoustic space".

"It doesn't intrude; it is there and you can pay attention or consider it background. Also you don't need to leave your workspace to interact with others in your group. You can choose when and how to participate".

Some of the most interesting insights in terms of social process had to do with defining the etiquette of the Media Space. Many of the typical interactions were conversations among individuals and groups across sites (Irwin, 1990). Certainly media space technologies could also be used for intensive but unobtrusive monitoring of workers. However, there was a strong inclination not to build controls into the technologies that might be negotiated socially. Some attention was placed on building the Media Space so that it encouraged the status quo of shared control. For instance, a person should always be able to know if someone else was looking at them; such a feature was built into an application for controlling the video/audio connections. Another notion was *ethical video,* which meant that the observed should always be able to observe the observer. In SCL, this meant that a camera was usually paired with a monitor but observers could choose to stand outside of camera range and still see the monitor.

4.4. THE NATURE OF MANAGEMENT CONTROL

The final aspect of learning and doing roles in the work group process is the nature of control. With certain types of tasks, milestones and deliverables may be highly specific and measurable so that individual performance can be easily determined. In many work groups, the only real control by either management or other work group members is pure observation ("He is never in his office. No wonder he isn't going to meet the deadline—he is never working".)

An adhocracy tends to support an egalitarian, frequently participative, management style. Thus the organization members themselves may set policy and direction. In many such organizations, the implicit culture strongly indicates what is acceptable behavior (including such mundane things as dress, punctuality, etc.) without any explicit rules or policies. Individuals are "expected to figure it out", and those who do not are either misfits (working on the wrong things) or feel uncomfortable in the environment and choose to leave.

Furthermore, the physical place of the organization exerts a direct, if not very efficient, form of control over individuals. When an employee enters the facility, his or her time is *owned* by the organization. Even if employees are not being very productive, their *time in* is the basic metric on which their performance is determined. This fact was brought home to one author in extensive research on "telework", where employees worked at home instead of going to the office. The primary obstacle to telework as an employee work option was management's discomfort with not being able to *see* that their employees were working, and furthermore that the employee was in an environment, the home, which was explicitly outside of the organization's control (Olson, 1987).

In a work group where members themselves determine task assignments and roles, it is more likely that at least some control is held by group members themselves. Thus if one group member is slacking off, peer pressure is an effective control process.

The lab's experience: What can be generalized from the Portland Experience regarding the nature of control over work? Systems that are intended to improve the efficiency of coordination are also implicitly about the control process. The work done in SCL is differentiated from these approaches specifically because it emphasized sharing control by increasing the capacity of reciprocal inter-dependence.

The social organization of SCL's management structure was relatively participatory. There were two levels of management (area managers and a lab manager), who took seriously the responsibility of handling administrative matters so that their subordinates could concentrate on research. Cross-site reporting was often debated and the area managers, while admitting it made sense as part of the "experience", generally felt unconfortable with it. Since there were few specific objectives or deliverables, individual performance was often determined in a fairly subjective *ad hoc* way. This is not unusual, but managers tended to discount their intuitions when the subordinate was not on-site. Managers in Palo Alto made frequent trips to Portland to "confirm a hunch" about a problem (e.g. a communication problem among subordinates) and then to deal with the problem face-to-face.

5. Conclusions

The question to be addressed here was what can be learned from the Portland Experience in terms of the process of collaboration in a distributed organization and the design and implementation of tools to support collaboration in a distributed organization. The group itself did not articulate what they learned about collaboration in a distributed organization. However, their work shows that, across a variety of projects with a variety of types of "design", the group focused on collaboration in the design activity and understood that, because of its high reciprocal interdependence, this activity had the greatest need for support tools. As to the second part of the goal, the group went a long way toward defining the support needs for design and actually implementing the tools. The group did not progress to the stage where, having the tools in place, it could enhance the collaborative design activity cross-site and over time, through their use.

There is a considerable amount of ongoing work on collaboration support that treats work groups generically. A major contribution of the SCL experience is that it focused on a specific type of work group collaboration which evolved to be identified as the design process. Their work, however, can be generalized to other types of collaborative work with the following characteristics:

• Collaboration in an intellectual effort;
• Information as the primary resource;
• Reciprocal interdependence of group members for information;
• Control primarily through example and peer pressure.

A second major contribution of the SCL work is that it forced the boundaries of social place to extend beyond the boundaries of physical place. The cross-site collaborations in SCL should be viewed not as something less than face-to-face but rather as a new "place" to be explored and examined. Continued work in similar spaces suggests that such places have much to offer (Root, 1988; Bulick, Abel, Corey, Schmidt & Coffin, 1989; Buxton & Moran, 1990). The Portland Experience did indeed act as a forcing function to contribute both appropriate tools for shared design and itself as an example of collaborative work in a geographically distributed organization.

Considerable appreciation goes to the members of SCL who participated in the Portland Experience and who contributed to this report through their work and interviews. We particularly thank those who took time to read drafts of this paper and provide modifications. Thanks also goes to Mark Abel, Steve Harrison and Scott Minneman for providing the timeline and videoswitch data in Figures 1 and 3.

References

ABEL, M. (1989). Experiences in an exploratory distributed organization. In J. Galegher, R. E. Kraut & C. Egido, Eds. *Intellectual Teamwork: The Sociological and Technical Bases of Cooperative Work*, 489–510. Hillsdale, NJ: Lawrence Erlbaum Associates.

BLY, S. A. (1988). A use of drawing surfaces in different collaborative settings. In *Proceedings of the Conference on Computer-Supported Cooperative Work*, Portland, Oregon.

BULICK, S., ABEL, M., COREY, D., SCHMIDT, J. & COFFIN, S. (1989). The US WEST advanced technologies prototype multi-media communications system. In *Proceedings of the IEEE Global Telecommunications Conference, GLOBECOM '89*, Dallas, Texas.

BUXTON, B. & MORAN, T. (1990). EuroPARC's integrated interactive intermedia facility (iiif): early experiences. In *Proceedings of the IFIP WG8.4 Conference on Multi-user Interfaces and Applications*, Heraklion, Crete.

DEAL, T. E. & KENNEDY, A. A. (1982). *Corporate Culture: The Rites and Rituals of Corporate Life*. Reading, MA: Addison-Wesley.

GOLDBERG, A. & ROBSON, D. (1984). *Smalltalk-80: The Language and Its Implementation*. Menlo Park, CA: Addison-Wesley.

GOODMAN, G. & ABEL, M. (1986). Collaboration research in SCL. In *Proceedings of the Conference on Computer-Supported Cooperative Work*, Austin, Texas.

GREIF, I. (1988). *Computer-Supported Cooperative Work: A Book of Readings*. Boston, MA: Morgan Kaufman.

HAGE, J. T. & AIKEN, M. (1979). Routine technology, social structure, and organizational goals. *Administrative Science Quarterly*, **14**, 366–377.

HARRISON, S. & MINNEMAN, S. (1990). *The Media Space, a Research Project into the Use of Video as a Design Medium*, Xerox PARC Technical Report.

IRWIN, S. (1990). Technology, talk and the social world: a study of video-mediated interaction. Ph.d Thesis, Michigan State University.

JOHANSEN, R., VALLEE, J. & VIAN, K. (1979). *Electronic Meetings*. Reading, MA: Addison-Wesley.

KELLEY, H. H. & THIBAULT, J. W. (1968). Group Problem Solving. *Handbook of Social Psychology*, **3**, 1–105.

MERROW, T. & LAURSEN, J. (1987). A pragmatic system for shared persistent objects. In *Proceedings of the OOPSLA '87 Conference*, Orlando, Florida.

MEYROWITZ, J. (1985). *No Sense of Place: The Impact of Electronic Media on Social Behavior*. New York: Oxford University Press.

MINTZBERG, H. (1979). *The Structuring of Organizations*. Englewood Cliffs, NJ: Prentice-Hall.

OLSON, M. H. (1987). *An Investigation of the Impacts of Remote Work Environments and Supporting Technology*, (NSF Grant No. IST-8312073, 9/83-8/85), Working Paper #161 (GBA #87-80). New York: Center for Research on Information Systems, New York University.

OLSON, M. H. (Ed.) (1989). *Technological Support for Work Group Collaboration*. Hillsdale, NJ: Lawrence Erlbaum Associates.

PUGH, D. S., HICKSON, D. J. & HININGS, C. R. (1969). An empirical taxonomy of work organizations. *Administrative Science Quarterly*, **14**, 115–126.

ROOT, R. W. (1988). Design of a multi-media vehicle for social browsing. In *Proceedings of the Conference on Computer-Supported Cooperative Work*, Portland, Oregon.

SHORT, J., WILLIAMS, E. & CHRISTIE, B. (1976). *The Social Psychology of Telecommunications*. New York: John Wiley and Sons.

SMITH, R., O'SHEA, T., O'MALLEY, C., SCANLON, E. & TAYLOR, J. (1989). Preliminary experiments with a distributed, multi-media, problem solving environment. In *Proceedings of the First European Conference on Computer Supported Cooperative Work*, London, UK.

STULTS, R. (1986). *Media Space*, Xerox PARC Technical Report.

STULTS, R. (1989). *Experimental Uses of Video to Support Design Activities,* Xerox PARC Technical Report #SSL-89-19.

THOMPSON, J. D. (1967). *Organizations in Action.* New York: McGraw-Hill.

TJOSVOLD, D. (1968). *Working Together to Get Things Done*: *Managing for Organizational Productivity.* New York: Lexington Books.

WEBER, K. & MINNEMAN, S. L. (1988). *The Office Design Project.* Xerox PARC videotape (28 min).

6

Power, ease of use and cooperative work in a practical multimedia message system

Nathaniel S. Borenstein

Chris A. Thyberg

The "Messages" program, the high-end interface to the Andrew Message System (AMS), is a multimedia mail and bulletin board reading program that novices generally learn to use in less than an hour. Despite the initial simplicity, however, Messages is extremely powerful and manages to satisfy the needs of both experts and novices through a carefully evolved system of novice-oriented defaults, expert-oriented options, and a help system and option-setting facility designed to ease the transition from new user to sophisticated expert. The advanced features of the system facilitate types of cooperative work that are not possible with other mail or bulletin board systems, but which would also be impossible in large heterogeneous communities if the system were not so easily used by both novices and experts. A major example of such cooperative work is the Andrew Advisor system, a highly-evolved and sophisticated system that uses the AMS to solve the problems of distributed support for a very diverse user community in a heterogeneous computing environment. The evolution of the Advisor system and its uses of the AMS mechanisms are considered as a detailed example of the power and limitations of the AMS.

Introduction

This paper describes one notably successful user interface program for reading and sending mail and bulletin board messages, the "Messages" interface to the Andrew Message System. This system is currently in use at hundreds of sites, and at some sites its use has become virtually ubiquitous. In such environments, where its advanced features can be universally relied on at both ends of the communication, it has facilitated new kinds of computer-based cooperative activities. In this paper, we will describe the Messages program in order to understand the factors underlying its success, both its popularity with users and its effectiveness as a tool for cooperative work. In particular, we will focus on the question of how it manages to accommodate the diverse needs of novices and experts alike. Finally, we will look at an example of how the system has been successfully used by an independent group to support a rather complex form of cooperative work, the Andrew Advisor system.

UNDERLYING DESIGN PRINCIPLES

A good user interface is, of course, always good news to the people who have to use it. All too often however, it has proven difficult or impossible to determine after the fact, what has made a user interface successful or popular. The lessons of popular user interfaces are often idiosyncratic and difficult to generalize, or just plain obscure, as noted in Borenstein and Gosling (1988). In the case of the Messages program, as with all others, a great deal of debate could be made over the reasons for its strengths and weaknesses, or indeed over the precise nature of those strengths and weaknesses. In this case, however, the program was initially built and subsequently remodeled on a clear foundation of assumptions and beliefs about user interface technology, so that the end product may justifiably be viewed as the result of an experiment, an empirical application of one set of user interface design principles. We will make these principles explicit before describing the program itself.

The principles put forward here were not explicitly stated or committed to print prior to the Andrew project, but they were certainly strongly held beliefs that were often expressed in conversation. One of the authors has recently produced an expanded attempt to enunciate these as general principles for user interface design (Borenstein, in press *a*). In that book, arguments are made to justify the principles. Here however, we will treat the principles as axioms, and will consider the resulting artifact, the Messages program, as empirical result of the application of these axioms. Or, to put it more simply, we describe the principles and the result in the hope that the connection between the two will tend to support the validity of the basic design principles involved.

Assumption 1: The actual utility of applications that promise to support Computer-Supported Cooperative Work (CSCW) cannot be judged in the absence of a real user community. Any system, therefore, that claims to make a contribution to CSCW, but has no significant base of regular users, is making an empty or unverifiable claim.

Assumption 2: Usability is an essential prerequisite for any software system with a significant user interface component, which includes all systems to support cooperative work. Even in "research" systems, if the focus of the research is on doing something for end users, as it necessarily must be in all CSCW research, then a highly polished and usable interface is essential. The absence of such an interface will make it nearly impossible to obtain a realistic user community, and will thus necessarily skew any research results in such a way as to make it nearly impossible to evaluate the underlying ideas.

Assumption 3: In user interfaces, there is *no* fundamental trade-off between power, complexity and usability. The most complex and powerful systems can also be the easiest to use, if designed properly, subject to ongoing, consciously evolutionary development.

Assumption 4: In a complex user interface, all defaults should be carefully tuned for the most common novice user responses and expectations.

Assumption 5: Powerful but potentially confusing user interface features should be turned off by default, so as to not conflict with novice learning.

Assumption 6: Mechanisms must be provided to ease the transition from novice to expert, especially in systems where powerful expert-oriented features are not made available without explicit user action to request them.

Assumption 7: Good user interfaces grow and evolve. The most essential part of the design process is the evaluation of, and improvement upon, previous versions of the interface, based on feedback from, and observation of real users of the system.

This paper views the Messages program as an uncontrolled field test of the above assumptions. The successes and failures of the system cannot be absolutely demonstrated to have resulted directly from these assumptions, but it is the authors' belief that a substantial connection does exist. At the very least, the principles provide the philosophical background against which the system should be understood.

Andrew and its message system

Besides the philosophical background, there is also a technical background that must be understood in order to have a clear understanding of the Messages program. Messages was produced as a part of the Andrew project, about which a brief explanation is in order.

The Andrew Project (Morris, Satyanarayanan, Conner, Howard, Rosenthal & Smith, 1986; Morris, 1988; Borenstein, in press *b*) was a collaborative effort of IBM and the Information Technology Center at Carnegie Mellon University. The goal of the Andrew project was to build a realistic prototype of a university-wide distributed computing environment. That is, particular emphasis was paid to the needs of the academic and research communities. The success of that effort can be measured in part by the fact that the prototype has been taken up and is now fully supported by the University's central computing organizations.

As the project evolved, it concentrated on three main parts. The Andrew File System (Howard, 1988; Howard, Kazar, Menees, Nichols, Satyanarayanan, Side-botham, & West, 1988; Kazar, 1988; Kazar & Spector, 1989) is a distributed network file system designed to provide the illusion of a uniform central UNIX file system for a very large network (10 000 workstations was the design goal).[†] The Andrew Toolkit (Palay, Hansen, Kazar, Sherman, Wadlow, Neuendorffer, Stern, Bader, & Peters, 1988; Borenstein, 1990) is a window-system-independent programming library to support the development of user interface software. It currently supports a number of applications, including a multi-media editor that allows seamless editing of text, various kinds of graphics, and animations.

The third main piece of Andrew is the Andrew Message System, or AMS. The AMS, which makes heavy use of the file system and the toolkit, provides a large-scale mail and bulletin board system. It transparently supports messages which include text, pictures, animations, spreadsheets, equations, and hierarchical draw-ings, while also supporting "old-fashioned" text-only communication with low-end machines such as IBM PCs and with the rest of the electronic mail world. The Andrew Message System has in recent years become widely available. While the Carnegie Mellon installation is still the largest by some measures, there are other

---

[†] The Andrew File System technology, AFS 3.0, is a product of Transarc Corporation.

large Andrew sites, one of which has a bulletin board system at least twice as large as Carnegie Mellon's. This paper primarily reflects experience with the system at Carnegie Mellon however, as that is where the system was developed, has been used for the longest time, and has been most readily observed by the authors.

There are many parts to the Andrew Message System, including several non-multimedia user interfaces for reading mail and bulletin board messages from low-end terminals and PCs. There are also several AMS subsystems that have relatively small user interface components, such as the distributed message delivery system. A detailed description of the Andrew Message System is beyond the scope of this paper and can be found elsewhere (Rosenberg, Everhart & Borenstein, 1987; Borenstein, Everhart, Rosenberg & Stoller, 1988; Borenstein & Thyberg, 1988; Borenstein, Everhart, Rosenberg & Stoller, 1989). This paper will concentrate on the high-end user interface, the "Messages" program, and on the manner in which it has proven to be particularly conducive to cooperative work.

Messages: the system functionality

Although the AMS is a complex system made of many parts, to most users the term "AMS" is virtually synonymous with the Messages user interface program, which is all they actually see of the AMS. Messages presents a basic user interface that is quite similar to many other mail and bulletin board readers, easing the learning process for many users. Hidden behind the superficial similarity, however, is a wealth of powerful features that await the interested user.

THE MESSAGES WINDOWS

Messages runs under any of several window management systems, the most common of which is the X11 window system from MIT (Scheifler & Gettys, 1987). The program can open multiple windows on the screen, but typically the novice user is confronted with the single window shown in Figure 1, in which the screen is divided into several subwindows for message bodies, message "captions" (one-line summaries), and the names of message "folders" (collections or directories of messages, analogous to mail classes in some other systems).

Within this main window, the novice user can do everything one might need to do in the course of *reading* mail and bulletin board messages. The most common actions—selecting a new message or folder—are accomplished by pointing and clicking. Other actions, such as deleting messages, are available via the standard Andrew pop-up menu mechanism. For the novice user, there is never any reason to touch the keyboard in the course of reading messages.

To send a message, a user may either choose the Send Message menu item or one of the *Reply* menus. This will cause a new "messages-send" window to appear on the user's screen, as pictured in Figure 2.

MULTIMEDIA FEATURES

A major area in which Messages offers more functionality than most mail and bulletin board systems is in the integrated manner in which it includes formatted text and multimedia objects. In Figure 3, for example, the user is reading a message that

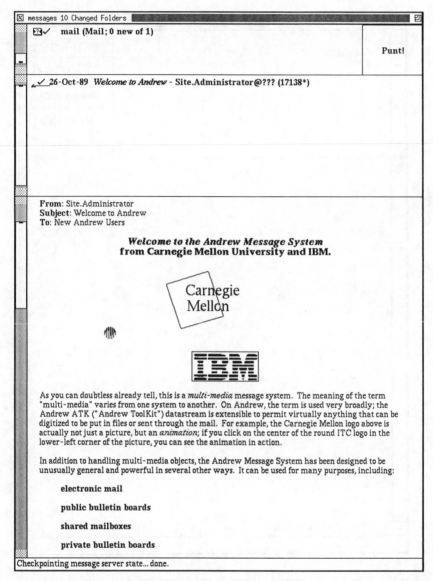

FIGURE 1. The main window of the Messages user interface as it might look to a new user receiving his first piece of multimedia mail.

contains a picture within formatted text. It is important to note that users can read, print, and otherwise manipulate such messages with absolutely no knowledge about the multimedia system. Multimedia messages are fundamentally no different from the user's perspective, to any other messages in the system, and the user need learn nothing new in order to read most of them, and only a few new things in order to compose them.

The multimedia capability of Messages has, perhaps not surprisingly, proven to be one of its most admired and successful features. Crucial to its success has been the

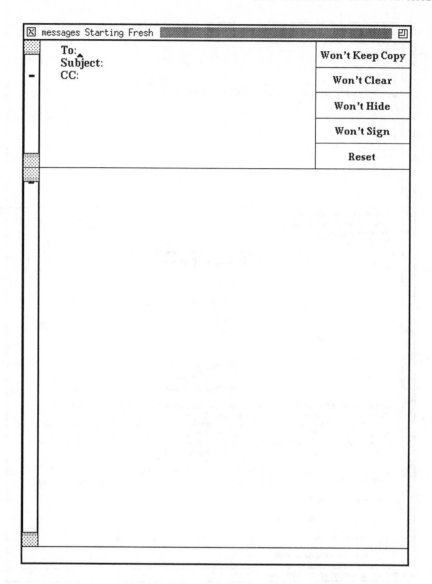

FIGURE 2. The message-sending window.

fact that novices can receive and appreciate multimedia features with essentially no extra effort or learning. Also critical has been the ease with which new and casual users can master a subset of the multimedia authoring capabilities and still get substantial benefit from that subset. Nearly all Messages users quickly learn, for example, the ease and value of using multiple fonts within mail messages.

ACTIVE MESSAGE FEATURES

Another aspect of Messages that has proven extremely useful and popular is a set of features known collectively as "active messages". These are a set of specialized

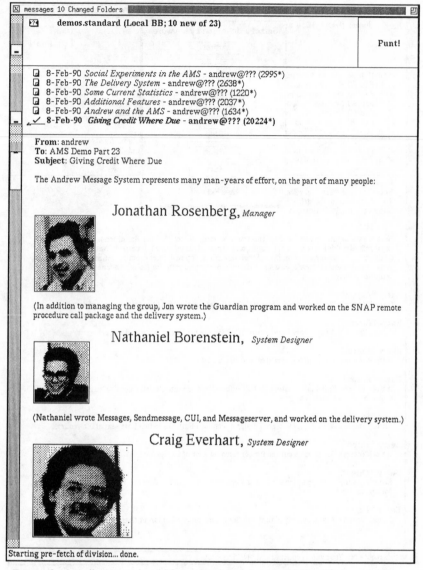

FIGURE 3. A mail message in which a raster image is embedded within formatted text.

message types that carry with them, in addition to a normal (and possibly multimedia) message body, information that directs a particular interaction with the user. For example, one type of active message is the "vote" message. Here special headers direct the user interface to ask the user a multiple choice question, the answer to which will be mailed to a designated address for collection and tabulation. Figure 4 shows a user reading a vote message. In addition to votes, the Andrew Message System supports four other types of active messages: return receipt requests, enclosures, folder subscription invitations, and redistribution notices. (See Borenstein *et al.*, 1989, for details on active messages).

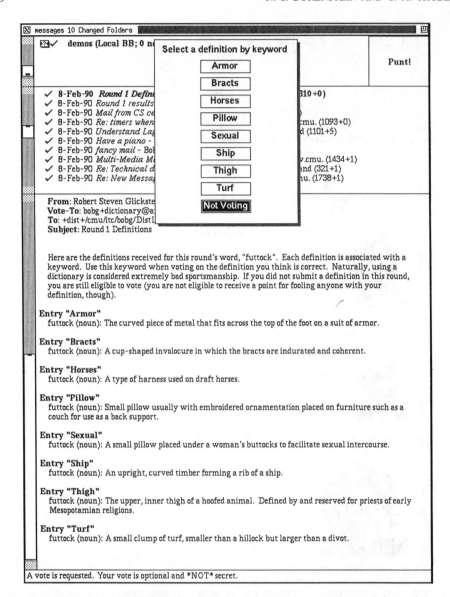

FIGURE 4. A "vote" message, inviting the reader to answer a question and have that answer automatically sent back to a specified destination.

As with multimedia messages, active messages require no special training to be of value to the receiver. For the receiver, they appear simply as messages that magically bring up dialog boxes and ask questions using mechanisms that are easily understood. The amount of expertise required to create an active message is also surprisingly small and is easily mastered by new users of the system.

It seems likely that the notion of "active messages" can be generalized substantially. This is the subject of recent research by Borenstein, unpublished data.

THE FLAMES MESSAGE FILTERING LANGUAGE

The AMS provides an embedded LISP-like language called FLAMES (Filtering Language for the Andrew Message System) that can be used to automatically classify new mail when it arrives. By default, new mail is placed in an automatically-created folder called "mail". However, a FLAMES program can sort incoming mail by keywords, by sender, or by any other aspect of the mail message, and can automatically place mail in the correct folder. (It is important, however, that the user "subscribe" to any folders in which mail is placed automatically, or the system will not automatically show the user the new messages in those folders.) Indeed, a FLAMES program can even reject mail by returning it to its sender, or it can automatically process the mail and send out an answer. The most common use for personal FLAMES programs is to automatically sort new incoming messages into folders. Beyond this, however, several complex FLAMES-based applications have been developed, and the Advisor system, to be described later in this paper, relies heavily on FLAMES for message processing.

PRIVATE BULLETIN BOARDS AND NEW BULLETIN BOARD CREATION

The Andrew Message System supports a rich and flexible set of protection and configuration options that facilitate group communication. In particular, the protection mechanisms permit the creation of public bulletin boards, private boards (readable and postable only by members of a group), official bulletin boards (readable by all, postable only by a few), administrative and advisory bulletin boards (postable by all, readable by only a few), administrative and advisory bulletin boards (postable by all, readable by only a few), and various hybrids thereof. In addition, the protection mechanisms can be (and are) used to allow, for example, a secretary to read and process someone else's electronic mail. (Indeed, a secretary could create something like a magazine for an employer, containing only those pieces of the employer's mail that the secretary thought the employer would really want to see.) The rich protection options make it possible to use message "databases" in innovative ways, as will be illustrated later in this paper.

CUSTOMIZATION OPTIONS

Most of the optional features that have been described are relatively easy to learn. Beyond this however, the Messages program is radically customizable using mechanisms that require substantially more expertise. The Andrew Toolkit, on which Messages is based, provides several such mechanisms, on several levels. In particular, it includes an "init file" mechanism, which offers a simple macro facility for creating compound commands. For situations where such a simple facility is inadequate, the toolkit includes Ness, an extension language described in Hansen (1990), which allows fully programmable customizations and extensions to the behavior of AMS, as well as the creation of powerful interactive objects that can be sent and received with Messages.

Though these mechanisms are complex enough to require substantial time and expertise to master, they are sufficiently useful and accessible to have been used on many occasions to create customized or extended versions of the AMS for specialized purposes, one of which will be discussed at some length later in this paper.

OTHER ADVANCED FEATURES

The AMS supports many other advanced features, too many to describe in detail here. These include:

- Electronic "magazines" which allow one user to act as an "information filter" for many other users and thus reduce the problem of "information flood".
- An unusually rich set of mechanisms for replying to messages.
- Support for easily including excerpts from one message in another in an aesthetically pleasing way.
- Heuristic validation of destination addresses.
- A rich set of variants on the basic notion of "subscribing" to a message folder.
- A large amount of functional support for manipulating message folders.
- Mechanisms for marking groups of messages and manipulating them as a group.

LEARNING ABOUT AND USING THE OPTIONAL FEATURES

As the Messages interface evolved, in every case where a choice had to be made between the needs of novices and the needs of experts, the default behavior of the program was targeted at novice users. The resulting program is undeniably easy for novices to use. For experts, the desire for extended functionality is accommodated through the use of options.

This in general, is a tricky and risky enterprise, because there is really no difference between a non-existent feature and a feature that the expert doesn't know about or can't figure out how to use. In order to successfully meet the needs of experts, it was important to ensure that no major expertise would be required in order to use the expert-oriented features.

The most important mechanism by which this is accomplished in the Messages program is the "Set Options" interface. In any message-reading window, the user can choose the Set Options menu option. When this menu action is initiated, the display is altered, as shown in Figure 5. Here the contents of the "captions" area have been replaced with a scrollable list of user-settable options, and the "bodies" area now displays a scrollable set of option-related information, including interaction objects that can be used to actually change the options.

Using the "Set Options" interface, users can easily learn about and use a large number of sophisticated options. By the time they have exhausted the potential of this interface, they are already expert Messages users by any reasonable definition. Beyond this point, further customization is still possible using more complex mechanisms, as previously mentioned. Although the Andrew help system provides significant assistance to users who want to master these mechanisms, they remain significantly harder than the "Set Options" mechanism. Most users never even attempt to learn to use the other mechanisms, so it is important that the needs of the majority of sophisticated and expert users be satisfied by the use of "Set Options".

The myth of the power/usability trade-off

There is a popular and widespread belief among programmers and end users alike that a fundamental trade-off exists between easy-to-use, novice-oriented programs on the one hand and very powerful and customizable expert-oriented programs on the

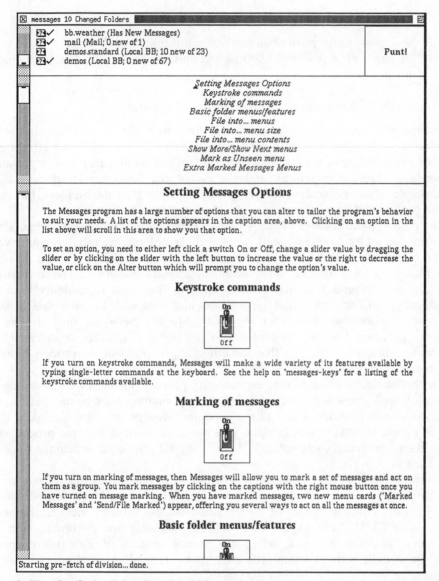

FIGURE 5. The "Set Options" interface, by which users gradually learn about and enable some of the more advanced capabilities of the system.

other. This belief persists in the absence of any really compelling evidence, and in spite of the existence of at least a few examples of programs that successfully "have it both ways".

Along with a handful of other programs, the Messages interface can be viewed as a proof-by-example of the fact that this is not a fundamental trade-off. There is no reason *in principle* why an interface cannot meet the needs of both experts and novice users. Indeed, doing so is startlingly simple in theory, though exceedingly difficult in practice. Basically, only three things are required:

(1) An easy-to-use, novice-oriented default interface.
(2) A large set of powerful features and options that are not visible or enabled for new users.
(3) A smooth, obvious and easy-to-use mechanism by which users can gradually learn about the more advanced features.

Of course, all three requirements are much more easily stated than done. In the case of Messages, these three requirements were successfully obtained only after a great deal of evolution, user testing, and independent evaluation. But it is important to understand that the popularity and success of the Messages interface was not attributable to any particular intuitive genius on the part of the builders, but rather to the process and environment in which the interface was developed.

The initial public releases of the Messages program in particular, satisfied almost none of the users. Novices found the screen layout of the initial version, which mixed folder names and the new messages within each folder in a single scrollable text region, to be confusing and unintuitive. Experts, meanwhile, were frustrated by the many features that had been omitted in the name of usability (and also expediency). In fact, the initial version was met with such hostility that it would have been reasonable to consider simply abandoning the whole project. The fact that the program was able to evolve into the popular interface described in this paper, is indicative of the fact that something did go right in the process by which the system evolved.

The first salient feature of that evolutionary process was the fact it was long and painful. It took about four years of full-time programming work by one person, with additional work by many others at many points. Most of this time was spent trying to get a great number of details right. It is not at all obvious how the process could have been significantly streamlined. There may simply be no substitute for sweat and hard work.

Another aspect of the evolution worth noting is that, from the second version on, the Messages program always had a large community of experienced users as a well as a continuous influx of novice users (in the form of incoming freshman students at CMU). The expert users helped guarantee the continuing accretion of expert oriented features, while the steady stream of new users ensured that the default settings would continue to be refined towards ease of use for novices.

Also crucial during this period, was the fact that Messages captured the attention of a number of non-technical specialists who helped to guide its evolution. The Andrew project was able to hire as consultants, a graphic designer to study the visual aspects of the program, technical writers to improve the documentation and interaction messages, and a human factors expert to study how novices and experts actually used the system and where they got stuck.

Most important, the Messages interface was able to evolve successfully because of the tenacity or stubbornness of many of the parties involved. The author bullheadedly proceeded from the assumption that nothing could possibly be wrong with the interface that couldn't be fixed with enough work—an attitude which, while it produced a good interface in the end, may well have produced a much bigger system than was strictly necessary. The managers supported the project unflaggingly, possibly fearing that the failure of the flagship application would produce domino-like conclusions of failure for the Andrew File System and the Andrew Toolkit, on which the message system was based. The funding had been secured for several years by the initial CMU/IBM contract, so there was essentially no one inclined to put the brakes on the project. Thus, a project that might have appeared to be headed for failure in the early years succeeded in some measure because it was given enough time to evolve naturally. Many other promising projects have surely died due to the absence of such patience and stability.

One useful practice that helped ensure that changes to Messages would be viewed as *positive* was that the author kept a permanent log of all functional changes made to the system. As the system matured through over one hundred releases of the software, this list became increasingly important. When changes were contemplated, the list could be used to determine why the current functionality worked the way it did. Without this list, it is easy to imagine an endless cycle of changes that undid each other to please diverse audiences. The list made it easier to relate new user feedback to the earlier feedback that had shaped the prior evolution of the system.

It is interesting to note that while the Messages interface grew into a form pleasing to experts and novices alike, it did not do this smoothly or continuously. After the disastrously unpopular first release in the spring of 1986, the next few versions were targeted explicitly at increasing the satisfaction of those who were currently using the system, and thus displayed an increasing bent towards expert users. Later, with the influx of new students in the fall, concern shifted abruptly to the difficulties experienced by new users of the system. This pattern continued for several years—expert-oriented refinements occurred in the spring and summer, and novice-oriented work was concentrated in the fall and winter. Good user interface projects are often driven by the needs of their users; in this case, the structure of the academic year was a fortunate coincidence that helped keep the Messages interface balanced between novice and expert concerns.

As the system developed, one of the last major pieces to be put in place was the "Set Options" interface. The evolutionary process just described had created a somewhat schizophrenic user base, with an artificially strong division between the novices and experts. Experts would request a new feature, it would be added, and an announcement would tell them explicitly what magic operation they had to perform in order to enable the new feature. But while established experts were able to assimilate one new bit of magic at a time, the growing body of such magic gradually became a major hurdle that prevented new users from growing into experts. That problem was substantially solved with the introduction of "Set Options".

Probably the hardest part of the evolutionary process was determining, whenever an expert-oriented change was made or contemplated, how that change would affect novices who were rarely part of the discussion about the functional change. It is very difficult for experts to predict how novices will react. Thus it is often hard to determine whether or not a new feature should be available by default. Indeed, the wrong decision was made on more than one occasion, though this was only found out via feedback from later novices. The only useful principle in this regard is to at least make an effort to view each new feature through novice eyes; this will catch many, though not all of the potential problems. The remainder simply have to be caught by experience with future novices.

To the authors, in hindsight at least, much of this appears to be little more than the application of common sense to practical user interface design. It is worth pausing, therefore, to consider why the myth of the power/usability trade-off is so widespread. Here too, the answer is mostly common sense: the above approach to interface evolution is quite costly, frustrating and time-consuming. It is so sufficiently hard and rare to build an interface that is exceptionally good for novices, or exceptionally good for experts, that most projects are more than satisfied with either achievement. For that reason, many users have rarely, if ever, been exposed to an interface that works well for both categories of user. The myth, then, is a simple case of unjustified extrapolation: "if I've never seen an elephant, then elephants must not exist".

Unfortunately, the analogy may apply equally to the future prospects for interfaces that work well for novices and experts. Like the elephants, which are being slaughtered wholesale for their ivory, such interfaces may be almost doomed to extinction by the laws of economics. It is far from clear that there is any substantial economic advantage to building programs that are tuned for both novices and experts, but it is all too clear that building them in such a way entails substantial extra costs. It seems sadly unlikely, therefore, that we will see a proliferation of such programs in the near future.

Putting it all together: cooperative work in the Andrew Message System

The Andrew Message System has proven to be exceptionally popular with its user community in general. Weekly statistics indicate that roughly 5300 people use it at Carnegie Mellon to read bulletin boards regularly. Even more users read their personal mail with the system. The AMS is also in use at over a hundred other universities and research sites. This would be indication enough that the system is a success; however, the greatest enthusiasm has in fact been found among those who are using the AMS for substantial cooperative activity. Most notable among these devoted users are the people who provide support services on Andrew at CMU. The Andrew Advisor is a singular example of real-life cooperative work, conducted with the Andrew Message System.†

THE ADVISOR SYSTEM

Centrally supported and distributed UNIX computing at CMU has a long and diverse history. The most recent milestone is the Andrew Project, as described above. Quite apart from the Andrew project is the much longer tradition of departmental UNIX computing, especially among such UNIX sophisticates as are to be found in the School of Computer Science. This tradition is a major influence on the development of centrally supported, distributed UNIX computing. Indeed, "collaboratively supported" is a better phrase than "centrally supported" since it indicates the (sometimes stormy) marriage of departmental and central facilities, systems administration, and user services.

† Substantially different versions of the following discussion of the Advisor electronic mail consulting service have appeared in Borenstein and Thyberg (1988) and Thyberg (1988).

The central computing organizations at Carnegie Mellon face unusual challenges in supporting their computing constituency. Four factors complicate the task. First, the distributed UNIX computing environment we provide has grown substantially beyond the Andrew project, and is now a complex assemblage of vendors' operating systems, the Andrew File System (now provided by Transarc Corporation), the X11 windowing environment from M, the Motif user interface offerings from the Open Software Foundation, third-party and campus-contributed software and, of course, the components of the Andrew project: ATK and AMS. Furthermore, this environment is provided for and supported by hardware from many manufacturers. Second, although the environment has been widely deployed and promoted, it is an ever developing, rapidly changing environment. As a result, it is not too inaccurate to characterize the computing environment as a 9000-user beta-test site. Third, campus computing expertise is widely, but unevenly, distributed. The users span the entire spectrum from technophobe to technophile. Fourth, the people involved in software development and maintenance, system administration, and user services belong to several organizations and work in different buildings.

To cope with these challenges, members of the Distributed Workstation Services group (DWS), with the help of the AMS group, developed an extensive electronic mail consulting service called "Advisor". Advisor presents the user with a single, private, and personal help resource for every conceivable problem a user might encounter in the complex system described above. The user simply mails a query to Advisor's account. In 24 to 48 hours, private mail comes back to the user from Advisor's account, prepared by a DWS staff member. In fact, however, Advisor is the front-end of a vast network of bulletin boards that enlist the cooperative efforts of all the professional staffs in the central computing organizations.

ADVISOR I

Advisor has been in use since January 1985. In the earliest days, it was simply another Andrew account. One person logged in as "advisor", read the incoming mail, handled it with what limited tools were available (online lists, hardcopy lists, hand written notes, and a good memory for the status of a given request), gathered information by talking with the programmers, and sent out replies to the user. This worked reasonably well during the deployment of Andrew when there were a small number of carefully selected users and the Andrew consultant had an office among the Andrew developers.

The first public Andrew workstation lab appeared in the spring of 1986. Shortly thereafter, Andrew accounts were made generally available. Advisor was immediately overwhelmed with mail. An additional consultant picked up Advisor duties, but there were always problems with how to divide the work between the two staff members and how to keep track of the status of any given message. A rudimentary method for classifying messages did exist, but the mechanism was clumsy, time-consuming and not that useful because all the messages were lumped together in one large, flat mail directory. The combination of the large volume of the easy questions and the genuine difficulty of the hard questions made it difficult to process Advisor mail in a timely fashion. We clearly required some way of getting almost immediate assistance from the right people in other organizations.

In the fall of 1986, the first version of what is now the Andrew Message System was released to campus. It marked a major advance in the integration of electronic communication. Personal mail and bulletin boards, though conceptually distinct, were now no longer different in kind. A public bulletin board and a user's private mailbox are both examples of message databases. The only real difference is the degree of accessibility to other users. As indicated above, the AMS supports a rich and flexible set of protection options that permit the creation of public bulletin boards, private bulletin boards, official bulletin boards, semi-private bulletin boards and shared mailboxes, and other variations on the theme. Furthermore, since message databases are built on top of the UNIX hierarchical directory structure, bulletin boards could now be nested within each other.

One of the authors hit on the idea of using bulletin boards as folders for classifying Advisor's mail. The authors created a suite of semi-private bulletin boards, postable by the whole community, but readable only by those in the central computing organizations, and wrote a program in a primitive stack-oriented language for automatically filing messages. (The stack-oriented language was the predecessor to the FLAMES language described earlier). The result was Advisor II.

ADVISOR II

Tom Malone, in his discussion of the Information Lens system (Malone, Grant, Turbak, Brobst & Cohen, 1987), has identified three fundamental approaches for handling large volumes of electronic information. The first approach, *cognitive filtering*, attempts to characterize the contents of a message and the information needs of the recipient. The system then matches messages about XYZ with readers who have expressed an interest in XYZ. The second approach, *social filtering*, focuses on the relationships between the sender and the recipient. In addition to the message's topic, the status of the sender plays a role in the reader's interest in the message. The final approach, *economic filtering*, looks at implicit cost-benefit analyses to determine what to do with a piece of electronic mail. Advisor II relied heavily on both cognitive and social filters as the criteria for automatic message classification.

Each message to Advisor that did not come from a member of a known set of Advisor "helpers" was assumed to be from a user requesting assistance. The message was then placed on a bulletin board called "*advisor.open*". The Advisor staff subscribed to this bulletin board and used it as an inbox for new questions. A copy of mail from the user was also placed in *advisor.trail*, to assist the staff in keeping track of requests, and to *advisor.qa,* to which answers would also eventually go, thus forming a repository of useful past work. Thus, the first criterion for sorting the mail was a social one—is the sender a helper or a user? The list of the helpers, that is, the staffs of the various computing organizations, had to be kept current as constants within the stack language program that did the automatic filing of messages.

An incoming question from a user was also copied to one of a series of subject-specific bulletin boards, according to keywords in the subject line. For example, if a subject line was "mail bug", the message was copied to *advisor.mail*. These bulletin boards, though not open to the public, were readable by the developers, system administrators, etc. who subscribed to the bulletin boards covering their areas of interest and responsibility. To continue the example, the AMS group members subscribed to *advisor.mail,* thereby increasing the likelihood of seeing only those messages generally relevant to them. Uninformative or nonexistent subject lines caused the message to be copied to *advisor.misc.* All good Advisor helpers were expected to subscribe to *advisor.misc,* in addition to their other subscriptions. Thus, the second criterion for sorting mail was a cognitive one—is the mail likely to be of interest to a particular group of people?

Cognitive and social filtering were combined at several critical junctures. For example, when the Advisor staff requested more information from the user, Advisor received a blind carbon copy of that request. Because the message was from Advisor, it did not go into *advisor.open* by virtue of the social filter which stipulated that Advisor was never to be taken as a user asking for help. Instead the message went to *advisor.trail* and to the relevant subject-specific bulletin board by virtue of cognitive filtering of the subject line. Another example was in the processing of contributions from Advisor helpers. A helper would see a question on some topical bulletin board. By choosing the Reply to Readers menu option (which prepends "Re:" to the same subject line as the user's initial post), the helper sent the answer, not to the user, but directly back to that subject-specific bulletin board. By virtue of social filtering, mail from helpers never went into *advisor.open,* but only to some topic-oriented bulletin board. And when a final answer was sent to the user, the blind carbon receipt once again bypassed *advisor.-open* because it was from Advisor and ended up on *advisor.trail* and the correct topical bulletin board. In addition, the Advisor would carbon copy the final answers to the *advisor.qa* bulletin board. Unfortunately, the questions and answers were not paired, but in chronological order, due to early limitations in the AMS.

To summarize: the Advisor staff answered questions from *advisor.-open* as they were able. They kept an eye on the relevant subject-specific bulletin boards for help with the difficult problems. Having collected the information from the helpers, the Advisors sent polished answers back to the users. As far as the users could see, they had sent mail to Advisor and received an answer from Advisor. The fact that there was additional internal consultation was kept behind the scenes.

EVALUATION OF ADVISOR II

The key feature of the first automated Advisor mechanism was the automatic filing of messages into subject-specific bulletin boards. The positive effect of this was two-fold. First, messages came to the immediate attention of the other technical groups. Often, the Advisor staff found that someone in another group had already answered the question before Advisor had even looked at it. This kind of pro-active assistance was greatly appreciated. Second, because requests for more information and final answers passed back to the subject-specific bulletin boards, the other groups could provide problem-solving advice and assure technical accuracy.

However, the negative effects outweighed the positive. First, poorly phrased questions from the users led to many "misclassifications". The message filing algorithm worked quite well, but so many subject lines were virtually contentless, e.g. "Help!", that far too many messages ended up on *advisor.misc*: close to 50%

of all mail to Advisor, according to the authors' estimate. Without better characterization of the message's content in the subject line, the Advisor staff were helpless to get the right mail to the right parties. The designers of Advisor considered the possibility of also searching the body of a message for sort keys, but the pre-FLAMES filtering language was not powerful enough to support free-text information retrieval techniques. Advisor settled for pattern matching on the subject line, rather than suffer too many false keyword hits.

Second, with every question going to a subject-specific bulletin board, the Advisor helpers had no easy way to distinguish between the questions the Advisor staff knew how to answer and those they didn't. Hence, they wasted time answering some questions unnecessarily and neglected other questions for which help really was required. In retrospect, it seems like a truism, but actual use of the mechanism vividly showed that cooperative work disintegrates if what is expected, and from whom, is not clearly articulated. Computer-supported methods can just as easily exacerbate the problem of undefined expectations as alleviate it.

Third, because every blind carbon from Advisor and every message from an Advisor helper also went to the subject-specific bulletin boards, these soon became too cluttered to be of much use. On the one hand, helpers got tired of wading through them. On the other, Advisor, at that time, had no way to show a message and all the replies to it in a single chain, so it was sometimes very hard to find the answers that were already available. There is nothing so deadly to cooperation as seeming to ignore another's efforts. Despite Advisor's best intentions, this problem appeared far too often.

Fourth, because every question and every answer went to *advisor.qa,* but the question and the answer were not adjacent messages, *advisor.qa* proved to be virtually worthless as a resource for the Advisor staff.

These four failings were compounded by the rapidly growing amount of mail being sent to Advisor. More staff were needed, contributing to difficulties working from a single inbox, and the helpers were becoming frustrated beyond their willingness to assist in the support of Andrew. It was clear that Advisor needed a significant overhaul.

ADVISOR III

The third version of the Advisor system was implemented in 1988, and, with the exception of the recent changes described below, Advisor III represents the current state of the system. In Advisor III, the only automatic sorting of incoming mail is by the day it arrived. This sorting is done by a FLAMES program. Mail goes into one of *advisor.inbox.monday, .tuesday,* etc. Student Advisors are each responsible for a particular day's worth of Advisor mail. They acknowledge every piece of user mail, handle most of the requests, and then cross-post the tough questions on topic-oriented bulletin boards with names like *"advisor.helpbox.mail"*. Figure 6 gives a sampling of the current suite of helpboxes. They are very similar to the "magazines" mentioned previously—they are, in essence, journals compiled by the Advisor staff of just those questions that require the help of some other group to answer. The technical staffs subscribe to appropriate helpboxes and to the parent bulletin board, *advisor.helpbox.* Posts to the parent bulletin board notify Advisor helpers of the

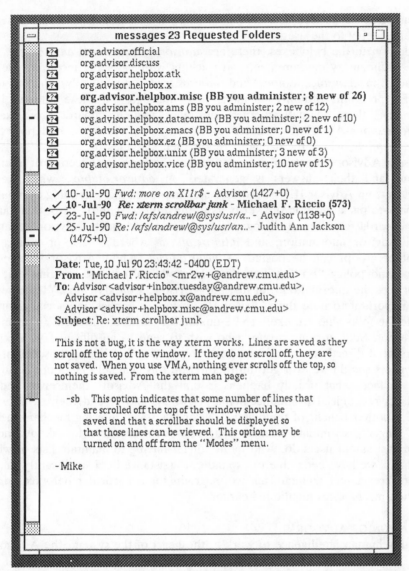

FIGURE 6. A partial listing of the Advisor suite of bulletin boards; a sampling of helpboxes.

creation of a new helpbox, give a synopsis of its purpose, and invite them to subscribe. All this is done automatically, via folder subscription invitations, one of the "active message" features mentioned above.

Some members of the technical staff prefer to receive as personal mail the postings to the helpbox they've agreed to monitor. FLAMES makes it trivial to combine any helpbox with a distribution list of interested individuals: these helpers get direct mailings while the bulletin board serves as a shared archive. The helpers' replies go back to Advisor' mailbox, where the FLAMES program processes them and, on the basis of a special reply-to header, places them on the correct helpbox and sends them to any associated distribution lists. The Advisor on whose day the question came in collects the information posted to the helpbox and sends a well-crafted reply to the user.

In addition to the helpboxes, there are *advisor.questions* and *advisor.trail* which provide rudimentary measurement and tracking. Copies of the incoming user mail get placed in *advisor.questions* and *advisor.trail* automatically, thanks to the FLAMES program. Monthly daemons take messages off these bulletin boards and archive them in date-stamped subsidiary bulletin boards, for example, *advisor.questions-Apr-1990.* There is even an Advisor bulletin board, *advisor.daemons,* where the daemons report their activities.

To assist Advisors in getting good answers to the users, a collection of interesting questions and their answers is generated on *advisor.outbox,* which replaces *advisor.qa* from Advisor II. The Advisor uses improved message-filing commands to move back-to-back question/answer pairs to the *advisor.outbox.* Also, there are two bulletin boards for internal dialog; *advisor.discuss,* for meta-Advisor debate and general Advisor information, and *advisor.official* where official pronouncements from other groups can be posted. *Advisor.official* is how Advisor receives such technical and policy "FYI" ("For Your Information") items, insuring that every Advisor sees the information, not just the Advisor on the day the FYI was sent.

It is important to note that Advisor III no longer applies any social filtering to separate the folks who are likely to be qualified to send us official FYIs from those who are not. Staff in other groups who wish to send us an official FYI are simply told to send it directly to the address "*advisor + official*".† We apply social pressure on our peers should we ever get information on this channel that is not accurate or useful. In fact, what usually happens is that the Advisors themselves and their supervisors see official pronouncements elsewhere and resend them to *advisor + official.* Another benefit of removing Advisor II's social filtering mechanism is that we no longer discriminate against staff; our peers are able to ask questions of Advisor just as our users do. And by no longer having to maintain lists of who are the helpers, we have been able to expand our assistance base significantly since it is trivial to create and maintain an access group for a particular helpbox using the protection mechanisms mentioned earlier.

EVALUATION OF ADVISOR III

By putting human intelligence to work at the heart of the system, the Advisor staff solved in one stroke several of the problems that troubled Advisor II. First, Advisor can support a far more fine-grained suite of helpboxes than it could with automatic filing. Poorly phrased subject lines are less of a concern because humans read the mail and digest its contents before passing it to a topical bulletin board. Second, when an Advisor staff member puts a question on a helpbox bulletin board, everyone knows this means help is genuinely needed. Third, because clutter does not automatically accumulate in the helpboxes, these have become "high-content" bulletin boards that the programmers and administrators feel are worth

---

† The Andrew Message System interprets any address of the form "userid + text" to be deliverable to the user named on the left of the " + " character. It is up to the FLAMES program processing that user's mail box to take whatever action the user would like, keying off the text to the right of the " + " character. If the user has no FLAMES program, or his FLAMES program doesn't recognize the text, the message is dropped off into the user's mail folder.

reading regularly. The pay-off for Advisor is a much more reliable information resource. And just in case there are a number of items pending on a given helpbox, the AMS now has a Mark Related Messages menu option which puts a marker beside all the messages in a given reply-chain. Advisor rarely misses a helper's contribution in the new scheme. Fourth, *advisor.outbox* is a useful repository of previously answered queries because the Advisors themselves decide to post only those question/answer pairs that are likely to be of future use. The questions are now adjacent to their answers with the addition of the message filing command, Append to Folder, which takes a set of marked messages and adds them to the end of a folder, rather than shuffling them into the folder in chronological order.

In summary, though Advisor III lacks the pro-active help and the quality assurance that was evident in Advisor II, the Advisor staff is better equipped to handle the load than before. Currently, Advisor receives, on average, 450 new messages per month; 714 messages received is the current single-month record. Note that these are new requests from users; the total number of messages that pass through the Advisor system, including help from Advisor helpers, requests for more information, and replies to users, averages 50 messages per day, or 1500 per month. The student Advisors do an admirable job of performing triage on incoming mail. Full-time DWS staff now function much more as Advisor supervisors, taking areas of technical responsibility, expediting helpbox requests, and insuring that the answers that go out from Advisor are timely and accurate. Messages in Advisor III filter up "manually" through different levels of expertise: the simplest questions are answered by the students, the harder ones are answered by the full-time consultants, and the hardest are tackled by the programmers and administrators themselves. At each level, humans work diligently and efficiently to minimize time-delays inherent in the system. But all parties involved feel that the Advisor scheme focuses and streamlines their efforts.

There were, however, some aspects of Advisor III that cried out for significant improvement. First, there was the problem of correctly routing follow-up mail to the inbox where the initial mail was placed. For example, if the first piece of mail about a particular problem came on Monday and thus was placed in *advisor.inbox.monday,* how would Monday's Advisor continue a dialog with the user on Tuesday, without having all that mail end up in the inbox of the Tuesday Advisor? If the follow-up mail is delivered to the Tuesday Advisor, parallel processing or deadlock can occur as both Tuesday's and Monday's Advisors try to figure out what's going on.

Second, we had no good way of tracking requests to Advisor. We would have liked to have been able to find out quickly, for any particular piece of mail from a user, when that mail arrived, who on the Advisor staff first handled it, who in some other organization was then working on it, what the current status of the item was, and so on. This was just one aspect of a larger need for good monitoring tools on Advisor. We needed ways to measure the flow of questions, their types, the steps taken to answer them, and the mean time to find an answer for a user.

Third, Advisor handles a huge load of routine items like requests for more disk quota. These are matters that rarely require attention from the Advisor staff, save to pass them along to a system administrator and send the users an acknowledgment of receipt. It would have been nice if it took little or no effort to handle such requests.

Fourth, routine filing operations were tedious and error-prone. For example, when closing an interesting exchange with a user, the Advisor had to move mail, one by one, into *advisor.outbox*. The messages that constituted the dialog were likely to be spread around in the inbox and were not necessarily connected by the same subject line. The Advisor would have to rummage around and find all the relevant messages, get them over to *advisor.outbox* in the correct order, and then delete the entire set from the inbox.

How the designers of Advisor have addressed these concerns, and what issues remain for future exploration, is discussed in the remainder of this paper.

ADVISOR TODAY

The Advisor III system was sufficiently successful to leave the basic scheme un-altered. Incoming messages are still classified primarily by the date of receipt, and then filtered upward as necessary through human action, allowing the simplest questions to be responded to by the least-expert Advisors. However, the authors believe that the powerful automatic classification features Messages provided encouraged over-automation. in Advisor II and that Advisor III was in large part a reaction against such over-automation. The further development of Advisor has been evolutionary, incremental, and in the direction of adding more automation back into the system. This time, automatic mail handling features have been added in a much more selective, principled, and informed way than was the case in the crude keyword-classification mechanisms of Advisor II. Automation has been added where it could solve specific problems in the Advisor mechanism, rather than attempting to automate the entire process at once.

Structuring routine advisor actions
While the Advisor designers were concerned to solve in a piecemeal fashion particular shortcomings with Advisor III, the authors believe that a pattern of development has been emerging which can be characterized as the application of the language-as-action paradigm (explicated in Winograd & Flores, 1986; Winograd 1988) to various aspects of the Advisors' actual work practices. This paradigm, along with the Information and Object Lens work of Malone, Grant, Lai, Rao and Rosenblitt, (1987) and Lai and Malone, (1988), has guided the Advisor staff toward the semi-formalizing of certain linguistic "steps" that Advisor frequently makes in the "language dance" from initial query to final answer.

We mentioned earlier that sorting Advisor mail by day creates the problem of how Monday's Advisor continues a dialog with a user on Tuesday, without getting in the way of the Tuesday advisor. This problem is solved with the Messages customization facilities mentioned earlier. The designers of Advisor have developed a suite of specialized message sending/replying commands on the *Advisor* menu card of the "messages-send" window as shown in Figure 7. These commands, which are also bound to keys, insert a special reply-to message header on the outgoing mail. That mail, and all mail in reply to it, get sorted into the correct day's inbox by virtue of that header. So even though the follow-up reply from the user comes in on Tuesday, it still goes to the Monday inbox, where Monday's Advisor is waiting for it. This mechanism is not foolproof. For example, a user may send in a piece of mail at 11:59 pm on Monday and follow it at 12:01 am on Tuesday with another piece of mail about the same matter, but with a completely different subject line. Since no reply from Advisor has come to the first message to provide the hook on which to hand subsequent dialog, the two messages are going to end up on different inboxes and the Monday and Tuesday Advisors are going to have to work it out. Still, the special reply-to header works in most cases to route extended mail exchanges correctly.

Notice in Figure 7 that these commands make no mention of any particular day of the week. The day-specific special message header is correctly inserted by virtue of an environment variable, *DAY,* which conditions the behavior of this single set of commands automatically and appropriately. This variable is set for each Advisor in a personal setup file he invokes whenever he logs into the Advisor account. Should this setup mechanism fail and the *DAY* variable be undefined, the sending/replying commands will prompt the Advisor for which day of the week it is that he is now answering. The Advisor can enter the day on the fly and can also set *DAY* for the rest of the session with the Change Advisor Day menu action. Staff members who work on more than one day's worth of incoming messages can, in a single Advisor session, trivially switch back and forth between, say, their identity as the "Tuesday advisor" and their identity as the "Wednesday advisor". With a single operation, they change all of the special header information that identifies and tracks their correspondence in these roles.

The second problem, tracking the actions that have been taken in response to a user's request for assistance, is one that Advisor continues to wrestle with. To provide the hooks for a solution, the Advisor staff introduced the notion of special message headers that indicate the "state" of each piece of Advisor mail in the progression from initial acknowledgment to closure. State is automatically set by use of the four sending/replying commands shown in Figure 7: Acknowledgment, Request for Information, For Your Information, and Final Answer, each of which marks the outgoing message with a distinct state message header: "ACK", "RFI", "FYI", and "ANS", respectively. A reply from the user to an Advisor message of a particular state can inherit the same state message header, which in turn can be processed by either Ness or FLAMES to generate rudimentary tracking and measurement. For example, one could go to advisor.trail, start with a user's initial request, and trace the entire exchange, noting Advisor's acknowledgment of the query, all requests for and provision of further information, and what Advisor believed to be the closing message. If the user replies to that "final answer" it indicates that the matter is still open. Unfortunately, there is currently no way to go back and change the state of Advisor's first "final answer" to something like "first try at an answer", "second try at an answer", and so on. As we have said, tracking a user's request is not yet fully developed in the current Advisor system.

The third area of concern in Advisor III is that of quickly handling the large volume of mail that requires nothing more than "message-shuffling" on Advisor's part. The most frequent request of this sort is the request for more disk quota. The Advisor neither dictates nor applies the quota policy and does not have the privileges required to actually change a user's quota. Thus, the Advisor does little more than acknowledge the user's request and pass it along to the Accounts group,

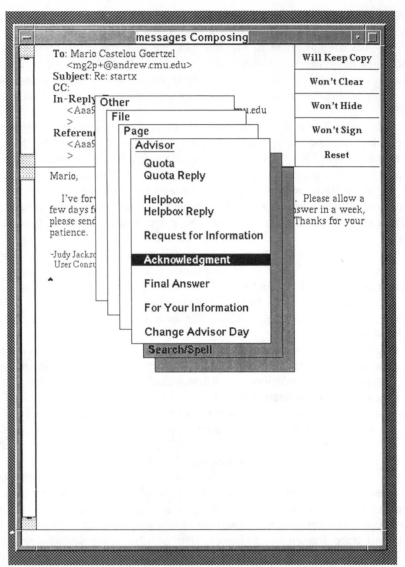

FIGURE 7. Custom Advisor commands for sending or replying to users' mail.

who makes the judgement whether additional quota should be granted and perform the necessary steps required to increase the user's quota. To streamline handling quota requests, the Advisor staff created the pair of menu actions Quota and Quota Reply, also shown in Figure 7. First the Advisor chooses the Forward menu action to create a message-sending window with the user's mail in it, giving the Advisor the opportunity to make annotations if warranted. Then the Advisor chooses Quota. The user's message is automatically addressed to *advisor.helpbox.quota*, and a command is run to generate some information about the requester's current disk usage. The results from this command, which are captured in a distinctive font, are prepended to the user's text and the resulting message is sent off with the state message header, "Quota", which gives us a hook for measuring the number of quota requests Advisor processes. The message also has a modified reply-to header so that both the user and Advisor will be notified by the Accounts group when the user's quota request has been processed. The Advisor acknowledges the user by using Quota Reply, which sends a message containing a prepared text about policy and current resource constraints.

The pair of commands, Helpbox and Helpbox Reply, are simply generalizations of the quota operation. After choosing the Forward menu action, addressing the mail-to-be-forwarded to the correct helpbox, and adding any commentary the Advisor thinks will be useful to the readers of that helpbox, the Advisor chooses the menu action, Helpbox. The state message header "Helpbox" is added to the message and the message goes to the specified helpbox. The state message header is a hook both for tracking Advisor's actions in getting an answer for the user, particularly to remind one of pending requests for assistance, and for measuring the frequency with which Advisor asks for help from the technical staff.

The fourth problem with Advisor III was the clumsiness of certain filing operations that Advisor frequently performed. Compound commands on the *Classify* menu card of the messages-reading window, shown in Figure 8, were created to make these actions easy. The menu action Current→ Outbox appends the currently displayed message to *advisor.outbox* and removes it from the inbox. The menu action Related→ Outbox gathers the messages that are in the same reply-chain as the currently displayed message, appends them to the outbox, and removes them from the inbox. If necessary, the Advisor can generate a reply-chain with the Mark Related Messages menu action, mark additional relevant messages by pointing and clicking, and then use the menu action Marked→ outbox to move the entire group of messages to the outbox, deleting them from the inbox.†

In summary, the four problem areas for Advisor III have been attacked by putting some structure into common Advisor behaviors. The designers of Advisor have made some investigation of the varying illocutionary implications of such linguistic actions as sending an acknowledgement or requesting more information. Though there is much more fruitful development to be done in this area, the authors are satisfied that this kind of approach is the right one for the principled addition of automation to the Advisor service.

Linking support groups
The Distributed Workstation Services group has for some time been exporting the Advisor concept and connecting the Advisor system to other help groups on campus. The most mature example to date is a bridge between the *advisor.helpbox.datacomm* bulletin board and a suite of bulletin boards attached to an account, dc0m, belonging to the Network and Communications group. Rather

---

† Another evolutionary change in the Advisor system has been the development of customized environments for each of the Advisor staff members. Staff members have developed their own auxiliary sub-systems, including additional bulletin boards for their own pending Advisor items, and have elaborately customized compound operations defined as well. The move-to-pending menu actions in Figure 7 are examples of a "personal" extension of the Advisor mechanism which has been adopted by all the Advisors.

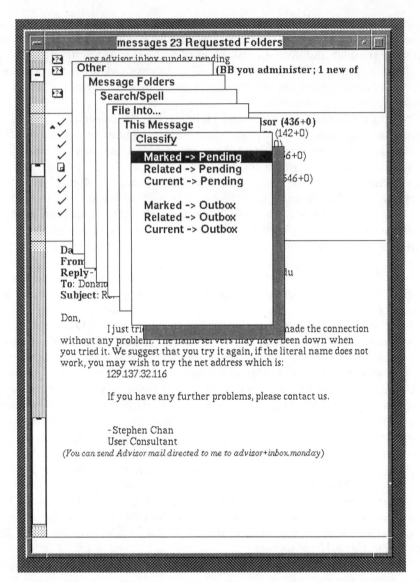

FIGURE 8. Custom commands for transferring Advisor mail into the *advisor.outbox*.

than have these folks subscribe to the Advisor helpbox as a second source of input to their group, the Advisor designers created a "hot link" between the two groups. When Advisor puts mail into its datacomm helpbox, it is automatically resent to dc0m with a special header. When someone in Data Communications replies to that mail, by virtue of that header, it comes back directly to Advisor's helpbox, just where the Advisor expects to find it. There are similar links to other groups who employ Advisor-like systems that we have exported for both academic and administrative use. In this way, DWS hopes to provide these groups with a common front-end to the community—mail to Advisor—while allowing them to use whatever internal consulting structures suit them best. It is our belief that a large part of Distributed Workstation Services' role is to enable this kind of distributed support.

Revealing Advisor's inner workings to users
Another subtle but useful change has been in making the hidden structure of the Advisor system more visible to sophisticated users. The Advisor system was heavily oriented from the very beginning to the notion that users would simply send mail to "advisor" and the right thing would happen automatically. That this is ideal for novice users is virtually self-evident. However, it has come to seem desirable to give expert users the ability to direct certain kinds of requests more specifically. (This is an interesting parallel to the general effort, in the Messages interface, to accommodate novices by default but to provide powerful and sophisticated features to those who want them.) Thus, for example, an expert can now send a security-related message to "advisor + security", and it will be delivered directly to the Advisor staff members concerned with security issues. In this case, not only is the message delivered more directly, it is also more private—fewer staff members will see what may be a rather sensitive message.

ADVISOR'S FUTURE

Structuring routine user actions
It would be nice if the Advisors did not have to handle such commodity services as quota requests, but had them forwarded immediately to the staff who do take care of such matters. However, the experience with automatic classification by keywords in Advisor II suggests that a simple keyword-based approach to routing such messages might well backfire. Instead, the Advisor staff is developing a combination of mail templates, Ness extension programs, and FLAMES programs that permit users to create semi-structured messages, similar in spirit though not in detail, to those of the Information Lens system (Malone, Grant, Turbak *et al.*, 1987), which can then be reliably routed automatically. For example, a user might type a command such as "more-quota" and be presented with a new mail-sending window, containing an interactive form containing various headers, fields, and relevant information, some of which may be filled in automatically. The data thus generated is then used by Advisor's FLAMES program to send an appropriate acknowledgment automatically and route the mail directly to the right place, rather than have it filter through the normal Advisor mechanism. Once we work out the kinks in a limited domain like quota requesting, the Advisor developers hope to follow this prototype with interactive templates and FLAMES parsings for bug reports, requests for new features, and the like.

Automatic Advisor "claim checks" and social filtering
We indicated earlier that we have not completely solved the problem of routing all mail from a user about a given problem to a single Advisor's inbox. It has been proposed that the FLAMES file which processes incoming Advisor mail immediately sends back to the user a confirming message which will ask the user to send Advisor any further messages about the matter at hand by replying to this "claim check" message. While such a claim check could be implemented today, the Advisor staff feel it makes more sense to introduce this after we have supplied some Advisor-submission templates, because then the claim check that is returned can be made apropos of the type of query Advisor received. It is here Advisor may introduce social filtering again. For example, if the submission mechanism can automatically

generate information about the status of the sender (e.g. faculty, staff, student, which department, etc.), then the handling of this mail, including the initial claim check, can be sensitive to the different needs of these constituencies and the (possibly) different computing policies that apply to various groups.

Structuring routine helper actions

Those who cooperate with Advisor by reading helpboxes and posting information there do so on a voluntary basis. It would be useful to develop tools for the helpers that semi-formalize their uptake of Advisor's requests for assistance. To design such tools will require careful thought about various illocutionary categories like directives—Advisor messages that attempt to get the helpbox reader to do something (e.g. answer the forwarded question), and commissives—helper messages that commit the helper to some action (e.g. fix some bug by a certain date). Furthermore, the helpers need some way to transfer ownership of a commitment, and both Advisor and the helpers need tools to facilitate the negotiation of help commitments, especially if they are subject to change as new information and technical and resource feasibilities warrant. Similarly, if the staffing model for Advisor changes significantly from that of an Advisor taking an entire day's worth of Advisor mail to a queue of requests that all the Advisors draw from, then there may be much greater need for internal mechanisms whereby different Advisor staff members can take up, transfer, and close responsibility for individual user requests. The work of Winograd and Flores, especially as it has begun to appear in software products like The Coordinator, is fundamental to our explorations in this area.

Tracking and measurement revisited

An experiment has been conducted with the Advisor system to use our FLAMES program to automatically generate an Informix database of tracking information about all the traffic through the Advisor system. This database, which was a course project for a group of students in the Social and Decision Science department, never went into full-scale use, largely due to a lack of programming resources. Nevertheless, the idea seems very promising, and also points strongly to the lack of database facilities as an underlying weakness in AMS. The Advisor staff is looking for additional resources to take up this project in earnest. The result will be a system parallel to Advisor's myriad bulletin boards that both the Advisors and their supervisors can use to get status on a particular user request, as well as to generate routine statistical measures and reports.

Question/answer service for users

The *advisor.outbox* is a fairly useful collection for Advisor's own use. But the notion of a database or a hyper-document of commonly asked questions and expert answers that grows in step with Advisor's question-answering is what we are aiming for. Such a tool would be enormously valuable to the Advisors themselves, their helpers, and other computing consultation services around campus. With careful user-interface design and expert system intelligence, it could also be most beneficial to the end user, provided that the information was timely, accurate, and easy to navigate. A recent example of the sort of system we would like to graft onto Advisor is the Answer Garden (Ackerman & Malone, 1990).

Other engines behind the AMS front-end

The infrastructure for the Advisor service was put together using AMS bulletin boards as much for the reason that was the tool we had available as for any intrinsic virtues of bulletin boards. Exploring other computer-based communication technologies would be a useful exercise. For example, computer conferences are a different breed of animal to bulletin boards. It would be very instructive to re-implement Advisor's helpboxes using an advanced conferencing system, one rich in mechanisms for assigning various roles and passing control of "the floor", in order to see how many of the tools for semi-formalizing Advisor and helper behaviors simply fall out as a consequence of the particular strengths of computer conferencing.

At a more fundamental level, it is clear to the authors that the Advisor service has nearly reached the limits of what current AMS bulletin boards can do as information repositories—AMS does not provide a general database mechanism, but Advisor often needs one. Then again, without AMS and its powerful kit of features and customization and extension mechanisms, the Advisor staff, who are neither academics nor researchers, but practising consultants and service providers, would likely never have pursued the vision of computer-supported cooperative consulting to the point where such limitations become apparent. When the son-of-AMS is available, whatever that might be, the designers of Advisors ars poised and ready to investigate the avenues of development outlined above.

Conclusions

The Messages interface has been highly successful as a user interface, easily learned and appreciated by novices, easily extended by experts, and powerful enough to support major cooperative work applications. Although one such program cannot be considered proof, it lends support to the notion that power and usability are not fundamentally incompatible. It demonstrates one approach to reconciling power and usability, which entails tailoring all default behavior to novices while providing a simple and graceful mechanism by which experts can extend its power.

The evolution of the Advisor system has taught its designers a great deal about computer-supported cooperative work. Our failed experiments have been the most instructive of all our experiences. But with each incarnation, Advisor feels more and more like an enduring technology for user support in times when central consulting services are lean and everyone looks to some form of distributed consulting to ease the load. We realize that we have only begun to scratch the surface, but we feel we are taking the right steps to exploit the ever-increasing power and sophistication of distributed computing in higher education. The Advisory staff, most of whom are not programmers, have proven able to use the expert-oriented features of the Andrew Message System to develop FLAMES programs, customized compound commands, hot links between support systems, Advisor-templates, and interfaces to alternative engines largely independent of the AMS developers. It is by virtue of putting these tools in the hands of cooperating workers that the Advisor system continues to be an interesting example of how the AMS supports a large, important, complex, "real-life" cooperative work application.

Messages is a part of the Andrew Message System, which was developed by Nathaniel Borenstein, Jonathan Rosenberg, Craig Everhart, Bob Glickstein, Adam Stoller, Mark Chance and Mike McInerny. Substantial parts of the Messages user interface reflect the suggestions and experiences of thousands of users, but most especially the suggestions of Dan Boyarski, Chris Haas, Chris Thyberg and Pierette Maniago, who devoted substantial time and effort to studying, deploying and extending the system. The Andrew Message System was built on top of the rich infrastructure provided by the Andrew File System and the Andrew Toolkit, which are themselves the product of a great deal of work by a great many top-notch software developers. The Andrew Message System and the Andrew Toolkit are part of the Andrew software as distributed on the X11R4 tape from MIT. They are freely available to all interested parties.

Advisor II was conceived by Chris Thyberg and implemented by Pierette Maniago, with help from Nathaniel Borenstein. Advisor III was designed and implemented by Chris Thyberg, Pierette Maniago, and Adam Stoller. Recent Advisor extensions are the work of Chris Thyberg, Wallace Colyer, Judith Jackson, Bob Glickstein and Michael Riccio.

Continued thanks also go to our frontline Advisors over the years. They are the real answer-givers and they have been an unfailing source of useful suggestions for the improvement of the Advisor mechanism and of distributed user support in general.

Finally, none of the work described here would have been possible without the encouragement and support of some very enlightened and visionary management at both CMU and IBM. This paper was written with the support of equally enlightened management at Bellcore.

Judith Jackson helped substantially with the description in this paper of the Advisor system. The paper also benefited greatly from the comments of several anonymous reviewers, as well as Terilyn Gillespie, Peter Clitherow, Bob Kraut and Steve Rohall.

References

ACKERMAN, M. & MALONE, T. (1990). Answer garden: A tool for growing organizational memory. In *Proceedings of the Conference on Office Information Systems,* Cambridge, Massachusetts. New York: ACM Press.

BORENSTEIN, N. S. & GOSLING, J. (1988). UNIX Emacs as a test-bed for user interface design. In *Proceedings of the ACM SIGGRAPH Symposium on User Interface Software,* Banff, Alberta.

BORENSTEIN, N. S., EVERHART, C. F., ROSENBERG, J. & STOLLER, A. (1988). A multi-media message system for Andrew. In *Proceedings of the USENIX 1988 Winter Technical Conference,* Dallas, Texas. Dallas, TX: USENIX Association.

BORENSTEIN, N. S. & THYBERG, C. (1988). Cooperative work in the Andrew Message System. In *Proceedings of the Conference on Computer-Supported Cooperative Work, CSCW 88,* Portland, Oregon.

BORENSTEIN, N. S., EVERHART, C. F., ROSENBERG, J. & STOLLER, A. (1989). Architectural issues in the Andrew Message System. In E. STEFFERUD, O.-J. JACOBSEN & P. SCHICKER, Eds., *Message Handling Systems and Distributed Applications.* Amsterdam: North-Holland.

BORENSTEIN, N. S. (In press *a*). *Software Engineering and Other Delusions.* Englewood Cliffs, NJ: Prentice Hall.

BORENSTEIN, N. S. (In press *b*). CMU's Andrew project: a report card. *Communications of the ACM.*

BORENSTEIN, N. S. (1990). *Multimedia Applications Development with the Andrew Toolkit.* Englewood Cliffs, NJ: Prentice Hall.

HANSEN, W. (1990). Enhancing documents with embedded programs: how Ness extends insets in the Andrew Toolkit. In *Proceedings of IEEE Computer Society 1990 International Conference on Computer Languages,* New Orleans.

HOWARD, J. (1988). An overview of the Andrew File System. In *Proceedings of the USENIX 1988 Winter Technical Conference,* Dallas, Texas.

HOWARD, J., KAZAR, M., MENEES, S., NICHOLS, D., SATYANARAYANAN, M., SIDEBOTHAM, R. & WEST, M. (1988). Scale and performance in a distributed file system, *ACM Transactions on Computer Systems*, **6**, (1).

KAZAR, M. (1988). Synchronization and caching issues in the Andrew File System. In *Proceedings of the USENIX 1988 Winter Technical Conference*, Dallas, Texas.

KAZAR, M. & SPECTOR, A. (1989). Uniting file systems, *UNIX Review*, March.

LAI, K.-Y. & MALONE, T. (1988). Object lens: a spreadsheet' for cooperative work. In *Proceedings of the conference on computer-supported cooperative work*, CSCW 88, Portland, Oregon.

MALONE, T., GRANT, K., TURBAK, F., BROBST, S. & COHEN, M. (1987). Intelligent information-sharing systems, *Communications of the ACM*, **30**, (3).

MALONE, T., GRANT, K., LAI, K.-Y. RAO, R. & ROSENBLITT, D. (1987). Semi-structured messages are surprisingly useful for computer-supported coordination. In I. GREIF, Ed., *Computer Supported Cooperative Work: A Book of Readings*. San Mateo, CA: Morgan Kaufman.

MORRIS, J., SATYANARAYANAN, M., CONNER, M., HOWARD, M., ROSENTHAL, D. & SMITH, F. (1986). Andrew: a distributed personal computing environment, *Communications of the ACM*, **29**, (3).

MORRIS, J. (1988). Make or take decisions in Andrew. In *Proceedings of the USENIX 1988 Winter Technical Conference*, Dallas, Texas.

PALAY, A., HANSEN, W., KAZAR, M., SHERMAN, M., WADLOW, M., NEUENDORFFER, T., STERN, Z., BADER, M. & PETERS, T. (1988). The Andrew Toolkit: an overview. In *Proceedings of the USENIX 1988 Winter Technical Conference*, Dallas, Texas.

ROSENBERG, J., EVERHART, C. & BORENSTEIN, N. (1987). An overview of the Andrew Message System. In *Proceedings of SIGCOMM '87 Workshop, Frontiers in Computer Communications Technology*, Stowe, Vermont.

SCHEIFLER, R. & GETTYS, J. (1987). The X window system, *ACM Transactions on Graphics*, **5**, (2).

THYBERG, C. (1988). Advisor—an electronic mail consulting service. In *Proceedings ACM SIGUCCS User Services Conference XVI*, Long Beach, California.

WINOGRAD, T. & FLORES, F. (1986). *Understanding Computers and Cognition*. Norwood, NJ: Ablex Publishing Corp.

WINOGRAD, T. (1988). A language perspective on the design of cooperative work. In I. Grief, Ed. *Computer Supported Cooperative Work: A Book of Readings*. San Mateo, CA: Morgan Kaufman.

Part 3

Computer-mediated communications
and group decision support systems

7

Electronic meeting support: the GroupSystems concept

JOSEPH S. VALACICH

ALAN R. DENNIS

J. F. NUNAMAKER JR.

In recent years, there has been a rapidly growing interest in the use of information technology to support face-to-face group meetings. Such Electronic Meeting System (EMS) environments represent a fundamental shift in the technology available for group meetings. In this paper, we describe the development and evaluation research conducted at the University of Arizona that has led to the installation of one EMS at more than 30 corporate and university sites around the world. Based on our experiences in working with student groups in controlled laboratory experiments and with organizational work groups in the field, we are convinced that EMS technology has the potential to dramatically change the way people work together by effectively supporting larger groups, reducing meeting and project time, and enhancing group member satisfaction.

1. Introduction

This paper provides a state-of-the-art description of the research and facilities to support electronic meetings developed at the University of Arizona. However, in its broadest context, group meeting support has been around for a long time. The Greeks and Romans had special purpose facilities for planning and decision making. Decisions are produced in special meeting rooms in the Senate and the House of Representatives of the United States and in other social institutions. Winston Churchill had a special decision room in London to chart progress and to plan strategy during World War II. Our objective is merely to improve this age old process through the use of information technology, i.e. an Electronic Meeting System (EMS).

An EMS is an information technology (IT)-based environment designed to support group meetings (Dennis, George, Jessup, Nunamaker & Vogel, 1988). These environments can include distributed facilities, computer hardware and software, audio and video technology, procedures, methodologies, facilitation and applicable group data. Although the University of Arizona has primarily focused on supporting face-to-face meetings, an EMS can be used to support groups distributed geographically and temporally. Group tasks can include communication, planning, idea generation, problem solving, issue discussion, negotiation, conflict resolution, systems analysis and design, and collaborative group activities such as document preparation and sharing.

EMS environments represent a fundamental shift in the technology available for group interaction. Huber (1990) has suggested that much of the theory for small group interaction and organizational design be re-examined in a computer-supported context, as the use of computer technology may profoundly affect group and organizational process, structure and outcomes (see also Finholt & Sproull, 1990). The next major section describes the developmental motivation of one EMS, the University of Arizona GroupSystems, and how its integration of facilities, software and procedures are used to enhance meetings. The third major section reviews previous evaluation research made by the University of Arizona which documents many of our empirical and self-evident truths (the ones we cannot prove but observe to be true), discovered in several laboratory experiments, field and longitudinal case studies. The paper concludes by providing recommendations to EMS developers and users based upon the experiences gained over the past several years developing, using and evaluating these technologies.

2. University of Arizona GroupSystems environment

Although no one theoretical perspective can fully explain all aspects of group work, we have chosen to build on the concept of process losses and gains (Steiner, 1966, 1972; Hill, 1982). As such, we view the actual productivity of a meeting as the result of a series of factors that act to increase productivity (i.e. provide process gains) and inhibit productivity (i.e. introduce process losses). Thus, the GroupSystems concept is quite simple: *reduce or eliminate the dysfunctions of the group interaction (i.e. process losses), so that a group reaches or exceeds (i.e. process gains) its task potential.* In this section we will first define several process losses and then present the GroupSystems environment—facilities, software and procedures—and describe how each of these factors provide opportunities for process gains by mitigating process losses.

2.1. PROCESS LOSSES

Process losses are described as dysfunctions in the group process, that inhibit the group from reaching their potential task performance (based upon the resources of the groups) (Steiner, 1972). There are countless group process losses. In this section we will define several important process losses that are relevant to the GroupSystems environment.

Process losses can arise from numerous dysfunctions in the group interaction process. *Production blocking,* defined slightly differently by several authors, generally refers to the fact that only one member of a group can speak at a time during verbal communication (Dunnette, Campbell & Jaastad, 1963; Lamm & Trommsdorff, 1973; Jablin & Seibold, 1978; Diehl & Stroebe, 1987). Production blocking has at least three effects on the group process. First, group members who are prevented from verbalizing their ideas as they occur may forget or suppress them because they seem less relevant or less original at a later time (attenuation blocking). Second, when waiting to verbalize an idea, group members focus on remembering that idea, rather than generating new ideas (concentration blocking). Third, listening to other members speak may preclude generating new ideas (attention blocking).

Another process loss is *unequal air time*. This process loss, closely related to production blocking, refers to the division of available verbal communication time among the group (Lamm & Trommsdorff, 1973). As groups get larger, the time available to each participant shrinks (Dunnette *et al.*, 1963; Lamm & Trommsdorff, 1973; Jablin & Seibold, 1978; Diehl & Stroebe, 1987). A third process loss, *evaluation apprehension,* refers to the fear of negative evaluation of ideas shared with the group which may cause individuals to withhold ideas and comments (Collaros & Anderson, 1969; Lamm & Trommsdorff, 1973; Harari & Graham, 1975; Jablin, Seibold & Sorenson, 1977; Jablin & Seibold, 1978; Diehl & Stroebe, 1987). *Free-riding* refers to the tendency of some group members to rely on the other members of the group to accomplish the task without their contributions (Kerr & Bruun, 1981, 1983; Harkins & Petty, 1982; Albanese & Van Fleet, 1985; Diehl & Stroebe, 1987). While free-riding may be caused by social loafing, the tendency for people to exert less effort when they pool their efforts toward a common goal than when they are individually accountable (Steiner, 1972; Kerr & Bruun, 1981; Harkins & Jackson, 1985; Diehl & Stroebe, 1987), it may also be affected by the need to compete for air time. Group members are also more likely to free-ride if they perceive their contributions to be less necessary for success (Diehl & Stroebe, 1987), and thus free-riding may increase in larger groups. Another process loss is *cognitive inertia,* which is the tendency of discussions to move along one line of thought without deviating from the current topic (Lamm & Trommsdorff, 1973; Harari & Graham, 1975; Jablin & Seibold, 1978).

Socializing refers to the tendency of groups to engage in dysfunctional non-task related behavior (Shaw, 1981). Although some socializing is necessary for effective functioning, too much will of course reduce meeting performance. *Domination* occurs when some group member(s) exercise(s) undue influence or monopolize(s) the group's time in an inefficient manner (Dalkey & Helmer, 1963; Van de Ven & Delbecq, 1971; Jablin & Seibold, 1978; Watson & Michaelsen, 1988). *Failure to remember* refers to the failure of members to fully listen to and remember the comments of others (Diehl & Stroebe, 1987; Jablin & Seibold, 1978). *Incomplete analysis* occurs when members fail to use information available and to challenge the assumptions held by others (Hirokowa & Pace, 1983).

2.2. GROUPSYSTEMS FACILITIES

The University of Arizona currently operates two EMS facilities, with two additional facilities scheduled to open in 1991. All facilities provide participant work areas (i.e. tables or desks) arranged to provide a central focus at the front of the room. Each participant is provided with a separate networked, hard disk-based, color graphics microcomputer workstation that is recessed into the work area. One or two workstations serve as the facilitator's consoles which are used to control the EMS. At least one large screen video display is provided as an electronic blackboard, with other audio-visual support also available (typically white boards and overhead projectors). Adjacent to the meeting room is a control room for the electronics, and a laser printer and copier to provide immediate hardcopy printouts.

The first EMS facility at Arizona opened in 1985. The main meeting room provides a large U-shaped table accommodating 16 participants. Building on the experience with this room, which demonstrated the need for a larger facility, Arizona's second facility was constructed in 1987 (Figure 1). This facility, the University of Arizona Collaborative Management Room, has 24 workstations arranged in two concentric tiered rows. For a more complete description of both facilities, see Dennis *et al.* (1988).

We believe that various design aspects of these rooms mitigate several group process losses. The networked workstations allow group process tools to be designed that allow all group members to contribute information simultaneously and for a consistent process related structure to be enforced (DeSanctis & Gallupe, 1987). This parallelism and structure, should reduce aspects of production blocking, unequal air time, domination and free riding. The large central group display can be used as a "group memory", and should help to both deliver process structure and mitigate failure to remember losses.

2.3. GROUPSYSTEMS SOFTWARE

The GroupSystems tools are used to deliver a process related structure to a meeting phase. There are three distinct styles of meeting process, which we term a *chauffeured* process, a *supported* process, and an *interactive* process. In a

FIGURE 1. The University of Arizona collaborative management room.

chauffeured process, only one person, either a group member or facilitator, uses the EMS. Group members verbally provide information to the "chauffeur" to enter into the group memory via a workstation connected to a large public display. In a *supported* process, groups use both the electronic and verbal communication. During supported activities, a mixture of both sequential (i.e. verbal communication) and parallel communication (i.e. electronic communication) is applied to activities that require multiple communication channels. In an *interactive* process, the electronic communication channel provided by the EMS is used for almost all group communication; virtually no verbal communication occurs.

Each meeting style addresses different process losses. The interactive process is the strongest intervention (but not necessarily the "best"), as it reduces aspects of production blocking, unequal air time, failure to remember, socializing, and domination by providing a parallel communication channel. Free riding may be reduced in an interactive process environment by lowering the "cost" to participate. Furthermore, the electronic channel can be configured to be anonymous, which may reduce evaluation apprehension and conformance pressure. However, anonymity may also increase free-riding and depersonalization/de-individuation, making it inappropriate for some situations.

A chauffeured process is the weakest intervention (but not necessarily the "worst"). This process primarily addresses failure to remember via the group memory of the public display. An increased task focus promoted by this process may also reduce socializing. Between these extremes is the supported process. Process losses reduced in supported environments will hinge upon the amount of electronic and verbal communication, and the extent of the use of the public display. Each GroupSystems tool is designed to use one of these meeting styles to support one of three types of group activity: idea generation, idea synthesis or prioritizing.

2.3.1. Idea generation

Idea-generation is often an early phase in many group activities (e.g. decision making, negotiations planning, information systems development, etc.), where various options and alternatives are surfaced (McGrath, 1984). The success of subsequent group task phases, such as choosing among alternatives, is often contingent upon the success of the idea-generation phase. During this phase, groups are typically encouraged to be creative and to focus solely on generating ideas, with the evaluation of ideas reserved for later group phases (see discussions on Brainstorming by Osborn, 1957, or the Nominal Group Technique by Van de Ven and Delbecq, 1974). In this section we describe two GroupSystems tools for idea-generation, that use an interactive process.

Electronic Brainstorming (EBS) provides an interactive process in which participants enter comments into many separate discussions contained in separate files that are randomly shared throughout the group. A high degree of process structure is imposed on the group by the random sharing of files in EBS. This file sharing facilitates the development of many separate discussions, which should address cognitive inertia losses. However, the random passing of files makes receiving feedback on comments more difficult. A sample EBS screen is shown in Figure 2. In EBS, prior comments are stored in the upper window of the screen and are viewed using a "read-only" editor. New comments are entered in the bottom window and

```
┌─────────────────────────────────────────────────────────────────────┐
│ ─────────────── ELECTRONIC BRAINSTORMING ───────────────             │
│ PRIOR COMMENTS: To Scroll PRIOR COMMENTS, Use PgUp, PgDn, Home, End   │
├─────────────────────────────────────────────────────────────────────┤
│   What are the key issues in technological support for group work?    │
│                                                                       │
│   7.1 Users believing that it is worth their time and effort to       │
│   change the way they now work and then invest in these technologies. │
│                                                                       │
│   7.2 We must determine those conditions for which GDSS is suitable,  │
│   or desirable, and those for which it is not.                        │
│                                                                       │
│   7.3 I agree with 7.2, we need to create a harmonious marriage of    │
│   both technical and behavioral considerations.                       │
│                                                                       │
│   7.4 What about cost and ease of use!                                │
│                                                                       │
│   7.5 The ease of use demand and flexibility issues are discussed in  │
├─────────────────────────────────────────────────────────────────────┤
│   YOUR COMMENTS (limit of 5 lines):                                   │
├─────────────────────────────────────────────────────────────────────┤
│   7.6 Certainly, this whole area comes under the heading of           │
│   organizational support systems. The purpose of this technology . . .│
│                                                                       │
│   PRESS F10 TO SUBMIT COMMENTS & CONTINUE              F1 = HELP       │
└─────────────────────────────────────────────────────────────────────┘
```

FIGURE 2. Sample electronic brainstorming (EBS) screen.

are saved by pressing a function key. After pressing the function key, the system appends the newly entered comment to the end of the current file and returns this file to the file server in exchange for another.

Topic Commenter (TC) also uses an interactive process for group idea generation, however, comments are collected from meeting participants using a task-specific structure. TC operates like a set of index cards, with each card having a name (Figure 3). Participants select a card by using the arrow keys to move a reverse video bar over card titles. Once a card is selected, participants can press one function key to enter comments, or another to read all prior group comments related to this topic. TC provides more structure to idea generation than EBS as comments are directed to specific conversations and are not randomly placed.

2.3.2. Idea synthesis

The purpose of idea synthesis is to identify, synthesize, formulate and consolidate ideas, proposals or alternatives that have been discussed in an idea generation tool. Using a multi-windowed display, participants can view comments developed during idea generation and the task specific functions of the synthesis tools. Idea synthesis typically uses a supportive process. For example, using the GroupSystems tool *Idea Organizer* (IO), each participant works separately to create a private list of idea categories which are submitted to the groups. Figure 4 displays a sample IO screen which has three windows. In the top window, one-line idea categories are entered. The bottom window is a "read-only" environment that contains prior comments developed using EBS (or some other tool). Users are instructed to browse the prior

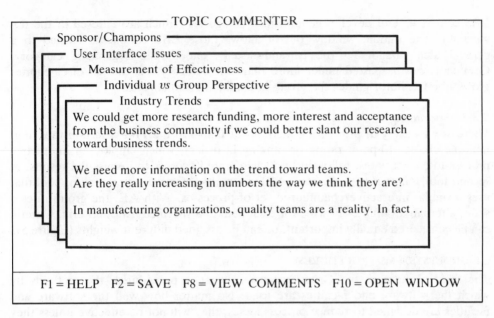

FIGURE 3. Sample topic commenter (TC) screen.

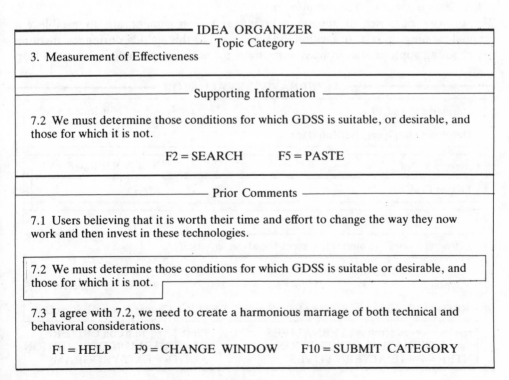

FIGURE 4. Sample idea organizer (IO) screen.

EBS comments and develop general idea categories (which are entered in the top window). The middle window of IO allows those EBS comments related to a general idea category to be cut-and-pasted "under" the organizing category. Comments can be pasted under more than one category. As the list of categories grows, the facilitator guides the group in combining similar ones.

2.3.3. Prioritizing

There are a variety of prioritizing methods available in the *Vote Selection* tool (e.g. multiple choice, 10-point rating or ranking in order), which employ an interactive process to collect votes, followed by a chauffeured process to discuss the results. A second tool, *Alternative Evaluator* (AE) is a multi-criteria decision making tool that uses a similar interactive/chauffeured set of processes. With AE, the group rates a set of alternatives on a 1–10 scale for each item in a specified list of criteria. Criteria can be considered equally important, or can be assigned different weights (Figure 5).

2.4. GROUPSYSTEMS PROCEDURES

The third element in the GroupSystems concept is procedures, the methods by which the software and facilities are used. No matter how well the software and facilities are designed to reduce process losses, they will not be effective unless they are used appropriately. The two key elements in GroupSystems procedures are session planning and management and meeting facilitation.

2.4.1. Session planning and management

The primary purposes of session planning and management are to establish a rational meeting agenda, to facilitate the following of this agenda during the meeting (by choosing appropriate GroupSystems tools for each agenda activity), and to help

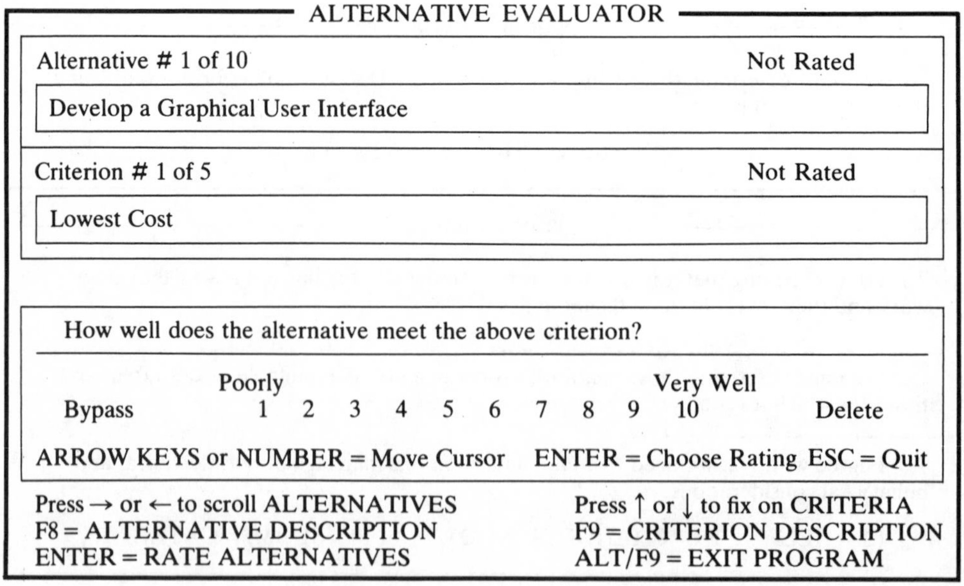

```
┌──────────────────── ALTERNATIVE EVALUATOR ────────────────────┐
│  ┌──────────────────────────────────────────────────────────┐ │
│  │ Alternative # 1 of 10                          Not Rated  │ │
│  │  ┌────────────────────────────────────────────────────┐  │ │
│  │  │ Develop a Graphical User Interface                 │  │ │
│  │  └────────────────────────────────────────────────────┘  │ │
│  │                                                          │ │
│  │ Criterion # 1 of 5                             Not Rated  │ │
│  │  ┌────────────────────────────────────────────────────┐  │ │
│  │  │ Lowest Cost                                        │  │ │
│  │  └────────────────────────────────────────────────────┘  │ │
│  └──────────────────────────────────────────────────────────┘ │
│                                                                │
│  ┌──────────────────────────────────────────────────────────┐ │
│  │  How well does the alternative meet the above criterion? │ │
│  │  ──────────────────────────────────────────────────────  │ │
│  │          Poorly                        Very Well         │ │
│  │  Bypass     1   2   3   4   5   6   7   8   9   10   Delete│ │
│  │                                                          │ │
│  │  ARROW KEYS or NUMBER = Move Cursor   ENTER = Choose Rating  ESC = Quit │ │
│  │  ─────────────────────────────────────────────────────  │ │
│  │  Press → or ← to scroll ALTERNATIVES    Press ↑ or ↓ to fix on CRITERIA │ │
│  │  F8 = ALTERNATIVE DESCRIPTION           F9 = CRITERION DESCRIPTION │ │
│  │  ENTER = RATE ALTERNATIVES              ALT/F9 = EXIT PROGRAM │ │
│  └──────────────────────────────────────────────────────────┘ │
└────────────────────────────────────────────────────────────────┘
```

FIGURE 5. Sample alternative evaluator (AE) screen.

organize post-meeting activities. A GroupSystems tool, Session Manager (SM), is used to support these activities. SM supports pre-meeting activities by ensuring that important planning information is not overlooked. The system is currently a "static" checklist questionnaire, however, an expert system to assist this stage is currently under development (Aiken, Motiwalla, Sheng & Nunamaker, 1990). The establishment of an agenda should help groups remain more task focused during a meeting (i.e. less socializing). During the meeting SM assists in following the agenda, as all tools must be initialized, started and ended via SM. An established agenda reduces coordination problems during the meeting, as more reliable meeting sequences are used (as suggested by SM). SM assists post-meeting activities by permanently recording meeting information as part of the group memory. Various components of the group memory can be indexed, stored and reported, which assists the integration of information across multi-session meetings (i.e. improve the group memory, Valacich, Vogel & Nunamaker, 1989).

2.4.2. Meeting facilitation

The role of the meeting facilitator in the GroupSystems environment is multifaceted. The facilitator provides technical support for using the environment, provides group dynamics support, assists in meeting agenda planning, and in on-going organizational settings, provides organizational continuity by setting standards for system use, training and system maintenance. During the meeting the facilitator is paramount in ensuring that a group follows their agenda (i.e. providing process structure). Effective group dynamics support will reduce numerous process losses, such as evaluation apprehension (by establishing a non-judgemental atmosphere), free riding (by encouraging participation), domination, socializing and cognitive inertia (by making sure the meeting "moves along").

3. Evaluation of use

Research evaluating GroupSystems has included both laboratory and field research, as we believe that multiple methods are needed to better understand the impacts of the technology. Our research has focused on the effects of those variables employed in prior group research (e.g. group size, group task) as well as those more common to computer-mediated environments (e.g. anonymity, proximity). We begin by examining laboratory research followed by field and case research.

3.1. LABORATORY RESEARCH

There are virtually countless group tasks that can be investigated in a EMS context. Our laboratory research has chosen to focus on two general types of tasks: idea generation and decision making. As briefly discussed above, for groups in a multi-phased meeting, the "success" of later group activities is often determined by the success (or failure) of earlier activities. Consequently, a large portion of our experimental research has focused on idea generation, a task that often precedes many subsequent group activities. The last activity in many meetings is the selection of some alternative(s) by the group (i.e. making a decision). As group members typically have differences in knowledge, skills, influence and values, some of which may be hard to reconcile, our decision making research focuses on trying to understand these differences so that we might effectively design technologies to support them. We first review our idea generation and then our decision making laboratory studies.

3.1.1. *Idea generation research*

The first controlled study on anonymity in the GroupSystems environment was conducted by Jessup, Connolly and Galegher (1990). This study examined the influence of anonymity on the group process of idea generating groups. Anonymous groups used the standard version of EBS, while a special version was developed to provide "identified" comments by attaching user names to each comment. Group members whose contributions were anonymous, generated more comments, were more critical and probing, and were more likely to embellish ideas proposed by others than were those whose contributions were identified by name. This suggested that anonymity could reduce evaluation apprehension even in student groups

TABLE 1

GroupSystems experimental studies related to idea generation

Study	Variables	Total number of comments	Number of unique solutions	Number of critical comments	Overall satisfaction
Jessup et al., 1990	Anonymity	More with anonymity	No effect	More with anonymity	—†
Jessup et al., 1988	Anonymity and proximity	More in anonymous and distributed groups	No effect	More with anonymity	Higher in proximate groups
Connolly et al., 1990	Anonymity and meeting tone	More in anonymous and critical groups	More in anonymous and critical groups	More in anonymous and critical groups	Higher in identified and supportive groups
Valacich et al., 1990b	Anonymity and group size	No difference per person	More in large groups	More in anonymous and large groups	Higher in small-identified groups
Dennis et al., 1990b	Group size	—	Increased with group size	—	Increased with group size
Valacich 1989	Group size and proximity	No difference per person	More in large and remote groups	—	No effect
Valacich et al., 1990a	Group size and group type	—	Increased with group size—more in "real" groups	—	Higher in "real" groups

† Variable not studied.

performing low threat tasks (see Table 1 for a summary of this and subsequent idea generation laboratory studies).

In a follow up study, Jessup, Tansik and Laase (1988) examined the influence of anonymity and the physical proximity of group members on group process and outcomes of idea generating groups. As above, anonymity was manipulated by using different versions of EBS. Proximity was manipulated by having groups work either on workstations in the same room or with each group member in a separate room. Group members working anonymously and apart generated the most comments, while those working in the same room had the highest satisfaction. The highest levels of perceived system effectiveness were reported by groups working under anonymous conditions. These results again suggested that anonymity could reduce evaluation apprehension.

Connolly, Jessup and Valacich (1990) evaluated the effects of anonymity and evaluative tone on group idea generation performance. Evaluative tone was manipulated through a confederate group member who entered supportive or critical comments into EBS. Groups working anonymously and with a critical confederate produced the greatest number of ideas and total comments. Identified groups working with a supportive confederate were the most satisfied and had the highest levels of perceived effectiveness, but produced the fewest ideas and total comments. The increased performance in the anonymous and critical conditions was likely due to reduced evaluation apprehension and more complete analysis (as ideas were more frequently challenged). However, as satisfaction levels were lower in these groups, anonymity and/or criticalness may also have negative side-effects.

Valacich, Dennis and Nunamaker (1990b) examined the combination of group size (3- and 9-member) and anonymity on group idea generation productivity. Contrary to prior non-computer supported idea generation research, larger groups were significantly more productive than smaller groups, in terms of the number and quality of ideas generated. Group members in all conditions made, on average, about the same number of comments. This finding suggests that group process losses (e.g. production blocking and unequal air time) were mitigated in conditions where prior non-computer supported group research has found these losses to increase. Members of large groups and anonymous groups, however, made more critical comments than did group members of small and identified groups, suggesting that anonymity may promote de-individuation and uninhibited behavior. Small-identified groups were the most satisfied and rated themselves more effective than group members from the other experimental conditions, yet members of all conditions shared very similar perceptions about the usefulness of the technology.

Dennis, Valacich and Nunamaker (1990b) studied three sizes of groups using the standard anonymous version of EBS: small (three members), medium (nine members) and large (18 members). Group productivity and member satisfaction increased with group size: large groups generated more ideas and were more satisfied than medium groups, who generated more ideas and were more satisfied than small groups. These findings contrast sharply with the productivity and satisfaction findings of previous non-EMS-supported studies, which have generally found larger groups to generate no more ideas than smaller groups, while being less satisfied. On balance, this suggests that EBS was able to moderate the negative effects of the many process losses that traditionally increase with group size (i.e. production blocking, air time, evaluation apprehension, etc.).

Valacich (1989) investigated the effects of group size (four and eight members), group member proximity, and the interaction of these two variables on the performance of idea generating groups using EBS. Group member proximity was manipulated by allowing proximate groups to work in a single meeting room, while members of distributed groups worked in separate rooms. Groups in all conditions contributed approximately the same number of comments and felt equally satisfied, but large groups were more productive than small groups for both idea quantity and quality. Small groups were, however, more productive than large groups on a per person basis, as increased group size yielded diminishing returns (i.e. redundant ideas). Remote groups were more productive than proximate groups and there were no interaction effects.

Another important and consistent finding of non-computer-supported group research relates to the performance of nominal and interacting groups. More than 80 past studies have compared the idea generating performance of nominal groups (i.e. groups constructed by pooling individual efforts—not to be confused with Van de Ven & Delbecq's, 1974, Nominal Group Technique) with interacting groups (see McGrath, 1984; Diehl & Stroebe, 1987, for reviews of this research). In this large body of research, the findings have been consistent: nominal groups consistently outperform interacting groups.

Valacich, Dennis, George & Nunamaker (1990a) conducted three experiments where interacting groups of various sizes were compared with nominal groups of equivalent sizes. The first experiment compared groups of three, nine and 18 members. The second experiment compared groups of four, eight and 12 members. The third experiment compared groups of six and 12 members. Although each experiment asked the same fundamental research question (i.e. could interacting groups supported by information technology outperform nominal groups for an idea generation task), each study was significantly different (e.g. the studies varied the group task, group performance incentives, group instructions, environment, etc.). The rationale for conducting multiple investigations of this general question in substantially different research designs was to ensure that the experimental results were not artifacts of the experimental procedures. The pattern of results was similar in all three studies; the performance of interacting groups increased with group size, and at a rate faster than that of nominal groups, such that large interacting groups (18 and 12 members) generated significantly more ideas than large nominal groups. Further, members of interacting groups were more satisfied than members of nominal groups. As large interacting groups outperformed large nominal groups, process gains must have outweighed process losses.

3.1.2. Decision making research

George, Dennis, Nunamaker & Easton (1989) compared the decision quality, the number of alternatives, member satisfaction and degree of consensus for computer-supported groups, that were permitted to develop their own group work process *vs* groups that followed a pre-specified agenda. In both cases, four and five member established groups (groups that had worked together in the past and which were expected to continue to work together) were studied. Groups that followed the agenda were less likely to reach consensus. While there were no other statistical differences between the two, the agenda-driven groups did generate more alternatives. Using an ANCOVA analysis to control for this difference in the number of alternatives, agenda-driven groups were still less likely to reach consensus, but produced decisions of greater quality (Table 2).

Easton, George, Nunamaker and Pendergast (1990) investigated the role of GroupSystems software characteristics on group decision making performance. One experimental condition used EBS, IO and Vote, while the second used a version of EBS that shared all group information with all group members simultaneously and incorporated similar functions as IO and Vote. The study found that while the original version of EBS helped generate more unique alternatives, the second version of EBS (the multi-purpose tool) produced better quality decisions. Thus the technique used by EBS to reduce cognitive inertia did result in more ideas, but made the discussion of those ideas leading to the decision, more difficult.

3.2. FIELD AND CASE RESEARCH

Our field investigations of the GroupSystems on organizational groups have a long history. Numerous groups, addressing various tasks have used our facilities over the past several years. Due to space and time limitations, this section will present but a fraction of these studies (see Table 3 for a summary of those reviewed here). Our objective will be to present a spectrum of groups and tasks in order to produce a more complete picture.

Nunamaker, Applegate and Konsynski (1987) report an early study of GroupSystems use by groups from seven organizations. The groups, ranging in size from six to 22 members (median size of 16) spent several sessions conducting a variety of strategic planning activities, such as idea generation, decision making, planning and evaluation, although the focus of the study was on idea generation. The use of EBS was reported to be more effective and more satisfying than traditional methods, as it appeared to reduce several process losses. The use of parallel communication enabled simultaneous generation and discussion of ideas, and prevented any one group member from dominating the meeting. Anonymity

TABLE 2

GroupSystems experimental studies related to decision making

	GroupSystems decision making laboratory research		
Study	Variables	Decision quality	Number of alternatives	Degree of consensus
George *et al.*, 1989	Agenda/no agenda	Higher in agenda-driven groups	Higher in agenda-driven groups	Lower in agenda-driven groups
Easton *et al.*, 1990	Degree of software tool integration	Higher in groups using multi-purpose tools	Higher in groups using EBS-only tools	—†

† Variable not studied.

TABLE 3
GroupSystems case and field studies

Study	GroupSystems case and field research Effectiveness	Efficiency	Satisfaction
Nunamaker *et al.*, 1987	Anonymity neutralized group status differences	Allowed for more equal participation	High levels reported
Dennis *et al.*, 1990*a*	Facilitated a larger and faster meeting	Saved months in the strategic planning process	High levels reported
Dennis *et al.*, 1989*a*	Rated higher than non-electronic meeting	Saved several months in the strategic planning process	High levels reported
Tyran *et al.*, 1989	Rated higher than non-electronic meeting	Reached consensus more rapidly	High levels reported
Dennis *et al.*, 1989*b*	Anonymity improved effectiveness	Rather higher than non-electronic meeting	High levels reported
Nunamaker *et al.*, 1989	Construction of additional facilities	Man-hour savings of over 51%	High levels reported

promoted more open and honest discussion and appeared to neutralize the effects of an authority hierarchy in the group.

Dennis, Heminger, Nunamaker and Vogel (1990*a*) reported on the use of GroupSystems by Burr Brown. Burr Brown is a publicly held international corporation which manufactures and sells electronic components to other electronics manufacturers in the USA, Europe and Japan. It has approximately 1500 employees and $150 million in annual sales. The computer-supported planning session was an annual part of Burr Brown's strategic planning process and was carried out over a three day period at the University of Arizona Collaborative Management Room in January 1988. Besides the CEO, participants in the session included 30 vice-presidents and senior managers of functional, product and geographic divisions. Prior to the three-day planning meeting, three pre-planning meetings were held with representatives of the company during which the company's goals for the sessions were refined and the agenda developed.

The group began by using EBS to generate ideas about expected corporate performance, which were then organized and sorted using Idea Organizer (IO). This was followed by a detailed examination and evaluation of each of the divisional one-year and five-year plans using Topic Commenter (TC). Each card in TC represented one aspect from which the plans were to be evaluated (e.g. capital requirements). EBS and IO were used to generate and organize specific plan elements to accomplish the next year's overall corporate objectives, which were then prioritized using the Vote module. These elements were ranked three times, first by overall benefit to the firm, second by time frame (short-term versus long-term) and third, feasibility. The top five issues from the benefit ranking were then entered into

TC for further group discussion. Finally, the participants broke into four smaller work groups to develop specific plans for the next three to 12 months. When asked about the effectiveness of GroupSystems on post-session questionnaires and in interviews held three months after the session, 85% of the participants rated electronic meetings (supported by GroupSystems) as more effective than traditional meetings, with the other 15% finding them to be as effective. Jim Burns, the CEO of Burr Brown, noted:

> The process allowed us to do in three days what would have taken months to do. In addition, if we had done it manually, we could not have brought more than 9 or 10 people into the process . . . and there would have been less interaction. A lot more people are on board with an understanding of what went on. Thus there is a stronger sense of understanding and agreement among the employees. A lot of education happened that previously hadn't happened . . . . People walked in with narrow perceptions of the company and walked out with a CEO's perception. This is the view that is sought in strategic planning, but is usually not achieved.

Twenty-nine managers from all management levels of Southwest Gas conducted a two-day computer-supported strategic planning retreat (Dennis, Paranka, Vogel & Nunamaker, 1989a). The CEO of more than 30 years and three other senior executives had recently left the firm, and therefore the new CEO, Mr. K. C. Guinn, felt it was time to re-examine the firm's goals and conduct some team-building. During an initial agenda planning session with the CEO and his staff, the GroupSystems tools were mapped to specific group activities. The strategic planning session began with Electronic Brainstorming to generate ideas about corporate goals, which were then sorted and organized. The one-year and five-year plans for each corporate division were then examined and criticized in sequence by the entire group using a structured framework which included such topics as capital requirements and profitability. Finally, more Electronic Brainstorming and Idea Organization was done to develop a list of specific plan elements to accomplish the next year's objectives. When asked about the effectiveness of GroupSystems use on post-session questionnaires and interviews, 94% of the participants felt that GroupSystems use was more effective than non-supported meetings. Mr. Guinn found that the meeting "saved us at least six months in the strategic planning process . . . . What we also got from the process was a renewed sense of comprehensiveness of staff. Those at the lower levels felt good because they had the chance to have equal input".

Greyhound Financial Corporation is a commercial lending firm that has used the University of Arizona Collaborative Management Room on several occasions for a variety of tasks, including developing a mission statement, building strategic objectives, strategy formulation, and individual evaluations of senior managers (Tyran, Dennis, Vogel & Nunamaker, 1989). Perhaps the most interesting task was developing a series of initiatives to improve the firm's competitive position. After discussing several competitive analysis techniques with senior management, a technique focusing on strengthening the links between the value adding activities of the firm was selected, and the results communicated throughout the firm.

In August, 1988, 30 managers from all departments within the firm travelled to the Collaborative Management Room for a one day competitive analysis session. The group broke for an early lunch, during which paper copies of all comments were prepared and distributed. The group reviewed the comments over lunch, with several managers informally discussing ideas with their staff and members of other departments. The rest of the afternoon was spent with the department heads individually addressing the group. Each first gave a brief summary of the innovations that had been proposed for the department and either committed to executing them, explained why they could not be implemented, or promised further study. Each manager then answered any questions that remained about the major proposals that had been prepared and discussed electronically.

Post-session questionnaires completed by all participants indicated that 88% of them felt that the use of GroupSystems was better than traditional meetings. The CEO, Mr. S. L. Eichenfield, agreed:

> Before using the . . . [GroupSystems] for a strategic planning session, I was unsure of its suitability for subjective rather than specific problem-solving purposes. But I found that we accomplished 100 percent of our objectives. People usually reluctant to express themselves felt free to take part, and we were surprised by the number of new ideas expressed. We also reached conclusions far more rapidly. Unabridged input from a variety of sources helped us to reshape our mental models of the organization and our perceptions of ourselves as a group.

In another case, a 14-member group from one Hughes Aircraft department used the system to brainstorm, organize and prioritize the weaknesses in the current performance appraisal system (Dennis, Tuchi, Vogel & Nunamaker, 1989*b*). Another 16 member plant-wide task force from Hughes used the system as part of their regular weekly meetings to identify ways to reduce the cycle time to get changes into products and product documentation. Members of both groups reported that the GroupSystems meetings were more effective, efficient and satisfying than regular meetings of these groups. Several reasons were identified. The parallel and simultaneous communication provided was seen as important. Members of both groups reported anonymity to be important, although members of the first group (all levels of one department) found it to be more important than members of the second (task force of peers).

The University of Arizona GroupSystems research and development project has been supported by a number of sponsors, both internal and external to the University. One especially effective relationship has been established between Arizona and IBM. Early in the GroupSystems project, IBM recognized the potential of the system to improve group meetings and organizational performance (Nunamaker, Vogel, Heminger, Martz, Grohowski & McGoff, 1989). The site selected for the initial IBM installation was a manufacturing plant with approximately 6,000 employees, located in a rural setting in upstate New York. The first phase of implementation began in the Spring of 1987 with a site visit and was concluded in December of 1987 with a corporate evaluative report. Tasks performed by groups using the facility were typically planning and problem solving tasks, such as strategic planning, process problems, and functional area data processing needs.

Post-session questionnaires indicated a strong agreement among the participants that the system improved meeting process effectiveness and was highly satisfying. Interviews with managers who had used the system produced similar findings. Prior to using the facility, each group leader was required to recommend and document a feasible project schedule for the accomplishment of his or her group's objectives, based on previous experience with similar projects. After completion of the project, expectations before use of the tools was compared with what actually occurred. Man-hours were saved in every recorded case, with an average per session saving of 51·15%. Based on these results, and its own internal studies, IBM built an additional 17 GroupSystems facilities sites by the end of 1989, with another 18 facilities planned for the end of 1990.

4. Recommendations for developers

In this section we discuss several of the lessons we have learned developing, using and evaluating groups and organizations using GroupSystems. Specifically we discuss issues related to the design of facilities, software and the management of electronic meetings.

4.1. FACILITIES

We have several recommendations for organizations and researchers contemplating the construction of EMS facilities. EMS facilities need to accommodate a variety of group sizes. As extensively documented above, we have repeatedly found that larger group sizes improve meeting effectiveness. However, the size of traditional non-EMS-supported meetings are often artificially constrained (see Thelen, 1949), as group enlargement "results in accelerating increases in process losses . . . and a size will eventually be reached beyond which group productivity will decrease" (Steiner, 1972, p. 95). In an EMS-supported meeting, this is no longer the case, as the optimal group size will be a function of the resources required to solve the task at hand. Consequently, our first facility supported 16 participants, our second 24, and our new facility under construction will support 30 participants.

In order to have strong interventions on several process losses, we contend that each group member should have their "own" workstation. Separate workstations allow all meeting participants equal opportunity to make contributions, regardless of their status or group size. Of course these workstations must be networked and the network must be "fast". We have tested the user response times for our tools using several network architectures and support software, and have found surprising differences between configurations (Dennis, Abens, Ram & Nunamaker, in press). Our experience has shown that users expect to receive sub-second response for all activities. Slow system response time may create production blocking, mitigating the potential benefits of the technology. Workstations should also be equipped with their own mass storage devise (i.e. a hard disk) to allow the EMS system software to be replicated on each workstation (not the server). The benefit of this approach is to lessen the network traffic, so that only shared data is passes and not applications. We have found that the speed of the network is the biggest determinate of system response time, and this becomes more of an issue as geographically dispersed members participate in electronic meetings.

To permit verbal discussion during supported and chauffeured processes, the public display must be positioned so that all group members have an unobstructed view of the group memory. Room layout options are constrained by the maximum group size, and as the maximum group size is increased, the positioning and location of workstations becomes much more complicated. For small groups, an oval board-room-type table can be used. For larger groups, a U-shaped table or concentric tiered rows of workstations (Figure 1—legislative layout) can be used. The boardroom and U-shaped layout supports verbal exchanges between group members better than the tiered row design, as all group members can easily see one another. Our observations suggest that practical group size limitations for these layouts are approximately eight to 12 participants for the boardroom and 12 to 16 participants for the U-shaped design. For very large groups (more than 16 participants), we have found the legislative layout to be effective. Although this design is not optimal for verbal group discussions, the use of swivel chairs for workstation seating allows participants to easily change their line of sight, facilitating verbal exchanges.

The public display needs to support various types of media in addition to presenting computer generated information. Support for other media such as slides, optical disks, videotape and transparencies provides flexibility during presentations and verbal meeting phases. Configurable seating and workstation layout (height and angle of keyboard) will also add to participant comfort during long meetings. Thus, the layout of the room is crucial and variables such as the number of workstations (i.e. group size), communication issues (so everyone in the room be easily heard during verbal communication), line of sight (between group members and the front display), environmental issues (e.g. lighting, noise, heating and air conditioning) and ergonomics must be considered, else the potential benefits of the EMS may not be realized.

4.2. SOFTWARE

The GroupSystems approach to EMS software development has been to focus on supporting generic activities (e.g. idea generation) and not specific task (e.g. strategic planning). The GroupSystems software can be described as a toolkit, similar to the concept of a DSS model base or tool set (Sprague, 1980), where numerous "generic" tools have been developed to support various meeting activities. The main advantage of the toolkit approach is flexibility. This approach provides the most flexibility and enables the support of a wider array of groups and tasks (i.e. an idea generation tool like EBS can be used by negotiating groups to generate alternatives, by system developers to generate a list of system requirements, or by strategic planners developing a list of "critical success factors").

By developing distinct tools for different meeting activities, tools can more easily apply different meeting processes (i.e. chauffeured, supported or interactive). Although each tool should have a similar "look and feel" (to ease participant learning), each can have its own personality based upon the requirements of the task. Another advantage of this flexible approach is that tools can be used in any order, allowing a customized solution for the unique problems that each group faces. This implies that information developed in one tool should easily transfer to a second tool for subsequent processing, regardless of the order the tools were used. While flexibility is important, it is also important to limit the type and number of functions available to participants at specific points in the meeting (Silver, 1990), so that groups use the system as intended by the group leader.

Another important issue relates to information ownership; once a participant shares information with the group it becomes part of the group memory. In

GroupSystems, only the facilitator (by the authority of the group) has the ability to change and/or delete public information. This is especially important for large groups with competing political factions. Yet for smaller or more homogeneous groups, this formal information control may not be a critical issue (e.g. Stefik, Foster, Bobrow, Khan, Lanning & Suchman, 1987). We chose this design because it assures that the group memory is not intentionally (or unintentionally) altered without the approval of the entire group. A final recommendation for developers is to design tools so that they may easily evolve and "grow" (Boehm, 1985; Brooks, 1987). For example, the concept for several of the GroupSystems tools has been to automate a structured group process as described in the small group literature, for example Osborn's (1957) brainstorming evolved to our Electronic Brainstorming tool. It is not uncommon for new functions and capabilities to be added to tools many months after they have begun to be used. We have found that most of our tools have evolved in this manner, and believe it to be one key to success in developing systems such as these.

4.3. MEETING FACILITATION AND PROCEDURES

Although some EMSs have been designed to be used without a meeting facilitator, we have found that a facilitator can play an important role in improving the meeting process and outcomes (Dennis et al., 1988; Nunamaker et al., 1987, 1988, 1989). The role of the facilitator during the meeting is the same as that of the room and software, to mitigate process losses by matching the facilitator's role with the characteristics of the group and their task. We believe that the technology alone, in the near term, will not lead to unfacilitated meetings; if no meeting facilitator is used, some member of the group (e.g. the group leader) will usually assume the role. We have found that the ability to lead groups is the most important determinate in being a good facilitator in an EMS environment, as this role is dynamic and multi-faceted. In contrast, the operation of the technology is generally very easy to learn.

An important part of a GroupSystems meeting is pre-session planning. By formally requiring group leaders to meet with the meeting facilitator and articulate the goals and objectives of the meeting, measures of meeting success can be determined and appropriate group activities can be selected. If the planning is incomplete and unclear, then the results of the meeting will most probably be unsatisfactory. Our recommendation here is straightforward, meetings (whether electronic or not) must be planned and managed.

Over the past five years, we have built, tested and re-designed a variety of GroupSystems facilities, software tools and meeting procedures, in an attempt to improve the productivity of group meetings. Based on our experiences in working with student groups in controlled laboratory experiments and with work groups from more than 150 organizations in the field, we are convinced that this technology has the potential to dramatically change the way people work together.

We would like to thank Jeff Hoffer and three anonymous reviewers for their many excellent suggestions for improving the paper. This research was partially supported by grants from IBM, the National Science Foundation, the U.S. Army AIRMICS, AT&T, and NCR Corporation. Additional funding was provided by the Social Sciences and Humanities Research Council of Canada.

References

AIKEN, M. W., MOTIWALLA, L. F., SHENG, O. R. L. & NUNAMAKER, J. F., JR. (1990). ESP: An expert system for pre-session group decision support systems planning. In *Proceedings of HICSS-23*, vol. 3, pp. 279–286.

ALBANESE, R. & VAN FLEET, D. D. (1985). Rational behavior in groups: the free riding tendency. *Academy of Management Review*, **10**, 244–255.

BOEHM, B. W. (1985). *A Spiral Model of Software Development and Enhancement*, TRW Technical Report 21-371-85, TRW Inc.

BROOKS, F. P., JR. (1987). No silver bullet. *IEEE Computer*, **20**, 10–19.

COLLAROS, P. A. & ANDERSON, L. R. (1969). Effect of perceived expertness upon creativity of members of brainstorming groups. *Journal of Applied Psychology*, **53**, 159–163.

CONNOLLY, T., JESSUP, L. M. & VALACICH, J. S. (1990). Effects of anonymity and evaluative tone on idea generation in computer-mediated groups. *Management Science*, **36**, 689–703.

DALKEY, N. & HELMER, O. (1963). An experimental application of the Delphi Method to the Use of Experts. *Management Science*, **6**, 458–67.

DENNIS, A. R., ABENS, T., RAM, S. & NUNAMAKER, J. F., JR. (In press). Communication requirements and network evaluation for electronic meeting systems. *Decision Support Systems*.

DENNIS, A. R., GEORGE, J. F., JESSUP, L. M., NUNAMAKER, J. F., JR. & VOGEL, D. R. (1968). Information Technology to Support Electronic Meetings. *MIS Quarterly*, **12**, 591–624.

DENNIS, A. R., HEMINGER, A. R., NUNAMAKER, J. F., JR. & VOGEL, D. R. (1990a). Bringing automated support to large groups: the Burr–Brown experience. *Information and Management*, **18**, 111–121.

DENNIS, A. R., PARANKA, D., VOGEL, D. R. & NUNAMAKER, J. F., JR. (1989a). *Electronic Meeting Support for Strategic Management*, Working paper, University of Arizona.

DENNIS, A. R., TUCHI, J. J., VOGEL, D. R. & NUNAMAKER, J. F., JR. (1989b). *A Case Study of Electronic Meeting System Use*, Working paper, University of Arizona.

DENNIS, A. R., VALACICH, J. S. & NUNAMAKER, J. F., JR. (1990b). An experimental investigation of group size in an electronic meeting system. *IEEE Transactions on Systems, Man and Cybernetics*, **20**, 1049–1057.

DESANCTIS, G. S. & GALLUPE, B. (1987). A foundation for the study of group decision support systems. *Management Science*, **33**, 589–609.

DIEHL, M. & STROEBE, W. (1987). Productivity loss in brainstorming groups: toward the solution of a riddle. *Journal of Personality and Social Psychology*, **53**, 497–509.

DUNNETTE, M. D., CAMPBELL, J. & JAASTAD, K. (1963). The effect of group participation on brainstorming effectiveness for two industrial samples. *Journal of Applied Psychology*, **47**, 30–37.

EASTON, G., GEORGE, J. F., NUNAMAKER, J. F., JR. & PENDERGAST, M. O. (1990). Using two different electronic meeting system tools for the same task. *Journal of Management Information Systems*, **7**, 85–100.

FINHOLT, T. & SPROULL, L. S. (1990). Electronic groups at work. *Organization Science*, **1**, 41–64.

GEORGE, J. F., DENNIS, A. R., NUNAMAKER, J. F., JR. & EASTON, G. K. (1989). *Experiments in Group Decision Making: Group Performance in an EMS Decision Room*, Working paper, University of Arizona.

HARARI, O. & GRAHAM, W. K. (1975). Tasks and task consequences as factors in individual and group brainstorming. *Journal of Social Psychology*, **95**, 61–65.

HARKINS, S. G. & JACKSON, J. M. (1985). The role of evaluation in eliminating social loafing. *Personality and Social Psychology Bulletin*, **11**, 457–65.

HARKINS, S. G. & PETTY, R. E. (1982). Effects of task difficulty and task uniqueness on social loafing. *Journal of Personality and Social Psychology*, **43**, 1214–29.

HILL, G. W. (1982). Group versus individual performance: Are $N + 1$ heads better than one? *Psychological Bulletin*, **91**, 517–39.

Hirokowa, R. Y. & Pace, R. (1983). A descriptive investigation of the possible communication based reasons for effective and ineffective group decision making. *Communication Monographs,* **50,** 363–79.

Huber, G. P. (1990). A Theory of the Effects of Advanced Information Technologies on Organizational Design. *Academy of Management Review,* **15,** 47–71.

Jablin, F. M. & Seibold, D. R. (1978). Implications for problem solving groups of empirical research on 'brainstorming': a critical review of the literature. *The Southern States Speech Communication Journal,* **43,** 327–56.

Jablin, F. M., Seibold, D. R. & Sorenson, R. L. (1977). Potential inhibitory effects of group participation on brainstorming performance. *Central States Speech Journal,* **28,** 112–21.

Jessup, L. M., Connolly, T. & Galegher, J. (1990). *The Effects of Anonymity on Group Process in Automated Group Problem Solving.* Working paper, University of Arizona.

Jessup, L. M., Tansik, D. A. & Laase, T. L. (1988). Group problem solving in an automated environment: The effects of anonymity and proximity on group process and outcome with a group decision support system. In *Proceedings of the Academy of Management Conference,* Organizational Communication Division, Annual Meeting, Anaheim, CA.

Kerr, N. L. & Bruun, S. E. (1981). Ringelman revisited: Alternative explanations for the social loafing effect. *Personality and Social Psychology Bulletin,* **7,** 224–31.

Kerr, N. L. & Bruun, S. E. (1983). Dispensability of member effort and group motivation losses: Free-rider effects. *Personality and Social Psychology Bulletin,* **44,** 78–94.

Lamm, H. & Trommsdorff, G. (1973). Group versus individual performance on tasks requiring ideational proficiency (brainstorming): a review. *European Journal of Social Psychology,* **3,** 361–388.

McGrath, J. E. (1984). *Groups: Interaction and Performance.* Englewood Cliffs, NJ: Prentice-Hall, Inc.

Nunamaker, J. F., Jr., Applegate, L. M. & Konsynski, B. R. (1987). Facilitating group creativity with GDSS. *Journal of Management Information Systems,* **3,** 5–19.

Nunamaker, J. F., Jr., Applegate, L. M. & Konsynski, B. R. (1988). Computer-aided deliberation: model management and group decision support. *Journal of Operations Research,* November-December, 826–848.

Nunamaker, J. F., Jr., Vogel, D., Heminger, A., Martz, B., Grohowski, R. & McGoff, C. (1989). Group Support Systems in practice: Experience at IBM, *Decision Support Systems,* 5:2, 183–196.

Osborn, A. F. (1957). *Applied Imagination: Principles and Procedures of Creative Thinking,* 2nd edit. New York: Scribners.

Shaw, M. (1981). *Group Dynamics: The Psychology of Small Group Behavior,* 3rd edit. New York: McGraw Hill.

Silver, M. S. (1990). Decision support systems: directed and non-directed change. *Information Systems Research,* **1,** 47–70.

Sprague, R. H. (1980). A Framework for the Development of Decision Support Systems, *MIS Quarterly,* **4,** (4) 1–26.

Stefik, M., Foster, G., Bobrow, D. G., Khan, K., Lanning, S. & Suchman, L. (1987). Beyond the chalkboard: computer support for collaboration and problem solving in meetings, *Communications of the ACM,* **30,** (1) 33–47.

Steiner, I. D. (1966). Models for inferring relationships between group size and potential group productivity. *Behavioral Science,* **11,** 273–83.

Steiner, I. D. (1972). *Group Process and Productivity.* New York: Academic Press.

Thelen, H. A. (1949). Group dynamics in instruction: principle of least group size. *School Review,* **57,** 139–48.

Tyran, C. K., Dennis, A. R., Vogel, D. R. & Nunamaker, J. F., Jr. (1989). *The Design and Evaluation of Electronic Meeting Systems to Support Strategic Management.* Working paper, Arizona University.

Valacich, J. S. (1989). *Group Size and Proximity Effects on Computer Mediated Idea Generation: A Laboratory Investigation* Ph.d. Thesis, University of Arizona.

VALACICH, J. S., DENNIS, A. R., GEORGE, J. F. & NUNAMAKER, J. F., JR. (1990a). *Electronic Support for Group Idea Generation: Shifting the Balance of Process Gains and Losses.* Working paper, Arizona University.

VALACICH, J. S., DENNIS, A. R. & NUNAMAKER, J. F., JR. (1990b). *Anonymity and Group Size Effects on Computer Mediated Idea Generation.* Working paper, Arizona University.

VALACICH, J. S., VOGEL, D. R. & NUNAMAKER, J. F., JR. (1989). Integrating information across sessions and between groups in group decision support systems. In *Proceedings of HICSS-22,* vol. 3, pp. 291–99, Kona, Hawaii.

VAN DE VEN, A. H. & DELBECQ, A. L. (1971). Nominal versus interacting group processes for committee decision making. *Academy of Management Journal,* **14,** 203–212.

VAN DE VEN, A. H. & DELBECQ, A. L. (1974). The effectiveness of nominal, delphi and interacting group decision making processes. *Academy of Management Journal,* **17,** 605–621.

WATSON, W. E. & MICHAELSEN, L. K. (1988). Group interaction behaviors that affect performance on an intellective task. *Group and Organizational Studies,* **13,** 495–516.

8

Computer-mediated communication, de-individuation and group decision-making

Martin Lea

Russell Spears

This paper discusses social psychological processes in computer-mediated communication (CMC) and group decision-making, in relation to findings that groups communicating via computer produce more polarized decisions than face-to-face groups. A wide range of possible explanations for such differences have been advanced, in which a lack of social cues, disinhibition, "de-individuation" and a consequent tendency to antinormative behaviour are central themes. In these explanations, both disinhibition and greater equality of participation are thought to facilitate the exchange of extreme persuasive arguments, resulting in polarization. These accounts are briefly reviewed and attention is drawn to various problematic issues. We provide an alternative model and explanation based on social identity (SI) theory and a re-conceptualization of de-individuation, which takes into account the social and normative factors associated with group polarization. Predictions from both sets of explanations are explored empirically by means of an experiment manipulating the salience of the discussion group, and de-individuation operationalized as the isolation and anonymity of the participants. In this experiment we were able to partial out the effects of the CMC technology which have confounded comparisons with face-to-face interaction in previous research. The results challenge the explanations based on persuasive arguments, while being consistent with our SI model. We discuss our approach in relation to other very recent research in group computer-mediated communication and offer a reinterpretation of previous findings.

Introduction

Computer support for group decision-making has become a central topic of concern in CSCW research and in this context the effects of computer-mediated communication (CMC) on the process and outcomes of group interaction are of particular interest. Numerous studies have attempted to evaluate the efficiency and quality of CMC in comparison with the face-to-face "standard" (see Hiltz & Turoff, 1978 and Rice, 1984 for reviews). Early work in this field was mainly descriptive and atheoretical, but more recently social psychologists in particular have begun to investigate the psychological processes that are involved. Research conducted by the Committee on Social Science Research in Computing at Carnegie–Mellon University has been especially influential in this regard (Kiesler, Siegel & McGuire, 1984; Kiesler, 1986; Siegel, Dubrovsky, Kiesler & McGuire, 1986; Sproull & Kiesler, 1986; McGuire, Kiesler & Siegel, 1987). Their account of the social psychological processes in CMC as applied to group decision-making was the impetus for the research reported here. We shall therefore begin by outlining their descriptions of these processes and address some of the important questions raised by this work. We then introduce an alternative approach, based on social identity theory and a recent re-conceptualization of de-individuation. The empirical section of the paper reports on a group-polarization experiment designed to address the relevant conceptual issues. Finally, we relate the results of the experiment to other recently reported work and offer a reinterpretation of the earlier studies in terms of our new approach.

The central thesis advanced by the Carnegie–Mellon team is that various technological features of electronic communication trigger psychological states and processes that result in less normative influences on individuals and groups and more deregulated and extreme behaviour. These tendencies are manifested in uninhibited behaviour such as "flaming" by individuals, and in more extreme or polarized decisions by groups. Kiesler et al. (1984) draw on a major account of group polarization, namely persuasive arguments theory, to support their line of reasoning. Persuasive arguments theory posits that polarization results from the exposure to a greater pool of arguments favouring the preferred pole, exchanged during discussion (Vinokur & Burnstein, 1974; Burnstein & Vinokur, 1977). Kiesler et al. (1984) suggest, for example, that if the exchange of information is greater and more evenly spread when communicating via computer, participants will be exposed to more extreme persuasive arguments.

The explanations identified in the Carnegie-Mellon account of CMC can be considered under five headings: (1) lack of social cues; (2) de-individuation; (3) difficulties of co-ordination and feedback; (4) depersonalization and/or attentional focus; and (5) conformity to a particular norm or etiquette associated with the computing subculture (Kiesler et al., 1984).

A central and recurring theme is the absence of social influence and contextual cues, and thus the reduced impact of social norms and constraints. For example, Siegel et al. (1986) suggest that "...the absence of social context cues in computer mediation will reduce normative influence, relative to informational influence" (p. 182). The lack of such cues also results in more equal participation, by masking cues to status and power, which allegedly leads to a greater exchange of extreme arguments. Furthermore, the absence of cues undermines leadership so that there are fewer constraints on uninhibited behaviour and hence the exchange of extreme arguments (Kiesler et al. 1984, p. 1125).

A second explanation invokes the concept of de-individuation which, classically defined, is the process whereby submergence in a group produces anonymity and a loss of identity, and a consequent weakening of social norms and constraints (e.g. Festinger, Pepitone & Newcomb, 1952; Zimbardo, 1969). Kiesler et al. (1984) observe that "Computer-mediated communication seems to comprise some of the same conditions that are important for de-individuation—anonymity, reduced self-regulation and reduced self-awareness" (p. 1126).

Because uninhibited behaviour is traditionally linked with de-individuation (Festinger et al., 1952; Zimbardo, 1969), this may once again explain the communication of more extreme views. Siegal et al. (1986) concur in identifying de-individuation as a possible explanation for uninhibited and antinormative behaviour. Kiesler et al. (1984) argue that disinhibition so derived may also contribute to the normative (social comparison) explanation of group-shifts in decision-making by supporting a more extreme group norm. Briefly, social comparison theory argues that polarization shifts result from conformity to a socially desirable but relatively extreme norm which only becomes apparent during group communication (Sanders & Baron, 1977).

A third explanation is that difficulties of communication arising from the lack of feedback from participants may cause uninhibited behaviour and polarization. Reflecting on the results of one experiment, Kiesler *et al.* (1984) suggest, "Perhaps it was frustrating for people to be discussing a problem inefficiently; they might have become angry and, hence, more extreme in decision-making and more uninhibited" (p. 1130). Absence of feedback may also help to explain the equality of participation thought to facilitate the persuasive arguments route to polarization (Kiesler *et al.*, 1984).

The fourth explanation of polarization shifts is in terms of depersonalization or a redirection of attention away from the audience. Kiesler *et al.* (1984) assert that participants are ". . .less responsive to immediate textual cues . . .and less bound by precedents set by societal norms" (p. 1130). Siegel *et al.* (1986) also maintain that the nature of CMC encourages participants to focus on the content and context of the message, rather than on the *social* context. They argue that a heightened self-consciousness or self-absorption in the message, may result in reduced sociability and relatively unrestrained and antinormative behaviour (p. 182). According to these authors, equality of participation (and hence uninhibited behaviour) may also depend on this focus of attention.

The fifth class of explanation advanced both by Kiesler *et al.* (1984) and Siegel *et al.* (1986) is based on a particular etiquette or norm apparently associated with the computing subculture ". . .which rejects conventionality and social restrictions" (Siegel *et al.*, 1986, p. 183).

To summarize, certain themes receive particular weight in the explanations that have been advanced, namely the absence of social cues, the breakdown of social constraint and regulation ("antinormative behaviour"), and the emphasis on informational influence as the agent of polarization. However, these explanations at times appear problematic and contradictory when taken both as a whole and in their elements. We will briefly consider the theoretical consistency between the ideas before going on to assess the support for specific explanations and the assumptions underlying them.

To begin at a general level, there is a potential conflict between the characterization of CMC as a potentially fast and efficient means of communication on the one hand, and the citing of the relative inefficiency of the system as a cause of frustration and uninhibited behaviour on the other. Clearly the concept of efficiency is a complex and multidimensional one which needs greater elaboration in the CMC context. The theme of "rationality" is similarly double edged in this regard; on the one hand CMC seems to be more rational, more equalized, and focused on hard information rather than "biasing" peripheral cues (cf. Petty & Cacioppo, 1986). Conversely, CMC is also characterized by a lack of rationality (disinhibition, deregulation) as invoked in the traditional concept of de-individuation (namely a loss of identity leading to an antisocial state). These two themes—the enhanced exchange and processing of information, and uninhibited and impulsive behaviour— sit rather uneasily together.

In terms of the relationship between efficiency and persuasive arguments, it seems that greater efficiency of electronic communication should lead to a fast and free flow of information, feeding persuasive arguments, unhindered by irrelevant social cues. Meanwhile, the communication inefficiencies associated with CMC (caused by lack of feedback and cues) also seem to kindle the generation of persuasive arguments by stimulating frustration and disinhibition, and by equalizing information exchange. This apparent flexibility clearly requires some attention to prevent the underlying concepts from losing their heuristic value.

The traditional concept of de-individuation used in this work also raises certain questions. First, employing the concept of de-individuation (submergence in a group leading to the weakening of social norms) to explain a classic group influence effect (group polarization) is not theoretically straightforward. Secondly, there is a serious problem in relation to the argument regarding focus of attention. Although de-individuation is associated with a lack of self-awareness, Siegel *et al.* (1986) argue for heightened self-consciousness in CMC. An elevated state of "private self-awareness" in CMC—precisely the opposite of the state predicted by de-individuation theory (Diener, 1980)—is also confirmed in other CMC research (Matheson & Zanna, 1988, 1989). Indeed, the increase in self-attention processes for people isolated at computer terminals could plausibly be argued to be "individuating" rather than de-individuating (Spears, Lea & Lee, 1990). In addition, the idea that people are somehow "submerged in the machine" (Kiesler *et al.*, 1984), or absorbed by the message (Siegel *et al.*, 1986) appears to be contradictory to the earlier observation; it is not clear how people can be both more self-aware and more absorbed by the information at the same time.

However, perhaps the greatest difficulties rest with the central argument concerning the lack of social cues and consequent weakening of social norms and standards in CMC. It may be noted that it is undermined by another suggestion, that uninhibited behaviour and thus extreme decisions may be due to a particular computing norm or etiquette. If people in CMC are impervious to social norms in general, it is not entirely clear how this particular norm penetrates through the system. Meanwhile, if it penetrates successfully, why don't other more pervasive norms as well?

More important is the problem of defining normative versus "antinormative" behaviour. The idea of a weakening of norms is clearly manifested in the concept of disinhibition associated with "flaming" in CMC. However, it could be argued that "antinormative" behaviour, where it has a clear and directional form precisely describes a "norm" (albeit an extreme of negative one). In group discussions, if behaviour was really socially deregulated as implied by the de-individuation principle, then a haphazard and random distribution of decision responses (or those favouring *both* extremes) should be expected, rather than the consistent favouring of a single decision extreme. Such deregulated behaviour should, almost by definition, result in group responses closer to the mid-point than to one polar extreme of a scale.

Again, many explanations of the group-polarization effect within social psychology are based on the role of social values or norms (Stoner, 1961; Sanders & Baron, 1977; Mackie, 1986; Turner, Hogg, Oakes, Reicher, & Wetherell, 1987). It seems therefore that there is an important distinction to be made between uninhibited behaviour or a state of disinhibition on the one hand and polarization in group decision-making on the other. The group-polarization literature has long since shown that decisions in the group can become more polarized in the direction of caution, as a result of group discussion—i.e. both more extreme and less risky or "uninhibited" at the same time (e.g. Fraser, 1971).

Empirically, the assumption that CMC is characterized by a weakening of social norms seems to have little direct or independent support. In fact it could be argued that an absence of social cues from other interacting individuals, together with the resulting uncertainty, forces people to resort to default social norms to guide their behaviour. Both our own and other research in this field indicates that people may be particularly susceptible to social norms in CMC, particularly when their group identity is salient (Hiltz, Turoff & Johnson 1989; Spears *et al.*, 1990).

One report by the Carnegie-Mellon group would seem to undermine the generality of their explanation of group polarization in CMC (McGuire *et al.*, 1987). In this study, as in Siegel *et al.* (1986), CMC participants actually produced a smaller volume of argumentation (due to the efficiency constraints of the system) compared with a *face-to-face* condition. This is then used to support a persuasive arguments explanation of polarization in face-to-face groups, whereas the same principle is cited in the previous work as mediating greater polarization in CMC groups. As we have seen, the earlier research invokes equalization of participation and thus argumentation to explain the generation of more extreme arguments, so there appears to be a shift away from this explanation to the importance of the *quantity* of arguments in McGuire *et al.* (1987).

Advocates of persuasive arguments theory do not refer to equality of participation so much as to the volume of new arguments exchanged (e.g. Burnstein & Vinokur, 1977). In fact, it could be argued that greater equality of participation would underlie a wider spread of advocated positions (reflected in arguments) leading to diffusion rather than polarization. Conversely, greater "floor-taking" by a particular participant could actually be argued to bias the decision in that person's preferred direction, leading to imbalance and greater polarization. Finally, while on the subject of persuasive arguments, it should also be noted that the exchange of arguments or information, is not necessary for group polarization to occur (see Wetherell, 1987). In sum, the link between equality of participation and polarization is not clearly established, and appears to be contradicted by the McGuire *et al.* (1987) study.

Hitherto, we have identified some important questions raised by the explanations that have been proposed for CMC decision-making phenomena. In the computer-mediated group decision-making experiment to be reported below, we attempted to explore some of these explanations and their underlying assumptions while advancing our own alternative position. Our theoretical approach is described in detail elsewhere along with a preliminary report of some of our findings (Spears *et al.*, 1990). In the present context our aim is to add some empirical support for the conceptual issues we have highlighted above. We will therefore present a brief recapitulation here and in addition present new data (derived from the message traffic log, content analysis of the group discussions and post-discussion responses) which are directly relevant to an evaluation of the explanations advanced by the Carnegie–Mellon group.

Essentially our view is that, rather than being of decreased importance, the social and normative contexts are of central relevance to decision-making in CMC. In making our case, we draw on a recent re-conceptualization of de-individuation which avoids many of the problems which seem to bedevil not only the work on CMC, but also the more general social psychological research on collective behaviour with which de-individuation is classically associated (for critiques see Reicher, 1987; Hogg & Abrams, 1988). Adopting an approach developed from social identity theory (Tajfel & Turner, 1986), Reicher (1984, 1987) argues that de-individuation or anonymity associated with immersion in a group does not weaken social norms, but can act to enhance the salience of the group and thus the relevant norms. He asserts that if people identify with a group, and that group membership is made salient to them, then they will be more likely to be influenced by the group under de-individuating conditions. This is because (visual) anonymity leads to a perceived reduction of intragroup differences, thereby further increasing the salience of the group. However, if one's group identity is not already salient, de-individuation can enhance one's sense of individuality, reducing the salience of group norms (Reicher, 1984).

Applying this point to the CMC context, Spears et al. (1990) predicted and found greater norm-directed social influence and polarization in de-individuating conditions (where the participants were in separate rooms and could not see each other) when group salience was high, but least (actually "depolarization") when participants' individuality was made salient. This pattern of findings is not explicable by any of the accounts proposed earlier. The finding that polarized group decision-making within CMC can be associated with an increased salience and influence of group norms has also been confirmed in other contemporaneous research. Hiltz et al. (1989) found greatest polarization under conditions of anonymity (a "pen-name" condition) which is consistent with our own results and explanation. Moreover, they arrive at a comparable reconceptualization of de-individuation to account for their findings.

Another related explanation for these results which should be considered turns on the role of self-attention processes (e.g. Carver & Scheier, 1981). As proposed by Siegel et al. (1986) and Matheson & Zanna (1989), social isolation in CMC is likely to be associated with high (private) self-awareness. However, again we argue that the effects of this will be to heighten the salience of particular norms given by the social context, rather than reduce them. If a participant's group identity is made salient, increased self-attention should enhance the influence of social norms associated with the group, whereas a more individual standard will be influential when the participant's individuality is already salient. This account draws on the idea in social identity theory that people have different identities, both as unique individuals or "personalities" on the one hand, and as members of social groups on the other. These various identities become salient as a function of the social context. In other words, self-attention and private-self awareness do not necessarily have to be "individualizing" in the sense of reducing adherence to social standards. Instead, we see this account as a complementary explanation based on the "socialized" conceptualization of de-individuation outlined above (for a more detailed discussion of this relation see Spears et al., 1990; Lea & Spears, in press). Matheson and Zanna (1989) also come to similar conclusions relating to self-awareness and the role of social factors.

To summarize then, a unifying theme for these two explanations which distinguishes them from those discussed earlier, is the provision made for the role of the social context, and the influence of social norms specified therein. This allows for a relatively parsimonious theoretical structure, which is nevertheless able to account for considerable variation in CMC behaviour. We argue that there has been a tendency to confound the form and content of behaviour in CMC in earlier explanations of group polarization whereby the form (disinhibition, "flaming") has been confounded with the content of group norms which underlie polarization. It seems to us that the content of these norms will depend more on the nature of the pre-existing group of CMC participants (i.e. degree of cohesiveness, ingroup identification, group salience and so on) than on features of the technology *per se,* although the technology may introduce certain conditions which crucially mediate its influence (e.g. anonymity, isolation).

In the following report we do not attempt to provide a definitive test of all the explanations outlined above, as this would be impossible within a single study. Also, given the number of explanations considered, the listing of competing hypotheses would not be an efficient use of space. However, the data reported here do speak to many of the explanations proposed, and this is followed up in the discussion.

In our design we manipulate what we see as two critically important social psychological variables independently of each other, namely whether the group or individual identity of participants is made salient, and whether participants are de-individuated by virtue of being isolated and anonymous as opposed to being co-present. This last point is important and requires some further elaboration. Previous relevant research in this area has, to our knowledge typically employed a conventional face-to-face discussion group as the comparison or control condition for the CMC group. However, because CMC by its very nature is not usually "face-to-face", this has in our view confounded the effects of the technology with an important socio-structural variable (namely whether or not participants are visible or anonymous during the discussion). So while this may have been an interesting and relevant comparison in practical terms, as can be surmized from the foregoing analysis this point is of crucial theoretical importance and remains unresolved. In the present study therefore, our face-to-face condition also communicated via computer, in order to control for the constraints and effects of the communication system.

Method

PROCEDURE

Forty-eight subjects were recruited by internal mail from a volunteer subject panel of first-year psychology students. Their initial (pre-discussion) attitudinal positions on four controversial topics were solicited (see Dependent measures). For the experimental sessions, which took place some days later, subjects were randomly placed in groups of three and assigned to one of four experimental conditions (see Experimental manipulations). Subjects learned *in situ* how to use a simple electronic mail system. Group discussions on four controversial issues were then conducted using the system. Each discussion lasted 10 minutes, with a two minute break in between during which time subjects consulted their "issues booklet" (see section on experimental manipulations). Messages sent by any individual were received by all subjects. After the discussions, subjects' attitudes on each topic were re-assessed, and additional measures were taken (see section on dependent measures).

EXPERIMENTAL MANIPULATIONS

Group immersion
Immersion in the group was manipulated through the description of the aims of the experiment, and by subjects' coded identities which appeared in the electronic mail message headers. Group identity was made salient (group condition) by introducing the study as one designed "to evaluate the efficiency of the communication system, to see if there are any differences between various groups in the way they communicate and to investigate social perception". Subjects were told that their group consisted exclusively of first-year psychology students, and that they were being tested as members of this group and not as individuals. Written instructions referred to the subject as a "group member", and the other subjects as "the rest of the group". Subjects were assigned a group membership number to refer to each other in the discussions. During the discussions they used their group membership identity in their message headers (e.g. "From: Group member 1"), and all messages which they received bore the group membership number as the only subject identity. This type of manipulation has been found to be sufficient to engender perceptions of group membership by subjects in previous social categorization studies (Turner, 1983; Turner *et al.*, 1987).

In the condition in which the group was required to be made less salient (individual condition) the aims of the study were described as being: ". . .to evaluate the efficiency of the communication system, to examine personal styles in the way individuals communicate, and to investigate person perception". Subjects were assigned a participant number and subjects identified themselves as participants in their message headers (e.g. "From: Participant 1").

De-individuation
De-individuation was operationalized by manipulating subjects' physical locations and social anonymity. In the de-individuated condition, participants received their instructions in separate rooms and were physically isolated from each other throughout the experiment. In the individuated condition, participants were seated two to three metres apart at separate desks in the same room and faced each other throughout. In other words, subjects were clearly visible to each other as in standard face-to-face interaction. They were instructed not to talk to each other, but to communicate using the electronic mail system.

Norm reference
Normative information about first year psychology students was provided through a four-page "issues booklet" which participants consulted prior to each discussion period. The discussion issues were chosen so that the same well-defined directional norm (i.e. a left-right political dimension) should underlie each issue (nuclear power; privatization of industry; government subsidy of the arts; positive

discrimination for minority groups). Responses on the issues could then be summed to provide a more reliable dependent measure than would be obtained from a single-issue discussion.† A survey of the same issues on a previous year's first-year psychology students had revealed a two-thirds majority to the left on these issues (Spears, unpublished data). In order to communicate and reinforce the norm, without specifying the actual positions on the rating scales that were used, the results of the survey were presented to subjects in tabular and histogram formats showing "percentage in favour" and "percentage against".

DEPENDENT MEASURES

Opinion measures were collected both before and after the experiment. These consisted of 9-point Likert-type rating scales on which subjects indicated their attitudinal positions on each discussion issue. The scales were counterbalanced and anchored at the extremes and at the mid-point (-4, very strongly disagree; 0, neutral/don't know; $+4$, very strongly agree).

The post-measures were collected in the context of a "computer communication questionnaire" in which the same rating-scales were presented in a different order and embedded among other items assessing subjects' impressions of the session and the other participants. These additional items included a set of social perception measures consisting of six seven-point scales (warm, dominant, uninhibited, responsible, likeable and competent), which have been previously used in research on CMC (Lea, Wilson & Young, 1989). Subjects were also required to estimate, using nine-point scales, the attitudinal positions of their co-participants on each discussion topic.

A message traffic log recorded the number of messages sent, the number of words sent, and the number of words per message from which measures of comparative participation rates and the amount of discussion were derived. After the experiment the two experimenters worked independently to code the discussion transcripts for three categories of remark. The definition of a remark was that used by Siegel *et al.* (1986). The three content-categories were discussion orientated remarks [$r(14) = 0.92, p < 0.0001$]; situation and system-orientated remarks [$r(14) = 0.94, p < 0.0001$]; socially-orientated remarks [$r(14) = 0.89, p < 0.0001$] (inter-rater reliabilities are presented in parentheses for each category). The transcripts were also coded for two categories of language use which have been previously used as indicators of uninhibited behaviour (Kiesler *et al.*, 1984; Siegel *et al.*, 1986). These were the number of uses of paralanguage [$r(14) = 0.68, p < 0.005$] and the number of incidences of swearing. The latter category of behaviour was observed too infrequently to permit further analysis.

Analysis and results

The results of the experiment are summarized in Table 1 and significant effects are illustrated in Figures 1A–H. Measures of polarization were derived by comparing

† Despite these precautions, subsequent examination of the transcripts of the discussions revealed a problem with the "government subsidy of the arts" topic with respect to the pre-established directional norm. Examination of responses and discussion content revealed the consistent emergence of a counter-acting norm, also founded on the right-left dimension. Given this emergent ambiguity, it was decided not to include the data from this topic in the overall attitude measures.

TABLE 1

Results of the group discussions by condition†

Dependent variable	De-individuation Group	De-individuation Individual	Individuation Group	Individuation Individual
Polarization‡	1·20[ac]	−1·51[bc]	−0·29[a]	0·75[b]
	(1·76)	(2·72)	(3·28)	(1·96)
Perceived agreement‡	9·83[a]	15·50	19·75[ab]	12·42[b]
	(7·91)	(6·52)	(9·17)	(6·10)
Number of messages	13·75	14	11·92	14·67
	(4·65)	(3·22)	(1·68)	(2·77)
Number of words§‖	274·58[a]	365·25[abc]	261·75[c]	286·25[b]
	(71·38)	(79·03)	(71·89)	(83·67)
Message length‡§	21·48[a]	26·40[abc]	21·82[c]	19·56[b]
	(6·52)	(3·82)	(4·50)	(4·84)
Number of remarks	53·88[a]	70·88[ab]	53·25[b]	56·88
	(11·91)	(11·15)	(11·85)	(5·22)
Number of discussion remarks‡‖	36·63[a]	67·38[ab]	48·75[b]	50·13[a]
	(4·70)	(12·11)	(8·53)	(8·16)
Number of social remarks‡	10·38[ab]	2·38[a]	0·88[b]	3·25
	(7·03)	(1·75)	(1·03)	(6·50)
+ve/−ve interpersonal evaluation	54·08	57·50	56·25	57·25
	(10·42)	(7·31)	(7·46)	(5·05)
Variance in person perception	1·33	0·92	1·08	0·92
	(1·44)	(0·99)	(0·90)	(1·08)
Paralanguage use	3·00	4·63	4·13	2·50
	(2·35)	(1·11)	(2·95)	(1·58)
Perceived uninhibitedness	9·67	10·50	9·08	9·25
	(2·46)	(1·62)	(3·37)	(2·34)
SD of words sent‡	66·80	41·32	36·74	84·08
	(29·82)	(16·94)	(38·66)	(38·65)
Average relative SD of words sent‡	0·026	0·005[a]	0·012	0·035[a]
	(0·024)	(0·005)	(0·016)	(0·028)

† Means (SDs) sharing the same superscript are significantly different ($p < 0.05$)
‡ Significant interaction ($p < 0.05$) between de-individuation and group immersion
§ Significant main effect ($p < 0.05$) for de-individuation factor
‖ Significant main effect ($p < 0.05$) for group immersion factor

the pre-discussion and post-discussion opinion measures for each discussion topic. Opinion scores on the scales were transformed so that positive change scores indicated convergence on the group norm. Subjects' opinion change on each discussion topic were calculated by subtracting their pre-discussion score from their post-discussion score. These were then summed to provide an overall change score for each subject. The change scores formed the dependent measure, and subjects' pre-discussion opinion scores were the covariate in a two-way between-groups analysis of covariance in which the de-individuation and group immersion manipulations formed the independent factors.

The results of the analysis of the polarization data were as follows. There was a significant interaction between the two factors, group and de-individuation [$F(1,39) = 5.12$; $p < 0.05$]. There were no significant main effects and no significant effects for the covariate. Comparisons of the mean scores (adjusted for the

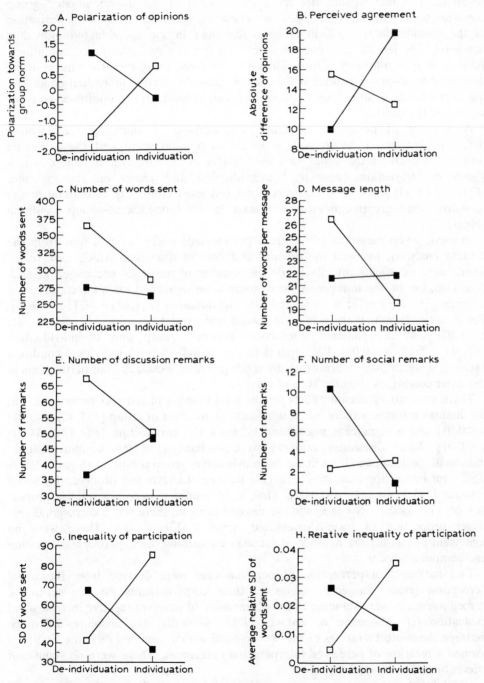

FIGURE 1. Significant effects by condition. Key: ■, group; □, individual. Reproduced with permission from The British Psychological Society. First published in the *British Journal of Social Psychology* 29(1), p. 129.

covariate) revealed significantly more polarization in the de-individuated–group condition than in the individuated–group condition and significantly less polarization in the de-individuated–individual condition than in the individuated–individual condition. The largest difference was between the two de-individuated conditions: subjects were significantly more polarized in the direction of the group norm in the de-individuated–group condition than in the de-individuated–individual condition; the corresponding difference between the two individuation conditions was not significant (Figure 1A).

A measure of perceived consensus was derived by summing the absolute difference between a subject's post-discussion opinion score and the perceived position of each of the other two participants in the discussions. There was a significant interaction between de-individuation and group on this measure $[F(1, 44) = 8.97; p < 0.005]$. Subjects perceived most consensus of opinion in the de-individuated–group condition and least in the individuated–group condition (Figure 1B).

In total, seven measures (three from the message traffic log and four from the content analysis), assessed the amount and type of discussion which took place. There were no significant effects for the number of messages exchanged in each condition, but on the number of words there were significant main effects of group salience $[F(1,44) = 6.77; p < 0.05]$ and de-individuation $[F(1,44) = 4.31; p < 0.05]$. For message length, there was a significant main effect of group $[F(1,44) = 4.81; p < 0.05]$ and a significant interaction between group and de-individuation $[F(1,44) = 5.90; p < 0.05]$. Participants in the de-individuated–individual condition exchanged significantly more words by sending longer messages than participants in the other conditions (Figures 1C and D).

There were no significant effects for the total number of remarks exchanged, but for discussion remarks there was a significant main effect of group $[F(1,12) = 13.41; p < 0.01]$ and a significant interaction between the two factors $[F(1,12) = 11.21; p < 0.01]$. Most discussion remarks were exchanged in the de-individuated–individual condition and least in the de-individuated–group condition (Figure 1E). A significant interaction indicating a reverse pattern of effects was observed for social remarks $[F(1,12) = 4.50; p < 0.05)$. That is, in conditions where a smaller proportion of remarks directly concerned the discussion topic, there was a correspondingly larger proportion of socially-orientated remarks (Figure 1F). There were no significant effects for the number of remarks concerning the experimental situation and computer system.

Two measures of perception of personal cues were derived from the social perception scales. Subjects' ratings of their co-participants on the six social perception scales were summed to form a measure of positive/negative interpersonal evaluation (cf. Matheson & Zanna, 1988). Secondly, the absolute difference between the subject's ratings of the two co-participants, summed over the six scales formed a measure of perceived interpersonal differences. There were no significant effects on either measure.

Uninhibited behaviour was measured by calculating the number of uses of paralanguage, and perceived uninhibited behaviour was measured by summing responses on the uninhibited scale of the social perception scales. There were no significant effects on either dependent variable.

Inequality of participation was measured in two related ways by taking the standard deviation of the number of words sent by participants within each condition and by calculating the average relative standard deviation of subjects' participation rates. The latter provides a standardized measure of inequality controlling for between group differences in the overall number of words sent (Siegel et al., 1986). The measure varies between zero (equal participation) and unity (maximum inequality). There was a significant interaction between the group and the de-individuation factors on both inequality measures (SD_{words}: $F(1,12) =$ 5·09; $p < 0.05$; average relative SD_{words}: $F(1,12) = 4.74$; $p < 0.05$). The mean contrasts between conditions did not reach significance on the SD_{words} measure, but on the average relative SD_{words} measure there was significantly greater inequality in the individuated–individual condition than in the de-individuated–individual condition (Figures 1G and 1H).

SUMMARY

The main focus for comparison is between the de-individuated–group condition and the de-individuated–individual condition. Subjects in the de-individuated–group condition were significantly more polarized in the direction of the group norm. Greater polarization was associated with the exchange of significantly fewer words, shorter messages and a significantly smaller proportion of remarks related to the discussion topic. Participation was also more unequal. Subjects in this condition exchanged more social remarks and perceived least disagreement among themselves after the discussions. Greater polarization was not associated with more uninhibited behaviour or the reduced perception of social cues.

Discussion

In making the comparison between CMC and face-to-face interaction, our experiment can be viewed as an attempt to separate for study some of the important social psychological variables from the physical and technical requirements of mediated communication. Thus, problems in the interpretation of media comparison studies which arise from differences in the time taken for speaking *vs* typing, and reading *vs* listening have been avoided (cf. Siegel et al., 1986). Instead, we assume that the individuation conditions in this study approximate in social psychological terms to face-to-face conditions. That is, while physical and technical requirements of the interaction medium were controlled for, the participants were nevertheless visually and physically co-present in the same room.

The reduced social cues model propounded by the Carnegie-Mellon team is essentially anormative and asocial. It predicts greater polarization in CMC due to the reduction or absence of social cues, de-individuation (defined as reduced self-awareness leading to antinormative behaviour), uninhibited behaviour, and more attentional focus on the task, which all feed by various routes in to the "persuasive arguments" explanation of group polarization. These psychological states and behavioural outcomes have come to be regarded by many as concomitant social psychological features of CMC. However, this study was designed to test the hypothesis that these features are not fixed attributes of CMC relative to face-to-face interaction, but that they can be manipulated experimentally, and by extension, in real-life. In particular we maintain that group norms can directly influence the outcome of group decision-making in CMC, under conditions of group salience.

From social identity theory we argue that group polarization is largely determined by prevailing group norms, in contradistinction to the primarily anormative explanations discussed earlier. We also employ a re-conceptualization of de-individuation such that an individual's social identity can be more salient than his or her individual identity under conditions of anonymity within a group. De-individuation, so defined, does not necessarily have to be conceived of as a deregulated state associated with uninhibited behaviour (unless that is a part of a prevailing group norm). Nor does de-individuation have to be contingent on the physical co-presence of the group. Following social identity theory (e.g. Tajfel & Turner, 1986; Turner et al., 1987; Brown, 1988; Hogg & Abrams, 1988), we argue that both one's group identity can be salient and influential in the absence of other group members, and that the co-presence of others can actually undermine group salience by facilitating the perception of intragroup differences. These arguments have been developed in more detail elsewhere (Spears et al., 1990).

In support of this view, we found greater group polarization in the direction of a pre-established group norm when members of a salient group were de-individuated. Greatest shift away from the group norm was obtained in the de-individuated condition where the participant's individuality was made salient (which we refer to here as "depolarization"; see Wetherell, 1987, p. 144). The latter result deserves some further explanation. We consider that in the individual conditions the prescribed norm is perceived to be individualism such that resisting the pre-established group norm may be the only means subjects have of expressing their individuality when they have been placed in conditions of social anonymity.

We also found that greater polarization in the de-individuated–group condition was not associated with uninhibited behaviour, nor with greater overall participation, nor with reduced perceptions of social cues. Polarization was associated with a greater proportion of social remarks and with more unequal participation. Depolarization, as in the de-individuated–individual condition, was associated with longer messages, greater equality and more discussion-orientated remarks.

How does this pattern of results fit with the previous accounts of group decision-making in CMC (e.g. Kiesler et al., 1984; Siegel et al., 1986)? We shall consider the positions relating to persuasive arguments, disinhibition and antinormative behaviour. However we can begin by dismissing the "computer culture" explanation for our data at least, because our subjects were using a CMCS for the first time and were not drawn from a population experienced in using computers.

First, in terms of the persuasive arguments explanation, polarization should be associated with the exchange of a greater number of discussion-orientated remarks, but as we have seen this was not the case. The condition in which most discussion remarks were exchanged exhibited least polarization (actually depolarization), and the condition with the greatest degree of polarization exchanged fewest discussion-orientated remarks. Similarly, the predicted relationship between equality of participation and polarization, as mediated by persuasive arguments, is not borne out. The condition with the greatest equality of participation (de-individuated–individual) actually exhibited the least polarization. There was also no relation between uninhibited behaviour and either polarization or depolarization in terms of our conditions. Thus to the extent that it could be argued that depolarization away from the group norm is actually "antinormative", no association with uninhibited behaviour was obtained. Finally, there was no evidence that polarization occurred because of reduced perceptions of social cues. This is evidenced both in specific dependent measures designed to tap such cues, and the fact that one of the de-individuation conditions (de-individuated–individual) still exhibited less polarization in comparison with the co-presence or individuated conditions, where social cues should be richest.

Turning to the putative relationship between polarization and antinormative behaviour, our results clearly argue for the converse: the greater polarization associated with CMC in the de-individuated group condition was norm directed. This finding is consistent with much work in the group-polarization paradigm generally (e.g. Sanders & Baron, 1977; Wetherell, 1987). The current finding that the number of social remarks exchanged was highest in the condition in which there was greatest polarization may also support a normative explanation, to the extent that such remarks contained norm-relevant information.

In regard to this assumed relation between an "antinormative" tendency and group polarization, we would argue that difficulties have arisen from conflating more extreme decisions (polarization) with disinhibition, and by employing a particular form of the group-polarization paradigm which focuses on *risky* decision-making (e.g. Lamm & Myers, 1978). However, as argued earlier, group polarization is not necessarily characterized by disinhibition because groups can polarize and become more "extreme" in the direction of caution (e.g. Fraser, 1971; Wetherell, 1987), depending on the initial group trend or norm. It may be that the phenomenon of "deregulated" and uninhibited behaviour in CMC can also ultimately be interpreted within a normative context. Certainly there seems to be mounting evidence that "flaming" is not a universal attribute of CMC as has been widely assumed (e.g. Hiltz *et al.*, 1989; Spears & Lea, in press).

To summarize, it would appear that no single explanation offered by the Carnegie-Mellon research can satisfactorily explain the present findings. In general, their position is not well equipped to explain the variations between the four conditions of the present experiment, and the diametrically opposed results of the de-individuation conditions in particular. We shall now turn to briefly reconsider their empirical findings in order to see whether our approach can shed light on some of the apparent contradictions in the reported data.

The conditions reported by Kiesler *et al.* (1984) and Siegel *et al.* (1986) in which group discussion members using CMC exhibited greater group polarization than face-to-face groups could be seen as comparable with the de-individuated–group condition of the present study. In the CMC condition participants were placed out of hearing and sight of each other, and the fact that subjects were drawn largely from a single homogeneous student pool would seem to guarantee a relatively cohesive and salient group context (the "individual" basis of the decision-making task was not emphasized as in the de-individuated–individual condition of our experiment). By contrast, in the face-to-face condition subjects were seated around a table and were tape-recorded, which arguably is a highly individuating manipulation similar to our individuated–individual condition. Given these factors, their polarization results seem broadly in agreement with our analysis. However, we should recall that the study by McGuire *et al.* (1987) obtained less (in fact no) polarization in the CMC condition as compared with a face-to-face condition. This may have been something to do with the experimental task, which diverged from the standard group polarization paradigm, nevertheless various features of the experiment can be viewed as having weakened the salience of the group, and accentuated the individuality of participants, in ways predicted to undermine the normative basis of polarization.

The particular social context which formed the background to the McGuire *et al.* (1987) study was not reported in any detail so it is unclear whether there was an historically pre-established group norm for the sample of managers and administrators who took part, which was stronger than that instituted experimentally. Such a norm may have been competitive and individualistic, which the instructional set used could have reinforced ("Imagine you are a manager of a firm. . ."). The fact that the majority of participants were familiar to each other, that they could see each other during the session, and that their names were displayed throughout, would also, in our terms, have had an "individuating" effect, further undermining the salience of the discussion group and any related normative basis for influence and polarization.

These features of the study would be expected to undermine group-level categorizations in themselves. However a second problem arises from the fact that participants were drawn from two sources, namely managers from the same organization ($n = 19$) and university administrators ($n = 29$). This meant that over half of the experimentally created groups comprised participants from the two different sources with the result that one level of group categorization (occupation) was cross-cutting another (the discussion group). It is possible to argue that competing group norms and loyalties may have been circulating which could favor intergroup polarization where one faction or group polarizes away from the other (cf. "bipolarization", Paicheler, 1977).

Finally, it is interesting to note that their analysis showed that the first advocate position in each discussion group was highly predictive of the course of the final group outcome or decision, and that this was markedly different for CMC groups as compared with face-to-face groups (going against the predicted norm in CMC). This first stated position could thus be interpreted as setting the standard for the norm within groups. Given the small sample size (16 groups in all) it cannot be ruled out that initial positions, which seem largely to determine the course of decision-making, differed by chance between the two conditions. Overall then, given the features of the design of the McGuire *et al.* study which diverge in important ways from the earlier studies, their results are not necessarily incompatible with our own model.

How does our model and the results of the present experiment compare with independent research carried out elsewhere? The Hiltz *et al.* (1989) study is particularly relevant to our own because it operationalized de-individuation in a similar way (through the provision of pen-names in one condition and the use of real names in another). Subjects were recognizably part of a group (they consisted of managers from the same company on a three-week residential course) and this group identity was highly salient (the attitudes and behaviour of the course attendees are reported in some detail). Furthermore, Hiltz *et al.* were able to identify from these and other observations a relevant directional group norm in favour of conservative decision-making. Arguably, the conditions in their study corresponded most closely to the de-individuated–group and individuated–group conditions of the present study and can be compared as such. Hiltz *et al.* found only weak and mainly insignificant effects for their de-individuation manipulation which they attributed to the powerful, conservative company-norm. For example, there was a floor effect for uninhibited behaviour and a ceiling effect for post-discussion consensus in both conditions. Nevertheless the reported trends in the data concur with our own findings for the same two conditions: there were no significant differences in the amount of uninhibited behaviour or inequality of participation, and there was a tendency for groups to make more conservative (i.e. more normative) decisions in the de-individuated condition.

A recent study by Matheson and Zanna (1989) is also of some relevance to the present research, although the experimental design diverged in important respects from the group-polarization paradigm. It should be recalled that in both that study and in an earlier one (Matheson & Zanna, 1988), CMC was found to be associated with enhanced private self-awareness, and therefore with greater attention to salient contextual standards (Carver & Scheier, 1981). Elsewhere it has been argued that self-attention processes may play a role in making either group or individual standards more salient within CMC, depending on the broader context, and that such processes can be incorporated within a social identity perspective (Hogg & Abrams, 1988; Spears *et al.*, 1990). Again, these independent findings call into question the explanations propounded in earlier work.

To sum up, the present study contributes to the mounting evidence which suggests that earlier research underestimated the role of social contextual factors and normative processes in CMC. Together with other recent research (Myers, 1987; Matheson & Zanna, 1988, 1989; Hiltz *et al.*, 1989; Spears *et al.*, 1990; Lea, in press; Spears & Lea, in press) our findings imply that, compared with face-to-face interaction, the social and normative context may be of even greater importance in computer-mediated communication.

Financial support was provided by a postdoctoral research fellowship in information technology to Martin Lea from the UK Science and Engineering Research Council and a Simon Marks research fellowship from the University of Manchester to Russell Spears.

References

BROWN, R. (1988). *Group Processes*. Oxford, UK: Blackwell.

BURNSTEIN, E. & VINOKUR, A. (1977). Persuasive argumentation and social comparison as determinants of attitude polarization. *Journal of Experimental Social Psychology*, **13**, 315–332.

CARVER, C. S. & SCHEIER, M. F. (1981). *Attention and Self-regulation: A Control Theory Approach to Human Behavior*. New York: Springer-Verlag.

DIENER, E. (1980). De-individuation: The absence of self-awareness and self-regulation in group members. In P. PAULUS, Ed. *The Psychology of Group Influence*. Hillsdale, NJ: Erlbaum.

FESTINGER, L., PEPITONE, A. & NEWCOMB, T. (1952). Some consequences of de-individuation in a group. *Journal of Abnormal and Social Psychology*, **47**, 382–389.

FRASER, C. (1971). Group risk taking and group polarization. *European Journal of Social Psychology*, **1**, 493–510.

HILTZ, S. R. & TUROFF, M. (1978). *The Network Nation: Human Communication via Computer.* Reading, MA: Addison-Wesley.

HILTZ, S. R., TUROFF, M. & JOHNSON, K. (1989). Experiments in group decision making, 3: disinhibition, de-individuation, and group process in pen name and real name computer conferences. *Decision Support Systems,* **5,** 217–232.

HOGG, M. A. & ABRAMS, D. (1988). *Social Identifications: A Social Psychology of Intergroup Relations and Group Processes.* London: Routledge.

KIESLER, S. (1986). The hidden messages in computer networks. *Harvard Business Review,* January–February, 46–58.

KIESLER, S., SIEGEL, J. & McGUIRE, T. (1984). Social psychological aspects of computer-mediated communication. *American Psychologist,* **39,** 1123–1134.

LAMM, H. & MYERS, D. G. (1978). Group induced polarization of attitudes and behavior. In L. Berkowitz, Ed. *Advances in Experimental Social Psychological Research,* vol. 2. New York: Academic Press.

LEA, M. (In press). Rationalist assumptions in cross-media comparisons of computer-mediated communication. *Behaviour and Information Technology.*

LEA, M., WILSON, P. & YOUNG, R. (1989). *Recommendations for Application, Further Development and Evolution of Cosmos.* Final Deliverable to the Alvey Directorate, London. Project No. MMI/109.

MACKIE, D. M. (1986). Social identification effects in group polarization. *Journal of Personality and Social Psychology,* **50,** 720–728.

MATHESON, K. & ZANNA, M. P. (1988). The impact of computer-mediated communication on self-awareness. *Computers in Human Behavior,* **4,** 221–233.

MATHESON, K. & ZANNA, M. P. (1989). Persuasion as a function of self-awareness in computer-mediated communication. *Social Behaviour,* **4,** 99–111.

McGUIRE, T. W., KIESLER, S. & SIEGEL, J. (1987). Group and computer-mediated discussion effects in risk decision making. *Journal of Personality and Social Psychology,* **52,** 917–930.

MYERS, D. (1987). "Anonymity is part of the magic": individual manipulation of computer-mediated communication contexts. *Qualitative Sociology,* **10,** 251–266.

PAICHELER, G. (1977). Norms and attitude change: 2. The phenomenon of bipolarisation. *European Journal of Social Psychology,* **17,** 5–14.

PETTY, R. E. & CACIOPPO, J. T. (1986). The elaboration likelihood model of persuasion. In L. BERKOWITZ, Ed. *Advances in Experimental Social Psychology.* New York: Academic Press.

REICHER, S. D. (1984). Social influence in the crowd: Attitudinal and behavioural effects of de-individuation in conditions of high and low group salience. *British Journal of Social Psychology,* **23,** 341–350.

REICHER, S. D. (1987). Crowd behaviour as social action. In J. C. Turner, M. A. Hogg, P. J. Oakes, S. D. Reicher & M. S. Wetherell, Eds. *Rediscovering the Social Group: A Self-Categorization Theory.* Oxford, UK: Blackwell.

RICE, R. E. (1984). *The New Media: Communication, Research and Technology.* Beverly Hills: Sage.

SANDERS, G. S. & BARON, R. S. (1977). Is social comparison irrelevant for producing choice shifts? *Journal of Experimental Social Psychology,* **13,** 303–314.

SIEGEL, J., DUBROVSKY, V., KIESLER, S. & McGUIRE, T. (1986). Group processes in computer-mediated communication. *Organizational Behavior and Human Decision Processes,* **37,** 157–187.

SPEARS, R. & LEA, M. (In press). Social psychological factors in computer-mediated communication. In M. LEA, Ed. *The Social Contexts of Computer-Mediated Communication.* Hemel Hempstead: Harvester-Wheatsheaf.

SPEARS, R., LEA, M. & LEE, S. (1990). De-individuation and group polarization in computer-mediated communication. *British Journal of Social Psychology,* **29,** 121–134.

SPROULL, L. & KIESLER, S. (1986). Reducing social context cues: electronic mail in organizational communication. *Management Science,* **32,** 1492–1512.

STONER, J. A. F. (1961). *A Comparison of Individual and Group Decisions Including Risk.* MA Thesis, Massachusetts Institute of Technology, School of Management.

TAJFEL, H. & TURNER, J. C. (1986). The social identity theory of intergroup behaviour. In S. WORCHELL & W. G. AUSTIN, Eds. *Psychology of Intergroup Relations*. Chicago: Nelson-Hall.

TURNER, J. C. (1983). Some comments on the measurement of social orientations in the minimal group paradigm. *European Journal of Social Psychology,* **13,** 351–367.

TURNER, J. C., HOGG, M. A., OAKES, P. J., REICHER, S. D. & WETHERELL, M. S. (1987). *Rediscovering the Social Group: A Self-categorization Theory*. Oxford, UK: Blackwell.

VINOKUR, A. & BURNSTEIN, E. (1974). The effects of partially shared persuasive arguments on group-induced shifts. A problem solving approach. *Journal of Personality and Social Psychology,* **29,** 305–315.

WETHERELL, M. S. (1987). Social identity and group polarization. In J. C. TURNER, M. A. HOGG, P. J. OAKES, S. D. REICHER & M. S. WETHERELL, Eds. *Rediscovering the Social Group: A Self-Categorization Theory*. Oxford, UK: Blackwell.

ZIMBARDO, P. G. (1969). The human choice: individuation reason and order versus de-individuation impulse and chaos. In W. J. Arnold & D. Levine, Eds. *Nebraska Symposium on Motivation. Volume 17*. Lincoln, NA: University of Nebraska Press.

9

Conversational flexibility in a computer conference used in professional education

Judith Weedman

In order to examine the ability of computer mediated conferences to provide variety in communication, data were gathered on task-related and non task-related uses of a computer-mediated conference in use at a research university. The conference was organized by the graduate students of a professional school to provide additional opportunities for communication between the students, faculty, staff and some professionals in the field. Data were gathered twice, in 1987 and 1989, and were of two types, printouts of the content of the conference and surveys of the participants. Four measures of content data were used: (1) the number of items (strings of entries forming discussions) originating with task-related and non task-related entries; (2) the lifespans of items; (3) the total number of entries falling into task and non-task categories; and (4) flexibility in moving between functions as indicated by opposite category responses. Three banks of questions from the survey instrument provided data concerning participants' perceptions of variety supported by the conference: (1) task-related and non task-related motivations for using the conference; (2) analogies to other communication; and (3) measures of the extent to which the conference provided interactions between people which did not take place otherwise.

Analysis of survey and perception data revealed variety and flexibility in patterns of interaction, with a higher level of non-task content than had been found in other studies. The computer conference environment was found to be very supple, supporting a wide range of topics and interactions between individuals who differed in status and in the degree to which they knew one another outside the conference.

1. Introduction

Professional schools within universities prepare future practitioners by teaching the knowledge and technical skills they will need, and also by socializing them into the attitudes and behaviors expected in members of the profession. These processes occur in several ways, including direct instruction by faculty, informal exchanges between faculty and students, communication among the students, and contact with professionals in the field. An additional avenue for communication and professional socialization is provided by computer mediated conferences. Many research universities now have available conferencing software which can be used by various groups within the university community. Such conferences are increasingly employed by individuals working on the same or related problems. Those which operate in asynchronous mode allow people to interact without the necessity of being in the same location at the same time; individuals can log on to the conference at any time and read everything contributed since they last logged on,

175

and add entries of their own. Computer conferences thus provide a great deal of flexibility to group communication.

However, since the inception of computer-mediated communication such as electronic mail and conferences, its effectiveness has been questioned. Studies have tried to ascertain what effects this particular medium has had on communication behaviour. Computer-mediated communication is often assumed to be lacking in social presence; because the individuals in communication are not in each other's presence, and such nonverbal and paraverbal cues such as facial expression and intonation are lost. In addition, behavior such as comments with socio-emotional content (e.g. "I see what you mean" or friendly kidding which serves to relieve tension) may not occur as easily when conversation has to be typed rather than spoken.

Studies of group process indicate that even in task-oriented interactions the social and emotional dimensions can contribute to, or detract from, the group's ability to function effectively (Bales, 1951). Thus if computer conferencing does indeed inhibit normal conversational asides and sociability there may be some forms of communication for which it is not an effective medium.

In order to further explore social and task-related dimensions of computer conferencing, data were gathered for this study from a computer conference which has been in existence for four years in a professional school in a large research university. The conferencing software resides on a mainframe computer, and many conferences are in use at the university by students, faculty, and other groups. This conference was begun for the use of students and faculty of the professional school and has attracted some local professionals in the field as well. The conference was organized by the students to provide an opportunity to become familiar with this tool for professional communication, and to provide an additional avenue of communication within the school.

This conference is particularly useful for analysis of task and non-task uses because it does not have a fixed agenda. Conversations thus are free to evolve in a natural manner, with no strict "stick to business" norms or pressure to complete a task by a deadline. There is thus more opportunity for social and emotional content to develop than in a conference originated to achieve a work-related goal.

2. Literature

The social dimension of computer conferences has been addressed in various ways. Researchers have studied the existence of uninhibited behavior, socially undesirable content, politeness strategies, perception of social presence, and socio-emotional content. No clear consensus has emerged, but the most frequent conclusions are that the medium is limited in its ability to perform a social function and may even encourage negative social behaviors.

Siegel, Dubrovsky, Kiesler and McGuire (1986) compared decision making in face-to-face interactions with that in computer-mediated interactions, both simultaneous conferences and electronic mail; the research design was experimental, using college students as subjects. They found significantly more uninhibited behavior, defined as instances of swearing, insults, and name calling, in computer-mediated discussions than in face-to-face discussions. They speculated that the fact that an individual participating in a computer-mediated discussion is not actually in the presence of the people with whom he is communicating may lead to a level of social anonymity, a focus on content rather than social context, and the existence of fewer social norms than have evolved for face-to-face interaction.

Kiesler and Sproull (1986) compared survey response data gathered from students and faculty with a written questionnaire, with responses gathered via electronic mail. They found electronic mail respondents provided answers which would be considered socially undesirable more frequently than paper questionnaire respondents.

Sproull (1986) administered a questionnaire in face-to-face interviews and through electronic mail, and found no difference in content of responses, but a larger number of responses falling at the extremes in the group receiving the questionnaire through electronic mail.

Sproull and Kiesler (1986) also found a deregulating effect in electronic mail used within a corporation, which led to more irresponsible behavior than occurred with face-to-face interactions. They also found, however, that use of an electronic mail system brought information to participants that did not come through other channels.

It is not entirely clear these findings do indicate that a computer provides a less satisfactory medium than face-to-face-interactions for social exchange, as their authors suggest. To the extent that these behaviors indicate lack of constraint by the medium and informality of tone, they may indicate the potential of computer communication to be quite expressive of social and emotional content. The increase in socially undesirable responses when an electronic rather than paper survey instrument is used, may indicate greater honesty and therefore more accuracy in responses. Sproull and Kiesler (1986) in fact suggest that the deregulating effect of electronic mail may lead to an increased flow of new ideas through an organization. The presence of swearing and insults may suggest informality and humor more than feelings of loss of identity and reduced sociability.

One factor which influences the use of computers for communication is the existence of social norms paralleling those which govern other types of communication. Siegel et al. (1986) discuss the lack of shared social norms and well developed etiquette resulting from the relative newness of computer communication to most people.

Chesebro (1985), Vallee and Johansen (1974), and Hiemstra (1982), however, all report the existence of such norms and expectations regarding etiquette. Chesebro cites conventions regarding length of messages sent and standard abbreviations such as "oic" for "Oh, I see!" Vallee et al. describe the evolution of different styles in different organizations using the same conferencing software. Hiemstra found that social norms and concern for face were strongly present in a work group which used a computer conference to produce a research report; more than 75% of the utterances he analysed contained "politeness strategies".

Several studies provide data on the quantity of social or socio-emotional content. Chesebro (1985) studied a public bulletin board on the commercial utility CompuServe and found that 30% of the messages were interpersonal in their central concern. Sproull and Kiesler (1986) analysed the content of electronic mail within a corporation and found that 40% of the messages had nothing whatever to do with work; in addition, many of the work-related messages had a high social content since the definition of the category included topics such as the company softball games. Vallee and Johansen (1984) found that 17% of the messages in the 10 conferences they studied were either irrelevant to the discussion in which they were embedded, or affective in nature; 83% were related to the task of the discussion. Rice and Love (1987) defined socio-emotional content as interactions which convey personal (as opposed to task-related) information or show solidarity, tension relief, agreement, antagonism, tension, or disagreement. In a public computer bulletin board, they found 71% of the sentences to be task-oriented, 28% to contain positive socio-emotional content, and 0·4% to contain negative socio-emotional content.

Despite the differing definitions of social content and different units of analysis used, all of these studies clearly demonstrate a substantial amount of social or non-task content in computer mediated communication. These findings hold, both in groups where there is no set task, and in those where there is a clear task or work-related agenda.

Finally, perceptions of the existence of social presence in computer conferences and electronic mail have been studied. Hiltz and Johnson (1989) surveyed users of four different systems, with differing capabilities and ease of use. On a scale ranging from 1 (impersonal) to 7 (friendly) the mean rating was 4·4, very close to the center of the scale. When asked if they were able to get an impression of personal contact while using the conference, respondents again gave a mean rating close to the scale's midpoint, 2·8, where 1 = always, 3 = sometimes, and 5 = never. Vallee, Johnson, Lipinski, Spangler and Thaddeus (1978) also reported middle range ratings on this question, 2·5 on the same scale. Their respondents also rated computer conferences as to how satisfactory they would be for several tasks. For the task of getting to know someone, respondents gave a mean rating of 3·5—again near the midpoint—on a scale where 1 = completely unsatisfactory and 7 = completely satisfactory. Another social function—keeping in touch—received a higher rating of 5·4. Less social tasks received higher mean ratings; 5·7 for exchanging opinions and 5·9 for exchanging information. The generation of new ideas was rated at 5·4.

Because of differing communication settings, definitions and methodologies, the studies discussed above cannot be directly compared with one another. Nevertheless, the general impression conveyed is that the ability of computer-mediated communication to convey social and personal content, is perceived as moderate at best, although a great deal of social and personal exchange does in fact take place.

3. Methodology

In order to examine further the issue of whether computer-mediated conferences allow the variety in communication needed for effective interaction, data were gathered on the use of a professional school's student-organized conference. Two types of data were gathered, transcripts of the content of the conference and survey data from conference participants. Analysis was thus possible of both the actual use of the conference and the perceptions of the individuals using it. Data were first gathered in 1987, one year after the conference was initiated, and again in 1989.

The structure of the conference consists of a series of chains of entries, each chain referred to as an item. An item is begun when an individual enters a comment or a request for information; anyone using the conference after that point can then choose to respond to it or not. The responses are linked to the original entry in chronological order, so that an individual sees the original entry followed by all responses; if he or she chooses to respond as well, that response is added to the chain and will be visible to subsequent users. Any number of items may be active concurrently.

3.1. CONTENT DATA

Data were gathered by signing on to the conference and printing off all items. The first transcript, printed in 1987, contained items back to the original one when the conference was begun 12 months earlier. The 1989 transcript, however, contained entries for only nine months; because conference use becomes increasingly cumbersome as entries accumulate, the conference is occasionally closed and restarted. A restart of the conference had occurred in July 1988. To ensure comparability of the two data sets, therefore, for the 1987 transcript only entries from the same span of months (July–April) have been analysed. Some items have been deleted from the 1987 conference. Conference organizers removed items which were outdated, such as job announcements and schedules. Since the intent of this study is to examine the conference as it existed at two points in time, these deletions do not distort the results as they would if the intent were to consider all conference interactions over a three-year period.

Content analysis was carried out with a two-category dictionary. The unit of analysis was the individual entry. The initial item entry and all subsequent responses were coded independently of one another into either the category *task* or the category *non-task*.

Task was broadly defined to include any text conveying a question, information, or opinion related to: (1) the students' professional education; (2) the profession itself; or (3) the tools and skills of the profession. Thus any entry concerning school policy, course offerings, schedules, or events would be coded into the task category. Entries relating to the profession included topics such as ethics and job hunting. The final aspect of the task category, tools and skills, included entries on computer applications, where to buy personal computers, resources and supplies needed for school (including such non-specialized items such as office supplies), and use of the computer conference itself. This broad definition of the task category follows Sproull and Kiesler's 1986 analysis of electronic mail in a corporate setting, but differs in that entries regarding strictly social events such as softball games were coded as non-task.

Entries were coded non-task if: (1) they were humorous only in intent, with no information content; (2) they concerned strictly social events such as parties; or (3) they were informative but not on a topic directly related to the profession. The latter category contained discussions for instance of political events, racism and local history.

If an entry had both task and non-task content, it was coded as task. Expressions of emotion or opinion in the context of a task-related discussion (e.g. "thank you" or "ugh") were coded as task entries if they served the purpose of extending or facilitating the discussion; they were coded as non-task if they were diversionary in nature, humorous asides, or parenthetical remarks. Items frequently contained both task and non-task entries, some remaining close to the intent of the author of the original item entry, others exhibiting the phenomenon known as "item drift".

It should be noted that no value judgement is contained in the terms task and non-task. The conference was established for the purposes of providing experience with the medium and extending the opportunities for communication within the school; these two goals were served by playful and humorous uses as as well as by discussion of professional concerns. In addition, many of the non-task items were substantive discussions of contemporary issues and concerns.

As is generally true with content analysis, many entries did not fall neatly into one or the other of the categories. Intercoder reliability on a random sample from the transcripts, however, was 95%.

3.2. SURVEY DATA

Questionnaires were mailed in April 1987 and 1989, to all individuals registered as participants in the conference on the dates on which the transcripts were printed.

In 1987 the population of registered participants was 139; 117 students, seven faculty members, two school staff members, and 18 working professionals. Eighty-four questionnaires were returned, for a 60·4% response rate. The response rate for students was 51·3%, for faculty 71.4%, for staff 100%, and for professionals 94·4%.

In 1989 the population of participants was 172; 142 students, five faculty, three staff, and 22 professionals. Ninety-two questionnaires were returned, a response rate of 53.5%. Student response rate was 52·8%, faculty 100%, staff 42·6%, and professionals 50·0%.

4. Findings

4.1. CONTENT DATA

The content data provided two indications of the ability of computer conferences to support both task and non-task communication, the extent to which the conference was actually used for each purpose, and the flexibility with which participants were able to change from one function to the other. Three measures indicated the extent of use for task and non-task communication: (1) the number of items which originated with task entries and with non-task entries; (2) the lifespans of items, measured by the number of responses which occurred and their duration in days; and (3) the total number of entries which fell into task and non-task categories. Flexibility was indicated by the number of items containing opposite-category responses and the total number of opposite category responses.

4.1.1. Number of items originating with task-related entries and with non task-related entries

The topics which users select for conference entries, provide one indication of the functions for which a conference is an effective environment. Early use of a conference will be somewhat experimental in nature; habits, expectations and norms will develop over time. The presence of both task and non-task topics indicates that both have been found to be effectively addressed through the medium of the conference.

TABLE 1
Number of conference items in-
itiated each year on task-related
topics   and   non-task-related
topics

		1987	1989
Task	%	86·1	60·6
	n	(105)	(40)
Non-task	%	13·9	39·4
	n	(17)	(26)
Total items	n	122	66

In both the 1987 and 1989 conference transcripts, more than half the items originated in task-related entries. However, the proportion of items originating with non-task entries almost tripled from 1987 to 1989. In the nine months analysed from the 1987 transcript, 86·1% of the items orginated with a task-oriented entry and 13·9% originated with an entry which was non-task in nature. In the transcript for 1989, 60·6% of the items originated with task-oriented entries, 39·4% with non task-oriented entries (Table 1).

In 1987, the earliest items provided information on useful features of the conference and on how to carry out various procedures. These were coded as task entries, because they related directly to the conference as a tool for school communication. Other items which originated with task-oriented entries concerned subjects such as the formation of study groups, Macintosh computer applications, books recently added to the school's library, an assertion that the workload for students in the program was unrealistic (the first response to which, from another student, was "Dig in. You can handle it"), a discussion of recent curriculum changes, the relative advantages of the mainframe's text formatting software and microcomputer word processing programs, and some part-time job announcements.

The items coded as having initial entries which were non-task related primarily concerned social events. One announced a Happy Hour gathering, another suggested getting together a group to attend an upcoming hockey game, another a Halloween party. The only non-task item which appeared to be entered for its interest/entertainment value alone was initiated eight months after the conference was begun. A student asked the question "Got any good words?" and followed it up with a discussion of how the trade name "Kodak" originated. Other words which came up for discussion on the item were "otorhinolaryngology", "dismantle", "limelight" and "bangs"; along the way a discussion of odd city names also arose briefly.

The 1989 task-related initial item entries were similar in character to the 1987 items. Conference use, a discussion of a recent professional association meeting, summer short courses, and résumé writing were among the topics.

There was an increase in the number of non-task items begun for entertainment value alone. One, for instance, was titled "The Quote Item" and consisted of participants' favorite quotations and occasional discussions spinning off from them.

Another representatively humorous item consisted of smiley faces which can be created with punctuation symbols. The initial entry demonstrated the common ":)", frequently used in computer communication to ensure that the reader will recognize the humorous intent of what preceded, and continued with the wink ";)". Other entries suggested a bearded smile ":)}" and a devilish smile ":}⟩". Another item rang changes on the "how many Xs does it take to change a lightbulb?" joke. Many of the entries on these items were only one line long, as opposed to task-oriented entries which were frequently 10–15 lines long, and occasionally much longer.

4.1.2. Lifespans of items originating with task-related entries and with non task-related entries

A collaborative medium also needs to support variety in the length of the discussion. Some topics may be resolved briefly; for others more extended interaction is appropriate. Two measures of lifespan were used, the number of responses accumulated by an item and the duration, the number of days from original entry to final entry. Both measures showed a great deal of variability; participants used the conference for protracted discussions as well as for brief announcements.

The number of responses ranged from zero to 208. In 1987, three task items had more than 50 responses, with 60 as the most; four non-task items had more than 50, with the highest being 86. In 1989, 10 task items had more than 50 responses, with 124 as the highest; 13 non task items exceeded 50 responses, with 208 as the highest. The mean task items was 13·6 and for non-task 35·3 in 1987; in 1989, 28·4 for task and 62·6 for non-task. The distribution was positively skewed.

The range in duration was from one day to almost 9 months; more than 40% of the items lasted more than a week but less than 2 months. The median durations for 1987 were 9 days for task and 29 days for non-task items; in 1989 the medians were 31 days for task and 23 for nontask. This distribution was also positively skewed (Tables 2 and 3).

4.1.3. Total number of task and nontask entries

For the two years combined, the entries were split almost evenly between task and non-task topics: 48 and 52% respectively. The distributions were quite different in

TABLE 2

Comparison of four studies of computer-mediated communication

Researcher	Unit of analysis	Categories	Percentages %	Medium
Chesebro (1985)	Message	(1) Information (2) Interpersonal	69·0 31·9	Public bulletin board
Sproull & Kiesler (1986)	Message	(1) Work (2) Non-work	60 40	Corporate e-mail
Vallee & Johansen (1974)	Message	(1) Task-related (2) Affective or irrelevant	88 17	Synchronous and asynchronous conferences
Weedman (1990)	Message	(1) Task (broad) (2) Non-task	47·9 52·1	Asynchronous conferences

TABLE 3

Number of responses on items originating each year with task and non-task entries

Number of responses	1987 Task %	1987 Non-task %	1989 Task %	1989 Non-task %
0	7·6	0·0	10·4	3·8
1–2	16·2	0·0	4·2	3·8
3–5	10·5	0·0	4·2	7·7
6–20	41·0	35·5	35·4	23·1
21–50	17·9	41·1	25·0	11·5
51–100	2·9	23·5	18·8	26·9
101–200	0·0	0·0	2·1	15·4
201–300	0·0	0·0	0·0	7·7
Mean n	13·6	35·3	28·4	62·6
Median n	9	30	16	52
	$n = 101$	$n = 16$	$n = 48$	$n = 26$

the two years, however. In 1987, 64·2% of the total number of entries were task-oriented and 35·7% were non task-oriented. In 1989, despite the fact that more items originated with task than with non-task entries, the total number of entries was highest in the non-task cateogry (63·7% as opposed to 37·2%).

Table 4 compares these data with those found by other researchers. Although the content analysis categories do not correspond exactly, the overall differences are clear. The current study is the only one to find a lower percentage of task-related material.

4.1.4. Flexibility in changing from one function to another: opposite cateogry responses

Because each response is linked to the original entry to which it was a reply, items tend to have identifiable topics. However, as with spoken conversations, topics evolve as one idea stimulates another. The evolution may be logical and gradual, or it may be quite abrupt. One indication of the flexibility of computer conferences as communication media is the occurrence of this evolution. The frequency with which non task-related responses appear in items which were originally task-related, and vice versa, provides a partial measure of flexibility.

In 1987, 29·5% of the items which originated as task-related contained non-task entries as well. (This does not necessarily mean the topic of the items completely changed; often the non-task responses were brief asides.) Interestingly, the items beginning with non-task entries showed the same level of variation; 29·4% contained task entries. In 1989, there was an increase in opposite category responses of both types; 58·3% of the originally task-related items contained non-task entries, and 38·5% of the non task-initiated items had task-related responses.

The variations were of several kinds. Some were humorous asides, play on words or teasing comments on typographical errors. These sometimes stimulated other non-task comments, and the item would veer from its original purpose. Other variations resulted from the association of ideas, when one entry would trigger a

TABLE 4

Duration of items originating each year with task and non-task entries

| | 1987 | | 1989 | |
Duration in days	Task %	Non-task %	Task %	Non-task %
1	12·9	0·0	8·1	7·7
n	(13)	(0)	(6)	(2)
2–7	26·7	0·0	18·8	19·2
n	(27)	(0)	(8)	(5)
8–14	19·8	31·3	10·4	7·7
n	(20)	(5)	(5)	(2)
15–30	12·9	18·8	6·3	19·2
n	(13)	(3)	(3)	(5)
31–60	11·9	12·5	25·0	19·2
n	(12)	(2)	(12)	(5)
61–99	6·9	37·5	6·3	3·8
n	(7)	(6)	(3)	(1)
100–199	8·9	0·0	16·7	7·7
n	(9)	(0)	(8)	(2)
200–269	0·0	0·0	4·2	15·4
n	(0)	(0)	(2)	(4)
Mean n	27·5	40·4	52·2	66·1
Median n	9	29	31	23
	$n = 101$	$n = 16$	$n = 48$	$n = 26$

related thought. The task entries on originally non-task items generally occurred when the topic under discussion had a potential impact on the profession (such as political events) or when some aspect of professional work was pertinent to the topic. Table 5 shows the opposite category responses as a percentage of all conference responses.

4.2. SURVEY DATA

Three banks of questions from the survey instrument provided data concerning the conference participants' perceptions of the conference. The first addressed task-

TABLE 5

Occurrence of opposite category responses, by category and year

	1987	1989
Non-task responses on task-initiated items	211	417
Percentage of all responses	9·8	19·4
Task responses on non-task-initiated items	33	102
Percentage of all responses	3·3	13·6
Total opposite category responses	244	519
Percentage of all responses	11·3	16·9

related and non task-related functions served by computer conferences and requested respondents to indicate the extent to which each function motivated his or her own conference use. The second provided analogies to other communication activities. The final explored the extent to which the conference provided interactions between people which did not otherwise take place.

4.2.1. Motivations for use of the conference

Participants were asked to rate 10 possible reasons for their use of the conference on the following scale: 4 = a major reason, 3 = a fairly important reason, 2 = a minor reason, 1 = not a reason. For students, the most highly rated reason was "feeling in touch with the school and what's going on". This was considered task-related, since it is concerned with the school, but it contains a socio-emotional component, stressing the individual's feeling rather than simply the information about the school. The second most highly rated reason was concerned specifically with factual information about the school—"notification of important dates and events". The third category was "intellectual stimulation—exchange of ideas, philosophies, knowledge". It includes but is not limited to professional topics. The next most important reason for use of the conference, however, was the "chance to discuss professional ideas, concerns, information". Fifth in order was "social exchange—chance to talk informally about a variety of things". All of these items were related as either 3 or 4 on the scale by more than 50% of the students.

The five lower-rated items were also mixed in their relationship to the task and non-task dimensions of the conference. In descending order, they were: "Asking for specific information about dates, events, assignments, etc.", "study break", "BS-ing", "Opportunity to express frustrations about the school in order to get something changed", and "Opportunity to express frustrations about the school".

Faculty, staff and professionals were, not surprisingly, somewhat different in their reasons for using the conference. Four of their top-rated five items were the same as the students', however, and they rated the same factor—the feeling of being in touch with the school—the most highly. The category in which the difference was most notable was that of "social exchange—the chance to talk informally about a variety of things". Whereas more than half the students rated this non-task function as of major importance or fairly important, only about a fourth of the non-students did so.

Table 6 provides this data and indicates the categories where differences between students and non-students were statistically significant. There was no significant difference between the two years in which the data was gathered.

4.2.2. Perceptions of the conference environment

In an attempt to better understand the participants' perception of the experience of communicating through a computer conference, a bank of questions provided several analogies. Respondents were asked to indicate which was most similar to using the conference. All of the analogies found some agreement, but none elicited a strong response. The largest percentage of respondents—32·4%—selected the option "Nothing else is really similar to using the conference". The next largest percentage—23·9%—selected "sitting in a lounge or lunch room and talking with people who wander in". Those who selected the "other" option were not similar in

TABLE 6

Reasons of students and non-students for using the conference

		Students	Faculty, staff, professionals
Feeling in touch			
Important†	%	88·5	85·7
	n	(116)	(36)
Minor†	%	11·5	14·3
	n	(15)	(6)
Notification of events			
Important	%	78·6	50·0
	n	(103)	(21)
Minor	%	21·4	50·0
	n	(28)	(21)
Intellectual stimulation			
Important	%	69·5	47·6
	n	(91	(20)
Minor	%	30·5	52·4
	n	(40)	(22)
Discuss professional concerns			
Important	%	65·2	57·5
	n	(84)	(23)
Minor	%	34·9	42·5
	n	(45)	(17)
Social exchange‡			
Important	%	57·3	27·5
	n	(75)	(11)
Minor	%	42·8	72·5
	n	(56)	(29)
Requesting information			
Important	%	32·1	40·5
	n	(42)	(17)
Minor	%	67·9	59·5
	n	(89)	(25)
Study break§			
Important	%	26·7	0·0
	n	(35)	(0)
Minor	%	73·3	100
	n	(96)	(40)
BS-ing§			
Important	%	19·4	0·0
	n	(25)	(0)
Minor	%	80·6	100
	n	(104)	(40)
Work for change in the school§			
Important	%	17·6	2·5
	n	(23)	(1)
Minor	%	83·4	97·5
	n	(108)	(39)
Express frustrations regarding the school§			
Important	%	16·8	0·0
	n	(22)	(0)
Minor	%	83·2	100
	n	(100)	(40)

†The two responses "a major reason" and "a fairly important reason" were collapsed into the category "Important". "A minor reason" and "not a reason" were collapsed into the category "minor".
‡ Significant at the 0·05 level.
§ Significant at the 0·01 level.

TABLE 7

Perceptions of the conference environment. Respondents were asked "which of the following seems to you to be most similar to using the conference?"

	%	n
(1) Sitting in a lounge or lunchroom talking with people who wander in	23·9	(42)
(2) Conversations before and after class	11·9	(21)
(3) The meeting of a club	8·0	(14)
(4) Reading the student newsletter	7·4	(13)
(5) Reading professional literature (journals, etc.)	1·7	(3)
(6) Nothing else is really similar to the conference	32·4	(57)
— Missing data	8·5	(15)

the analogies they suggested. The responses to this question provided no grounds for asserting either that the experience of using a computer conference is unique among communication media or that it is very similar to other media. Table 7 summarizes the responses to the analogies.

4.2.3. Extent to which the conference provided unique interactions

The relationship between conferees' knowledge of one another inside and outside the conference environment is of interest because it sheds light on the ability of computer conferences to support extended exchanges between individuals who may have little contact otherwise.

As one measure of the extent to which the conference provided communication not occurring through other channels, three assertions were provided and respondents were asked to check all those with which they agreed. Nearly three fourths agreed with the statement: "The conference gives me a chance to interact with people I would not have much or any contact with otherwise". The statement "The conference gives me a chance to interact with people I would see anyway, but in ways that would not occur otherwise" was true for more than 40% of the respondents. Only 13·1% agreed with the statement: "The conference gives me a chance to interact with people I would see anyway, and our interaction is pretty much the same as it is away from the conference". There was no statistically significant difference between students and non-students, or between the 1987 and 1989 data. Table 8 displays the data.

As a second measure of the extent to which the conference provided interactions not otherwise occuring within the school, participants were asked to estimate how many of the people they knew through the conference they also knew personally. To the first question, "Of the people whose names are familiar to you from the conference, how many do you talk to in person frequently?" more than half replied "none or practically none". Fewer than 10% of the respondents talked to 50% or more of the familiar participants frequently. In response to a question asking how many of the participants whose names they were familiar with from the conference they would recognize by sight, nearly 50% indicated not more than 25%. Table 9 displays the responses to these items.

TABLE 8

Extent of unique interactions. Respondents were asked to indicate whether or not they agreed with the following statements

	Percentage of respondents agreeing
(1) The conference gives me a chance to interact with people I would not have much or any contact with otherwise.	72·7
(2) The conference gives me a chance to interact with people I would see anyway, but in ways that would not occur otherwise.	43·2
(3) The conference gives me a chance to interact with people I would see anyway, and our interaction is pretty much the same as it is away from the conference.	13·1
	$n = 173$

TABLE 9

Percentage of individuals whose names are familiar from the conference known personally by the participants

		None	Approx. 25%	Approx. 50%	Approx. 75%	All or almost all
Would recognize by sight	%	14·2	34·1	22·2	21·0	6·3
	n	(25)	(60)	(39)	(37)	(11)
Talk with occasionally	%	24·4	42·6	19·9	9·7	1·1
	n	(43)	(75)	(35)	(17)	(2)
Talk with frequently	%	52·3	36·9	6·8	1·1	0·0
	n	(92)	(65)	(12)	(2)	(0)

The number of familiar participants who would be recognized by sight was the only one of this bank of questions on which non-students differed significantly from students; as would be expected, since most of them were professionals not directly involved in the school, they generally knew fewer of the participants than did the students.

5. Discussion

Variety and vigor of communication are important to successful collaboration. The medium of speech allows and even encourages such variety because multiple messages are transmitted simultaneously, through words, facial expressions, intonation, and the ability to interrupt a thought with parenthetical remarks or a change in the direction of the conversation. If computer conferences are to be used in cooperative work, it is essential that they be sufficiently flexible to allow an acceptably full range of information exchange. A conference must permit exchange of single facts, complex opinions, subtle distinctions, and nuanced arguments.

Sustained cooperation also involves the establishment and maintenance of a group identity. More than a shared task is necessary; ease in interaction is also important.

Lack of inhibition in expressing ideas depends in part upon the communication medium's ability to include tension-relieving mechanisms such as humor and disclaimers. If personality can be conveyed and there is a social dimension to the group's communication, the ability to work together is enhanced.

Other researchers have found ratings of the social presence of computer-mediated communication to be only around the midpoints of the scales provided (Hiltz & Johnson, 1989; Vallee et al., 1978). Moderate social presence is probably inadequate for cooperative work of any complexity. However, this study indicates that a computer conference need not be fatally limited in its range of social nuance.

Content analysis indicated that users of this conference found it an appropriate and suitable medium for exchange on topics related to the students' professional education, and for humor and social interactions as well. In 1989, three years after the conference was instituted, the proportion of items originated on professional education topics and those originated for non-task topics was roughly two thirds to one third. Topics ranged from discussions of ethics to St. Patrick's Day parties. There was variety in the pattern of interactions as well, from single-entry items to items remaining active more than three months with well over 100 responses. The conference contained both narrowly focused exchanges and lengthy, complex discussions. Conference participants were able to change the direction of discussions, makes asides and engage in group maintenance behavior such as supportive statements and teasing.

Opposite category responses provided further evidence of conversational flexibility. Both items which originated with task and non-task entries received responses of the opposite type. Many of these responses were the kinds of parenthetical remarks which contribute to positive affect within a group; others were apparently intentional playful diversions. The presence of task-related responses in items originally not task-related in intent appears to reflect the group's immersion in professional education and concerns.

Extensive discussion of conference etiquette and social norms is outside the scope of this report, but there were numerous indications in the conference text that they did exist. There were examples of explanations of the tone intended, and of clarification when subsequent entries revealed that an entry had been misinterpreted. Explicit discussions of etiquette did occur within the conference occasionally; one example was triggered when a new participant entered a response with the caps lock key on. The next response pointed out that her entry was all in capital letters and asked her to toggle it off in the future, since in the conference, capitals were interpreted as shouting. (Electronic emphasis is generally indicated with *asterisks*.)

There was no indication of the type of hostility and social alienation that Siegal et al. (1986) found in their study of decision making via electronic mail and synchronous computer conferences. While the conversational behavior in this school-wide conference could indeed be described as "uninhibited", this took the form of playfulness and was positive rather than negative in affective tone.

Analysis of the content of the conference thus reveals both substantive discussion and group maintenance behaviors. The survey data reflect those dimensions as well. The primary reason given for using the conference indicated both a task-related and a social value, namely that it provided a sense of feeling in touch with the school.

Other major reasons were intellectual stimulation and the chance to discuss professional concerns.

Participants in the conference did not all know each other well outside the conference environment. Around half of the respondents to the survey indicated that they talked to practically none of the other participants frequently. The conference created new contacts between people and also provided different kinds of interactions with people already known to one another.

Norms and expectations govern, to a large extent, the way in which technology is integrated into an environment. The stated purposes of the conference were very broad, to allow students to learn to use the medium and to provide additional communication within the school. The conference therefore was not shaped by specific external expectations but was able to evolve in response to its own internal momentum; the increase in non-task entries and opposite category responses over the two-year period indicate that participants were discovering and putting to use the conversational flexibility of the medium. The findings here suggest that the elasticity of a communication medium is determined in part by the expectations of the users and their willingness to experiment. The conference analysed in this study proved to be a very supple medium, capable of supporting a wide range of topics and interaction patterns.

References

BALES, R. F. (1951). *Interaction Process Analysis: A Method for the Study of Small Groups*. Cambridge: Addison-Wesley.

CHESEBRO, J. W. (1985). Computer-mediated interpersonal communication. In B. D. RUBEN, Ed. *Information and Behavior*, vol. 1, 202–222. New Brunswick: Transaction Books.

HIEMSTRA, G. (1982). Teleconferencing, concern for face, and organizational culture. In M. BURGOON, Ed. *Communication Yearbook* **6**, pp. 874–904. Beverly Hills: Sage Communications.

HILTZ, S. R. & JOHNSON, K. (1989). Measuring acceptance of computer-mediated communication systems. *Journal of the American Society for Information Science*, **40**, 386–397.

KIESLER, S. & SPROULL, L. S. (1986). Response effects in the electronic survey. *Public Opinion Quarterly*, **50**, 402–413.

RICE, R. E. & LOVE, G. (1987). Electronic emotion: socio-emotional content in a computer-mediated communication network. *Communication Research*, **14**, 85–108.

SIEGEL, J., DUBROVSKY, V., KIESLER, S. & McGUIRE, T. W. (1986). Groups processes in computer-mediated communication. *Organizational Behavior and Human Decision Processes*, **37**, 157–187.

SPROULL, L. S. (1986). Using electronic mail for data collection in organizational research. *Academy of Management Journal*, **29**, 159–169.

SPROULL, L. & KIESLER, S. (1986). Reducing social context cues: electronic mail in organizational communication. *Management Science*, **32**, 1492–1512.

VALLEE, J. & JOHANSEN, R. (1974) *Group Communication Through Computers. Volume 2: A Study of Social Effects*. Menlo Park: Institute for the Future.

VALLEE, J., JOHANSEN, R., LIPINSKI, H., SPANGLER, K. & WILSON, T. (1978). *Group Communication Through Computers. Volume 4: Social, Managerial, and Economic Issues*. Menlo Park: Institute for the Future.

Part 4

Novel and innovative groupware technologies

10

Multidimensional audio window management

MICHAEL COHEN

LESTER F. LUDWIG

This paper proposes an organization of presentation and control that implements a flexible audio management system we call "audio windows". The result is a new user interface integrating an enhanced spatial sound presentation system, an audio emphasis system, and a gestural input recognition system. We have implemented these ideas in a modest prototype, also described, designed as an audio server appropriate for a teleconferencing system. Our system combines a gestural front end (currently based on a DataGlove, but whose concepts are appropriate for other devices as well) with an enhanced spatial sound system, a digital signal processing separation of multiple sound sources, augmented with "filtears", audio feedback cues that convey added information without distraction or loss of intelligibility. Our prototype employs a manual front end (requiring no keyboard or mouse) driving an auditory back end (requiring no CRT or visual display).

1. Introduction

This paper presents a virtual workspace that employs gestural control of multiple audio sources. We call such an organization of presentation and control "audio windows". Audio windows anticipate new dimensions in user interfaces, allowing the user to manage sound through a presentation system as easily and as richly as graphics are managed with a window-based workstation. This paper surveys the basic ideas underlying audio windowing, and describes our implementation of an enhanced spatial sound system with hand gesture recognition and feedback based on "filtears", audio feedback cues that convey added information without distraction or loss of intelligibility. We develop the conceptual framework of spatial sound, audio windows, and gestural input (section 2), survey telecommunications applications (section 3), and then describe the prototype of our system exploring some of these concepts: output/presentation (section 4), input/control (section 5), and architecture (section 6). We go on to discuss the problems and performance (section 7) of the system as we have crafted it. We frame our research in the context of past work (section 8) and describe some fertile lines of future research (section 9), concluding with a summary of the important ideas introduced by our investigations (section 10).

2. Conceptual background

2.1. SPATIAL SOUND

Spatial sound projects audio media into space by manipulating sound sources so that they assume virtual positions, mapping them from 1-space (the source channel) into 3-space (the perceptual envelope around the listener). These virtual positions allow auditory localization, a listener's separation in space of the channels, via space-domain multiplexing. By creating psychoacoustic effects with DSP (digital signal processing), scientists are developing ways of generating this 3D sound imagery (Chowning, 1977; Blauert, 1983; Kendall & Martens, 1984; Kendall, Martens, Freed, Ludwig & Karstens, 1986a, 1986b; Martens, 1987; Kendall & Freed, 1988; Wenzel, Wightman & Foster, 1988; Scott, 1989; Bernardini & Otto, 1989), sometimes called "sonic holography". Spatial sound takes theatre-in-the-round and turns it inside-out, embedding the listener in a landscape of sound.

Current audio systems project only a one-dimensional arrangement of the real or mixed sources. Our display research involves technology that allows sound sources to have not only a left–right attribute (as in a conventional stereo mix), but up–down and back–forth qualities as well. It is related, but goes beyond, systems like quadraphonics and Surround Sound.† Augmenting a sound system with a spatial attribute opens new dimensions for audio; spatial sound is a rich audio analog of three-dimensional graphics.

Part of listening to an admixture of conversation or music is being able to appreciate the overall blend while also being able to hear the individual voices or instruments separately. This synthesis/decomposition dual is the opposite effect of masking: instead of sounds hiding each other, they are complementary and individually perceivable. (For instance, musical instruments of contrasting color are used against each other.) Localization effects contribute to this anti-masking, by helping the listener distinguish separate sources, be they instruments in an ensemble or voices in the cacophony of a cocktail party (Cohen, 1987).

Mature spatial sound, made available through emerging technologies (Kendall & Martens, 1984; Wenzel, Wightman & Foster, 1988), promises a fertile source of new applications. Speech, music and other sound will affect spatial gestures as naturally as physical objects fill reality. Potential telecommunication and other applications of spatial sound are described elsewhere (including in Section 3 and Cohen, 1988). This section introduces a taxonomy of such applications.

Computer-aided exploitation of the use of audio may well cooperate and compete with computer-aided video. The idea of a placing sound in space leads to the idea of giving sound motion, so the positions of the listener and sound sources may be constantly changing as they move around each other and the room.‡ Issues of exactly who has permission to move the sources and sinks are discussed in section 9.4.

Table 1 organizes spatial sound applications according to a matrix of generator (source) and listener (sink) mobility, each quadrant of which is described by a following subsection. Since any spatial sound application can be augmented with full source and sink motion, these distinctions are fuzzy, but they are still useful for their characterization of modalities. The applications are characterized in terms of their distillations, the minimum functionality needed to realize them. Each quadrant of the table shows applications characteristic of the taxon combination, headed by a *perspective label*,§ and footed by a **descriptive metaphor**.

† Surround Sound 360 and THX are two commercial examples of theatrical audio systems, as Circle Vision 360 and Omnimax are examples of analogous visual systems.

‡ The difference between simple relative motion between a listener and source and movement by both in the context of a virtual room is the effect of room acoustics.

§ Words in text in italics denote perspectives; in roman, applications; and in bold, metaphors.

TABLE 1
Perspectives, applications and metaphors of audio window modes†

| | | Generators (sources) | |
		Stationary	Moving
Listeners (sinks)	Stationary	*Fixed perspective* Spotlight **Monaural radio**	*Egocentric perspective* Cursor Throwing voice/Bouncing sound **Theatre**
	Moving	*Orientation Perspective* Horizon Compass **Museum**	*Dancing perspective* Teleconferencing **Cocktail party**

† Words in italic denote perspectives; in roman applications; and in bold metaphors.

Stationary sources; stationary listener (*fixed perspective*: **monaural radio metaphor**): Degenerately simple spatial sound systems allow neither the sources nor the sinks to move. This kind of configuration is still useful for separating channels and, in fact, offers a good checkpoint to spatial sound applications under development; i.e. the several participants in a conference call would project distinct sound images to each other, consistent with their relative virtual (if static) locations. An unsophisticated demonstration of this functionality on a conventional system features three users, each with two phones, calling each other cyclically, as illustrated in Figure 1. By each user holding the calling and called handsets to different ears they demonstrate one application of stereotelephonics (Cohen, 1987), the use of stereo effects in telephones. One tool that might be useful in such a domain is an (*audio*) *spotlight* (described further in section 4.2.1), a way of highlighting a channel.

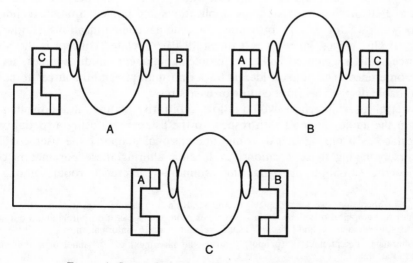

FIGURE 1. Stereotelephonics and three-way cyclic conferencing.

Stationary sources; moving listener (*orientation perspective*: **museum metaphor**): A system in which the sources are stationary, but the listeners move about (like visitors at a museum) would be useful for providing orientation. For instance: the sources might always come from North, serving as an audio compass, or they might always "point" down, acting like a (sonic) horizon; protégés might cluster at a mentor's ankles, disciples might swirl around masters.

Moving sources; stationary listener (*egocentric perspective*; **theatre metaphor**): An egocentric perspective (like that employed by our prototype, described in sections 4–6) allows the sources to move around a static listener, as if the user were attending a theatre performance or movie. Applications of this class might include the *audio cursor* (section 4.2.1), a pointer into 3-space to attract the static user's attention. Conferencing tools (such as InfoSound (Sonnenwald, Gopinath, Haberman, Keese & Myers, 1990) would allow users to throw their voices (Cohen, 1987), and musical applications may eventually feature bouncing and dancing sound, putting the band on the wagon.

Moving sources; moving listener (*dancing perspective*; **cocktail party metaphor**): A "dancing" perspective is a system in which the objects are simultaneously generators and listeners (simulating, for instance, circulation around a cocktail party) and requires full mobility for both sources and sinks. This class also describes a general spatial data management system, in which users can browse through a dataworld of moveable objects. Groupware applications (such as teleconferencing video windows (section 9.3) are perhaps the most obvious example, but more fanciful modes of dance or social intercourse are easily imagined. Like the children who followed the *Pied Piper,* or the characters who floated up to the ceiling in *Mary Poppins,* users might use the space to exhibit their mood—flights of fancy in a Disco Tech.

2.2. AUDIO WINDOWS

Audio windows are an implementation of a user interface ("front end") to an enhanced spatial sound system. The Integrated Media Architecture Laboratory (IMAL) at Bellcore has been studying applications and implementation techniques of audio windows for use in providing multimedia communications (Ludwig & Pincever, 1989; Ludwig, Pincever & Cohen, 1990). A related concept is the notion of a "perceptually segmented" mix of multiple simultaneous audio sources, such as in a teleconference. The general idea is to permit multiple audio sources to coexist in a modifiable display† without clutter or user stress.

A powerful user interface would allow arbitrarily setting and adjusting the position of the audio channels with respect to the listener. By using a spatial sound user interface as a mixing board, a multidimensional panpot,‡ the user could set parameters reflecting these positions. A listener altering these parameters could experience the sensation of wandering around a conference room, among the

---

† Throughout this paper, we use "display" in a general sense to denote presentation—output in any medium (not just graphical or video). In fact, since our prototype is based on purely audio output, we employ no visual media at all, and "display" usually refers to auditory information.

‡ A "panormanic potentiometer" (panpot) controls the placement of a channel in a conventional (left-right stereo) mix.

teleconferees. Members of the audience at a (live or recorded) concert could actively focus on a particular channel by sonically hovering over the shoulder of the respective musician in a virtual concert hall. Sound presented in this dynamically spatial fashion is as different from conventional mixes as sculpture is from painting.

As described in sections 4 to 6, we have implemented a subset of this interface. Our prototype is of the "moving source/stationary listener: *egocentric perspective* (**theatre metaphor**)" type, allowing a single user to arrange sources around his or herself with direct manipulation.

2.3. GESTURAL RECOGNITION

Our system is motivated (literally and figuratively) by gestures, i.e. spatial motions that convey information. We use gestural recognition as input to our spatial sound system, and so manipulate virtual sound sources in a full three-dimensional presentation. Our prototype front end is based on a DataGlove (described in section 6), but the notion of gestural recognition applies equally well to other input devices (section 9.1). By using a posture† characterizer to recognize intuitive hand signs along with full motion arm interpretation, we can gesturally indicate, select, highlight and relocate these sound sources, mapping the work envelope around the user into the (much larger) perceptual space.

3. Telecommunications and groupware applications

Audio windowing tools offer both immediate utility and vast long-term potential, and telecommunications is one of many possible application domains. The generally increasing bandwidth of the telephone network invites groupware applications that are made possible by enhanced spatial sound technology. The functions and applications of telephony, home entertainment and personal computing are converging. Emerging high-fidelity stereo telephone systems present compelling opportunities for integrated audio windowing systems. The next sections survey some of these potential applications. The sections are ordered inductively, each subsuming those before it.

3.1. ASYNCHRONOUS

Asynchronous applications could profitably employ audio window and enhanced spatial sound systems. Consensus styles of decision making lead itself to collective documents—sources layered with levels of annotation and comments. Electronic mail ("e-mail") and voice mail ("v-mail") encompass these multimedia documents, and invite spatial extensions, especially when there are several commentators or levels of emendation. Spatial metaphors will prove useful for structuring these comments. For example, forwarded voice mail could be augmented by having a commentary envelope localized separately from the substrate. Even dynamic effects would be desirable, as programmed auditory gestures could prove to be a significant rhetorical device, in the same way that voice projection is a significant oratory device.

---

† We have adopted the convention of calling the DataGlove's recognized static positions "postures", reserving the term "gestures" for the sequential composition of multiple postures.

3.2. SYNCHRONOUS

Imagine, for instance, the power of spatial sound technology to enhance conference calls: each participant would be arrayed in virtual 3-space, perhaps around a (virtual) conference table, projecting an aural image to the other conferees. Consistent with their relative virtual locations, the conversants will each have a unique audio location. Speaker identification, even among speakers with similar voices, would be subconscious and automatic, since a listener would have associated an aural position with each.

As an extension of the increasingly popular "gablines", teleconferencing invites introduction of a dynamic spatial notion, allowing participants to move around. One can imagine a vast telecommunity of physically remote users circulating about: temporarily joining conversations, then moving to other parts of the room or building, like conventioneers or minglers at a cocktail party—an electronic fête (hence the moniker *Partyline*) on a virtually unlimited scale (Cohen, 1988). If a caucus wanted to meet privately, its participants could adjourn to an adjacent private chamber. Visual icons could be displayed in a pattern corresponding to their owners' positions. (We envision that eventually the system might be augmented by a three-dimensional visual display, but the audio effects alone suffice to transcend conventional modes of static un- or uni-dimensional teleconferencing.)

Of course, musical expression will also benefit from spatial sound's ability to bring people together electronically. Musicians will be able to rehearse or perform together, using audio window technology as a sort of distributed mixing board.

3.3. TERMINAL AUDIO MANAGEMENT†

A user at a workstation may need to manage several audio sources in the course of participating in a conference or working on a multimedia document. Audio from various multimedia databases, editors, and message systems will have to be presented in an environment that also includes other application output and prompts along with collaborative teleconferences. A graphical interface might feature a map of the spatialized source virtual locations, and a mouse could be used to reposition sources, by dragging their respective icons, as the perceived source location dynamically tracks along. For sound-annotated documents, the voice-over should be localized to the same place as the corresponding visual window.

4. Output: presentation via spatializer and filtears

This research is concerned with the presentation of multiple simultaneous audio sources. Our system is designed to declutter the cacophony of a teleconference, by introducing axes of audio presentation along which the respective channels may be distributed. It forms the foundation for a user interface that perceptually separates the user utterances.

We are using spatial sound and *filtears*—signal processing that exploits psycho-acoustic effects to superimpose information on audio signals—as critical elements of the user interface.‡ The functionality of both spatial sound and filtears is described below (in sections 4.1 and 4.2, respectively). What makes them especially useful for

† This section is adapted from Ludwig *et al.* (1990), section 5.1.

‡ As we have implemented it, spatial sound could be considered a filtear. But since one imagines a purely mechanical (if contrived) implementation of spatial sound, we draw a (perhaps artificial) distinction.

the user interface is the fact that, unlike an audio zoom feature (Addeo, Gelman & Massa, 1987) that simply makes the chosen speaker louder, the extended attributes introduced by spatial sound and filtears are separate from conventional dimensions of control and they can be adjusted independently.

At a physical gathering with many simultaneous conversations, a mingler can follow any particular exchange by filtering according to continuity of speaker attributes: position, voice quality and subject (semantic) matter. This "cocktail party" effect (Blauert, 1983, p. 257) can be simulated in a teleconference by differentiating according to virtual position (via spatial sound) and ensuring that voice differences are preserved (via filtears). Of course the words being spoken cannot be controlled, but the way they are presented can be manipulated.

4.1. SPATIAL SOUND

We stimulate spatial hearing by assigning each source a virtual position with respect to each listener and simulating the positional cues. This requires dynamic selection of filter parameters presented to a convolution engine (Wenzel *et al.*, 1988), creating psychoacoustic localization effects by introducing stereo spatial cues into the original monaural speech. A Polhemus Isotrak (Polhemus, 1987) dynamically provides 3-space coordinates to a geometry-parameter calculation system employing a Transputer chip. The hardware-based convolution engine implements FIR (finite impulse response) audio digital filters whose output signals are presented to stereo headphones. The resulting system synthesizes a three-dimensional distribution of stationary or moving sound sources, whose acoustics reflect the user's head orientation at each moment.

4.2. FILTEARS

While the channels are "perceptually segmented" by virtual location, it is still useful to have other attribute cues, independent of direction and distance. We employ active audio filters to implement these orthogonal attribute cues. Our cues are related to earcons (Blattner, Sumikawa & Greenberg, 1989), audio messages used to provide feedback about computer entities. But unlike pure earcons, our cues are transforming, rather than transformed, hence their moniker *filtears*. The name was chosen for being onomatopoeic—pronounced self-descriptively. "Filtear" ('fil-tEr) is meant to sound as close to "filter" ('fil-tir) as possible without being indistinguishable. This is a useful property for filtears themselves—to be "just noticeable", right over the edge of perceptibility. We don't want to bury the source channels under mountains of effects. Filtears should be transparent unless the user is actively seeking them.

Filtears can be thought of as sonic typography: placing sound in space can be likened to putting written information on a page, with audio highlighting equivalent to italicizing or boldfacing. We want to be able to project, reverberate, embolden and italicize audio channels.

We have implemented three types of filtears: (1) spotlight; (2) muffle; and (3) accents, described in the following sections.

4.2.1. Telepointers: (audio) cursor and spotlight

Once audio channels are distributed in space, a user-controlled pointer within that space becomes useful. In visual domains, eyegaze selects the focus of attention;

there is no direct analog in audio domains since audition is more omnidirectional than vision. A method of focusing or directing auditory attention is needed to extend the paradigms of graphical indication into audio conferencing.

One could simply instantiate another independent sound source, an "audio cursor", to superimpose on the selected sources—for instance, a pure tone, steady or pulsed. But this has the disadvantage of further cluttering the auditor's space, especially if multiple cursor positions are allowed. In any case, this feature is available intrinsically: user-movable sources can be used as audio cursors "for free" (except for the loss of a channel). User-programmable sources could be the basis of the horizon or compass mentioned earlier (section 2.1). Like a mythical Siren, sound endowed with the ability to move about can also entice users to follow it. Such a "come-hither" beacon might be used to draw attention to a particular place or workstation window in the office, to "catch someone's ear".

We also explicitly implemented a perhaps a better solution: an *audio spotlight*, a highlighting of one or more channels. Highlighting might comprise any combination of the suite of effects used by audio exciters and aural enhancers: echos and reverberation, equalization, pitch shifting, amplitude-dependent harmonic empha- sis, and frequency-dependent phase shift. This highlighting can be likened to sonic italicization, an audio shimmering that draws attention to the emboldened source(s) without overpowering the others. However, a spotlight, unlike a cursor, can only highlight an active channel, and therefore is less useful as a general pointing device.

We use a spotlight to confirm selection of one or more channels, as a prelude to invoking some action (like amplification, muting or repositioning), or the selection can be an end unto itself, since the highlighting makes the selected object(s) more prominent. The idea is to create a "just noticeable difference", an acoustic enhancement that is both noticeable and ignorable, unambiguous but unintrusive.†

In practice, as the user sweeps his or her hand around the room, pointing at the localized sources, he or she gets confirmation of the direction by having the indicated source highlighted with a spotlight. This is analogous to title bar emboldening in the visual window domain. An audio spotlight is a way of specifying a subset of the channel mix for special consideration—a way of focusing auditorily, bringing a chosen channel out of background cacophony, and selecting it as the object of a subsequent operation.

4.2.2. Muffle

We use a *muffle* filtear to suggest the grabbing of a source. As the user grabs a channel, as a prelude to moving or accenting, its sound is muffled, imitating the effect of his or her hand closed around it. This aural confirmation of a gesture fulfills the user interface principle of compatibility (Sanders & McCormick, 1987, p. 54–57). The muffling effect is accomplished with a lowpass filter, since a covering hand tends to attenuate the high-frequency components of a sound source. Again, the filtear quality of just-noticeability is important in order to avoid loss of intelligibility‡ in the selected channel.

---

† Different users will probably prefer different styles and degrees of effects. An advanced system might employ configuration files for each user, containing tuned calibration and preference data.

‡ A filtear to mute the channels of boring or boorish speakers might be called a *muzzle*. Perhaps for this type of filtear, loss of intelligibility wouldn't be so bad.

4.2.3. Accents

Accents are a way of emphasizing audio channels, of endowing them with a perceptual prominence. Accents are like an ordered ladder of spotlight-like effects that can be associated with channels. Since they are linked to pointing direction, spotlights can't be locked on a source, but accents, which are closely related, may be. Unlike spotlights or muffles, accents persist beyond pointing or grabbing. We use them to impose a perceptual hierarchical organization on an emsemble of channels (Ludwig & Pincever, 1989). The feedback is implicit in the effect.

5. Input: control via gestural recognition (glove at first site)

Our system recognizes and obeys gestural commands from a DataGlove. The gestures (and their feedback filtears) include:†

- indicating/pointing (confirmed by audio spotlight)
- grasping (confirmed by muffle on) to enable
  —repositioning (tracked by moving source)
  —accenting (reflected by hierarchical enhancement)
- releasing (confirmed by muffle off)

Pointing at a source indicates it, as a prelude for selection by grasping. Grasping and releasing are delimiting duals, enabling and disabling both repositioning and accenting. Repositioning is grasping accompanied by movement. Accenting is grasping accompanied by a hierarchical specification, represented by extended fingers. Since repositioning and accenting are orthogonal, a grasped object may be simultaneously moved and accented.

These gestures are captured by a front end based on the DataGlove. We employ posture recognition, as parametrized with the VPL-supplied "gesture editor" (VPL, 1988), along with our own full arm interpretation. The display operators provide immediate feedback, confirming the various operations.

5.1. INDICATING/POINTING

In our prototype, indication direction is determined via LOS (line of sight): extrapolating from the user's head, along the visual line of gaze, past the outstretched hand to aim at sound targets. (Wrist orientation, which might be preferable eventually due to its economy of motion, was unreliably measured because of ambient electromagnetic noise.) The direction of the pointing is quantized to the object nearest to the suggested line; that is, the nearest source is selected by minimizing the angular (rather than absolute) distance from the source and the suggested semi-infinite line, i.e. selected by the criterion

$$\min_{i=1}^{|sources|} \cos^{-1}\left(\frac{source_i \cdot \overline{LOS}}{|source_i||LOS|}\right) \tag{1}$$

where $\overline{LOS} = \overline{hand} - \overline{head}$, and the source vectors are normalized with respect to (the user's) $\overline{head}$. As feedback to the user, an audio spotlight (described above in section 4.2.1) is cast upon the nearest source. The choice of the nearest source results implicitly in a postfix ("noun–verb" or "object–action") command syntax.

† Additionally, several other gestures were implemented as auxiliary (and filtear-less) commands, including: (1) calibrate; (2) help; and (3) stop.

5.2. GRASPING AND RELEASING

Sound objects may also be moved around perceptual space. The recognized gestures are tightly constrained to avoid spurious event generation. To disambiguate the gestures, we employ the notion of closure (Buxton, 1987, p. 372), a deliberate (muscular) tension that delimits the extent of the action. The tension of the grasping, a deliberate curling of the fingers, indicates a non-ambiguous gestural action, avoiding a subjective interpretation of the user's hand motion. Specifically, grasping signifies that the nearest (spotlighted) object is to be relocated and/or accented, and releasing disengages the action. (Relocating with the DataGlove can be likened to dragging with a mouse: grasping is like mouse button down, and releasing is like mouse button up.) To provide further feedback, when an object is grasped, its sound is slightly muffled (without loss of comprehensibility) to suggest the effects of the hand around it (as described in section 4.2.2).

5.2.1. Repositioning

A user repositions a source by grasping a channel and dragging it to a new location. This feature is important for mnemonic spatial data organization, since a user is most likely to know where something is if she put it there herself.

The Cartesian coordinates of the DataGlove are mapped into spherical coordinates to give the user an egocentric perspective. To avoid complications imposed by room geometry, the sound sources are constrained to move spherically: azimuth is adjusted horizontally circularly (as opposed to rectilinearly), elevation is adjusted vertically circularly, and distance is adjusted radially (with respect to the user). Azimuth and elevation track the user's hand, and distance (which maps to gain in this dry (no reverberation, see section 9.2) is adjusted proportionally to the radial distance difference between the onset and completion of the relocation, measured from the head to the hand.

$$azimuth = \tan^{-1}\left(\frac{hand_y - head_y}{hand_x - head_x}\right) - \frac{\pi}{2} \tag{2}$$

$$elevation = \tan^{-1}\left(\frac{hand_z - head_z}{\sqrt{(hand_x - head_x)^2 + (hand_y - head_y)^2}}\right) \tag{3}$$

$$distance\,^* = \frac{|\overline{hand(t_2)} - \overline{head(t_2)}|}{|\overline{hand(t_1)} - \overline{head(t_1)}|} \tag{4}$$

The position of the source is tracked continuously during repositioning. Audio panning is subsumed by spatial sound, and gain or volume is controled by closeness/distance effects. For example, if the user indicates an object, grabs it and pushes away, the object will recede. In effect, the reachable work envelope is magnified to span the auditory space, giving the user a projected telepresence from physical into perceptual space. The closer an object is to the user, the finer the proximal/distal adjustment. Since the azimuthal and elevational control and presentation spaces for a (DataGlove-manipulated) spatial sound domain are the same, their C/R (control/response) ratio $\equiv 1$. And with a variable radial C/R ratio, the near-field work envelope maps gracefully into the entire perceptual space, finessing the issues of scale.

5.2.2. Accenting

The user may specify a hierarchical accent level (described in section 4.2.3) for a selected object by grasping it and extending 1 (index), 2 (index and middle), or 3 (index, middle and ring) fingers. Sound objects are sonically highlighted by employing the audio enhancement techniques described in Ludwig and Pincever (1989). The enhancement is not one of proximity or loudness, but of conspicuousness, relative to the other, unaccented, sources.

6. Architecture

Figure 2 below illustrates the architecture of our system. Generally in the schematic, digital control data goes down the left, and analog audio signals go up the right.

We are exploring ways of exploiting emerging three-dimensional I/O devices (Cohen, Mann, Littlefield & Sloan, 1988). The user interface of our prototype uses

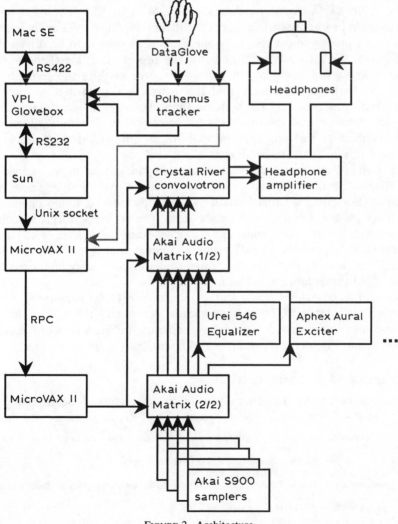

FIGURE 2. Architecture.

a DataGlove (VPL, 1987) which is coupled with a Polhemus 3-Space Isotrak (Polhemus, 1987). The DataGlove/Polhemus system senses the position and orientation of the wearer's hand† and the posture of the user's fingers.

Three-dimensional tracking products like the coupled Polhemus employ a physically stationary standing wave generator (electromagnetic or ultrasonic) and one or more movable sensors. The resulting systems provide 6 parameters in real-time (the $x/y/z$ of the sensor's physical location and roll/pitch/yaw of the sensor's orientation). Finger posture is calculated by measuring flex-induced leakage in fiber optics laid across the finger joints. With a device like a DataGlove, a user can point and gesticulate using a three-dimensional workspace envelope. In our system, the DataGlove postures and positions are strobed by a Sun, and integrated into gestures which are used to drive the output. A graphical display module could be interfaced across the same backbone architecture.

Sound sources (for simulation) are provided by four samplers (Akai Professional‡), synchronized by a MIDI daisy chain, and cued by a MIDI synthesizer. We use a digital patch matrix (Akai Digital§), driven via an RPC-invoked (remote procedure call) server, to switch in the filtears. Since the number of channels in our prototype is fixed, only one channel at a time can be driven through the spotlight or the muffle filtears, and (for the prototype at least) the effects are mutually exclusive (i.e. grabbing an indicated source disables the spotlight as the muffle is enabled), we effectively fold the matrix and regard it as two logical matrices. The front end of our system, then, becomes a scheduler, (literally) handling the dynamic reallocation of the filtear resources. The *spotlight* and *muffle filtears* (described above) are implemented by an aural exciter (Aphex¶) and a lowpass filter (Urei, 1980), respectively.

The back end of our prototype is an enhanced spatial sound system based on the Crystal River Convolvotron, an (IBM AT-based) convolution engine (Wenzel, Wightman & Foster, 1988) that spatializes sound by filtering audio channels with transfer functions that simulate positional effects. The device performs a mathematical convolution or arbitrary (non-sine) signals, such as voices, with the filter coefficients that "place" the signals within the perceptual 3-space of the user. By using the DataGlove to drive the Convolvotron, we can manipulate virtual sound sources in a full three-dimensional auditory display.

The control (DataGlove box) and presentation (Convovolvotron) processes communicate via internet (UDP) Unix‖ sockets across an Ethernet.†† The distributed architecture was designed to modularly separate the client (gestural recognition data model) from the server (spatializer and filtear).

7. Problems and performance

This project demonstrates the general possibilities of gesture recognition and spatial sound in a multi-channel conferencing system. The technology employed, however,

---

† Since the DataGlove is a fully three dimensional input device, it is sometimes likened to a bat, a flying mouse.
‡ S900 Midi Digital Sampler Operators Manual. Fort Worth, Texas.
§ DP 32000 Audio Digital Matrix Patch Bay. Fort Worth, Texas.
¶ Aphex Systems LTD. Aural Exciter Type C Model 103A Operating Guide. North Hollywood, California.
‖ Unix is a trademark of AT&T Bell laboratories.
†† Ethernet is a trademark of Xerox.

is perhaps better suited for a concept demonstration than for general deployment. It is expensive and slightly unwieldy: the glove itself does not interfere with other tasks (including writing and typing), but the cables are cumbersome. Further, ambient electromagnetic noise, reflected by metal surfaces in our lab environment, make reliable operation of the Polhemus tracker difficult beyond a short range and measurement of orientation, impossible. Elevation data is obscured by vertical Polhemus noise, making a two-dimensional auditory display more practical.

The response of the system is somewhat restricted by the speed of our processors and the high bandwidth requirements, forcing the user to be deliberate in manipulating sound objects. The system is tuned using a choke, a parameter specifying how many postural events to coalesce before transmission. Averaging, debouncing, and hysteresis (to clean up noisy data) are adjusted to match the environment.

There are two user-specific sets of data which should be individually calibrated for each user: the ear maps, modeling the HRTFs of the user, and the posture characteristics, calibrating the various hand positions. In practice, without individually tailored HRTFs, the ear maps are not very precise, and a visual display is useful for confirmation of source placement. (In a commercial deployment, each user might have a characteristic profile initialize their calibration tables.)

8. Related work

This project incorporates elements of numerous (proposed and/or implemented) multimedia systems, including Cohen (1987), Ludwig and Pincever (1989), Ludwig *et al.* (1990). It is related to various experiments involving mapping gesture to sound or music, including Cohen *et al.* (1988). It also recalls the *Put That There* (Bolt, 1984) system, with several major differences: (1) The objects are virtual sound sources, rather than visual icons; (2) The domain is three-dimensional auditory space instead of a 2D screen; and (3) We rely purely on gestural input, rather than using voice input. The auditory interfaces crafted by InfoSound (Sonnenwald *et al.*, 1990) are also related to filtears, although they were developed independently.

9. Future work

We hope to incorporate our work into a "real" application to do usability testing and to demonstrate general utility. We are ready to implement a few extensions, and have identified some longer-term research goals:

- porting our gesture recognition to a non-DataGlove device (like a mouse, joystick or trackball);
- incorporating reverberation;
- integrating our prototype with the IMAL teleconferencing system;
- exploring scalability issues and applicable floor control protocols;
- feeding back headtracker data for pointing calibration.

A survey of the scope of these extensions and research goals follows.

9.1. OTHER INPUT MEDIA

The ideas explored in this research apply not only to DataGlove-driven systems, but also to more conventional input modalities. Virtual sources can be indicated, selected, and repositioned with less exotic devices. Economic reasons encourage the development of inexpensive alternatives to the DataGlove for recognizing gestural enhanced spatial sound operations. The standard pointing device in a window/icon/menu/pointing device (WIMP) system is a mouse. A mouse, trackball (a mouse on its back), or joystick would suffice for positioning objects in 2-space.† As long as visual tokens for the teleconferees are accessible through the workstation, they can be manipulated through the operations described above. For example, a mouse-based system might find analogs to indicating/highlighting/relocating in pointing/clicking/dragging. A speaker might be singled out for special attention by clicking on their picture, which would throw a spotlight on their voice.

9.2. REVERBERATION

We plan to incorporate reverberation by generating an early reflection (echo) off the floor, spatialized to the same direction as the incident source. By varying the ratio of direct to indirect sound (Kendall & Martens, 1984), we expect to strengthen distance cues. This is a first step to strengthening our acoustic room model.

9.3. IMAL CONFERENCING

Exploiting the generality and intuitiveness of hand gestures to control the three-dimensional sonic imagery, this auditory display capability could be integrated with the IMAL conferencing system, into a full multimedia windowing network (Ludwig & Pincever, 1989).

One approach establishes a coupling between the video windows on the CRT and the virtual positions of the audio sources. The 2×2 video mosaic used in the current IMAL conference bridge can be thought of as a birds-eye‡ view of a planar arrangement of the participants. Then, if the workstation is directly in front of the user, the voice of the teleconversant in the top right of the mosaic will come from the right front (at an azimuth of $-45°$§) of the user's office, the bottom left of the mosaic will map to the left rear (135°), and so on. Alternatively, a vertically aligned plane, perhaps with exaggerated geometry, could be used to display a side projection.

Such a prototype might incorporate both a mouse- and a DataGlove-based interface, the better to compare the modalities. If the video windows used in the mosaic could be decoupled and moved around separately, they could be dynamic icons, positional representations of the positions of the instantiated audio sources. The mouse-based system would work as described above, with teleconferees iconified by full-motion or static video images (preferably some icon that moves when the respective user is talking) which can be selected, manipulated and repositioned by the workstation user.

---

† One can imagine direct control of position (with for example a mouse, trackball or DataGlove, say), steering control (with a return-to-center joystick, perhaps), or programmed control (automatic circulation).

‡ Azimuth discrimination is easier than elevation discrimination (Wenzel, Wightman and Foster, 1988). Just as our eyes have more range horizontally than vertically since they are positioned left-right (hence landscape-shaped movie and TV screens, instead of portrait-shaped), our ears are more attuned to angular than vertical cues.

§ Directly in front of the subject, the azimuth is 0°, increasing counter-clockwise.

9.4. FLOOR CONTROL

Floor control is a protocol for negotiating control of a (time domain multiplexed) multicast channel, i.e. the conventions for sharing auditory space. Since our prototype is for a single user, we avoided floor control issues, like having to choose between shared and private data models. One area ripe for exploration is the impact of dynamically repositioned sound sources on multiuser floor control (Cohen, 1987). Aweighing the anchors of rigid displays permits teleconferees to (virtually) circulate, throwing their voice to anywhere in the perceptual space. For instance, a speaker might want to wander among the other conference participants, mingling in and out of sub-conversations. Or a user might want a voice to emanate from a particular place to call attention to a window. A useful metaphor would have each user controlling (at least) the position of their own voice with respect to all the other users, circulating around a virtual conference room, or diving into dataspace to sit inside a workstation (for example, behind some display of interest). Cohen (1988) explores some extensions of private position models with potential for dynamic conferencing and control contention.

One model that might be useful for large-scale conferences is a two-tiered system, representing a panel and an audience. The panel functions as an inner coterie who moderate their conversation with normal anarchy social voice protocol (i.e. multiple access/collision detect with discretionary back-off conventions), and the audience is an outer group of muted (voiceless) listeners. To gain entrance to the inner group, members of the outer set might appeal from "off to the side", i.e. in some alternate audio space.

9.5. INDICATION DIRECTION CALIBRATION FROM HEAD TRACKER DATA

An important effect in stereophonic localization is the ability to "triangulate" the position of a sound source by moving one's head back and forth. Since the virtual sources don't actually exist but are simulated by two channels of audio, the simulated system must be aware of the position of the listener's head in order to faithfully emulate the desired sound image.

One way to detect this position is to use a headtracker (Thurlow & Runge, 1967; Wenzel et al., 1988; Martens, 1989), a sensor attached to the user's head [perhaps as part of an (audio) headset or a head-mounted (visual) display, Foley (1987), Pollack (1989)]. The orientation data selects a (stereo) pair of finite impulse responses, which are used to filter the sound sources. Counter-intuitively, once the stimulus/response behavior of localization effects are charted, virtual sources could be localized with more accuracy than real ones, assuming the convolution engine employs idealized HRTFs (head-related transfer functions).

But the data from the head tracker could be used in another way, to calibrate the indication direction. Recall that we employ a LOS (line of sight) method of selection, extrapolating from the user's head past his outstretched hand. Currently we employ an initialization phase, in which the user identifies the position of his eye by raising their DataGloved hand to it. If we could feedback the positional data (as opposed to the orientation data) from the headtracker, this calibration phase would be unnecessary.

10. Conclusion

Our prototype demonstrates the potential of audio windows as a way of decluttering acoustic space, and the recognition of gestures as a natural front end to such a system. The models we have been exploring give users a telepresence into metaphorical space. Our system exploits our innate localization abilities, our perception of spatial attributes, and our intuitive notions of how to select and manipulate objects distributed in space. Everything in our system is manifest, and objects and actions can be understood purely in terms of their effect on the display. Some of the features we have implemented find close approximation in visual or physical media; others elude analogy. But since we rely on perceptual rather than symbolic processing, our system requires minimal instructions or training.

An important characteristic of our prototype is that its input is gestural (requiring no keyboard or mouse) and its output is auditory (requiring no CRT or visual display); it can be used by blind people as well as by sighted. We were able to achieve this purity by employing filtears, active audio filters that can flag voices in a "just-noticeable" way (perceivable if the user is receptive, and otherwise ignorable). Filtears exploit, extend, and enhance the audio bandwidth.

Audio windowing for teleconferencing is like sonic cubism: it presents several audio perspectives on an assembled conference simultaneously. When one gives sound a physical manifestation, it can become an icon for anything imaginable. By networking users into a shared virtual environment, we can allow spatially multidimensional communications. Encouraging users to interactively position themselves with respect to others will enhance their perception of where they are. With such an audio windowing system, speaker identification is automatic, and orientation is felt, rather than understood.

As more and more audio and multi-media messages and sessions are sent and logged, the testimony of voice will come to rival that of writing. Our prototype provides a testbed for exploring the immediate potential of the emerging technology's application to teleconferencing and for researching the relevant human factors issues.

This project would not have been possible without the help of the Bellcore IMAL group. Sarah Martin and Laura Pate helped with the switching matrix. Natalio Pincever implemented the accent effects. Sherri Hiller, Kai Kwok, Ron Plummer, and Ying Wu provided general assistance.

Thanks also to Toni Cohen, Diane Sonnenwald, and anonymous referees for their comments on drafts of this paper. Ed Frankenberry, of BBN, offered technical advice. Phil Stone, of NASA/Ames, provided much of the Convolvotron interface code. Scott Foster, of Crystal River Engineering, developed the idea of using a convolution engine to produce spatial sound using empirically measured impulse response catalogs, and provided the Convolvotron and its software.

References

ADDEO, E. J., GELMAN, A. D. & MASSA, V. F. (1987). *An Experimental Multi-Media Bridging System*. Technical Memorandum, Bell Communications Research.
BLAUERT, J. (1983). *Spatial Hearing: The Psychophysics of Human Sound Localization*. Cambridge, MA: MIT Press.

BERNARDINI, N. & OTTO, P. (1989). TRAILS: An Interactive System for Sound Location. In *Proceedings of the International Computer Music Conference*, pp. 29–33. San Francisco, CA: Computer Music Association.

BOLT, R. A. (1984). *The Human Interface*. Lifetime Learning Publications (Van Nostrand-Rinehold).

BLATTNER, M. M., SUMIKAWA, D. A. & GREENBERG, R. M. (1989). Earcons and icons: their structure and common design principles. In *Human–Computer Interaction*, **4**, 11–44, L–540.

BUXTON, W. (1987). There's more to interaction than meets the eye: some issues in manual input. In R. M. Baecker & W. A. S. Buxton, Eds. *Readings in Human–Computer Interaction: A Multidisciplinary Approach*, pp. 357–392. Los Altos, CA: Morgan Kaufmann.

CHOWNING, J. M. (1977). The simulation of moving sound sources. *Computer Music Journal*, **1**, 48–52.

COHEN, M., MANN, S., LITTLEFIELD, R. & SLOAN, K. (1988). *3D I/O*, Technical Report 88-06-01. Seattle, WA: University of Washington, Department of Computer Science.

COHEN, M. (1987). *Stereotelephonics*, Internal Memorandum IM-000-21460-87-04, Bell Communications Research.

COHEN, M. (1988). *Holoistics*. Winning Paper, Honeywell Futurist Competition.

COHEN, M. (1989). *Multidimensional Audio Window Management*, Technical Memorandum TM-NPL-015362, Bell Communications Research.

FOLEY, J. D. (1987). Interfaces for Advanced Computing. *Scientific American*, **257**, 126–135.

KENDALL, G. S. & FREED, D. J. (1988). *Scientific Visualization by Ear*, Technical report. Evanston, IL: Northwestern Computer Music, Northwestern University.

KENDALL, G. S. & MARTENS, W. L. (1984). Simulating the cues of spatial hearing in natural environments. In *Proceedings of the International Computer Music Conference*. Computer Music Association.

KENDALL, G. S., MARTENS, W. L., FREED, D. J., LUDWIG, M. D. & KARSTENS, R. W. (1986a). Spatial processing software at Northwestern Computer Music. In *Proceedings of the International Computer Music Conference*, pp. 285–292. San Francisco, CA: Computer Music Association.

KENDALL, G. S., MARTENS, W. L., FREED, D. J., LUDWIG, M. D. & KARSTENS, R. W. (1986b). Image model reverberation from recirculating delays. In *Proceedings of 81st Convention of the Audio Engineering Society*. New York: Audio Engineering Society.

LUDWIG, L. F. & PINCEVER, N. C. (1989). *Audio Windowing and Methods for its Realization*, Technical Memorandum TM-NPL-015361, Bell Communications Research.

LUDWIG, L. F., PINCEVER, N. C. & COHEN, M. (1990). *Extending the Notion of a Window System to Audio. IEEE Computer (Special Issue on Voice in Computing)*, **23**, (8).

MARTENS, W. L. (1987). Principal components analysis and resynthesis of spectral cues to perceived direction. In *Proceedings of the International Computer Music Conference*.

MARTENS, W. (1989). Spatial image formation in binocular vision and binaural hearing. In *Proceedings of 3D Media Technology Conference*.

POLHEMUS NAVIGATION SCIENCE DIVISION (1987). *3SPACE ISOTRAK™ User's Manual*. Colchester, VT: McDonnell Douglas Electronic Company.

POLLACK, A. (1989). What is artificial reality? wear a computer and see. *The New York Times*, CXXXVIII **138**, (47,836), 1,27.

SANDERS, M. S. & McCORMICK, E. J. (1987). *Human Factors in Engineering and Design*, 6th edit. New York: McGraw-Hill.

SCOTT, D. (1989). A processor for locating stationary and moving sound sources in a simulated acoustical environment. In *Proceedings of the International Computer Music Conference*, pp. 277–280, San Francisco, CA: Computer Music Association.

SONNENWALD, D. H., GOPINATH, B., HABERMAN, G. O., KEESE III, W. M. & MYERS, J. S. (1990). InfoSound: an audio aid to program comprehension. In *Proceedings of the Hawaii International Conference on System Sciences*.

THURLOW, W. R. & RUNGE, P. S. (1967). Effect of induced head movements on localization of direction of sounds. *Journal of the Acoustic Society of America*, **42**, 480–488.

UREI (United Recording Electronics Industries) (1980). *Dual Parametric Equalizer Model 546 Operating Instructions*, 1980. Sun Valley, C.A.

VPL (Visual Programming Language) *DataGlove Model 2 Operating Manual*. Redwood City, CA: Research, Inc.

VPL (Visual Programming Language) (1987). *DataGlove Model 2 Test and Calibration Software Operating Manual*. Redwood City, CA: Research, Inc.

VPL (Visual Programming Language) (1988). *DataGlove Model 2 Gesture Editor Software, Version 1.69*. Redwood City, CA: Research, Inc.

WENZEL, E. M., WIGHTMAN, F. L. & FOSTER, S. H. (1988). A virtual display system for conveying three-dimensional acoustic information. In *Human Factors Society—32nd Annual Meeting*, pp. 86–90.

11

Liveware: a new approach to sharing data in social networks

IAN H. WITTEN

HAROLD W. THIMBLEBY

GEORGE COULOURIS

SAUL GREENBERG

While most schemes that support information sharing on computers rely on formal protocols, in practice much cooperative work takes place using informal means of communication, even chance encounters. This paper proposes a new method of enabling information sharing in loosely-coupled socially-organized systems, typically involving personal rather than institutional computers and lacking the network infrastructure that is generally taken for granted in distributed computing. It is based on the idea of arranging for information transmission to take place as an unobtrusive side-effect of interpersonal communication. Update conflicts are avoided by an information ownership scheme. Under mild assumptions, we show how the distributed database satisfies the property of *observational consistency*.

The new idea, called "Liveware", is not so much a specific piece of technology as a fresh perspective on information sharing that stimulates new ways of solving old problems. Being general, it transcends particular distribution technologies. A prototype database, implemented in HyperCard and taking the form of an electronic directory, utilizes the medium of floppy disk to spread information in a (benign!) virus-like manner.

1. Introduction

The information communication needs of individual computer users are frequently quite different from the large, highly-structured, shared databases that have been developed for corporate applications. Moreover, although many individuals now operate personal computers whose power rivals that of mainframes, they lack the infrastructure of support that accompanies larger computer installations.

Informal communication of non-critical information is vitally important for many information workers (Kraut, Egido & Galegher, 1988). The present paper asks how such information can best be communicated in an environment devoid of organized network support, at low cost, and with little effort for the user. We introduce an information distribution concept, called "Liveware", that is not so much a specific piece of technology as a fresh perspective on information sharing. Liveware stimulates new ways of solving old problems.

Here are three information sharing problems that are inadequately addressed by existing software and distribution mechanisms.

Problem 1: At the Apple kiosk of the human–computer interaction conference CHI'89, 1800 attendees had the opportunity to have their digital picture taken and enter information about themselves—interests, address, e-mail, etc. The database was to be distributed on CD-ROM one year later. Although interesting, the database is of limited value because no mechanism for correcting, updating or adding entries is possible due to the read-only nature of the medium. Much of the information will clearly become stale very quickly. But suppose the storage medium was writeable. The problem of tracking changes in individuals' information would be formidable. It is hard to see how any mechanism other than a sizeable central administration could permit such updates, and this would introduce such delays and overheads that people would probably not bother to contribute.

Problem 2: Consider the plight of those who have identical personal computers at both home and work. While trivial conceptually, the problem of keeping both filestores consistent is in practice horrendous. The common solution is to carry a floppy disk to and fro and transfer files manually. This poses a tremendous cognitive burden. If a disk or a file gets forgotten, the two filestores diverge. Problems escalate as the number of machines grows beyond two, or the number of people involved grows beyond one!

Problem 3: Recently a freeware Apple HyperCard document by Jakob Nielsen has been widely circulated. This interesting hypertext, described by Nielsen (1990), incorporates a number of attractive and unusual features. It records each person's track through the database in the form of a "history list", and users are requested to mail a copy of their disk to Nielsen when they have finished browsing, for analysis of usage patterns. But how many actually do? It would be better if the distribution mechanism retained old histories when the disk was passed on, to maximize the information gained on the rare occasions when a disk is actually returned. However, the history list is personal information, which raises the question of how to impose a degree of information security in a distributed environment.

These three scenarios illustrate different information distribution requirements. The first involves sharing personal information within a community, and necessitates distributed update. The second concerns the communication of information between machines controlled by one person. In the third, information is transmitted from the community to a particular individual.

This paper describes a technique that allows cooperation to take place in loosely-coupled socially-organized systems involving personal rather than institutional computers. The idea is technically very straightforward and involves a mixture of social convention and software support. It can solve diverse problems of information sharing, including those above, for which conventional techniques of data distribution would be extremely cumbersome to administer. Despite its simplicity, Liveware does not yet seem to have been put into practice. We describe a specific example of a Liveware system for an application very similar to Problem 1 above, though on a smaller scale. Sufficient implementation detail is included for the work to be replicated.

2. The idea of Liveware

The idea of Liveware is to arrange for information transmission to occur as a side-effect of interpersonal communication. It is designed for a communication environment, where connections are like chance meetings or casual encounters: they do not occur regularly and, when they do, maximum advantage must be taken of the opportunity to exchange information. This contrasts sharply with other protocols for computer communication, which are invariably predicated on the assumption that—except in cases of breakdown—information can be transmitted whenever the system finds a need to do so, an assumption which requires a permanent communications infrastructure.

2.1. DESIGN PRINCIPLES

Liveware was designed around three principles:

(1) *Symmetry:* exchange of information should always be two-way;
(2) *Transitivity:* users should act as carriers of other users' information; and
(3) *Transparency:* communication for information exchange purposes should be as unobtrusive as possible, and require negligible personal effort.

The first principle helps to ensure that maximum advantage is taken of every communication opportunity. When information is distributed in a conventional system, it is copied from source to receiver and no communication takes place in the reverse direction, except perhaps acknowledgements dictated by the protocol used. However, when connections are rare it makes sense to maximize the flow of information by transmitting information both ways. Both parties partially update each other's database, since in general each will have something to offer the other. This has the side-effect of simplifying the user's conceptual model of communication. It becomes symmetric: each party brings itself up-to-date whenever possible, and after an interchange both are in the same state.

The second principle is also intended to increase overall information flow. When communication opportunities are rare and fortuitous, it may be that the only way two parties can exchange information is through a chain of intermediaries. Interpersonal communication often takes advantage of this, although human fallibility makes it somewhat unreliable. Computer media are well suited to indirect communication because they can store information indefinitely and recall it accurately—information transfer is a transitive operation.

The third principle is intended to ensure that use is made of every available communication opportunity, in keeping with Kraut *et al.*'s (1988) requirements for successful casual interaction. It is most important that users are not tempted to turn off communication because it interferes with their own priorities. Although they may have nothing immediate to gain from the interchange, the quality of the information sharing service as a whole is maximized if every available opportunity is used. This indicates that use of the Liveware system should be as transparent as possible. The implications of these three principles are explored below.

2.2. MANAGING DISTRIBUTED INFORMATION

The information in a Liveware database is created and modified in a distributed fashion, at different sites and at different times. When two databases meet, a symmetric update is performed to bring both to the same state. This merge operation, which forms the core of any Liveware system, should (whenever possible) be accomplished automatically to minimize intrusion.

To ensure that update conflicts can be resolved automatically, databases are split into units of information, each of which has a unique identification code, a single owner who alone can alter it, and a time stamp. Given this information, the minimal set of updates that are required to bring two databases to the same, updated state can easily be determined.

The way that Liveware works means that information ownership must apply regardless of whether the information is personal or not. Precisely one person must be responsible for each unit of information; that person is charged with ensuring that any update supersedes all previous versions. This is the only way—apart from manual intervention in the merging process—to circumvent the multiple-update problem where one update is overwritten by a different one made at a different place. Owners may make updates anywhere, to any version of the database, so long as they intend only the last change made to survive—for that will eventually replace all alterations made elsewhere. No locking of information is necessary (for owners can only be in one place at a time).

Some applications must disobey this information ownership rule and allow information to be updated by more than one person. For example, an address list may be shared by a group of users, and any address may be updated by any member. In this case the Liveware mechanism must flag duplicate entries during the merge operation and allow the user to decide how to treat them. Here the merging process supports a useful degree of data validation; if two or more users take responsibility for entering critical new information, any discrepancies are identified when their versions are merged.

In any case, additional access control rules might be desirable, depending on the situation. For example, in Problem 3 above where usage information is to be transmitted to the originator of a hypertext, read permission should be restricted to the information creator and the originator.

Liveware applications may permit new information owners to join in and contribute information anywhere, at any time. In this case it is necessary that owners are known publicly by their names to avoid subsequent ownership conflicts. It is insufficient merely to check that a new registrant's name is not duplicated in the database, for two people of the same name may register at different places and the problem is only detectable during merging, when the two versions meet. Hence full names, possibly supplemented to ensure uniqueness, should be used instead of abbreviated "computer style" log-in names.

2.3. THE COMMUNICATION ENVIRONMENT

We have so far deliberately avoided discussing the communication environment, because the idea of Liveware transcends any particular distribution technology. In our present implementations, the distribution device is a floppy disk. Users carry a disk containing their version of the database with them wherever they go. One user might visit another and plug in his disk, causing bidirectional information sharing; on returning to his own site he will insert the disk once again to update his personal computer. Ideally information transfer would not involve the user at all, but take place as an immediate side effect of the disk being inserted into the drive. A group of users might meet and swap disks, or users might correspond by mail in an individual and uncoordinated fashion. Effective distribution relies on a rich interconnection structure where interchange occurs frequently, but it does not assume any particular organization. If people realize that their information is getting out of date, they will naturally make a special effort to communicate with others who are likely to be better connected. Social mechanisms will tend to ensure that information gets distributed as widely and as quickly as the need dictates, as they do conventionally in gossip circles and grapevines.

Of course, personal computer users exchange floppies at present. Unfortunately, manual procedures for updating files from floppy disks are notoriously unreliable. The difference with Liveware is that updates are performed entirely automatically, based on the timestamps associated with information units.

Liveware is in some respects like a virus, an observation that evokes both fascination and horror (Witten & Thimbleby, 1990). Indeed, the success and rapidity that has been observed in the spread of computer viruses—and the extreme difficulty of *avoiding* infection—provide a testament to the power of social networks to support information distribution. However, while Liveware systems strive to minimize any disruption caused by the fact that communication occurs, no attempt is made to conceal the fact that it occurs. Their use is discretionary: they only infect volunteers who want to share information.

Manual exchange of disks is by no means the only possible distribution mechanism. Others could be equally effective, or more so, depending on the means of communication available. Indeed, any way that can be used to spread viruses can be used to spread Liveware. For example, distribution could be piggybacked on e-mail or bulletin boards—the Liveware mechanism automatically determines minimal updates, so the bandwidth consumed need not be excessive. Or whenever a user connects to a distant host for remote login or file transfer, a mechanism could be invoked to see if advantage might be taken of that connection to update Liveware databases unobtrusively.

2.4. OBSERVATIONAL *VS* GLOBAL CONSISTENCY

A shared database must be sufficiently timely to remain relevant for shared work. If users do not communicate their information with others, the database will inevitably get out of date and different versions of it will disagree. If you really need guaranteed consistency, you must pay for the infrastructure it requires. For many purposes people will be prepared to trade currency off against cost—particularly the ongoing administrative and communications cost associated with conventional distributed databases. Liveware is still considerably better than a paper file or card index; the fact that paper has severe problems—and none of the advantages of automatic updating—has never stopped people from using it effectively. Liveware is certainly good enough for many applications: it does a far better job than conventional media, and at a far lower cost than conventional computer solutions.

Liveware enjoys the property of *observational consistency*. So long as users carry their information around with them, they cannot observe inconsistency in the database. This property holds when no one travels faster than their information, as certainly happens if they are using e-mail or carrying it in their pocket on a floppy disk. As soon as a user encounters an inconsistent database, Liveware sorts it out before he can use it. Although one may *believe* the database to be inconsistent, one can never *observe* it.

Observational consistency can also constitute a limited security measure. Consider automated teller machines (ATMs) that place cash withdrawal limits on their customers. During periods of heavy load (e.g. over lunch time) these machines run in batch mode. On the assumption that a customer can only be in one place at a time and that the time to get from one machine to another exceeds the period that the machine is in batch mode, customers cannot overdraw their limit. They cannot tell if the system is batch (like Liveware) or real time (fully distributed). Of course, criminals copy cash-cards, and organized groups can masquerade as a single customer in many different places and withdraw many times the cash limit.

Whether Liveware is any good for a particular purpose depends on whether or not observational consistency is adequate for that purpose. In many information sharing situations, real global, moment-to-moment consistency is either unnecessary, or a luxury that will not be missed. Besides, on those occasions when consistency is required, a group of Liveware users could easily arrange for a disk to be passed around the group twice—the first pass collecting the information, the second distributing it. This procedure guarantees total consistency so long as updates do not occur while it is taking place (though often it will be overkill).

In general, global as opposed to observational consistency is only required when a group of people are working on a single object that is visible to the world at large, for example, a monolithic report. Observational consistency is always sufficient when users are working collaboratively but "doing their own thing"—as when members of a group are assigned their own tasks and it is not important whether other members observe them performing those tasks straight away.

3. Example: an electronic directory

Consider Problem 1 from the Introduction, namely to establish a database that records information about each member of an interest group. In fact our example concerns the community of human-computer interface researchers in Scotland; the purpose of the database is to facilitate cooperation by ensuring that at least people will know what others are doing, and how to get in touch with them. Setting up a conventional database would require identifying the members of the group, soliciting information from them all, encouraging them to respond, collecting data, collating and distributing it.

Some of the clerical work could be avoided by circulating a questionnaire on disk and encouraging interested people to pass it on to colleagues, returning completed forms for central, automated collation. Furthermore, if collation can really be automated, it can take place at any site, not just centrally—this is the idea of Liveware.

A Liveware database can act as both questionnaire and information directory. People fill it out and pass it to others who may be interested. As it spreads it accumulates useful information from everyone who contributes. When run on a machine that already has a copy, the databases merge and update each other as appropriate. The need to return disks is eliminated, for collation is automatic. It is not even necessary to identify the target group in advance, for people can pass the system to their colleagues and anybody can join in. Updates can be done anywhere, at any time, and will percolate throughout the community. This scheme has been implemented as a HyperCard stack.†

3.1. THE DATABASE

Viewed as an ordinary hypertext document, the Scottish HCI Database is a standard HyperCard application with two principal components: personal records of participants; and an electronic noticeboard.

Each person has a card (like that shown in Figure 1) on which he or she records name, address, phone number, email address, and a list of one-line phrases describing research interests. An **Add a new person** button on the front page (not shown) allows new owners to register with the database. They enter a dialogue that solicits their name and initial password, and a blank card is created that they can fill out.

The second component is an electronic noticeboard on which any user can post notices. Entries have an expiry date after which they are automatically deleted. A facility is provided so that individual notices may be hidden: having been seen by one user they will not be shown to him again, but are retained in the database and will be passed on to others.

Two indexes are maintained automatically. A list of all people represented is collected on a separate card; clicking on an entry brings up that person's card. A

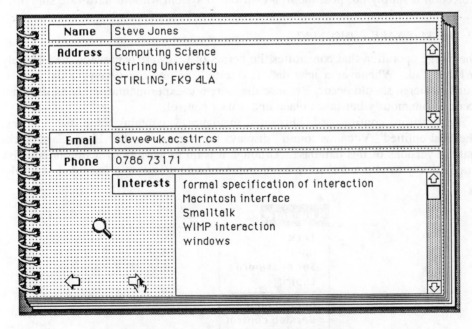

FIGURE 1. An entry in the Scottish HCI Database.

† HyperCard is a product of Apple Corporation (Apple, 1987). It has the advantage of being oriented towards the end user, and is widely available because it comes free with all Macintosh computers.

complete list of every person's interests is automatically compiled on another card; clicking on a line of this index cycles through the cards of people who have declared that interest. The stack contains a few cards owned by the stack creator that give information and help about the database and about Liveware, and a brief summary is included of the social conventions on which the system relies.

What has been sketched so far is a standard application of hypertext. The following sections describe the Liveware component, beginning with the means of enforcing information ownership—which, as noted above, is absolutely necessary for distributed update to work with fully-automatic merging.

3.2. SECURITY

A new pulldown menu, shown in Figure 2, is added to the HyperCard menu bar to give controlled access to the hidden Liveware control information. It allows the owner of particular cards within the database to log in (called "unlock" in the menu), change password, or change the expiry date of those cards he owns.

Passwords are used to impose a degree of integrity on the information. They are encrypted on entry by HyperTalk's† built-in "ask password" facility and stored (invisibly) on each card. The same password is stored on all cards that belong to a given owner; thus cards are self-contained and can be treated independently. In practice, the security mechanism can be circumvented fairly easily by anyone acquainted with the HyperTalk language, since the code is stored in source form and can be read by all. Although more complex schemes could be implemented, real protection is simply not possible in a distributed system without hardware support.

3.3. THE LIVEWARE COMPONENT

The merge operation that constitutes the kernel of Liveware is implemented entirely in HyperTalk. Whenever a new disk is inserted, or another Liveware database is found, a merge should occur. Because the system is experimental, merging does not occur autonomously but takes place under user control.

The Liveware control card, illustrated in Figure 3, contains three dialog boxes. The field entitled "Versions found" displays the names of other HyperCard stacks that are versions of this database. Although it is quite feasible to scan a floppy disk automatically to check for versions of the database, scanning a hard disk can take

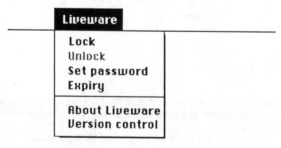

FIGURE 2. The Liveware menu.

† HyperTalk is the language of Hypercard.

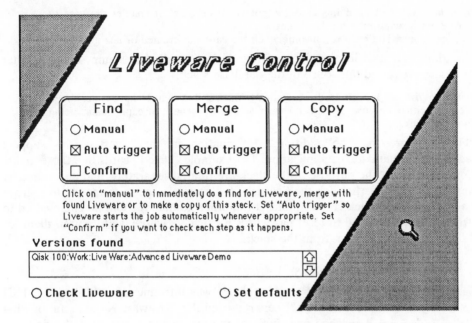

FIGURE 3. The Liveware control card.

some time. To avoid inordinate delays whenever the system is entered, users can add new names to the list manually with the "Find" dialog box.

The "Merge" dialog box permits one to initiate the merge operation manually. Alternatively it can be triggered automatically whenever a new version of the database is entered into the "Versions found" field. The "Copy" box allows the user to make new copies of the database without leaving HyperTalk—we want to encourage copying as much as possible. Checking the "Confirm" box will request user confirmation before carrying out auto-triggered actions.

3.4. THE HYPERCARD IMPLEMENTATION

The information necessary for Liveware to operate correctly is called the *Livestamp*. Normally of no especial interest to the user, it is stored in a hidden field. Different forms of Liveware have different methods for merging, and hence different Livestamp requirements. Each card in the Scottish HCI Database requires the following information within its Livestamp.

- *Signature:* A code unique to the owner of the card. It consists of the owner's actual name, combined with a machine-generated identifier (to "uniquify" the name so that collisions can at least be detected during the merge operation) and an encrypted password (to avoid impersonation).
- *Identification code:* Each card (for a given signature) has a unique code—easily provided by the computer's clock.
- *Expiry date:* Used to destroy the card when it has exceeded its useful life.
- *Dormancy flag:* Set to true if the current user is not interested in the card, but nevertheless wants to share the information with other users. (The alternative is to delete the card: then, of course, it cannot be shared.)

- *New flag:* Set to true if this card has not yet been seen. It enables the user to locate newly acquired information easily.
- *A time stamp:* The most recent time when the card was created or last modified.

In addition to this information maintained in a card's Livestamp, there is other information required only once in the database stack:

- *Deletion list:* A list of cards, previously shared, but which have since been deleted, either because of explicit owner action or because of expiry dates being brought back.

Finally, there may be additional information in the Livestamp to support mechanisms specific to the application. For example, "fixed" cards like those giving information about the purpose of the stack are treated separately, and are owned by the stack's creator. Although the Scottish HCI Database permits anyone to register as a new user, the stack creator alone (or another nominee) could be empowered to introduce new users and to reset passwords for owners who have forgotten them, or who have been withdrawn from the stack.

3.5. THE SCOTTISH HCI DATABASE IN USE

A Liveware form of the Electronic Directory was introduced to the Scottish HCI community in the spring of 1990. Users reported that Liveware is successful in what it tries to do, and it reached over 70% of the target audience within the first few weeks. Its replication over this short time was clearly effective, matching the exponential behaviour expected of a computer virus.

Longer term use of the Electronic Directory was not as promising. Users now report that since the directory information in the database has become relatively stable, there is insufficient motivation to carry it around at all times (except for larger organized meetings). This in turn reduces penetration of the database into the remaining unreached community.

This preliminary experience suggests that Liveware as a technology can work (as seen by its initial rapid growth), but that its overall success or failure will depend upon the cost/benefit trade-offs perceived by users. In this case, the Electronic Directory failed to live up to the *principle of transparency,* which demands that information exchange be unobtrusive and require negligible effort. While the early rapid growth of the database gave community members enough incentive to update their database frequently (and thus update other databases), the diminishing returns given to them in the older and relatively stable system made the effort of carrying the database around too costly.

4. Controlling resource usage

Replicated databases can be expensive to store, and Liveware databases tend to grow monotonically in terms of the data they contain (although stability may set in once the target population of users has been reached). There is no doubt that Liveware is intrinsically resource-hungry. However, its growth can be controlled—at least to some extent—in three ways: deleting information; filtering information; and restricting the user community.

It is easier to add information to Liveware than to remove it. Deleting a unit of information locally has only a temporary effect, for unless it is removed in concert from all versions of the database it will eventually be restored through the merging operation. Instead a record must be kept of the unit's identification so that it can be deleted whenever it appears again. A different mechanism for permanent deletion, also illustrated in the Scottish HCI Database, is to furnish information units with expiry dates. Another, inspired by Jefferson's (1985) notion of "virtual time", is to arrange for cards to be chased by "anti-cards" that annihilate them. This could perhaps be expedited by having Liveware record the immediate recipients of information in order that anti-cards might seek the same route, although we have not seriously considered such protocols.

So far, we have assumed that each copy of the database ideally contains the same information. Instead, a scheme of user profiles could be implemented to permit greater selectivity when picking up and dispensing information. The merge operation would require the user to log in and would then respect his profile, inserting only those cards that match it. Extensive use of profiles will mean that the spread of information is socially moderated by the group as a whole: what people are interested in will disseminate rapidly, specialist information will not propagate. The requirement of automatic merging means that users will have to *describe* the information they want, rather than look for it directly; indeed the question of specifying user profiles automatically is a topic of current research (e.g. Malone, Grant, Turbak, Brobst, Cohen, 1987; Chen, Ekberg & Thompson, 1989).

Systems like the Scottish HCI Database that let new users register and contribute in a completely uncontrolled manner are likely to become polluted by unwanted users. Fortunately, Liveware can be used to implement elaborate schemes for club membership. For example, existing card-owners may be empowered to introduce new ones, or several may have to collaborate to propose a new one. Liveware may enforce collaboration in a single interactive session, or permit nominations to be stored on cards owned by the proposers to distribute the process in time and place. In the latter case the nominee could take his Liveware disk round potential proposers until he has collected the requisite number of nominations. Moreover, each owner's nominations may be stored to allow limits to be placed on the number of introductions that owners may participate in. All of these possibilities are quite simple to implement; the chief problem is in deciding which scheme is suitable for any particular purpose.

Whenever physical interchange of disk is the transmission medium, Liveware will be limited by the storage capacity of common interchangeable media. While it may never be suitable for really large databases, it seems likely that current advances in removable optical disk storage (Freese, 1988) will open up a wide range of potential applications.

5. Conclusions

A method has been described that allows information sharing to take place in loosely-coupled socially-organized systems involving personal computers. Conventional means of information sharing on computers are expensive. Liveware, in contrast, is cheap and intrinsically intertwined with social conventions of spreading information. A practical and easy-to-use prototype has been implemented in HyperCard and was recently introduced to the Scottish HCI community; it is still too early to document its course of evolution. More generally, the idea has many applications, from public domain databases, through facilitating the exchange of information in interest groups, to providing identical environments on several computers controlled by a single person.

We believe that the idea of casual information sharing with low administrative overhead is timely and reflects many human to human interchanges. The increasing use of laptop portable computers underscores the need for effective, yet informal, mechanisms of multiway information distribution, as does the burgeoning complexity of computer systems. For example, Liveware might permit users to automatically pick up updates to software. How many times have you wished you had the most recent bug fixes from the supplier, or even bug reports from other users? Liveware is a step in the right direction.

The solution we propose has the technical merit of replicating the database on as many machines as are involved (and on all disks used for transport); it has the economic merit of costing nothing and requiring no wiring or other installation. Because there need not be any technical infrastructure such as networking, nor the usual geographical restrictions of networks (e.g. being in a single building), the sharing mechanism meets the needs of many mobile and flexible social work groups.

It is a pleasure to acknowledge valuable input by Stuart Anderson, Ann Burnie, Jean Dollimore and Steve Jones.

References

APPLE COMPUTER, INC. (1987). *HyperCard User's Guide.* Cupertino, CA.

CHEN, J. C., EKBERG, T. W. & THOMPSON, C. W. (1989). Querying an object-oriented hypermedia system. In *Proceedings Hypertext II,* University of York, UK.

FREESE, R. P. (1988). Optical disks become erasable. *IEEE Spectrum* **25,** 41–45.

JEFFERSON, D. R. (1985). Virtual time. *ACM Transactions on Programming Languages and Systems* **7,** 404–425.

KRAUT, R., EGIDO, C. & GALEGHER, J. (1988). Patterns of contact and communication in scientific research collaboration. In *Proceedings ACM Conference on Computer-Supported Cooperative Work,* Portland, Oregon, September, pp. 1–12.

MALONE, T. W., GRANT, K. R., TURBAK, F. A., BROBST, S. A. & COHEN, M. D. (1987). Intelligent information-sharing systems. *Communications of the ACM* **30,** 390–402.

NEILSEN, J. (1990). The art of navigating through hypertext. *Communications of the ACM* **33,** 296–310.

WITTEN, I. H. & THIMBLEBY, H. W. (1990). The worm that turned. *Personal Computer World,* July, 202–206.

12

rIBIS: a real-time group hypertext system

GAIL L. REIN

CLARENCE A. ELLIS

This paper describes rIBIS, a real-time group hypertext system, which allows a distributed set of users to simultaneously browse and edit multiple views of a hypertext network. At any time, rIBIS users can switch back and forth between tightly coupled and loosely coupled interaction modes. The paper describes the high-level architecture and user interface of the rIBIS system. Early use of the rIBIS system by a software system design team suggests that users' acceptance increases as they continue to use the tool. We conclude that rIBIS effectiveness is affected by both people and implementation issues.

1. Introduction

The process of software system design, our domain of interest, is becoming more and more of a social activity. Today's complex systems require the cooperative effort of many specialists to design, build and maintain. This is confirmed by DeMarco and Lister (1987) in their Santa Teresa study, which found that a typical computer system developer spent 70% of his time on a large project working with others. In general, as Johansen (1988) points out, US businesses are becoming increasingly team-oriented. This suggests that if people are going to work more productively with others, the tools they use in their work should have an awareness of groups.

There is growing recognition that hypertext is a suitable data model on which to base a support environment for the system design process. Its open structure especially fits the informality that is characteristic of the upstream of the design process (Conklin and Begeman, 1988), which consists of information such as early design notes and sketches, and discussions among team members about the merits of various design and implementation alternatives. Conklin appropriately calls information of this sort *design rationale*.

This paper describes rIBIS,† a real-time group hypertext system. With rIBIS a distributed set of users can simultaneously browse and edit multiple views of a hypertext network. At any time, rIBIS users can switch back and forth between tightly coupled and loosely coupled interaction modes. The tightly coupled interaction mode is GROVE-like (Ellis, Gibbs & Rein, 1990), meaning that many actions are reflected immediately on the screens of all participants who have chosen the tightly coupled mode. The loosely coupled interaction mode is gIBIS-like (Conklin & Begeman, 1988) in that a participant's actions are done "in private" and most results are not immediately visible to others.

rIBIS has been used in both face-to-face sessions in the Electronic Blackboard

Room at MCC, and in distributed sessions where the users are working from machines in their offices and using a conference call on speaker phones for voice communication. Work sessions using rIBIS have received mixed reports from frustrating and unproductive to satisfying and productive, with the more "successful" sessions happening as users gained experience with the tool. We have found that rIBIS can provide a good environment for helping people to learn how to use the tool. Because the prototype lets a knowledgeable session participant control all the screens in a session, new users can learn how to use the tool by watching a more experienced user during the tightly coupled interactions.

The remainder of the paper is organized as follows: section 2 discusses related work by other researchers; section 3 describes rIBIS' roots and its connection with other Software Technology Program prototypes; section 4 is a description of the rIBIS tool, including its high-level functions, implementation approach, and user interface; and section 5 describes what we have learned from everyday use of the rIBIS system in our research program.

2. Related work

The work presented in this paper describes a real-time group hypertext system. There is some literature about hypertext that is aimed at supporting groups of people (typically non real-time) and literature about real-time groupware for various applications (typically not hypertext). One novel contribution of this paper is that it combines these two areas. In this section we describe related work in the hypertext area, and then describe related work in the groupware and desktop conferencing areas.

There has been a recognition that large hypertext systems will naturally be used by groups of people, and that group use of these systems introduces special problems (Nelson, 1967). In NLS, the pioneering hypertext system of Engelbart (Engelbart & English, 1968), there were groupware capabilities similar to some of today's research prototypes, including on-line conferencing and multiple views. In more recent work (Akscyn, McCracken & Yoder, 1988), there is an explicit attempt to address some of the (non real-time) problems of group usage of hypertext. At MCC, the gIBIS work has recognized the need to pay careful attention to the group aspects of hypertext (Conklin & Begeman, 1988). The missing ingredient in many of these systems is the real-time groupware environment element.

Several real-time groupware systems have been built to explore some of the elements of groupware environments which are of direct concern in a system such as rIBIS. Work at Xerox PARC (Stefik, Foster, Bobrow, Kahn, Lanning & Suchman, 1987a) was exploring interaction structuring tools within a face-to-face environment in which each participant had a workstation, and there was a large display visible to all. This work defined important terms of telepointer and WYSIWIS. Similarly, work at the University of Arizona (Applegate, Konsynski & Nunamaker, 1986), the EDS Center for Machine Intelligence (Mantei, 1988), and other institutions has been investigating ideas for group decision support within a face-to-face meeting environment. The Nick meeting room at MCC (Cook, Ellis, Graf, Rein & Smith, 1987) was investigating the software design process within a face-to-face context. All of these efforts have contributed to our groupware understanding.

Desktop conferencing systems have tried to use the computer workstation to provide technology to support real-time, non face-to-face work group interactions. An example of desktop conferencing is the MMConf system (Forsdick, 1986), which provides a shared display of a multimedia document as well as channels for voice and shared pointers. Another example is the Rapport multimedia conferencing system (Ahuja, Ensor & Horn, 1988), which supports various forms of interaction from simple telephone-like conversation to multi-party shared display interaction. These systems have helped expose some of the real-time problems and solutions within the groupware communications backbone.

3. What is rIBIS?

As Figure 1 shows, rIBIS evolved from a number of other prototypes developed by the Software Technology Program (STP) at MCC. In fact, rIBIS is actually a modified version of Germ (Bruns, 1988) that is infused with many of the real-time groupware ideas first tried in a group outline editor named GROVE (Ellis *et al.*, 1990). Germ is a direct descendent of gIBIS (Conklin & Begeman, 1988), an application-specific hypertext system that was designed to facilitate the capture of early design decisions using the method of Issue Based Information Systems (Kunz & Rittel, 1970), which we'll describe shortly.

Germ is a generalization of the gIBIS tool. Whereas gIBIS supported hypertext networks only in the form of Issue Based Information Systems (IBIS) networks, Germ operates on a variety of hypertext networks. Germ achieves its flexibility through a user-defined schema, which contains a data schema as well as definitions of the visual properties of the objects defined in the model. For example, a schema for data flow diagrams would contain definitions of data and process entities, would define their input and output relationships, and would specify that a process is to be displayed as a circle and a data structure as a rectangle. For each schema there can be a number of Germ folios,† each containing some nodes and links.

Although we based rIBIS on the more general Germ prototype, and not on the older gIBIS prototype, we decided to name the prototype rIBIS to emphasize the fact that we were interested in developing a real-time groupware tool that supported

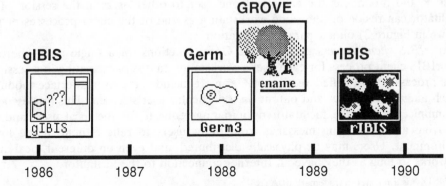

FIGURE 1. rIBIS genealogy.

† A hypertext network in Germ (and rIBIS) is called a *folio*.

a group using the IBIS model and process. The IBIS process requires the articulation of the key issues of a design problem, along with the positions that respond to these issues, and the supporting or objecting arguments for the positions.

One might ask two related questions: (1) Why is it important to capture design rationale? and (2) Why should the design rationale be in the form of issues, positions and arguments? Design rationale is especially important on large software-intensive systems because such systems are fundamentally difficult to understand and to maintain. The actual process of capturing the rationale helps designers' clarify their thoughts about the complex systems they are building, and the product of the process (the resulting captured rationale) serves to document design decisions for people who need to understand the design at some later time (Conklin & Yakemovic, 1990). The IBIS form (i.e. issues, positions and arguments) is a natural, intuitive form for expressing rationale (Hashim, 1990).

Even though our focus in using rIBIS has been primarily within the context of the IBIS process and method, it is important to note that rIBIS is a general, real-time, group hypertext tool. Since rIBIS is based on Germ, it can be used with any Germ schema file and hence is not restricted to hypertext networks of IBIS structures.

4. The rIBIS system

In this section we describe the rIBIS tool. We begin with a high-level description of the tool's functions and a brief discussion of the implementation approach and end with a detailed description of the user interface and the tool's functions.

4.1. HIGH-LEVEL FUNCTIONALITY AND IMPLEMENTATION APPROACH

A goal of the design of rIBIS was to minimize changes to Germ. The rIBIS prototype is written in C and runs under UNIX† on a network of Sun Workstations‡ using Internet TCP for communications. Like Germ, the user interface is built on top of the SunView§ window system. When running, rIBIS consists of two or more main processes as shown in Figure 2.

The *Germ facilitator process* performs the necessary functions that enable or facilitate interactions among rIBIS users. For example, the facilitator (shorthand for Germ facilitator process) adds users to the rIBIS session, removes users from the session, and broadcasts the actions of one user to other users in the session. The facilitator can reside on the same workstation as one of the client processes or (as shown in Figure 2) on a separate workstation.

An *rIBIS client process* performs the Germ functions for a single user—there is one rIBIS client process for each user's workstation that is participating in a session. This process is a modified version of Germ. It includes the user interface modules which manage the input and output on a particular user's screen. This process also communicates with the facilitator by initiating requests for the local user, and by receiving and processing messages from other users to reflect them in the local environment. Users may be physically distributed, and even on different local area networks so long as they have an Internet connection to the facilitator.

† UNIX® is a registered trademark of AT&T.
‡ Sun Workstation® is a registered trademark of Sun Microsystems, Inc.
§ SunView is a trademark of Sun Microsystems, Inc.

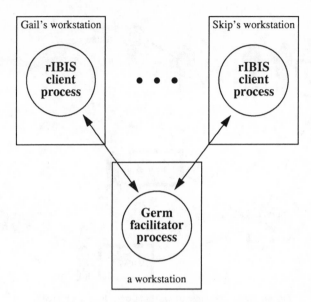

FIGURE 2. The rIBIS system.

An *rIBIS session* is a set of users working together on the same Germ folio via the same facilitator. At any time, a user can choose one of two different interaction modes with the other people in the session: loosely coupled (LC) mode or tightly coupled (TC) mode. LC mode supports parallel activity; TC mode is for highly focused activity and provides an environment in which the group can see the same subgraph, discuss a selected node, and edit an item in real time.

In LC mode, several people can be active in the folio at the same time, and some of their operations (node movement, deletion and addition) are broadcast to all the Germ's in a session. Most operations, however, are not broadcast. Locking occurs automatically when a user edits a node or link, and is maintained until the user indicates completion. The effect is that if one is working in the same part of the folio as others, one sees objects in the browser move, appear and disappear as others are active. If person A tries to edit a node that person B is editing, a message informs A that another user has the object at the moment and rIBIS prevents A from also editing it.

In contrast, in TC mode people take turns controlling the tool. A turn-taking protocol was chosen for this mode because it provides an environment conducive to highly focused activity, appropriate for getting group consensus and feedback on specific items in the folio. The person in control is called the *group mouser* or *mouser*. Almost everything done by the mouser results in a broadcast to all the Germ's in the session. The interface is as WYSIWIS† (What You See Is What I See) as we could make it. Thus, when the mouser moves the view finder in the browser, everyone's view finder moves. When the mouser opens a node for inspection or editing, the node appears for everyone as though they had done the operation themselves. Everyone can watch the mouser as he edits or highlights text.

† WYSIWIS is a term coined by Stefik, Bobrow, Foster, Lanning & Tatar (1987b).

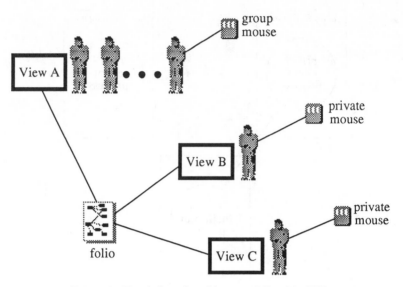

FIGURE 3. Users' view of working on a folio with rIBIS.

Figure 3 shows rIBIS from the users' perspective. Three people are working together as a group in tightly coupled mode, and one person has the group mouse and is interacting with the folio for the group, managing the group view (i.e. View A). Two other people are working on the same folio in loosely coupled mode, each using their own mouse in their own personal views (i.e. Views B and C) of the folio.

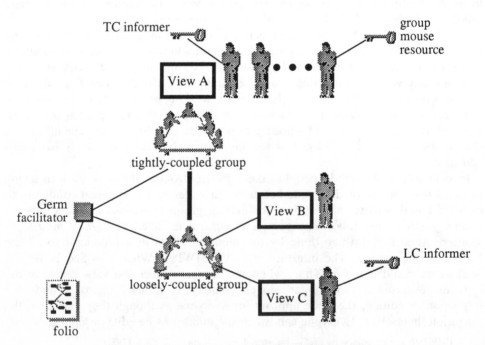

FIGURE 4. System view of working on a folio with rIBIS.

In a sense, from the users' perspective the tightly coupled group is like another loosely coupled user.

Figure 4 shows rIBIS from an implementation or system perspective. The system achieves its goal of supporting multiple users by imposing the Germ facilitator between the users and the folio. There are two kinds of group users: a tightly coupled group whose members are all working together in TC mode, and a loosely coupled group whose members are working on the same folio but in LC mode. Every person in the tightly coupled group is also a member of the loosely coupled group—this is indicated in Figure 4 by the *thick* link connecting the tightly coupled and loosely coupled groups. An rIBIS session supports one LC-group and one TC-group (possibly empty, when no participants are in TC-mode).

From the system's perspective, the person controlling the group mouse owns the *group mouse resource.* Another person's rIBIS client process serves as the *TC informer,* invisible to the actual user. This client has the added responsibility of sending TC state information (such as mouse moves) to the facilitator for the benefit of the other rIBIS's in the tightly coupled group. Yet another person's client process serves as the *LC informer,* also invisible to the actual user. This client has the added responsiblities of saving the folio, maintaining shared variables (such as a new node identifier), and sending LC mode state information (such as node moves) to the facilitator for the benefit of the other rIBIS's in the loosely coupled group.

4.2. USER INTERFACE

Figure 5 shows Germ and rIBIS as they each appear on start-up. At first glance, they look the same. Focusing first on the Germ screen layout (upper half of Figure 5), we remark briefly on some of its features. For a more complete description of Germ functionality, see Bruns (1988).

The large window on the far left is the empty browser with the global world view and view finder in its lower right-hand corner. After a folio is loaded, the browser will provide a visual presentation of the folio structure. The window in the upper right is the index window, where folio objects (such as all nodes or links or the results of a query) can be listed. The control panel is below the index window, and below it is an inspection window where the contents of opened folio objects will appear. Below the inspection window is another very tiny window, the edit window. At most, two objects in the browser can be opened at the same time: one for inspection (read only) and another for editing. When both the inspection and edit areas are active, they occupy approximately equal amounts of the combined space allotted to both windows. When only one of the inspection or edit areas is active, it grows to occupy most of the space allotted to both windows.

Now, comparing the rIBIS screen (shown in the lower half of Figure 5) to Germ, one notices that rIBIS has several interface differences: (1) a new window at the upper right is used for displaying pictures of the session members who are in TC mode;† (2) in the control panel there is a toggle switch that lets people change back and forth between TC and LC interaction modes; and (3) to the right of the toggle switch there is a mouse hole which indicates whether or not the group mouse is

† The use of people's pictures to indicate their presence in a session is a carry-over from GROVE (Ellis, Gibbs & Rein, 1990).

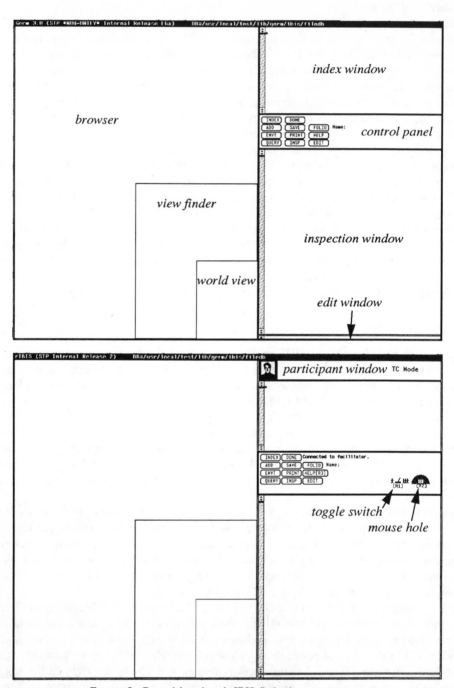

FIGURE 5. Germ (above) and rIBIS (below) on start up.

free (i.e. not currently owned). As we shall see, when rIBIS is in action there are even more differences.

The rest of this section describes details about the user interface. In Figures 6 to 9 rIBIS is shown from one user's—Gail's—point of view.

Interaction mode switch: At any time, users can toggle a switch to move back and forth between TC and LC interaction modes. The toggle switch is controlled by hitting the R1 function key. TC mode is the default when a user starts up rIBIS. When rIBIS is in TC mode the toggle switch points to the right to the multiple person icon (see Figure 5), reminding the user that she is now using a shared view. When in LC mode the toggle switch points to the left to the single person icon, reminding the user that she is the only person using this view.

Floor-passing protocol: Similar to several conferencing systems (Greif & Sarin, 1986; Lantz, 1986; Ahuja *et al.*, 1988), the TC interaction mode uses a floor-passing (or turn-taking) protocol. This means that only one person at a time can control rIBIS. More specifically, only one person at a time can use the group mouse (described shortly) or edit nodes. Other participants in TC mode are observers. Thus, when the person in control changes the browser view or selects a node and edits it, all other participants who are in TC mode immediately see all of these actions.

The group mouse is requested by hitting the R2 function key. If the group mouse is free when R2 is hit, then the mouse is granted immediately. If the group mouse is in use, the request is ignored. If the group mouse is currently owned by someone, but has been idle for five seconds or more (easily changed to some other time interval), the group mouse is freed (i.e. returned to the mouse hole). Hitting the R2

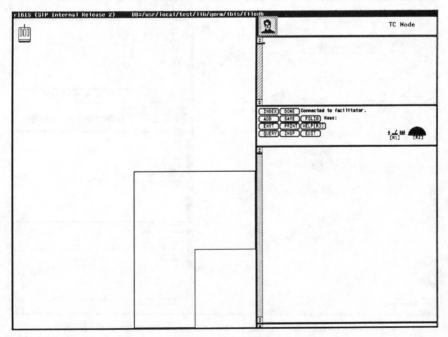

FIGURE 6. Gail requests the group mouse.

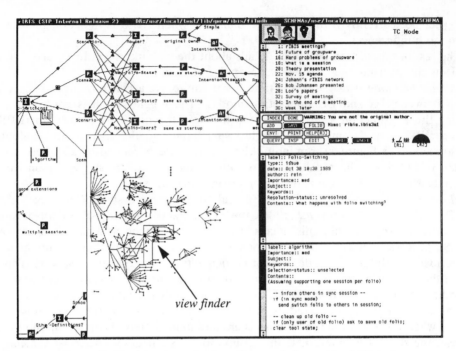

FIGURE 7. At a later stage after two other people have entered TC mode.

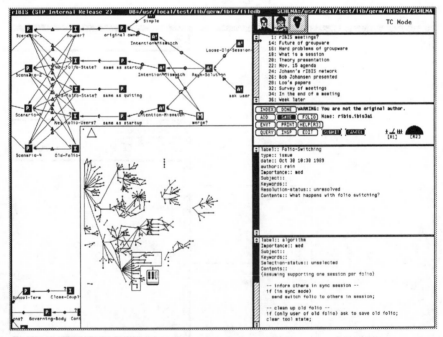

FIGURE 8. Skip is moving the view finder to another part of the folio.

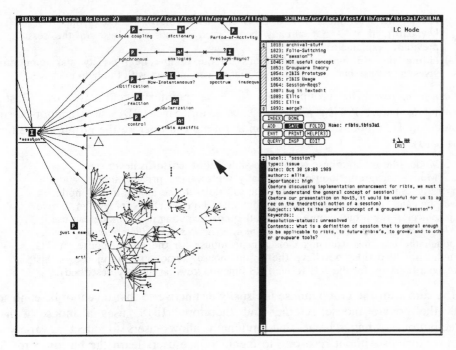

FIGURE 9. Gail switches to LC mode.

key again, grants the mouse if no one else asks for it first.† This preemptive feature was added because we discovered it was too easy for the mouser to get involved in the conversation and forget he had the group mouse. It was disruptive and annoying to hear people constantly saying "please free the mouse—I want to use it".

Private mouse: Each rIBIS user may, at times have a private mouse, meaning that he can use his mouse (and keyboard) independently of other users and that he is the only one who sees his mouse's cursor on the screen. The private mouse cursor looks just like the Germ cursor (an arrow).

- LC Mode—the mouse and keyboard is fully functional; in fact, the same as in Germ except that one cannot change folios (since all rIBIS users in a particular session are working on the same folio, only the mouser can change folios).
- TC mode—the mouse is semi-functional: holding down the right mouse button will bring up the rIBIS window menu ("Close", "Move", "Resize", "Front", "Back", "Redisplay", and "Quit"). All other mouse actions are disabled. A user can interact with rIBIS in only three other ways through three functions keys on the keyboard.:
  (1) Hitting the R1 function key switches the user to LC mode, and gives him a fully functional mouse and keyboard.

† The group mouse has two states: "free" and "busy". Two hits are required to effect a preempt: the first hit changes the state from busy to free, and the second hit changes the state from free to busy. A better interface might be to require only one R2 hit, effectively hiding these internal state changes from the end user. However, there have been instances when someone simply frees the group mouse, and then decides not to take it immediately. Therefore it is not always desirable to make these state changes atomic at the user interface.

(2) Hitting the R2 function key gives the user control of the group mouse (and keyboard), if it is not already being used by someone else in the session, as previously explained.
(3) Hitting the R3 function key brings up the on-line help facility and temporarily gives the mouse back to the user so that he can interact with the help package.

Group mouse: The group mouse is a telepointer (Stefik, Bobrow, Foster, Lanning & Tatar, 1987*b*) with mouse behavior. Since rIBIS uses a floor-passing protocol in TC mode, only one person at a time can operate the group mouse (and keyboard).

• LC Mode—the group mouse is not accessible and its cursor is never seen.
• TC Mode—the group mouse functionally replaces the private mouse, and the operator can do anything with it that he can do with the mouse in LC mode. In fact, he can even switch to LC mode, but when he does rIBIS forces him to give up control of the group mouse so that others participating in TC mode can use it. *When a user has control of the group mouse, he has no private mouse*—it is as though the user has exchanged his private mouse for the group mouse. A TC mode user who does not have the group mouse cannot use his mouse or his keyboard (except for the R1, R2 and R3 function keys, as already described).

The cursor for the group mouse is visually distinctive so that it cannot be confused with the private mouse. Germ, and therefore rIBIS, uses a mouse with a three-button cording scheme that optionally allows users to effect a variety of browser actions without resorting to menus. Once users learn the button cords for various actions, the information as to what buttons are depressed is a significant clue to the mouser's intentions. Consequently, the group mouse has a real-time, simulated mouse (Myers & Buxton, 1986) for its cursor, which allows everyone to see where the group mouse is at all times and what buttons the mouser is pushing. This level of feedback helps others anticipate the changes that occur to their screens as a result of the mouser's actions.†

Some screen dumps: Figure 6 shows the rIBIS user interface after Gail took over the group mouse (by hitting the R2 function key). Note that the mouse hole is now empty, that Gail's cursor has been replaced by the group mouse cursor (in the upper left corner of the browser), and that Gail's picture has been highlighted to indicate that she has control of the group mouse.

Figure 7 shows the user interface at a later time. Gail has loaded a folio, and two other people have joined the session. Users' pictures appear in the participant window in the order in which people enter TC mode. Thus we can see that Gail was first, then Joel, and Skip joined most recently.

Focusing on the browser in Figure 7, we see that the world view (in the lower right corner of the browser) shows a view of the entire folio. The view finder is the up-side-down L-shaped polygon in the world view, and it indicates which part of the world view is visible in zoomed-in detail in the browser. The view finder can be dragged to various parts of the folio within the world view, effectively allowing one to scroll the browser to any particular area of interest. If the view finder is dragged into any boundary of the world view, this action causes the virtual display space to increase in size by 10% (the default, but the user can set to other percentages),

† In fact, the simulated mouse is such an effective user feedback mechanism that many rIBIS users find they miss the simulated mouse when they go to LC mode. Thus, not only is it a useful feedback mechanism in group situations, but also it could satisfy a real need in single-user situations.

adding the extra space at that boundary. Thus the folio can be grown gradually and dynamically as the group adds more nodes to the network.

In Figure 7, Gail has just selected the node labeled "Folio-Switching" for inspection. Its icon, near the group mouse, is highlighted with horizontal bars above and below the icon, and its contents are displayed in the inspection text window immediately below the control panel. Another node labeled "algorithm" was previously selected for editing and is still open. Its icon, below the group mouse, is highlighted with vertical bars on either side of the icon, and its contents appear in the edit text window below the inspection window. The SUBMIT and CANCEL buttons appear only when a node is being edited, as these functions relate only to editing.

In Figure 8, Skip has taken control of the group mouse, and he is showing the group another part of the folio that he's interested in discussing. Notice that now Skip's picture is highlighted to indicate that he is controlling the group mouse. Gail (and Joel) can watch as Skip moves the view finder to another part of the folio. She can anticipate Skip's actions, because the group mouse cursor indicates that Skip is depressing the left and middle mouse buttons (the cord for moving an object in the browser). Everything on Gail's screen changes as if she were operating rIBIS herself.

In Figure 9, Gail has switched to LC mode (by hitting the R1 function key). This is indicated by the toggle switch that is now to the left, pointing to the single person icon to remind her that she is the only person using this view. Also there are no longer any pictures in the participant window. The private mouse is now activated, and her cursor is the familiar Germ cursor (the arrow in the world view).

Gail can toggle between LC and TC modes at any time by hitting the R1 function key. Notice several implications of this:

- When Gail switches to TC mode, the browser and text windows on her screen may immediately change to show the view that all other participants in TC mode see.
- When Gail switches back to LC mode, the browser and text windows do not change—these windows simply do not respond immediately to the operations of other participants, and Gail's operations are not immediately visible on other participants' screens. However, in LC mode rIBIS notifies users of others activities—for example, new nodes/links appear and deleted nodes/links disappear. If Gail tries to edit a node or link being edited by someone else, rIBIS informs her that someone else is editing it and prevents her access.

5. Early usage

Table 1 lists the early rIBIS sessions where the prototype was used for actual work; that is, sessions that were for other than debugging and testing of the prototype. The table shows the date of the session, session type (whether planned or spontaneous, face-to-face or distributed), the number of people participating, and the main topic of discussion.

Since mid-October 1989 we've been using rIBIS to record design and implementation deliberations about the rIBIS prototype. Most of the sessions were with the four members of the Groupware Project team, and all but one of the two-person sessions involved a subset from this team. The two-person session on 2 November involved a person from the Groupware Project and a person from the Design

TABLE 1
rIBIS work sessions

Date	Session type	Number of users	Main topic
10/10/89	Planned (F)†	4§	rIBIS process issues
10/11/89	Planned (F)	4§	rIBIS process issues
10/12/89	Spontaneous (F)	2	rIBIS process issues
10/12/89	Planned (D)‡	4§	rIBIS process issues
10/18/89	Planned (F)	4§	November workshop
10/19/89	Planned (F)	4§	rIBIS demonstration for workshop
10/20/89	Planned (D)	2	rIBIS demonstration for workshop
10/20/89	Planned (F)	4§	Multiple session support
10/25/89	Planned (D)	4	Workshop To Do List
10/30–11/10/89¶	Spontaneous (D)	2–3	rIBIS sessions
11/02/89	Planned (D)	2	rIBIS Project Folio form
11/03/89	Spontaneous (D)	2	New entries in rIBIS Project Folio
11/12/89	Spontaneous (D)	2	Seed folio for NSF all day meeting
11/16/89	Planned (F)	11‖	NSF project update and plans
11/17–12/20/89¶	Spontaneous (D)	2–3	rIBIS enhancements & refinements
12/06/89	Spontaneous (D)	3	Remote rIBIS sessions

† (F), Face-to-Face session in the Electronic Blackboard Room at MCC/STP.
‡ (D), Distributed session using office workstations and conference call.
§ Sessions with fewer workstations than people (two people shared one workstation).
¶ Many sessions.
‖ rIBIS used in the background on one machine by a "technographer".

Journal Project. In the 16 November session, rIBIS was used very much in the background (operated by a member of Groupware Project team, serving as "technographer") during an all day meeting in the Electronic Blackboard Room with NSF grant collaborators from the University of Michigan and Arthur Andersen Consulting. The 6 December session involved an MCC shareholder visitor.

The early rIBIS sessions were planned, face-to-face sessions in the Electronic Blackboard Room where there are three Sun color workstations.† The more recent sessions have been distributed sessions, where rIBIS is used from the machines in peoples' offices in conjunction with a conference call over speaker phones. We have had as many as four rIBIS clients in a session, and as few as two.

5.1. rIBIS PROCESS MODEL

We designed rIBIS expecting that it would be used for two activities common in group work: (1) group brainstorming; and (2) issue resolution or group decision making. During brainstorming people produce ideas as quickly as possible, sharing them with others without passing judgements on the ideas. During issue resolution, people review and discuss the argumentation associated with the issues, possibly clarifying them or even adding new positions and arguments, and then make

† We saw the same usage pattern with the earlier GROVE prototype. We suspect that new groupware tools are first tried in a face-to-face setting rather than a distributed setting, because it is easier to work out ways of using a new tool in a face-to-face setting. Debugging, a common activity in early sessions, is also easier.

decisions about the options. Even without technology, the accomplishment of both activities frequently involves intense, real-time interactions among team members.

In the rIBIS process model, brainstorming is the first stage in the generation of an issue net, and we expected that rIBIS would facilitate the sharing of ideas, resulting in a "seeding" of the issue net. During the next stage, people work with the seeded issue net independently, identifying the issues, posting positions to the issues, and identifying and organizing arguments to these positions. This phase can last hours, days or even weeks, depending on the complexity of the problem. At times during this "filling-out of the net" stage, people may work together in pairs or small subgroups to discuss things and record their discussion using rIBIS. At times, we expected the entire group would plan marathon rIBIS sessions where they would work hard to resolve and record their decisions about issues of concern to all.

5.2. TYPES OF SESSIONS

Consistent with the rIBIS process model, rIBIS sessions can be considered to be either planned or spontaneous. We characterize each type of session, then describe the different usage patterns characteristic of each.

Planned sessions are those where people agree ahead of time to use rIBIS for a specific purpose at a specific time (i.e. for group brainstorming, issue resolution and decision making). These sessions often have a written statement of purpose and sometimes an agenda or plan for accomplishing their goals. These are rIBIS "meetings".

Spontaneous sessions are those where either one person initiates a session without any prior planning with others, or two or more people happen to be using rIBIS at the same time and begin to interact with each other. These sessions tend to happen during "the filling-out of the net" stage of the process model.

Planned sessions—usage patterns: The planned sessions, with the exception of the 20 October session, have been mostly unsatisfying and frustrating. In the 20 October session, rIBIS was used effectively as a presentation tool—everyone stayed in TC-mode for most of the session, and one person used the group mouse almost the entire time to present and discuss a folio that he had prepared before the meeting.

In all the other planned sessions we tried to use rIBIS in the spirit of the process model for issue resolution; i.e. to capture the discussion as issues, positions and arguments in real time as the discussion ensued. We have had only little success so far with issue resolution in planned sessions. Arguments, especially, have been hard for us to capture—in fact our project folio had very few areas where the IBIS structures were fully developed. On the positive side, these sessions had a rich mix of LC and TC-mode interactions, demonstrating that the mode switch feature is valuable.

Spontaneous sessions—usage patterns: rIBIS has proved to be most satisfying and productive for those spontaneous sessions where interactions happen because they need to happen. The first spontaneous session (12 October) was an accident—two people happened to be using rIBIS at the same time and began to interact through the tool without ever actually establishing a voice link through a conference call. Most of the other spontaneous sessions have been initiated by one person to discuss something urgent or important at the moment and get consensus quickly.

The most satisfying and productive session was on 12 November when two people worked together to seed a folio for the NSF session on 16 November. This session was initiated by one person suggesting the session to the other by phone. The session lasted half an hour, during which a skeleton folio was produced from scratch. The group modeled the folio after the rIBIS Project Folio so structuring was straightforward. The content for the folio was evolved from an e-mail message of the meeting agenda that had been prepared a few days earlier. This session had an effective mix of LC and TC-mode interactions. LC-mode was used predominantly with short TC-mode episodes to synchronize and agree upon refinements. The session was unusual in that the use of the tool was almost even, each person contributing about the same number of nodes and links.

5.3. PLANNED VERSUS SPONTANEOUS SESSIONS

Spontaneous sessions have two characteristics that account for their success over planned sessions: first, they have fewer people (usually two, sometimes three people); and secondly, they are of shorter duration (30 min maximum vs two hours for planned sessions, not to mention the eight-hour session on 16 November). Thus, spontaneous sessions tend to be highly focused, serving the needs of the moment.

We must not, however, be hasty in placing too much importance on these observations in favor of spontaneous sessions. Firstly, we are inexperienced in the IBIS method. It is difficult to learn how to capture discussion as issues, positions and arguments. Perhaps with more practice, this will become easier and more natural and we will be able to use the method successfully for long, planned work sessions.

Secondly, the Germ interface inherited by rIBIS is not easy to learn. It takes many hours of working with the tool to learn how to use it to its full potential. However, in several situations, rIBIS has proved to be an unexpectedly good environment for helping people learn how to use Germ. Since the prototype lets a knowledgeable session participant control all of the sceens in a session, new users can learn how to use the tool by watching a more experienced user during the tightly coupled interactions.

5.4. USER ACCEPTANCE

No statistical analysis of the questionnaires designed to capture each participant's reaction to each IBIS session was performed, although a trend can be observed: for any given individual, the ratings have been improving over time. Using rIBIS was at first disappointing—the tool seemed frustratingly to hinder rather than help us capture the key points of the conversation. Yet through persistent use, and by trial and error, we have begun to learn how to use effectively groupware tools as complex as rIBIS.

6. Conclusion

rIBIS is a prototype group hypertext system that allows people to have a (typically distributed) work session in real-time. The prototype was developed to help system design teams capture their design rationale. Consequently, most rIBIS usage has employed an IBIS schema, meaning that the system uses the IBIS model to help a group structure their conversation. Other schema files can be used and/or defined that provide the foundation for other group process models. We say "foundation" because a complete process model requires the evolution of complementary social protocols—those mutually understood, agreed upon ways of interacting that allow people to work together.

rIBIS' target user population is assumed to be heavy computer users, people who use computers for a large portion of the day and who are themselves adept at making computers do new things. rIBIS has a rich set of functionality that requires time for even experienced computer users to fully master. rIBIS is more than a "toy" system—it provides enough functionality that people can work on complex tasks and use the system for real problems.

At any time, a user can choose one of two different interaction modes with the other people in the session: loosely coupled mode or tightly coupled mode. Loosely coupled mode supports parallel activity; tightly coupled mode is for highly focused activity and provides an environment conducive to group participation in which the group can see the same subgraph, discuss a selected node, and edit an item in real time, useful functions for getting immediate group feedback and consensus.

Early use of the rIBIS system by a system design team, mainly, the implementers, suggests that users' acceptance increases as they continue to use the tool. We conclude that future rIBIS effectiveness is affected by both people and implementation issues. Small changes, such as the addition of a preemptive mechanism for requesting the group mouse, have had big payoffs for increasing user acceptance. However, rIBIS is a complex application, and not all improvements will come so easily. We have much to learn about *how to use* the tool effectively; and we have much to learn about *how to make* the tool more effective.

The prototype has been used with a maximum of four rIBIS clients in a session. Although, there is no architectural limit on the number of potential users in a rIBIS session, it is not clear that the tool as it exists today could *effectively* support 100 (to be extreme) simultaneous users, or even 10 for that matter. As we consider what would be required to coordinate larger numbers of people engaged in an IBIS discussion, we have no experience to suggest what additional or different support features the tool should provide. This dimension could be an exciting area for future research with potentially high pay-off. The research issues are, again, both *how to use* the tool effectively and *how to make* the tool more effective.

In the more immediate future, some decisions will be made concerning the enhancement or re-implementation of rIBIS. The current prototype supports only a portion of Germ's functionality in the tightly coupled mode. For example, user specificable environment settings that control the size of the windows and the colors used in the browser, aggregate creation, and queries are not supported in a WYSIWIS fashion. Thus, people in tightly coupled mode can have different sized windows, colors and information on their screens—this can be very confusing. There are also many functional deficiencies that we noticed in the first rIBIS session, most notably the need for several inspection and edit windows.

There are difficult issues to resolve to coordinate people's subscription lists to folios. A subscription list is a file specifying the path names of the folios that a person wishes to access through Germ. If peoples' subscription lists are not the same, when the group moves to a different folio some Germ clients may not be able to visit that folio.

Finally, there are the issues of what is a session, and how multiple sessions should be supported. The current prototype requires one to be in tightly coupled mode and own the group mouse in order to change folios; and then, even those people who are in loosely coupled mode are forced to change folio. This is not the desired functionality!

In the near future rIBIS will be used for remote sessions between researchers at MCC/STP and shareholders at their sites. This will be a unique opportunity to see if long distance distributed rIBIS sessions can accelerate IBIS research. This real world use of the prototype will also serve as invaluable input to the resolution of the longer term issues.

We thank Les Belady, Pete Cook, Bill Curtis and Michael Begeman for encouraging and supporting groupware research at MCC. rIBIS could not have been done without the prior work of Michael Begeman (the gIBIS prototype), Glenn Bruns (the first Germ), and Peter Marks and David Creemer (today's enhanced Germ). The Germ facilitator was designed and implemented by Joel Loo. We would have given up trying to use rIBIS for serious work without the continual encouragement, tutoring, and insights from Jeff Conklin and Safaa Hashim on IBIS process and method.

References

AKSCYN, R. M., McCRACKEN, D. L. & YODER, E. A. (1988). KMS: a distributed hypermedia system for managing knowledge in organizations. *Communications ACM*, **31**, 820–835.

AHUJA, S. R., ENSOR, J. R. & HORN, D. N. (1988). The Rapport multimedia conferencing system. In *Proceedings of the Conference on Office Information Systems*, pp. 1–8. New York: ACM.

APPLEGATE, L. M., KONSYNSKI, B. R. & NUNAMAKER, J. F. (1986). A group decision support system for idea generation and issue analysis in organization planning. In *Proceedings of the Conference on Computer-Supported Cooperative Work*, pp. 16–34. New York: ACM.

BRUNS, G. (1988). *Germ: A Metasystem for Browsing and Editing*, MCC Software Technology Program Technical Report STP-122–88.

CONKLIN, J. & BEGEMAN, M. (1988). gIBIS: a hypertext tool for exploratory policy discussion. In *Proceedings of the Conference on Computer-Supported Cooperative Work*, pp. 140–152. New York: ACM.

CONKLIN, J. & YAKEMOVIC, K. C. B. (1990). *A Process-oriented Paradigm for Design Rationale*, MCC Software Technology Program Technical Report STP-269–90.

COOK, P., ELLIS, C., GRAF, M., REIN, G. & SMITH, T. (1987). Project Nick: meetings augmentation and analysis. *ACM Transactions on Office Information Systems*, **5**, 132–146.

DeMARCO, T. & LISTER, T. (1987). *Peopleware: Productive Projects and Teams*. New York: Dorset House Publishing.

ELLIS, C., GIBBS, S. & REIN, G. (1990). Design and use of a group editor. In G. COCKTON, Ed. *Engineering for Human-Computer Interactions*, pp. 13–25. Amsterdam: North-Holland.

ENGLEBART, D. C. & ENGLISH, W. K. (1968). A research center for augmenting human intellect. In *Proceedings of the Fall Joint Computer Conference*, pp. 395–410. Reston, VA: AFIPS.

FORSDICK, H. C. (1986). Explorations in real-time multimedia conferencing. In R. P. UHLIG, Ed. *Computer Message Systems—85*, pp. 331–347. Amsterdam: North-Holland.

GREIF, I. & SARIN, S. (1986). Data sharing in group work. In *Proceedings of the Conference on Computer-Support Cooperative Work*, pp. 175–183. New York: ACM.

HASHIM, S. (1990). *WHAT: Writing with a Hypertext-based Argumentative Tool,* MCC Software Technology Program Technical Report STP-270-90.

JOHANSEN, R. (1988). *Groupware: Computer Support for Business Teams.* New York: The Free Press, Macmillan, Inc.

KUNZ, W. & RITTEL, H. W. J. (1970). *Issues as Elements of Information Systems,* Technical Report S-78-2 of the Institut fur Gundlagen der Planung I.A., Universitat Stuttgart, Keplerstrasse 11, 7000 Stuttgart 1, Germany.

LANTZ, K. (1986). An experiment in integrated multimedia conferencing. In *Proceedings of the Conference on Computer-Supported Cooperative Work,* pp. 267–275. New York: ACM.

MANTEI, M. (1988). Capturing the capture lab concepts: a case study in the design of computer supported meeting environments. In *Proceedings of the Conference on Computer-Supported Cooperative Work,* pp. 257–270. New York: ACM.

MYERS, B & BUXTON, W. (1986). Creating highly-interactive and graphical user interfaces by demonstration. *Computer Graphics,* **20,** 249–258.

NELSON, T. H. (1967). Getting it out of our system. In G. SCHECHTER, Ed. *Information Retrieval: A Critical Review,* pp. 191–210. Washington, DC: Thompson Books.

STEFIK, M., FOSTER, G., BOBROW, D. G., KAHN, K., LANNING, S. & SUCHMAN, L. (1987a). Beyond the chalkboard: computer support for collaboration and problem solving in meetings. *Communications ACM,* **30,** 32–47.

STEFIK, M., BOBROW, D. G., FOSTER, G., LANNING, S. & TATAR, D. (1987b). WYSIWIS revised: early experiences with multiuser interfaces. *ACM Transactions on Office Information Systems,* **5,** 147–186.

13

Modelling groupware in the electronic office

STEVE COOK

GARY BIRCH

ALAN MURPHY

JOHN WOOLSEY

This is a report on a project now completed, to explore ideas for a distributed software system intended to enhance people's ability to communicate effectively and conveniently, to give them information about each others' status and whereabouts, and to support them in planning and executing various kinds of computer-supported office tasks both alone and in collaboration. The purpose of the project was to explore architectural issues, user-interface issues, and the definition of possible future products. The approach taken was to create software models of scenes written by a multi-disciplinary team, and to create performances using these models. The paper reviews the objectives of the project, discusses the approach, architecture and implementation, and draws conclusions both about the approach adopted and the ideas explored.

1. Introduction

The origins of the project lay in the conjunction of several observations of the development of computer hardware and software technology, and of the activities of so-called white-collar workers i.e. executives, managers, professionals and secretarial/clerical staff.

First, we observed the extremely rapid growth of all kinds of computer networks. The rate of installation of local area networks is now growing by at least 50% per annum in the USA, according to Baker (1989). Several other kinds of network are being rapidly developed, including satellite, broadband, X25, ISDN, and the intelligent telephone network. Connectivity is the order of the day.

We recognized that object-orientation is emerging strongly as a technology both for user-interface development and for the integration of heterogeneous technologies. The use of object-orientation for user interfaces goes back to the Smalltalk system, described in Goldberg and Robson (1983), and is currently demonstrated by window systems such as X Windows, described in Scheifler and Gettys (1986), and frameworks such as MacApp, described in Schmucker (1986), and ET++, described in Weinand, Gamma and Marty (1988).

Object-orientation provides a powerful method for the integration of heterogeneous technologies by virtue of its support for expressing high-level generic abstractions and binding these dynamically to different implementations, using the mechanisms of instantiation and inheritance.

243

This power has been recognized by developers of object-oriented database management systems (OODBMS), which allow encapsulated abstractions, such as those found in object-oriented programming languages, to be stored and retrieved across program executions. According to Maier (1989), OODBMS are particularly useful for supporting design applications, particularly those involving graphics or multiple media. They are also finding an increasing role as repositories for life cycle information in computer-aided systems engineering (CASE) systems. The Object Management Group is a consortium of several major vendors of computer technology whose objectives are stated in OMG (1989) to include "enabling co-ordination among applications across heterogeneous networked systems in a multinational, multilingual environment". The OMG is developing an object management system designed to achieve substantially increased application integration by exploiting object-oriented methods.

Our third observation was that a growing number of heterogeneous devices exist which are capable of being connected to networks of computers. These devices include workstations with displays of text, graphics, images and video, video cameras, sound recording and playback, speech synthesis and recognition facilities, telephones, scanners, printers, fax machines, optical disks, and so on. Multi-media is increasingly fashionable, and a multitude of products are now reaching the marketplace.

Finally, we observed that the large majority of time spent by professional office workers is spent on "unstructured communication tasks", such as speaking on the telephone, attempting to make contact by telephone or another information medium, and having organized or ad-hoc meetings. According to Teger (1983):

> Since white-collar workers spend 80 to 95 percent of their time communicating and managing information, improvement in communications processes has enormous potential leverage on operating expense control, as well as substantial potential for improving the inputs to decision making for managers.

Taken together, these observations indicate a range of opportunities for software products which support unstructured communication tasks for professional office workers on a variety of heterogeneous devices and information media. With these opportunities in mind, a project was started with the objective of exploring the application of object-oriented technology in supporting a range of unstructured communication tasks over a range of devices and media. It was anticipated that the work would lead to insights into architectural issues, user-interface issues, and the definition of possible future products, as well as producing artifacts which would serve to introduce ideas about computer-supported co-operative work (CSCW) to a wider audience.

The remainder of this paper is organized as follows. Section 2 discusses the overall setting of our work in design terms, and defines the problems we set out to solve. Section 3 states our approach. Section 4 presents a set of dimensions which we use to evaluate our work. In sections 5 and 6 we discuss the development of our model. Section 7 describes the architecture in more detail, and section 8 gives details of the scenes. Section 9 gives a brief presentation of the implementation. In section 10 we assess the work from various points of view. Section 11 includes and summarizes the paper.

2. Paradigms

We believe that the emergence of products exploiting the increased power and connectivity of computer technology will be complemented by the emergence of new paradigms for the user. In his seminal book *The Structure of Scientific Revolutions,* Kuhn (1970) uses the word *paradigm* to refer to the background of culture and tradition which guides the work of research scientists. We use the word here in a parallel sense, to mean the background of culture and tradition which guides the way people use computers. Kuhn refers to a paradigm shift in science as a *transformation of vision,* and we think that users of highly connected systems will perceive them and their purpose very differently to the way in which today's personal computers are seen by their users. In particular, systems will be regarded as primarily for communication, rather than primarily for computation. Johansen (1984) supports this point with surveys of computer users.

We want to participate in the creation of the new paradigms, and discover what will be the equivalents of *applications, objects, operating system,* and *desktop* in this transformed vision of the technology. Our aim is to translate our view of the emerging paradigms into a detailed understanding of the architectures and services which will provide the generic infrastructure for applications built within the new framework.

Our thinking here is restricted to the next stage of development, when personal computers will be multi-media and highly connected, but still recognizably personal computers. We are not looking decades ahead, to a future where "telepresence" and "virtual reality" may be commonplace for ordinary users. We still operate in a world of windows, icons, menus, pointers and cut-and-paste; in this context the differences we are looking for result from increased connectivity, sharing, integration and choice of medium.

We are aware that there are many fundamental technological, sociological, ergonomic and political difficulties in creating an integrated information architecture which successfully connects a wide range of people together. We anticipate that the value of the emerging paradigms will result from the combination of many functional areas. We believe that the attributes which will make the next generation of systems valuable will be emergent, rather than inherited attributes. That is to say, they will be present because of the combination of all parts into an integrated whole, rather than because of the attributes of any particular vertical application.

The difficulty with emergent attributes is predicting them with any accuracy before they have emerged. To address this difficulty we have tried in this project to build and understand a very simplified version of the *whole system,* rather than concentrating on any single technological objective. We call this a *model.* The purpose of our model is to be able to prioritize issues and questions, discover any important missing functional areas, generate ideas for possible future product areas, and create videos for initial end-user feedback. *Model* is distinguished from *prototype.* A prototype would have a different purpose, namely to ensure the practical viability of a particular approach having already decided on a specific product.

Using language chosen by Ehn (1988) in his challenging examination of the design process, our model, demonstrations and video are *design artifacts* which act as *paradigm* cases. A major goal of creating these artifacts has been to generate a *practical understanding* of how an end-user might experience an integrated computer system aimed at optimizing communication within a networked environment.

3. Approach

Our approach has been to build software models demonstrating a set of fictitious scenes, and to create performances of those scenes. Each scene focused on a particular type of situation, defined in terms of the participants in the scene, their relationships and their tasks. For example,

> Alan, a colleague of Steve from a separate workgroup, comes into Steve's office in his absence, in order to arrange a meeting with Steve and to leave some confidential papers.

The focus of our work was the personal computer. We assumed that each user of the system will have their own workstation, connected to a variety of devices such as video camera, scanner, printer, microphone and loudspeaker, and to a variety of networks, including LAN and telephone.

Our overall approach proceeded by iterating a cycle. The starting-point of each cycle was the creation by brainstorming and discussion of several scenes to be considered as candidates for modelling. Scenes were selected according to how well-defined they were, and how practical it would be to model them within our constraints. The selected scenes were refined in parallel with the development of architectural ideas, finishing up with a detailed description of a proposed implementation of the scenes, together with an architecture which would support the implementation. The scenes were then implemented in software, with a focus on providing a complete performance of the scene, with as much as possible of the architecture realized in software. "Cheating", i.e. demonstrating unimplemented facilities, was allowed as long as a thoroughly plausible proposal for implementation could be provided. The fully implemented scenes were demonstrated, recorded on video, and assessed before starting a further iteration.

During the three years we completed two complete iterations of this cycle. The first iteration, which was carried out using a single workstation, was mainly concerned with developing user-interface techniques and had no significant "groupware" content. The examples and details in the remainder of this paper refer to the second of these iterations, when we had two interconnected workstations.

We are painfully aware that more than two workstations would have given us much more scope for realistic modelling of groupware scenarios; unfortunately we were limited in this by factors outside our control. By the same token, our ability to explore the consequences of multiple media were severely limited by the lack of availability of suitable hardware.

4. Dimensions

We chose the following set of dimensions for evaluating our work: support for real-time remote co-operative working, integration across differing tasks, availability of personal secretary function, co-ordination and time management, use of multiple media, and end-user programming. We felt strongly throughout the project that a system which fully supported all of these elements would satisfy the opportunity identified in our original observations. The following rationale supports each of these elements.

Support for *real-time remote co-operative working* using the WYSIWIS (What You See Is What I See) principle is considered to be an essential component of the system. The ability for several remotely located people to see the same objects, and to watch each other point and refer unambiguously to them by words such as "this", provides a fascinating opening into a shared virtual reality. Experiments by Smith, O'Shea, O'Malley, Scanlon and Taylor (1989) with Shared ARK (Shared Alternate Reality Kit) indicate that this mode of working can be highly effective, and can even reduce the *social distance* between collaborators in comparison with a conventional face-to-face encounter. Rather than imposing *strict* WYSIWIS, where everybody would see exactly the same image, we relax the principle in various specific ways described later.

Integration across differing tasks refers to our attempt to reduce the walls between different applications, by substantially raising the level and diversity of the objects provided as part of the shared environment, to include such entities as representations of users and their relationships, generic frameworks representing classes of similar applications, and building-blocks representing components used by application.

Personal secretary function refers to the ability of the system to protect its users from unnecessary disruptions while permitting essential interruption, to take messages where necessary, to authenticate callers and control access to facilities, to provide "while-you-were-out" services, etc. This facility is notionally built upon a database kept by the system of all of its users, together with their current physical location, relationships to others users, diary, current availability, commitments etc.

Time management facilities will allow users of the system to manage their own diary, and to refer to (and in some cases to alter) the diaries of others, for the purpose of scheduling meetings, calls and so on. *Co-ordination*† refers more generally to facilities for making stored communications (such as e-mail), for keeping track of the state of a group project, recording commitments made by individuals and issuing reminders.

The use of *multiple media* is justified on the grounds that we are multi-sensory beings living in a multi-media world. We are restricted by the availability of practical technology to handling text, images, video and sound. The best use of each medium for any particular task is largely unknown, and we hope to gain some insights in this area.

End-user programming is an ideal which we consider is of paramount importance if computer systems for co-operative work are to be accepted into real working situations. A system should provide simple facilities which enable users to express their own requirements. End-user programming is the way we propose to make the "secretarial" facilities "personal".

We also consider that computer systems in general, and systems to support co-operative work in particular, should be *non-prescriptive,* in the sense that they

---

† Some authors use the term "co-ordination" in a more specific sense, referring to systems which support the making and managing of commitments by explicit representation of speech acts. Our use of the term here has a somewhat wider interpretation.

should rarely if at all commit a user to any particular course of action. As a general rule, our design goal is to maximize end-user choice while retaining simplicity.

A further ideal is that the system should be *transparent,* in the sense that users should be able to determine very easily what is going on and predict the outcomes of their actions. We rule out proposals which attempt to reorganize a schedule, or make decisions automatically, on the basis of rules which cannot be transparently understood and altered by an end-user.

5. Development of scenes

The development of the scenes proceeded in stages. Initially they were created from ideas generated by brainstorming and discussion. The first refinement was to articulate the scenes, as far as possible, in a technology-independent form. Thus, for instance, the following description of a transaction between Gary and Steve:

> Gary requests a communication with Steve. Steve agrees and they communicate. Gary discusses a document he is creating. They both look at it. Steve gets Gary's permission to make changes. Steve moves a paragraph, adds a new one, gets a picture from a folder, and adds this picture to the document. Gary watches him do this and agrees to each change. Gary puts the document away. They finish the communication.

The only technology-dependent references here are to documents, paragraphs, pictures and folders, which are assumed to be concepts sufficiently abstract to survive a wide range of different technologies. In particular, there is no statement about the relative location of Steve and Gary, although with paper technology the description would not make sense unless they are in the same physical location.

It might be argued that this description, although independent of specific electronic technologies, is at the wrong level of abstraction, and that a more appropriate formulation would refer to Steve and Gary's real intentions in the interaction, e.g. the collaborative preparation of a presentation. Although we have some sympathy for this argument, we have specifically avoided any attempt to represent users' goals and intentions in this work, and concentrated instead on our objective of revealing *generic* (application-independent) architectures for co-operative working, based on familiar metaphors where possible. Even if abstractions such as paragraph, document, picture and folder may not ultimately be the best for collaborative working, we think it is valid to use them as a starting-point.

Before the development of the description above can be taken any further towards an implementation, two areas of context needed to be explored in some detail. The first concerned the nature of the relationship between Steve and Gary. To say "Gary requests a communication with Steve" begs many questions, such as: Do they know each other? Do they have a working relationship? Do they have a formalized organizational relationship (e.g. Steve is Gary's boss)? How do they get on? Is Steve busy now? Does Gary have permission to interrupt Steve? When did they last communicate? How far are they apart? And so forth. These questions strongly influence the kind of technological solution that might be proposed for implementing "Gary requests a communication with Steve".

For example, an obvious present-day solution is the telephone. However, if Steve is very busy but is still willing to accept an interruption from a small set of people including Gary, the telephone in its existing form is not a very appropriate solution.

Intelligent network services, as discussed in Weinstein (1986), may provide a solution to this particular problem. This would, however, be a solution tied to one particular technology, whereas we would prefer to allow Steve to be able to express the concept "I'm busy" and have his integrated workstation handle all aspects of the solution.

Other possible solutions include an intercom, e-mail, a paging device, flashing messages on the screen, and appearing in a real or simulated office. Each of these might be most appropriate, depending on the relationshp between the participants, their moment-to-moment availability, emotional state, preferences and so on. The overall system design goal is to maximize the choice and expressive power provided for users to express their preferences between these alternatives, given a range of underlying technological possibilities.

For the model we address the issue of relationships between the participants by inventing a fictitious organization. This is a moderately-sized company, with around 100 employees grouped into *workgroups* of about 10 people. Employees within a single workgroup are called *colleagues,* whereas other people are called *strangers.* Workgroups can have *visitors.* Workgroups have a hierarchical management structure internally. Within the organization each individual has an *availability,* which can be set to *busy* or *free.* Each individual also has a set of time commitments, in particular a *time-when-free* if the individual is busy, and a *time-when-back* if the individual is absent from the office.

Inventing this structure allows some of the questions raised above to be formalized: if Gary and Steve are in the same workgroup, then they know each other, they have a working relationship, and they have a formalized organizational relationship. The meaning of *busy* is defined on an individual basis; for example, it might mean "only allow my boss to interrupt me".

It is clear that a much more powerful structure than this would be necessary to represent the relationships between individuals for an effective general-purpose system. People's relationships are associated with projects, activities and events, and roles within these. Within each relationship there may be several conversations in progress, including the *conversations for action* described by Winograd and Flores (1986), comprising specific commitments made in time, or contingent on particular events.

The second area of context which impacts strongly the interpretation of a technology-independent description is the technological infrastructure: the range of media which exist in the outside world, such as the telephone, postal service, TV, the existence and development of specific software, networks, network services and standards, and so on. Within the project we sidestepped this issue, largely for pragmatic reasons to do with the limited availability of particular equipment, and simply set all our scenes within the context of a single workgroup and its visitors, and in the present day. Obviously, however, the technological infrastructure has a major bearing on the design of any serious system of this kind.

6. Development of architecture

The second stage in the cycle was to create an architectural framework enabling the transformation of fragments of description such as that above into storyboards, i.e.

sequences of screen images with surrounding descriptions indicating how the scenes are implemented. The development of this architecture involved the synthesis of a number of ideas taken from existing systems and from the literature. The architecture is described in more detail in section 7, but the fundamental ideas are the following:

- Shareable objects in a distributed address space
- Views, icons, and direct manipulation
- WYSIWIS via views, perspectives (rooms) and Doors
- Private and shareable layers
- Visual editing of views
- Activity model
- Object naming and behaviour
- Integration of multiple media
- Ownership and authentication
- A standard working environment
- Use of colour to indicate information ownership

The main architectural ideas were developed concurrently with the scenes. During this process we spent most time drawing and discussing pictures of what might appear on the screen during each scene. Our experience was that it was important that people from both computer systems and human factors disciplines were present while developing these ideas.

One difficulty we encountered during this process was separating the user interface decisions from the architectural decisions. Many of the user interface decisions, for example the actual appearance of windows and icons, or the precise way of selecting between options, were of little interest to us, except that we had to decide on something. We considered that the correct way to make a fully informed user interface decision would be as the result of a properly-conducted evaluation in context. At the stage of modelling an architectural design, much of the context for user-interface evaluation does not yet exist, and so we made decisions on the basis of a number of *ad hoc* guidelines. These were:

- Use whatever already exists wherever possible.
- Favour push buttons, pop-up menus, dialogue boxes and intelligent forms.
- Aim for a "chunky" and "cartoon-like" feel.

Another, rather more subtle, area of difficulty had to do with choosing the concepts to be represented explicitly in the interface. The approach of using real-world analogies was superficially appealing, and was adopted in many cases. Hence the model has an icon representing the telephone, another representing the intray, another representing the postbox, and so on.

One difficulty with this approach arises when areas of functionality are considered which do not fit cleanly into this naive real-world metaphor. For example, "creating and sending a voice memo". Is this part of the functionality of the telephone or not? Another more abstract example is "becoming busy", where part of becoming busy involves switching on some kind of answering machine. Is this answering machine part of the telephone, part of the intray, part of the e-mail system, or something separate? If something separate, what kind of interface does it provide to the telephone, the intray and the e-mail system?

A further difficulty concerns the "piece of wire" communications architecture which is suggested by the appearance of objects such as a telephone and intray. In a "transparently distributed address space" or "virtual reality" architecture, a more suitable representation might be an object representing the other person, providing a range of services including the ability to speak, send and receive messages etc.

There are some subtle and complex design trade-offs here, involving efficiency of representation, ease of learning and ease of use, as well as interworking with existing software and hardware solutions, and we do not claim to have any concrete solutions to them. Detailed answers to these issues become of great importance when considering the requirement for end-user programming. If an end user is to be able to configure whatever "becoming busy" means to him or her, without having to resort to writing programs, the system must provide effective and intelligible representations of the resources available.

In general, in formulating the architecture for our model we permitted a certain amount of cheating. For example, although we did not implement any coherent policy for authorization and access control, we included elements in the scenes which suggested that such facilities existed. Our criterion for the inclusion of an element was that we could justify it by a plausible description of how to do it using existing technology. Such elements as real time speaker-independent natural language understanding, for example, which would have been extremely useful in building an intelligent answering machine, were outlawed by this principle. Another outlawed element was a "tidy-up-your-mess" agent.

An interesting part of the process of developing the architecture was the revealing of covert assumptions. For example, with regard to the topology of the system, some members of the team had a definite "piece of wire" mindset, and described the scenes in those terms; whereas other members of the team had a "large

```
┌─────────────────────────────────────────────────┐
│ Office procedures                                │
│    Getting approval for a trip                   │
│    Creating a remind assistant                   │
├─────────────────────────────────────────────────┤
│ Controlling interrupts                           │
│    *Becoming busy                                │
│    The intelligent intray                        │
│    Creating an interrupt profile                 │
├─────────────────────────────────────────────────┤
│ Office integrity                                 │
│    *Visitor enters the office                    │
│    *Owner enters the office                      │
│    *Stored voice communication                   │
├─────────────────────────────────────────────────┤
│ Meetings                                         │
│    *A one-to-one meeting                         │
│    Setting up a meeting of more than two         │
│    Having a meeting of more than two             │
├─────────────────────────────────────────────────┤
│ Ad hoc communications                            │
│    Sending an annotated sketch                   │
└─────────────────────────────────────────────────┘
```

FIGURE 1. Areas and scenes. Scenes implemented are marked with an asterisk.

transparently-distributed address space" mindset. The basic problem was the difficulty of talking about the new in terms of the old. Ehn (1988) refers to this contradiction as *the dialectics of tradition and transcendence in design and use,* and considers it a crucial and fundamental aspect of design philosophy. A considerable amount of our discussion was concerned with making our assumptions explicit, and attempting to work out their areas of applicability, and the parameters which determine them. The result was a compromise, in some cases an uneasy one.

No doubt there are further assumptions waiting to be revealed. As we have indicated, we are aware that building our conception around the notion of a workstation may in itself be an assumption to be overturned in the future, but we are willing to overlook this possibility in the light of the practical goals of the project.

The overall process described in this section produced detailed descriptions of 12 scenes, divided into five functional areas. Figure 1 shows the list of scenes and areas. These scenes were further prioritized according to an assessment of how they measured up to the criteria in section 4, leading to the final decision to implement the scenes marked with an asterisk.

7. Architecture

In this section the main architectural framework which underpins the model is described in more detail.

7.1. SHAREABLE PERSISTENT OBJECTS IN A DISTRIBUTED ADDRESS SPACE

The system is uniformly object-oriented. This means that all data and behaviour is clustered around concrete units called objects, often having real-world counterparts. For example, a person's home address and current location are not stored separately, but together in a *person* object. These objects are thought of, at least by the user, as existing in a global distributed address space transparently accessible from all of the workstations. We expect this address space to be co-extensive with the organization in which the system is installed, and to correspond to the domain of a single local area network. Objects are also thought of as persistent. There is no concept of a separate non-volatile store into which objects must be put to ensure they are kept. This requirement raises a whole host of technical issues, such as those raised in Grief and Sarin (1987), which we have not addressed in any detail.

7.2. VIEWS, ICONS AND DIRECT MANIPULATION

Views are visual representations of one or more objects. Views exist in an expanded or collapsed form, and in the collapsed form are called icons. Views can be moved around the screen, expanded or collapsed, resized and re-ordered by simple direct manipulations using a conventional mouse. Pop-up menus associated with icons, views and parts of views provide a general means of interacting with the objects attached to views.

Each view is constructed from a number of component subviews, selected from a small library of standard components including buttons, text views, labels, pictures, icon containers and sliders.

Border colour is used to indicate the state and ownership of a view. We found that it was helpful when views created by several people are simultaneously visible to be able to distinguish them according to ownership. This bears out the suggestion of Bannon and Schmidt (1989), that representation of information ownership is an important factor for successful systems for supporting cooperative work.

7.3. WYSIWIS VIA VIEWS, PERSPECTIVES AND DOORS

Views are grouped into screen-sized workspaces called perspectives. Each perspective may be displayed on one or more workstations simultaneously. Views in perspectives displayed on more than one workstation look the same on each workstation, and support the WYSIWIS (What You See Is What I See) abstraction first introduced in the Colab project at Xerox PARC and described in Stefik, Foster, Bobrow, Kahn, Lanning and Suchman (1987). *Strict* WYSIWIS, with every user seeing exactly the same displayed image, is too inflexible for most purposes as well as being potentially computationally expensive, as pointed out in Stefik, Bobrow, Foster, Lanning and Tatar (1987). We have relaxed strict WYSIWIS in three ways: grain size, multiple cursors, and private *vs* shared objects.

Progressive changes (such as dragging or sliding) which go through many intermediate positions between a starting and a finishing point are not replicated on remote workstations. Instead, the remote item simply jumps to the end-point on completion of the move. This grain-size restriction saves considerably on the use of bandwidth and does not seem to detract unduly from the illusion of WYSIWIS.

Our model adopts a simple token-passing floor control policy at the level of views, whereby only one user may have control of any one view at a time. A user gets control, if it is available, by moving his cursor into the view, and relinquishes it by moving the cursor out of the view.

Multiple cursors are not supported. Each work station supports its own cursor, and the cursors of other users cannot be seen: a further violation of strict WYSIWIS. The cursor changes shape to indicate gaining control of the object underneath the cursor. In this way the user can tell whether he has control himself, but cannot tell who else has control if he does not. This we found quite satisfactory for interactions between two people, who could simply ask each other for control if necessary. However, we predict it would not be satisfactory for larger numbers of people interacting with the same object. In this case there are several different problems to be resolved, including knowing who is active in the perspective, knowing who has control of any particular window, and relinquishing control; and we are not convinced that multiple cursors provide the most satisfactory solution to any of these problems. Other ideas, such as the use of icons, multiple pointers, colour coding and control timeouts, appear to hold out some promise, although further work is needed.

A user shifts from one perspective to another by interacting with an icon called a Door, which looks like a physical door. Each Door provides a menu option *enter* (occasionally *exit,* depending on context), which when selected causes the workspace currently viewed on the screen to change. To indicate which perspective is currently occupied, the screen background colour is different for each perspective: we sometimes think of this as "wallpaper" for the rooms, or as a "coloured tablecloth" for a shared desktop.

Each Door has a fixed name created when the Door is created. Some Doors are thought of as entrances, and others as exits; the rationale for this distinction is rather subtle, and seems to depend upon a notion of "privateness" or "distance from the outside" which we have not articulated very clearly. Doors are created explicitly: in any perspective it is possible to create a Door to that perspective, name it, and move it to where it is required. There are no "Back Doors" created automatically to ensure a user can get back to a previous perspective; instead a user is expected as a matter of policy to keep Doors to important places in a private perspective (see below), so they are always accessible.

As so far described, our perspectives are very similar to the Rooms concept introduced in Henderson and Card (1986), and the combination of WYSIWIS and Rooms which was proposed in Stefik, Bobrow *et al.* (1987) as a suitable approach for computer-supported meetings and processes associated with large groups. However our approach differs in the sense that we propose this abstraction not only as a paradigm for conducting multi-user meetings, but much more widely as a paradigm for conducting all use of the workstation. Eventually we see it as a possible replacement for the "desktop" metaphor, destined to become as widespread in the networked environment as today's window/icon/menu interfaces are in the PC environment, in which spontaneous and informal *electronic meetings* will take place between remote users with the minimum of technical or organizational overhead.

7.4. PRIVATE AND SHAREABLE LAYERS

Every workstation always displays two perspectives, one in front of the other. The front perspective contains private information, and only appears on one workstation. The rear perspective is shareable, and may appear on many workstations. The act of going through a Door causes the shareable perspective to change, leaving the private one unaltered. The background colour, or wallpaper, is associated with the shareable perspective. We often call the private perspective the *Shelf*, and the shareable one the *Desk*; the analogy on which this is based is a transparent shelf on which private papers are kept, positioned over a desk for the more public papers.

Views on the Shelf always appear in front views on the Desk, and are visually distinguished. Figure 2 shows two screens, both displaying the same Desk perspective with views 1, 2 and 3, and each showing a different Shelf perspective,

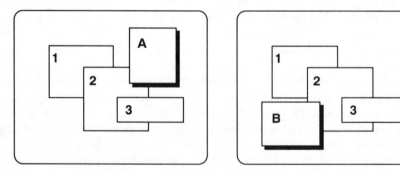

FIGURE 2. Shawing a desk.

with views A and B. Our proposal is that translucent drop shadows should be attached to the views on the Shelf, to reinforce the analogy. Time defeated our attempt to implement such shadows convincingly in our full colour system.

Moving views between shareable perspectives is accomplished by lifting them to the Shelf, going through the Door, and dropping them back to the Desk. Although this may sound cumbersome, in practice it is simple and transparent as long as it is immediately visually obvious whether a view is on the Shelf or the Desk, and quick to move from one to the other. Lifting and dropping views were felt to be such useful operations that they are accomplished by a mouse chord in our model. This use of the Shelf fulfils the functions of both *baggage* and the *pocket* in the Rooms system described in Henderson and Card (1986).

Another possible mechanism for moving views between perspectives which we thought of but didn't implement is to iconize a view and drop it "through the door", in the same way as icons can be dropped into a postbox for mailing, or a wastebin for trashing, in our model. This mechanism has the advantage that the user need not follow the view through the door, counterbalanced by the disadvantages that the view must be iconized before moving, and a decision is needed on where it will materialize in the destination perspective.

A shareable perspective has a special icon called the Pointer. The purpose of the Pointer is to draw attention to features of the shared material. The Pointer may be moved around by any of the participants. The Pointer always appears in front of everything in the Desk and behind everything in the Shelf.

Shareable perspectives do not have to be shared. The question of who has permission to go through a Door and operate in a perspective is a separate issue, and a shareable perspective may in fact never be shared because only one user has the right to operate in it.

The simultaneous presence of two perspectives for every user explains why we have adopted the name *perspective* rather than the name *room*. We consider that always being in two rooms at once is stretching the analogy too far. However, we did find it appropriate to name several perspectives as though they were rooms. We justify this apparent inconsistency by distinguishing between perspectives as a *mechanism* for sharing information, and rooms as an *interpretation* of that mechanism which applies for some, but not all, perspectives.

7.5. VISUAL EDITING OF VIEWS

A view can be switched into *editing mode*. In this mode, components can be moved around and cloned, their attributes such as shape, size and behaviour can be altered, new components can be introduced, and the icon, menus, titles, colours and other attributes associated with a view can be altered. When editing is complete, a view can be switched back into *run mode,* and will operate normally. Views can be made by cloning *templates* kept in a special perspective called the Warehouse. The way views are created and edited follows to some extent the philosophy espoused by Smith (1986) in the Alternate Reality Kit, and by Ungar and Smith (1987) in the language Self.

Our editable, shareable views, operating within perspectives, can be thought of as a kind of multi-user HyperCard-like system.† They provide the ability to create easily new kinds of object, representing a wide variety of information, such as messages, tools, devices, documents and forms.

7.6. ACTIVITY MODEL

The co-ordination and time management aspects of the model are supported by an activity model which represents the people known to the system, their location, activities, relationships and commitments. Each person is represented by an object which encapsulates information including their name, postal and electronic mail address, telephone number, picture, current location, schedule of activities, relationships to other people, set of commitments, and current state of availability. A schedule of activities is represented simply as diary appointments, which are associations of text strings with times. In the model the only relationships represented are organizational relationships in the workgroup hierarchy, and the only commitments are those related to a person's next change of location.

Messages between users are represented as views with a "mailability" attribute, allowing them to be accepted by the message delivery service, which will deliver them to the recipient's in-tray.

7.7. OBJECT NAMING AND BEHAVIOUR

Objects have names in nested environments. *Workgroup global* names are valid everywhere within the workgroup; examples are the names of objects representing the people in the workgroup. *Workstation global* names are valid within a single workstation, and include names for objects representing the owner of the workstation, the current operator, and the current perspectives. Within any perspective there are names for the views, and within views names for the components of the view.

Object behaviour results from the execution of scripts, caused by the arrival of events at objects. System events are sent whenever significant changes occur, such as the user going through a door, moving or resizing a view, pressing a button, lifting the handset etc. User-defined events can be sent from scripts.

Every script has two parts: a *global* and a *local* script. The global script causes changes which should appear everywhere, such as changes of state in a globally accessible object. The local script causes changes which should only occur on the workstation where the event is generated, such as going through a Door.

7.8. A STANDARD WORKING ENVIRONMENT

Every workstation has an owner, and a current user who may not be the owner. Each owner has a standard configuration of perspectives. The standard Desk perspectives in the model are the Office (for the owner), the Temporary Office (for visitors), and Nowhere (for when there is no current user). The standard Shelf perspectives are the Shelf (for the owner's private views) and the Lobby (for whenever the user is not the owner). This configuration simulates the idea of the workstation acting as a receptionist, for a visitor who wishes to gain access to the

† HyperCard is an application for the Apple Macintosh described in Goodman (1987).

workstation. The visitor can be given limited facilities, customized according to the owner's preferences.

In addition to the standard perspectives for each owner, there are a number of well-known public Desk perspectives, notably the Meeting Rooms and the Warehouse. We also imagined but did not implement the Corridor, the Outside, the Bulletin Board, and the Lounge.

In a real system there would be many more perspectives than the simple configuration in this model. Each owner would have several Desk perspectives for different projects and tasks, and there would be shared Desk perspectives for group projects, *ad hoc* meetings, reading public bulletin boards, and so on.

7.9. INTEGRATION OF MULTIPLE MEDIA

Objects can represent information in several media including text, graphics, image, forms, video and speech. These media are integrated wherever appropriate, so for example a message in the intray might consist of any combination of media. This integration results as a natural consequence of the polymorphism provided by object-orientation. Cox (1986) discusses the application of object-orientation to applications like this.

Video in our model is implemented in a rather crude way, with a single television camera connected into the workstation via a slow interface, essentially providing only the ability to take snapshots of people's faces and display them in windows on the screen. The model supports telephony, via a small PABX, and provides facilities to record speech from the telephone or a microphone, and replay it on the telephone or a loudspeaker.

7.10. OWNERSHIP AND AUTHENTICATION

The model does not implement any fundamental architectural concept of ownership, authentician and access protection. Instead, the script associated with going through a particular Door may validate access depending on the current operator of the workstation, thus giving the illusion of access protection at the level of Doors. An alternative policy would be to associate access with possession of the Door, and validate requests to obtain Doors instead of requests to enter them.

Once inside a perspective, all users have equal rights in our model. It might be desirable to have a further level of protection on views, so that only certain users have the right to perform particular operations: some users might have read-only access, for example. This should not be taken too far. It seems unreasonable, for example, to have views which are invisible to some users in a perspective, if only because their presence and maybe even their contents could be guessed from the activities of other users. It would also be an extreme violation of strict WYSIWIS.

8. Scenes

The completed demonstration comprises four scenes in full. The action in these scenes takes place in one of four physical locations, namely Steve's office, Charlie's office, Gary's office, and a public telephone box. There are five speaking characters,

Steve, Charlie (Steve's boss), Gary and Trish (colleagues of Steve), and Alan (from another workgroup). The content of each scene is outlined below, together with the system attributes which the scene demonstrates.

8.1. SCENE 1: ALAN VISITS STEVE

Story

It is 8.30 am. Alan, who works in another department, wishes to give Steve some information to help him write his progress report. As Alan happens to be passing Steve's office, he decides to go in. Once inside, Alan discovers that Steve has not yet arrived, so he decides to use Steve's workstation to leave him a message requesting a meeting. The workstation asks Alan to record his personal details (including his picture) on a multi-media form, before granting him access to temporary facilities. These include a view of Steve's diary and the ability to send messages, in particular a semi-structured message called a *request for diary entry* which he creates by cloning a template of such messages.

Alan also wishes to return some confidential documents borrowed from Steve's department. Alan does not want to leave them unattended, and decides to consult Steve's boss. However, Alan does not know who Steve's boss is. Alan uses a diagram of Steve's worksgroup to locate Charlie, Steve's boss, telephone him and arrange a meeting. Alan then leaves Steve's office.

Attributes demonstrated

(1) Steve's workstation knows where Steve is and when he will return.
(2) The workstation provides strangers with limited access to search for information, look in Steve's diary, leave messages and make telephone calls.
(3) The workstation allows browsing of the workgroup structure.
(4) Multi-media forms are used, to record Alan's personal details, and his request for a diary entry. The act of cloning in context allows the system to determine some values for the form; in this case, that the sender is Alan and the recipient is Steve.

8.2. SCENE 2: STEVE ENTERS HIS OFFICE

Story

Steve arrives in his own office on schedule at 9 am. He signs on to his workstation, and examines his diary to review his engagements. So that the can open his mail undisturbed, he sets his availability to "busy", causing the machine to handle interruptions. He looks at his mail, and sees a message from Alan requesting a meeting. After reading the message, he accepts the request, whereupon the entry in the diary is made automatically and Alan informed. While he continues with the remainder of his mail, other events unfold.

Attributes demonstrated

(1) The workstation supports an abstract concept of "busy", and adjusts its response to interruptions accordingly.
(2) The *request for diary entry* contains enough information for Steve to accept it with a single act, whereupon a commitment will be made, automatically inserted in the diary and a message of confirmation sent to the requestor. Note that Alan does not have the ability to insert commitments in Steve's diary directly.

8.3. SCENE 3: TRISH CALLS FROM A PUBLIC PHONE

Story

It is 9.30 am. Trish has been delayed on the way to work and decides to telephone Steve to let him know. Steve's workstation answers the call, using synthesized voice messages. Trish keys a code which tells the machine who is calling. The machine tells Trish where Steve is, that he is busy, and when he will be free. She decides to send him a voice message, telling him what has happened.

Steve has finished going through his mail. He is informed that a voice message has arrived. He listens to it. He tells the workstation that he is prepared to accept interruptions again. Meanwhile, in another office, Gary is having problems with a boat he is designing.

Attributes demonstrated

(1) The system can be accessed from a public telephone using the key tones to drive the responses.

(2) Telephony is fully integrated with the system's view of the current state of affairs.

8.4. SCENE 4: STEVE AND GARY COLLABORATE

Story

Gary is working on his boat design and wants to consult Steve about a technical detail. He decides to interrupt him. Steve gets the interruption and accepts it. He and Gary are placed in voice contact. Gary explains his problem, and suggests they work on it together in the "Green Meeting Room" perspective. Steve agrees, and goes through the appropriate Door. Gary lifts his boat design documents to his Shelf and goes through the Door into the Green Meeting Room, where he drops the documents, which become visible on Steve's workstation. They discuss the problem, using the meeting room Pointer to draw each other's attention to particular points.

Steve remembers he has some tables back in his office which will help and goes to fetch them. Dropping them into the Meeting Room they becomes visible to Gary. They help with the problem, and Gary decides he would like a copy. He asks Steve's permission, which is granted, and Gary clones the tables. They each pick up their documents and return through Doors into their offices.

It is now nearly 11 am and Steve leaves his office for a meeting, telling the workstation where he will be.

Attributes demonstrated

(1) Perspectives and WYSIWIS are used for two colleagues to set up an *ad hoc* meeting in which they work together remotely on visual material.

Each scene has a theatrical aspect and a software aspect. The software aspect consists of an implementation of the system services implied by the script of the scene. Building the software involved a balancing act between the two objectives of implementing the very specific detailed behaviour required by the script, and implementing the general behaviour implied by scenes in the context of the architecture. Where there was a conflict, the specific was normally favoured over the general.

A demonstration of the completed model is a theatrical exercise which requires learning and rehearsal. Each demonstration requires an introduction to set the scene, so that the audience can grasp the meaning of what happens on the screens, followed by a performance with simultaneous commentary.

9. Implementation

The model is implemented in the Smalltalk-80 programming environment running on 80386-based colour workstations, using the BrouHaHa interpreter described in Miranda (1987). Smalltalk-80 was used because of its uniformly object-oriented approach, and because considerable local expertise was available. Approximately 300 classes were added in all. The basic Smalltalk-80 image was substantially extended in several areas, as follows:

- Support for colour, with a colour model designed to allow the state and ownership of views to be represented simply, as well as the ability to display full colour icons and grey-scale renditions of video images;
- Direct manipulation of views, using mouse clicks and drags;
- Support for overlapping colour pixmaps of any shape, with concurrent updating of obscured pixmaps and double buffering for smooth animation;
- High-level network support, including remote invocation of methods, and the establishment of remote pipes;
- Improved process scheduling; and
- Binary object storage.

On top of the enhanced Smalltalk system we built the perspective management system, and the classes implementing shareable, editable views and their components.

The illusion of operating in a shared distributed object space was created by the view objects. The model is started by running an identical Smalltalk-80 image, containing the starting configuration of views in perspectives, on all nodes of the network. Each view in this configuration is connected by network pipes to its counterparts at all nodes, using protocols which ensure that all changes to the view are synchronized everywhere. Each workstation displays one shareable and one private perspective at any time, and workstations can change perspectives independently of each other. Views in non-displayed perspectives are invisible, but are still updated if they are being altered elsewhere.

Floor control between multiple users of a single view is administered by a master workstation, which responds to requests for control by only allowing one workstation to have control at a time.

Input events generated by the controlling user at the level of view components are transmitted one-by-one to the remote views, using a protocol related to the component type. For example, for text components events are transmitted for each keystroke; for button components, on each press or release; for components such as sliders which respond to a continuous motion input, an event is only transmitted at the end of the motion, so only the end result appears remotely.

Input such as collapsing, resizing, and moving which causes changes at the level of whole views, is broadcast according to a similar principle, so that remote views end up in the same final state without going through intermediate values.

As stated earlier, local and global scripts associated with events implement the detailed behaviour of the individual views. Local scripts implement changes which only occur on the local workstation, such as going through a Door. The script for going through a Door causes the Desk perspective on the local workstation to change, but has no effect on remote workstations. Global scripts implement changes which occur on all workstations, such as typing into a text component.

10. Assessment

Having built the model, and performed the scenes in front of several audiences and on video, we state here the main things that we believe have been learnt from the project. These fall into three categories: what worked, what didn't work, and what is missing. We have not carried out any empirical evaluation with users, so these assessments should be considered as speculative, with considerable further research required.

10.1. WHAT WORKED

WYSIWIS: WYSIWIS, modified as we have indicated, is a powerful and compelling idea, and once observed in action generates a host of new ideas and possibilities, particularly when combined with ideas like video conferencing and stereo sound. There are two sides to WYSIWIS: representation of the shared material, and representation of the sharers themselves. We think that WYSIWIS as a principle only applies to the shared material itself, subject to issues of granularity.

Private and shareable layers: The idea of shareable (Desk) and private (Shelf) perspectives works well. It provides a transparent way of distinguishing between shared and private information, organizing information into personal and group projects, and moving information between perspectives. Several issues remain to be resolved, in particular the best way of visually distinguishing between the two perspectives, and the best way of ensuring that shared material is not inconveniently obscured by private material.

Watching the video of our model, there is a very telling moment when Gary and Steve have finished their remote meeting and return to their own office perspectives, taking their respective views with them. There is a strong sense of them "going somewhere and taking something". We see this as evidence of the potential power of the perspectives concept. We also see it as indicative of an important paradigm shift, which we think of as follows: the computer ceases to be an *agent,* and becomes instead an *opening onto a place* in a shared, structured space.

The pointer: We found that the Pointer provides a workable solution to the problem of how to refer to features of shared material, although even with two participants there was occasionally some contention and uncertainty over the use of the Pointer.

Activity model: The activity model was essential. The central database of information about individual people gave both long-term information such as various addresses, and transient information such as their current location, state of availability, current schedule and so on. The creation of an agent to answer the telephone usefully in a person's absence was made simple by having the information available. Issues of authentication and access are brought to the forefront by this exercise.

Forms: The use of electronic forms to implement semi-structured messages, such as a *request for diary entry,* is potentially surprisingly powerful, as suggested in Malone, Grant, Lai, Rao and Rosenblitt (1987). The power is derived from the richness of the activity model in which the messages are interpreted. Tagging messages as requests and promises provides the potential to track *conversations for action,* as described in Winograd and Flores (1986), within the activity model. Reminders and to-do lists can be generated automatically from the activity model.

Group structure: Our decision to invent an organizational structure with work-groups cast light on how to implement abstractions like *busy* and *available* for individual users, as well as the concept of a visitor, which had a substantial bearing on our default working arrangement of perspectives. Our experience indicates that the concept of *group* is a fundamental aspect of the system architecture, with people being able to belong to many groups.

Event programming: Event-driven programming worked quite well. An example is the creation of a new "request" message by cloning a template. The new message responds to the event of being created by looking at the context of its creation (Who created me? Where and when am I being created?) to determine sensible defaults for its contents, minimizing input and mistakes for the user.

Object-orientation: The principles of object-orientation pervaded our entire approach. It is difficult to imagine how we would have thought about the project in any other way. Every part of the design is formulated and documented in terms of objects, and their classes, behaviour and relationships. At the user level, template objects and cloning were satisfying ideas which fulfilled our objective of transparency.

The fundamental philosophy of Smalltalk-80 provided a good platform for exploring these ideas. Exploratory programming, re-usability and integration was very much in tune with our requirements.

10.2. WHAT DIDN'T WORK

Script Language: The language we developed for writing the scripts associated with views and their components was not very successful. We used an imperative language, in which component scripts could directly change the value of other components. This proved unmanageable, because of the difficulty of finding out where any particular component is changed. In retrospect, we had simply ignored all the good advice of object-orientation. Instead we should have made each component responsible as far as possible for its own changes, using a more declarative approach.

The distinction between local and global scripts proved difficult to manage in practice. Because scripts could have side-effects, including generating events, obscure distributed recursions could be set up. We still consider the basic idea to be necessary and workable, but further work is needed to see how to make it work cleanly with the more declarative approach suggested above.

Limitations of Smalltalk: Many detailed aspects of Smalltalk took considerable work to overcome. Limitations of the user interface and window manager had to be solved. The network support had to be written. Our scripts, kept as BlockContext objects, were not recorded on the change log file and so we had to be very careful not to lose a lot of work through system crashes.

Sometimes we spent too much time on detailed user-interface issues. It is often tempting when inventing a design such as this to go down side alleys, wondering about the specific format of menus, icons, push buttons etc. On reflection these issues are orthogonal to the architectural themes which form the focus of this study. If Smalltalk had made more decisions for us, we could have adopted these and concentrated more on the deeper issues.

10.3. WHAT IS MISSING

Perhaps the most important contribution is the list of what is missing, since identifying what would be needed to do the job properly was one of our main objectives. Here we set out the most important results in this area.

Applications: Our model does not define any separation between what is considered to be generic software, and what is considered to be application-specific. A real system would need to define and provide support both for new applications which take advantage of the groupware facilities, and for existing ones which are designed to run under a more conventional operating system.

Authentication: We have not implemented any scheme for authentication and access control. In any real system such facilities would be absolutely essential. An attractive idea is the use of "SmartCards", electronically readable credit-card sized devices which can be used to authenticate a person simply and reliably. These would obviate the typing of passwords, and in a suitable secure environment would provide the equivalent of electronic signatures, permitting "sign-offs" to be made.

Floor control: Our token-passing floor control scheme is simplistic and would probably become cumbersome if used by more than two participants. The problem occurs when a participant fails to relinquish control, a common occurrence. The problem could be solved by allowing control to be pre-empted after a short time-out, and we think this would provide an effective solution with the right time constant.

Presence indication: We do not provide any explicit indication of the presence of a user in a perspective. This means that it is possible for a user to enter a perspective and observe what is happening covertly. In general this is probably a poor idea, and we suggest that the presence of a new participant in a perspective should be indicated at least by the appearance of an icon, and possibly also be an explicit announcement. One promising idea is to have a Pointer for each user, which would automatically appear in the current Desk perspective for that user, and could only be moved by its owner. This would both give an explicit representation of the user's presence, as well as resolving the pointer contention problem which arose with a single Pointer.

Activity model: Our activity model is very primitive. Having completed the modelling exercise, we think that a fuller model should represent at least the following classes of object: Message, Person, Group, Relationship, Activity, Promise, Event, Action and Role, as well as supporting classes such as Date, Time and Trigger.

The class Message would define all objects sent from one user (or group) to another. All messages would be semi-structured, with some attributes interpreted in the context of the activity model, and other attributes consisting of free text, images, speech or other information. Each message structure would have a type, such as requests for diary entries or information, announcements of seminars or meetings, and so on. Messages can also be classified according to their importance and urgency, and whether they are personal. Each user would set up rules for how each of these structures would be interpreted in their own personal environment, causing diary entries to be made, information to be filed, messages to be acknowledged, forwarded or discarded, and so on. The transparency of such rules for users is a matter for further research.

The classes Person, Group and Relationship would provide the basis for a model of organizational structure, enabling locating and addressing of people and groups, automatic interpretation of messages, and establishing the availability and preferences of individuals.

The class Activity would provide a mechanism for associating events, promises and actions with ongoing projects. An activity might be associated with a perspective, or group of perspectives, to retain a visual record of progress.

Each Promise object would represent a promise made by a person to another person or group. Different kinds of promises are promises for actions to be carried out by a certain time, promises which come into effect when a certain event occurs, and promises to do something at a specific time for a specific duration, e.g. attend a meeting. Promises would have the ability to generate reminders and carry out actions on completion or non-completion.

Event objects would represent diary entries. They would often, but not necessarily, be associated with promises to attend. There would be one-off and repeated events, and many *types* of event such as meetings of various kinds, conferences, seminars, presentations, lectures, travelling etc. Users would also define their own event types. Each event could generate actions and reminders both before and after the event.

Action objects would represent specific atomic actions, such as telephone calls, sending messages, and writing letters. Some action objects would represent actions wholly or partly amenable to automation; for example sending a message might be completely automatic, whereas a telephone call action could dial the number and attempt to place the call, and a letter-writing action could invoke a word-processor with the right address and letter format filled in. The idea is to provide a smooth transition between the fully automated and the completely manual in the same activity model.

The class Role would distinguish between people and the roles that they play within various activities and events. For example, a meeting has a convener and a chairman, a project has a leader, and so on. Roles were discussed by Anatol Holt in work cited by De Cindio, De Michelis, Simone, Vassallo and Zanaboni (1986). Roles in message systems were investigated by Tsichritzis and Gibbs (1987), and roles and activities were explored by Dollimore and Wilbur (1989) in the COSMOS project.

There is an immense amount of work to be done in the details of the activity model and its user interface, including applications such as diaries, calenders, schedules, to-do lists and commitments. A complex activity model, although potentially very powerful, is unlikely to be accepted by users unless the user interface makes it both complete (in the sense that it can be relied on at all times for all activities) and transparent.

Multiple media: Our provision for the use of video and sound was very restricted. In particular we had no hardware to integrate colour video images with colour digital images, so we could not display video in real time on the screen. We believe that the provision of a full video network, with sufficient bandwidth for each user of the system to see other users and their work, could transform the experience of each user. The provision of such facilities would raise many important questions, including whether video images should always share the same screen as other objects. If not, should they all be on a separate screen, or should some be separate and some integrated? If video images are integrated with other objects, where should they be located in the perspectives system? How can eye-contact be established between video users? SharedARK, as described by Smith *et al.* (1989), uses a "video tunnel" constructed with a half-silvered mirror set at 45° to the screen to ensure eye contact. We wonder if it is feasible to build such facilities into a workstation.

The use of sound could be extended much further. The telephone provides point-to-point circuits of speech quality, and used in conjunction with recording and playback, voice synthesis and recognition, and integrated with an activity model, still has a great deal of scope for development. The provision of high fidelity stereo sound would open up completely new areas, music being an obvious one. However, even in the area of ordinary office work the provision of high-quality shared *sound spaces* would add a new dimension to remote co-operative working. For example, every user could have their own stereo image of the participants in an electronic meeting. Reverberation could be used to give depth to the image, and perhaps even to distinguish *sotto voce* remarks from public statements. Sound spaces could be associated with perspectives, so that entering a perspective would automatically connect a user into the appropriate sound space.

11. Conclusion

In this project we built a model of a groupware system, and used it to explore and assess the requirements for an infrastructure capable of supporting future networked applications.

The main contribution of our work has been to throw further light on the architectural requirements for an integrated groupware infrastructure, which would provide the operating foundation for general workstation applications in a networked office environment. We believe we now know enough to define a programme to build a real prototype version of the integrated system we set out to explore.

The approach of writing detailed scenes, creating an architecture based on those scenes, implementing them in full, and demonstrating and videoing the implementations gave a vivid sense of the issues involved. We strongly recommend this approach to others who wish to evaluate ideas for complex multi-user software.

This project has deliberately not set out to investigate the organizational consequences of introducing a system such as the one described. In the terms of Bannon and Schmidt (1989) we are probably "strict constructionists": we are certainly implementors, interested in building widgets and looking for novel applications. However our focus is not simply on supporting our own work; we are equally interested in seeing how these novel applications can be brought to the marketplace, which is where the success or otherwise of novel applications will become apparent.

The project has convinced us that technology such as this has the potential to provide a host of new opportunities, for increasing productivity, democracy in the workplace, and the flexibility of the working location.

Many thanks for creative participation go to Ron Bird, Mike Davis, John Francis, Mike Garrett, Kerry LeClue, Eliot Miranda, Doug Turner, Trish Tustin and Nik Shaylor. Thanks for careful reviewing of this paper go to Bruce Anderson, and the anonymous referees. This project was funded by IBM UK Laboratories Ltd, Hursley Park.

References

BAKER, G. (1989). Best Sellers. *LAN Magazine,* **March**.

BANNON, L. J. & SCHMIDT, K. (1989). CSCW: four characters in search of a context. In J. BOWERS & S. BENFORD, Eds. In *Proceedings of the First European Conference on Computer Supported Cooperative Work,* pp. 358–372. Computer Sciences Company.

COX, B. J. (1986). *Object Oriented Programming: an Evolutionary Approach.* Reading, MA: Addison-Wesley.

DE CINDIO, F., DE MICHELIS, G., SIMONE, C., VASSALLO, R. & ZANABONI, A. M. (1986). Chaos as coordination technology. In *CSCW'86 Proceedings of the Conference on Computer-Supported Cooperative Work,* pp. 325–342. Austin, TX: ACM Press.

DOLLIMORE, J. & WILBUR, S. (1989). Experiences in building a configurable CSCW System. In J. BOWERS & S. BENFORD, Eds. In *Proceedings of the First European Conference on Computer-Supported Work,* pp. 215–225. Computer Sciences Company.

EHN, P. (1988). *Work-Oriented Design of Computer Artifacts.* Stockholm: Arbetslivscentrum.

GOLDBERG, A. & ROBSON, D. (1983). *Smalltalk-80: The Language and its Implementation.* Reading, MA: Addison-Wesley.

GOODMAN, D. (1987). *The Complete Hypercard Handbook.* Bantam Books.

GRIEF, I. & SARIN, S. (1987). Data sharing in group work. *ACM Transactions on Office Information Systems,* **5**, 187–211.

HENDERSON, A. D. & CARD, S. K. (1986). Rooms: the use of multiple virtual workspaces to reduce space contention in a window-based graphical user interface. *ACM Transactions on Graphics,* **5**, 211–243.

JOHANSEN, R. (1984). *Teleconferencing and Beyond.* New York: McGraw-Hill.

KUHN, T. S. (1970). *The Structure of Scientific Revolutions,* 2nd edit. University of Chicago Press.

MAIER, D. (1989). Making database systems fast enough for CAD applications. In W. KIM & F. H. LOCKOVSKY, Eds. *Object-Oriented Concepts, Databases, and Applications,* pp. 573–582. New York: ACM Press.

MALONE, T. W., GRANT, K. R., LAI, K.-Y., RAO, R. & ROSENBLITT, D. (1987). Semistructured messages are surprisingly useful for computer-supported coordination. *ACM Transactions on Office Information Systems,* **5**, 115–131.

MIRANDA, E. (1987). BrouHaHa—a portable smalltalk interpreter. In N. MEYROWITZ, Ed. In *Proceedings of the 1987 Conference on Object-Oriented Programming Systems, Languages and Applications. ACM Sigplan Notices* **22**(12), 354–365.

OMG (1989). *By-laws of object management group, Inc.* Framingham, MA: Object Management Group.

SCHEIFLER, R. W. & GETTYS, J. (1986). The X Window System. *ACM Transactions on Graphics,* **5,** 79–109.

SCHMUCKER, K. J. (1986). *Object-Oriented Programming for the Macintosh.* Hayden Book Company.

SMITH, R. B. (1986). The alternate reality kit: An animated environment for creating interactive simulations. In *Proceedings of the 1986 IEEE Computer Society Workshop on Visual Languages,* pp. 99–106.

SMITH, R. B., O'SHEA, T., O'MALLEY, C., SCANLON, E. & TAYLOR, J. (1989). Preliminary experiments with a distributed, multi-media problem solving environment. In J. BOWERS & S. BENFORD, Eds. *Proceedings of the First European Conference on Computer Supported Cooperative Work.* pp. 19–34. Computer Sciences Company.

STEFIK, M., BOBROW, D. G., FOSTER, G., LANNING, S. & TATAR, D. (1987). WYSIWYS revised: early experiences with multiuser interfaces. *ACM Transactions on Office Information Systems,* **5,** 147–167.

STEFIK, M., FOSTER, G., BOBROW, D. G., KAHN, K., LANNING, S. & SUCHMAN, L. (1987). Beyond the chalkboard: computer support for collaboration and problem solving in meetings. *Communications of the ACM,* **30,** 32–47.

TEGER, S. L. (1983). Factors Impacting the Evolution of Office Automation. *Proceedings of the IEEE,* **71,** 503–511.

TSICHRITZIS, D. & GIBBS, S. J. (1987). Etiquette specification in message systems. In D. TSICHRITZIS, Ed. *Office Automation Concepts and Tools,* pp. 93–113. Berlin: Springer-Verlag.

UNGAR, D. & SMITH, R. B. (1987). Self: the Power of Simplicity. In N. MEYROWITZ, Ed. *Proceedings of the 1987 Conference on Object-Oriented Programming Languages, Systems and Applications. ACM Sigplan Notices,* **22**(12), 227–242.

WEINAND, A., GAMMA, E. & MARTY, R. (1988). ET++—an object oriented application framework in C++. In N. MEYROWITZ, Ed. *Proceedings of the 1988 Conference on Object-Oriented Programming Systems, Languages and Applications. ACM Sigplan Notices* **23**(11), 46–57.

WEINSTEIN, S. B. (1986). Personalized services on the intelligent wideband network. *Proceedings of the 1986 International Zurich Seminar on Digital Communications,* pp. 13–18.

WINOGRAD, T. & FLORES, F. (1986). *Understanding Computers and Cognition: A New Foundation for Design.* Norwood, NJ: Ablex Publishing.

Part 5

Removing rigidity from groupware

14

Post-mechanistic groupware primitives: rhythms, boundaries and containers

PETER JOHNSON-LENZ

TRUDY JOHNSON-LENZ

We are exploring a middle path bridging two prevailing but polar opposite approaches to groupware: (1) mechanism—making groups work through the use of explicit forms and procedures; and (2) context or open space—allowing groups to self-organize. A group is a living system, and its work is a creative, dynamic process. Appropriate forms come and go. Computer-supported groups need groupware that provides more than procedural mechanisms and open space. They need groupware that can be tailored for their changing needs and evolving purposes. Life is organized in rhythms, boundaries and containers. Using tailorable groupware of our own design, we have implemented *post-mechanistic* groupware primitives that bridge the prevailing approaches to groupware in six steps: open space (context), timing, rhythms, boundaries, containers and procedures (mechanism). In the laboratory of our on-line learning community, we tailor the groupware to support the purpose and flow of a variety of educational activities. In the years ahead, nearly all organizations will be affected by rapid and fundamental change. Those that thrive will be in a state of continuous, accelerated learning regardless of their purpose. We believe that the educational principles of *purpose-centered* groupware explored here potentially apply to *any* computer-supported group work. As the virtual reflection of developing society, purpose-centered groupware is an essential part of the necessary transition to a vital, sustainable culture.

Groupware as a co-evolving human–machine system

Groupware† is *computer-mediated culture*. It is an embodiment of social organization in *hyperspace*—that asynchronous, aspatial place where people meet via computer (Johnson-Lenz, 1989c). Since many pressing global problems are widely recognized as symptoms of limitations inherent in the passing mechanistic world view (among others Bateson, 1972, 1979; Berman, 1981), groupware which is effective in these turbulent times will necessarily reflect more sustainable cultural patterns than those which are breaking down.

To provide background, we begin with the relationship between the human and machine subsystems of groupware, how they co-evolve, and how the software is most appropriately tailored to support evolving group purpose. Two prevailing approaches to groupware (mechanism and context) are described and then integrated into a broader approach that embodies the new emerging world view.

As culture, groupware is a single system integrating co-evolving human and tool systems. Our original definition of groupware (Johnson-Lenz, 1980, 1982) was "intentional group processes plus software to support them". It has both *computer* and *human* components: software of the computer and "software" of the people using it. The human component is a shared "mental model" of what the group is doing (purpose) and how it is doing it (process). Recently this definition has been extended to include other more expressly cultural factors including myth, values and norms (Johnson-Lenz, 1989a). The computer software should reflect and support a group's purpose, process and culture. Like well-designed co-processes in a cooperating network server and workstation, the matched co-processes of computer and group software join the machine and biological "hardware" in a creative whole.

As co-evolving systems, the human and machine components augment each other's capacity, and provide a context for each other's development. They function like a rope climber's two hands, each pulling the system always one step more beyond itself. As the system evolves to higher levels of organization, it increases its creative capacity to respond with the requisite wisdom.

As early as 1962, Engelbart recognized the power of this co-evolutionary approach applied to knowledge work (Englebart, 1962) and proposed a "bootstrapping strategy" whereby each generation of groupware technology is used as the creative context within which the next generation is designed and implemented.

> Inherent in the Bootstrapping Strategy is the explicit co-evolution of the Human-System and the Tool-System as one holistic system. As the complexity and urgency facing today's organizations increases exponentially, the need for this Co-Evolution approach becomes absolutely critical (Englebart, 1988, p. 5).

Tailoring groupware to fit group purpose

> In times ahead we should find ourselves more able to understand institutional structure itself not as truth, but as a context for creative process . . . In other words, we should find people increasingly adapting structures to fit their purposes, rather than tailoring their lives to fit structures (Johnston, 1988, p. 10).

We developed our early ideas about groupware while working with Murray Turoff and Roxanne Hiltz via EIES®,† the Electronic Information Exchange System housed at the New Jersey Institute of Technology. Turoff's uniquely *tailorable* toolchest and concept of "structured communication" (Turoff, 1971; Hiltz & Turoff, 1978) drew us to EIES. From our early experiments there we learned two fundamental lessons: (1) some structure is needed by most on-line groups; and (2) different structures serve different purposes. We began to realize the software component of groupware is best tailored in response to the needs of the human component, rather than the other way around. While this may be obvious, it is neither widely understood nor practised.

Today, except for Turoff's second-generation TEIES®/EIES2®† (Turoff, Hiltz, Foster & Ng, 1989) and our own system (Johnson-Lenz, 1988a), we are unaware of any other truly tailorable groupware that: (1) offers a *variety* of communication structures; (2) supports easily modified paths guiding users through the system; and (3) can be tailored by those using it without reprogramming. Given the obvious utility of different structures for different purposes and the variety of groupware forms that already exist, this lack is puzzling.

† EIES, EIES2 and TEIES are trademarks of the New Jersey Institute of Technology.

Limited tailoring of menus and dictionaries is available on some systems, but they provide only a single communications structure, leaving users with no choice but to work within the designer's assumptions about group communication. Benston (1990) describes how system structures determine the types of possible communication, and how most systems are biased toward the exchange of abstract ideas rather than authentic human contact. In the absence of an established theory of asynchronous group dynamics, including fundamental organizing principles and group process *primitives,* each designer is left to intuition, personal bias and trial and error to discover appropriate structures.

Values and cultural assumptions are incorporated into each and every groupware design. As Turoff notes:

> It is possible to design, via the computer, almost any variation from a free and open communication process to a complete dictatorship. . . . The list of possibilities for imposing control are rather large . . . . In that sense, this technology is a rather unique two-edged sword (Turoff, 1982, p. 255).

Designers may be wise enough to create structures which empower, and that may be a necessary first step in the "bootstrapping" process, but a better solution is to involve users in the design process. Interest in this approach is growing as indicated by the recent Participatory Design Conference (PDC '90), sponsored by Computer Professionals for Social Responsibility.

Better yet is a design that allows its users to pattern their own communications by providing tools for those directly involved (facilitators, managers and even users) to tailor the system to their purposes and processes. Our early tailoring experiences on EIES opened us to the possibilities of evolving a system over time in response to user feedback (Johnson-Lenz, 1981), but the tools required too much technical expertise, took too long to tailor, and reflected our limited understanding of group dynamics via computer. We had yet to discover the appropriate primitives for human interaction via computer.

To understand the primitives described below, it is useful to review the two prevailing—and polar opposite—approaches to groupware.

Groupware as mechanism

Groupware as mechanism is the most common approach to groupware. It is based on the social theory that human interaction can be modeled as a machine with deterministic interactions among separate parts, such as hierarchical chains of command, bureaucracies and Robert's Rules of Order. This social theory is a reflection of the mechanistic world view that rose into dominance during the Age of Reason and the Industrial Revolution. If the universe is a machine, so is society.

From this point of view, the computer's role in groupware is to provide well-defined mechanisms for interaction. Much of the groupware available for the corporate market falls into this category, including many computer-supported cooperative work systems. The most common examples are systems for shared authoring, project management, and shared calendars that regulate interactions within a limited, task-specific focus.

More ambitious designs seek to encompass a broader range of tasks with a general-purpose mechanism. Winograd and Flores' The Coordinator (Winograd,

1986) is the first of a genre of systems that define specific communication acts—requests for action and commitments to fulfill them. All interaction is required to fit within that framework, and the computer monitors the fulfillment of all commitments. Transaction groupware, as defined by Dyson (1989), breaks complex tasks into replicable subtasks of transactions. Its purpose is to improve efficiency by making all transactions explicit and automating the routine parts.

Social coherence in these systems is "caused" by a mechanism that *determines* the outcome through explicit rules and algorithms. The causal principle is mechanistic, or what we call *right-handed* causality, popularly known as "cause and effect". Such groupware designs focus on the basic units of interaction among people cooperating on well-specified tasks. They are designed to keep the group on task, enforce roles and commitments, *make* the group efficient and productive, and *make* it behave in a certain predefined way.

The implicit values often underlying such groupware are control and adherence to rules, at the expense of individual autonomy and freedom of choice. Often their inflexible structures trigger organizational and individual resistance, effectively *reducing* the creative capacity of the group rather than increasing it. Zuboff (1988) criticizes the use of computer technology to monitor workers, warning of the potential danger of electronic sweatshops. Reder and Schwab postulate:

> Automated attempts to "pin people down" and thereby enhance accountability may not bring about better communication or enhanced productivity. It is very likely such attempts, if they are accepted by users, will change the "rules of the game", and certain types of critical conversations will move to contexts in which the tool will not be used, thereby altering the nature of the communication which does take place through the new technology (Reder & Schwab, 1988, p. 367).

While these criticisms are sometimes warranted, it is most often when the groupware has taken the mechanistic model to the extreme. There is an important and useful place for groupware as mechanism. It is part of effective groupware, but something more is needed. The critics point the way. More flexible patterns that encourage personal initiative are just as important as well-defined group procedures.

The description of these systems is oversimplified here in order to highlight the dominant causal principle in their designs. Most do include some flexibility. For example, recent versions of The Coordinator have added more open-ended communication act categories. This only serves to make the point.

Groupware as context

Groupware as context is the popular "alternative" approach to groupware. It is the polar opposite of groupware as mechanism. It is based on the social theory that human systems are self-organizing and arise out of the unrestricted interaction of autonomous individuals. This social theory has emerged in response to the limitations of hierarchical, mechanistic styles of organization and is part of a much broader challenge to the mechanistic world view in virtually every field.

Much has been written about this social theory applied to management. Several works are particularly relevant here. Ackerman (1984) has developed a theory of "flow state management" in which the primary management task is removing blocks to the natural flow of energy. Peters (1987) describes the advantages of actively engaging with chaos as a creative source rather than trying to control it. Owen (1987) writes about creating "open spaces" with few, if any, forms to pattern interactions and within which people organize themselves.

From this point of view the computer's role is to provide open space for people to meet and self-organize. Most computer conferencing systems such as CompuServe, The WELL, the Santa Monica Public Electronic Network (PEN), and America Online embody this approach. They use variations on a simple two-tiered structure originally developed on the Confer system (Zinn, Parnes & Hench, 1976) that allows participants to organize themselves into topics or special interest groups.

In some of the more sophisticated systems, the computer also provides tools to support this self-organizing activity. Incorporating precursors to Sculley's (1987) vision of a knowledge navigator, two levels are usually involved: (1) collective knowledge structuring tools; and (2) personal interface tools for navigating those structures. Knowledge structures provide forms within which communications can be organized into more useful patterns using hierarchical file systems, keywords, and hypertext. User interfaces support pull-down menus and point-and-click hypertext links.

Engelbart's (1962) Augment pioneered most of these concepts. Newer commercial systems including Connect and America Online incorporate some of them. The recently released Lotus Notes system is a derivative of the Xerox NoteCards system (Trigg, Suchman & Halasz, 1986) which extends many of these ideas. Our system (Johnson-Lenz, 1988a) includes simple hypertext tools similar to those in the original Augment system. Turoff's EIES2 goes a step further with group and personal organizing tools using a "list processing" metaphor (Turoff, Hiltz, Foster & Ng, 1989). Even low-end conferencing and bulletin board systems such as Coconet, HyperBBS, and TeamMate are beginning to reflect some of this sophistication by including hypertext capability and point-and-click interfaces.

The causal principle of social formation in these systems is non-mechanistic, or what we call *left-handed* causality. It assumes that social coherence will emerge from individual interactions. It is the polar opposite of mechanistic causality which seeks to *produce* coherence. Left-handed causality creates space for coherence to emerge and then *allows* it to happen. At the group level, this is non-mechanistic. However, at the levels of knowledge organization and user interfaces, it *is* mechanistic. Groups form as the result of individuals using personal knowledge navigation tools interacting through a vast knowledge building mechanism.

These systems focus on the user interface and structure of knowledge, rather than the dynamics of group process and interaction. They are designed to give each user as much freedom as possible. Rather than focusing on commitments and support for keeping them, such systems offer the polar opposite—complete freedom to come and go at will, to do whatever one wants, whenever one wants to do it. The implicit values embedded in these systems are individual autonomy and freedom of choice at the expense of the commitment and responsibility to others necessary for social coherence. This is not really groupware. If groups do emerge, it happens *without* much support from the software. The results are often disappointing, or at least sporadic. Sometimes there is a lot of activity, but conversations tend to be scattered and of uneven quality. Small islands of creative interaction do occur, but they are infrequent (Johnson-Lenz, 1989b, 1989c).

This approach is an important alternative to the mechanistic approach, but ultimately it reduces social interaction either to chance meetings or to the mechanical accumulation of knowledge. The open space approach offers another part of effective groupware for these times, but still only a part, even when taken together with the mechanistic approach. A user interface is but a single membrane in a rich and complex living social system. Routine transactions and explicit commitments can lack meaning. What and where is the deep structure?

The vital missing link

> What is missing? There are many ways it could be put, but perhaps most simply, what is missing is *life*. In Newtonian/Cartesian reality the universe and all within it are like a great clockworks, an immense and wondrous piece of machinery. A mechanical paradigm can offer us many amazing things. But no matter how great a machine's complexity, it can never be more than just that, a machine (Johnston, 1986, p. 7).

A social theory is beginning to emerge that bridges the opposites of mechanism and context discussed so far. It reflects a new world view broad enough to include both right- and left-handed causality. It integrates mechanism into a larger framework. Rather than viewing reality as a machine, a rule-driven, deterministic system of fixed, independent parts, it views reality as a creative process, essentially interconnected, multiply determined, inherently uncertain, and constantly changing (Johnston, 1991). Rather than measuring the effectiveness of a system in mechanistic terms alone, such as productivity or efficiency, it uses more inclusive measures or referents such as its capacity to be creative, to be alive.

Johnston identifies three "waves" of this new world view emerging during the last 100 years (Johnston, 1991). Each wave bridged previously separate realms. The first included Darwin's bridging of humanity and nature with an encompassing model of evolution and Einstein's bridging of energy and matter, space and time, and the observer and observed. The second wave brought Plank, Bohr and Heisenberg's quantum physics which bridged certainty and uncertainty, and cause and effect; Hegel's dialectic synthesis of opposites; and Whitehead's bridging of being and doing, rational and irrational, and determinate and indeterminate. The third wave in the last 30 years brought systems thinking with von Bertalanffy's exploration of wholes, Jantsch and Lazlo's evolutionary dynamics in living systems, and Bateson's bridging of mind and nature.

This integral world view and the social theory that reflects it are the foundation of our conceptual framework for groupware. They provide a way of thinking about group process via computer which encompasses mechanisms and forms to support group work as well as context and open spaces in which group life can emerge. They provide powerful conceptual tools for integrating these two approaches into a single, creative whole.

While beyond the scope of this paper, we describe elsewhere (Johnson-Lenz, 1990b) two bodies of work that have been particularly influential in the development of our framework: Mindell's process-oriented psychology (Mindell, 1985) and Johnston's bridging of left- and right-handed causality as *creative causality* (Johnston, 1986) (Figure 1). The latter shows how bridging opposites by framing

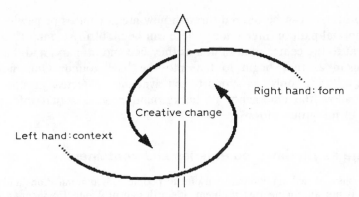

FIGURE 1. Left and right hands of creative causality.

questions in terms of "both-and" rather than "either/or" polarities, results in something larger, dynamic, and more creative. Bridging context and form results in the process of creative change.

Groupware as creative process

Effective group work requires a shared understanding of what the group is doing (its purpose) and how it is doing it (its process). This shared form occupies the foreground of group attention. Without it nothing would happen. But that form is an output of the living, creative process of group work, not the process itself. The process also includes background processes—the vague dissatisfactions, inchoate preferences, or senses of what could be better—some of which may emerge to challenge the foreground process. These are a vital source of new directions and creative power for the group. To support a group's creative process, groupware must at times support the current forms and at others expedite moving them out of the way to support new processes emerging from the background, the context.

Effective groupware must have the capacity to support: (1) foreground *and* background processes; and (2) the entire creative cycle whereby new processes/forms emerge from and return to the background/context (Johnson-Lenz, 1990*b*). While back channels like e-mail and places for debriefing or evaluating group work provide a similar function, they separate background process from the group. Reder and Schwab (1988) have shown that users spontaneously select different channels for different communication purposes. But isolating background processes in other channels does not provide a way for them to emerge into primary form within the group. Other tools are needed to invite their expression *within the group* and support them in influencing the direction of the group, rather than keeping them in the background.

At least two kinds of tools serve this purpose: (1) tools which give users choices along their path through social spaces; and (2) tools which allow facilitators, managers and group members to tailor new forms quickly. With such tailoring tools emergent processes can be offered through new menu choices or new choice points along the normal path of interaction. These can be inobtrusive and off to the side at first, brought to the center of attention as they become primary, and then moved to the side again as they begin to fall into the background. Only flexible, very easy-to-use tailoring tools can support such dynamics. Effective groupware is open enough to allow the emergence of background processes that inform the next generation of foreground forms.

Groupware as rhythms, boundaries and containers

> The problem of making computers useful to people as communications and information devices is not an engineering problem, it's a design problem. Engineers are trained to eliminate the subjective factors. But it's clearly the subjective factors that are critical here (Kapor, 1990, p. 85).

All living systems are rhythmic. Everything turns in cycles within cycles. The daily rhythm of sunrise and sunset is contained within the broader cycle of the seasons. The rhythms of our heartbeats and breathing give us life. Living systems are contained within vessels with flexible, permeable boundaries. The biosphere contains all life on the planet. Our bodies contain our organs which contain cells which contain cell nuclei and so on. Rhythms, boundaries and containers are *primitives*—universal, fundamental patterns from which all life is built—including our social life. Face-to-face contacts often occur in regular rhythms. Boundaries of many sorts pattern when and where people connect and when they don't. Physical and social containers frame and hold meetings. The skillful use of these tools is second nature to experienced group facilitators. Could groupware based on these primitives more effectively support creative group life?

By seeing group work as a living system and looking for ways the machine can embody organic processes which support it, we can begin to integrate groupware as context and groupware as mechanism. The group has a life of its own and yet needs the form of virtual rhythms, boundaries and containers to guide its creative process. The computer's role is to provide space within which those forms can emerge, and the capacity to create appropriate forms within it. Groupware is not merely the forms, but the *capacity* to create them. The greater its capacity, the more it can support.

Rhythms, boundaries and containers are patterns that connect groupware mechanisms and germinal open spaces in a creative whole—fundamental, dynamic patterns to hold group life in hyperspace, and on whose foundation other forms are built. This approach to groupware is more like art than science, more like using graphics than numerical analysis. It necessarily involves subjective, even intuitive judgements on the part of groupware designers, tailors, group facilitators and managers. In our work we begin by observing naturally occurring patterns of human interaction, which by their nature bridge the polarities of mechanism-context and commitment-autonomy. These patterns are embodied in the groupware as rhythms, boundaries and containers, as forms to persuade rather than control, to hold that life in a flexible way. Sensitive to the life of the group, we feel for how alive and creative it is, and then tailor and adjust the forms to fit the group as it evolves.

Virtual learning community™† as a living laboratory

In the fall of 1988, after a year of prototyping and pilot testing, we convened our Virtual Learning Community for self-development education. It uses a computer-mediated communications system and tailorable groupware of our own design. In this on-line community, we are exploring appropriate rhythms, boundaries and containers for creative group work via computer. While the focus is self-development education, we believe these primitives apply to almost any asynchronous group work.

Members connect to our UNIX host via modem at 1200 or 2400 baud. Because members have a wide variety of personal computing equipment, the interface uses the popular VT100 display standard that supports visual editing and simple graphics. More than half of the current members are outside the Portland, Oregon metropolitan area. The system is available 24 hours a day, seven days a week. Activities are asynchronous; members participate at times of their choosing in an evolving variety of on-line activities.

In this paper, groupware for three selected activities is discussed:

- Right Livelihood Workshop, September to December, 1988: a 12-week workshop with 14 participants looking for more meaning and fulfillment in their work
- The Creative Exchange, November 1989 through April 1990: an open-space activity with 26 participants who self-organized into small groups to explore common personal and work issues
- Living on Purpose Workshop, March 1990: a four-week workshop with 14 participants exploring their personal life purposes

Our groupware toolchest

To support our learning community and action research, we have developed our own tailorable groupware. Written in C and running under UNIX, it includes:

- **items:** text objects
- **exchanges:** named containers for exchanging items which are organized in a hierarchy of sub-exchanges with levels separated by periods; examples: right livelihood.circle, creative.talk, purpose.1.sharing
- **actions:** commands for performing operations on items and exchanges; examples: view ⟨item⟩, select ⟨exchange⟩, download new ⟨exchange⟩
- **permissions:** on/off switches for an exchange, permitting specific classes of actions within it; examples: view items, change own items only, create sub-exchanges
- **roles:** named roles for an exchange with associated permissions; examples: convener, facilitator, member
- **members:** users permitted by role to perform actions within an exchange
- **markers:** pointers for a member to last item viewed, created, or responded to
- **group markers:** pointers for an exchange marking a range of currently active items
- **settings:** on/off switches for an exchange, specifying structures and governing interactions within it; examples: private membership, pen named/anonymous items allowed, items named rather than numbered
- **arrangements:** named, commonly used patterns of roles and settings; examples: meeting, topics, circle

† Virtual Learning Community is a trademark of Awakening Technology.

- **scripts:** items containing procedures written in a structured, high-level interpreted programming language which includes actions and variables for accessing the above parameters
- **menus:** items containing menu text and commands that map abbreviations (menu choices) to specific actions and which adapt the displayed menu text to the user's situation (intelligent menus)
- **agents:** scripts that act on behalf of facilitators, either at predetermined times or in response to certain events

All of these can be configured and modified at any time by any permitted user.

Arrangements

Just as the arrangement of furniture and other objects in a room has a significant effect on how people interact, the arrangement of objects in hyperspace governs our interactions there. Benston (1990) notes how software "furnishings" set the stage for social interaction via computer. Successful facilitators pay careful attention to how the space is arranged so that it fits and supports the group's process needs. They need tools that allow them to rearrange the furniture.

Unlike most systems which provide only a single arrangement, our toolchest provides a variety of arrangements, some which emulate the most common structures available on other systems, and some which are unique. Spaces can be rearranged by facilitators without reprogramming. The three arrangements of particular importance here are:

- **meeting:** an exchange of sequentially numbered text items; the system keeps a marker for each member showing the last item viewed; users may enter any number of items whenever they want; the simplest form of asynchronous conferencing
- **topics:** an exchange of sequentially numbered text items called topics plus a sub-exchange for each with sequentially numbered responses; the system keeps a marker for the last topic viewed and the last response viewed within each topic; users may enter new topics or responses whenever they want; two-level conferencing
- **circle:** an exchange of sequentially numbered text items called rounds plus a sub-exchange for each with responses identified by user name; the system keeps a marker for the last round responded to and the last response viewed within each round; users may enter only one response to each round and may respond only to certain rounds at any given time

Each of these is similar to arrangements found on other systems. The basic EIES structure is similar to a meeting. Topics-like structures are found in many systems including Confer (Zinn, Parnes & Hench, 1976), VAXNotes, Caucus and EIES2 (Turoff *et al.*, 1989). EIES2 uses a question-response structure for its Virtual Classroom®† (Hiltz, 1986) that is similar to some aspects of the circle arrangement. While not discussed here, our system also includes arrangements for unlimited branching similar to Participate. However, instead of allowing users to add branches wherever they wish, branching arrangements are used to organize exchanges and items within certain activities.

† Virtual Classroom is a trademark of the New Jersey Institute of Technology.

Post-mechanistic groupware primitives

> Information is a derivative of the relationship, not the other way around . . . . Instead of asking, "What is the information that matters and how do we most effectively manage it?" companies must start asking, "What are the relationships that matter and how can the technology most effectively support them?" (Schrage, 1990).

Using the above tools for building blocks, we have implemented six groupware primitives adapted from Johnston's (1991) "bag of tools" for change agents. We call these *post-mechanistic* since they move beyond a mechanistic approach to groupware into a more organistic, process-oriented approach. They bridge groupware as context and groupware as mechanism with four intermediate steps. These primitives are:

- **white space (context):** creative incubation; context for form, time to reflect
- **timing:** appropriate tools for current stage of group evolution; to punctuate transitions, beginnings, endings
- **rhythms:** patterns for periodic contact and participation
- **boundaries:** to define group membership, delineate group identity; mark rhythms, beginnings, endings
- **containers:** to hold group energy, life, identity, "presence"; give meaning and purpose to group life
- **procedures (mechanism):** to sequence events; manage rhythms and boundaries

White space and procedures are the prevailing groupware approaches of context and mechanism already discussed, but the four others are new. They form a bridge between the poles, providing a continuum of functionally distinct and yet intermediate process tools to choose from. We call them *primitives* because they are fundamental and orthogonal. They cannot be explained in terms of simpler constructs without losing their functionality. While complex patterns can be built by combining them, their functions are mutually exclusive. Figure 2 shows how they array themselves within the frame of creative causality.

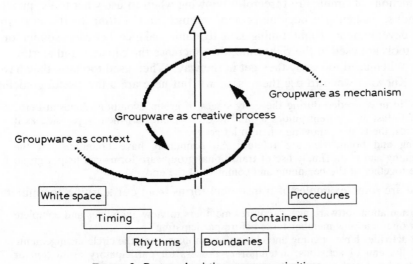

FIGURE 2. Post-mechanistic groupware primitives.

The effective use of each of these process tools involves one or more dynamic balances—constantly changing points on a continuum. Below they are described in terms of their functions, the dimensions along which they vary and within which dynamic balances are required, and our experience with them.

White space

The function of white space, or context, is creative incubation. It is the germinal source of form. Spatially it provides a context for creation to emerge. Temporally it provides time to reflect, to let the answer come.

The most effective amount of white space depends on the situation. If an existing form seems rigid and stuck, more space may allow new forms to emerge. If lively interactions are not occurring frequently enough, a smaller space may gather the energy together. If the group is grasping for answers, more time may allow new insights to emerge. If people are scattered, shorter timelines may focus their activity.

The Creative Exchange is an example of open space. Using the topics arrangement, it offers a context within which members self-organize into mutual interest groups. However, it is not just open space. As detailed in later sections, a variety of initial forms were designed to get things going.

The groupware also provides temporal white space, or open time, by reminding members to take time to relax and reflect. Optional guided imagery and pauses in text to display selected words and phrases slowly and rhythmically offer "time medicine" for reducing stress and finding the calm center in the midst of busy, pressured lives (Dossey, 1982). Participants frequently report getting much more from the workshops and other activities when they follow such reminders and take time to allow their creative process to unfold (Johnson-Lenz, 1988b).

Timing

The functions of timing are threefold: knowing when to use what tools; punctuating transitions, particularly beginnings and endings; and shifting to the next stage of group development. Right timing is a dynamic balance between sooner or later. When tools are used at the right time, they increase the capacity and alertness of the group. When used too early they get in the way. When used too late, they have little effect. Knowing when to use them is an art, but here are a few useful guidelines:

- More form is needed during the early stages of group evolution (Johnson-Lenz, 1990b). Just as a parent guides a child's development and then steps aside as it matures, the trick is knowing when to let go.
- Timing and boundaries are related. All containers have boundaries at the beginning and end. Timely use of transitional groupware forms can help a group come together at the beginning and complete at the end.

Here are some examples of transitional forms from our learning community:

- An orientation software agent requires members to view guidelines and complete other one-time new member tasks before participating.
- Most activities have opening and closing ceremonies using the circle arrangement.
- Near the end of activities, a temporary process for participatory evaluation or negotiation of next steps is often begun.

Rhythms

The function of rhythms is to provide appropriate patterns for periodic contact and participation. Most face-to-face meetings occur in rhythms that are taken for granted, whether daily, weekly or even yearly. Gibb (1978) has written that rhythm and flow are essential for creating high-trust groups. Rhythm is an embodiment of commitment to relationship.

Rhythms are particularly important for meeting via computer. The advantage of asynchronous group work is that meetings do not need to be scheduled for specific times. However, if interaction is too infrequent, group life does not flow. Unlike face-to-face meetings where rhythms must coincide precisely if people are to be there at the same time, hyperspace meetings challenge us to learn a new kind of "fuzzy" rhythm that is somewhere between synchrony and asynchrony. Liberation from the limitations of synchronous meetings confronts us with the responsibility of creating vital rhythms within the unbounded reaches of asynchronous hyperspace. Effective rhythms are a dynamic balance between slow and fast. If members do not feel connected with each other, a faster rhythm may bring them closer. If too much is happening, a slower rhythm may work better. Effective rhythms are both a tonic and an antidote for overload.

Boundaries

The functions of boundaries include defining group membership, delineating group identity, and marking group rhythms, beginnings and endings. Living boundaries are inherently dynamic, varying along the dimensions of permeability and flexibility. A permeable boundary is one that allows things to flow through it. A flexible boundary is one that changes over time. This applies to both spatial and temporal boundaries.

An appropriately permeable boundary retains the identity of the group while allowing enough flow in and out to keep it alive. If a boundary is too permeable, if it's too easy to join or leave a group, or if the beginning or ending is unclear, energy may leak away. If a boundary is not permeable enough, if joining or leaving is difficult, or if beginnings and endings are too rigidly enforced, some individuals may resist or break the boundaries anyway. The right balance depends on the situation.

Most asynchronous conferencing systems have *lurkers,* participants who read but never express themselves, who "lurk" in the background. This common phenomenon exemplifies the situation-dependent balances necessary for effective group boundaries. In open spaces such as the Creative Exchange, where groups are self-organizing and their boundaries are highly permeable, there will be lurkers. If the purpose is to allow self-forming groups to emerge, some lurking is inevitable and not a problem.

In contrast, if the purpose is to involve everyone, lurking is a signal of leaky boundaries. Equal participation is expected in our workshop circles. Group boundaries are clear. Commitments to participate are required. However, the price of full involvement is resistance. Boundaries *always* create resistance, which is a sign they are functioning in a living system.

Containers

The function of containers is to hold the energy, life, identity and "presence" of the group. They must be big enough to hold the group in the most creatively alive way, but not too big. Containers hold both the white space within which the group develops as well as the procedures which support that development. They also serve symbolic, mythical purposes. Bay (1986) has written that giving participants a background "sense of the whole" helps maintain a group. Appropriate containers give meaning to group life and remind the group of its purpose and identity through celebrations, ceremonies and rituals.

An effective container is a dynamic balance between the forces holding the group together and pulling it apart. It embodies the group's commitment and other holding forces while resisting the diversity of impulses that do not contribute to the group's purpose. It can remind and persuade members to participate, but if the strength of their actual commitment is significantly less than that embodied in the container, more resistance will be generated than it can hold. The primary form will give way to the secondary process of the group coming apart. If the strength of commitment exceeds that of the container, the group will probably acknowledge it by creating a new container that embodies the emerging secondary process of deepening commitment.

Procedures

While procedures are fundamental to computing, in our work they serve several functions directly related to the five other post-mechanistic groupware primitives. These include sequencing events and managing boundaries and rhythms. Most of these procedures are embodied in scripts and agents. Many of them provide functions similar to what is commonly thought of as groupware.

The dynamic balance central to effective use of procedures involves knowing when to use them and when to let the life of the group manage itself. Too much procedure and the group rebels. Too little and nothing happens. In our experience, they work best in collaboration with the natural life of the group, nudging, guiding, persuading or reminding users rather than controlling them. For example, the design of the circle agent has evolved from one that controlled to one that persuades. Rather than forcing anything, it invites members into new spaces and reminds them of incomplete tasks which they can choose to do or leave incomplete.

On the other hand, certain procedures are enforced without exceptions. For example, the orientation software agent assures that new members view the guidelines, view and agree with the community covenant, and complete their membership directory entry before participating in the workshops.

Scripts as agents for group facilitators

We use scripts to manage the sequence of events and to maintain boundaries and rhythms. Easily modified as needed, scripts serve as rule-driven, artificial intelligence *agents* acting on behalf of facilitators, performing functions with accuracy and speed while freeing facilitators to handle subtler tasks requiring human judgement.

Others have used agents as part of computer-mediated communications systems.

Hiltz, Johnson and Turoff (1982) used an "iterative group preference aggregator" to gather opinions from group members, compute a group mean, and then ask those with the most divergent opinions to share their points of view with the group. Object Lens (Lai & Malone, 1988) provides agents for filtering the flow of communications and managing other routine functions.

The boundaries of most activities within our system are handled by agents that manage the sequence of events on the way into the activity. For example, the easily modified script agent that guides participants into the Creative Exchange:

- checks to see if they have viewed all the guidelines, and if not asks them to;
- welcomes them to the exchange and displays the quote of the week;
- checks for the existence of timely special-purpose containers like those for evaluation and transition ceremonies, whether participants have responded in those places, and if not, asks if they want to;
- involves them in a brief exchange of asynchronous one-line messages expressing how they are feeling at the moment (since most of the activity in the exchange is in self-selected groups, this gives everyone in the exchange at least this brief contact with everyone else);
- offers them a summary of new topics and new responses to topics in which they are participating;
- displays the Creative Exchange menu which includes choices for reviewing the guidelines, participating in any special-purpose evaluation or ceremony, raising a new topic, participating in an existing topic, leaving the exchange, and other actions;
- displays a friendly parting message on their way out of the exchange.

Another agent manages circle rhythms in the workshops. It encourages participants to keep up with the group by reminding them to view new items or respond to current rounds. While its behavior varies according to certain exchange settings as detailed elsewhere (Johnson-Lenz, 1990b), it normally encourages without forcing completion of tasks in order to provide flexible rhythms. By its design it manages turn taking, inviting response while making sure that each person responds only once.

Virtual Circle™†

At the heart of each of our workshops is a "virtual circle", based on a group process found in many native cultures. For millennia, people have gathered in circles around a fire and passed a "talking stick" or other object symbolizing the sacred. As the object passes from hand to hand, each person takes a moment to share his or her truth while others listen with respect. There may be several rounds in a sitting. Each person responds once and only once to each round.

This egalitarian pattern and the time-honored spiritual meaning of the circle drew us to adapt the circle process to hyperspace. Our purposes were: (1) to create equal participation in groups by encouraging lurkers to express themselves; (2) to create a reflective atmosphere; and (3) to persuade people to take time to discover what really matters to them and then express it in the respectful presence of others.

† Virtual Circle is a trademark of Awakening Technology.

These virtual circles are supported by a complex of software tools that includes the following components:

- twelve exchange settings that allow dynamic reconfiguration of the circle process
- three group markers that define the circle rhythm boundaries
- three circle arrangements that represent the most frequently used configurations
- a circle agent action written in C that facilitates the process
- a graphic that displays the names of members in a circle
- boundary agents tailored to the needs of each circle group that manage transitions in and out of the circle container
- background agents that move group markers according to schedule

Spatial circle boundaries

The membership of each on-line circle is clearly defined. Except for special cases such as dropouts there are few, if any, lurkers. Virtual Circle dynamics work best with at least seven and no more than 16 participants. Groups of less than seven do not work well. Like a chain-reaction with subcritical mass, they rarely get enough interaction going. Groups of more than 16 overwhelm participants with 16 or more times as much text as they enter.

Participation is organized into weekly rounds. Everyone responds once and only once to each round. Each week the round consists of one or more evocative questions or self-discovery processes. Their purpose is twofold: (1) to focus the group on a shared issue; and (2) to invite participants to consider what is true for them. Participants often connect early in the week to read the question and live with it for several days before responding in the circle.

Even though the circle agent encourages rather than enforces equal participation, the distribution of responses across participants in the circles is nearly flat, quite unlike the typical draw-down or Zipf curve (Zipf, 1949) found in most asynchronous group work. Figures 3 and 4 show representative response distributions from two of these activities. Participants are ordered along the bottom axis by decreasing percentage of total responses entered. Figure 3 plots responses in a space called Creative Talk, an adjunct to the Creative Exchange. It used the meeting

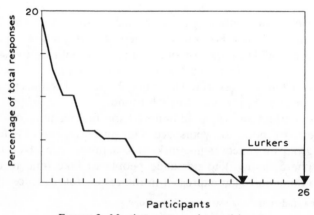

FIGURE 3. Meeting responses by participant.

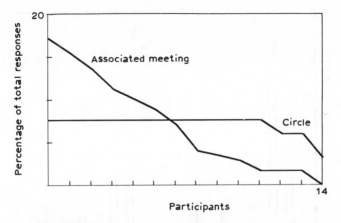

FIGURE 4. Circle and associated meeting responses by participant.

arrangement. It exemplifies the skewed distribution typical of asynchronous groups in which a few participants contribute most of the responses while many others lurk.

In contrast, Figure 4 plots responses in both containers of one of the Right Livelihood workshops, the circle and sharing. The workshop included a total of 14 rounds over 12 weeks. The number of rounds to which each member responded is shown. Note the nearly flat distribution for the circle. Two participants missed one round and a third dropped out of the workshop after only six rounds due to a change in life situation. Figure 4 also includes the distribution of responses in the sharing exchange that accompanied the circle. It used the meeting arrangement in which participants may respond at will. Note that while the distribution is not flat like the circle, it is not nearly as skewed as that for "creative talk" in Figure 3. There is only one lurker! We have observed similar patterns in most of the workshops. Apparently the equalizing effect of the circle spreads to the associated sharing exchange. The rhythm of the circle is felt in nearby containers.

Circle rhythms and temporal boundaries

Most computer-supported meetings have skewed participation patterns. They also have irregular, arrhythmic distributions when plotted over time. The typical pattern has bursts of activity separated by periods of relative inactivity. Figure 5, a plot of responses over time in Creative Talk, shows this pattern.

To nudge the group into a more rhythmic pattern, the circle process uses a temporal boundary, or *gate*, that prevents members from moving on to the next round until it is opened. This gate marks a point on the group timeline by which everyone is encouraged to respond. Figure 6 plots responses in the circle from a recent Living on Purpose workshop. While an arrhythmic pattern emerges the first week, by the second week responses are beginning to cluster just before the gate. The group "heartbeat" begins to appear in response to the "pacemaker" of rhythmic gates. The smaller number of responses to the last round is due to several members' inability to participate (travel, illness, equipment problems) at the end of the workshop.

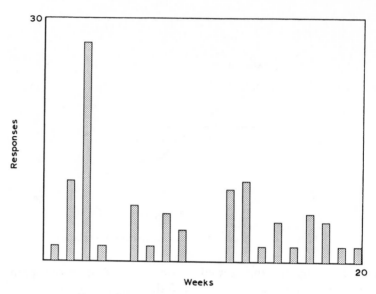

FIGURE 5. Arrhythmic participation over time.

This group "heartbeat" is a subtle, elusive phenomenon demonstrating participants' commitment to participate more than software enforcement. It was observed only after months of experimenting and incorporating user feedback. Initial approaches were too coercive and created resistance. Later attempts were too formless and participation was spread too thin. Finally, with a complex of 12 exchange settings and three markers, we observed the above rhythm. It requires a delicate balance between persuading participants to respond during the time window scheduled for responses and then taking a round out of circulation when its time has passed. The details of this and two other variations of the circle arrangement that support other purposes are reported elsewhere (Johnson-Lenz, 1990b).

Rhythms, boundaries and containers each contribute something unique and vital to the process of supporting group work. When taken together they become a

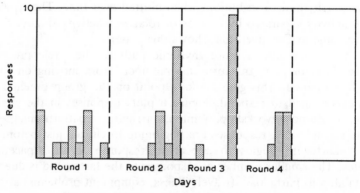

FIGURE 6. Rhythmic response clustering with gates.

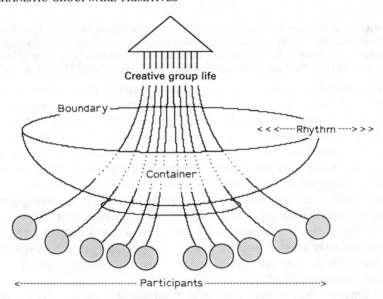

FIGURE 7. Rhythmically bounded container supporting creative group life.

potent creative whole that is more effective than any one by itself. The container holds the group life, the boundary delineates and protects its identity, and the rhythmic "heartbeat" gives it duration through time. This creative process is graphically depicted in Figure 7.

Evolving tools for groupware design and tailoring

While these experiences strongly suggest that rhythms, boundaries and containers are effective primitives for groupware, our designs and implementations are crude when compared with what lies ahead. We are convinced that these tools are essential for supporting creatively potent group work, but they are just a beginning. We imagine powerful, graphically based tools that allow group facilitators and members to see rhythms, boundaries and containers in action and to watch group life flow and unfold through them. With expressive gestures, they sketch shared images of the shape of the group they see emerging, negotiating the next steps in its evolution. Perhaps they will use groupware design tools similar to the participatory architectural design tools in Janus (Fischer, Girgensohn, Lemke & McCall, 1990) which provide critical feedback based on past experiences of how proposed patterns have worked. Then, satisfied with their design choices, with a mouse click they change the permeability of a boundary, open a new container, or nudge the flow into livelier, more creative rhythms.

Purpose-centered groupware

In a technologically advanced society where production of sufficient goods and services can be handled with ease, employment exists primarily for self-development, and is only secondarily concerned with the production of goods and services . . . . In the "learning society" the occupational focus of most people is learning and developing in the broadest sense (Harman, 1988, pp. 146–147).

> The new purpose must be purpose itself. In a "quality of life" reality, the heart of education must be the art of addressing questions of value: learning to identify and ask the important questions, both personal and cultural, and developing appropriate skills to affect one's world. The new education must be purpose-centered (Johnston, 1988, p. 6).

To respond effectively to the urgency and complexity of these turbulent times, we need to be as creative as possible. This means bringing all of our creative capacity to our collaborative group work, becoming individually and collectively whole (Johnson-Lenz, 1990a). This is achieved by educating (drawing out) and encouraging what is most vital, alive and creative for each of us, learning to ask and live with the difficult questions, and developing greater capacity for effective action under conditions of fundamental uncertainty—purpose-centered education.

This may seem a limited purpose for groupware since it focuses primarily on developing the creative capacity of individuals, but we believe that purpose-centered education is also in the long-term interests of business and society in general. While our work is expressly educational, we believe the principles of self-development we are exploring, will become an essential part of the foundation of many groupware systems in the decades ahead (Johnson-Lenz, 1989b).

This fundamental shift in purpose is a cultural sea change, already recognized in many spheres:

- Michael *et al.* (1980) describes the new competence for organizations as learning systems.
- Engelbart (1988) proposes that corporations institutionalize an evolutionary learning process into their structure.
- Harman (1988) writes that our survival depends on redefining the purpose of work from production to self-development.
- Johnston (1988) articulates a new purpose-centered purpose to education itself.
- Nelson (1989) describes the necessity of learning how to learn and of becoming a learning society.
- Theobald (1987) writes of learning to navigate the rapids of change and of becoming social entrepreneurs.
- Milbrath (1989) describes a strategy for envisioning a sustainable society by learning our way out.

In the turbulent years ahead, nearly all organizations will be profoundly affected by rapid and fundamental change. Regardless of their purpose, those that thrive will learn how to achieve a state of continuous, accelerated learning. For this reason, we believe that the educational principles of purpose-centered groupware we are exploring potentially apply to *any* computer-supported group work. As the virtual reflection of the coming learning society, purpose-centered groupware is an essential part of the necessary transition to a vital, sustainable culture.

The creative imperative

> We are being challenged not just to the creative uncertainty inherent to any next step in growth, but to a whole new relationship to uncertainty .... The critical new questions are demanding a bigger view of things. They are demanding that we take responsibility in a reality without external absolutes, to make our passage into our mature adulthood as a species. It's a big step (Johnston, 1988, p. 8).

Never before in history have we been confronted as a species with the freedom and awesome responsibility of consciously creating the social systems within which we live and work. In the past these were provided by the culture and passed on generation after generation. Instead of engaging creatively with this challenge, it is tempting to grasp for easy answers—either tighter mechanisms of social control or its polar opposite—refusal to make responsible choices. Neither works by itself. Either too much or too little form exacerbates social breakdown. After a while, the way forward reveals itself as a dynamic balance between form and formlessness that varies from one situation to another, depending on its unique needs. At all levels of society, from the household to the computer-mediated culture of groupware, *some* form of rhythms, boundaries and containers emerges as the embodiment of vital and sustainable culture. The paradox of freedom is that it obliges us to choose.

References

ACKERMAN, L. (1984). *Managing in the Flow State: A New View of Organizations and Leadership*. McLean, Virginia: Linda Ackerman Inc.

BATESON, G. (1972). *Steps to an Ecology of Mind*. New York: Ballentine.

BATESON, G. (1979). *Mind and Nature: A Necessary Unity*. New York: E. P. Dutton.

BAY, D. (1986). Sense of the whole: computer support for collaboration. Presented at the *Sixteenth Annual Information Exchange of the Organization Development Institute*, Williams Bay, Wisconsin.

BENSTON, M. (1990). Participatory design by non-profit groups. In *Proceedings of the 1990 Participatory Design Conference*. Palo Alto, CA: Computer Professionals for Social Responsibility.

BERMAN, M. (1981). *The Reenchantment of the World*. Ithaca, NY: Cornell University Press.

DOSSEY, L. (1982). *Space, Time and Medicine*. Boston: Shambhala Publications.

DYSON, E. (1989). Groupware. *Whole Earth Review*, Fall, 105–108.

ENGELBART, D. (1962). *Augmenting Human Intellect: A Conceptual Framework*. Stanford, CA: Stanford Research Institute.

ENGELBART, D. (1988). Bootstrapping and the handbook cycle. Presented at *CSCW '88, Conference on Computer-Supported Cooperative Work*, Portland, Oregon.

FISCHER, G., GIRGENSOHN, A., LEMKE, A. & McCALL, R. (1990). Conceptual frameworks and innovative system designs for participatory design. In *Proceedings of the 1990 Participatory Design Conference*. Palo Alto, CA: Computer Professionals for Social Responsibility.

GIBB, J. (1978). *Trust: A New View of Personal and Organizational Development*. Los Angeles: Guild of Tutors Press.

HARMAN, W. (1988). *Global Mind Change: The Promise of the Last Years of the Twentieth Century*. Indianapolis, IN: Knowledge Systems.

HILTZ, S. R. & TUROFF, M. (1978). *The Network Nation: Human Communication Via Computer*. Reading, MA: Addison-Wesley.

HILTZ, S. R., JOHNSON, K. & TUROFF, M. (1982). *The Effects of Formal Human Leadership and Computer-Generated Decision Aids on Problem Solving Via Computer: A Controlled Experiment*. Research report no. 18, Computerized Conferencing and Communications Center, New Jersey Institute of Technology.

HILTZ, S. R. (1986). The virtual classroom: using computer-mediated communication for university teaching. *Journal of Communication*, Spring, 95–104.

JOHNSON-LENZ, P. & JOHNSON-LENZ, T. (1980). Groupware: the emerging art of orchestrating collective intelligence. Presented at the *World Future Society's First Global Conference on the Future*, Toronto, Canada.

JOHNSON-LENZ, P. & JOHNSON-LENZ, T. (1981). *The Evolution of a Tailored Communications Structure: The TOPICS System*, Research report no. 14, Computerized Conferencing and Communications Center, New Jersey Institute of Technology.

JOHNSON-LENZ, P. & JOHNSON-LENZ, T. (1982). Groupware: the process and impacts of design choices. In KERR & HILTZ, Eds. *Computer-Mediated Communication Systems*. New York: Academic Press.

JOHNSON-LENZ, P. & JOHNSON-LENZ, T. (1988a). *Synapse: The Awakening Technology Integrated Conferencing and Knowledge Software*. Lake Oswego, Oregon: Awakening Technology.

JOHNSON-LENZ, P. & JOHNSON-LENZ, T. (1988b). *Computer Support for Some Forgotten Aspects of Cooperation*, Research report no. 1, Awakening Technology, Lake Oswego, Oregon.

JOHNSON-LENZ, P. & JOHNSON-LENZ, T. (1989a). Connecting with the heart of matters in a virtual learning community. Presented at the *Electronic Networking Association Conference, "Groupware: The Next Wave"*, Allentown, Pennsylvania.

JOHNSON-LENZ, P. & JOHNSON-LENZ, T. (1989b). *Computer Support for Sustainable Culture*, Research report no. 2, Awakening Technology, Lake Oswego, Oregon.

JOHNSON-LENZ, P. & JOHNSON-LENZ, T. (1989c). Humanizing hyperspace. *Context*, Fall, 52–57.

JOHNSON-LENZ, P. & JOHNSON-LENZ, T. (1990a). Islands of safety for unlocking human potential. In *Proceedings of the Third International Guelph Symposium on Unlocking Human Potential via Computer-Mediated Communication*, University of Guelph.

JOHNSON-LENZ, P. & JOHNSON-LENZ, T. (1990b). *Rhythms, Boundaries, and Containers: Creative Dynamics of Asynchronous Group Life*, Research report no. 4, Awakening Technology, Lake Oswego, Oregon.

JOHNSTON, C. (1986). *The Creative Imperative*. Berkeley, CA: Celestial Arts.

JOHNSTON, C. (1988). Beyond knowledge—toward wisdom. *Noetic Sciences Review*, Winter, 4–11.

JOHNSTON, C. (1991). *Necessary Wisdom: Meeting the Challenge of a New Cultural Maturity*. Seattle, WA: Institute for Creative Development.

KAPOR, M. (1990). In K. Wright, The road to the global village. *Scientific American*, March, 84–94.

LAI, K. & MALONE, T. (1988). Object lens: a "spreadsheet" for cooperative work. In *Proceedings of the 1988 Conference on Computer-Supported Cooperative Work*. New York: Association for Computing Machinery.

MICHAEL, D. N., LARSON, M. A., VAN DER HORST, B. & WILSON, I. (1980). *The New Competence: The Organization as a Learning System*, Technique Report, Values and Lifestyles Program. Stanford, CA: Stanford Research Institute.

MILBRATH, L. W. (1989). *Envisioning A Sustainable Society: Learning Our Way Out*. Albany, NY: SUNY Press.

MINDELL, A. (1985). *The Dreambody in Relationships*. London: Routledge & Kegan Paul.

NELSON, R. F. W. (1989). *Learning to Sustain Learning: The Key to Our Future, An Exploration of Personal, Organizational and Societal Learning*, Working Paper No. 8. The Post-Industrial Future Project, Square One Management, Ltd., Canmore, Canada.

OWEN, H. (1987). *Spirit: Transformation & Development in Organizations*. Potomac, MD: Abbott Publishing.

PETERS, T. (1987). *Thriving on Chaos: Handbook for a Management Revolution*. New York: Knopf.

REDER, S. & SCHWAB, R. G. (1988). The communicative economy of the workgroup: multi-channel genres of communication. In *Proceedings of the 1988 Conference on Computer-Supported Cooperative Work*. New York: Association for Computing Machinery.

SCHRAGE, M. (1990). In information technology, the key is good relationships. *The Wall Street Journal*, March **19**, A18.

SCULLEY, J. (1987). *Odyssey: Pepsi to Apple... A Journey of Adventure, Ideas, and the Future*. New York: Harper & Row.

THEOBALD, R. (1987). *The Rapids of Change: Social Entrepreneurship in Turbulent Times*. Indianapolis, IN: Knowledge Systems.

TRIGG, R. H., SUCHMAN, L. A. & HALASZ, F. G. (1986). Supporting collaboration in NoteCards. In *Proceedings of the 1986 Conference on Computer-Supported Cooperative Work*. New York: Association for Computing Machinery.

TUROFF, M. (1971). Delphi and its potential impact on information systems. In *AFIPS '71 Conference Proceedings*. Montvale, NJ: AFIPS press.

TUROFF, M. (1982). Management issues in human communications via computer. In R. LANDAU, J. H. BAIR & J. H. SIEGMAN, Eds. *The Management and Evolution of Electronic Office Systems*. Norwood, NJ: Ablex Publishing.

TUROFF, M., HILTZ, S. R., FOSTER, J. F. & NG, K. (1989). Computer mediated communications and tailorability. In *Proceedings of the 22nd Annual Hawaii Conference on Systems Science*, IEEE Computer Society.

WINOGRAD, T. (1986). A language/action perspective on the design of cooperative work. In *Proceedings of the 1986 Conference on Computer-Supported Cooperative Work*, New York: Association for Computing Machinery.

ZINN, K. L., PARNES, R. & HENCH, H. (1976). Computer-based educational communication at the University of Michigan. In *Proceedings of the 31st ACM National Conference*. New York: Association for Computing Machinery.

ZIPF, G. (1949). *Human Behavior and the Principle of Least Effort*. Reading, MA: Addison-Wesley.

ZUBOFF, S. (1988). *In the Age of the Smart Machine: The Future of Work and Power*. New York: Basic Books.

15

Structure and support in cooperative environments: the Amsterdam Conversation Environment

ELIZABETH A. DYKSTRA

ROBERT P. CARASIK

This paper discusses theory and concepts in designing a synchronous shared workspace to support human interaction, and a description of such a system. The Amsterdam Conversation Environment (ACE) supports group interaction in face-to-face meetings. ACE does not, however, support meeting process; instead it is designed to support conversation and stimulate interaction among group participants.

The ACE design emerges from design conversations seeded with several specific concepts. One is the notion of semi-structured computer applications, which leave room for the development, by users, of group conventions to structure how the group interfaces with the computer support environment. A related topic is the difficulty of setting "support" boundaries: what should the machine do or enable *vs* what are the structure and function responsibilities of user group members themselves? Another concept is the development of user-languages as a reflection of group experience and coherence. A third concept is the transition away from group-member equivalence within computer-mediated conversation (a currently favored view in the design of "democratic" computer systems) toward encouraging variety and stimulating "next actions" among users. Using these and other concepts, we create an overall conceptual picture of what ACE does, how it feels, and how the user interface looks and works, which we call the "design image". We conclude with some thoughts about the next steps in the project.

Introduction

This paper discusses the social issues and the design process of a computer-supported cooperative work (CSCW) application that supports group-structured interaction in a shared workspace. We submit that given the opportunity, users can provide for themselves a significant amount of the task-oriented structure inherent in most computer applications, creating not only ownership of the process but also evolving the group's competence to structure their own shared workspace, visually and functionally. We present a snapshot of the continuing design of the Amsterdam Conversation Environment (ACE), an application which provides an object-oriented shared workspace for synchronous interaction over a network of Macintoshes.

ACE takes a distinctive approach to CSCW by providing users with a common workspace through which they can share and manipulate individual products, where the focus is on stimulating interaction rather than on producing a product out of the interaction. ACE is a semi-structured application that is non-task specific; it is a *conversation* environment rather than a *production* environment. Given initial conditions which impose some constraints, we incite users to increase their competence to collectively develop their own constraints and to structure their interaction, instead of relying on the structure provided by a task-oriented application.

Support systems, process and structure

The Amsterdam Conversation Environment is a project to develop groupware for laboratory study of collective support systems and group behavior at the Center for Innovation and Co-operative Technology (CICT), University of Amsterdam. The organization of the project reflects its group-owned design with the primary role distinction that between designers/users and designer/builders, since only two of the project team are programmers.

CSCW is an approach to the design of systems which are deeply embedded in human interactions and which may profoundly change the pattern of these interactions (Carasik, Eveland & Grantham, 1988). There is frequently in system design a trade-off between task specificity and support of the affective aspects of groups, which can be expressed in a hyperbolic curve; one goal of groupware is to push this curve further along the affective axis. ACE is designed to support group work through technology, rather than using technology to replace or automate activities. ACE is not domain specific; it differs fundamentally from applications built to support specific tasks in areas such as accounting or making airline reservations. ACE also differs fundamentally from individual productivity tools such as word processors and spreadsheets. We submit that CSCW applications should support the non-deterministic aspects of work processes by focusing on supporting group interaction, instead of group process. ACE therefore does not seek to drive work processes toward closure. It aims instead to provide an avenue for mutual conversation; closure can be reached elsewhere in the work process.

It appears that most CSCW applications are built to support a specific process or category of processes normally conducted with two or more people. For example, collaborative authoring is supported in the form of multi-access single file text editors, e.g. DocuForum and Bellcore's Quilt (Leland, Fish & Kraut, 1988); issue or problem formulation and resolution is supported in the form of multi-access single file graphic representations, as in gIBIS (Conklin & Begeman, 1988). We decided to integrate text and graphic editing capabilities into an environment to support what we assumed people do when they get together for a meeting and are open to using computers to support their collaborative work. As we began to develop the look and feel of the system, we started to question what it was that we really wanted to support: processes or people?

While reviewing the potential activities that could be supported through the computer, one thing became clear: applications designed to support a specific activity encourage people to have a pre-conceived start-point, agree to the process embedded in the software, and decide on a targetted end-point. What if we built an environment where the focus is on interaction itself, without a specific process in mind, and without a predetermined conclusion? How do you create an open interaction system that encourages participants to continue to take action, address variety, share viewpoints and data, without dictating when the action "should" cease? Rather than forcing contributions, encouraging "next steps" (and its corollary, discouraging closure) breaks paralysis. This led us toward exploring how interaction itself can be supported.

We use "support" here in a very specific sense. Our definition of support is "non-dependency-creating enablement". Working within this definition, a support system is a collection of resources constituted in such a way that the user finds his or her own way toward extending the boundaries of a problem space. This requires the system of support to be flexible in its view of the user, and not only encourages but requires that the user develop new distinctions. Designers often base their CSCW systems on how they believe people should work and behave. They frequently succumb to design according to what they have constructed in their heads as a "model of the user". Designing by creating a model of the user, limits the potential of the users, the software, and their interaction by imposing assumptions. Providing a model *for* the user, on the other hand, gives an example that is not essentially limiting or controlling. ACE declines by its nature as a semi-structured application to provide a fixed model of the user, nor does it allow the user a fixed model of the system. Its user documentation, on the other hand, provides several examples of use which serve as models for users.

The type of support system under discussion does not necessarily lead a user to solve problems. A system which assists the user to mechanically reduce a problem to manageable proportions works in the reductionist paradigm. A system can assist the user to operate holistically, expanding a problem to include enough new elements to require a substantially different perspective. However, our view of a support system moves the user away from the objective of problem resolution as the desirable end-state, and toward a process of continuous incremental improvement requiring interaction and barring end-state finality. The effects-in-use of such a support system thus include a new capability to develop distinctions; a higher degree of interaction; an increased exchange and negotiation of viewpoint; and a richer variety in the conversations among users—without creating a dependency on the software.

The ACE environment supports conversation instead of process, aiming overall for an increase in the *individual competence* of its users, and protecting against the decrease of *collective competence* within a group. An individual competence is the ability of an individual to perform an activity. However, where a support system may increase competence in one area, it may decrease competence in another area; when a support system prevents such a decrease, it is said to support collective competence. What participants expect in a conversation is not what they do alone; they show their variety and base their next events on each other, thus increasing their competence. An increase in competence is not the same thing as "learning", but does imply "improvement". It is this idea of increasing competence that we wish to support. Our goal is to support groups in such a way as to increase individual and collective competence.

Working from basic conversation theory (Pask 1976) namely that meaningful conversation conveys both *content* and *intent,* we decided to create a "conversation space", an open, loosely structured environment with two basic functions and one primary objective. The functions are: (1) a synchronous shared mixed media workspace; with (2) a variety of "discussion channels" for associating commentary about what's happening in the workspace and for communicating with other group participants. The objective is to support people in continuing their interaction *in their choice of activity,* allowing the group itself to provide the structure for the activity in a way that they see fit. Thus we call our system a *conversational support system,* the Amsterdam Conversation Environment.

So what exactly is a conversational support system? It is a system which allows the expression and preservation of people's views as distinctions which are fluid and flexible, while not obstructing their thinking. It is suggested but not substantiated that linear-format applications obstruct associative thinking, while hypertext, a networked method of associating ideas, does not. A conversational support system evolves the clearly non-linear record of human exchange, with its persuasion, dialogue, and negotiation. Developing such a record captures a group's memory-in-progress. However, the record as such is not the focus of ACE, as it is with MCC's gIBIS. Rather more important is the way in which the use of a shared workspace serves as a focusing mechanism for the group's interaction. The history of the interaction actually structures the group's process.

A conversational support system should not aim at institutionalizing conversation space; formalized methods of conversation lead to bureaucracy, "empty talk", and rules that stop conversation. What a conversational support system *should* do is facilitate the construction of new concepts and behavior. It should help people invent relations between concepts, and encourage the formation of general concepts or abstractions which relate to the network of concepts through analogy, metaphor and abstraction. Above all, a conversational support system *should not* direct attention toward itself. We provide in ACE multiple channels of communication and a hypertext-like layered method of representation, but do not limit the interaction to what can happen "inside the computer".

The intention of ACE is to provide a conversational background that, because it has little inherent procedural structure, causes users to exercise their own preferences and creativity in how they choose to use the system. While avoiding a rigid model of the user may be important to remember in developing requirements for a computer-supported conversational environment, equally important is the notion that users themselves carry models of each other, the tasks in which they are engaged, and the support elements they use. These "models" are notions of conscious preference or subliminal predisposition. We propose that the more choices that designers confer on users, the more successful the systems are in actual use.

Design concepts

HUMAN FACTORS IN SEMI-STRUCTURED APPLICATIONS

In his discussion of the Information Lens electronic mail system, Tom Malone presents a definition of "semi-structured", in regard to message types: "We define semi-structured messages as messages of identifiable types with each type containing a known set of fields, but with some of the fields containing unstructured text or other information" (Malone, Grant, Lai, Rao & Rosenblitt, 1986). This definition does not address the inevitable overlap of content and structure. By contrast, we define a semi-structured application as one which not only exhibits a given degree of user-modifiability, but is built with the intention of extension and development by those who use it (Forsgren, 1989; Carasik & Dykstra, 1989). In semi-structured applications, there are no longer vivid distinctions between the designer, builder and user.

The ACE design is based on the notion of semi-structured applications which are: (1) not process-bound to a rigid set of procedures, leaving the process to the users; and which are (2) user-extensible. In an interview reported in *The Road to the Global Village,* Lucy Suchman is quoted as discovering "two ingredients of technology that can win people's enthusiasm: familiarity and flexibility". She emphasizes that all technology requires some investment on the part of learners. However, when the technology is totally unfamiliar, users are not convinced that the pay-off will be worth the investment. She states that "users need to be able to accommodate a design to their specialized requirements" and "design processes would improve if engineers and programmers observed how their wares were used after the devices left the lab" (Wright, 1990). We propose that our approach, developing user-extensible applications, means that engineers and programmers provide a substantial platform upon which users can build a familiar and useful set of action routines that serve their own purposes. In other words, flexibility is the key to assuring that users find value in the software they use; familiarity is the key to their continued investment in it, and what better route to familiarity than returning control of the process to the user? This essentially means tackling the problems of group applications from an interface perspective, rather than a process perspective.

Semi-structured applications do have built-in constraints; it is the source and control of constraint, rather than the amount of it, that is important. A completely unconstrained environment is uninspiring. Constraints are useful; consider a meeting that is deadlocked. Introduce new rules, give a role to someone, do something to lead people with more variety, and the conversation can continue. The point is to make variety a part of the whole procedure so that selection can happen. We would like groups to think of their own strategies to control and maintain variety, to add variety or decrease it, rather than assert control via the computer through implicit or imposed stopping rules. All kinds of crazy constraints should be implementable within ACE, but the source and location of the constraint is important—while there will inevitably be constraints inside the application, they are ultimately the responsibility of the user.

There's a real limit to how much a designer should make the software do the job that the group should be doing. ACE attempts to handle this by using a semi-structured construction. There are, of course, dangers in both overstructure and understructure. A group can be paralyzed through equality. We submit that even if the group has no explicit notions of their own about structure, their structure will quickly become apparent in their actual use of the system, regardless of what the stated purpose of their tools and techniques might be.

GROUP-DEVELOPED USER LANGUAGES

Taking language as the primary dimension of human cooperative activity, the language/action perspective of Winograd focuses on how people "act through language". The language/action perspective emphasizes not the form of language, but what people do with it (Winograd, 1986). However, we suggest that action and language grow out of each other. One thing that makes a group a group is their sharing of experience, which is necessarily couched in language (Carasik & Dykstra, 1989). Experience itself creates a "user language". The interchangeability of the interpretation and observation parts of a user language is an essential property. Without this property, viewpoints could not change; new actors and new neighborhoods would be excluded from the system. Therefore, a useful criterion for the recognition of a user language in practical contexts is that its observation/interpretation distinctions are not permanently anchored (de Zeeuw & Robinson, unpublished data).

User languages can be created as social support systems. A practical requirement of a user language is that it should simply be an advantage. It should result in a more flexible interaction, and hence in a more flexible organization. It should break the cycle of institutional closure that locks around a model of the user—without the organization becoming "confused", directionless, or ineffective (de Zeeuw & Robinson, 1989). As collaborators work together, they mutually create language/ action experience that structures how they relate to each other and their work. Group-specific uses of language evolve with or without conscious design. The local language developed and used among groups as they work with support systems confirms their experiences and names new experiences, developing competence with the system and in turn, developing the system. In our semi-structured shared workspace, we want to lend full expression to the language groups development as they share experiences, and not limit it by process. We set initial constraints by employing the Macintosh idiom, in a way that allows users to transfer their experiences with Macintosh applications to the ACE environment. However, we seek to support rather than direct the evolution of group language by introducing as few language formalisms as possible, and encouraging groups to capture their conversations—their thinking processes—in on-screen objects and commentary on objects.

DEMOCRACY, EQUALITY AND CONTROL

Increasing publicity has been given to the notion of democratic support systems. This concept is well-known in Scandinavian countries where an ethic of management/labor cooperation prevails in the practice of participatory design (Bødker, Knudsen, Kyng, Ehn & Madsen, 1988). This idea of democracy in the workplace, and in the systems that support working, is sometimes misconstrued. Participation and collaboration overlap, but are not the same thing. Democracy and equality overlap, but are not the same thing. While most people are confident that they know what democracy is and that there is a standard definition, it must be remembered that democracy is defined in context.

It is politically correct to assume that a collective group of users are roughly equivalent in their access to and transformation of resources. To refer to a support system as a "democratic, participatively designed system" says something about the way it was produced, but not necessarily anything about how people behave with it. Joint design by users and developers to support a domain-specific task in a way that "designs out" some of the problems of cooperative work (in deference to a "democratic" model of the users) concentrates on removing inequalities in power and control. "Good" group process practices follow from a human resource tradition of facilitation. There is a tendency to "rein in" strong personalities and practices of domination, "for" everyone else.

There are at least two dangers in this. First, strong participants may have something good to say; second, this practice of "reining in" creates a dependency within the group on the facilitating mechanism. Well-intentioned intervention with the intention of equality is not a good thing; an electronic environment which perfectly constrains domination is not only difficult to implement, but destructive as well. The ideal of facilitating empowerment is implementable without going to the extreme of giving up the ideal of equality and democracy. We believe that systems should be capable of imposing constraints, but that the locus of control, of choosing and generating constraints, should remain with the users, not in the system.

Providing equal access to resources, enforcing identical procedural constraints, and requiring collaboratively owned task boundaries are three of the means of ensuring that all system participants have control, but this is not the same as attempting to alter the power relationships which are determined outside of the computer support space. We are not opposing the idea of altering power relationships; not opposing the idea of working towards more equality in groups; what we are saying is that only a certain amount of that can reasonably be done in software.

A conversational support system should be a medium of negotiation but not take an "active role". The system is not a critic, apprentice, reviewer, "intelligent agent" or project manager—it is a medium for interaction. These notions can be built and layered onto a system by the system users as extensions, but the "critiquing" or intelligent agency should be under individual control. To do otherwise results in an essentially dishonest pseudo-delegation to an artifact which necessarily reflects a designer's agenda more than a user's.

It is charming but unrealistic to suppose that we can build systems that change people's behavior to other than ways they want to behave. The design of some CSCW systems embodies a desired behavioral/organizational structure which might be quite different from the structure users prefer; e.g., The Coordinator (Carasik & Grantham, 1988). Imposing artificial equality is as inappropriate as imposing artificial hierarchy; therefore we want to avoid as much as possible having to embody one structure or another. This implies that a lot of roles are not defined from within the system, but the system is allowed to reflect what the users see as roles. Grudin maintains a qualifying characteristic of CSCW applications is that they support user role distinctions (Grudin 1988). His comment derives from the frequently neglected difference in the approach to an application by, for example, a manager as opposed to a secretary. He warns that an application's success is impaired if its design does not balance user's investments and benefits. By not imposing a "model of the user" on the user, the issue of equal benefit rests with the users. ACE makes very few assumptions about its prospective users, save for the expectation that users should be comfortable with the idea of computer support, and they must be willing to take responsibility for how they use the system and how they treat each other while doing so.

Design process: iterative prototyping and participatory design

The ACE development team includes four designer/users, two designer/builders, and the entire CICT research staff as users/testers. The roles of designer, programmer and user were quite clear at the beginning of the project, but have become less rigid as the project continues. The programmers could not begin building ACE until sufficient specifications existed using the appropriate technical terminology for standard Macintosh applications. However, as the designers learned the correct idiom, the programmers began to contribute significantly to the design. As users begin to test the prototype, the design evolves further. We believe that a key to the integration of the three roles, designer, user and builder, is that all participants must find an interesting challenge. ACE presents some interesting problems in group behavior, design for collaborative work, and the protocol necessary for computer supported shared workspaces. Openness to challenge (and indeed, the challenge itself!) is critical for multiple, incrementally rich prototype iterations.

It is by now well understood that the design and development of systems is not a linear, but an iterative process. Various techniques ranging from prolonged meetings between users and developers, to source code and screen generators (software tools) have been used to speed up the iteration of design and development (Vaske & Grantham, 1990). Prototyping is frequently an effective method of system design. System users are usually not able to articulate or fully perceive the needs to be satisfied by a system under development without experiencing some artifacts which represent the proposed functionality of the system. Prototypes can be seductive; users become very comfortable and attached to the prototype on which they have collaborated, want to take it live, and then experience "horribleness" because it is only a first prototype. Developers are seduced by prototypes because prototypes can freeze assumptions about what the system should be like; a prototype can be "enhanced into viability" when the design is unstable and immature.

The iteration of prototyping is itself valuable. However, we suggest that series of iterations should each involve the use of radically different tools, such as screens drawn with software prototypers, hand-drawn diagrams, and conversational scenario-building and analysis. Whatever the method, such a design-building process must include multiple participants. It is extremely easy to come up with a workable image of a certain element of functionality and become rather attached to it, just because it exists.

The design process for ACE began with a set of basic functional requirements. As those requirements were "brought to life" through iterative prototyping, the requirements themselves changed. The following system description is a result of four design iterations. Throughout the design discussions, an emphasis was placed on functional requirements that could provide a challenge to our programmers' computing skills and similar challenges to the design of experiments in user observation and behavioral analyses. It should be noted that as implementation proceeds, we anticipate that further (and perhaps more radical) design changes will emerge.

CREATING THE ACE DESIGN IMAGE

Our "design image" is the conceptual overall picture of what ACE does, how it feels, and how the user interface looks and works. The goal of ACE is to provide an environment for synchronous communication of large groups (we specified 21 as a suitable "large" size) with a central projected view of the workspace. Using ACE, group participants can share and modify products from a variety of external tools. The "feel" is intended to be determined by the users in real time through the tool's extensibility. Later phases of the project will explore how different kinds of users cope with this unstructured environment; we expect to be able to draw some parallels to Mantei's observations in analysing user behaviors in the Capture Lab (Mantei, 1988). The "look" of ACE conforms to the standard Macintosh interface. For example, we describe below a simple mechanism for annotating ACE window objects; given contextual support, this mechanism can encompass the substantive, annotative, and procedural types of comments identified in (Trigg & Halasz 1986).

ACE is a networked Macintosh application providing unlimited multi-user windows as shared workspaces which function analogously to a whiteboard, although this metaphor's usefulness is limited.† ACE windows are kept in a designated server machine which maintains links among versions of objects, identifies users, and provides an "etiquetted simultaneity". Any kind of text or graphic "object" can be placed on an ACE window using the standard Copy-Paste operation from another Macintosh application. Each object has a number of attributes, such as its type, location, authorship and permissions.

In addition to the shared workspace, ACE provides a method for capturing commentary about and between objects. Objects can be annotated in an associated window; these windows-related-to-objects behave the same as the window in which the object is found. Conversation *about* objects can be carried on using a related

† The whiteboard metaphor suggests the kind of blank space we intend, but does not have the dimensionality of recursion and connection provided for in ACE. Our metaphor evolved from the chalkboard metaphor of facilitating group display and changeable group display in a non-computer supported WYSIWIS manner. With the introduction of electronic whiteboards, we achieve a more changeable, flexible medium for group display, distributable in hard copy, yet one-dimensional. With a computer supported whiteboard, we add a dimension; we have a distributable, changeable group display medium which is highly manipulable with endless instant versioning capability, import capability, and implied security (saving, locking, etc.). The computer supported whiteboard has a "back room" aspect of work that the computer performs to serve the users, including linking and commenting facilities that provide a second "conversational channel" for what is immediately visible. This we could call two-dimensional, similar to a landscape whose surface alone is navigable.

An object-oriented implementation of the computer supported whiteboard brings us into a three-dimensional world that isolates ideas, pieces of conversation, and illustrations into "things in the virtual world" that have attributes (such as authorship, ownership, position, relation) and behaviors (they can move, make sound, rearrange, reorganize). We start to see possibilities of structure and identity changing how we approach ideas as "things in the (shared) virtual world". Our three-dimensional "landscape" has the richness of levels; what you can see, and what you can access to explain what you see. This is a new metaphor entirely. We are no longer limited to a single conversational boundary or landscape "plane". We are not limited to what is above, on, and below the horizon; these become artificial distinctions which may or may not be valid, as we determine how many planes there are in our own constructed virtual networks of objects. We may construct our own paths and define our own hierarchies, and negotiate those constructs with others in order to similarly interpret and process what we share. The problems of navigation common to hypertext systems apply here, with the exception that we are encouraging groups to find meaningful constraints together. We have yet to determine in the design of ACE whether or not there will be navigational aids such as exist in some hypertext systems as "virtual world maps".

window, or through public mailing which acts as a bulletin board for continuous conversation, or through e-mail capability (speaking "in parentheses").

FIRST ITERATION: PROTO-ACE

The initial design of ACE evolved out of a simulation exercise conducted by one of the authors at a seminar with researchers at the CICT in Amsterdam. We wanted to expose ACE in its infancy to criticism of its purpose and exploration of its potential; introduce an experimental environment and watch the behavior of this group as it performed a given task; and learn a little, through structured activity, what this particular group considers to be a "support system".

The exercise centered on the meaning (to the CICT members) of "support". We presented a hypothetical support system: Proto-ACE. "Proto-ACE" is a heavy cardboard purple cube 12″ square. On the front of the box is a gray mylar "screen" the exact size of a Macintosh screen, with a white "menu" bar along the tope edge. Below the "screen" on the left is the word ACE in press-on letters, and to the right, a thick line representing a disk drive. Inside each box are five large paper airplanes constructed with a "message compartment". Each plane has a paper-streamer "tail" stapled to its end, with the paper-streamer tucked inside the compartment. In addition to the airplanes, each box holds an additional ten streamers, five sheets of legal-sized paper (for more planes), a pencil, a small notepad, and a plastic bag holding a toy-like plastic stapler, extra staples, and two or three little clothes-pin style clips. A box was placed under each chair before the seminar, one for each of the fifteen attendees.

We suggested to the group that we use P-ACE as the medium for a discussion about support systems. Following is a first-person report of what happened during the seminar, from the author's role as "leader":

> I took my box from under my chair, opened it, and described the contents. I did NOT give the group any instructions about what to do with the box itself. As I went through the inventory of contents, each participant mimicked what I did with my box: they placed it in front of themselves, opened it up, and handled the articles inside.
>
> I introduced the pencil as the "input device", the notepad as the "communications medium", the airplanes as the "communications protocol", and the bag of staples and clips as the "hardware support package". I demonstrated an "anonymous message": a note written on a piece of notepad paper, and flown in an airplane with the paper streamer still tucked inside, to someone across the room. I also demonstrated a "traceable message", one whose paper streamer "tail" unfurled as it flew across the room. People perked up (mostly, I think, because this was very colorful and looked like fun).
>
> I asked the group to discuss the meaning of "support", giving examples for "What is a good support system?" and "What is a bad support system?" Having been assured that all opinions were to be considered equally valid, they were asked to conduct this discussion via P-ACE. The group started immediately. After a few moments of consideration, everyone started writing notes and flying them across the room. I occasionally received messages that said, "Stop?" and "Why computers?" Otherwise, there were few comments sent to me *about* the activity; I sent several comments about the topic under discussion, and I received several replies. I started to tape notes I had received to the blackboard behind me. Once I had begun to tape up the notes, I received messages that indicated an exchange of comments; the group evidently decided that once an exchange had taken place, the task was completed, and the result could be flown up to the blackboard. More and more people looked to me for direction and finally someone

asked if we were finished. I said I guessed we were finished when we stopped, and if I had all the airplanes and could put up all the notes we could stop. People started to send airplanes directly into my box, and two or three people helped collect notes and passed them to me for posting. The exchange of paper airplanes lasted about fifty minutes.

The "users" of P-ACE had a very limited "model" of what they were to do and how they were to behave. Although the subject of the task and a method were suggested, the only request made was that participants engage with each other.

In the exchanged messages, people wanted to know *about* the task: when it would stop, why this topic, what the purpose of the task was. However, no one asked verbally and publicly about the task. The process was not challenged; the group exhibited significant trust that aspects such as purpose, duration, and stopping rules were designed in, although they were not talked about in advance. *No-one* invented or took initiative to change the fundamental task on more than an individual level (inside their own exchanges with other people).

This group appeared to quickly conform to an "activity model" consisting of write, note–send note, and sometimes write, note–send, note–receive, reply–continue. Although they seemed to be surprisingly obedient, it is worth noting that the initial request, that participants develop an exchange of ideas about support systems, was not the primary task with which these people were engaging. They were primarily captivated by the activity "send" because it was fun. This illustrates a central issue in the design of group support systems; the artifacts have a way of becoming the focus of the discussion. Learning how to manipulate a support system does not in itself indicate an increase in competence.

The subject of conventions for closure, a type of "management ritual", was purposely avoided in the construction of the task. Some participants felt that there should have been more "closure" to what they *expected* to have happened. Interestingly, no one specifically requested more closure or a review or summary, much less invented a process for doing so. On reflection, we feel that there is usually a push for closure only when a group is expected to continue at another time with the same or a similar task, and needs to feel a firm starting ground for the next time the group begins work.

One of the tests we wanted to make was to see how people behave with a physical obstacle in front of them. An uncomfortable aspect of computer supported meetings is the physical visual impediment of the hardware itself in front of each participant. Given no instructions in this regard, we wanted to see how the group behaved with an easily removable obstruction in front of them. At the end of the exercise, of the fifteen participants, only three had removed the box from immediately in front of them. Many people used the boxes as targets for their airplanes. There was a great deal of commotion as the exercise progressed; although a process obstacle had been imposed (participants had been asked to communicate their ideas about support via written notes) and was for the most part obeyed, there was a great deal of simultaneous discussion about getting the planes to fly right, to whom messages were directed, comments about each other, etc. Neither the visual obstacle nor the process obstacle impeded conversation, although the process obstacle *directed* conversation away from the discussion topic and toward commentary about things going on in the room. With repetition and increased complexity (had the exercise continued longer, had further conventions been established, or had repetitions of this type of exercise been planned), we presume that the group would have invented local language—terminology specific to the environment.

SECOND ITERATION: ACE 0.0

The second round of design prototyping was done in software. Using a Macintosh prototyping tool, we created an environment of layered menus and command structures in standard Macintosh format. We built a version of a public window as well as menu access to software tools, and a facility for group member identification by personalized icon. This second attempt at building a system image provided a turn in the overall direction of ACE.

Developing a software prototype has advantages and disadvantages. The primary advantage here was that many implementation ideas as well as problems quickly surfaced. Once we decided to conform to the Macintosh development paradigm, we found that we had some obvious constraints on the system. We wanted to keep modality and command structures to an absolute minimum, and therefore had to change some of our ideas. We negotiated design ideas through the prototyping tool, and got a fairly accurate view of the complexity of adding certain functions, as well as the user-activities necessary to accomplish some tasks. For example, "I want each user to be able to develop or choose their own graphic icon to use as their "signature" when posting work to a common workspace or when sending messages" sounds easy but becomes a non-trivial mesh of commands which may require more user process-steps than users are likely to want to perform. In this example, the benefit of having handy, personal icons with some measure of identification integrity "costs too much". Providing the icons is relatively simple. Ensuring that they are securely linked to an author, and can *move with the author* from machine to machine, is much more difficult.

The upper limits of computer-supported prototyping are soon reached if no actual code is being developed. For a richly connected command structure, some code must be developed in order to get a realistic view of how the application will work. Now that we had a better idea of Macintosh interface standards, we were ready for a third try at conceptualizing the overall image of ACE.

THIRD ITERATION: ACE ON THE DRAWING BOARD

The third design approach was literally a drawing-board approach. Armed with what we had learned in the previous two attempts, we put together a series of overlaying transparencies to simulate the ACE windows and their relationships. With designers and developers mutually respecting theoretical and technical aspects, this time the picture "clicked", and we could begin technical refinements.

Overhead transparencies are a particularly valuable way of showing layered windows, even when a projector is not used. The visual impact of "this is what you could see when you do *x*" carries significantly more weight than a verbal description of the same thing. We drew up a progression of screen additions with each transparency addressing one desired function of ACE, done in different colors. The design team sat around a table with the transparencies in the middle, doodling and making notes on fresh transparencies laid over the design set. This was a good way to annotate the design, gave everyone a sense of flexibility, and recorded design changes in the same kind of workspace that we were trying to create. While the previous prototype (second iteration) was more of a throw-away learning experience, we often referred back to these transparencies as a visual "anchor".

FOURTH ITERATION: ACE 0.1

ACE 0.1 was our first demonstration version, and included ACE windows and object-oriented data structures. ACE windows are standard Macintosh windows which include the title bar, size box, close box, zoom box, scroll bars, and a special Monitor pane. Multiple views of the same ACE window are supported on the individual machines; while the entire window (four times the standard Macintosh window size) may be projected as a central view, individual machines may reorganize their views independent of the central view-of-record. Individual machines can independently scroll through their view of the projected window.

As new ACE windows are created, it is important as a matter of user orientation to name them distinctively. We leave the setting of naming conventions to the users, with the constraint that duplicate names are not allowed. Users may subscribe to multiple ACE windows by selecting one window at a time through the Open file operation. Since it is possible to share multiple windows, the group may wish to designate one as the primary shared workspace.

New ACE windows can be initiated by any user. A user opens a new ACE window and names it. The initiator is the "owner" of the window, and may lock it, indicating that it is private and participation in it is by invitation only. The owner of a window can use the messaging facility to suggest that other users subscribe to the named window. We call this type of subgroup shared space activity a "caucus". Users who wish to learn more about restricted ACE windows must inquire directly of other users, via the messaging capability (or by asking participants in the room, if ACE is being used in a face-to-face situation).

Multiple windows present at least two kinds of navigation problem in group work, especially where each user may navigate independently. One is "how do I know how to get where I want to go?" Another is, "how do I find out where everyone else is?" This first problem is addressed through the conventions of naming windows and look-up lists of windows. There is currently no back-tracing as exists in hypertext. We felt that the second problem is more interesting and somewhat more sensitive due to the privacy issues brought up in ownership of windows and objects. A "Monitor" pane attached to each window indicates the number of users subscribed to it, as well as how many of those subscribers have this window active on their screen; this gives a rough idea of the engagement of users in any particular conversation, but does not differentiate between active participants and passive observers.

Text, graphics, and even sounds can be copied from other applications and inserted on the ACE window via standard Macintosh Copy-Paste operations. The content of each Paste operation to the window is treated as a single object and is a representation of the original, and as such is not fully operational. Only minor text editing to each object is allowed on the shared window; new text objects can be created through the text editing facility. To edit non-text objects, the object must be copied back from the ACE window into an application where it can be fully manipulated, and repasted to the ACE window. Objects pasted to the ACE window can be PICT or text, and are pasted to the window from the user's Clipboard (a Scrapbook is a handy storage place for multiple objects).

Pasted to a window, objects can be moved in several ways, resized, and edited (with limitations). Because the window is intended as a conversation space, more importance is placed on the ability to share displays of personal contributions and talk about them, than on sharing entire documents. However, a single user can easily paste an object onto the ACE window that would take up the entire available space; this is not programmatically discouraged.

The connectivity of ACE windows and its messaging facilities allow users to share their thoughts about what is going on in the work space; it is intended that if users wish to manipulate each other's objects fully, they may inquire of the author for more detail. For example, a spreadsheet object cannot be manipulated on the ACE window, and the author may wish to share only a portion of the spreadsheet. If other non-authoring participants in this window want to work with the numbers shown on the spreadsheet object, they may copy the object to an application on their machine and the object will carry with it the associated formulas. If a user other than the author wants to manipulate the entire spreadsheet, the spreadsheet should be requested of the author, who may send it as a file to the requestor over the messaging facility.

Standard Macintosh selection operations are supported. When an object is selected, information about the object can be displayed by choosing the Get Info . . . menu item from the Edit menu. Choosing this item brings up a dialog box with an identifier for the object; a view of the object; authorship (who pasted the object to the ACE window, "ownership" of the object, and its home location); linked-to information; update/read rights (for content and location); and its change history. At present, multiple selection is only supported for objects of the same type.

Double-clicking on an object brings up a new blank window "related" to the object. There is no structure imposed on any window. A text object can be created on a blank window to comment or annotate the object to which it is attached, using the provided basic text editing facilities. A new window initially appears in the lower right-hand corner of the screen, can be moved, closed, and resized, and when closed and re-opened will reappear in its most recent screen position. (At this time, deselection of the object automatically closes the attached window.) While a window may be opened attached to an object, a copy of that object may also be placed in its referent window. Because there are no structural limitations on what may appear where, it will be interesting to observe how users navigate these layered and related windows.

ACE will incorporate an existing messaging system (such as Quickmail or Broadcast) to allow users to send messages to any other participant on the network. Messages may be sent to single individuals, designated groups, or specified window subscribers. Additionally, through the server, a message can be sent to all participants in all active windows. Participants may choose to be identified or remain anonymous.

Next steps

The first working prototype of ACE is designed for face-to-face synchronous interaction. However, we want to consider relaxing the constraint that ACE window subscribers must all be present during a session, and explore bulletin board usage as well.

As our project continues, we are designing testing procedures and beginning to test both the development process and the product. Primarily, we want to see how groups feel about computer support that they structure themselves, and how they behave. We would like to see if the lack of rigid process induces "process paralysis" or encourages the group to establish its own process conventions. We want to observe what people do in an environment where they choose and generate constraints, whether they will feel pressured to bring structure to it, and if this experience of collaborative building influences whether users see themselves as members of a group. We are also interested in what kind of constraints may be necessary to build in to support continuation. Secondarily, we are interested in observing the production of group-structured artifacts, the record of the interaction.

A significant design dilemma is the amount of user orientation that any particular function will require. We would like to keep the requirement for role differentiation in the user domain, and not in the system: e.g., if operating ACE becomes too elaborate, a facilitator with special training will be required to assist groups. In keeping with low learning-curve overhead, we wish to avoid forcing a role distinction that demands a special competence that is not shared by the group. We also wish to keep user documentation to an enjoyable minimum, and have designed it in three parts. The first section is a brief functional description of ACE in standard Macintosh documentation format (a model of the system). The second part is a collection of different scenarios, essentially short stories, that describe groups of people from an observer point of view as they work on different tasks using ACE (a series of models for the user). The third section is a cross-reference to the scenarios, describing how to prepare for and follow through the described activities using ACE.

We anticipate that users will choose to see ACE in different ways, some of which it can be expected to support, and some of which it will not. For example, multiple contiguously-placed text objects can look like an outline or a set of connected paragraphs in a single-document context. Although ACE is not designed to serve as a co-authoring tool, it can do so, if the group establishes sufficient conventions. We hope that users will make use of the annotation and layering abilities that multiple windows provides, and work in more than the two dimensions suggested by collaboration in a single window.

We would also like to see if the introduction of a computerized medium for conversation changes how people converse. It is widely recognized that e-mail users adopt highly informal language when using a communication medium that is fairly anonymous. ACE offers both identification and anonymity, but we wonder how much anonymity is possible or desired when an established group works together on a shared task. We anticipate that groups using the ACE shared workspace will make use of the opportunity to develop a richer conversation and improve their ability to work together. We also want to test whether the documentation capabilities of ACE suffice as records of group memory for meetings; people accustomed to having scribes in meetings may not record enough objects to make up for this lack.

As we build ACE our product and our design evolves. As our project team works together and we exchange ideas, we become more capable of understanding each other's goals and challenges, and what each of us finds an "interesting problem".

We hope that in the end, groups using ACE will similarly be able to converse, to discover, and to encourage new ideas to emerge.

We wish to acknowledge, in particular Prof. G. de Zeeuw, Director of the CICT; Dr M. Robinson; and G. Hulstein and R. Pixley, ACE's designer/builders. We also thank the following members of the CICT for their theoretical and conceptual contributions: Dr H. van Haaster, Dr C. Meeuwissen, Dr T. Meijers, Dr H. Riper, Dr M. Vahl; and D. Schechter of Pacific Bell.

E. Dykstra is on loan from the Technology Laboratories division of Pacific Bell to the Center for Innovation and Co-operative Technology at the University of Amsterdam for the ACE project.

References

BØDKER, S., KNUDSEN, J. L. KYNG, M., EHN, P. & MADSEN, K. H. (1988). Computer support for cooperative design. In *Proceedings of the Conference on Computer-supported Cooperative Work,* Portland, Oregon, September 26–28, pp. 377–394.

CARASIK, R. P. & GRANTHAM, C. E. (1988). A case study of CSCW in a dispersed organization, In *Proceedings of CHI '88: Conference on Human Factors in Computing Systems,* Washington D.C., May 15–19, pp. 61–65.

CARASIK, R. P., EVELAND, J. D. & GRANTHAM, C. E. (1988). *A Strategy for Computer-supported Cooperative Work,* Working Paper. May 1988, pp. 2–4. San Francisco, CA: Pacific Bell Applied Research and Development.

CARASIK, R. P. & DYKSTRA, E. A. (1989). Requirements for a semi-structured graphics communication medium for CSCW. In *Proceedings of the First European Conference on Computer-supported Co-operative Work,* London, England, September 13–15.

CONKLIN, J. & BEGEMAN, M. (1988). gIBIS: A hypertext tool for exploratory policy discussion. In *Proceedings of the Conference on Computer-supported Cooperative Work,* Portland, Oregon, September 26–28, pp. 140–152.

FORSGREN, O. (1989). The first CO: a prototype of a learning co-constructor. In *Proceedings of the 33rd Annual Meeting of the International Society for the Systems Sciences,* Edinburgh, Scotland, 2–7 July, pp. 92–97.

GRUDIN, J. (1988). Why CSCW Applications Fail: problems in the design and evaluation of organizational interfaces. In *Proceedings of the Conference on Computer-supported Cooperative Work,* Portland, Oregon, September 26–28, pp. 85–93.

LELAND, M. D. P., FISH, R. S. & KRAUT, R. E. (1988). Collaborative document production using quilt. In *Proceedings of the Conference on Computer-supported Cooperative Work,* Portland, Oregon, September 26–28, pp. 206–215.

MALONE, T. W., GRANT, K. R., LAI, K.-Y., RAO, R. & ROSENBLITT, D. (1986). Semi-structured messages are surprisingly useful for computer-supported coordination. In *Proceedings of the Conference on Computer-supported Cooperative Work,* Austin, Texas, December 3–5, pp. 102–114.

MANTEI, M. (1988). Capturing the capture lab concepts: a case study in the design of computer-supported meeting environments. In *Proceedings of the Conference on Computer-supported Cooperative Work,* Portland, Oregon, September 26–28, pp. 257–270.

PASK, G. (1976). *Conversation Theory: Applications in Education and Epistemology,* pp. 1–16. Amsterdam: Elsevier.

TRIGG, R. H. & HALASZ, F. G. (1986). Supporting colloboration in notecards. *In Proceedings of the Conference on Computer-supported Cooperative Work,* Austin, Texas, December 3–5, pp. 153–162.

VASKE, J. J. & GRANTHAM, C. E. (1990). *Socializing the Human–Computer Environment,* pp. 1–33. Norwood, NJ: Ablex.

WINOGRAD, T. (1986). A language/action perspective on the design of cooperative work. In *Proceedings of the Conference on Computer-Supported Work,* Austin, Texas, December 3–5, pp. 203–220.

WRIGHT, K. (1990). The road to the global village. *Scientific American,* March, 57–66.

Part 6

Participatory design

16

Obstacles to user involvement in software product development, with implications for CSCW

Jonathan Grudin

This paper addresses one particular software development context: large product development organizations. It describes common obstacles that product developers face in obtaining knowledge about actual or potential users of their systems and applications. Many of these obstacles can be traced to organizational structures and development practices that arose prior to the widespread market for interactive systems. These observations apply to user involvement in human–computer interface development in general, but have particular relevance to CSCW and groupware development.

Introduction

The need for the developers of interactive systems to understand the eventual users and their work is well known. The difficulty of acquiring that knowledge indirectly has led to an emphasis on direct user contact during the development process. Although good human-computer interfaces can be found, the difficulty of developing them is substantial. This paper explores the underlying problems in one systems development context: large product development organizations. Because most of these companies were formed before the human–computer interface attained its present prominence, little or no consideration was given to the particular needs of interface development in establishing their organizational structures and development processes. The result was several common difficulties in achieving and benefiting from user involvement in development—the topic of this paper.

These obstacles affect the development of any interactive system. Their particular relevance to CSCW and groupware development is described in the next section and returned to periodically in the paper. However, there is a higher-level reason to address these issues in this setting. While today's practitioner may best address the problems outlined in this paper by being aware of them and seeking constructive paths around them, to overcome the organizational constraints and forces will ultimately require organizational change. CSCW researchers and developers are uniquely endowed with the interests and skills to understand and guide such organizational change.

This paper draws on the growing literature in the field of human–computer interaction, much of which originates in product development companies. It also makes use of surveys and interviews of over 200 interface designers in several product development companies (Grudin & Poltrock, 1989; Poltrock, 1989a), my experiences in product development, and thousands of conversations with fellow developers over the years. Of course, organizations vary considerably. Reliable, industry-wide data are difficult to find. The obstacles described here are encountered, but are not universal. The hope is that the forewarned reader will be better able to anticipate, recognize and respond to these and similar challenges if and when they appear.

USER INVOLVEMENT AND CSCW

In examining interface design in product development organizations, we are clearly engaged in the study of *Cooperative Work*. Furthermore, by specifically considering the prospects for user involvement, we are focused on possible degrees of participatory or collaborative design. However, what about the *Computer Support*? In this section, I describe five strong connections between the conditions for user involvement in product development and the application of CSCW. Although the paper will then focus on user involvement and interface design, frequent reference will be made to the particular concerns of CSCW.

CSCW and groupware development are primarily product development
The formation of the discipline of CSCW represents in part a shift of attention of some product developers to applications that support group work. The issues of computer support for groups and organizations long pre-dated the coining of the terms "CSCW" and "groupware" and the conferences of the mid-1980s, but the earlier work came less from a product development orientation and more from an internal or in-house development perspective, where the introduction of large systems into organizations was examined. Only recently have the conditions of technology and price emerged that may support "mass-marketed" applications designed to support groups. *The CSCW'86 and '88 Conferences were heavily attended by employees of large product development companies.*†

User involvement in development is especially *important for groupware*
To succeed, much groupware will have to be used by most or all group members. This means appealing to people with differing roles, backgrounds and preferences. In addition, group dynamics can be complex, can vary widely from setting to setting, and are not well understood. Any one person's intuition will be a less reliable guide than has been true for single-user applications. Developers will need more information about prospective users and more feedback from actual users. It is unlikely that indirect information flow will be enough. Recognition of this has led to a strong emphasis on participatory or collaborative design at CSCW conferences.

Human-computer interface design is especially *important for groupware*
A single-user application can satisfy a fairly narrow user population and succeed by appealing to one segment of the market. CSCW and groupware force designers to attend to individual differences, part of the reason being the aforementioned need to be accepted by entire groups; an even more significant factor is the inherent asymmetry of benefits that groupware almost inevitably provides (Grudin, 1988; 1990a; 1990c). Very often, some people will be required to do more work to

---

† 35–45% of registrants, if the 5% associated with telephone operating companies are included. A further 10% were from smaller product development companies and 25–30% were from academic institutions. Most of the remaining 25–30% were from government, consulting companies, or the information systems departments of large companies.

support a CSCW application, while others will be the principle beneficiaries. To minimize resistance and to offer some hope for success, it will be crucial to optimize the interface for the users who are *not* the principal beneficiaries, something we are not in the habit of doing as developers. This cannot be overemphasized. And the most widely endorsed approach to interface optimization is iterative development based on continuous user involvement (e.g. Gould & Lewis, 1983).

Several of the obstacles are particularly *grave for groupware development*
As the obstacles to user involvement are described, it will be evident that some of them pose special challenges for CSCW researchers and developers. For example, while it may be difficult for individual users to find the time to contribute meaningfully, obtaining the cooperation of a group for a significant period could be far more difficult.

Implications for one CSCW focus: computer support for systems development
One area in which group support applications have made progress is in support of software development itself: code management systems that support version control and patching and the integration of complex systems. Here, developers' intuitions are obviously better, user involvement is readily accessible, and the user population is technically sophisticated and relatively homogeneous. However, by understanding the communication and coordination problems that are encountered, such as those described below, we may see how to extend these "object management" systems to better support developers. Some suggestions in this direction conclude the paper.

PRODUCT DEVELOPMENT ORGANIZATIONS

Our focus is on large companies that develop and market interactive software systems and applications: systems with a human–computer dialogue or interface. Projects resulting from specific contracts and internal development groups within large organizations are not addressed. Contract and internal development, which do not result in externally marketed products, have different advantages and disadvantages in developing interactive systems (Grudin, in press). Of course, a company may straddle categories: a product development company may bid on government contracts, an internal development group may decide to market a system built initially for internal use, and so forth. In addition, *small* product development companies may not experience the problems described here, while companies of moderate size may experience some and not others.

Although product development accounts for only a fraction of interactive systems development, it is an influential fraction. Large product development companies are visibly concerned with usability and "look and feel". They have hired and trained many user interface specialists, recruiting heavily from research universities. These specialists dominate the conferences and journals in the fields of human–computer interaction and CSCW, especially in the United States.

These companies matured in the 1960s and 1970s, making their money selling or leasing hardware. Software functionality was secondary and the human-computer interface received little attention. Since then, software has come to rival hardware in importance—many of the successful new product development companies of the 1980s primarily sold software. The focus was on functionality and price, not on the interface—until the success of the Macintosh in the late 1980s. Now, the interface is increasingly important.

Attitudes may be changing, but the current business operations and development procedures of most large product development companies were formed when hardware and software functionality were the only considerations. It is therefore not surprising that existing organizational structures and processes do not facilitate interface development. In fact, they often systematically *obstruct* the design and development of good interfaces.

DEVELOPMENT PROJECTS

The process of defining a product can be separated into two parts: the events before the project is launched and those occurring during development. An ongoing development project can generally provide a neat time line showing a start date, a projected completion date, and a few milestones along the way. Reality may be less precise, with one event flowing into another. Rather than a decision being made at one point in time, those involved may gradually realize that a decision had emerged sometime earlier. Nevertheless, teams are formed, assignments announced, budgets allocated. Some projects use a number based on the month and day of initiation as their first working name.

The product definition, consisting of the high-level functionality to be developed or implemented, precedes the project start date. While implementing that functionality, the team designs and develops the necessary low-level functions and other aspects of the human–computer dialogue or interface. It is notoriously difficult to draw a line between software functionality and its "user interface", and potential users have a substantial interest in *both*. However, we can distinguish between the high-level description of the product that precedes project initiation and the low-level aspects of the design that are worked out later. This paper will generally apply the expressions "human–computer interface" or "interface" to the latter. For example, the interface to a word processor will define not only the "look and feel" but also whether a one-step "move" or a two-step "cut" and "paste" is provided. In addition, the "interface" is defined broadly to include documentation, training, hot-line support, or other elements that directly affect the users' experiences.

Different groups are involved in these two phases. A management group, with representation from development, works out product definition. Companies vary in the degree to which they are driven by their engineering or marketing divisions, but marketing often has a particularly strong influence at this stage. Once the project is assembled, this group may recede from view, monitoring progress through documentation and management reviews.

Potential product users are sometimes involved in each phase. During product definition, market research and focus groups may provide contact. Typically, these will seek out *customers,* rather than users—information system specialists from large companies whose job it is to represent user requirements (as well as management requirements and other factors influencing purchase decisions). During development, experimental studies of design alternatives and prototype testing may involve users.

An interesting question is whether greater user participation in product definition would be useful. What form of user involvement might be optimal at that stage? Better to sample a wide range of potential users or to work closely with a small number? Open-ended needs-finding—involving users without any preconceptions— is rare, though not unheard of. It might lead to good product ideas, but other forces are at work defining products. Most companies operate within a restricted product range to begin with. They generally have existing products that are in clear need of improvement. Indirect channels through sales, marketing, and consultants are a source of product ideas. Other ideas are formulated by responding to competition and monitoring technological innovation. A dearth of product ideas is not usually a problem.

A second question is whether user participation might continue across both the product definition and product development phases. Given the way many product development companies operate, the answer is no—there is remarkably little carryover of the *company's* personnel from one phase to the next. This may be based on the contract model of system development—the belief that a written requirements specification is enough to communicate a product idea. It may also lead to some of the faults of contract development: a product being delivered by developers that is not quite what those defining it had in mind.

While there may be room for experimentation, product development does generally begin with a product idea defined primarily in terms of high level functionality (although as the interface gains prominence, attempts to define it will move forward in time, creating new challenges). This paper concentrates on the period after the baton is passed to the development team; in particular, on the process of defining and developing the human–computer interface.

INTERFACE DEVELOPMENT AND USER INVOLVEMENT

Product developers can acquire an understanding of computer users without making direct contact. Many mediators exist to facilitate the flow of information between computer users and developers. These include marketing and sales organizations, consultants, information systems specialists, users groups, standards organizations, trade magazines and journals. Of course, the calls for direct user involvement question the effectiveness of these intermediaries—and the demands on them are escalating.

As computer users become less technical and more diverse, developers have more need to obtain information about them and their work environments. Also, as competition increases in some markets, increased knowledge about users is needed to fine-tune products. Finally, as noted above, groupware will require far more information about users and their environments than did single-user products, in order to support a wider range of users and a greater percentage of users in a given setting. Given the limits to any one person's intuition, more information must be gathered about users and their work environments, both to support design and development, and to support product adoption, where a range of potentially deadly problems must be avoided (Grudin, 1990c). As noted, mediators may be unable to meet the challenge of providing this information, necessitating direct contact between developers and potential users.

The most direct and extensive form of user engagement is participatory or collaborative design, enlisting potential users as full members of the design team (e.g. Bjerknes, Ehn & Kyng, 1987). A limited form of this is obtained by hiring people from user organizations to work in development groups as "domain experts". More common but also more circumscribed user involvement is provided by limited-duration studies of existing or potential users, or individuals presumed to be much like them.

In the context of product development, Gould and Lewis (1983) made an early, forceful argument for participatory design, eschewing reliance on mediators and more limited empirical approaches. They wrote: "we recommend that *typical users* (e.g. bank tellers) be used, as opposed to a 'group of expert' supervisors, industrial engineers, programmers. We recommend that these potential users become part of the design team *from the very outset* when their perspectives can have the most influence, rather than using them *post hoc* to 'review', 'sign off/on', 'agree' to the design before it is coded". Their message has been repeated in several prominent papers since then (Gould & Lewis, 1985; Gould, Boies, Levy, Richards & Schoonard, 1987; Gould, 1988) and is widely cited, yet it is rarely adopted. Gould and Lewis (1985) allude to unexplored "obstacles and traditions" that stand in the way. This paper explores those obstacles and traditions.

Obstacles to user involvement

The inherent nature of product development, in which a broad market is sought and the actual users are not known until after development is completed, presents challenges to involving users effectively. Additional obstacles to bringing developers into contact with existing or potential users can be traced to the division of labor within the organization (see Figure 1).† Existing assignments of responsibility may serve useful purposes, but they separate software developers from the world outside. With non-interactive systems this was not a major problem, but it is a problem now and is likely to get worse as user requirements and expectations increase. Contact with customers and users is the province of groups or divisions outside of development: sales, marketing, training, field support, and upper management. The people assigned these tasks are not primarily concerned with the interface, their relevant knowledge is not systematically organized, and they are often located far from the developers. They have a limited sense of what information would be useful or to whom to forward it. Groupware development will tax these indirect communication channels even further, being new, different, and with many concerns that are difficult to recognize and characterize. After discussing these structural impediments, we will examine difficulties that can be traced to standard software development procedures and techniques.

CHALLENGES IN MOTIVATING DEVELOPERS

Success may require most or all members of the development team to commit to user involvement. One person can work with users and try to introduce the results

† Many small and large variants of this organizational structure are found. To take one example, functions such as Quality Control and Performance Analysis may be handled centrally.

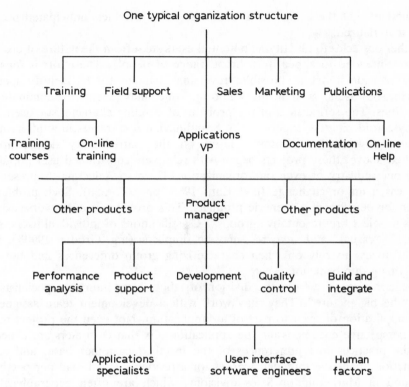

FIGURE 1. Organization chart showing separation of user-related functions. Adapted from Poltrock (1989c).

into the process, but iterative development requires a broader commitment, prototyping and testing may require software support, the results have to be valued, and so forth. Management must be willing to invest the resources, and the help of others may be needed to smooth contacts with users.

Although most developers would agree to user involvement in principle, it requires a greater commitment to make it work. Engineers and other team members may not follow through for several reasons. They may lack empathy or sympathy for inexperienced or non-technical computer users. When developers and users meet, they may find that different values, work styles, even languages get in the way of communicating. Developers tend to be young, rationalistic and idealistic, products of relatively homogeneous academic environments. They often have little experience or understanding of the very different work situations and attitudes of many system users. The best of intentions can succumb to these factors, especially in the face of the slowness and imprecision that often accompanies user involvement.

CHALLENGES IN IDENTIFYING APPROPRIATE USERS AND GROUPS

Developers may have a market in mind, but the actual users of a product are not known until the product is bought. The fate of many products, both negative and positive, are reminders of the inherent uncertainty in product development. The IBM PC is an example of a product with wider than expected appeal, while we can be confident that the designers of countless failed products anticipated users who never materialized.

Further obstacles to identifying potential users stem from the nature of developing products intended to appeal to a broad range of people. The effort is focused on casting as wide a net as possible; reversing gears to try to identify specific or characteristic users is difficult. Choosing one may seem to eliminate other possibilities. The seriousness of the problem of defining characteristic users can be seen by considering the experience of Scandinavian researchers in a different, *more favorable* development context. Based on the participatory design approach described above, these projects began with relatively constrained user populations, within one industry or even one organization. Even so, selecting "representative" users was a major challenge (e.g. Ehn, 1988, pp. 327–358). Such problems are greater for developers of generic products. This problem is even worse when the goal is to select "representative groups". Classifications of individual users, such as "novice", "casual" and "expert", may be simplistic (e.g. Grudin, 1990*b*), but we have even less to rely on when characterizing group differences and the factors underlying group behavior.

Obstacles also arise from the division of labor. User interface specialists rarely have "the big picture". They may work with a development team assigned to a single application or even to part of an application. Not even the project manager has a perspective encompassing the application mix that customers are expected to use, the practices and preferences of the installed customer base, and strategic information about the intended market for a product. This broad perspective may be found in Marketing or Sales divisions, which are often geographically and organizationally distant from the development groups. The projected market—the identity of the future users—may be closely guarded by upper management due to its competitive importance.

In large companies, marketing and sales representatives become species of "users" of products emerging from development. They also consider themselves to be internal advocates for the customers. Since the customers are often information specialists or managers, rather than "end-users", the chain of intermediaries lengthens. Low levels of contact and mutual respect between marketing and development (e.g. Kapor, 1987; Grudin & Poltrock, 1989; Poltrock, 1989*a*) can further reduce the value of this very indirect link between developers and users. Another complication in identifying appropriate users is that a system is often modified substantially after the development company ships it but before the users see it. This is done by software groups within customer organizations and by "value-added resellers" who tailor products for specific markets, for example. These developers are in a real sense "users" of the product—perhaps among the most important potential users. It may be more appropriate for *them* to involve the actual "end-users". In any case, the initial development team must discover which aspects of their design are likely to be "passed through" to users. Third-party intermediaries represent an opportunity, but their role also complicates the selection of "representative end-users".

CHALLENGES IN OBTAINING ACCESS TO USERS

Once candidates have been identified, the next challenge is to make contact with them. Obstacles may arise within either the users' organization or the development organization. Contacts with customers are often with managers or information system specialists, rather than with the computer users themselves. Getting past them may not be easy: their job is precisely to represent the users. In addition, the employers of prospective users may see little benefit in freeing them to work with an outside development group.

Within the product development company, *protecting (or isolating) developers from customers is traditionally a high priority.* The company cannot afford to let well-intentioned developers spend all of their time customizing products for individual users—priority is given to developing generic improvements to benefit scores or hundreds of users. Wise customers are well aware of the value of having the phone number of a genial developer, and barriers erected to keep users from contacting developers also prevent developers from easily connecting with users: the relationships and channels are not there.

The development company's sales representatives may be reluctant to let developers meet with customers. A developer, coming from a different culture, might offend or alarm the customer, or create dissatisfaction with currently available products by describing developments in progress. Similarly, a marketing department may consider itself to be the proper conduit into the development organization for information about customer needs, and may fear the results of random contacts between developers and users. In one company, developers, including human factors engineers, were prevented from attending the annual users' group meeting. Marketing viewed it as a show staged strictly for the customers.

Sometimes the potential user or group is *within* the development company. Convenient, but a dangerous special case to rely on. The company is not in business to build products for itself, and user environments are becoming less likely to resemble development environments.

CHALLENGES IN MOTIVATING POTENTIAL USERS

In an in-house development project, the product developers share the same management (at some level) with the potential users. This is not true in the case of product developers and external users, which may make it more difficult for the users to obtain time away from their jobs. In addition, the potential users may be less motivated, knowing that they may not end up actual users of the final product. The problems of sustaining user involvement have been recognized as substantial even in internal development projects. Of course, for contacts of limited duration, many computer users and their employers are pleased to be consulted.

Potential users may be less motivated if they do not see how the planned product could possibly benefit themselves. This is particularly a problem for some large systems and for the many groupware applications that selectively benefit managers, such as project or work management applications, decision support systems, meeting scheduling and management systems, and even some voice applications. In fact, it is noteworthy that the more successful applications that are sometimes categorized as groupware, such as e-mail, code management systems, and databases, do not selectively benefit managers (Grudin, 1990c). Of course, the situation is even worse when the potential users feel that their jobs might be threatened by a product that creates greater efficiency.

CHALLENGES IN BENEFITING FROM USER CONTACT

Given an uncertain identity of future users and a wide range of conceivable candidates, assessing one's experiences with a small number of possible users can be difficult. The Scylla of over-generalizing from a limited number of contacts is accompanied by the Charybdis of bogging down when users disagree. Finally, if user involvement succeeds in producing design recommendations, the work has just begun. Design ideas, whatever their source, must be steered through a software development process that is typically fraught with obstacles to interface optimization. User involvement may increase the odds of successfully navigating this course, but the journey is rarely easy, for reasons described below.

CHALLENGES IN OBTAINING FEEDBACK FROM EXISTING USERS

Feedback from users may be collected informally or through bug reports and design change requests. The latter generally focus on the basics and on what is of primary importance in the marketplace—e.g. hardware reliability and high-level software functionality—and not on interface features. As to features supporting groups, it may not even be clear who would be in a position to make such a determination. Even the little information that *is* collected rarely gets back to developers. Field service or software support groups shield developers from external contacts by maintaining products and working with customers on specific problems. The original product developers move on to new releases or product replacements, are reassigned to altogether different projects, or leave the company for greener pastures.

The extent of feedback may vary with the pattern of marketing and product use. A company such as Apple, with a heavy proportion of "discretionary" purchases initiated by actual users rather than by management or information systems specialists, *benefits* from having a particularly vocal user population. In general, though, the lack of user feedback may be the greatest hindrance to good product interface design and among the least recognized defects of standard software development processes. System developers cannot spend *all* of their time fielding requests from customers, but their overall lack of experience with feedback is an obstacle both to improving specific products and to building an awareness of the potential value of user participation in design. Developers rarely become aware of the users' pain.

This point deserves emphasis. Engineers are engaged in a continuous process of compromise, trading off among desirable alternatives. Interface improvements will be given more weight if engineers are aware of the far-reaching, lasting consequences of accepting an inferior design. Consider some typical trade-offs: "This implementation will save 10K bytes but be a little less modular." "This design will run a little faster but take a month longer to complete." "This chip provides two more slots but adds $500 to the sales price." Each requires a decision. Once the decision is made, the price in development time, memory size, or chip expense is paid and the matter is left behind. In this environment, the interface is just one consideration among many. "This interface would be nicer, but take two months longer to design." Without feedback from users, once this decision is made, it too can be forgotten. The decision may adversely affect thousands of users daily for the life of the product, but the developer remains unaware of this. The interface *is* special, but developers do not recognize that—once it is built and shipped, they are on to the next job, and other people (including users) must do the sweeping up.

The lack of feedback from the field is a particular problem for CSCW research and development. Collecting and analysing information about group use is more time-consuming and difficult than it is for single-user applications. Group processes are slower and environmental variables play a much larger role. Both successes and failures are much more difficult to understand. As a result of this inability to learn from experience, the same expensive failures are experienced repeatedly (Grudin, 1988; 1990*a*; 1990*c*).

TRYING TO FIND THE DESIGN TEAM

User involvement would be easier if one group had responsibility for all aspects of usability, as recommended by Gould (1988). But the "user interface", broadly defined, is not often the province of one recognizable team in a large product development company. The hardware is designed by one group, the software by another, the documentation by a third, and the training by a fourth. Representatives from other groups may have periodic involvement—reviewing design specifications, for example. A product manager with little direct authority over developers may coordinate scheduling. Individuals from several different marketing groups, such as competitive or strategic analysis† and international marketing, may contribute. Members of support groups such as human factors or performance analysis may participate, although not necessarily throughout the project. Several levels of management may monitor the process and comment at different stages. In concert, these people contribute to defining a computer user's experience with the system or application, yet communication among them may be surprisingly sparse. With whom are users to participate? In addition, turnover in project personnel is common, a further obstacle to sustained user involvement.

Matrix management is one approach to overcoming organizational separation. Representatives of a subset of these groups are given temporary assignment to a project. However, due to the perception or the reality that the contribution of "support roles" is limited to certain phases of a project, such assignments are often of limited duration or effectiveness. (An example of a matrix management effort succumbing to these forces is described in Grønbæk, Grudin, Bødker & Bannon, 1991.)

The general neglect of on-line help illustrates how divided responsibility can affect interface design. A good help system might save the company a substantial amount of money in customer "hand-holding", service calls, printed documentation, and so forth. The savings would be in the budget of, say, the Customer Service Department. But the effort and expense would have to come from Development, who may get more credit for devoting their resources to new functionality instead. Missing is the "affirmative action" needed to promote on-line help in the face of possible lack of developer empathy with less experienced users, re-enforced by the

† Competitive analysis may seem to be a logical ally of a development organization. However, in practice their concern may be the effective marketing of existing products against competition, rather than the planning of future products.

lack of mutual contact. Thus, help systems often end up with a low development priority.

THE SOFTWARE DEVELOPMENT PROCESS

This section turns from the structural aspects of product development organizations to consider the influences on interface development of some widely used software development processes and methods. These were developed when interactive systems were rare. Many were developed in the context of contract or internal development projects, not product development. As a result, they may obstruct rather than facilitate the development of usable interactive systems.

Computing resources were initially too expensive to devote much to the interface. Nor was the demand great: most computer users were engineers who understood the system or were willing to learn it. The computer use environment was similar to the computer development environment. Thus, the interface that emerged during development and debugging was often adequate or even *appropriate* for use—when the interface reflects the underlying architecture the engineer need learn only one model.

One legacy of this era is the persistence of the belief that the interface can be ignored or tidied up at the end of development. Late involvement in the software development process is a common complaint of members of support groups such as human factors and technical writing (Grudin & Poltrock, 1989). They are the project members most likely to advocate user involvement. If management is unaware of the need for *their* early and continual involvement, how much support will their calls for early and continual *user* involvement receive?

Over time, the original "engineering interfaces" are being replaced by interfaces developed for increasingly diverse user populations, following a pattern seen in other maturing technologies (Gentner & Grudin, 1990). Software development methods did not anticipate this change. New approaches to development are emerging (e.g. Boehm, 1988; Perlman, 1989), but have yet to be proven or widely adopted. One source of inertia is that insufficient information about user environments reaches developers: the degree to which development and user environments have diverged is not appreciated.

"Waterfall" models of software development arose in the context of large government projects. By their nature, competitively bid contracts emphasize written specifications: contact with the eventual users may be forbidden or discouraged following the initial requirements definition, occurring prior to the selection of the developers. Separate contracts may be awarded for system design, development and maintenance. Approaches to development emerging from this tradition included structured analysis, where the task "establish man–machine interface" is relegated to one sub-phase of system development (De Marco, 1978), and Jackson System Development, which "excludes the whole area of human engineering in such matters as dialog design . . . it excludes procedures for system acceptance, installation and cutover", (Jackson, 1983). Because such methods do not specify user involvement in design, project plans do not anticipate it. Development organizations are not structured to facilitate it and often work against it. This is obviously not ideal for interactive systems development, where early and continual user involvement has been an early and continually recommended principle for developing usable systems. A "Catch 22" is that even *late* user involvement is blocked. Once the underlying software code is frozen, a fully functioning system is available for user testing—but at that very moment, documentation moves into the critical path toward product release. Since it is the software interface that is being documented, the interface is also frozen—before a user can try it out!

Prototyping and iterative design are recommended by every developer cited here as proposing innovation in technique or methodology—Bjerknes *et al.* (1987), Gould and Lewis (1985), Boehm (1988), Ehn (1988), Perlman (1989). These go hand in hand—there is little point to prototyping if the design cannot be changed. Unfortunately, the high visibility of the interface works against iterative design in three ways: (1) the interface is grouped with aspects of the product that must be "signed off" on early in development; (2) support groups, such as those producing documentation, training and marketing are strongly tied to the software interface and are affected by changes; and (3) iteration or change in the interface is noticed by everyone, which can create uneasiness, especially in an environment with a history of stressing early design.

The emphasis on careful early design makes sense for non-interactive software, with its relatively predictable development course. It works less well for the interface, where design uncertainty is inevitable—the motivation for prototyping and iterative design in the first place. As the interface grows in importance, the desire to see it alongside the proposed functionality in the preliminary design will grow, and once management has "signed off" on a design, changes require approval. Poltrock (1989*b*) observed the unique problems that high visibility and dependencies create for the interface development process. One developer summed it up:

> I think one of the biggest problems with user interface design is that if you do start iterating, it's obvious to people that you're iterating. Then people say, "How is this going to end up?" They start to get worried as to whether you're actually going to deliver anything, and they get worried about the amount of work it's creating for them. And people like (those doing) documentation are screwed up by iterations. They can't write the books. Whereas software, you can iterate like mad underneath, and nobody will know the difference.

Interface development is distinct from other software development. Gould and Lewis (1985) summarized it this way:

> "Getting it right the first time" plays a very different role in software design which does not involve user interfaces than it does in user interface design. This may explain, in part, the reluctance of designers to relinquish it as a fundamental aim. In the design of a compiler module, for example, the exact behavior of the code is or should be open to rational analysis ... Good design in this context is highly analytic, and emphasizes careful planning. Designers know this. Adding a human interface to the system disrupts this picture fundamentally. A coprocessor of largely unpredictable behavior (i.e., a human user) has been added, and the system's algorithms have to mesh with it. There is no data sheet on this coprocessor, so one is forced to abandon the idea that one can design one's algorithms from first principles. An empirical approach is essential.

Solutions to these problems can be found—and *will* be found—but the problems are new and adopting the solutions will require changing the way we work.

Unfortunately, an innovative process proposal is unlikely to leave management as comfortable as a detailed product design specification.

THE ROUTINIZATION OF DEVELOPMENT

As competition and the pace of change increase, product development companies are pressured to turn out enhancements and new products in a timely, predictable fashion. Consider this analysis: "Ashton-Tate's decline began with what is becoming a well-worn story in the industry: failure to upgrade a market-leading product. Dbase III Plus went for almost three years before being upgraded, while competitors' products were upgraded as often as twice in that time" (Mace, 1990). A similar pattern of predictable new releases is found in other maturing markets, from automobiles to stereo systems. The result is pressure for a predictable and controllable software development process: for routinization of development. Parker (1990) describes a perceived solution to the problem described in the previous quotation:

> Lyons (an Ashton-Tate executive) responds that he can keep customers by providing predictable if not always exciting upgrades. "Customers don't want to be embarrassed; they want their investment to be protected. If you are coming out with regular releases, even if they skip a release because a particular feature is missing, they will stay (with the product) because the cost of change is large."

This perceived need for controlled development creates difficulties for design elements or approaches that have uncertain duration or outcome. Interface design in general has a relatively high level of uncertainty, and user involvement can increase development time and introduce the possibility of changing its direction. This is the intent, of course—to produce a better design—but it nevertheless works against these powerful pressures for predictability.†

Once again, groupware development faces particularly severe problems. To understand the dynamics of computer use in group contexts requires time, whether it is done to assess the need for computer support, to determine the factors affecting adoption success, or to understand the organizational effects of use. Product development companies are only slowly adjusting to human factors engineers, whose studies of single-user applications take hours to complete. These companies are far from ready to adopt the much slower and less certain approaches applied by social scientists and anthropologists to understand group processes that unfold over days or weeks.

ASSISTANCE FOR USER INVOLVEMENT IN LARGE PRODUCT DEVELOPMENT COMPANIES

To end on a note of optimism, these companies also provide some *support* for involving users in interface design, primarily through putting the interface itself in the spotlight. A better interface is one way to distinguish a product and to increase its acceptance in a competitive marketplace. Applications are reaching out to "discretionary" users, people who have the choice of whether or not to

---

† Friedman (1989) discounts claims of a trend toward routinization and deskilling of programming. Perhaps he is right, but his focus is on internal software development centers on large corporations, not on software product development. The competitive and marketing pressures that might lead to efforts to increase control of development are less evident in the environments he studies.

use a computer, and the greater availability of alternatives further increases buyer discretion. Computer users are likely to consider usability in exercising discretion. Large product development organizations often have considerable resources to devote to usability—development costs are highly amortized. As noted above, these companies are major employers of human-factor engineers and interface specialists.

There is a positive side to the relatively frequent upgrades and product replacements: developers can break out of "single-cycle" development. Evaluation of existing product use can feed into the design of later versions and good ideas arriving too late for use on a specific development project can be retained for later use (Grudin, Ehrlich & Shriner, 1987). Product development efforts may have a large supply of potential users, and the fate of a product doesn't depend so heavily on the situational factors that operate in any one given site. Finally, while inertia may develop, software product development companies were founded on change and recognize at a deep level that they must change to survive, leading to some openness to experimentation.

Overcoming the obstacles

To one working within a large product development organization, the obstacles sometimes seem insurmountable. But as noted above, the company has a powerful incentive to improve product interfaces. Ease of learning and use becomes a more important marketing edge as software products mature. Adding a new bell or whistle may not help much if the already available functionality is under-utilized. In addition, declining hardware and software costs permit more resources to be directed to the interface. These forces have already pushed large product development companies into the forefront of human factors research and development in the United States. In the long term, organizational structures and development processes may evolve, institutionalizing solutions to the problems described here. The forces in development companies that work systematically *against* user involvement stand in the way of product optimization and success.

The directions that these companies will take are not obvious. As the focus of development shifts from generic products to systems and applications that meet the needs of different specific markets, companies may have to choose between working closely with independent developers, working with value-added resellers who in turn work with "end-users", or working with the diverse computer users themselves. Each alternative will benefit from "user involvement"—but the identity of the "users" will vary.

In the meantime, where can developers look for approaches to overcoming these obstacles? Persistence should not be underestimated. There are examples of successful case studies and general approaches, such as the development of the Olympic Message System at IBM (Gould *et al.*, 1987) and the contextual interview approach at Digital (Whiteside, Bennett & Holtzblatt, 1988).

Another promising source of new techniques is the experience derived from other development contexts, notably European projects based more on internal or in-house development. In part because some of the obstacles described in this paper are encountered in a muted form or not at all in such contexts, user involvement is more often achieved. Several of these projects and approaches are described in the Proceedings of CSCW'88; see also Bjerknes *et al.* (1987). Of course, transferring what has been learned from internal development to product development is not always easy or even possible.

The UTOPIA project (described in Ehn, 1988) explicitly applied some of these approaches to a product development effort. In this project, a small set of potential users was heavily involved with the developers, while techniques including a newsletter were used to involve a much broader selection of potential system users on a more limited basis during design and development.

Experiments with prototype testing and iterative development are increasing our understanding of when and how they are most effectively used. Boehm's (1988) spiral model of development builds these techniques into a disciplined software engineering methodology. He is one of several writers encouraging an explicit change of focus in development from the current "product focus" to a focus on process *per se* in development. Grønbæk *et al.* 1991 describe a project that succeeded only after this shift occurred in mid-course.

Due to the growing demand for more usable systems, practitioners may find a climate for limited experimentation with these and other approaches. But even to *begin* working effectively requires a clear awareness of the obstacles, an understanding of why they are there, and a tolerant recognition that their source is in institutional constructs, not in unsympathetic individuals.

COMPUTER SUPPORT FOR COOPERATIVE DEVELOPMENT

One CSCW topic receiving considerable attention is support for software development. It is impossible to say anything that has not been said before, but these analyses permit us to re-emphasize particular points. Rapid prototyping tools are of course critical; even better will be prototyping tools that are explicitly designed to facilitate cooperation among computer users and developers in design. (See the discussion in Grønbæk, 1991.) Just as code management systems have proven useful in multi-programmer environments, so single-user rapid-prototyping tools may benefit by adopting features designed to support the collaborative nature of most product development.

Improved capabilities for transferring multi-media documents will help. Video is likely to be useful in two ways—to enable developers to communicate more effectively across distances, and perhaps more importantly, to communicate aspects of users' experiences and work environments to developers. It is difficult to overestimate the impact video can have in conveying the specific details as well as the general richness of work environments.

This need to bridge the information gap between development and use environments is so great that the computer should come to play a direct role in making it happen, by communicating information about computer use directly to developers. Issues of privacy and confidentiality will have to be worked out carefully; in some environments it will not be possible. But the potential advantages are so great, for both computer developers and computer users, that efforts to find a mutually satisfactory arrangement will be amply rewarded.

This work profited immeasurably from interactions over the years with Susan Ehrlich and Steve Poltrock. Numerous reviewers, most of them anonymous, helped refine the paper. MCC and its Shareholders supported some of the research, and Aarhus University provided two key ingredients: an external perspective from which to view the product development environment and the time to write.

References

BJERKNES, G., EHN, P. & KYNG, M. (Eds.) (1987). *Computers and Democracy: A Scandinavian Challenge.* Brookfield, VT: Gower Press.

BOEHM, B. (1988). A spiral model of software development and enhancement. *IEEE Computer,* **21**(5), 61–72.

DE MARCO, T. (1978). *Structured Analysis and System Specification.* New York: Yourdon Press, Inc.

EHN, P. (1988). *Work Oriented Design of Computer Artifacts.* Stockholm: Arbetslivcentrum.

FRIEDMAN, A. L. (1989). *Computer Systems Development: History, Organization and Implementation.* Chichester, UK: Wiley.

GENTNER, D. R. & GRUDIN, J. (1990). Why good engineers (sometimes) create bad interfaces. In *Proceedings of CHI'90 Human Factors in Computing Systems,* Seattle, April 1–4.

GOULD, J. D. (1988). How to design usable systems. In M. Helander, Ed. *Handbook of Human-Computer Interaction.* Amsterdam: North-Holland.

GOULD, J. D., BOIES, S. J., LEVY, S., RICHARDS, J. T. & SCHOONARD, J. (1987). The 1984 Olympic Message System: A test of behavioral principles of system design. *Communications of the ACM,* **30,** 758–769.

GOULD, J. D. & LEWIS, C. H. (1983). Designing for usability—key principles and what designers think. In *Proceedings CHI'83 Human Factors in Computing Systems,* pp. 50–53.

GOULD, J. D. & LEWIS, C. (1985). Designing for usability: Key principles and what designers think. *Communications of the ACM,* **28,** 300–311.

GRUDIN, J. (1988). Why CSCW applications fail: Problems in the design and evaluation of organizational interfaces. In *Proceedings CSCW'88 Conference on Computer-Supported Cooperative Work,* Portland, September 26–28. Published (1989) in slightly expanded form as: Why groupware applications fail: Problems in design and evaluation. *Office: Technology and People,* **4,** 245–264.

GRUDIN, J. (1990a). Groupware and cooperative work: problems and prospects. In B. LAUREL, Ed. *The Art of Human–Computer Interface Design.* Reading, MA: Addison-Wesley.

GRUDIN, J. (1990b). interface. In *Proceedings CSCW'90 Conference on Computer-Supported Cooperative Work,* Los Angeles, October 7–10.

GRUDIN, J. (1990c). Seven plus one challenges for groupware developers. In *Two Analyses of CSW and Groupware,* Technical report DAIMI PB-323, Department of Computer Science, Aarhus University, Denmark

GRUDIN, J. (in press). The development of interactive systems: Bridging the gaps between developers and users. *IEEE Computer.*

GRUDIN, J., EHRLICH, S. F. & SHRINER, R. (1987). Positioning human factors in the user interface development chain. In *Proceedings CHI + GI'87 Human Factors in Computing Systems,* Toronto, April 5–9.

GRUDIN, J. & POLTROCK, S. (1989). User interface design in large corporations: communication and coordination across disciplines. In *Proceedings CHI'89 Human Factors in Computing Systems,* Austin, April 30–May 4.

GRØNBÆK, K., GRUDIN, J., BØDKER, S. & BANNON, L. (1991). Cooperative system design: shifting from a product to a process focus. In SCHULER, D. & NAMIOKA, A. Eds. *Participatory Design.* Hillsdale, NJ: Lawrence Erlbaum Associates.

GRØNBÆK, K. (1991). Extending the boundaries of prototyping—towards cooperative prototyping. *Scandinavian Journal of Information Systems,* **2,** 3–24.

Jackson, M. (1983). *System Development.* Englewood Cliffs, NJ: Prentice-Hall.

Kapor, M. (1987). Interview. *INC. Magazine,* January, 1987.

Mace, S. (1990). Defending the Dbase turf. *InfoWorld,* **12,** 2 (January 8), 43–46.

Parker, R. (1990). Bill Lyons' task: incremental moves to consistency. *InfoWorld,* **12,** 2 (January 8), 44.

Perlman, G. (1989). Asynchronous design/evaluation methods for hypertext technology development. In *Proceedings Hypertext'89,* pp. 61–81, Pittsburgh, November 5–8.

Poltrock, S. E. (1989a). *Participant–Observer Studies of User Interface Design and Development,* MCC Technical Report ACT-HI-125-89.

Poltrock, S. E. (1989b). Innovation in user interface development: obstacles and opportunities. In *Proceedings CHI'89 Human Factors in Computing Systems,* Austin, April 30–May 4.

Poltrock, S. E. (1989c). *Participant–Observer Studies of User Interface Design and Development: Communication and Coordination,* MCC Technical Report ACT-HI-162-89.

Whiteside, J., Bennett, J. & Holtzblatt, K. (1988). Usability engineering: our experience and evolution. In Helander, M. Ed. *Handbook of Human–Computer Interaction.* Amsterdam: Elsevier Science Publishers B. V. (North-Holland).

17

Cooperative prototyping: users and designers in mutual activity

Susanne Bødker

Kaj Grønbæk

In most development projects, descriptions and prototypes are developed by system designers on their own utilizing users as suppliers of information on the use domain. In contrast, we are proposing a *cooperative prototyping* approach where users are involved actively and creatively in design and evaluation of early prototypes. This paper illustrates the approach by describing the design of computer support for casework in a technical department of a Danish municipality. Prototyping is viewed as an ongoing learning process, and we analyse situations where openings for learning occur in the prototyping activity. The situations seem to fall into four categories: (1) Situations where the future work situation with a new computer application is simulated to some extent to investigate the future work activity; (2) situations where the prototype is manipulated and used as a basis for idea exploration; (3) situations focusing on the designers' learning about the users' work practice; (4) situations where the prototyping tool or the design session as such becomes the focus. Lessons learned from the analysis of these situations are discussed. In particular we discuss a tension between the need for careful preparation of prototyping sessions and the need to establish conditions for user and designer creativity. Our conclusion is that users and designers should prepare to learn from breakdowns and focus shifts in cooperative prototyping sessions rather than trying to avoid them.

1. Introduction: background and motivation

The ideas behind cooperative, collaborative, participatory, or participative design, are not new. In fact, a conference entitled *Systems Design For, With and By the Users,* held in Italy in 1982 was dedicated to the topic "Participative design" (Briefs, Ciborra & Schneider, 1983). Similar ideas have, however, received new and more widespread attention in recent years. A conference held in Seattle, USA, 1990 (Namioka & Schuler, 1990) was dedicated to the topic "Participatory design". One aim of this conference was to explore the possibilities of conveying the so-called "Scandinavian model" of user involvement in system design to North-American settings. Also within the CHI and CSCW communities, ideas about participatory design have been of growing concern, notable in contributions such as (Bødker, Ehn, Knudsen, Kyng & Madsen, 1988; Blomberg & Henderson, 1990; Grudin, 1990; Johnson, 1990).

This paper documents research within this particular field of CSCW which is more and more commonly denoted "Cooperative design". We have our roots in a Scandinavian tradition of system development, and in a three year period we have been engaged in a research program *Computer Support for Cooperative Design and Communication*. Within this program we have undertaken several field studies of cooperative design, in particular prototyping. From such field studies we have discussed how, in current system design, descriptions and prototypes are developed by system designers utilizing users only as sources of information concerning the use domain (Grønbæk, 1989; Bødker & Grønbæk, 1991). However, we see prototyping with *active* user involvement as a way of overcoming problems that current approaches have in developing computer applications that fit the actual needs of the users. Such prototyping using wood and paper mock-ups, was successfully applied in the UTOPIA project (Bødker, Ehn, Knudsen, Kyng & Sundblad, 1987; Bødker, 1991). In several subsequent smaller projects this approach was applied using computer-based prototyping (Bødker & Grønbæk 1989; Trigg, Bødker & Grønbæk, in press and this paper). Experiences from these projects led to proposals for a so-called *cooperative prototyping* technique (Bødker & Grønbæk, 1989; Grønbæk, 1990). Cooperative prototyping is meant to combine the use of computer-based tools for exploratory prototyping (Floyd, 1984) with approaches to design that allow users to participate in the modification of wood and paper mock-ups as described in Bødker *et al.* (1987).

The cooperative prototyping approach aims to establish a design process where both users and designers are participating *actively* and *creatively* based on their differing qualifications. Analysis and design activities are more closely coupled by rapid development of one or more prototypes early in the development process. The initial prototypes help make the participants' visions concrete. This requires them to relate to core work tasks, i.e. users' current skills must be confronted with new technical possibilities. These alternative, possible prototypes can then be modified, thrown away, or built anew in an iterative process that increases the participants' understanding of technological possibilities related to the users' work tasks. The activities may serve one or both of the following goals: (1) Idea generation and exploration; and (2) work-like evaluation of the prototypes. When serving the first goal, the focus is on the cooperative use of the prototyping tool and existing building blocks to create a prototype or extend an existing one. When serving the second goal, the designers must somehow let the users experience a fluent work-like situation with a future computer application. This can be done in a simulated future work situation or, even better, in a real use situation if a fairly robust prototype has been prepared. The users first get introduced to its use and then an evaluation based on work-like use of the prototype is undertaken. Breakdowns (Winograd & Flores, 1986; Bødker, 1991) in this use caused by faulty design, lead to immediate modifications of the prototype. Breakdowns due to other causes are handled in other ways; for example, lack of training is handled by further training and by setting up training programs for future users. Ideally, cooperative prototyping should be performed by a small group of designers and users with access to flexible computer-based tools for rapid prototype development and modification. The (possibly simulated) functionality provided, should make it possible to envision future work tasks (Bødker *et al.*, 1987; Bødker & Grønbæk, 1989; Grønbæk, 1990). In the project described in this paper, the primary prototyping tool used was HyperCard for the Apple Macintosh.†

This paper discusses experiences from a project that was set up to further

† All trade marks are acknowledged.

investigate cooperative prototyping in realistic settings, in this case so-called casework in a Danish municipal office. Primarily, the project aimed to develop ways for users and designers to experience future use situations. The outcome of the project was not as anticipated, since it turned out that setting up ways for the users to experience future use was much more difficult than in our previous cases. However, the prototyping sessions did stimulate creative cooperation between users and designers, which will be discussed below.

Our process was well documented by means of notes, audio and video tape. In this paper we will focus primarily on prototyping sessions where the users and designers work with a fairly advanced prototype. These sessions were video taped, and the recordings analysed (see also Trigg, Bødker & Grønbæk, 1990) where we applied interaction analysis techniques.

Since our primary interest is in developing tools and techniques for cooperative prototyping, we have set up a framework to analyse the various situations and roles that users, designers, prototyping tools, prototypes and sample data get, in and between prototyping sessions. This yields a much more detailed analysis than we have achieved in our previous work.

2. The project: designing computer support for casework

This section briefly describes the cooperative approach to prototyping used in the project. The design project was undertaken together with architects, engineers and draftspeople in a technical department of a Danish municipality.

2.1. CASEWORK

A technical department has responsibility for tasks such as long-term urban planning, environmental inspection and advice, and so on. Besides these tasks, a number of smaller requests from citizens are treated on a day-to-day basis. The architects, engineers and draftspeople call their tasks *cases* and we use the term "casework" to describe their work. Thus, we call the architects, engineers and draftspeople, "caseworkers". There is one caseworker in charge of a case. He or she handles external contacts and brings in a number of people with specific skills. The department currently possesses three different kinds of computer equipment. They use terminal connections to a common mainframe running shared databases for a number of municipalities. PC's are used for small budget and environmental inspection calculations and Xerox Viewpoint† workstations are used for advanced text and picture processing. The different kinds of computer equipment are badly integrated and the caseworkers feel that better computer support could improve their work.

2.2. THE DESIGN PROCESS

Together with the caseworkers from the technical department we went through a process, designed to take their practice as the starting point and involve them cooperatively in system design to influence technology development in their work environment. Elements of this process included studies of the workplace, brain-storming on problems and ideas, and cooperative prototyping activities. For a

† All trade marks are acknowledged.

of such techniques refer to (Greenbaum & Kyng, 1991) which strongly inspired us when setting up the project.

Using a previous contact in the technical department we presented a project proposal aimed at trying out our cooperative approach to system design. The benefit for the department was that it would receive an analysis of the possibilities for integrated computer support for casework. The caseworkers agreed to participate in order to gain insight into possibilities for improving their work, although they did not at the time have money to start an actual development project.

We started by improving our understanding of the work tasks. In this round we interviewed most employees from the urban planning and environmental offices and sent summaries of our impressions to all interviewed participants. We arranged the workshops according to the results of the interviews. The caseworkers chose among themselves five representatives to participate. We denote these caseworkers A, B, C, D and E in the following analysis. Caseworkers A, C and E are from the urban planning office, and B and D are from the environmental office.

We used the future workshop idea (Jungk & Müllert, 1987) as a frame for the two first workshops. The first day dealt with the critique and vision phases.† The participants were each asked to focus specifically on a central work task from their daily work in the presentations. Before the second workshop we tried to focus the discussions by suggesting some specific problem areas. The caseworkers chose one of these, and in the second workshop we continued with the realization phase: The visions were made more specific with respect to the selected problem realizable in a prototype.

Following this, two initial prototypes‡ were set up, one for each of the groups: environmental caseworkers and urban planning caseworkers. The idea of making two prototypes was to focus on the specific needs of each group, as well as to get mutual inspiration from two rather different prototypes. The initial prototype for the environmental caseworkers was partly made by a group of students who had also attended the workshops.

The environmental prototype was first tried out by B and D in two consecutive half-day sessions. The urban planning prototypes were similarly tried out by A, C and E in one half-day session. The prototypes were augmented cooperatively in the workshops and again revised by the designers between sessions. Following this, the prototypes were revised again and built together into one. This prototype was given to each caseworker to try out for one hour. They were to start out from the work tasks that they had chosen as representative earlier in the processs. These tasks thus framed the evaluation, and we call them *frame tasks* throughout the paper. The researchers/designers were present in the sessions. In each session, one of the designers had the role as *primary designer,* i.e. he or she sat close to the caseworker(s) and the machine, taking responsibility for the interaction with both caseworker(s) and prototype. The *secondary designer* sat in the background observing, taking notes and intervening in the design activity when appropriate.

Inspired by (Suchman & Trigg, 1991) the five sessions from the final

† Refer to Greenbaum and Kyng (1991) for a discussion on the use of the technique in a system design setting.

‡ The prototypes were built by means of Hypercard, Reports, a word-processor and a spreadsheet application that could be linked together using Hypercard.

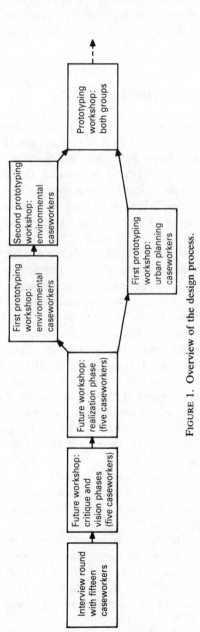

FIGURE 1. Overview of the design process.

prototyping workshop were all video-taped to make it possible to analyse the problems and prospects of the prototyping approach. Results from the design process were documented in a report that was given to the caseworkers in the technical department, and it was approved that the caseworkers could get access to the prototypes if they wanted.

3. Breakdowns and focus shifts

As in the following analysis we use the terms *breakdown* (Winograd & Flores, 1986) and *focus shift* frequently, they deserve an introduction in the context of prototyping. In Bødker and Grønbæk (1989) we described cooperative prototyping as sessions in which users primarily experienced the future use situation and secondarily participated in modifying the prototypes when breakdowns required it. We distinguished between two levels of breakdowns present in the situation: those related to the use process, and those related to the in-session modification of the prototype. *Breakdowns* in the use process occur when work is interrupted by something, e.g. that the tool behaves differently from what was anticipated. In these situations the tool as such becomes the object of our actions. *Breakdowns* in relation to the modification of the prototype occur when the fluent conduction of the design situation is interrupted, e.g. because the user loses interest in what is happening. By *focus shifts* we mean breakdowns as well as changes of focus that are more deliberate than those caused by breakdowns. For instance, a designer or a user may have prepared to raise some issues in the session. Openings, e.g. pauses, in the session may allow for a participant to deliberately shift focus.

The participating caseworkers each had their frame task to work on in the sessions. These tasks were representative of the work done by the caseworkers, and we aimed to create prototypes which would simulate support for these selected work tasks. From the outset we aimed to have the prototypes tried out in a *work-like situation* lasting for an hour, following an introduction to and a demonstration of the prototype. We did not set up evaluation in the real work setting, because we knew that our example material was far too limited for that. We found that while the structure of the protype was sufficient to support parts of the work tasks, the sample data was too limited to keep the illusion of a work-like situation going for a longer period.

In retrospect, viewing what went on in the prototyping sessions as a real work process is of little value: Only one or two of the caseworkers started out on "their" frame task. Rather the evaluation can be characterized as a step-wise hands-on evaluation of the prototype using the frame task as a guide for the evaluation. The sessions appeared as a mixture of caseworkers expressing expectations and trying out single features, and designers guiding the caseworkers through the structure of the prototype. There was an on-going vivid discussion between the designers and the caseworkers participating in the session. The activities ranged from guided tours of prototypes, where the caseworker asked questions and came up with proposals, but touched the keyboard and mouse only when asked, to situations focused on the design of computer-based materials—forms, reports, plans, check-lists, etc.—used in the work processes.

The caseworkers in general never engaged in long-lasting fluent simulated use situations. Thus, our analysis shows few of the breakdowns in simulated use suggested by Bødker (1991). One example is that we used an asterisk "*" as a hypertext link icon attached to a word, but to follow the link, the word marked with the "*" needed to be selected. Often the caseworkers selected the "*", and got an error message, confusing them. Other breakdowns occurred, as mentioned above, when the users lost patience with the designers' attempts to fix something in the prototype. This issue will be discussed later.

Although the project activities dispered slightly from our expectations, our material shows a richness of openings for learning that can be analysed in terms of breakdowns and focus shifts. But restricting ourselves to the kinds of breakdowns mentioned previously is far too simple to help us explain the rich variety of learning openings. Rather we look for different kinds of potentials for focus shifts and breakdowns in prototyping situations than described in our earlier works. Focus shifts and breakdowns reveal the unpredictability of prototyping sessions that cannot be avoided. In most cases they are not just "failure" indicators, but rather they lead to new insight and trigger new ideas to be explored. We will give a number of such examples from our prototyping sessions.

4. The theoretical framework

Our analysis of the prototyping situation is inspired by the application of activity theory to situations that range from empirical studies of physicians work (Engeström, Engeström & Saarelma, 1988; Engeström & Engeström, unpublished data), to Bisgaard, Mogensen, Nørby and Thomsen's (1989) application of the framework to system development. The key idea is that the design activity is a learning activity. The future work activity of the users, here the caseworkers, is its main object. Prototyping is a part of this, where, in our case, the detailed conduct of the work tasks-to-be are in focus.

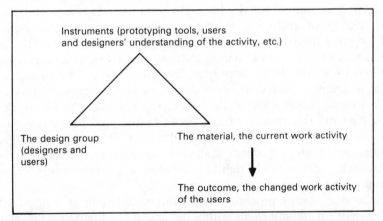

FIGURE 2. The design activity. Designers and users act together with the mutual purpose of changing the work practice of the users by introducing a computer application. The instruments of this change include prototypes and prototyping, programming and programming facilities, and so on, as well as the participants' mutual language, and their pre-understanding of the use and design activity.

Some of the fundamental concepts from activity theory are necessary to qualify our understanding: *Human work activity* is the basic component of the theory. A human being takes part in a number of activities when working: getting food and clothes, making an urban plan, etc. Activity is bound to a purpose and it gives meaning to each concrete *action,* through which any activity is conducted. These actions are conducted consciously by individual human beings. Each action is implemented through a series of *operations.* Each operation corresponds to the concrete material (physical or social) conditions for conduction of the actions, and it is triggered by meeting with specific concrete material conditions. Operations are carried out by a human being in a specific situation, without conscious thought, to perform the actions which he or she is consciously aware of. This framework is elaborated on by Bødker (1991). At the same time we can look at the activity, action and operational aspects of any human undertaking, by asking *why* it takes place, *what* goes on, and *how* it is carried out (Bærentsen, unpublished data).

In Engeström and Engeström (unpublished data) patients' sessions with doctors are confrontations of two activities in quest for a mutual goal: to diagnose a certain illness based on the symptoms of the patient. The doctor in his or her diagnosis uses instruments such as X-rays, lab tests, the understanding of different diseases, and maybe even medical literature. The patient has access to the symptoms, the pain, and so on, but he or she may also interpret these in terms of folklore medicine, etc.

We find many similarities between this situation and our prototyping sessions. The common goal of the prototyping situation is to develop a computer application to function in work. The designers use instruments such as the prototyping tool, interview techniques, etc. They have an understanding of numerous technical issues relevant to the process and product, and some understanding of the work practice. The caseworkers, on the other hand have access to the instruments and materials that they employ in their current work situation. They have an understanding of this, plus ideas for how they want things done differently. We see this framework as one application of the general understanding illustrated by Figure 2.

We have found it fruitful to look at the actions that the different actors involved take as part of their mutual activity [in some cases there is a very subtle difference between a cluster of such actions and a separation into several activities, as described by Engeström and Engeström (unpublished data, figure 3)]. In general we find issues of sharing or not sharing instruments as well as an understanding of the intentions of actions to be important for our analysis. For example, when a caseworker is deeply involved in some details of his or her work tasks, and the designer is looking impatiently at the clock, we interpret the caseworker to be focused on the work situation and the designer on the prototyping session. We will identify situations based on the intentions and foci by which they are characterized. We see roles as a cluster of actions that share an actor as well as focus/intention. Sometimes, such a cluster could rightfully be seen as a separate activity, similar to what is done in the doctors' case.

When observing change processes in organizational settings, Engeström (1987) bases his analysis on *contradictions* within the activity and between this activity and surrounding activities, since they constitute the basis for change: he looks at contradictions in how tools, objects and subjects are seen. He suggests studying the contradictions found between the tools currently used and the object created for

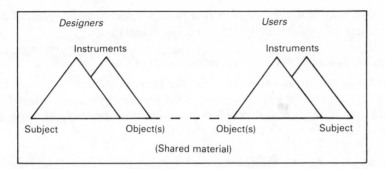

FIGURE 3. Activity theory description of design situations. In our case, several caseworkers, as well as several designers, can appear on the scene. In some situations, the designers, for example, take action together, in some they do not. Actions have intentions and contribute to the goal of the activity. Operations always take place under certain material conditions, and both, as well as the activity as such, are mediated by instruments.

example, or between the norms that are part of praxis and the division of work. We use the idea of contradictions to understand changes in the design situation. The types of contradictions that are relevant for our above triangle—beside from those already mentioned, where for example the designer feels both part of a collective subject, and a need to act as an individual—are contradictions for one of the groups, between the instrument applied and the object on which one is focusing. In the doctor's case, this could be situations where the symptoms of a patient do not fit the models of diseases the doctor has in mind.

In our analysis we will look both for such contradictions, and for situations where a shift of focus occurs. In a breakdown situation, the object or focus of a certain actor changes (Winograd & Flores, 1986; Bødker, 1991). In our case, a breakdown often happens to one party, resulting in a change of this actor's focus, e.g. when the designer is changing the prototype. Something happens, causing the designer to focus on the syntax of the programming language. This shift causes a later contradiction when the focus has become different for the two parties (e.g. the caseworker believes that they are still designing screen images, while the designer is fighting to correct the syntax).

Breakdowns are openings for learning, and in our unhampered daily activity, we can see some breakdowns causing a focus shift by which a daily activity becomes the object of our learning activity (Engeström, 1987; Bisgaard et al. 1989). Learning can take place in deliberate learning actions as well, where for example one of the actors teaches some other actor about his or her work practice. In the same way, the design activity can become the object of our activity.

5. Prototyping sessions: situations and focus shifts

In this section we apply the framework on a variety of situation types and focus shifts experienced in the project. We illuminate examples of openings for learning that occur in cooperative prototyping sessions. We claim that these types of openings are worth paying attention to in cooperative design in general. The examples are grouped under headings that point to more general types of situations, but do not span all possible cooperative design situations.

5.1. FOCUS ON SIMULATING FUTURE WORK ACTIONS

This section focuses on situations in which the primary focus is on the prototypes as a medium for establishing work-like evaluation sessions by means of simulation. We discuss the conditions for, and problems in, setting up prototyping sessions where users pretend to be in a future work situation.

5.1.1. Fluent play of work-like actions

Our goal in cooperative prototyping is to evaluate prototypes in simulated work situations. Bødker and Grønbæk (1989) describe working with dental assistants to evaluate a prototype patient record system. But the current project differs from this earlier case with respect to the success of establishing fluent work-like evaluation.

The caseworker sessions, produced only short passages that resemble a fluent simulation of future work. In one such situation, the urban planning caseworkers (A, C and E) were trying to navigate in the hypermedia structure, combining maps and physical data on a certain area under consideration for buildings renovation. Caseworker A clicked with the mouse on compass arrows and buttons attached to scanned maps (Figures 4–6). The quality of the scanned maps was too poor for actual use, but he had no problem in pretending that he was navigating real digitalized maps linked to textual information. Later when the caseworker had left the maps he wanted to quickly pick up the most detailed map again. This was, however, not possible to do directly; he had to follow the links from the overview map and go several levels down. This breakdown led to a proposal for a facility to by-pass the map hierarchy. This facility was built into the next version of the prototype. It proved to be useful in situations where caseworkers were

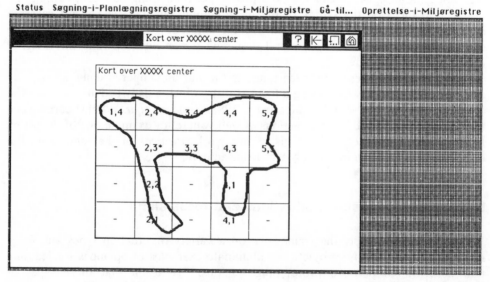

FIGURE 4. Sketch of top level map for simulation of map navigation.

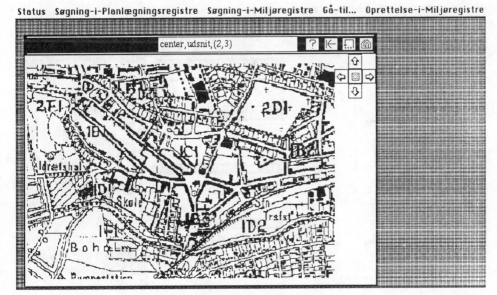

FIGURE 5. Scanned map for simulation of map navigation.

resuming work on cases for which they could remember labels of detail maps. The hierarchical navigation was useful when they had to find a detailed map for the first time.

The illusion of a fluent work-like situation only lasted for a short period of time; therefore discourses caused by breakdowns in the simulated use in such situations were few.

One explanation of the difference between experiences from the two projects could be that the prototypes used in the dental assistants sessions were simpler than the ones developed in this project. But we see a more important difference in the characteristics of the work task and the need for sample data to get a work-like evaluation going. In the dental patient record system, little initial sample data was needed to get started on a work task. Also, registering patient data is a considerable part of a dental assistant's work. This implied that an important work task with the prototype was data entry, which meant that the dental assistants bootstrapped the prototype with sample data when evaluating it. In the dental assistant project, the material conditions to make a work-like evaluation take place, were more easily brought about than in the case of the municipal caseworkers: Most casework in the technical department was concerned with the use of existing information that had to be gathered from paper files and computer databases. Entering new data into these files is a minor part of daily work. To let a caseworker get started on, for instance, modifying a local area plan required having access to nearly all of the long-term plans in the hypertext structure that we had built. These long-term plans consisted of several hundred pages of text.

5.1.2. Point-wise play of work-like actions

When one of the caseworkers, A, went through his frame task with the prototype at the second prototyping workshop, it was clear that he was not in a fluent simulated

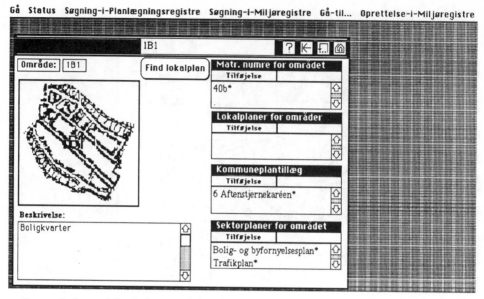

FIGURE 6. Scanned detailed map and data fields for simulation of map and database navigation.

work situation. Rather, we saw a performance of a sequence of actions, that the caseworker associated with the frame task. The caseworker used an important instrument in the prototyping situations, namely his understanding of how the information he worked on was organized in the real work situation. This understanding encompassed both structure and content of a large body of text. While looking for information in the prototype, a fluent work situation broke down because sample data was missing. But the caseworker performed an advanced play, where he used terms from his work domain only when referring to the prototype. For instance he said "I need to look at the 'preconditions section' of the municipality plan" when he pushed a link icon† and jumped to the place in the structure where he expected to find that section. He was also able to abstract from some kinds of breakdowns that happened in performance of such actions. This can be seen from A's reactions in a situation where the designers had entered sample data in wrong places of the structure. He said "let's just pretend that it was swapped . . .".

Caseworker A maintained a focus on the frame task throughout the whole session. When he tried to perform an action that was not supported in the prototype, he continued on his own initiative a discussion of what he wanted to do with the prototype using concepts belonging to the work domain (these issues are discussed further in a later section). For instance he said at one point: "At this place I would like to be able to bring up a list of tasks that I have to do when treating a case (on a local area plan) . . . and I would like to be able to mark the task I have already done". Only in a few places breakdowns in actions were turning the

† "Link icon" is the hypertext term (Conklin, 1987) for the button to push when the user wants to follow a link to a destination node in the network.

focus to the prototype as an object detached from the frame task. These are cases where he needed instructions for how to continue. For instance he at some point wanted to follow a hypertext link backwards, and asked "which button should I push?" and when he got the answer he pushed the button and replied: "Oh, it is this arrow I have to push".

5.1.3. Discussion

The sessions with A show that a fluent work like performance of the work task was difficult to set up at this early stage in the project, mainly due to lack of sample data. However, evaluation activities based on the frame task helped maintain a focus on the work task in a prototyping session. The close focus on work tasks brought up important issues such as the deficiencies of the hierarchical map navigation.

The fact that the overall activity was design and not use, did not seem to disturb A. To some extent he used his paper-based materials when the materials were not available on the computer. There is no doubt that he knew he was in a learning situation, and not all the material conditions were as they should be, but the setting allowed him to try out certain future actions anyway. Thus we consider the future work situations with computer support much closer than is found in traditional evaluation. For instance Baecker and Buxton (1987) and Monk (1987) propose controlled experiments to collect data on specific features of prototypes. They take the prototype and its individual facilities as the starting point, not the work task which it is going to support.

Our general conclusion from the two examples is that it is important to simulate aspects of the future use situation to some extent. The main purpose of this is to try out the future material conditions set up by the computer application. It is less important though to make this simulation work-like in all respects. Actually, we have seen demonstrated that a play-like situation may be useful.

5.2. FOCUS ON IDEA EXPLORATION

Some situations from the prototyping sessions resemble brainstorming carried out by caseworkers and designers using the computer and prototype as instruments.† The prototype and computer are used to explore technological possibilities and for experimenting with design possibilities. In all such situations the caseworkers are articulating their work tasks rather than doing them.

5.2.1. Augmenting the current prototype

The session with one of the caseworkers, B, quickly turned from a work-like evaluation to idea generation and augmentation of the prototype. The frame task was an environmental case: checking hidden oil tanks and drinking water conditions on a site. To get started on the task, B found the data of a fictitious site with a key-word search on the database. She examined the sample data already there and said "how do I find the site map?" We explained that we had not prepared, i.e. scanned, a site map for this task. Instead she explained how she would examine the site map, and she entered some fictitious notes reflecting the examination of the site

† Jordan, Keller, Tucker & Vogel (1989) introduced the term "software storming" for a mixture of rapid prototyping and brainstorming techniques.

map and related data. In the middle of her formulation of a request for the name of the owner of the site, she said: "In general we would like to be able to subtract a 'list of requests' on house owners—nowadays we have to remember the requests ourselves". B on her own initiative also took the mouse and attempted to use the existing key-word search function to search for house-owners who have had a demand given to them by the environmental office. Now the focus shifted from the frame task to a discussion of how a reminder facility could be designed. A first attempt on designing the facility was made by the primary designer who picked up the mouse, entered "Design mode" in the tool,† reorganized existing fields/buttons, and added two new fields "Deadline for fulfilling request" and "Description of request" to the current screen image. B tried to reformulate the request and used the fields. Then it was proposed that for a following session we prepare a report to generate the list of reminders on requests with deadlines in the current month. We also noted that the reminder facility might be useful in general for the tasks that the other environmental caseworker, D, was performing. But, B did not know at what level D made his request, thus we decided to discuss this issue with D in another session. We turned the focus back to the initial frame task.

Later in the same session B needed information from the Building File, a file currently kept on paper. B pushed the button that brought her to the current representation of the Building File in the prototype. B examined the data on the screen and realized that there was no representation of the change applications/permissions that had been made for a building. B explained that each applications/permissions case consisted of a folder with letters and architectural drawings sent in by the various house owners. According to B it would be of no use to enter this extensive material into the computer, but it would be nice to have a list of all the cases on a building and for each case a brief abstract describing the case and telling where to find the material in the paper files. We started to design that facility. The primary designer entered "Design Mode", and used some existing application-oriented objects. One of these objects was a scrollable item list field that could be used as an index of abstracts for the applications/permissions cases. An instance of this object was placed on the screen. B suggested a prototypical headline for an applications/permissions case. We added an "abstract" screen carrying this headline and linked that to the item on the list. Now the abstract could be brought up by a single click on the item in a list on the overview screen. B tried that operation and seemed satisfied with the solution.

The example described here shows that B, the caseworker, got a number of ideas when confronting the frame task with a sketchy prototype that was supposed to support her work. The focus shifts in the session were not caused by breakdowns in the simulated use situation, but rather by ideas that came to B when she had to imagine the prototype being part of her future workplace. This way, the prototype was used to create visions concerning the future computer application and changed

† We had customized our HyperCard environment with a "Status" menu that allowed us to make quick switches between "Design mode" and "Use mode". In "Use mode" the environment was restricted to consist of only menus and windows that were familiar to the caseworkers. In "Design mode" two windows and some menus that among other things made a number of application oriented and general objects available for reuse/specialization in the session. Unfortunately HyperCard did not allow us to remove all the system menus, such as "File", "Edit", and "Go" that were not familiar to the caseworkers. But in "Use mode" the complexity of the screen-layout was reduced considerably.

work practice. Some of the proposals and ideas might have come across in a paper-based design session, but it seems as if the confrontation with the prototype triggered a more extensive idea generation. One explanation could be that the prototype was viewed as an object to be developed in conjunction with investigation of the frame task and not viewed as something complete that was brought into the office.

5.2.2. Going beyond the current prototype

In the first urban planning workshop with the caseworkers (A, C, E) we were designing computer support for urban and area planning. We considered A's frame task on local area planning for an area where the building of a small airport was proposed. The initial prototype was made to try out how to organize the information in database fields on a series of screen images.

A general issue was raised by A: when working with a local area plan it was often necessary to look up certain issues in the long-term plans. These were kept as textual/graphical descriptions in paper folders. In general the caseworkers found it hard to trace particular issues throughout these folders. Moreover, it was necessary to keep track of changes made between major revisions of the long-term plans. Such changes often had implications for a number of paragraphs, tables and figures throughout the plans. It would be useful for the caseworkers to be reminded of such add-ons when retrieving information. This general issue coined a discussion on how to represent large text and graphics documents in combination with a conventional database design. For the designers it seemed obvious that some kind of hypertext system was needed and one of the designers went to the blackboard and showed how sections and regions within sections of the long-term plan could be linked together as hypertext. At the same time, the other designer had opened a Guide hypertext document on the workstation.† A brief demo of Guide was given and one of the caseworkers tried to follow some links in the document. This example shows that it was possible for the caseworkers to relate already articulated problems concerning the material conditions and instruments of the work activity to the use of a prototype, and to be creative with respect to changing the situation. The conclusion of this session was that the designers, for the next session, should design a hypertext structure representing the long-term plan. In the second prototyping workshop the caseworkers were provided with this hypertext structure representing the long-term plan and they worked rather painlessly with hypertext facilities without much further introduction.

5.2.3. Discussion

The situations described in this section can be seen as examples of what Ehn (1988, pp. 451–453) calls creative transcendence of tradition. The caseworkers were able to go beyond their traditional skills when confronted with new technological possibilities such as prototypes and example applications. Moreover, the situations show that the caseworkers often take the initiative to transcend their own skills in such prototyping sessions.

† Guide is a hypertext system running on the Apple Macintosh. We acknowledge all trade marks. Compared with HyperCard it is better to illustrate hyper*text*, because it resembles a word-processor extended by linking facilities. It mainly supports replacement links and pop-up notes as discussed in Conklin (1987) and Bannon and Grønbæk (1989).

In the prototype modification situations the prototype had the role of an instrument to facilitate a concrete discussion of visions. Both caseworkers and designers were pointing at objects in the prototype and various facilities were discussed. Instead of using terms from the application domain there was a higher frequency of computer-oriented terms such as "screen image", "fields", "buttons" and "arrows". This distance to the frame task was reduced a bit when reusing parts of the prototype already familiar to the caseworkers, but rarely were the parts to be reused referred to with a name familiar to the caseworkers. For instance B could recognize how to use the scrollable item list field when she saw it, but she did not have a name for it, because it did not correspond to something familiar to her.

When hypertext was introduced the caseworkers easily adapted to the idea of browsing through text, using buttons, instead of key-word search facilities that were otherwise more common in the computer systems they were familiar with. The designers' introduction of hypertext represented a more advanced form of text representation than what the caseworkers themselves knew about, or would have imagined to be implementable, on the computer. At the same time, however, there was a clear need to impose a structure on the current texts to support efficient traversal and to remind of crossing dependencies.

5.3. FOCUS ON CURRENT WORK PRACTICE

In several situations the focus is on the caseworkers current work practice. These are situations where caseworkers and designers use prototypes as instruments to trigger a further investigation of the current work practice. In these situations the caseworkers were articulating their work tasks rather than performing them.

5.3.1. Talking through the frame tasks

C, B and D did not simulate the future use of the prototype very much. Rather the frame task was talked through while the prototype was examined. The role of the prototype became that of an object that was brought in to illustrate how certain parts of the frame task could be supported with a computer. The prototype never became an instrument for work actions.

An example of such situations was seen in sessions with D who did environmental inspection of companies in the municipality. D's frame task for the session was "collecting information before an inspection visit at a company". The sessions started out with the designer giving a brief guided tour in the relevant part of the prototype. Then the initiative was given to D by the designer asking: "Show what you would start out with when you collect information for an inspection visit?". D then took over and said "First I'm checking whether the company has a 'Chapter 5 approval' and then I check whether I have made an earlier inspection visit at the company . . . —I guess I'll enter this 'Chapter 5 approval' file". D clicked the mouse on the corresponding item in the table of contents menu of the prototype. When the screen image came up D sat thinking for a while and said: "This is only an overview of approvals given—how do I find the detailed information? There ought to be information about heating technology, chimney size and the like!" The designer thought for a short while and said: "But this information is kept in the file of 'inspection visit reports'—have a look!" The designer grabbed the mouse and jumped to the file of 'inspection visit reports'. D said: "Oh here they are . . . but this information is really needed in both places, because we have approvals on companies we haven't formally inspected yet!". This way we recognized a need for making links between "Chapter 5 approval" documents and "inspection visit reports", and it was discussed how this could be done after the session.

From this breakdown the session shifted to talking through the frame task as D could recall it, detached from his performance of the work. During this talk-through we experienced other focus shifts that moved us into other kinds of situations. On the one hand we moved into situations where we modified and augmented the prototype. On the other hand we also experienced the need for getting more information on D's current frame task. This led to an interview-like situation with very little focus on future work; the kind of situation discussed in a following section.

In these talk-through situations the caseworker primarily demonstrated his own current role when going through a typical work task—the frame task, by thinking aloud. This kind of thinking aloud is slightly different from the way it is practised in human-interface studies by for example Mack, Lewis and Carroll (1987). In those studies the designers define a new task that the users are going to learn and the designers want to study how they learn the task, e.g. by using a word processor. In our prototyping sessions the caseworkers were going through a task they were already familiar with, even though they were detached from their normal perfor-mance of the task. The designers on the other hand were listening to understand the work task, to ask questions, and to introduce relevant parts of the prototype. Focus shifts or breakdowns typically occurred when contradictions in the case-workers and the designers understanding of the frame task occurred. Some of these contradictions related to the prototype as described above, but they occurred as well when the caseworker progressed in the detailed talk-through of the frame task.

With the frame task it is possible to go through the work actions and articulate and investigate not only questions of what has been done, or should be done, but also questions of how and why.

5.3.2. Caseworkers teach designers about their work practice

In some situations the focus shifted from design towards more analysis-like situations, because of contradictions between the participants' understanding of the frame task.

An example of such a situation occurred in the session with D when he was examining the "inspection visit reports". He realized that space was only allocated for making one query per visit. D explained that he typically made a number of queries on particular aspects such as chimney size or heating. The current forms used did not support this use and D made notes on the margin. This showed a misconception in the designers understanding of the queries. The focus of the session shifted to a situation where the caseworker was teaching the designers about his work. The designers were listening and occasionally questioning the caseworker about the different ways in which queries were used.

In Trigg, Bødker and Grønbæk (1990) a more detailed video analysis of the session with caseworker E is used. Among other things studied, was how a confrontation with a prototype inspired E to tell short anecdotes from her work. These anecdotes illustrated her daily work more generally than the frame task. This was a similar but more indirect way of teaching the designers about her work practice.

5.3.3. Discussion

In the above situations the frame task and the prototype were used in different ways to help the caseworkers articulate problems with their current work practice. The situations were different with respect to the role of the prototype and the frame task. In the first one, the prototype was used to provoke articulation of work actions closely related to the frame task. In the second, the caseworkers taught the designers about their work. In these situations the designers got a pupil's role. The prototype received the role of an instrument to trigger the caseworkers' teaching and story-telling about their current work practice. These examples also show situations where it could have been useful to supplement the prototyping technique with other means to better document the caseworkers' articulation of their work. For instance, the anecdotes could easily be overheard by the designers, and making basic investigations of current work practice in front of the prototype can cause premature changes to the prototype.

5.4. FOCUS ON THE PROTOTYPING TOOL OR THE SESSION

We often experienced breakdowns in the session, such as breakdowns that moved all participants' foci towards the conducting of the session, the prototype, or the prototyping tool. These focus shifts are of little use as openings for learning with respect to the actual system to be designed. But with respect to improving the designers' understanding of how to prepare prototypes and improve prototyping tools they can be quite useful. We give examples of this kind of focus shifts. In several situations we also see focus shifts when the designers are concerned about getting the session moving. These shifts are necessary to keep within time limits, but they can, as we shall see, easily disturb the prototyping activity.

5.4.1. Lacking tool support

In situations where the prototype was augmented, breakdowns occurred due to a mismatch between the designers ability to make modifications and the caseworkers needs. An example of such a situation happened with respect to use of prepared objects in the prototype. We had prepared a number of general objects such as general search buttons that could be parametrized, and fields with special hypertext supporting features. These objects were intended to be used in already existing screen images,† but a breakdown occurred when we wanted to start from scratch with the design of a new screen image. We needed a blank HyperCard screen that inherited properties similar to already existing screens. However, the tool was set up in such a way that it was not possible to get a blank screen, preserving for instance the browsing capabilities that all the screens in the application were supposed to have. One would either get a blank screen with no functionality, or a screen with contents similar to the current screen in use. This breakdown taught us to be better prepared for following sessions by providing blank screen images that preserved operational properties for each screen type we could expect to reuse for design from scratch.

† "Cards" in HyperCard.

5.4.2. Bugs in prototypes or sample data

Breakdowns due to regular programming bugs and misplaced sample data occurred as well. Some of these were simple bugs in details that caused little trouble. Either the fixing was simple or the bug could be ignored when continuing the session while still focusing on the users' frame task. In a session with one of the architects we had swapped two pieces of sample data in the hypertext structure, but after realizing that it was not his fault he said on his own initiative: "let's just pretend they are swapped". Other bugs though were more serious. For instance breakdowns happened (see also Bødker & Grønbæk, 1989) when we were evaluating a report design made before the session. The report generator would not select the data requested in the query. After three attempts, the report generator created a system bug that required reinstallation of the program in order to get started again. Meanwhile, the caseworker, who at the beginning was interested and active, became more and more passive as the designer moved into areas of the prototype that the caseworker did not understand. In that situation we were forced to shift focus and jump to another part of the prototype and continue evaluation there.

The focus shifts described here give the prototype the role of an instrument that does not function well; neither as support for casework nor as a medium for the design activity. The designer becomes a repair person, a programmer, who uses only computer specific instruments to solve problems outside the scope of the case-workers understanding. The caseworkers become passive observers who watch a professional completing a compilated task. These kind of breakdowns are not very productive with respect to improved understanding of computer support for casework. In this project the prototype was not aimed at becoming part of a final working system; hence fixing the programming bugs had little impact on the final system implementation. Thus these kinds of breakdowns should ideally be kept to minimum in cooperative prototyping sessions. Careful preparation and good understanding of what can be done in sessions to get around such breakdowns without spoiling the purpose of the session is needed on the designer's side of the table. This issue is developed further in section 6.

5.4.3. Conducting the session

In several situations we saw focus shifts towards the conduction of the session. Frequently the designer who had the secondary role in the session realized that the session activities did not serve their purpose and started intervening into the situation.

In one example, the caseworker A was deeply involved in typing some piece of information into a text node of the hypertext structure, whereas the designers got impatient and finally interrupted the caseworker. The caseworker was concerned with correctness of spelling and language. In contrast, the secondary designer was concerned about time frames and the evaluation of such: this was a pity as the caseworker spent the whole time typing away on details, instead of entering into some of the more "interesting" aspects of the prototype.

In other situations the designers "pulled" the caseworker away from his or her focus, either because they wanted to get through the agenda for the session or simply because they were eager to explore some particular features of the prototype. In these situations the designer often intervened and encouraged the caseworker to "have a look at this", "try this . . " or "try to write something here". This kind of designer intervention was not planned from the outset but often happened in situations where there was a break, a moment of silence, in which one of the designers lost his or her patience.

5.4.4. Discussion

We have seen various types of situations where the design situation as such has become the focus for the participants. When focus moved away from the frame task towards the sessions as an object, this usually did not lead to learning about the caseworker's work or the computer system under design. However, we learned how to plan and conduct sessions. In one of the situations a breakdown occurred in the activity of the designers: the prototyping tool stopped working. This breakdown caused the designers to move away from the common activity, leaving the caseworker in a state of irresolution. In the other situation, one of the designers was reminded of his role as conductor of a session with limited time resources. This caused the designer to try to pull the caseworker out of the actions that were then being carried out, and so arresting the fluent acting.

One lesson learned from these focus shifts, was that taking time limits seriously, is useful for evaluating future work-like situations in a theatre and movie-like fashion, where a scene indicates that some activity begins and quick scene shifts give the illusion that some long lasting activity has taken place. Activity then continues in a following scene assuming that time has passed and things are changed. We are actually facing a more general problem of how to reduce the complexity of real work tasks without losing the important points that lead to good design. Up until now we have not had concrete experiences with this issue, but find it important to consider when setting up simulated work situations.

6. Preparing prototyping sessions

We have discussed several types of situations that we have observed in cooperative prototyping sessions. These situations have helped shed some light on the different learning actions going on in cooperative prototyping. Learning with respect to the activity, the actions and the operations of the users, both with respect to the limitations of the current work practice, and to the possible changes when a computer application is introduced. But there is of course more to cooperative prototyping than what goes on in front of a prototype in sessions together with users. Before sessions, preparation and planning is needed; between sessions clean up and reconstruction of the prototype is needed; after a series of sessions results need to be collected and documented in order to propagate them to continuing development activities. In this section we briefly discuss lessons from the analysis with respect to setting up sessions, and the activities that go on before and between sessions.

Each session needs to be prepared according to the current stage of the design process. Issues concerning preparation of protoyping sessions were discussed at a general level in Grønbæk (1989), where the consideration of the following questions for preparation is suggested: What is the purpose of the session? How stable should the prototype be in advance? To what extent should in-session modifications be made? What setting should be chosen? How should the outcome be documented or evaluated? The analysis in this paper has improved our understanding of the richness of cooperative prototyping sessions. We have seen that prototyping sessions are somehow unpredictable due to inherent properties of creative activities. Although sessions were prepared to be rooted in a certain frame task, the focus shifted due either to breakdowns or more or less deliberate "pulling" of the focus by participants. We have analysed a number of such situations and focus shifts. From these analyses we conclude that users and designers should view focus shifts as openings of learning in the prototyping sessions rather than trying to avoid them. Of course it is not all kinds of focus shifts that are particularly fruitful openings for learning, as pointed out.

We have pointed to a tension between careful preparation of sessions and the inherent unpredictable character of the prototyping sessions. Being aware of such a tension, a contribution from our analysis is an improved understanding of the variety of situations that may occur in prototyping sessions. This understanding can be utilized in preparation of sessions—not to put a tighter steering on the session, but to prepare to handle better the most common and important types of situations and focus shifts. We briefly discuss a few examples of focus shifts to prepare for.

6.1. EXAMPLES OF LESSONS LEARNED WITH RESPECT TO PREPARATION

A first example is from the situations discussed in section 5.1. We saw that extensive sample data was equally important as the prototype in order to establish fluent work-like evaluation. We find it important to pay attention to sample data early in a prototyping process. Since the long-term municipal plans in this case did not exist in computer-readable form, our only realistic possibility here was to scan parts of the material into the prototype. This would help in situations where the caseworkers were navigating in existing information. But it would not help much in situations where the caseworkers needed to modify the material. Another lesson could be to be less ambitious in cases where it is hard to provide sample data, and only aim at a pointwise fluent performance of actions, as described in section 5.1.

A second example is when ideas move the focus towards technological solutions beyond the current prototype, as described in section 5.2. We experienced a quite successful example of such a focus shift where we jumped out of the prototyping tool and experimented with the Guide hypertext system.† Guide happened to be installed on the computer that we were using in the prototyping session. We were not prepared for such a focus shift, but in this situation it worked quite well. We got a shared hypertext example before we actually built tailored facilities aimed at the particular work of the caseworkers. In this case this happened by coincidence. More generally we would support preparing enough to go beyond the current prototype. Such preparation requires some good guessing on behalf of the designers, for it is of course impossible for them to keep all sorts of example applications and be familiar with those. Thus, during preparation of sessions it is necessary to think of a repertoire of good example applications to have in stock for the next sessions. This corresponds to an attempt to anticipate the potential direction of development of the group in the following sessions. Such anticipation is generally hard and cannot

† All trade marks are acknowledged.

be directed by general guide-lines. But based on the understanding of the work practice studied in the actual project, it may not be equally hard for designers to make good guesses with respect to potential example applications in stock.

There are other ways of being prepared for such situations. We see less fancy prototyping means such as mock-ups, see for example Kyng (1989); Bødker (1991) as a handy support. What we are thinking of is using anything from simple paper screen images to more advanced slide- or video-based simulations to support design. Vertelney (1989) describes the use of a range of tools from simple drawings in flip-books to advanced video-based animations for storyboard prototyping. Earlier projects (Bødker *et al.*, 1987) have shown that often mock-up simulations are more easily set up for illustration than are computer-based prototypes. A disadvantage of mock-ups, however, is that it is harder for users to *experience* dynamic aspects of the future system than it is with a computer-based prototype simulation.

A third example of a type of situation/focus shift that we could have handled differently in the project, is the situation where caseworkers teach their work practice as described in section 5.3. In this we realized that the designers needed to learn more about casework. The action changed from design to analysis. In one of the sessions, however, we kept sitting by the prototype mixing the caseworkers teaching of his work practice with interview-like inquiries. This took place without proper tools and techniques to undertake and document such activities. In order to be better prepared the designers could set up the sessions in a room equipped with pens and white cardboard or a flip-over. From our experience with future workshops, it seems to be a good idea to have simple means like white cardboard to write on, because it can easily be carried away as documentation. To designers, a computer-based tool might be appropriate, but to our experience users generally are more comfortable when using simpler means such as paper and pens to illustrate aspects of their work. Moreover, the designers should be prepared to move temporarily away from the prototype even though that is not always the best solution.

A fourth example of a situation type that the designers could be prepared for is when, as described in section 5.4, the focus shifts towards conducting the session. In that kind of situation it is typically one of the designers that starts acting to get the process going. It is important that the designers on beforehand share an understanding of what they do when for instance time limits seem to be violated in the session, or when either one of the users or one of the designers jumps to a level of detail that seems to be irrelevant for the session. Having discussed such issues previous to sessions may help smooth possible adjustments in the sessions.

It is difficult to give general guide-lines for what to do in the situations. But for the preparation there are important issues to consider: The number of participants and their roles are important to discuss. In the project described by Bødker and Grønbæk (1989) a single designer was working together with two to four dental assistants in the sessions. In the current project we always arranged sessions with two designers and a varying number of caseworkers. From these experiences we conclude that it is clearly an advantage to have two (or more) designers participating in the sessions. Documenting the process and maintaining the session when states of irresolution occurred became much easier when, in the current project, the secondary designer took responsibility for some of these tasks. The primary designer could concentrate on the interaction with the caseworker(s), and the prototyping tool when modifications to the prototype were needed. The conclusion with respect to the number of users is less clear. When the focus is on establishing work-like situations the nature of the frame task to some degree directs the number of participants. However, it may be an advantage to have several users participating when the focus is on idea exploration and current work practice. The confrontation between the users' different understanding of the current work and the direction of development of the prototype can uncover issues that the designer would not realize from having contact with the users individually. A disadvantage of having more than one user participate in the session may be that some participants are too dominant and thus suppress important contributions from their participants. In the current project we observed that the draftspeople were generally more active when they were *not* together with architects or engineers in the sessions.

In section 5.4 we also pointed to the possibility of making deliberate focus shifts like scene shifts in a movie to progress through the frame task in a condensed form due to time limits. The use of so-called storyboard prototyping as suggested by Vertelney (1989) and Andriole (1989) seem to provide good and flexible means for this.† Storyboards can be used to identify individual scenarios to be tried out with a prototype. Shifts to other scenarios can be discussed with direct reference to the storyboard. The storyboard techniques are inspired both from scripting and storyboard techniques used in setting up movies and dance shows. The technique seems intriguing with respect to getting a representation of the use of scenarios to be considered in the evaluation. But a very strict planning of the scenarios may violate the idea of open-endedness (Trigg, Bødker & Grønbæk, 1990) which is an important feature of cooperative prototyping.

A final example of situations for which it is hard to be extensively prepared for are situations where the focus moves towards the prototyping tool (see section 5.4). This happens in situations where we reach the limits of the prototyping tool or when regular bugs are found. Bugs cannot be totally avoided and no prototyping tools are without constraints. It can, however, be discussed beforehand what the designers should do when such focus shifts are about to happen. For instance questions such as: "When is it worth fixing a bug in-session? When and how should unsuccessful programming attempts be stopped?" could be considered. Focus shifts that have previously been experienced may lead to more general ideas of how to prepare subsequent sessions. For instance we experienced several breakdowns because we could not pick a blank screen with certain inherited properties. We prepared the next session by making it possible to pick a blank screen for all the different categories in the prototype. Another issue is to be able to anticipate certain types of breakdowns. In Bødker and Grønbæk (1989), we discuss when to stop an in-session modification, when the situation has become meaningless to the users, and too complicated for the designers to get out of within a reasonable amount of time. In this case study, we have seen situations where the designers support each other in getting out of the situation, and situations where they do not. The roles of the

† Both Andriole (1989) and Vertelney (1989) use the term storyboard prototyping. But Andriole (1989) is, unlike Vertelney (1989), only sketching the actual screen images of the human–computer interface in his storyboards and not the scenarios of use as Vertelney (1989) proposes.

designers should clearly be discussed in advance. Often it is the secondary designer who can feel when the user is loosing her or his patience. Clearly the decision about when to stop must be held up against the importance of the change, but generally the designers can avoid serious breakdowns in the sessions as such by understanding the extent to which in-session modifications make sense. Limitations in the current prototyping tool may also trigger consideration of different tools. Grønbæk (1990) discusses a variety of tools to support cooperative prototyping.

The above examples do not claim to span the space of all possible situations and focus shifts, but they illustrate how focus shifts in prototyping sessions can be viewed as openings of learning. Taking such openings seriously they can make us improve our understanding of the cooperative design process in general. With respect to specific projects this understanding can improve our ways of setting up following cooperative prototyping sessions.

7. Conclusion

As pointed out in the introduction there is more to prototyping than rapid development of prototypes and demonstration of their features. To benefit from prototyping it needs to be carried out cooperatively by users and designers (Grønbæk, 1989). This kind of cooperation is a confrontation between two groups of subjects that from the outset possess different kinds of instruments and work on different kinds of objects aiming at different purposes. However, we claim that the purpose of designing computer support is that new objects tailored to the users' needs, have to be temporarily shared between the two groups, or two skills. This implies that we as designers need to develop our instruments in a direction that make us able to deal with the objects of design as objects for a shared purpose. This is not easy, but techniques to perform cooperative system design experimentally is, from our point-of-view, the best attempt. This is similar to the observation that the best way to improve the understanding of the usability of design proposals is to have prototypes tried in use. The project that we have set up and analysed can be seen as a contribution to make the development of designer instruments go in a cooperative direction. In particular we have discussed a tension between needs for careful preparation of prototyping sessions and establishing good conditions for user and designer creativity. The message with this respect is that we need to be open to learn from focus shift in sessions and not try to avoid them.

Compared with our previous work, the present study has illustrated a variety of situations where prototypes can be related closely to frame tasks. These are situations where point-wise performance of work actions take place, where ideas are explored, and where designers learn about the users work practice, etc. This is the case although work-like evaluation in early prototyping may be hard to get to in some settings. To maintain the idea of work-like evaluation the meaning of "work-like" needs to be modified somewhat. We find it inspiring to think of the prototyping activities as plays, where the participants act out some situations, but skip others. The timing of which situations to act out, and which to skip or condense in time seems to be of major importance for the development of this idea. In future research we will try out the emerging storyboard prototyping techniques.

This work was supported by the Danish Natural Science Research Council, FTU grant no. 5.17.5.1.30. The municipal caseworkers, students and colleagues at Aarhus University are kindly acknowledged for their help with the project. Randy Trigg has played an important role in the later phases of our analysis, and Jonathan Grudin has helped out with language and other comments in the final, critical state. Finally we thank the anonymous referees for their constructive comments.

References

ANDRIOLE, S. J. (1989). *Storyboard Prototyping—A New Approach to User Requirements Analysis*. Wellesley, MA: QED Information Sciences, Inc.

BAECKER, R. & BUXTON, W. (1987). Empirical evaluation of user interfaces. In R. M. Baecker & W. A. S. Buxton, Eds. *Readings in Human–Computer Interaction*: *A Multidisciplinary Approach*, pp. 131–134. Los Altos, CA: Morgan Kaufman.

BANNON, L. & GRØNBÆK, K. (1989). Hypermedia: support for a more natural information organization. In H. Clausen, Ed. In *Proceedings of the Seventh Nordic Conference for Information and Documentation*, Lyngby, Denmark, Dansk Teknisk Litteraturselskab.

BISGAARD, O., MOGENSEN, P., NØRBY, M. & THOMSEN, M. (1989). *Systemudvikling som lærevirksomhed, konflikter som basis for organisationel udvikling* (Systems development as a learning activity, conflicts as the origin of organizational development), DAIMI IR-88. Århus: Aarhus University.

BLOMBERG, J. & HENDERSON, D. A. (1990). Reflections on participatory design: lessons from the Trillium experience. In J. C. Chew & J. Whiteside, Eds. *Conference Proceedings Empowering People CHI '90* pp. 353–359. New York: ACM.

BØDKER, S. & GRØNBÆK, K. (1989). Cooperative prototyping experiments—users and designers envision a dental case record system. In J. Bowers & S. Benford, Eds. *Proceedings of the first EC-CSCW '89*, UK, Computer Sciences Company.

BØDKER, S. & GRØNBÆK, K. (1991). Design in action: From prototyping by demonstration to cooperative prototyping. In J. GREENBAUM & M. KYNG, Eds. *Design at Work*: *Cooperative Design of Computer Systems*. Hillsdale, NJ: Lawrence Erlbaum Associates.

BØDKER, S. (1991). *Through the interface—a Human Activity Approach to User Interface Design*. Hillsdale, NJ: Lawrence Erlbaum Associates.

BØDKER, S., EHN, P., KAMMERSGAARD, J. KYNG, M. & SUNDBLAD, Y. (1987). A Utopian experience. In G. Bjerknes, P. Ehn & M. Kyng, Eds. *Computers and Democracy*: *A Scandinavian Challenge*, pp. 251–278. Aldershot, UK: Avebury.

BØDKER, S., EHN, P., KNUDSEN, J. L., KYNG, M. & MADSEN, K. H. (1988). Computer support for cooperative design. In *Proccedings of Conference on CSCW, Portland, Oregon, September 1988*, pp. 377–394. New York: ACM.

BRIEFS, U., CIBORRA, C. & SCHNEIDER, L. (Eds.) (1983). *System Design for, with, and by the Users*. Amsterdam: North-Holland.

CONKLIN, J. (1987). Hypertext: an introduction and survey. *IEEE Computer*, **20**, 17–41.

EHN, P. (1988). *Work-Oriented Design of Computer Artifacts*. Falköping: Arbetslivscentrum/-Almqvist & Wiksell International.

ENGESTRÖM, Y. (1987). *Learning by Expanding*. Helsinki: Orienta-Konsultit.

ENGESTRÖM, Y., ENGESTRÖM, R. & SAARELMA, O. (1988). Computerized medical records, Production pressure and compartimentalization in the work activity of health center physicians. In *Proceedings of Conference on CSCW, Portland, Oregon, September 1988*, pp. 65–84. New York: ACM.

FLOYD, C. (1984). A systematic look at prototyping. In R. Budde, K. Kuhlenkamp, L. Mathiassen, & H. Züllighoven, Eds. *Approaches to Prototyping*, pp. 1–18. Berlin: Springer Verlag.

GREENBAUM, J. & KYNG, M. (Eds.) (1991). *Design at Work*: *Cooperative Design of Computer Systems*. Hillsdale, NJ: Lawrence Erlbaum Associates.

GRUDIN, J. (1990). Obstacles to participatory design in large product development organizations. In A. Namioka & D. Schuler, Eds. *Proceedings of the Participatory Design*

Conference PDC'90, Seattle, WA, March 31–April 1. Palo Alto, CA: Computer Professionals for Social Responsibility, Workplace Project.

GRØNBÆK, K. (1989). Rapid prototyping with fourth generation systems—an empirical study. *OFFICE: Technology and People,* **5,** 105–125.

GRØNBÆK, K. (1990). Supporting active user involvement in prototyping. *Scandinavian Journal of Information Systems,* **2,** 3–24.

JOHNSON, J. (Moderator). (1990). Panel on participatory design of computer systems, In J. C. CHEW & J. WHITESIDE, Eds. *Conference Proceedings, Empowering People CHI'90* pp. 141–144. New York: ACM.

JORDAN, P. W., KELLER, K. S., TUCKER, T. W. & VOGEL, D. (1989). Software storming: combining rapid prototyping and knowledge engineering. *IEEE COMPUTER* **22,** 39–48.

JUNGK, R. & MÜLLERT, N. (1987). *Future Workshops: How to Create Desirable Futures.* London, UK: Institute for Social Inventions.

KYNG, M. (1989). Designing for a dollar a day. *Office, Technology and People,* **4,** 157–170.

MACK, R. L., LEWIS, C. H. & CARROLL, J. M. (1987). Learning to use word processors: Problems and prospects. In R. M. BAECKER & W. A. S. BUXTON, Eds. *Readings in Human–Computer Interaction: A Multidiscriplinary Approach.* Los Altos, CA: Morgan Kaufmann.

MONK, A. (1987). How and when to collect behavioural data. In R. M. BAECKER & W. A. S. BUXTON, Eds. *Readings in Human–Computer Interaction: A multidisciplinary Approach,* pp. 138–142 Los Altos, CA: Morgan Kaufman.

NAMIOKA, A. & SCHULER, D. (Eds.) (1990). In *Proceedings of the Participatory Design Conference PDC' 90, Seattle, WA, March 31–April 1.* Palo Alto, CA: Computer Professionals for Social Responsibility, Workplace Project.

SUCHMAN, L. & TRIGG, R. (1991) Understanding practice: video as a medium for reflection and design. In J. Greenbaum & M. Kyng, Eds. *Design at Work: Cooperative Design of Computer Systems.* Hillsdale, NJ: Lawrence Earlbaum Associates.

TRIGG, R. H., BØDKER, S. & GRØNBÆK, K. (1990) A video-based analysis of the cooperative prototyping process. In R. HELLMAN, M. RUOHONEN, & P. SØRGAARD, Eds. *Preeedings of the 13th IRIS conference, Report on Computer Science & Mathematics no. 108,* Åbo Akademi University, Finland, pp. 453–474.

VERTELNEY, L. (1989). Using video to prototype user interfaces. *SIGCHI Bulletin,* **21,** 57–61.

WINOGRAD, T. & FLORES, F. (1986). *Understanding Computers and Cognition: A New Foundation for Design.* Norwood, NJ: Ablex.

Part 7

Literature sources for CSCW and groupware

18

An annotated bibliography of computer-supported cooperative work

Saul Greenberg

Computer-supported cooperative work (CSCW) is a new multi-disciplinary field with roots in many disciplines. Due to the youth and diversity of this area, few specialized books or journals are available and articles are scattered amongst diverse journals, proceedings and technical reports. Building a CSCW reference library is particularly demanding, for it is difficult for the new researcher to discover relevant documents. To aid this task, this article compiles, lists and annotates some of the current research in computer-supported cooperative work into a bibliography. Over 300 references are included.

1. Introduction

An important part of any new research venture is building and maintaining a reference collection of relevant publications. This article provides a bibliography of computer-supported cooperative work (CSCW). Many entries are annotated with a brief description derived from snippets from the original abstract, my personal notes, and from commentaries written by other people. Annotations also include a keyword list for topic disambiguation, where each keyword is selected from the limited set shown in Table 1. The article also includes an overview of the general sources that publish CSCW works (Section 2), and a list of groupware systems and concepts indexed to the bibliography (Section 3).

The bibliography is available in both an EndNote† database and a Refer database. Those wishing to have an electronic version of this bibliography can obtain it in two ways. The EndNote database and a Microsoft word copy of this document are available by writing to the author at the above address (please enclose a 3.5 inch Macintosh disc and a self-addressed stamped envelope). The Refer database and other related files are available via anonymous ftp from *cpsc.ucalgary.ca* in the directory *pub/CSCWbibliography*.

2. General CSCW sources

Due to the youth and diversity of CSCW, there are only a handful of specialized books available. Most of the literature is scattered amongst many journals, proceedings of conferences and workshops, and technical reports. This section is a resource guide for readers interested in tracking the relevant published literature in CSCW and groupware‡.

---

† EndNote is a Macintosh-based bibliographic package available through Niles & Associates Inc.
‡ With special thanks to Jonathan Grudin, who provided a contents list of several books and proceedings, and where selected articles had been republished.

TABLE 1

Keywords used to annotate the bibliography entries and their meanings

Keyword	Meaning
asynchronous conferencing	Different time, different place meetings. Also known as computer-mediated communication, computer conferencing, and bulletin boards
collection	A collection of papers, readings, essays, etc.
conceptual	High-level discussion of CSCW
critique	General analysis and assessment of CSCW
data sharing	Sharing of common data (files, etc.)
decision support	Group decision support systems (GDSS)
education	CSCW applied to education
email	Electronic mail
evaluation	A formal study by controlled experiment, questionnaire, field study, observations, etc.
face-to-face meetings	Meetings in the same place and at the same time
hypertext	Hypertext and Hypermedia
idea processors	Idea processors, outliners, brainstorming tools
implementation	A description of an implemented system or a commercially available product
informal meetings	Explicit recognition of informal encounters and meetings and technical support of them
multimedia	Multiple types of media (graphics, voice, video, text, rasters, etc.)
organizational concerns	Organizational issues in the use/acceptance of groupware
overview	An overview/survey of an area within CSCW
participatory design	Users are involved as part of the design team. Article describes how to do it, or describes tools supporting it, or discusses implications to CSCW
protocols	Person to person communication protocols such as speech acts
remote meetings	Meetings held at the same time, different location
report	Report on a workshop or conference
semi-structured messages	Template-based textual communication with some free text
shared views	Shared views and serial interaction with single-user systems
shared workspace	Shared workspaces, usually supporting simultaneous participant activity
social impact	Social science theory and social issues in the use of CSCW systems

Keyword	Meaning
software design	Design and development of groupware including both design process and toolkits
video	Video is used as a component of the CSCW system or for data analysis
virtual environments	Shared virtual environments or ideas related to it
virtual hallways	Social real-time interaction in a virtual world

2.1. BOOKS

Perhaps the best selection of CSCW articles is provided by Irene Greif's *Computer Supported Cooperative Work* (Greif, 1988)§. Her collected readings span from the earliest visions of CSCW to present day theory and practice. On the groupware front, Johansen's *Groupware: Computer Support for Business Teams* is a very readable layman's book detailing current approaches and applications of groupware to business environments (Johansen, 1988). Two recent CSCW collections cover social and technological support for work group collaborations: *Intellectual Teamwork* by Galegher, Kraut and Egido (1990); and *Technological Support for Work Group Collaboration* by Olson (1989). *Computer-supported, Cooperative Work and Groupware* (Greenberg, 1991c) collects 16 articles previously published in a two-part special edition of the *International Journal of Man Machine Studies*, as well as this bibliography.

2.2. CONFERENCES

The major conference for CSCW is the bi-annual ACM-sponsored *Conference on Computer-Supported Cooperative Work*. The first conference was held in 1986 in Austin, Texas (ACM Press, 1986). Although its proceedings are no longer in print, many of the articles have been reprinted in revised form in the books and journals mentioned in this section. Proceedings of the 1988 Portland Oregon conference and the 1990 Los Angeles California conference (ACM Press, 1988, 1990) are available from the ACM Order Department, PO Box 64145, Baltimore, MD 21264, USA. These proceedings are of excellent quality, with collected papers covering most contemporary work.

The *European Community Conference on Computer Supported Cooperative Work* is the European counterpart to the ACM conference. The first was held on September 13–15 in Gatwick, London, UK (EC-CSCW, 1989), with a second conference scheduled for the autumn of 1991 in Amsterdam, The Netherlands. Proceedings are available from the Computer Sciences Company, Computer Sciences House, Brunel Way, Slough, SL1 1XL, UK.

§ The annotated references to books and proceedings include a list of section or conference session names and, in some cases, ordering information.

Several other important conferences deserve mention. The *IFIP WG8.4 Conference on Multi-User Interfaces and Applications* was recently held in Crete (Gibbs & Verrijn-Stuart, 1990). The *Symposium on Computer Conferencing*, once centred around distance education and asynchronous conferencing, now has broader coverage more in line with CSCW (University of Guelph, 1987, 1990). ACM's *SIGCHI Conference on Human Factors in Computing Systems* and the *SIGOIS Conference on Office Information Systems* normally have special sessions, panels or papers on CSCW.

2.3. JOURNALS

There are no dedicated journals for CSCW. Still, the ones listed below do publish occasional papers of interest.

ACM Transactions on Information Systems has had several special editions on CSCW. These tend to republish selected and revised papers previously presented at the ACM-sponsored CSCW conferences. In particular, see Volumes 5(2) 1987 and 6(3 and 4) 1988. A forthcoming edition will feature several articles from the CSCW '90 conference.

The *International Journal of Man Machine Studies* has formalized its interest in CSCW in its reorganization of the editorial board into topic areas, one being CSCW. A two-volume special edition on CSCW and Groupware containing 16 new articles on a variety of topics was published in February/March of 1991. Academic Press has republished the collection as this book.

The December 1988 issue of *Byte* had a special section devoted to CSCW papers, and the odd high-quality article has appeared in *Communications of the ACM* and *IEEE Computer*. ACM's *SIGCHI Bulletin* and *SIGOIS Bulletin* occasionally contain relevant articles and summaries of conferences and workshops. Other mainstream human–computer interface and management-oriented journals also have the odd article on CSCW. These include *Behaviour and Information Technology; Decision Support Systems; Human Computer Interaction; Interacting with Computers; Management Science;* and *Office: Technology and People.*

2.4. MAJOR COLLECTIONS INCLUDED IN THE BIBLIOGRAPHY

The bibliography contains a large mix of references. While some come from the "gray literature" of unusual journals, research reports, and unpublished papers, most come from the sources listed above. The following list shows which major collections of CSCW papers are *completely* included in this bibliography.

- Proceedings of the 1986, 1988, and 1990 *ACM Conference on Computer Supported Cooperative Work* (ACM Press, 1986, 1988, 1990)
- *Proceedings of the 1989 European Community Conference on Computer-Supported Cooperative Work* (EC-CSCW, 1989).
- *Proceedings of the 1990 IFIP WG8.4 Conference on Multi-User Interfaces and Applications* (Gibbs & Verrijn-Stuart, 1990)
- *Intellectual Teamwork: Social and Technical Foundations of Cooperative Work* (Galegher, Kraut & Egido, 1990)
- *Computer Supported Cooperative Work: A Book of Readings* (Greif, 1988)
- *Technological Support for Work Group Collaboration* (Olson, 1989)
- *International Journal of Man Machine Studies Special Editions on CSCW and Groupware* (February and March 1991), republished in Greenberg (1991c)

- *ACM Transactions on Information Systems Special Editions on CSCW*, Volumes 5(2) 1987, 6(3) and 6(4) 1988.

3. Index to groupware systems and CSCW concepts

Name	Citation
ACE (Amsterdam Conversation Environment)	Dykstra (1991)
AMIGO model	Danielsen (1986)
Andrew Messaging System	Borenstein (1988a, b, 1991)
Animating Interfaces	Wulff (1990)
Aplex project	Bodker (1988)
ArgNoter	Stefik (1987a, b)
Audio windows	Cohen (1991)
Augment/NLS	Engelbart (1963, 1968, 1982, 1984, 1988, 1990)
Banyan	Jackson (1989)
BITNET	Jarrell (1986), Pliskin (1989)
BoardNoter	Stefik (1987a, b)
Callisto	Sathi (1986)
CAVECAT	Mantei (1991)
Cantata	Chang (1986, 1987a, 1989)
Capture Lab	EDS (1988); Halonen (1989); Losada (1990); Mantei (1988, 1989)
CATeam Room	Ferwanger (1989); Lewe (1990)
CHAOS	De Cindio (1986)
ClearFace	Ishii (1991)
CoAuthor	Hahn (1989)
Cognoter	Foster (1986); Stefik (1987a, b); Tatar (1991)
CoLab	Foster (1986); Stefik (1987a, b); Tatar (1991)
Collaboratory	Lederberg (1989)
Commune	Bly (1990); Minneman (1990, 1991); Tang (1990)
Confer	Fanning (1986)
Contexts	Delisle (1987)
Cookbook	Ishii (1990b)
Coordination theory	Malone (1988, 1990)
Coordinator	Bair (1988); Erickson (1989); Winograd (1986, 1988a, b)
Cosmos	Bowres (1988)
Cruiser	Fish (1989); Root (1988)
DHSS Large Demonstrator Project	Storrs (1989)
Dialogo	Lantz (1986, 1989); Lauwers (1990a, b)

Name	Citation
Diamond	*see MMCONF*
DistEdit	Knister (1990)
Earth Lab	Newman (1988)
Electronic Brainstorming System	Applegate (1986)
Envisioning Machine	Singer (1988)
EuroPARC Multi-media Environment	Moran (1990); Buxton (1990); Heath (1991)
gIBIS	(*see also rIBIS*) Conklin (1988); Lee (1990a); Yakemovic (1990)
GroupSketch	Greenberg (1991)
Grove	Ellis (1988a, b)
Hypermate	Ellis (1988b)
ICICLE	Brothers (1990)
Intermedia	Garrett (1986); Landow (1990)
InVision	Kass (1989)
KMS	Yoder (1989)
Liveware	Witten (1991)
Liza	Ellis (1988b); Gibbs (1989)
MAFIA	Lutz (1990)
MBlink	Sarin (1985)
Mermaid	Watabe (1990)
MIAC conferencing system	Clark (1989)
MMCONF	Crowley (1987, 1989, 1990); Lison (1989), Thomas (1985)
Mosaic	Garcia-Luna-Aceves (1988)
NETLIB	Dongarra (1987)
Notecards	Halasz (1988); Trigg (1986, 1988)
NSF EXPRES	Olson (1990)
Object Lens, Information Lens	Crowston (1988b); Lia (1988); Mackay (1989, 1990); Malone (1986, 1987a, 1989); Tarazi (1989)
Office design project (Xerox)	Harrison (1989); Stults (1988)
Open Hyperdocument System	Engelbart (1990)
PAGES	Mantyla (1990)
Polyscope	Borning (1991)
Portland Experiment	Abel (1990a); Goodman (1987b); Olson (1991)
PREP editor	Neuwirth (1990)
Project Nick	Begeman (1986); Cook (1987); Ellis (1988b); Rein (1989)
Quilt	Leland (1988)
RandMail	Eveland (1987)
Rapport	Ahuja (1990); Ensor (1988, 1989)
Rendezvous	Patterson (1990)

Name	Citation
rIBIS	Rein (1991)
RTCal	Sarin (1985)
SharedARK	Smith (1988, 1989)
SharedX	Garfinkel (1989); Gust (1988, 1989)
Share	Greenberg (1990b, 1991d)
SIBYL	Lee (1990a)
Simple Simon's GesturePad	Gerrissen (1990b)
Slate (BBN)	*See MMConf*
Speech filing system	Gould (1983, 1984)
STRUDEL	Shepherd (1990)
SYNVIEW	Lowe (1986)
Talking Heads	MIT (1983a)
TeamWorkstation	Ishii (1990a, c, 1991a, b)
Timbuktu	Farallon (1988); Guttman (1989)
Together	Quinn (1990)
Trillium	Blomberg (1986)
University of Arizona GDSS	Valacich (1991); Vogel (1990)
Unix customization files	Mackay (1990)
US West Tele-collaboration Project	Abel (1990b); Corey (1989); Bulick (1989)
VideoDraw	Tang (1989, 1990)
VideoWhiteboard	Tang (1991)
VideoWindow	Fish (1990)
Video wall (Xerox)	*See Portland Experiment*
Virtual Environments	Cohen (1991)
Visual Schedular	Beard (1990)
Vmacs	Lakin (1990)
Vrooms	Borning (1991)
XSketch	Lee (1990b)

Bibliography

ABEL, M. (1990a). Experiences in an exploratory distributed organization. In J. GALEGHER, R. E. KRAUT & C. EGIDO, Eds, *Intellectual Teamwork: Social Foundations of Cooperative Work*, pp. 489–510. Hillsdale, New Jersey: Lawrence Erlbaum Associates.
(virtual hallways, video, information meetings, evaluation) Abel describes a case study of a video wall used to create permanent links between two geographically-distributed research labs to support informal interaction. The system is described as adequate (but just barely so) for creating a joint sense of place and culture.

ABEL, M., COREY, D., BULICK, S., SCHMIDT, J. & COFFIN, S. (1990b). The US West Advanced Technologies TeleCollaboration research project. In G. WAGNER, Ed., *Computer Augmented Teamwork*. Van Nostrand Reinhold.
(virtual hallways, video, informal meetings) This chapter provides an overview of the US West TeleCollaboration project. The emphasis is on supporting day-to-day interaction

among individuals, especially informal, spontaneous interaction. Motivation, technical infrastructure, and lessons learnt are provided. A good sequel to Xerox's Portland experiment.

ABEL, M. J. & REIN, G. L. (1989). Report on the collaborative technology developers' workshop. *SIGCHI Bulletin,* **20**(3), pp. 86–89, January. Also published in ACM SIGOIS 1989, 10(1).
(report, software design) This brief report summarizes the 1988 CSCW workshop held for developers building collaborative technologies. Several issues were raised: 1) personalized views versus what you see is what I see (WYSIWIS); 2) synchronous versus asynchronous interaction; 3) navigation and visual metaphors; 4) single vs multi-user applications; 5) social protocols and the niche for sociologists. The workshop was part of the CSCW '88 conference.

ACM Press (Ed.) (1986). Proceedings of the 1986 Conference on Computer-Supported Cooperative Work. ACM Press. December 3–5, Austin, Texas.
(collection) Session titles were: 1 Supporting face-to-face groups; 2 Empirical studies; 3 Supporting distributed groups; 4 Hypertext systems; 5 Underlying technology for collaborative groups; 6 Collaboration research; 7 Interfaces: Multimedia and multi-user; 8 Industrial experience with computer-supported groups; 9 Coordination and decision-making. Although proceedings are no longer available, many of the articles have been reprinted/revised in: Trans Office Information Systems 1987 5(2) and 1988 6(3); Human–Computer Interaction 3(1); Office: Technology and People 1987 3; Computing Surveys 1988 20(2); and Greif (1988).

ACM Press (Ed.) (1988). Proceedings of the 1988 Conference on Computer-Supported Cooperative Work. ACM Press, September 26–28, Portland, Oregon.
(collection) Session titles were: 1 Remote communication; 2 Work settings and applications; 3 Perspectives on evaluation; 4 Structured communication technologies; 5 Practical experiences in system development; 6 Enabling technologies and environments; 7 Synchronous communication; 8 Collaborative learning; 9 Electronic mail; 10 Perspectives. A few articles have been revised/reprinted in: Trans Office Information Systems 1988 6(4); Office: Technology and People 1989 4(2) and 4(3). Proceedings available from ACM Order Department, PO Box 64145, Baltimore, MD 21264, or phone 1–800–342–6626.

ACM Press (Ed.) (1990). Proceedings of the 1990 Conference on Computer-Supported Cooperative Work. ACM Press. October 7–10. Los Angeles, California.
(collection) Session titles were: 1 Shared video spaces; 2 Experimental studies in CSCW; 3 Supporting structured communications; 4 CSCW within and across organizations; 5 Cooperative support and customization; 6 User interfaces in the CSCW context; 7 (CS)CW in the field; 8 Systems infrastructure for CSCW; 9 Issues and perspectives on CSCW. Proceedings available from ACM Order Department, PO Box 64145, Baltimore, MD 21264, or phone 1–800–342–6626.

ADRIANSON, L. & HJELMQUIST, E. (1988). Group processes in face-to-face and computer-mediated communication. Department of Psychology, University of Gotenborg.
(evaluation, decision support, face-to-face meetings, remote meetings, protocols) This study reports results from an experiment investigating different aspects of communication pattern and communicative outcome. The experiment was a 2×2×2 ANOVA. Factors were mode of communication (face-to-face vs computer mediated), problem type (human relation vs technical ranking problem) and experience (experienced vs inexperienced). Results show no differences in decision quality depending upon medium, but more consensus decisions in face-to-face. No equilization of participants was seen in computer-mediated communication, contrary to previous research.

AHUJA, S. R., ENSOR, J. R. & LUCCO, S. E. (1990). A comparison of applications sharing mechanisms in real-time desktop conferencing systems. In *Proceedings of the Conference on Office Information Systems,* pp. 238–248. Boston, April 25–27.
(shared views, software design, implementation) This paper contrasts three architecturally different versions of a shared window system (Rapport): a single-site centralized approach,

a multi-site distributed approach, and a combination of the two. Performance issues were discussed, and the single-site approach was recommended.

ALLEN, R. B. (1990). User models: Theory, method, practice. *Int J Man Machine Studies,* **32**(5), pp. 511–544, May.
(asynchronous conferencing) This paper describes the use of user models to select and filter information sources for readers of information services. Results suggest that prediction of preferences are straightforward for general categories of news articles, but difficult when specific news reports are desired.

ANCONA, D. G. & CALDWELL, D. F. (1990). Information technology and work groups: The case of new product teams. In J. GALEGHER, R. E. KRAUT AND C. EGIDO, Eds, *Intellectual Teamwork: Social Foundations of Cooperative Work*, pp. 173–190. Hillsdale, New Jersey: Lawrence Erlbaum Associates.
(organizational concerns, social impact) The focus is on groups which face the highly interactive and complex task of developing new products. A description is presented of the activities in which these teams engage, and moves from that data to suggest how information technology might better be used to support the work of those teams. The work is premised on the belief that an in-depth understanding of the group's complex tasks is necessary to realize the full capabilities of technology.

APPLEGATE, L. M., KONSYNSKI, B. R. & NUNAMAKER, J. F. (1986). A group decision support system for idea generation and issue analysis in organizational planning. In *Proceedings of the Conference on Computer-Supported Cooperative Work*, pp. 16–34. Austin, Texas, December 3–5, ACM Press.
(decision support, idea processors, face-to-face, evaluation) The idea generation and management process has been chosen as the domain for the study of the design and implementation of a GDSS to support complex, unstructured group decision processes within organizations. Results of research conducted in the MIS Planning and Decision Laboratory on the use of the Electronic Brainstorming System with over 100 planners are presented. Planners reported high levels of satisfaction with the process and rated the computer brainstorming tool as much better than manual brainstorming.

ATTEWELL, P. & RULE, J. (1984). Computing and organizations: What we know and what we don't know. *Comm ACM,* **27**(12), pp. 1184–1192. Reprinted in Greif, 1988.
(organizational concerns) This paper analyses the earlier literature on the effects of computing in organizations. The literature is found to be inconsistent and inconclusive.

AUSTIN, L. C., LIKER, J. K. & McLEOD, P. L. (1990). Determinants and patterns of control over technology in a computerized meeting room. In *Proceedings of the Conference on Computer-Supported Cooperative Work (CSCW '90)*, pp. 39–52. Los Angeles, California, October 7–10, ACM Press.
(face-to-face meetings, evaluation) Groups completed a priorization task in a "low structure" computerized meeting room. All group members had equal access to a public screen used to complete the task. The authors studied how groups distributed control of the technology, the determinants of which group members took control, and the consequences of control. They noticed that proficiency with the computer interface and the social influence are factors which predicted who will take control. Dedicated versus non-dedicated scribes are also discussed.

BAIR, J. H. (1987). CSCW '86. *ACM SIGOIS Bulletin,* **8**(3), pp. 3–13.
(report) A review of the CSCW '86 conference.

BAIR, J. H. (1989). Supporting cooperative work with computers: Addressing meeting mania. In *Proceedings of the 34th IEEE Computer Society International Conference–CompCon Spring*, pp. 208–217. San Francisco, CA, February 27–March 3.
(overview, face-to-face meetings, critique) This paper argues that CSCW is a renewed recognition of user needs for extensions to current communication media. A taxonomy of communication media is provided; four levels of user needs—informing, coordinating,

collaborating and cooperating—are presented; limits of current media are raised; and extensions of electronic media are proposed. A good overview of the area, its problems, and directions to follow.

BAIR, J. H. & GALE, S. (1988). An investigation of the Coordinator as an example of computer supported cooperative work. Hewlett Packard Laboratories, California. Unpublished.
(semi-structured messages, protocols, critique, evaluation) This paper describes an extensive investigation of the Coordinator and the suitability of speech-act systems in organizations. Conclusions and recommendations are included.

BANNON, L., BJORN-ANDERSEN, N. & DUE-THOMSEN, B. (1988). Computer support for cooperative work: An appraisal and critique. In H. J. BULLINGER, Ed., *Eurinfo '88. Information Systems for Organizational Effectiveness*. Amsterdam, North-Holland.
(critique)

BANNON, L. J. & SCHMIDT, K. (1989). CSCW: Four characters in search of a context. In *Proceedings of the 1st European Conference on Computer-Supported Cooperative Work (EC-CSCW '89)*, pp. 358–372. Gatwick, UK, September 13–15. Computer Sciences House, Slough, UK.
(conceptual, critique) This paper highlights the inadequacies of the CSCW acronym. A framework for approaching the issue of cooperative work and computer support is provided; core issues are identified; and the fields prospects are outlined.

BEARD, D., PALANAPPIAN, M., HUMM, A., BANKS, D. & NAIR, A. (1990). A visual calendar for scheduling group meetings. In *Proceedings of the Conference on Computer-Supported Cooperative Work (CSCW '90)*. Los Angeles, California, October 7–10, ACM Press.
(face-to-face meetings, evaluation, organizational concerns) This paper discusses a comprehensive group meeting scheduling system called "Visual Schedular" that summarizes available information for quick, flexible, and reliable scheduling. A controlled experiment shows the automated system to be faster and less error-prone than manual scheduling, and a field study shows the Visual Schedular to be generally useful. An interesting paper, as it contradicts previous studies that suggested that automated scheduling systems do not work in practice.

BEAUDOUIN-LAFON, M. (1990). Collaborative development of software. In S. GIBBS & A. A. VERRIGHN-STUART, Eds, *Proceedings of IFIP WG8.4 Conference on Multi-User Interfaces and Applications*, Crete. North Holland.

BEGEMAN, M., COOK, P., ELLIS, C., GRAF, M., REIN, G. & SMITH, T. (1986). Project NICK: Meetings augmentation and analysis. In *Proceedings of the Conference on Computer-Supported Cooperative Work (CSCW '86)*, pp. 1–6. Austin, Texas. December 3–5, ACM Press.
(face-to-face meetings) See Cook (1987) for an expanded version of this paper.

BENFORD, S. (1989). Requirements of activity management. In *Proceedings of the 1st European Conference on Computer-Supported Cooperative Work (EC-CSCW '89)*. Gatwick, UK, September 13–15, Computer Sciences House, Slough, UK.

BENSON, I., CIBORRA, C. & PROFFITT, S. (1990). Some social and economic consequences of groupware for flight crew. In *Proceedings of the Conference on Computer-Supported Cooperative Work (CSCW '90)*. Los Angeles, California, October 7–10, ACM Press.
(organizational concerns, evaluation) Groupware can never substitute for the social and organisational integration of team members, but it can fill many of the inevitable logistical, knowledge and communication gaps that always arise, especially in large and/or dispersed teams performing complex tasks. Within this context, a case study of 3000 flight crew from a major European airline is described.

BERLIN, L. M. & O'DAY, V. L. (1990). Platform and application issues in multi-user hypertext. In S. GIBBS & A. A. VERRIGHN-STUART, Eds, *Proceedings of IFIP*

WG8.4 Conference on Multi-User Interfaces and Applications, Crete. North Holland.

BERMANN, T. & THORENSON, K. (1988). Can networks make an organization? In *Proceedings of the Conference on Computer-Supported Cooperative Work (CSCW '88)*, pp. 153–166. Portland, Oregon, September 26–28, ACM Press.
(participatory design, evaluation, organizational concerns, social impact) The authors share their experience of a cooperative systems development project involving centralization of several previously independent surgical departments in a hospital. A few simple cases illustrate that the conventional development process is wrought with conflicts, contradictions and challenges. In particular, the design of a cooperative system can neither be pushed by technology, nor by the workers' view of what they require. Rather, the process is collaborative, where both designer and end user forward and evaluate ideas during system development. The work is an example of the "Scandinavian approach" to design.

BHANDARU, N. & CROFT, B. (1990). Architecture for supporting goal-based cooperative work. In S. GIBBS & A. A. VERRIGHN-STUART, Eds, *Proceedings of IFIP WG8.4 Conference on Multi-User Interfaces and Applications*, Crete. North Holland.

BIGNOLI, C. & SIMONE, C. (1989). AI techniques for supporting human to human communication in CHAOS. In *Proceedings of the 1st European Conference on Computer-Supported Cooperative Work (EC-CSCW '89)*. Gatwick, UK, September 13–15, Computer Sciences House, Slough, UK.

BIKSON, T. K. & EVELAND, J. D. (1990). The interplay of work group structures. In J. GALEGHER, R. E. KRAUT & C. EGIDO, Eds, *Intellectural Teamwork: Social Foundations of Cooperative Work*, pp. 245–290. Hillsdale, New Jersey: Lawrence Erlbaum Associates.
(email, asynchronous conferencing, evaluation) The paper reports a field experiment using email and computer conferencing to support a task force writing retirement policy. The study shows that computer-based communication can empower otherwise isolated people by providing them with the resources needed to accomplish their tasks, including access to information and other people. Barriers to social interaction are reduced, and leadership roles broadened.

BJERKNES, G. & BRATTETEIG, T. (1988). The memoirs of two survivors: Or the evaluation of a computer system for cooperative work. In *Proceedings of The Conference on Computer-Supported Cooperative Work (CSCW '88)*, pp. 167–177. Portland, Oregon, September 26–28, ACM Press.
(participatory design, evaluation, organizational concerns) The authors describe their experiences with the "ultimate test" of a CSCW system built according to the Scandinavian approach by evaluating its use several months after installation. Through a series of flashbacks of diary clips and analysis, they bring us through the design process, giving the reader insight as to what happened and why things were designed a certain way. The result of their ultimate test did more than show a system in active use, for it described several surprising work habits that had developed.

BLOMBERG, J. (1986). The variable impact of computer technologies on the organization of work activities. In *Proceedings of the Conference on Computer-Supported Cooperative Work (CSCW '86)*, pp. 35–42. Austin, Texas, December 3–5, ACM Press. Republished in revised form in Greif, 1988.
(organizational concerns, software design, participatory design) New computer tools are affecting the ways in which work is accomplished and, in turn, existing patterns of social interaction are shaping the evolution of these highly malleable tools. This paper explores the interplay between a computer-based design environment employed in the creation of machine interfaces and the "users" of this tool, including the user interface designers and the software engineers supporting the technology. The use of this has resulted in the restructuring of the social organization of the design tasks. An ethnographic study of a computer-based design environment called Trillium is used as an example.

BLY, S. (1988). A use of drawing surfaces in different collaborative settings. In *Proceedings of the Conference on Computer-Supported Cooperative Work (CSCW '88)*, pp. 250–256. Portland, Oregon, September 26–28, ACM Press.
(shared workspace, evaluation, video) Bly observed designers communicating through three different media: face-to-face; over a video link that included a view of the other person and their drawing surface; and over the telephone. From her observations, she hypothesizes that the actions, uses, and interactions on a drawing artifact are as important to the effectiveness of many design collaborations as viewing the final artifact. Also, allowing designers to share drawing space activities increases their attention and involvement in the design task. When interaction over the drawing surface is reduced, the quality of the collaboration decrease.

BLY, S. A. & MINNEMAN, S. L. (1990). Commune: A shared drawing surface. In *Proceedings of the Conference on Office Information Systems*, pp. 184–192. Boston, April 25–27.
(shared workspace, evaluation, remote meetings) The authors describe Commune, a shared drawing surface, and their observations of two-person use. Commune stresses people's ability not only to make marks simultaneously on the workspace, but to use cursors to support gesturing.

BODKER, S., EHN, P., KNUDSEN, J., KYNG, M. & MADSEN, K. (1988). Computer support for cooperative design (invited paper). In *Proceedings of the Conference on Computer-Supported Cooperative Work (CSCW '88)*, pp. 377–394. Portland, Oregon, September 26–28, ACM Press.
(participatory design, social impact, critique) The authors outline their theoretical perspective on design as cooperative work, and exemplifies the approach with reflections from the Aplex project. Historical roots of the Scandinavian approach to design are covered, and critical reflections made.

BODKER, S. & GRONBAEK, K. (1991). Cooperative prototyping: Users and designers in mutual activity. *Int J Man Machine Studies*, **34**(3), pp. 453–478, March. In the special edition on CSCW & Groupware. Republished in Greenberg, 1991c.
(participatory design) Given an environment conducive to participatory design, how does one go about doing it? The authors describe one method called cooperative prototyping. These involve sessions where users experience the future use situation, and then participate with designers in modifying the prototypes when usage breakdowns required it. Their article is especially valuable as it provides a theoretical framework, a practical guide for managing cooperative prototyping sessions, and an example of how cooperative prototyping develops in a real situation.

BODKER, S. & GRONBAEK, K. (1989). Cooperative prototyping experiments: Users and designers envision a dental case record system. In *Proceedings of the 1st European Conference on Computer-Supported Cooperative Work (EC-CSCW '89)*. Gatwick, UK, September 13–15, Computer Sciences House, Slough, UK.

BONFIGLIO, A., MALATESA, G. & TISATO, F. (1989). Conference Toolkit: A framework for real-time conferencing. In *Proceedings of the 1st European Conference on Computer-Supported Cooperative Work (EC-CSCW '89)*. Gatwick, UK, September 13–15, Computer Sciences House, Slough, UK.

BORENSTEIN, N., EVERHART, C., ROSENBERG, J. & STOLLER, A. (1988a). A multi-media message system for Andrew. In *Proceedings of the USENIX Winter Conference*, pp. 37–42. Dallas, Texas, February 9–12.
(multimedia, asynchronous conferencing, email) The Andrew Messaging System supports multi-media messages, which may include line-drawings, hierarchical drawings, spread-sheets, rasters, animations, and equations. It is explicitly designed to support a huge database of messages and an enormous user community. It also supports advanced features such as voting, private bulletin boards, shared mailboxes, and automatic classification of incoming mail. It is easily ported, can have multiple interfaces, and is distributed.

BORENSTEIN, N. & THYBERG, A. (1988b). Cooperative work in the Andrew message system. In *Proceedings of the Conference on Computer-Supported Cooperative*

Work (CSCW '88), pp. 306–323. Portland, Oregon, September 26–28, ACM Press.
(multimedia, asynchronous conferencing, email)   The Andrew Messaging System is built on the premise that mail is more than just text. Its important points are that it is a combined mail/bulletin board facility, and that it is multi-media. One can, for example, transmit line drawings, rasters, animations, and spreadsheets; ask for responses to a message via mail that asks its reader to select from a list of choices; and compile articles into magazines for further distribution on the bulletin board. Through the examples of how Andrew was actually used at Carnegie Mellon University, the authors leave a positive impression of what advanced email technology could offer.

BORENSTEIN, N. S. & THYBERG, C. A. (1991). Power, ease of use, and cooperative work in a practical multimedia message system. *Int J Man Machine Studies*, **34**(2), pp. 229–260, February. In the special edition on CSCW & Groupware. Republished in Greenberg, 1991c.
(asynchronous conferencing, multimedia, implementation, evaluation)   The Andrew Message System (AMS) is a powerful multimedia mail and bulletin board system. This paper discusses two parts of AMS. First, advanced features of the Messages program—a high-end interface to AMS—are described, emphasising how it facilitates types of cooperative work that are not possible with other less powerful systems. Second, the Andrew Adviser system is provided as an example of the way that AMS can help solve problems of distributed support for a very diverse user community.

BORNING, A. & TRAVERS, M. (1991). Two approaches to casual interaction over computer and video networks. In *ACM SIGCHI Conference on Human Factors in Computing Systems*. New Orleans, April 28–May 2, ACM Press.
(casual interaction, video)   Authors describe two systems that use interactive computer-controlled video for shared awareness and casual communication. Polyscope lets users monitor a large number of video-sources simultaneously, where screens are collections of frame-grabbed or animated bitmapped images. Vrooms employs a strong spatial metaphor, where users can enter and leave virtual rooms.

BOWRES, J. & CHURCHER, J. (1988). Local and global structuring of computer mediated communication: Developing linguistic perspectives on CSCW in Cosmos. In *Proceedings of the Conference on Computer-Supported Cooperative Work (CSCW '88)*, pp. 125–139. Portland, Oregon, September 26–28, ACM Press.
(protocols)   This paper is concerned with the development of a language/action perspective in the Cosmos project. The authors emphasize the importance of seeing cooperative work in terms of participants' communicative actions as embedded in dialogical contexts.

BRANDT, R., DEPKE, D. A., LEWIS, G., HAMMONDS, K. & HAWKINS, C. (1989). The personal computer finds its missing link. *Business Week*, pp. 120–128, June 5.
(overview)   This is a popular press article on networking, with some discussion of groupware.

BROTHERS, L., SEMBUGAMOORTHY, V. & MULLER, M. (1990). ICICLE: groupware for code inspection. In *Proceedings of the Conference on Computer-Supported Cooperative Work (CSCW '90)*. Los Angeles, California, October 7–10, ACM Press.
(face-to-face meetings, shared views, shared workspace)   ICICLE (Intelligent Code Inspection Environment in a C Language Environment) is a system intended to augment the process of formal code inspection. While it offers assistance in a variety of activities, the paper is directed towards the groupware issues encountered. ICICLE code inspection occurs within a face-to-face environment, where a view of the code is displayed on everyone's screen. Readers of the code can have synchronized shared views, or can choose to scroll independently through different parts of the code. Textual comments can be created, shown, and acted upon by participants.

BULICK, S., ABEL, M., COREY, D., SCHMIDT, J. & COFFIN, S. (1989). The US West Advanced Technologies prototype multimedia communication system. In *Proceedings of the IEEE Global Telecommunications Conference (GlobeCom)*,

pp. 1221–1226, November.
(virtual hallways, video, informal meetings) This is another paper that provides an overview of the US West Telecollaboration project. The most prominent feature is the way video is used to link two remote laboratories.

BULLEN, C. V. & BENNETT, J. L. (1990a). Groupware in practice: An interpretation of work experience. Research report CISR WP 205, Sloan WP No. 3146-90, Center for Information Systems Research, MIT, Cambridge, Mass., March.
(evaluation, email) This study of 223 people using groupware systems offers an early examination of how people are using personal computers for electronic exchanges via networking. The paper concludes that complex interactions of social and technical factors affect the use of groupware systems in organizations. Issues for developers and managers of groupware systems are raised.

BULLEN, C. V. & BENNETT, J. L. (1990b). Learning from user experience with groupware. In *Proceedings of the Conference on Computer-Supported Cooperative Work (CSCW '90)*. Los Angeles, California, October 7–10, ACM Press.
(email, asynchronous conferencing, organizational concerns, evaluation) This study examines how people are using personal computers for electronic exchanges that link people into task-oriented teams. Conclusions are presented in two ways: from a design perspective, which offers findings which designers of groupware systems should consider; and from an organizational perspective, whose findings should be considered by managers when planning for and implementing groupware systems.

BUSH, V. (1945). As we may think. *Atlantic Monthly,* **176**(1), pp. 101–108, June. Reprinted in Greif, 1988.
(conceptual, hypertext, data sharing)   This early paper is considered *the* seminal article for both CSCW and hypertext. Bush describes his vision of the microfilm-based "Memex," a way of structuring and leaving trails through a large, shared information store.

BUXTON, B. & MORAN, T. (1990). EuroPARC's Integrated Interactive Intermedia Facility (IIIF): Early experiences. In S. GIBBS & A. A. VERRIGHN-STUART, Eds, *Proceedings of IFIP WG8.4 Conference on Multi-User Interfaces and Applications*, Crete. North Holland.
(virtual hallways, video, informal meetings)   This paper describes the EuroPARC "Media Space" setup.

CALDWELL, R. G., VAN NEST, W. D., TYNAN, A. A. & LEACH, R. A. (1987). Conferencing selection and implementation: University of Arizona case history. In *The Second Guelph Symposium on Computer Conferencing*, pp. 209–222. Guelph, Ontario, Canada, June 1–4, University of Guelph.
(asynchronous conferencing, organizational concerns)   This paper summarizes the University of Arizona's selection and implementation of an asynchronous conferencing system. The selection criteria and the implementation plan are reviewed. A checklist for successful implementation is provided. The paper is useful for seeing a large organization's strategy for bringing in a conferencing system.

CASHMAN, P. & STROLL, D. (1987). Achieving sustainable complexity through information technology: Theory and practice. *Office: Technology and People, ***3**. An earlier version appeared in CSCW '86.
This paper describes a theoretical framework which sheds some light on the relationships between the levels of complexity with which managers deal, the value of information at each level, and the resulting information system requirements. A real-life experiment is described that uses advanced information technology to support strategic business unit management within a large corporation.

CHALFONTE, B., FISH, R. S. & KRAUT, R. E. (1991). Expressive richness: A comparison of speech and text as media for revision. In *ACM SIGCHI Conference on Human Factors in Computing Systems*. New Orleans, April 28–May 2, ACM Press.
(data sharing, evaluation) Authors constructed an experiment in which participants were required to make either written or spoken annotations to a document to help a fictional

co-author revise it. The results provide strong evidence that a richer expressive medium is especially valuable for the more complex, controversial, and social aspects of a collaborative task. Voice was preferred for dealing with the higher-level issues in the document, while text was preferred for communicating the lower-level problems (eg. spelling).

CHANG, E. (1986). Participant systems. *Future Computing Systems,* **1**(3), pp. 253–270.
(protocols, remote meetings, data sharing, implementation) This paper presents the paradigm of Participant Systems that supports collaborative intellectual tasks among a number of persons, possibly distributed in different locations. To do so, it must support communications, multiple views, common data, common action and common cognitive space. Such a system must coordinate access to a common problem representation, and contain sufficient knowledge and expertise in the problem domain to integrate the activity of the users, and even to participate as one of the experts. The Cantata implementation is briefly described.

CHANG, E. (1989). Protocols for group coordination in participant systems. In M. M. TAYLOR, F. NEEL & D. G. BOUWHUIS, Eds, *The Structure of Multimodal Dialogue,* pp. 229–247. North-Holland: Elsevier Science Publishers B.V.
(remote meetings, protocols) This paper describes the notion of participant systems; the experiences gained with Cantata; and briefly describes related work by other people.

CHANG, E., KASPERSKI, R. & COPPING, T. (1987a). Group coordination in participant systems. Department of Advanced Computing and Engineering, Alberta Research Council, Calgary, Alberta, Canada. Unpublished.
(protocols, remote meetings, data sharing, implementation) This paper introduces the paradigm of Participant Systems. It describes the Cantata participant system in detail: a) the shared terminal; b) the multi-person real-time text messaging system; c) the shared blackboard; and d) the participant construct system. It lists Cantata's features and how physically distributed groups that operate in real time are supported.

CHANG, S. K. & LEUNG, L. (1987b). A Knowledge-Based Message Management System. *ACM Trans Office Information Systems,* **5**(3), pp. 213–236, July.
(email, implementation) The design approach of a knowledge-based message management system is described. A linguistic message filter is used to filter out junk messages. Relevant messages are then processed by an expert system, driven by user-defined alerter rules. An alerter rule base for a secretarial office is illustrated.

CHAPANIS, A. (1975). Interactive human communication. *Scientific American,* **232**(3), pp. 36–42. Reprinted in Greif, 1988.
(evaluation, remote conferencing, video) Chapanis describes an important empirical study on the channels and modes through which people converse: voice, handwriting, typewriting, video, and their combinations. The results suggest that while voice and text gives substantial improvement to communication over text alone, adding video gives only a minor improvement.

CIBORRA, C. & OLSON, M. H. (1988). Encountering electronic work groups: A transaction costs perspective. In *Proceedings of the Conference on Computer-Supported Cooperative Work (CSCW '88),* pp. 94–101. Portland, Oregon, September 26–28, ACM Press.
(organizational concerns) The goal of this paper is to investigate the organizational context of cooperative work through the transaction cost approach. Implications for system and organizational design are provided.

CICOUREL, A. V. (1990). The integration of distributed knowledge. In J. GALEGHER, R. E. KRAUT & C. EGIDO, Eds, *Intellectual Teamwork: Social Foundations of Cooperative Work.* Hillsdale, New Jersey: Lawrence Erlbaum Associates.
(social impact) The paper discusses the importance of coupling information to its source. In collaborative medical diagnosis, the diagnosis arises out of social interaction as physicians exchange observations. Because physicians learn to assess the value of medical information on the basis of its association with a trusted human source, information systems designed to aid medical decision making must somehow incorporate evidence of their own credibility.

CLARK, W. J. (1989). The MIAC audiographic conferencing system: A practical implementation of the audiovisual service infrastructure. In *Multimedia '89: Proceedings of the 2nd International Workshop on Multimedia Communications*. Montebello, Quebec, April 20–23.
(remote meetings, multimedia, implementation)   The authors discuss the layout and implementation of the MIAC remote conferencing system.

CLEMENT, A. (1990). Cooperative support for computer work: A social perspective on the empowering of end users. In *Proceedings of the Conference on Computer-Supported Cooperative Work (CSCW '90)*. Los Angeles, California, October 7–10, ACM Press.
(organizational concerns, evaluation)   This paper explores the question of empowerment through computerization by looking at common problems of computer use in the context of office group work. In particular it examines the difficulties that secretaries confront when attempting to master desktop computing and the cooperative solutions they have developed to overcome them. Based on the findings, the paper outlines proposals for the design and implementation of CSCW applications intended to enhance the power of clerks and secretaries, office workers who are relatively resource-weak.

CLEMENT, A. & GOTLIEB, C. C. (1987). Evolution of an organization interface: The new business department at a large insurance firm. In *Proceedings of the ACM SIGCHI+GI Human Factors in Computing Systems*. Toronto, Canada, April 5–9. Reprinted in Greif, 1988.
(organizational concerns)   This study looks at the interaction dynamics between a work and a computer organization in a large life-insurance firm. The dynamics of the interaction between the two is explained in terms of "the economic incentive to reduce the length of transaction processing chains and the more political goal of extending managerial control."

COHEN, M. & LUDWIG, L. F. (1991). Multidimensional audio window management. *Int J Man Machine Studies,* **34**(3), pp. 319–336, March. In the special edition on CSCW & Groupware. Republished in Greenberg, 1991c.
(virtual environments, remote meetings, implementation)   Recent developments in interactive Virtual Environments has sparked interest in spatially-located three-dimensional sound. Cohen and Ludwig describe an audio management system called audio windows that integrates spatial sound, audio emphasis, and gestural input recognition. While this exciting use of computer-controlled sound can be applied to any aspect of the human–computer interface, the article suggests new enhancements this technology can bring to tele-conferencing.

CONKLIN, J. (1987). Hypertext: An introduction and survey. *IEEE Computer,* **20**(9), pp. 17–41. Reprinted in Greif, 1988.
(hypertext)   An excellent introduction and survey to hypertext systems. Features of many implementations are contrasted.

CONKLIN, J. (1988). gIBIS: A hypertext tool for exploratory policy discussion. In *Proceedings of the Conference on Computer-Supported Cooperative Work (CSCW '88)*, pp. 140–152. Portland, Oregon, September 26–28, ACM Press.
(semi-structured messages, protocols, decision support, hypertext)   This paper introduces gIBIS, a hypertext system that captures early design deliberations on large complex problems. It is based upon the Issue Based Information Design (IBIS) methodology that views design as a rhetorical process, with a set of issues that can be generalized, specialized, responded to, questioned, argued and so on. gIBIS is based to a large part on semi-structured messages. Participants propose and respond to issues in structured ways that eliminate unconstructive moves such as name-calling and argument by repetition. The authors also evaluate and criticize their work based upon preliminary observations of its use.

COOK, P., ELLIS, C., GRAF, M., REIN, G. & SMITH, T. (1987). Project NICK: Meetings augmentation and analysis. *ACM Trans Office Information Systems,* **5**(2), pp. 132–146, April.

(face-to-face meetings) This paper investigates meetings for the early part of some design process. Face-to-face meetings are an important activity since they provide a medium for direction, exploration, and consensus building. Project Nick is attempting to apply automated facilities to the process, conduct, and semantic capture of the design meetings. Primary topics covered are meeting analysis, meeting augmentation, and a model of meeting progression. The overview (including references) is good. The meeting tool itself deserves a better description.

COOK, S. & BIRCH, G. (1991). Modelling groupware in the electronic office. *Int J Man Machine Studies,* **34**(3), pp. 369–394, March. In the special edition on CSCW & Groupware. Republished in Greenberg, 1991c.
(implementation, remote meetings) This is a report on a project to explore ideas for a distributed system that: enhances convenient and effective communication; gives information about each other's status and whereabouts; supports people in planning and execution of various kinds of office tasks. Architectural and user interface issues are discussed.

COREY, D., ABEL, M., BULICK, S. & SCHMIDT, J. (1989). Multi-media communication: The US WEST advanced technologies prototype system. In *Fifth IEEE Workshop on Telematics.* Denver, Colorado, September 17–21. Submitted paper.
(informal meetings, virtual hallways, video) This paper describes the US WEST virtual hallways system, a fairly elaborate video connection between two distance-separated sites.

CORNELL, P. AND LUCHETTI, R. (1989). Ergonomic and environmental aspects of computer supported cooperative work. In *Human Factors Society 33rd Annual Meeting,* pp. 862–866.

CROWLEY, T., BAKER, E., FORSDICK, H., MILAZZO, P. & TOMLINSON, R. (1990). MMConf: An infrastructure for building shared applications. In *Proceedings of the Conference on Computer-Supported Cooperative Work (CSCW '90).* Los Angeles, California, October 7–10, ACM Press.
(shared views, shared workspace, implementation) This paper describes MMConf, a system supporting computer teleconferencing and the way it has been used to support shared applications.

CROWLEY, T., FORSDICK, H., LANDAU, M. & TRAVERS, V. (1987). The Diamond Multimedia Editor. In *Proceedings of the Summer Usenix 1987 Conference.*
(multimedia) This paper describes the Multimedia editor behind the Diamond Multimedia conferencing system.

CROWLEY, T. & FORSDICK, T. (1989). MMConf: The Diamond Multimedia Conferencing System. In *Groupware Technology Workshop,* Palo Alto, California, August.
(remote meetings, shared views, implementation) This paper describes implementation details of the Diamond Multimedia conferencing system, a replicated shared-view system. It includes floor control, all the conference primitives, a telepointer, recording a conference for playback, and its existing packages. Disadvantages and advantages of the replicated architecture are raised.

CROWSTON, K., MALONE, T. & LIN, F. (1988a). Cognitive science and organizational design: A case study of computer conferencing. *Human Computer Interaction,* **3**(1), pp. 59–85. Reprinted in Greif, 1988. An earlier version was published in CSCW '86.
(organizational concerns, evaluation) The authors characterize information processing in terms of the kinds of messages people exchange. This method is used to analyse the introduction of a computer conferencing system to an organization.

CROWSTON, K. & MALONE, T. W. (1988b). Intelligent software agents. *Byte Magazine,* pp. 267–271, December.
(semi-structured messages, email, asynchronous conferencing) This is a popular introduction to Malone's Object Lens and how it differs from his earlier Information Lens system. A list of other groupware systems that use AI techniques is provided.

CULNAN, M. J. & BAIR, J. H. (1983). Human communication needs and organizational productivity: The potential impact of office automation. *Journal of the American*

Society for Information Science, **34**(3), pp. 215–221.
(conceptual, social impact)   This article defines communication, identifies the potential benefits to be realized from implementing office automation, and offers caveats related to the implementation of office automation systems. Realization of the benefits of office automation depends upon the degree to which new modes of communication may be successfully substituted for traditional modes.

DANIELSEN, T., PANKOKE-BABATZ, U., PRINZ, W., PATEL, A., PAYS, P., SMALLAND, K. & SPETH, R. (1986). The Amigo project: Advanced group communication model for computer-based communications environment. In *Proceedings of the Conference on Computer-Suppported Cooperative Work (CSCW '86)*, pp. 115–142. Austin, Texas, December 3–5, ACM Press.
(asynchronous conferencing)   This paper discusses and elaborates on the conceptual requirements as well as the tools of the General AMIGO Model for group communication. Features of the model are examined with particular reference to the social and ethical implications in the communication process. Applicability of the model is demonstrated by examples.

DE CINDIO, F., DE MICHELIS, F., SIMONE, C., VASSALLO, R. & ZANABONI, A. (1986). CHAOS as a coordination technology. In *Proceedings of the Conference on Computer-Supported Cooperative Work (CSCW '86)*, pp. 325–342. Austin, Texas, December 3–5, ACM Press.
(protocols)   Cooperation, to the extent that it is made up of communication and coordination, can be fully characterized under the assumption that an office is a special linguistic game, constituted by a set of rules defining the conversations possible within it, continuously changing under the perturbation created by the speech acts its members do performing the conversation. Within this context, the CHAOS prototype aims both at supporting the conversations and at improving coordination of the office activity.

DE KOVEN, C. & RADHAKRISHNAN, T. (1990). An experiment in distributed group problem solving. In S. GIBBS & A. A. VERRIGHN-STUART, Eds, *Proceedings of IFIP WG8.4 Conference on Multi-User Interfaces and Applications*, Crete. North Holland.

DELISLE, N. & SCHWARTZ, M. (1987). Contexts: A partitioning concept for hypertext. *ACM Trans Office Information Systems,* **5**(2). An earlier version appeared in CSCW '86.
(hypertext)   A hypertext system makes a good information management system for a software development environment. However, existing hypertext systems provide poor support for collaboration among members of the development teams. Authors examine several modes for forming partitions in a hypertext database and define a notion of "contexts", a partitioning scheme that supports multi-person cooperative efforts.

DESANCTIS, G. & GALLUPE, R. B. (1987). A Foundation for the Study of Group Decision Support Systems. *Management Science,* **33**(5), pp. 589–609, May.
(decision support, overview)   This paper presents a conceptual overview of group decision support systems based on an information-exchange perspective of decision making. Three levels of systems are described, representing varying degrees of intervention into the decision process.

DEWAN, P. (1991). Flexible user interface coupling in collaborative systems. In *ACM SIGCHI Conference on Human Factors in Computing Systems*. New Orleans, April 28–May 2, ACM Press.
(remote meetings, evaluation)   An important issue in collaborative systems is the kind of sharing or coupling among the various windows displaying a shared workspace (ie how and which components of the windows are shared across people). The paper describes an architecture to an interface toolkit supporting shared views that allows designers to express the degree of coupling between the interface components.

DOLLIMORE, J. & WILBUR, S. (1989). Experiences in building a configurable CSCW system. In *Proceedings of the 1st European Conference on Computer-Supported*

Cooperative Work (EC-CSCW '89), Gatwick, UK, September 13–15, Computer Sciences House, Slough, UK.

DOLLIMORE, J. R. T. & COULOURIS, G. (1990). Towards a language for defining structure in message-based cooperative work. In S. GIBBS & A. A. VERRIGHN-STUART, Eds, *Proceedings of IFIP WG8.4 Conference on Multi-User Interfaces and Applications*, Crete. North Holland.

DONGARRA, J. J. & GROSSE, E. (1987). Distribution of Mathematical Software Via Electronic Mail. *Comm ACM*, **30**(5), pp. 403–407, May.
(email, data sharing, implementation) This paper describes how distributed researchers can search for and retrieve items from a network library through NETLIB, a distribution system that handles requests made to it across an electronic mail system.

DYKSTRA, E. A. & CARASIK, R. P. (1991). Structure and support in cooperative environments: The Amsterdam Conversation Environment. *Int J Man Machine Studies*, **34**(3), pp. 419–434, March. In the special edition on CSCW & Groupware. Republished in Greenberg, 1991c.
(social impact, software design) Dykstra argues that while systems should nourish conversation and stimulate interaction amongst group participants, they should not directly regulate the actual meeting process. Instead, the technology should be supple enough to allow the group itself to define its own (perhaps changing) conventions, structures, and constraints. Several iterations of the Amsterdam Conversation Environment, a system supporting groupware as context, are described.

EC-CSCW (Ed.) (1989). Proceedings of the 1st European Conference on Computer-Supported Cooperative Work. Brunel Way, Slough, UK, SL1 1XL, Computer Sciences Company, Computer Sciences House. Conference took place September 13–15 at Gatwick, London, UK.
(collection) Session titles were: 1 Human sciences and empirical methods; 2 Applications; 3 Organizational issues in CSCW; 4 Underlying technologies; 5 General issues in CSCW. Proceedings available from Pam Knibb, Conference Secretariat at the above address.

EDS (1988). The Capture lab. EDS Centre for Machine Intelligence, Ann Arbor, Michigan. Videotape.
(face-to-face meetings, shared views) A video of what is perhaps the best-realized (but incredibly expensive) architecture for a face-to-face conferencing room—the Capture Lab.

EGIDO, C. (1988). Video conferencing as a technology to support group work: A review of its failures. In *Proceedings of the Conference on Computer-Supported Work (CSCW '88)*, pp. 13–24, Portland, Oregon, September 26–28, ACM Press.
(video, organizational concerns, remote meetings) There are only about 100 video conferencing (VC) sites world-wide, a figure that falls far short of the expected promise. Egido gives two main reasons for this failure. First, vendors gave VC an ill-conceived image as a replacement for face-to-face meetings. Second, VC is based on inadequate needs assessment methodologies. Most formal interactions are not suitable for video conferencing, and travel is not reduced. Rather, Egido notices that VC actually increases the physical face-to-face meetings, and argues that it is best viewed as a supplement, rather than a replacement of the normal meeting process.

EGIDO, C. (1990). Teleconferencing as a technology to support cooperative work: Its possibilities and limitations. In J. GALEGHER, R. E. KRAUT & C. EGIDO, Eds, *Intellectual Teamwork: Social Foundations of Cooperative Work*, pp. 351–372. Hillsdale, New Jersey: Lawrence Erlbaum Associates.
(remote meetings, video, evaluation) This paper covers the pitfalls of teleconferencing and video conferencing by reviewing and analysing existing literature. A spectrum of situations are identified where video conferencing succeeds, offers little, or outright fails.

ELLIS, C. (1989). CSCW '88 report. *ACM/SIGOIS Bulletin*, **10**(1), pp. 2–4, January.
(report) A brief trip report of the 1988 ACM Conference on Computer-Supported Cooperative Work, held in Portland.

ELLIS, C., GIBBS, S. J. & REIN, G. (1988a). Design and use of a group editor.

Technical report STP-263-88, MCC, Austin, Texas, September.
(idea processors, implementation, evaluation) GROVE is a prototype outline editor specifically designed for use by a group of people working simultaneously on the same text outline. It has been used in work sessions by several groups, both in face-to-face and distributed modes, for a variety of design tasks. This paper describes the function of GROVE and presents some of the important observations from these work sessions.

ELLIS, C., GIBBS, S. J. & REIN, G. (1988b). The Groupware project: An overview. Technical report STP-033-88, MCC, Austin, Texas, January.
(face-to-face meetings, implementation, experiment, critique) This paper is an overview of the Groupware Project at MCC. The goals and design philosophy of three prototype systems are presented, including: highlights of past work on Project Nick; a summary of key findings from an extensive empirical study of Project Nick; and brief descriptions of HyperMate, Liza, and Grove.

ELLIS, C. A., GIBBS, S. J. & REIN, G. L. (1991). Groupware: Some issues and experiences. *Comm. Acm,* **34**(1), pp. 38–58, January. (overview) A good overview of current CSCW.

ELLIS, C. & NUTT, G. (1980). Office information systems and computer science. *ACM Computing Surveys,* **12**(1), pp. 27–60. Reprinted in Greif, 1988.
(overview) This paper gives a general (although now dated) survey of computer science research in office information technology.

ENGELBART, D. (1963). A conceptual framework for the augmentation of man's intellect. In P. HOWERTON, Ed., *Vistas in Information Handling,* **1**, pp. 1–29. Washington, DC, Spartan Books. Reprinted in Greif, 1988.
(conceptual organizational concerns, social impact) Engelbart discusses his framework for understanding how human capabilities can be augmented through use of artifacts, language and training. Through a systems-engineering approach, he says that people and the computer system must be "designed together," so that people can incrementally master new skills.

ENGELBART, D. (1982). Towards high-performance knowledge workers. In *OAC '82 Digest: Proceedings of the 1982 AFIPS Office Automation Conference,* pp. 279–290, San Francisco, California, April 5–7. Reprinted in Greif, 1988.
(implementation, shared views, data-sharing, face-to-face meetings) This paper is an updated restatement of Engelbart's 1963 framework paper. He also includes an architectural overview of the NLS/Augment implementation.

ENGELBART, D. (1984). Authorship provisions in Augment. In *Proceedings of the IEEE Computer Society International Conference—CompCon.* Reprinted in Greif, 1988.
(implementation, shared workspace, data-sharing, face-to-face meetings) This is one of the several papers that discuss the implementation of the now-visionary Augment/NLS system.

ENGELBART, D. & ENGLISH, W. (1968). A research center for augmenting human intellect. In *Proceedings of the Fall Joint Computing Conference,* **33**, pp. 395–410, Montvale, NY, AFIPS Press. Reprinted in Greif, 1988.
(implementation, shared views, data-sharing, face-to-face meetings) This is one of the several papers that discuss the visionary Augment/NLS system.

ENGELBART, D. & LEHTMAN, H. (1988). Working together. *Byte,* December.
(implementation, shared workspace, data-sharing, face-to-face meetings) This paper gives a popular review of the NLS/Augment system, discussing it in terms of document development, production and control; research intelligence; community handbook development; computer-based instruction and shared screens; meeting and conferences; community management; and special knowledge work by individuals and teams.

ENGELBART, D. C. (1990). Knowledge-domain interoperability and an open hyper-document system. In *Proceedings of the Conference on Computer-Supported Co-operative Work (CSCW '90).* Los Angeles, California, October 7–10, ACM Press.
(organizational concerns, hypertext) This paper is concerned with the "interoperability

between knowledge domains", ie that knowledge in different fields (and in different forms) should be integrated within one coherent source. An "open hyperdocument system" is suggested as the backbone for interoperability. Issues concerned with this type of hypertext system are raised, and its essential elements provided.

ENGESTROM, Y., ENGESTROM, R. & SAARELMA, O. (1988). Computerized medical records, production pressure and compartmentalization in the work activity of health center physicians. In *Proceedings of the Conference on Computer-Supported Cooperative Work (CSCW '88)*, pp. 65–84. Portland, Oregon, September 26–28, ACM Press.
(participatory design, social impact)   This paper examines some aspects of communication between physicians in a group practice, focusing on the medical record as a communicative artifact. The role of computerized medical records are discussed in this light.

ENSOR, J. R. (1989). Rapport: A multimedia conferencing system. *The ACM SIGGRAPH Video Review Supplement to Computer Graphics,* **45**(5). ACM Press, Baltimore, MD. Videotape.
(remote meetings, shared views) This videotape illustrates the Rapport multimedia conferencing system.

ENSOR, J. R., AHUJA, S. R., HORN, D. N. & LUCCO, S. E. (1988). The Rapport multimedia conferencing system–a software overview. In *Proceedings of the 2nd IEEE Conference of Computer Workstations*, pp. 52–58. Santa Clara, March 7–10.
(remote meetings, shared views)   Rapport is a multimedia conferencing system that supports interactive, real-time, distributed conferences among two or more people. Rapport provides basic mechanisms to create, manage, and terminate conferences (data and voice is supported over the network). Existing programs can be shared. The paper discusses Rapport software: the user interface, the conference server, and its system levels.

ERICKSON, T. (1989). An eclectic look at CSCW '88. *ACM SIGCHI Bulletin,* **20**(5), pp. 56–64, July.
(report)   This report provides another review of ACM's 1988 CSCW conference, held in Portland, Oregon. In particular, Erickson looks at problems with existing systems in general and the Coordinator in particular, real world case studies, and laboratory prototypes.

EVELAND, J. D. & BIKSON, T. (1987). Evolving electronic communication networks: An empirical assessment. *Office: Technology and People,* **3**. An earlier version was published in CSCW '86.
(email, evaluation, organizational impact)   The paper presents the results of an analysis of the communication patterns that characterize The Rand Corporation's use of RandMail, its electronic messaging system. The goal of the work was to explore and assess the development of electronic messaging systems in the context of expanding use. A variety of quantitative properties of these communication networks are presented, including both sociometric structures and network metrics.

EVELAND, J. D. & BIKSON, T. K. (1988). Work group structures and computer support: A field experiment. In *Proceedings of the Conference on Computer-Supported Cooperative Work (CSCW '88)*, pp. 324–343. Portland, Oregon, September 26–28, ACM Press.
(evaluation, email)   This excellent study considered two slightly different groups in a natural office setting. Both groups comprised two types of people: normal employees who worked in the office, and ex-employees (retirees) who were usually at home. The overall interpretation is that email significantly and directly affects the outcomes and the process of cooperative work.

FAFCHAMPS, D., REYNOLDS, D. & KUCHINSKY, A. (1989). The dynamics of small group decision making over the e-mail channel. In *Proceedings of the 1st European Conference on Computer-Supported Cooperative Work (EC-CSCW '89)*, Gatwick, UK, September 13–15, Computer Sciences House, Slough, UK.
(asynchronous conferencing, evaluation)   A coding scheme was used to explore the dynamics of email discussions in a design team who used it for decision making support.

Findings suggest that discussions display similar group task activities but few group-centered strategies seen in face-to-face meetings; and that verbal devices may serve a different function when used in email discussions. The role of the discussion leader is raised.

FANNING, T. & RAPHAEL, B. (1986). Computer teleconferencing: Experience at Hewlett Packard. In *Proceedings of the Conference on Computer-Supported Cooperative Work (CSCW '86)*, pp. 291–306. Austin, Texas, December 3–5, ACM Press.

(asynchronous conferencing, evaluation, organizational concerns) This paper describes Hewlett-Packard's experience with the large-scale introduction and use of Confer, an asynchronous conferencing system. Discussed is its role in the corporate communications environment; some examples of prominent successes and failures; some heuristics for how to make the best of the technology; and some suggestions for future capabilities that would make such systems more widely useful.

FARALLON (1988). Timbuktu user's guide. Farallon Computing Inc., Berkely, California. User's manual.

(shared views) This manual describes Timbuktu, a system that allows geographically dispersed users to share views and serial interactions with their Macintosh-based application programs.

FELDMAN, M. (1987). Constraints on communication and electronic messaging. *Office: Technology and People*, **3**. An earlier version was published in CSCW '86.

(email, organizational concerns, evaluation) The author suggests that some new communication occurs in large organizations that have electronic mail, because it allows people to find other people with common interests at low cost to either party. This new communication creates links between people who would otherwise not share information. Granovetter's work on "weak ties" is discussed in this context.

FERWANGER, T., WANG, Y., LEWE, H. & KRCMAR, H. (1989). Experiences in designing the Hohenheim CATeam Room. In *Proceedings of the 1st European Conference on Computer-Supported Cooperative Work (EC-CSCW '89)*. Gatwick, UK, September 13–15, Computer Sciences House, Slough, UK.

FINHOLT, T., SPROULL, L. & KIESLER, S. (1990). Communication and performance in ad hoc task groups. In J. GALEGHER, R. E. KRAUT & C. EGIDO, Eds, *Intellectual Teamwork: Social Foundations of Cooperative Work*, pp. 291–326. Hillsdale, New Jersey: Lawrence Erlbaum Associates.

(email, evaluation, organizational concerns) The use of electronic mail in student work groups is evaluated, where groups had similar tasks but used email to different degrees. Groups that frequently used email out-performed those that did not, especially by making coordination easier. Further, email changes the pattern of work, not just the output of work. The paper speculates on the larger organizational implications.

FISH, R. S. (1989). Cruiser: A multi-media system for social browsing. *The ACM SIGGRAPH Video Review Supplement to Computer Graphics*, **45**(6). ACM Press, Baltimore, MD. Videotape.

(informal meetings, virtual hallways) This videotape describes the motivations behind, and the key features of the Cruiser interface, a system for creating audio and video links through a virtual hallway.

FISH, R. S., KRAUT, R. E. & CHALFONTE, B. L. (1990). The VideoWindow system in informal communications. In *Proceedings of the Conference on Computer-Supported Cooperative Work (CSCW '90)*, pp. 1–11. Los Angeles, California, October 7–10, ACM Press.

(video, informal meetings, virtual hallways, evaluation) VideoWindow is a very large screen, full duplex teleconferencing system used to support informal communication. The VideoWindow links two common rooms, allowing people in each area to communicate through it. The authors evaluate and discuss implications about the system in terms of transparency (how different it is from face-to-face), reciprocity (that people across the space can both see and hear each other), privacy, environmental context, social context, conversational regulation, and social relationships.

FOSTER, G. & STEFIK, M. (1986). Cognoter: Theory and practice of a Colab-orative tool. In *Proceedings of the Conference on Computer-Supported Cooperative Work (CSCW '86)*, pp. 7–15. Austin, Texas, December 3–5, ACM Press.
(idea processor, face-to-face meetings)   Cognoter is a program used in the Xerox CoLab that helps a cooperating group of people organize their thoughts for a presentation. It provides a multi-user interface and a structured meeting process. An annotated graph of ideas is built up by the group in three stages: brainstorming, ordering, evaluation.

GABARRO, J. J. (1990). The development of working relationships. In J. GALEGHER, R. E. KRAUT & C. EGIDO, Eds, *Intellectual Teamwork: Social Foundations of Cooperative Work*, pp. 79–110. Hillsdale, New Jersey: Lawrence Erlbaum Associates.
(social impact)   The paper describes both the affective and instrumental components of relationships with co-workers, focusing on the stages through which work relationships move and the establishment of trust among members of a work team. Elements underlying personal relationships that also apply to work relationships are also identified.

GALE, S. (1989). Adding audio and video to an office environment. In *Proceedings of the 1st European Conference on Computer-Supported Cooperative Work (EC-CSCW '89)*. Gatwick, UK, September 13–15, Computer Sciences House, Slough, UK.

GALEGHER, J., KRAUT, R. & EGIDO, C. (Eds) (1990a). Intellectual teamwork: Social and technological foundations of cooperative work. Hillsdale, NJ: Lawrence Erlbaum Associates.
(collection)   This important book of nineteen collected readings emphasizes intellectual teamwork. It covers the social and behavioural processes about groups and organizations, as well as the technological expertise required to build supporting systems. Chapter headings are: 1 Basic social processes; 2 Field studies of collaborative work; 3 Experiences with technology for cooperative work; and 4 Technology for cooperative work.

GALEGHER, J. & KRAUT, R. E. (1990b). Computer-mediated communication for intellectual teamwork: A field experiment in group writing. In *Proceedings of the Conference on Computer-Supported Cooperative Work (CSCW '90)*. Los Angeles, California, October 7–10, ACM Press.
(asynchronous conferencing, social impact, evaluation)   This paper is concerned with intellectual teamwork, where people work together over substantial periods of time to create information-intensive products. The variations of the members' needs over time suggest that different communication modalities may be useful at successive stages in the life of a long-term project. Computer-mediated communication (CMC) is often used for some of these stages. To access the utility of CMC for the various types and phases of intellectual teamwork, an experiment was conducted in which participants carried out complex collaborative writing project. Assessed were the effect of task divisibility and communication modality on work processes, group performance, and individual experiences, as well as the extent to which group members felt that the group was a viable and cohesive social identity.

GALEGHER, J. & KRAUT, R. E. (1990c). Technology for intellectual teamwork: Perspectives on research and design. In J. GALEGHER, R. E. KRAUT & C. EGIDO, Eds, *Intellectual Teamwork: Social Foundations of Cooperative Work*, pp. 1–20. Hillsdale, New Jersey: Lawrence Erlbaum Associates.
(overview, report)   This paper introduces Galegher, Kraut and Egido's 1990 book on Intellectual Teamwork. Social science knowledge about groups and organizations could be extremely valuable in designing tools to help people communicate and structure their work, yet this knowledge is under-used, for reasons presented in the paper. The authors recommend that social scientists should become actively and directly involved in design.

GARCIA-LUNA-ACEVES, J. J., CRAIGHILL, E. J. & LANG, R. (1988). An open-systems model for computer-supported collaboration. In *Proceedings of the 2nd IEEE Conference of Computer Workstations*, pp. 40–51. Santa Clara, March 7–10.
(shared view, decision support) In this paper, the authors explore the functions and structure of systems for CSCW; describe MOSAIC, a model for CSCW systems that provides, amongst other things, a shared view; and discuss a prototype designed to support collaborative decision making.

GARFINKEL, D., GUST, P., LEMON, M. & LOWDER, S. (1989). The SharedX multi-user interface user's guide, version 2.0. Research report STL-TM-89-07, Hewlett-Packard Laboratories, Palo Alto, California, March.
(shared views, implementation) SharedX is a multi-user environment that enables users to collaborate dynamically with others via their workstations. SharedX allows users to share existing X based applications by replicating the window interface among users. The system is described and some issues reported.

GARRETT, L. N., SMITH, K. & MEYROWITZ, N. (1986). Intermedia: Issues, strategies and tactics in the design of a hypermedia document system. In *Proceedings of the Conference on Computer-Supported Cooperative Work (CSCW '86)*, pp. 163–174. Austin, Texas, December 3–5, ACM Press.
(hypertex, multimedia) Hypermedia provides a tool for cooperative work by allowing writers and designers to share a network of linked documents where they can create documents, link their own and others' documents together, and leave notes for one another. This paper discusses issues that designers need to address in the development of hypermedia, eg what kind of linking, contexts, and visual modeling the system provides. A variety of solutions are presented, including the ones implemented in Intermedia.

GASPAROTTI, P. & SIMONE, C. (1990). A user defined environment for handling conversations. In S. GIBBS & A. A. VERRIGHN-STUART, Eds, *Proceedings of IFIP WG8.4 Conference on Multi-User Interfaces and Applications*, Crete. North Holland.

GERRISSEN, J. F. & DAAMEN, J. (1990a). Inclusion of a 'sharing' feature in telecommunication services. In *13th International Symposium HFT '90 Human Factors in Telecommunications*. Torino, Italy, September 10–14.
(shared workspace, remote meetings, evaluation) This paper contrasts human performance and communicative behaviour when using a shared fused video workspace (where participants have a shared work and gestural space) versus a traditional videophone setting (where participants can only see the others work space and gestures, but cannot share it). The workspace stimulated patterns of communicative expressions and employment of multimodal information exchange which are present in face-to-face situations but absent in traditional telecommunication use.

GERRISSEN, J. F., ITEGEM, J. V. & DAAMEN, J. (1990b). Simple-Simon's GesturePad: A puppet for added expressiveness in communication and interaction. In *SIGCHI'90: Conference on Human Factors in Computing Systems*. Seattle, Washington, April 1–5. Poster presentation.
(shared workspace, remote meetings) The authors describe how a limited number of on-screen hand postures (gestures) can be invoked from a keypad. The gestures not only add a few interaction techniques to the interface, but are also useful for supporting computer-mediated communication between people, for example remote sharing of a workspace.

GIBBS, S. & VERRIGHN-STUART, A. A. (Eds) (1990). Proceedings of IFIP WG8.4 Conference on Multi-User Interfaces and Applications (Crete). Amsterdam, North Holland.
(collection) Session titles included: 1 Multi-user interface design; 2 Cooperative development of software; 3 Shared environments; 4 Desktop conferencing and multi-user editing; 5 Messaging; 6 Experiences with multi-user applications; and 7 Coordination.

GIBBS, S. J. (1989). LIZA: An extensible groupware toolkit. In *Proceedings of the SIGCHI Human Factors in Computing Systems*, pp. 29–35. Austin, Texas, April 30–May 4, ACM Press.

(remote meetings, shared workspace) This paper presents a model of group tools based on active objects. The model has been applied to the design and implementation of an extensible groupware toolkit known as LIZA. The architecture and group tools available in LIZA are described, and multi-user design problems noted.

GOODMAN, G. & ABEL, M. (1987a). Collaboration research in SCL. *Office: Technology and People,* **3**. An earlier version was published in CSCW '86.
(remote meetings, evaluation) This paper reports on the second year of Xerox PARC's investigation of the support and enhancement of collaboration, with emphasis on the two-site distributed organization of the System Concepts Laboratory (the Portland Experiment).

GOODMAN, G. & ABEL, M. (1987b). Communication and collaboration: Facilitating cooperative work through communication. *Office: Technology and People,* **3**(2), pp. 129–146.
(informal meetings, video, virtual hallways) This report describes the Xerox video wall between Portland and Palo Alto.

GORRY, G. A., BURGER, A. M., CHANEY, R. J., LONG, K. B. & TAUSK, C. M. (1988). Computer Support for Biomedical Work Groups. In *Proceedings of the Conference on Computer-Supported Cooperative Work (CSCW '88),* pp. 39–51. Portland, Oregon, September 26–28, ACM Press.
(semi-structured messages, hypertext) The paper examined how members of a biomedical research group could coordinate efforts and share information. The authors' aim is to allow a researcher to scan, filter and manage information, to use the information for decision-making, and to disseminate it to the rest of the team and to outsiders through a "web" of interactions. In their implementation, users can structure or filter their information and their collaborations through sets of templates (structured messages), each tailored to fit a task. Templates exist, for example, for searching on-line medical databases and for sending and selectively receiving mail. Through templates, a uniform interface is created between group members and sources of information. Furthermore, all information can be pasted and presented in a hypertext system which allows its users to share information to the degree appropriate to their activities.

GOULD, J. D. & BOIES, S. J. (1983). Human factors challenges in creating a principal support office system—The speech filing system approach. *ACM Trans Office Information Systems,* **1**(4), pp. 273–298. Also published in Baecker & Buxton, 1987.
(email, multimedia) This paper describes the key behavioural challenges in designing the speech filing system, a voice store and forward message system with which users compose, edit, send, and receive audio messages using telephones as terminals.

GOULD, J. D. & BOIES, S. J. (1984). Speech filing—An office system for principles. *IBM Systems Journal,* **23**(1), pp. 65–81. Also published in Baecker & Buxton, 1987.
(email, multimedia, social impact) This paper describes the purpose behind the speech filing system and its user interface.

GRAY, P. (1987). Group Decision Support Systems. *Decision Support Systems (North-Holland),* **(3)**, pp. 233–242.
(decision support, face-to-face meetings, overview) The paper focuses on one type of group decision support system, a decision room in which computers and communications are used by participants during their deliberations. The paper introduces the concepts of private work, public screen, and chauffeur. It also reports on the experimental evidence of use, with special attention given to the potential of using gaming.

GREENBAUM, J. (1988). In search of cooperation: An historical analysis of work organization and management strategies. In *Proceedings of the Conference on Computer-Supported Cooperative Work (CSCW '88),* pp. 102–114. Portland, Oregon, September 26–28, ACM Press.
(participatory design, social impact) Greenbaum offers a historical perspective of work organization and management strategies. In essence, she argues that the Scandinavian view of user participation in the design process is part of building democracy in the

workplace. She indicates two central issues in the move to workplace democracy. First, democracy needs to be viewed as active participation in planning and decision-making, thus making worker involvement far more than techniques for improved human–computer interfaces. Second, CSCW means that computer systems need to reinforce forms of cooperation that enhance the chance for a more democratic workplace. For example, information flow in a CSCW application could emphasize lateral movement, as opposed to the top-down flow through authority normally seen in management. Planning functions could then move from current rule-based bureaucratic realms to situations where groups assume the stronger role.

GREENBERG, S. (1989). The 1988 Conference on Computer-Supported Cooperative Work: Trip Report. *ACM SIGCHI Bulletin,* **20**(5), pp. 49–55, July. Also published in Canadian Artificial Intelligence, Volume 19, April.
(report)   This report provides a comprehensive review of ACM's 1988 CSCW conference, held in Portland, Oregon.

GREENBERG, S. (1990a). Feasibility study of a national high speed communications network for research and development: Future applications. Research Report, Learning and Collaboration Group, Advanced Computing and Engineering Department, Alberta Research Council, Calgary, Alberta.
(overview)   This report is part of a large study investigating the feasibility of a national high speed communications network supporting researchers and developers. It emphasizes the future applications made of this network, with much discussion of the many different kinds of CSCW-styles of applications. Some of its sections are: computer support for real-time remote conferencing; casual real-time interaction; asynchronous messaging; bulletin boards and asynchronous conferencing; access and operation of distributed resources; digital libraries, and application areas.

GREENBERG, S. (1990b). Sharing views and interactions with single-user applications. In *Proceedings of the ACM/IEEE Conference on Office Information Systems*, pp. 227–237. Cambridge, Massachusetts, April 25–27.
(shared views, overview, implementation)   This report discusses several roles and responsibilities of view-sharing software that must be considered during its design and evaluation: view management, floor control, conference registration by participants, and handling of meta-level communications. A brief survey of existing shared view systems is provided, and several innovative new directions are described.

GREENBERG, S. (1991a). An annotated bibliography of computer supported co-operative work. *SIGCHI Bulletin*, July and in Greenberg (1991c). Continually updated versions are available as Research Report, Dept of Computer Science, University of Calgary, Calgary, Alberta.
(overview, report)   This report provides a bibliography of computer supported cooperative work. Most of the over 300 entries are annotated with a brief description derived from snippets from the original abstract, personal notes, and from commentaries written by other people. Annotations also include a keyword list for topic disambiguation. The report also includes an overview of the general sources that publish CSCW works. A list of groupware systems and concepts are listed and indexed to the bibliography.

GREENBERG, S. (1991b). Computer supported cooperative work and groupware: An introduction to the special edition. *Int J Man Machine Studies,* **34**(2), pp. 133–143, February. In the special edition on CSCW & Groupware. Republished in Greenberg, 1991.
(collection, overview)   This article introduces a special edition on CSCW and groupware (published across two journal numbers). CSCW and groupware are introduced and an overview of the sixteen articles is provided. A "further readings and sources" section is included. See Greenberg, 1991c.

GREENBERG, S. (Ed.) (1991c). Computer supported cooperative work and groupware. A book in the *Computer and People Series*. London: Academic Press.
(collection)   This edited book contains the following articles, most of which were originally published in the February/March 1991 issues of the *International Journal of Man Machine*

Studies special edition on CSCW and groupware. (1) Computer-supported cooperative work and groupware, Greenberg; (2) Findings from observational studies of collaborative work, Tang; (3) Twinkling lights and nested loops: distributed problem solving and spreadsheet development, Nardi; (4) Design for conversation: lessons from Cognoter, Tatar; (5) The Portland Experience: a report on a distributed research group, Olson; (6) Power, ease of use and cooperative work in a practical multimedia message system, Borenstein; (7) Electronic meeting support: the GroupSystems concept, Valacich; (8) Computer-mediated communication, de-individuation, and group decision-making, Lea; (9) Conversational flexibility in a computer conference used in professional education, Weedman; (10) Multidimensional audio window management, Cohen; (11) Liveware: a new approach to sharing data in social networks, Witten; (12) rIBIS: a real-time group hypertext system, Rein; (13) Modelling groupware in the electronic office, Cook; (14) Post-mechanistic groupware primitives: rhythms, boundaries and containers, Johnson-Lenz; (15) Structure and support in cooperative environments: the Amsterdam Conversation Environment, Dykstra; (16) Obstacles to user involvement in software product development, with implications for CSCW, Grudin; (17) Cooperative prototyping: users and designers in mutual activity, Bødker; (18) An annotated bibliography of computer-supported cooperative work, Greenberg.

GREENBERG, S. (1991d). Personalizable groupware: Accommodating individual roles and group differences. To be published in *Proceedings of the 2nd European Conference on Computer Supported Cooperative Work (EC-CSCW '91)*, Amsterdam. Also available as Research Report 90/404/28, Dept of Computer Science, University of Calgary, Alberta, Canada.
(conceptual, shared views) For groupware to be considered successful, it must be usable and acceptable by every member of the group. Yet the differences present between group members—their varying roles, needs, skills—and the differences between groups are a serious obstacle to achieving uniform acceptance of the groupware product, especially when the product treats all people and groups identically. This paper discusses the consequences that may occur as a result of not accommodating individual differences, and then offers a possible solution to the problem. First, instances of groupware failure are described: the inability of the group to reach a critical mass; the unequal accessibility of the groupware by participants; the failure to accommodate the different roles participants may play; the failure to balance the work done against the benefits received; and the failure of groupware to evolve with the needs of the group. Second, the notion of *personalizable groupware* is proposed, defined as a system whose behaviour can be altered to match the particular needs of group participants and of each group as a whole. Finally, the paper presents a working example of personalized groupware. *Share* is a shared screen system that offers its users a flexible choice of floor control models to help them mediate their interactions with the shared application.

GREENBERG, S. & BOHNET, R. (1991). GroupSketch: A multi-user sketchpad for geographically-distributed small groups. In *Proceedings of Graphics Interface '91*, Calgary, Alberta, July. Also available as Research report 90/414/38, Dept of Computer Science, University of Calgary, Alberta, Canada.
(shared workspace, implementation, evaluation) A workstation-based tool called Group-Sketch has been developed that allows a small geographically-distributed group to list, draw, and gesture simultaneously in a communal work surface, supporting interactions similar to those occurring in the face-to-face process. The design principles behind GroupSketch are discussed as well as the architecture of its implementation. Observations of use indicated that people use GroupSketch in much the same way they use face-to-face communal sketchpads.

GREENBERG, S. & CHANG, E. (1989). Computer support for real time collaborative work. In *Proceedings of the Conference on Numerical Mathematics and Computing*. Winnipeg, Manitoba, September 28–30. Available in Congressus Numerantium vol 74 and 75.
(overview, face-to-face meetings) A large portion of an office worker's time involves real time collaboration with fellow associates. Many traditional tools assist this process, such

as telephones, meeting rooms, specialized media such as whiteboards, and so on. This
paper is concerned with the potential of the computer as a tool to further enhance the
group work process through direct support of real time communication needs and the
specific collaboration requirements of the group. General computer support for four styles
of real-time interactions are distinguished and surveyed: 1) face-to-face meetings; 2) remote
conferencing; 3) casual real time interaction; and 4) multi-user applications. Each topic is
introduced, motivations discussed, and the key technical systems and related research
described.

GREIF, I. (1988). *Computer-supported cooperative work: A book of readings*, Morgan
Kaufmann Publishers Inc: San Mateo, California.
(collection)   This book is perhaps the best collection of previously-published (and
sometimes hard to get) papers on computer-supported cooperative work. The book is
divided into three major parts: visions and first steps; new technologies for CSCW; and
CSCW design theories.

GREIF, I. & SARIN, S. (1987). Data sharing in group work. *ACM Trans Office
Information Systems*, **5**(2), pp. 187–211, April. Reprinted in Greif, 1988. An
earlier version appeared in CSCW '86.
(data sharing)   This paper discusses issues in data sharing in group work from a data
management requirements. Support technologies range from conventional data base
management systems for regular information to object management systems for irregular
information storage and retrieval. This paper examines the data management requirements
of group work applications on the basis of experience with three prototype systems—two
calendar systems and one collaborative document editing system. Unresolved issues of
access control and concurrency are raised.

GRUDIN, J. (1988a). Perils and pitfalls. *Byte*, December.
(critique, organizational concerns)   Grudin describes the perils and pitfalls of groupware
design. In particular he describes why applications can fail. This paper is a popular version
of the excellent one presented in the 1988 CSCW conference and his 1988 MCC technical
report.

GRUDIN, J. (1988b). Why CSCW applications fail: Problems in the design and
evaluation of organizational interfaces. In *Proceedings of the Conference on
Computer-Supported Cooperative Work (CSCW '88) (CSCW '88)*, pp. 85–93.
Portland, Oregon, September 26–28, ACM Press.
(critique, organizational concerns)   Grudin discusses why CSCW applications fail. First,
there is a disparity between those who will benefit from a CSCW application and those
who must do additional work to support it. Second, there is a decision-making failure that
leads to ill-fated development efforts, due to the lack of management intuition for these
applications. Third, there is a failure to learn from actual experience because it is extremely
difficult to evaluate these applications. Grudin suggests that we must be aware of these
problems if we are to overcome them.

GRUDIN, J. (1989a). CSCW '88: Report on the conference and review of the
proceedings. *ACM SIGCHI Bulletin*, **20**(4), pp. 80–84.
(report)   A review of ACM's 1988 CSCW conference, held in Portland, Oregon.

GRUDIN, J. (1989b). Why groupware applications fail: Problems in design and
evaluation. *Office: Technology and People*, **4**(3), pp. 245–264.
(critique, organizational concerns)   Grudin describes three reasons why groupware
applications can fail. This paper is an expanded version of the excellent one presented in
the 1988 CSCW conference. See also his December 1988 Byte article.

GRUDIN, J. (1990a). Groupware and cooperative work: Problems and prospects. In
B. LAUREL, Ed., *The art of human–computer interface design*, pp. 171–185.
Reading, Massachusetts: Addison-Wesley.
(overview, critique)   The first half of the chapter describes problems that have led to
expensive, repeated failures of groupware development efforts. In the second half, a
groupware success story demonstrates the importance of focusing our analysis on the work
setting and provides a basis for speculating about the future.

GRUDIN, J. (1990b). interface. In *Proceedings of the Conference on Computer-Supported Cooperative Work (CSCW '90)*. Los Angeles, California, October 7–10, ACM Press.

(critique) This is an essay on the "user interface" to a computer and "the computer interface" to a user or users. It also addresses a "user's or group's interface" to a computer and a "computer's interface" to a user or users. After noting the further distinction of users' interfaces to their work, it concludes with a discussion of "the designer" and designers' "models of users." A delightful essay on what is really meant or implied by interface terminology.

GRUDIN, J. (1991a). CSCW: The convergence of two disciplines. In *ACM SIGCHI Conference on Human Factors in Computing Systems*, New Orleans, April 28–May 2, ACM Press.

(conceptual, social impact) This essay provides an excellent discussion/review of the CSCW field, its early roots and derivations, what it is and isn't, and how it is perceived by today's community. In particular, CSCW is discussed as the convergence of two development disciplines, one concerned with small-groups, and the other with large systems. It provides a much-needed perspective on the CSCW "paradigm".

GRUDIN, J. (1991b). Obstacles to user involvement in software product development, with implications to CSCW. *Int J Man Machine Studies,* **34**(3), pp. 435–452, March. In the special edition on CSCW & Groupware. Republished in Greenberg, 1991c.

(participatory design, organizational concerns, software design) While participatory design has generally succeeded for software development targetted to producing systems specific to an in-house organizational context, it has not really been applied to product development organizations that design mass-produced off-the-shelf products. Grudin suggests that in spite of the benefits participatory design may offer for improving a system interface (particularly for groupware systems), there are several serious obstacles to user involvement. Most stem from organizational structures and development practices that arose prior to the current market for interactive systems.

GRUDIN, J. (1991c). A tale of two cities: Reflections on CSCW in Europe and the United States. *SIGCHI Bulletin*, July.

(report) This essay contrasts ideas about CSCW in Europe and in America by focusing on the different viewpoints in the EC-CSCW and the ACM CSCW conference.

GUST, P. (1988). SX: An experiment with using shared windows to support cooperative work. Hewlett-Packard Laboratories, California, February. Unpublished draft.

(shared views, implementation) This is an early draft paper on the SharedX window system.

GUST, P. (1989). Multi-user interfaces for extended group collaboration. In *Proceedings of the Groupware Technology Workshop*. Xerox PARC, Palo Alto, California, August.

(shared views) Gust describes SharedX in the context of a venue-agile system.

GUTEK, B. A. (1990). Work group structure and information technology: A structural contingency approach. In J. GALEGHER, R. E. KRAUT & C. EGIDO, Eds, *Intellectual Teamwork: Social Foundations of Cooperative Work*, pp. 63–78. Hillsdale, New Jersey: Lawrence Erlbaum Associates.

(organizational concerns, social impact) Structural contingency theory, which suggests that an effective organization or work group must fit its technology to the structure of its tasks, can be used to guide research on computer use in cooperative work. The theory is explained and used as a framework for analysing the influence of information technology on work group effectiveness.

GUTTMANN, S. (1989). Farallon: Building the ultimate network. *MicroTimes,* **6**(7), July.

(implementation) Steve Guttman interviews Reese Jones of Farallon Inc. Jones discusses cheap networking on PC's, the screen/sound recorder, multimedia, and groupware via shared views in the Timbuktu program.

HAHN, U., JARKE, M., KREPLIN, K. & FARUSI, M. (1989). CoAUTHOR: A hypermedia group authoring environment. In *Proceedings of the 1st European Conference on Computer-Supported Cooperative Work (EC-CSCW '89)*. Gatwick, UK, September 13–15, Computer Sciences House, Slough, UK.

HAHN, U., JARKE, M. & ROSE, T. (1990). Group work in software projects. In S. GIBBS & A. A. VERRIGHN-STUART, Eds, *Proceedings of IFIP WG8.4 Conference on Multi-User Interfaces and Applications*, Crete. North Holland.

HALASZ, F. G. (1988). Reflections on Notecards: Seven issues for the next generation of hypermedia systems. *Comm ACM,* **31**(7), pp. 836–852, July.
(hypertext, multimedia)   This article presents NoteCards as a foil against which to explore some of the major limitations of the current generation of hypermedia systems, and characterizes the issues that must be addressed in designing the next generation systems.

HALONEN, D., HORTON, M., KASS, R. & SCOTT, P. (1989). Shared hardware: A novel technology for computer support of face to face meetings. In *Proceedings of the Groupware Technology Workshop*. Xerox PARC, Palo Alto, California, August 24–25. Also available as Report CMI-89-015, Center for Machine Intelligence, Ann Arbor, MI.
(face-to-face meetings, shared views)   The Capture Lab supports a shared hardware approach to groupware where meeting participants with their own private machines can access and transfer material to a public computer whose screen is being displayed at the front of a room. Advantages and limitation of this simple approach are briefly described.

HARPER, R. R., HUGHES, J. A. & SHAPIRO, D. Z. (1989). Working in harmony: An examination of computer technology in air traffic control. In *Proceedings of the 1st European Conference on Computer-Supported Cooperative Work (EC-CSCW '89)*. Gatwick, UK, September 13–15, Computer Sciences House, Slough, UK.

HARRISON, S. (1989). The office design project. *The ACM SIGGRAPH Video Review Supplement to Computer Graphics,* **45**(4). Videotape.
(informal meetings)   This videotape illustrates a team of three architects collaborating together over a video/audio/computing link.

HARRISON, W., OSSHER, H. & SWEENEY, P. (1990). Coordinating concurrent development. In *Proceedings of the Conference on Computer-Supported Cooperative Work (CSCW '90)*. Los Angeles, California, October 7–10, ACM Press.
Development of any large system or artifact requires coordination of many developers who often work concurrently. The goal of coordination is to enhance, not restrict, developer productivity while ensuring that concurrent development activities do not clash with each other. The paper presents a formal model of concurrent development, where development consists of a collection of modification activities that change files, and merges that combine the changes. The notion of coordination consistency ensures that changes are not inadvertently destroyed and that changes are correctly propagated to subsequent modification activities.

HART, P. & ESTRIN, D. (1990). Computer integration: A co-requirement for effective inter-organization computer network implementation. In *Proceedings of the Conference on Computer-Supported Cooperative Work (CSCW '90)*. Los Angeles, California, October 7–10, ACM Press.
(organizational concerns)   Inter-organization networks (IONs) provide significant opportunities for improving coordination between firms engaged in mutually dependent activities. The paper focuses on how IONs affect information processing requirements, and production and transaction costs when they interconnect firms with internally integrated computer systems and when they are used only as substitutes for conventional media.

HASLETT, B. (1987). Structural pragmatics: Managing conversations. In *Communication: Strategic Action in Context*, pp. 47–72. Hillsdale, New Jersey: Lawrence Erlbaum Associates.

(social impact) This chapter focuses on casual conversation. In particular, it discusses how we manage conversations successfully, with emphasis placed on turntaking.

HEATH, C. & LUFF, P. (1991). Disembodied conduct: Communication through video in a multi-media environment. In *ACM SIGCHI Conference on Human Factors in Computing Systems*. New Orleans, April 28–May 2, ACM Press.
(informal meetings, video, evaluation) Authors discuss findings concerning the organization of video-mediated communication in collaborative work in a dispersed, multi-media office environment. They describe the ways in which the technology transforms nonverbal and verbal conduct, introducing certain asymmetries into the social interaction between users. It is argued that such communicative asymmetries may facilitate, rather than hinder, certain forms of collaborative work.

HELLMAN, R. (1990). User support: Illustrating computer use in collaborative work contexts. In *Proceedings of the Conference on Computer-Supported Cooperative Work (CSCW '90)*. Los Angeles, California, October 7–10, ACM Press.
(organizational concerns, hypertext) It is relevant for users of a computerized information system to perceive the organizational context of collaborative work and corresponding information process. A theoretical framework for the realization of a context support system is presented, with four types of modules: images of information media; descriptions of jobs composed of task lattices; illustrations of physical work units; and visualizations of databases. Hypermedia is used as a potential implementation environment.

HENNESSY, P. (1989). Information domains in CSCW. In *Proceedings of the 1st European Conference on Computer-Supported Cooperative Work (EC-CSCW '89)*. Gatwick, UK, September 13–15, Computer Sciences House, Slough, UK.

HILTZ, S. R. (1988). Collaborative learning in a virtual classroom: Highlights of findings. In *Proceedings of the Conference on Computer-Supported Cooperative Work (CSCW '88)*, pp. 282–290. Portland, Oregon, September 26–28, ACM Press.
(education, evaluation) Hiltz describes a "virtual classroom." Goals included improving access and effectiveness of college-level courses through collaborative learning. On average, students report a better learning experience.

HOLAND, U. & DANIELSON, T. (1989). The psychology of cooperation – Consequences of descriptions, the power of creative diaglogues. In *Proceedings of the 1st European Conference on Computer-Supported Cooperative Work (EC-CSCW '89)*. Gatwick UK, September 13–15, Computer Sciences House, Slough, UK.

HUTCHINS, E. (1990). The technology of team navigation. In J. GALEGHER, R. E. KRAUT & C. EGIDO, Eds, *Intellectual Teamwork: Social Foundations of Cooperative Work*, pp. 191–220. Hillsdale, New Jersey: Lawrence Erlbaum Associates.
(social impact, organizational concerns) This paper provides a specific instance of intellectual teamwork: team navigation on board of ships. For example, the physical layout of the control room provides opportunity for crew members to observe each other at work, contributing to partial redundancy in their knowledge of each others work and maintenance of the group over time.

ISHII, H. (1990a). Cross-cultural communication and Computer Supported Cooperative Work. In H. RHEINGOLD, Ed., *Whole Earth Review*, pp. 48–52. Sausalito, California.
(social impact) This essay argues that groupware produces "cultural tools" that embody the protocol of a culture. Ishii argues that we should try to understand the nature of cross-cultural communication and to design systems to facilitate the cross-cultural communication process.

ISHII, H. (1990b). Message-driven groupware design based on office procedure model: OM-1. Research report, NTT, Yokosuka-Shi, Kanagawa, Japan, June. Reprinted from the Journal of Information Processing, Information Processing Society, Japan.
(organizational concerns) A design methodology for asynchronous groupware is proposed

that can control and keep track of the progress of cooperative tasks among office workers who are geographically distributed. The methodology is based on COOKBOOK: cooperative work support based on organizational knowledge.

ISHII, H. (1990c). TeamWorkStation: Towards a seamless shared space. In *Proceedings of the Conference on Computer-Supported Cooperative Work (CSCW '90)*, pp. 13–26. Los Angeles, California, October 7–10, ACM Press.
(shared workspace, video, remote meetings, implementation) Team WorkStation is a real-time shared workspace. Its key ideas are the overlay of individual workspace video images and the creation of a shared drawing surface. Because each co-worker can continue to use his/her favorite application programs in the virtual shared workspace, the cognitive discontinuity between individual and shared spaces is greatly reduced. The technique of fusing workspaces is also described and compared with other approaches.

ISHII, H. & ARITA, K. (1991a). ClearFace: Translucent multiuser interface for TeamWorkstation. Research report, NTT Human Interface Laboratories, Kanagawa, Japan, January. Submitted to EC-CSCW '91.
(shared workspace, video, remote meetings, implementation) Because of the limitation of screen size, it is hard to secure space for a shared drawing window large enough for effective use on one screen together with all face windows of the group members. A new solution, called ClearFace, is proposed, where translucent face windows are overlayed onto shared workspace windows. ClearFace is implemented in the TeamWorkstation prototype.

ISHII, H. & MIYAKE, N. (1991b). TeamWorkStation: Towards an open shared workspace. Submitted to *Comm ACM*. Also available from NTT Human Interface Labs, Kanagawa, Japan.
(shared workspace, video, remote meetings, implementation) This paper integrates the CSCW '90 and IFIP WG8.4 Conference papers on TeamWorkstation.

ISHII, H. & OHKUBO, M. (1990a). Design of TeamWorkstation: A realtime shared workspace fusing desktops and computer screen. In S. GIBBS & A. A. VERRIGHN-STUART, Eds, *Proceedings of IFIP WG8.4 Conference on Multi-User Interfaces and Applications*, Crete. North Holland.
(shared workspace, implementation) Another in the series of articles describing Team Workstation.

ISHII, T., KUZUOKA, H., TAKAHARA, T. & MYOI, T. (1990b). Collaboration system for manufacturing system in the 21st century. In *International Conference on Manufacturing Systems and Environment*. Tokyo, Japan, May 28–June 2, Japan Society of Mechanical Engineers. Submitted.
(video, remote meetings, implementation) Voice and video tools for informal communication between geographicaly distributed sites are described. Discussions include: superimposing a mouse cursor on a TV monitor and sharing a field of vision. A software toolkit to support groupware development is also offered.

JACKSON, S. L. (1989). Hypertext for computer conferencing. Research Report STL-89-8, Hewlett-Packard Laboratories, Palo Alto, California, June. From an MIT Master's thesis.
(asynchronous conferencing, hypertext, evaluation) This thesis proposes that a hypertext interface be used to represent the messages in a computer conferencing system, with links connecting messages and replies. A prototype system called Banyan was designed and tested.

JARRELL, N. F. & BARRETT, B. (1986). Network-based systems for asynchronous group communication. In *Proceedings of the Conference on Computer-Supported Cooperative Work (CSCW '86)*, pp. 184–191. Austin, Texas, December 3–5, ACM Press.
(asynchronous conferencing, multimedia, implementation) This paper presents an architecture for a network-based system that models communication as group access to shared multimedia objects. It also describes the features of a computer conferencing system that was implemented for Bitnet.

JOHANSEN, R. (1988). *Groupware: Computer Support for Business Teams*, The Free Press, Macmillan Inc.; New York.
(overview, collection) A very readable layman's book detailing current approaches and applications of groupware to business teams. Still the best introduction to the groupware area now available.

JOHANSEN, R. (1989). Groupware: Future Direction and Wild Cards. In *Proceedings of the Conference on Organizational Computing, Coordination and Collaboration*, Austin, Texas, November 13–14, 1989.
(conceptual) This paper offers Johansen's personal speculations on where groupware is going over the next five years.

JOHANSEN, R. & BULLEN, C. (1984). Thinking ahead: What to expect from teleconferencing. *Harvard Business Review*, pp. 4–10, March/April. Reprinted in Greif, 1988.
(remote meetings, asynchronous conferencing, overview, critique, video) Several remote conferencing installations are reviewed and technologies discussed: audio, still video, text, full-motion video, and live video. Some benefits of using these restricted modes over face-to-face meetings are provided. However, the impact of these technologies has not been as great as the authors expected.

JOHNSON, B. M., WEAVER, G. M., OLSON, M., DUNHAM, R. & McGONAGILL, G. (1986). Using a computer based tool to support collaboration: A field experiment. In *Proceedings of the Conference on Computer-Supported Cooperative Work (CSCW '86)*, pp. 343–352, Austin, Texas, December 3–5, ACM Press.
(email, evaluation, organizational concerns) This report describes a field experiment which focuses on the adaptation in work practices when groups of people are introduced to electronic communication tools (email) to support their collaborative work.

JOHNSON-LENZ, P. & JOHNSON-LENZ, T. (1991). Post-mechanistic groupware primitives: rhythms, boundaries and containers. *Int J Man Machine Studies*, **34**(3), pp. 385–418, March. In the special edition on CSCW & Groupware. Republished in Greenberg, 1991c.
(software design, social impact) Today's approach to groupware is mechanistic, ie based upon some social theory of human interaction or task-oriented approach that can be modelled by a machine. This article considers a "post-mechanistic" approach, where the model of group behaviour is not rigidly codified into the system but evolves with the group. An implementation considered post-mechanistic is described. It is particularly intriguing not only for technical reasons, but because the subject domain is "self-help", a far cry from the usual business-oriented applications emphasized by developers.

JOINER, R. & BLAYE, A. (1989). Mechanisms of cognitive change in peer interaction: Implications for the design of computer supported cooperative learning environments. In *Proceedings of the 1st European Conference on Computer-Supported Cooperative Work (EC-CSCW '89)*, Gatwick, UK, September 13–15, Computer Sciences House, Slough, UK.

KARBE, B. & RAMSPERGER, N. (1990). Influence of exception handling on the support of cooperative office work. In S. GIBBS & A. A. VERRIGHN-STUART, Eds, *Proceedings of IFIP WG8.4 Conference on Multi-User Interfaces and Applications*, Crete. North Holland.

KASS, R., BARNHART, G., DIMERCURIO, M., GOTTS, J. & SCOTT, P. (1989). InVision: Augmenting communication in a large organization by modelling Its Members. In *Proceedings of the Fourth Annual Rocky Mountain Conference on Artificial Intelligence*. Also available as technical report CMI-89-004. Center for Machine Intelligence, Ann Arbor, Michigan.
InVision is a project that focuses on improving the coordination of work in a large organization by modelling the knowledge and information needs of its members. A "Yellow Pages" service is used to indicate which individuals in the organization are knowledgeable about particular parts. The model can be exploited by a mail routing system to help direct and filter messages that potentially affect individuals in a wide range of jobs.

KEDZIERSKI, B. (1982). Communication and management support in system development environments. In *Proceedings of the ACM SIGCHI Conference on Human Factors in Computer Systems*, pp. 163–168. Gaithersburg, MD, March 15–17. Reprinted in Greif, 1988.
(protocols)   Speech acts are specialized to recognize the communications between people when developing and maintaining a software system.

KEISLER, S., SIEGEL, J. & McGUIRE, T. W. (1984). Social psychological aspects of computer-mediated communication. *American Psychologist, 39*, pp. 1123–1134. Reprinted in Greif, 1988.
(evaluation, asynchronous conferencing)   This paper looks at the application of social science methods to research the issues raised by computing and technological change. Their own study of a computer-mediated system is described.

KNISTER, M. J. & PRAKASH, A. (1990). DistEdit: A distributed toolkit for supporting multiple group editors. In *Proceedings of the Conference on Computer-Supported Cooperative Work (CSCW '90)*. Los Angeles, California, October 7–10, ACM Press.
(software design, implementation)   DistEdit is a toolkit for building applications that support collaboration between people in distributed environments. In particular, it allows one to build interactive group editors and has the ability to support different editors simultaneously. The toolkit allows existing single user editors to be modified slightly to become a multi-user system.

KOSZAREK, J. L., LINDSTROM, T. L., ENSOR, J. R. & AHUJA, S. R. (1990). A multi-user document review tool. In S. GIBBS & A. A. VERRIGHN-STUART, Eds, *Proceedings of IFIP WG8.4 Conference on Multi-User Interfaces and Applications*, Crete. North Holland.

KRAEMER, K. & KING, J. (1988). Computer-based systems for group decision support: Status of use and problems in development. *Computing Surveys, 20*(2), pp. 115–146. An earlier version appeared in CSCW '86.
(decision support, overview)   Application of computer and information technology to cooperative work and group decision-making has grown out of three traditions: computer-based communications, computer-based information service provision, and computer-based decision support. This paper provides an overview of the various kinds of systems that have been configured to meet the needs of groups at work, evaluates the status of these systems in the USA, evaluates the experience with them, and assesses barriers to their further development and use.

KRAEMER, K. L. & PINSONNEAULT, A. (1990). Technology and groups: Assessments of the empirical research. In J. GALEGHER, R. E. KRAUT & C. EGIDO, Eds, *Intellectual Teamwork: Social Foundations of Cooperative Work*, pp. 373–404. Hillsdale, New Jersey: Lawrence Erlbaum Associates.
(decision support, overview, evaluation)   The paper provides an up-to-date portrait of the state of our knowledge about group decision support systems (GDSS). Five major research implications are offered: the lack of research on some important "formal" factors of groups; the lack of knowledge of the impact of GDSS on the informal dimensions of a group; the need to move away from the lab towards real field studies; the relation between group development and how it affects GDSS; and how the structure imposed by technology affects group processes.

KRASNER, H. (1987). CSCW '86 conference summary report. *ACM/SIGCHI Bulletin, 19*(1), pp. 51–53.
(report)   A review of the CSCW '86 conference.

KRAUSS, R. M. & FUSSELL, S. R. (1990). Mutual knowledge and communicative effectiveness. In J. GALEGHER, R. E. KRAUT & C. EGIDO, Eds, *Intellectual Teamwork: Social Foundations of Cooperative Work*, pp. 111–146. Hillsdale, New Jersey: Lawrence Erlbaum Associates.
(social impact, evaluation)   Mutual knowledge occurs when people develop some idea of what their communicating partners know and don't know in order to formulate what they

have to say to them. Speakers come to conclusions about their partners' states of knowledge through a number of mechanisms: by listening to what they themselves have said, by making inferences from their partner's category membership, or by relying on feedback. Experimental research illustrating mutual knowledge is described, and implications to communications technology is offered.

KRAUT, R., EGIDO, C. & GALEGHER, J. (1988a). Patterns of contact and communication in scientific collaboration. In *Proceedings of the Conference on Computer-Supported Cooperative Work (CSCW '88)*, pp. 1–12. Portland, Oregon, September 26–28, ACM Press.
(evaluation, informal meetings) This paper describes the influence of physical proximity on the development of collaborative relationships between scientific researchers and on the execution of their work. These descriptions provide the foundation for a discussion of the actual and potential role of communications technology in professional work, especially for collaborations carried out at a distance. Communication between people is shown to have an exponential decay with distance.

KRAUT, R., GALEGHER, J. & EGIDO, C. (1988b). Relationships and tasks in scientific research collaborations. *Human Computer Interaction*, 3(1), pp. 31–58. Reprinted in Greif, 1988. An earlier version was published in CSCW '86.
(evaluation, informal meetings) This paper uses the results of studies of research collaborations among scientists to suggest design guidelines for computer technology aimed at supporting such collaboration. It shows that a great deal of emphasis will have to be placed on how researchers form and maintain their personal relationships.

KRAUT, R. E., EGIDO, C. & GALEGHER, J. (1990). Patterns of contact and communication in scientific research collaborations. In J. GALEGHER, R. E. KRAUT & C. EGIDO, Eds, *Intellectual Teamwork: Social Foundations of Cooperative Work*, pp. 149–172. Hillsdale, New Jersey: Lawrence Erlbaum Associates.
(informal meetings, evaluation, social impact) The paper describes the influence of physical promixity on the development of collaborative relationships between scientific researchers and on the execution of their work. Key aspects supporting developing relationships include the importance of informal communication, the quality of communication, and the personal cost. Implications to technological support are offered.

KREIFELTS, T., VICTOR, F., WOETZEL, G. & WOITASS, M. (1989). A design tool for autonomous group agents. In *Proceedings of the 1st European Conference on Computer-Supported Cooperative Work (EC-CSCW '89)*. Gatwick, UK, September 13–15, Computer Sciences House, Slough, UK.

KURBEL, K. & PIETSCH, W. (1990). A cooperative work environment for evolutionary software development. In S. GIBBS & A. A. VERRIGHN-STUART, Eds, *Proceedings of IFIP WG8.4 Conference on Multi-User Interfaces and Applications*, Crete. North Holland.

KYNG, M. (1988). Designing for a dollar a day. In *Proceedings of the Conference on Computer-Supported Cooperative Work (CSCW '88)*, pp. 178–188. Portland, Oregon, September 26–28, ACM Press.
(participatory design, software design) Kyng offers a design methodology. He steps through the Scandinavian experiences with end user participation, and reviews several tools and techniques which will: 1) establish possibilities of alternative forms of work within the workplace: 2) evolve the local work situation through a cycle involving situation analysis, goal discussion, and investigation of possible courses of actions; 3) create a vision of new and different uses of technology; and 4) view the design through mock-up simulations.

LAKIN, F. (1988). A performing medium for working group graphics. In J. GREIF, Ed., *Computer-supported cooperative work: A book of readings*. San Mateo, California: Morgan Kaufmann Publishers Inc. An earlier version was published in CSCW '86.
(shared workspace) This paper analyses the role in a meeting of shared text-graphic displays. He develops the notion of "text-graphic performance" that captures changes over

time of the images. The results are important to the design of computerized shared workspaces.

LAKIN, F. (1990). Visual languages for cooperation: A performing medium approach to systems for cooperative work. In J. GALEGHER, R. E. KRAUT & C. EGIDO, Eds, *Intellectual Teamwork: Social Foundations of Cooperative Work*, pp. 453–488. Hillsdale, New Jersey: Lawrence Erlbaum Associates.

(shared workspace, implementation)   A visual language can give group members a way to visualize an aspect of group work so they can better understand and perform it. Lakin describes a computer graphics system called "vmacs" that has the potential to allow people to move seamlessly between individual and group modes of work, between graphic and text work objects, and between casual and formal representations of objects.

LANDOW, G. P. (1990). Hypertext and collaborative work: The example of Intermedia. In J. GALEGHER, R. E. KRAUT & C. EGIDO, Eds, *Intellectual Teamwork: Social Foundations of Cooperative Work*, pp. 407–428. Hillsdale, New Jersey, Lawrence Erlbaum Associates.

(hypertext, multimedia, education)   When used in an educational context, hypermedia encourages undergraduate students to move beyond passive learning to active, generative scholarly work. The experiences of Intermedia use are described.

LANTZ, K. (1986). An experiment in integrating multimedia conferencing. In *Proceedings of the Conference on Computer-Supported Cooperative Work (CSCW '86)*. Austin, Texas, December, ACM Press. Reprinted in Greif, 1988.

(shared views)   This paper describes Lantz's experience in designing a centralized shared view system.

LANTZ, K. A., LAUWERS, C., ARONS, B., BINDING, C., CHEN, P., DONAHUE, J., JOSEPH, T. A., KOO, R., ROMANOW, A., SCHMANDT, C. & YAMAMOTO, W. (1989). Collaboration technology research at Olivetti Research Centre. Research report, Olivetti Research Centre, Menlo Park, California.

(overview, conceptual)   This paper describes the goals and premises behind the Olivetti Research Center's work in collaboration technology.

LAUWERS, J. C., JOSEPH, T. A., LANTZ, K. A. & ROMANOW, A. L. (1990a). Replicated architectures for shared window systems: A critique. In *Proceedings of the Conference on Office Information Systems*, pp. 249–260. Boston, April 25–27.

(shared views, software design, evaluation)   This paper documents the problems of replicated architectures used in shared window systems, and indicates how synchronization problems can be solved and how other limitations removed. The need for general systems support is addressed, and the advantages gained by making applications and servers "collaboration-aware" described.

LAUWERS, J. C. & LANTZ, K. A. (1990b). Collaboration awareness in support of collaboration transparency: Requirements for the next generation of shared window systems. In *Proceedings of the ACM/SIGCHI Conference on Human Factors in Computing*. Seattle, Washington, April 1–5, ACM Press.

(shared views, critique)   This report describes the problems/issues that existing shared window systems have come up against, and lists the requirements that the next generation of shared window systems should have. Issues addressed are: spontaneous interactions; workspace management; floor control; user customizability; annotation and telepointing; and performance.

LAZAROV, G., LILOV, V. & NIKOLOVA, M. (1990). The "User Illusion" method in multiuser interface design. In S. GIBBS & A. A. VERRIGHN-STUART, Eds, *Proceedings of IFIP WG8.4 Conference on Multi-User Interfaces and Applications*, Crete. North Holland.

LEA, M. & SPEARS, R. (1991). Computer-mediated communication, deindividuation and group decision making. *Int J Man Machine Studies*, **34**(2), pp. 283–302, February. In the special edition on CSCW & Groupware. Republished in Greenberg, 1991c.

(decision support, evaluation) Technology changes the way people within a group behave. Lea and Spears discuss how computer-mediated communication affects deindividuation, the anonymity and loss of identity that occurs when people are submerged in a group. If deindividuation does exist, we would expect the social norms and constraints of people's behaviour to be weakened, which would have serious consequences on how decisions made by the group should be interpreted. The authors question past findings on how electronic communication changes the group's psychological states, and then present their own study and alternate view of the role of deindividuation.

LEDERBERG, J. & UNCAPHER, K. (1989). Towards a national collaboratory. The Rockefeller University, March 17–18.
(overview, social impact) This is a report of an invitational workshop whose mandate was to develop recommendations for a research agenda leading to a "National Collaboratory", a resource that would use networking and computer technology to support collaboration independent of distance and by increasing productive access to scarce and expensive assets. Definitely a "must read" for all those interested in the future directions of CSCW.

LEE, J. (1990a). SIBYL: A tool for sharing knowledge in group decision making. In *Proceedings of the Conference on Computer-Supported Cooperative Work (CSCW '90)*. Los Angeles, California, October 7–10, ACM Press.
(semi-structured messages, protocols, decision support, hypertext) SIBYL is a system that supports group decision making by representing and managing the qualitative aspects of the decision-making processes: alternatives, the goals to be satisfied, and the arguments evaluating the alternatives with respect to these goals. SIBYL is described and compared with other systems with similar objectives (eg gIBIS), and an example session provided. SIBYL is claimed to be a knowledge-based system which uses a semi-formal representation, whereas gIBIS is mainly a hypertext system with semantic types.

LEE, J. J. (1990b). Xsketch: A multi-user sketching tool for X11. In *Proceedings of the Conference on Office Information Systems*, pp. 169–173. Boston, April 25–27.
(shared workspace, remote meetings, implementation) Lee describes work in progress on a multi-user sketching tool called xsketch. Requirements and design goals are provided, plus details of the prototype implementation. A list of known problems, shortcomings and possible extensions are included.

LELAND, M. D. P., FISH, R. S. & KRAUT, R. E. (1988). Collaborative document production using Quilt. In *Proceedings of the Conference on Computer-Supported Cooperative Work (CSCW '88)*, pp. 206–215. Portland, Oregon, September 26–28, ACM Press.
(data sharing, hypertext, implementation) Quilt is a tool for collaborative document production that emphasizes and supports the communication vital to good collaboration. For example, links may be structured hypermedia links that allow people to attach text and voice annotations to the document. These may be specialized as revision suggestions, public comments, and directed messages. The necessary coordination between collaborators is enhanced via activity logging, notification and triggering mechanisms. Access permissions can be set by the author to reflect the varying roles of collaborators (as writers, commentators, reviewers), while user-customizable definitions for such things as document and annotation types make the system both flexible and extensible.

LEWE, H. & KRCMAR, H. (1990). The CATeam meeting room environment as a human–computer interface. In S. GIBBS & A. A. VERRIGHN-STUART, Eds, *Proceedings of IFIP WG8.4 Conference on Multi-User Interfaces and Applications*, Crete. North Holland.

LIA, K.-Y. & MALONE, T. W. (1988). Object Lens: A "spreadsheet" for cooperative work. In *Proceedings of the Conference on Computer-Supported Cooperative Work (CSCW '88)*, pp. 115–124. Portland, Oregon, September 26–28, ACM Press.
(semi-structured messages, hypertext) This paper introduces Object Lens, a second-generation version of their Information Lens. Object Lens contains two fundamental ideas. First, passive information can be represented as semi-structured objects, where each object is defined as part of an inheritance hierarchy, eg "Thing, Message, Action-request,

Meeting-proposal." By defining and modifying templates for these objects, users can represent and interact with many different kinds of information. Second, active rules for processing information are represented as semi-autonomous agents. When creating these agents, users specify rules for automatically processing information in different situations. A rule triggered by incoming news from a bulletin board may, for example, sort the interesting and topical news into appropriate folders, discarding the rest. With these two ideas, Object Lens integrates object-oriented databases, hypertext, and electronic messaging with intelligent routing.

LICKLIDER, J. C. R. & VEZZA, A. (1978). Applications of information networks. *Proceedings of the IEEE,* **66**(11), pp. 1330–1346. Reprinted in Greif, 1988.
(overview)   This early paper briefly examines 30 "office of the future" applications and the network capabilities they require. Several political, social, and economic issues are then considered.

LIM, F. J. & BENBASAT, I. (1991). A communication-based framework for group interfaces in computer-supported collaboration. In *Proceedings of the 24th Hawaii Conference on System Sciences.* Kauai, Hawaii, January 8–11.
(decision support)   The paper presents a framework which outlines the various dimensions of communication in group interfaces. An analysis of communication flows is provided along four dimensions: concurrency, content, path, and channel.

LINDE, C. (1988). Who's in charge here? Cooperative work and authority negotiation in police helicopter missions. In *Proceedings of the Conference on Computer-Supported Cooperative Work (CSCW '88)*, pp. 52–64. Portland, Oregon, September 26–28, ACM Press.
(evaluation, social impact)   Linde questions the common (and perhaps naive) assumption that the authority status of participants within an organization is fixed. Through extensive videotapes, she observed a flight officer and pilot on board a helicopter engaged in police missions. The pilot is responsible for all on-craft decisions, while the officer is responsible for the actual police mission. She observed a quite complex social structure. In particular, the "authority status" of crew members was subject to moment to moment negotiations, invoked as a normal, unremarked background condition of the ongoing daily operations. Linde suggests that negotiating authority is quite common in most collaborative work, and that it would be a mistake to rely only upon the formal organizational hierarchy when deciding upon the authority of participants.

LISON, H. & CROWLEY, T. (1989). Sight and Sound. *Unix Review,* **7**(10), pp. 76–86.
(remote meetings, shared views, multimedia, implementation)   This paper describes the BBN/Slate package.

LOSADA, M., SANCHEZ, P. & NOBLE, E. E. (1990). Collaborative technology and group process feedback: Their impact on interactive sequences in meetings. In *Proceedings of the Conference on Computer-Supported Cooperative Work (CSCW '90).* Los Angeles, California, October 7–10, ACM Press.
(face-to-face meetings, evaluation, social impact)   The authors analysed group collaborative behaviour by detecting patterns of interactive sequences in face-to-face meetings using time series analysis (the room used was the Capture Lab). If group process feedback is given to people participating in a computer-supported meeting, the number of socio-emotional interactive sequences increases significantly above the expected level. With no feedback, the level is substantially less than the expected. The findings have implications for the efficient use of computer technology in terms of maximizing its collaborative potential.

LOUIE, G., MANTEI, M. & SELLEN, A. (1991). Making contact in a multi-media environment. Research Report, Dept of Computer Science, University of Toronto, Toronto, Ontario, February 2. Presented at the Ann Arbor HCI Consortium on Computer-Supported Cooperative Work.
(remote meetings)

LOWE, D. (1986). SYNVIEW: The design of a system for cooperative structuring of information. In *Proceedings of the Conference on Computer-Supported*

Cooperative work (CSCW '86), pp. 376–386. Austin, Texas, December 3–5, ACM Press.
(decision support)   The SYNVIEW system implements cooperative structuring of information through an explicit representation for debate between the users of the system and through a voting mechanism for resolving disputes.

Lu, I. & MANTEI, M. (1991). Idea management in a shared drawing tool. Research report, Dept of Computer Science, University of Toronto, Toronto, Canada. EC-CSCW '91.
(shared workspace)

LUBICH, H. & PLATTNER, B. (1990). A proposed model and functionality definition for a collaborative editing and conferencing facility. In S. GIBBS & A. A. VERRIGHN-STUART, Eds, *Proceedings of IFIP WG8.4 Conference on Multi-User Interfaces and Applications*, Crete. North Holland.

LUTZ, E., V. KLEIST-RETZOW, H. & HOERNIG, K. (1990). MAFIA – An active mail-filter-agent for an intelligent document processing support. In S. GIBBS, & A. A. VERRIGHN-STUART, Eds, *Proceedings of IFIP WG8.4 Conference on Multi-User Interfaces and Applications*, Crete. North Holland.

LYNCH, K. J., SNYDER, J. M., VOGEL, D. R. & McHENRY, W. K. (1990). The Arizona Analyst Information System: Supporting collaborative research on international technological trends. In S. GIBBS & A. A. VERRIGHN-STUART, Eds, *Proceedings of IFIP WG8.4 Conference on Multi-User Interfaces and Applications*, Crete. North Holland.

MACK, L. A. (1989). Technology for computer-supported meetings. In *Human Factors Society 33rd Annual Meeting*, pp. 857–861.

MACKAY, W. (1988). More than just a communication system: Diversity in the use of electronic mail. In *Proceedings of the Conference on Computer-Supported Cooperative Work (CSCW '88)*, pp. 344–353. Portland, Oregon, September 26–28, ACM Press.
(email, evaluation)   Email users were studied and rated into several categories, each with quite different habits and objectives. Prioritizers concentrate on the problem of managing incoming messages. Archivers concentrate on archiving information for subsequent use, and delegators delegate mail by passing it on to others. Mackay's study indicates that mail use is strikingly diverse, and that designers of email should recognize this diversity by designing systems that provide flexibility over a wide range of users.

MACKAY, W., MALONE, T. W., CROWSTON, K., RAO, R., ROSENBLITT, D. & CARD, S. K. (1989). How do experienced Information Lens users use rules? In *Proceedings of the ACM Conference on Human Factors in Computing Systems*. Austin, Texas, April 30–May 4, ACM Press.
(email, asynchronous conferencing, evaluation)   The Information Lens provides electronic mail users with the ability to write rules that automatically sort, select and filter their messages. This paper describes experiences of 13 volunteer users of the rules facility. In particular: people without significant computer experience can create and use rules; useful rules can be created based on the fields present in all messages; rules are used for both prioritizing and sorting messages; delete rules are used primarily to filter out messages from low-priority distribution lists.

MACKAY, W. E. (1990). Patterns of sharing customizable software. In *Proceedings of the Conference on Computer-Supported Cooperative Work (CSCW '90)*. Los Angeles, California, October 7–10, ACM Press.
(data sharing, organizational concerns, evaluation)   The act of customizing software is generally viewed as a solitary activity that allows users to express individual preferences. In this study, users were found to actively share their customization files with each other, which allowed members of each organization to establish and perpetuate informally-defined norms of behaviour. A small percentage of people were responsible for most of the sharing: highly skilled software engineers who were the first to experiment with and to

customize any new software; and "translators" who interpreted the needs of the rest of the organization and created customization files tailored to those needs (usually founded upon the customization files of the highly-skilled). Implications of the results are offered.

MACKAY, W. E. & TATAR, D. G. (1989). Special issue on video as a research and design tool. *SIGCHI Bulletin,* **21**(2), October.
(collection, video, evaluation)   This special issue contains several articles on how video can be used as a research tool for collecting and analysing data, and as a design tool.

MALONE, T. W. (1988). What is Coordination Theory? Research report SSM WP#2051-88, Sloan School of Management, MIT, Cambridge, Mass., February. Presented at the NSF Coordination Theory Workshop.
(conceptual)   Coordination theory is the study of coordination, ie how the activities of separate actors can be coordinated. Coordination theory is introduced, and its importance to "coordination technologies" (systems that help people coordinate their activities) is offered.

MALONE, T. W. & CROWSTON, K. (1990). What is Coordination Theory and how can it help design cooperative work systems? In *Proceedings of the Conference on Computer-Supported Cooperative Work (CSCW '90).* Los Angeles, California, October 7–10, ACM Press.
(conceptual)   Coordination theory is the study of coordination, ie how the activities of separate actors can be coordinated. Coordination theory is introduced, and its importance to "coordination technologies" (systems that help people coordinate their activities) is offered. Previous examples of coordination theory and CSCW are described.

MALONE, T. W., GRANT, K. R., LAI, K.-Y., RAO, R. & ROSENBLITT, D. (1987). Semi-structured messages are surprisingly useful for computer-supported coordination. *ACM Trans Office Information Systems,* **5**(2), pp. 115–131, April. Reprinted in Greif, 1988. An earlier version was published in CSCW '86.
(semi-structured messages, implementation)   This paper argues that using a set of semistructured message templates is surprisingly helpful in designing a variety of computer-based communication and coordination systems. The system provide aids for: 1) composing messages to be sent, 2) selecting, sorting and prioritizing messages that are received, 3) responding automatically to some messages, and 4) suggesting likely responses to other messages. The implementation, called "Information Lens" is described. An important paper.

MALONE, T. W., GRANT, K. R. & TURBAK, F. A. (1986). The Information Lens: An intelligent system for information sharing in organizations. In *Proceedings of the SIGCHI Human Factors in Computing Systems,* pp. 1–8. Boston, Mass., April 13–17, Association for Computing Machinery. Reprinted in Olson (1989).
(semi-structured messages)   This paper describes Information Lens, an intelligent system to help people share and filter information communicated by computer-based messaging systems.

MALONE, T. W., GRANT, K. R., TURBAK, F. A., BROBST, S. A. & COHEN, M. D. (1987a). Intelligent information-sharing systems. *Comm ACM,* **30**(5), pp. 390–402, May.
(semi-structured messages, email)   The Information Lens is a prototype intelligent information-sharing system that is designed to include not only good user interfaces for supporting the problem-solving activity of individuals, but also good organizational interfaces for supporting the problem-solving activities of groups.

MALONE, T. W., YATES, J. & BENJAMIN, R. I. (1987b). Electronic markets and electronic hierarchies. *Comm ACM,* **30**(6), pp. 484–497, June.
(conceptual)   By reducing the costs of coordination, information technology will lead to an overall shift toward proportionately more use of markets – rather than hierarchies – to coordinate economic activity.

MALONE, T. W., YU, K. & LEE, J. (1989). What good are semistructured objects? Adding semiformal structure to hypertext. Research report CCSTR #102, SSM WP #3064-89-MS, Sloan School of Management, Cambridge, Mass., June.

(semi-structured messages, hypertext, implementation)   This report suggests that adding semantic structure to hypertext nodes can provide significant benefits for summarizing the contents of objects and their relationships, and automatically searching and manipulating collections of objects. Object Lens is used as an example. The report also suggests that the objects should be semi-structured, instead of rigidly structured. An overview of Object Lens is provided.

MAMRAK, S. A., KAELBLING, M. J., NICHOLAS, C. K. & SHARE, M. (1987). A Software Architecture for Supporting the Exchange of Electronic Manuscripts. *Comm ACM,* **30**(5), pp. 408–414, May.
As electric-manuscript exchange becomes more prevalent, problems arise in translating among the wide variety of electronic representations. The optimum solution is a system that can support both the use and the creation of translation tools.

MANTEI, M. (1988). Capturing the Capture concepts: A case study in the design of computer-supported meeting environments. In *Proceedings of the Conference on Computer-Supported Cooperative Work (CSCW '88),* pp. 257–270. Portland, Oregon, September 26–28, ACM Press.
(face-to-face meetings, shared views, evaluation, social impact)   The Capture lab is a face-to-face meeting room that included a computer console for every participant and a shared electronic blackboard. Mantei discussed three seemingly trivial but ultimately important design decisions made: seating arrangements; inter-viewing distances between participants; and access protocols to the shared blackboard. Mantei's lesson is that CSCW is much more than software, and must also cover political, physical and social processes. Even a seemingly trivial detail can change the nature of meetings held in a room.

MANTEI, M. (1989). Observations of executives using a computer supported meeting environment. *Decision Support Systems,* **5**, pp. 153–166, June.
(decision support, face-to-face meetings)

MANTEI, M., BAECKER, R. M., SELLEN, A. J., BUXTON, W. A. S. & MILLIGAN, T. (1991). Experiences in the use of a media space. In *ACM SIGCHI Conference on Human Factors in Computing Systems,* New Orleans, April 28–May 2, ACM, Press.
(remote meetings, video, implementation)   CAVECAT is a media space system that uses integrated video, audio, and computers to allow spatially and temporally separated individuals and groups to work together. The paper presents and summarizes initial use of CAVECAT, including unsolved technological obstacles encountered, and its psychological and social impact.

MANTEI, M. M. (1988). Groupware: Interface design for meetings. Research report CMI-88-001, Center for Machine Intelligence, Ann Arbor, Michigan, February 28.
(face-to-face meetings, collection)   This article provides the position taken by four panelists at a CHI '88 conference panel session: Suchman (Xerox) DeSanctis (U of Minnesota), Applegate (Harvard U) and Jarvenpaa (U of Texas). Mantei introduces face-to-face meeting environments and asks several very interesting research questions.

MANTYLA, R., ALASUVANTO, J. & HAMMAINEN, H. (1990). PAGES: A testbed for groupware applications. In S. GIBBS & A. A. VERRIGHN-STUART, Eds, *Proceedings of IFIP WG8.4 Conference on Multi-User Interfaces and Applications,* Crete. North Holland.

MARKUS, M. L. & CONNOLLY, T. (1990). Why CSCW applications fail: Problems in the adoption of interdependent work tools. In *Proceedings of the Conference on Computer-Supported Cooperative Work (CSCW '90).* Los Angeles, California, October 7–10, ACM Press.
(critique, organizational concerns)   This paper extends Grudin's 1988 study on why CSCW applications fail. In particular, failure occurs even when: there are no asymmetries between those who benefit from an application and those who do extra work; and decision makers do not confuse their own personal benefits with the collective benefit. The authors argue

that failure may also be due to interdependence in the payoffs derived, where payoffs to one user may depend on the behaviour of others.

McCARTHY, J. C., MILES, V. C. & MONK, A. F. (1991). An experimental study of common ground in text-based communication. In *ACM SIGCHI Conference on Human Factors in Computing Systems*. New Orleans, April 28–May 2, ACM Press.
(remote meetings, evaluation)   An experiment was performed to examine predictions from Clark's contribution theory of discourse. Pairs were asked to use a text-based synchronous messaging system to solve a problem. Contribution theory suggests that in such text-only communication common ground will be difficult to achieve. This was shown to be the case. A parallel system, where participants could use a common report space in addition to the messaging space, significantly reduced these problems.

McCARTHY, J. C. & MILES, V. C. (1990). Elaborating communication channels in conferencer. In S. GIBBS & A. A. VERRIGHN-STUART, Eds, *Proceedings of IFIP WG8.4 Conference on Multi-User Interfaces and Applications*, Crete. North Holland.

McCARTHY, J. C.,, MILES, V. C., HARRISON, M. D., DIX, A. J. & WRIGHT, P. C. (1991). Four generic communication tasks which must be supported in electronic conferencing. *ACM SIGCHI Bulletin*, **23**(1), pp. 41–43, January. Poster presentation.
(remote meetings)   Four generic communications tasks must be supported by electronic conferencing: synchronizing communication; maintaining conversational coherence; repairing conversational breakdown; maintaining shared focus.

McDONNELL, D. & RAYMOND, J. (1987). Integration of the electronic blackboard and the electronic overhead projector. In *The Second Guelph Symposium on Computer Conferencing*, pp. 193–197. Guelph, Ontario, Canada, June 1–4. University of Guelph.
(remote meetings, shared workspace)   This paper describes a distance-education course-delivery system that uses a "real" electronic blackboard, slow-scan tv, an electronic overhead projector, and a fax machine. It is interesting in that it does not seem as workstation-based as the traditional systems seen in CSCW.

McGRATH, J. E. (1990). Time matters in groups. In J. GALEGHER, R. E., KRAUT & C. EGIDO, Eds, *Intellectual Teamwork: Social Foundations of Cooperative Work*, pp. 23–62. Hillsdale, New Jersey: Lawrence Erlbaum Associates
(social impact)   The paper provides a theoretical analysis of the small group. There are two themes. First, group functioning is multidimensional, and that the actions of individuals, groups and organizations have implications for outcomes on each of these dimensions. Second, the temporal sequence of behaviour in groups (stages of group development, phases of group task performance . . .) is both a function and a determinant of group effectiveness. The themes then provide the foundation for a speculative discussion of the effects of information technologies, and how they might help or hinder the temporal flow of communication and work in groups.

MINNEMAN, S. L. & BLY, S. A. (1990). Experiences in the development of a multi-user drawing tool. In *The 3rd Guelph Symposium on Computer Mediated Communication*, pp. 154–167, Guelph, Ontario, Canada, May 15–17, University of Guelph Continuing Education Division.
(shared workspace, evaluation, remote meetings)   Authors describe Commune, a multi-user drawing tool that allows users collaborating remotely to share a common drawing surface. The system is described and early observations of use provided.

MINNEMAN, S. L. & BLY, S. A. (1991). Managing a trois: A study of a multi-user drawing tool in distributed design work. In *ACM SIGCHI Conference on Human Factors in Computing Systems*, New Orleans, April 28–May 2, ACM Press.
(shared workspace, video, evaluation, remote meetings)   The authors evaluate a multi-user drawing tool called Commune (including video link) in a three-person distributed

design exercise. Tool use was augmented by a video/audio link and audio only. They observed no difficulties in 3 people over 2 people using the shared drawing surface use. Audio-only connections appeared to adequately support this work activity, but details of the interactions in the exercise raised questions about video support that deserve further studies.

MIT (1983a). Talking heads. In *Discursions*. Boston, Mass., Architecture Machine Group, MIT. Optical disc.
(remote meetings) A video of what is perhaps the best-realized telepresence remote conferencing system. Once described as a "very scary system" by a person involved in its design.

MIT (1983b). Zero bandwidth video. In *Discursions*. Boston, Mass., Architecture Machine Group, MIT. Optical disc.
(remote meetings) A video of a telepresence remote conferencing system. Rather than sending a video image down the wire, this version uses a speech recognizer to animate images of participants in a video conference.

MORAN, T. P. & ANDERSON, R. J. (1990). The workaday world as a paradigm for CSCW design. In *Proceedings of the Conference on Computer-Supported Cooperative Work (CSCW '90)*. Los Angeles, California, October 7–10, ACM Press.
(conceptual, critique, multi-media) Xerox EuroPARC is developing an integrated multi-media environment as an integral part of its formal and informal working environment. The authors suggest from their initial experiences with this kind of technology that it exhibits qualitatively different properties, which seem to call into question many of our ideas about what computer systems are and how people relate to them. A paradigm called the "Workaday World" is offered, that distinguishes between technology, sociality, and work practice. EuroPARC's multi-media environment is discussed within this paradigm.

MURREL, S. (1983). Computer communication system design affects group decision making. In *Proceedings of the ACM/SIGCHI Human Factors in Computing Systems*, pp. 63–67. Boston, December 12–15.
(remote conferencing, protocols, evaluation, decision support) This research explored the impact of two synchronous systems which vary in the role of immediacy of interaction and feedback on group decision making. One system is message-oriented, requiring a conferee to complete a message before interacting with others. The other displays what each group member is typing as it is typed in a separate window on the screens of all participants. Groups were asked to solve a problem. All groups produced decisions superior to the average initial individual solutions. Window system groups improved more, produced significantly higher quality decisions, and spent less time discussing how to organize the system and task efforts.

NARDI, B. A. & MILLER, J. R. (1990). An ethnographic study of distributed problem solving in spreadsheet development. In *Proceedings of the Conference on Computer Supported Cooperative Work (CSCW '90)*. Los Angeles, California, October 7–10, ACM Press.
(evaluation, social impact) A shorter version of Nardi and Miller's 1991 Int J Man Machine Studies article.

NARDI, B. A. & MILLER, J. R. (1991). Twinkling lights and nested loops: Distributed problem solving and spreadsheet development. *Int J Man Machine Studies, 34*(2), pp. 161–184, February. In the special edition on CSCW & Groupware. Republished in Greenberg, 1991c.
(evaluation, social impact) Nardi and Miller's ethnographic study is on spreadsheets, long considered a good example of a well-designed "single user" application. Much to their surprise, they observed that spreadsheet co-development was the rule, not the exception. They saw a high degree of cooperation in sharing program expertise; transferring domain knowledge; debugging; training; and face-to-face work in meetings. The general implication is that cooperative work happens all the time, in spite of the inherent limitations of the software.

NECHES, R. (1988). Tools help people cooperate only to the extent that they help them share goals and terminology. *ACM Trans Office Information Systems*, **6**(3). An earlier version was published in CSCW '86.
This paper describes two pieces of work on support tools: one for the construction of consistent and principled human–computer interfaces and the other for the construction of AI knowledge bases. The knowledge-based approach to interface construction illustrates how it would apply to detecting design conflicts and inconsistencies stemming from two different kinds of team communication failure.

NEUWIRTH, C. M., KAUFER, D. S., CHANDHOK, R. & MORRIS, J. (1990). Issues in the design of computer support for co-authoring and commenting. In *Proceedings of the Conference on Computer-Supported Cooperative Work (CSCW '90)*. Los Angeles, California, October 7–10, ACM Press.
(data sharing, hypertext, implementation) The paper reports on a project to develop a "work in preparation" editor, or PREP editor, to study co-authoring and commenting relationships. Three issues in designing computer support for co-authoring and commenting were identified: support for social interaction; support for cognitive aspects of co-authoring and external commenting; and suport for practicality in both types of interaction. The approach taken by the PREP editor is described.

NEWMAN, D. (1988). Sixth graders and shared data: Designing a LAN environment to support collaborative work. In *Proceedings of the Conference on Computer-Supported Cooperative Work (CSCW '88)*, pp. 291–305. Portland, Oregon, September 26–28, ACM Press.
(education, evaluation) This paper describes the Earth Lab project—a computer-supported collaboration on a science project between sixth graders. Students were seen to use the social organization of the classroom activities as a frame of reference.

NIELSON, J. (1987). Computer-supported cooperative work: Trip report. *ACM/SIGCHI Bulletin*, **19**(1), pp. 54–61.
(report) A review of the CSCW '86 conference.

NYLUND, A. (1989). Aspects of cooperation in a distributed problem solving environment. In *Proceedings of the 1st European Conference on Computer-Supported Cooperative Work (EC-CSCW '89)*. Gatwick, UK, September 13–15, Computer Sciences House, Slough, UK.

OLSON, G. M. (1989). The nature of group work. In *Human Factors Society 33rd Annual Meeting*, pp. 852–856.

OLSON, G. P. & ATKINS, D. E. (1990). Supporting collaboration with advanced multimedia electronic mail: The NSF EXPRES project. In J. GALEGHER, R. E. KRAUT & C. EGIDO, Eds, *Intellectual Teamwork: Social Foundations of Cooperative Work*, pp. 429–452. Hillsdale, New Jersey; Lawrence Erlbaum Associates.
(email, multimedia) A specific example of co-authorship is the joint planning, writing, and submission of research proposals to funding agencies. In the paper world, the document will include scotch-taped text, figures, tables, notes, and so on. The NSF EXPRES email system supports this model by allowing co-authors to bundle together text, outlines, graphics and spreadsheets into a single electronic document.

OLSON, J. S., OLSON, G. M., MACK, L. A. & WELLNER, P. (1990). Concurrent editing: The group's interface. In D. DIAPER et al., Ed., *Proceedings of Interact '90*, pp. 834–840. Elsevier Science Publishers B.V.
An issue-raising article on concurrent text editing activity.

OLSON, M. H. (1989). *Technological support for work group collaboration*. Lawrence Erlbaum Associates: Hillsdale, New Jersey.
(collection) Titles in this collection include: 1) User approaches to computer-supported teams. Johansen. 2) Assumptions underlying systems that support work group collaboration. Dhar & Olson. 3) How is work coordinated? Implications for computer-based support. Johnson. 4) The information lens: An intelligent system for information sharing and coordination. Malone, Grant, Lai, Rao & Rosenblitt. 5) Flexible interactive technologies

for multi-person tasks: Current problems and future prospects. Bikson, Eveland, Gutek. 6) Organizational architecture for distributed computing: The next frontier in system design. Pava. 7) Developing the management systems of the 1990s: The role of collaborative work. Cashman & Stroll. 8) Toward portable ideas. Stefik & Brown. 9) A method for evaluating work group productivity products. Floyd & Turner.

OLSON, M. H. & BLY, S. A. (1991). The Portland Experience: A report on a distributed research group. *Int J Man Machine Studies,* **34**(2), pp. 211–228, February. In the special edition on CSCW & Groupware. Republished in Greenberg, 1991c.

(remote meetings, virtual hallways, video, evaluation) Xerox developed a cross-site environment called Media Space – a network of video, audio, and computing technologies – to connect two distance separated research laboratories: the large Palo Alto lab and a much smaller site in Portland. The Portland laboratory was intentionally developed to force its group to focus on interpersonal computing in a geographically distributed organization (ie to keep in close touch with Palo Alto). This paper summarizes observations of the Portland experience made by an outside observer. Insight into remote work in a distributed organization is provided and the use of the collaborative tools discussed.

OPPER, S. (1988). A groupware toolbox. *Byte,* December.

(implementation) Opper provides a catalog of commercially available groupware products. Some of her topics include: document editing, forms centered applications (coordination), team development and workgroup communication management.

ORR, J. (1986). Narratives at work: Story telling as cooperative diagnostic activity. In *Proceedings of the Conference on Computer-Supported Cooperative Work (CSCW '86),* pp. 62–72. Austin, Texas, December 3–5, ACM Press.

(social impact) The diagnostic process for copiers involves narration of the process, including a description of the state of the machine. This follows from the fact that the problem in diagnosis is not so much the testing of components as keeping track of the tests and making sense of their results. The anecdotal re-telling of this narrative to one's associates constitutes the mechanism for incorporating the diagnostic experience into the community expertise.

PATTERSON, J. F., HILL, R. D., ROHALL, S. L. & MEEKS, W. S. (1990). Rendezvous: An architecture for synchronous multi-user applications. In *Proceedings of the Conference on Computer-Supported Cooperative Work (CSCW '90).* Los Angeles, California, October 7–10, ACM Press.

(software design, implementation) Rendezvous is an architecture for creating synchronous multi-user applications. It consists of two parts: a run-time architecture for managing the multi-user session (based on a UIMS), and a start-up architecture for managing the network connectivity.

PENDERGAST, M. O. & VOGEL, D. (1990). Design and implementation of a PC/LAN-based multi-user text editor. In S. GIBBS & A. A. VERRIGHN-STUART, Eds, *Proceedings of IFIP WG8.4 Conference on Multi-User Interfaces and Applications,* Crete. North Holland.

PETTERSSON, E. (1989). Automatic information processes in document reading. A study of information handling in two intensive care units. In *Proceedings of the 1st European Conference on Computer-Supported Cooperative Work (EC-CSCW '89).* Gatwick, UK, September 13–15, Computer Sciences House, Slough, UK.

PITURRO, M. C. (1989). Computer conferencing: Brainstorming across time and space. *Management Review,* pp. 43–40, August.

(asynchronous conferencing, overview, implementation) This popular article introduces asynchronous computer conferencing. It describes how to get started, lists several success stories and lists the commercial products available.

PLISKIN, N. (1989). Interacting with electronic mail can be a dream or a nightmare: a user's point of view. *Interacting with Computers,* **1**(3), pp. 259–272, December.

(email, evaluation) BITNET email encounters are reviewed from a user's point of view.

Interaction difficulties such as addressing problems, unreliability issues, medium limitations and interface problems are raised.

POOLE, M. S., HOMES, M. & DESANCTIS, G. (1988). Conflict management and group decision support. In *Proceedings of the Conference on Computer-Supported Cooperative Work (CSCW '88)*, pp. 227–243. Portland, Oregon, September 26–28, ACM Press.
(evaluation, decision support) This paper discusses group decision support systems (GDSS) and conflict management. The authors contrast three groups: those with computer supported GDSS, those with a manual GDSS, and those with neither.

POSNER, I., BAECKER, R. & MANTEI, M. (1991). How people write together. Research report, Dept of Computer Science, University of Toronto, Toronto, Canada. Submitted to EC-CSCW '91.

POSTEL, J. B., FINN, G. G., KATZ, A. R. & REYNOLDS, J. K. (1988). An Experimental Multimedia Mail System. *ACM Trans Office Information Systems,* **6**(1), pp. 63–81, January.
(email, multimedia, implementation) An experimental multimedia mail system that allows the user to read, create, edit, send, and receive messages containing text, images, and voice is discussed.

POWRIE, S. E. & SIEMIENIUCH, C. E. (1990). IBC and cooperative working in the automotive industry. In S. GIBBS & A. A. VERRIGHN-STUART, Eds, *Proceedings of IFIP WG8.4 Conference on Multi-User Interfaces and Applications*, Crete. North Holland.

PRINZ, W. & PENNELLI, P. (1989). Relevance of the X.500 directory to CSCW applications: Directory support for computer based group communication. In *Proceedings of the 1st European Conference on Computer-Supported Cooperative Work (EC-CSCW '89)*. Gatwick, UK, September 13–15, Computer Sciences House, Slough, UK.

QUINN, R. (1990). A coordination environment: A new way of working together. Product blurb, Coordination Technology, Inc., 35 Corporate Dr, Trumbull, Connecticut.
(implementation, protocols) This paper gives some background to "Together", a commercial product that allows people to coordinate their activities through a "coordination environment".

REDER, S. & SCHWAB, R. G. (1988). The communicative economy of the workgroup: Multi-channel centres of communication. In *Proceedings of the Conference on Computer-Supported Cooperative Work (CSCW '88)*, pp. 354–368. Portland, Oregon, September 26–28, ACM Press.
(social impact, critique) There are many channels of communication available to people within a work group. As a consequence, a CSCW system will assume a variety of socio-functional niches, competing with other electronic or traditional communications systems. When multiple communication channels are available, people should be expected to—and will—switch between them. The authors argue that the choice of the communication channel and the switching between them are a natural part of a person's communication strategies and tactics, and must be considered when installing a new CSCW system in the workplace.

REDER, S. & SCHWAB, R. G. (1990). The temporal structure of cooperative activity. In *Proceedings of the Conference on Computer-Supported Cooperative Work (CSCW '90)*. Los Angeles, California, October 7–10, ACM Press.
(organizational concerns, evaluation) The research considers the relationship between individual work and group work activity. In particular, it asks how the characteristic temporal and spatial patterning of behaviour in the work environment relates to the modes of cooperative behaviour. A theoretical framework is suggested, that begins with the observation that individuals in office settings must routinely resolve conflicts between having uninterrupted periods of time in which to get their own work done, and being accessible for communication with others with whom they work.

REIN, G. L. & ELLIS, C. A. (1989). The NICK experiment reinterpreted: Implications for developers and evaluators of groupware. *Office: Technology and People,* **5**(1). (face-to-face meetings, evaluation) The Nick experiment was an empirical study conducted to explore and increase the understanding of prototype meeting support technology usage by software design teams working on unstructured, high-level design problems. The paper interprets the experimental data, and accounts for interactions among the three main effects of technology, team and task. The salient findings were: 1) the electronic messaging facility emerged as a potentially effective way for group members to attain more equality and to influence the direction of the meetings; and 2) group focus and attention on completing the task was increased for groups using an electronic blackboard.

REIN, G. L. & ELLIS, C. A. (1991). rIBIS: A real-time group hypertext system. *Int J Man Machine Studies,* **34**(3), pp. 349–368, March. In the special edition on CSCW & Groupware. Republished in Greenberg, 1991c.
(data sharing, hypertext, remote meetings, implementation) Hypertext developers now recognize that hypertext documents will be used and updated by large groups of people. This paper takes the next logical step by combining both real-time with asynchronous hypertext manipulation in their rIBIS system. An rIBIS session is a distributed meeting where participants can be in a "tightly-coupled" or "loosely-coupled" mode. In the first, tightly-coupled members all see the same thing, and take turns controlling and manipulating the hypertext display. In the second, a person works semi-privately by editing a portion of the hypertext—only large-grained changes are broadcast to other members. The result is a system valuable not only for storing information, but also for allowing people to actively capture and structure critical aspects of a meeting process.

RICE, R. E. & SHOOK, D. E. (1990). Voice messaging, coordination, and communication. In J. GALEGHER, R. E. KRAUT & C. EGIDO, Eds, *Intellectual Teamwork: Social Foundations of Cooperative Work,* pp. 327–350. Hillsdale, New Jersey: Lawrence Erlbaum Associates.
(email, multimedia, evaluation, organizational concerns) Voice mail is shown to have advantages similar to email. In addition, voice mail provides a channel that makes it possible to communicate the emotional intensity of the message as well as its substantive content. The effect of task complexity and peer/supervisor relationships on voice mail use is also raised.

RODDEN, T. & SOMMERVILLE, I. (1989). Building conversations using mailtrays. In *Proceedings of the 1st European Conference on Computer-Supported Cooperative Work (EC-CSCW '89).* Gatwick, UK, September 13–15, Computer Sciences House, Slough, UK.

ROOT, W. R. (1988). Design of a multi-media vehicle for social browsing. In *Proceedings of the Conference on Computer-Supported Cooperative Work (CSCW '88),* pp. 25–38. Portland, Oregon, September 26–28, ACM Press.
(virtual hallways, video) This paper focuses explicitly on tools to enable unplanned, informal social interaction through a "social interface" which provides direct, low-cost access to other people through the use of multi-media communications channels. A prototype desktop browser called "Cruiser" is described.

SARIN, S. & GREIF, I. (1985). Computer-based real-time conferencing systems. *IEEE Computer,* **18**(10), pp. 33–45. Reprinted in Greif, 1988.
(shared views, shared workspace, remote meetings, implementation) This paper discusses design tradeoffs for shared workspaces in a remote conferencing setting. Several example systems are described. Mblink is a shared bitmap system, and RTCAL builds a shared workspace of information from participants' on-line calendars.

SATHI, A., MORTON, T. E. & ROTH, S. F. (1986). Callisto: An intelligent project management system. *AI Magazine,* pp. 34–52, Winter. Reprinted in Greif, 1988.
(implementation) Callisto is a project management system for building large engineering prototypes. It facilitates the documentation of the expertise related to the prototyping effort so that it can be transferred to future projects.

SCOTT, P. D. (1988). Formal models of protocols for computer supported meetings.

Research report CMI-88-002, Center for Machine Intelligence, Ann Arbor, Michigan, February 29.
(face-to-face meetings, protocols) This paper introduces turntaking protocols used by people at face-to-face meetings and how software should represent these protocols. The thrust is the set of formal specifications Scott uses to represent the protocols.

SHEFFIELD, J. (1989). The Effects of Bargaining Orientation and Communication Medium on Negotiations in the Bilateral Monopoly Task: A Comparison of Decision Room and Computer Conferencing Communication Media. In *ACM/SIGCHI Conference on Human Factors in Computing Systems*, pp. 43–48. Austin, Texas.
(decision support, asynchronous conferencing, evaluation) Pairs of subjects with either a competitive or an integrative bargaining orientation completed the Bilateral Monopoly Task in one of four communication media: text-only, text plus visual access, audio-only, and audio plus visual access. The audio mode led to a higher joint outcome. The support for negotiation offered by decision room and computer conferencing technologies is compared based on the efficiency and richness of the communication media available in each.

SHEPHERD, A., MAYER, N. & KUCHINSKY, A. (1990). Strudel – An extensible electronic conversation toolkit. In *Proceedings of the Conference on Computer-Supported Cooperative Work (CSCW '90)*. Los Angeles, California, October 7–10, ACM Press.
(semi-structured messages, protocols, implementation) Authors describe the conceptual model of Strudel, a toolkit of generic components for conversation and action management. To empower work groups to more effectively conduct their computer-based communication, coordination, and information sharing activities. Strudel packages within a simple model of task and action the semi-structured message, active message and conversation management paradigms. To facilitate acceptance and use within varying work cultures, the model is defined in terms of a set of extensible components.

SINGER, J., BEHREND, S. & ROSCHELLE, J. (1988). Children's collaborative use of a computer microworld. In *Proceedings of the Conference on Computer-Supported Cooperative Work (CSCW '88)*, pp. 271–281. Portland, Oregon, September 26–28, ACM Press.
(education, evaluation) This paper discusses a framework and methodology for understanding the use of computers in collaborative learning. The system used is the "Envisioning machine," where students learn by communicating their ideas and coordinating their actions.

SMITH, H. T., HENNESSY, P. A. & LUNT, G. (1989). The activity model environment: An object oriented framework for describing organisational communication. In *Proceedings of the 1st European Conference on Computer-Supported Cooperative work (EC-CSCW '89)*. Gatwick, UK, September 13–15, Computer Sciences House, Slough, UK.

SMITH, R. B. (1988). A prototype futuristic technology for distance education (working draft). In *NATO Research Workshop on New Directions in Education Technology*. Cranfield, England, November.
(education, virtualworlds, video) The shared alternate reality kit is described as a prototype for distance education. The system is based on a shared world model. Users may roam around, encountering each other to act together in a collaborative task while communicating over an audio-video link. Motivations, visions and issues are described.

SMITH, R. B., O'SHEA, T., O'MALLEY, C., SCANLON, E. & TAYLOR, J. (1989). Preliminary experiences with a distributed, multi-media, problem environment. In *Proceedings of the 1st European Conference on Computer-Supported Cooperative Work (EC-CSCW '89)*. Gatwick, UK, September 13–15, Computer Sciences House, Slough, UK.

SPROULL, L. & KIESLER, S. (1986). Reducing social context cues: Electronic mail in organizational communication. *Management Science, 32*(11), pp. 1492–1512. Reprinted in Greif, 1988.

(email, evaluation, social impact)   This paper describes an empirical study on email, particularly on the effects of email's limited social context cues. This lack of cues is an advantage and disadvantage, depending upon the situation.

STANCHEV, P. & SABEV, V. (1990). CNLS – Computer Network Lecturing System. In S. GIBBS & A. A. VERRIGHN-STUART, Eds, *Proceedings of IFIP WG8.4 Conference on Multi-User Interfaces and Applications*, Crete. North Holland.

STASZ, C. & BIKSON, R. (1986). Computer-supported cooperative work: Examples and issues in one federal agency. In *Proceedings of the Conference on Computer-Supported Cooperative Work (CSCW '86)*, pp. 318–324. Austin, Texas, December 3–5, ACM Press.

(critique)   This paper discusses five issues as examples of the kinds of issues that organizations may face in their attempts to successfully implement computer-supported work: training, dissemination, hierarchical vs network communications, centralized vs decentralized decision making, and work sharing between different technologies and systems.

STEFIK, M., BOBROW, D. G., FOSTER, G., LANNING, S. & TATAR, D. (1987a). WYSIWIS revised: Early experiences with multiuser interfaces. *ACM Trans Office Information Systems*, **5**(2), pp. 147–167, April. An earlier version appeared in CSCW '86.

(face-to-face meetings, shared workspace, idea processor)   WYSIWIS (What You See Is What I See) is a foundational abstraction for multiuser interfaces that expresses many of the characteristics of a chalkboard in face-to-face meetings. This excellent paper describes two WYSIWIS systems used in CoLab. Boardnoter imitates a chalkboard, while Cognoter is a multi-person ideas processor. The design issues encountered are described (particularly in problems dealing with multiple windows and foci of attention), along with their tentative solutions.

STEFIK, M., FOSTER, G., BOBROW, D., KAHN, K., LANNING, S. & SUCHMAN, L. (1987b). Beyond the chalkboard: Computer support for collaboration and problem solving in meetings. *Comm ACM*, **30**(1), pp. 32–47. Reprinted in Greif, 1988.

(shared workspace, implementation)   This paper describes CoLab, a shared workspace for face-to-face meetings. Three systems are described: Boardnoter (an electronic chalkboard), Cognoter (a multi-person ideas processor), and Argnoter (an argumentation spreadsheet for proposals). Conceptual and programming issues are described as well.

STEVENS, C. H. (1986). Electronic organization and expert networks: Beyond electronic mail and computer conferencing. Working paper 90s: 86-021, Sloan School of Management, Massachusetts Institute of Technology, Cambridge, Massachusetts, May.

STORRS, G. (1989). Group working in the DHSS Large Demonstrator Project. In *Proceedings of the 1st European Conference on Computer-Supported Cooperative Work (EC-CSCW '89)*. Gatwick, UK, September 13–15, Computer Sciences House, Slough, UK.

STULTS, R. (1988). Experimental uses of video to support design activities. Xerox PARC, Palo Alto, California.

(remote meetings, virtual worlds, video)   This report provides the origins and description of four projects that used video to support design activity. These are: a) the distributed design studio; b) the cross-site workspace, c) studio with design journal; and d) the office design project.

SUCHMAN, L. & TRIGG, R. (1986). A framework for studying research collaborations. In *Proceedings of the Conference on Computer-Supported Cooperative Work (CSCW '86)*, pp. 221–228. Austin, Texas, December 3–5, ACM Press.

(evaluation)   This paper describes a methodological and topical framework for studying collaboration in research settings. The framework is intended to capture the central activities and issues in research collaboration, and to represent them in a way that can inform the design of computer support. The starting premises for studying collaboration are presented, the use of qualitative and naturalistic methods described, and preliminary findings reported.

SUOMI, R. (1989). Inter-organisational information systems as a tool for computer-supported cooperative work. In *Proceedings of the 1st European Conference on Computer-Supported Cooperative Work (EC-CSCW '89)*. Gatwick, UK, September 13–15, Computer Sciences House, Slough, UK.

SUZUKI, T., TANIGUCHI, H. & TAKADA, H. (1986). A real-time electronic conferencing system based on distributed Unix. In *Proceedings of the Usenix 1986 Summer Conference*, pp. 189–199. Atlanta, Georgia, June 9–13.

(shared views, implementation)   This paper describes a real-time electronic conferencing service constructed on distributed Unix. Identical contents are displayed in windows on each participant's work station and updated simultaneously. Any Unix service can be run without any modification. Some mechanisms included are access-rights, shared cursor, and a voice channel through a parallel PBX system.

TANG, J. C. (1990). Observations on the use of shared drawing spaces. Videotape, Xerox PARC, Palo Alto, California.

(shared workspace)   The videotape uses clips of small group design meetings to illustrate how people collaborate through shared drawing spaces. Clear and convincing.

TANG, J. C. (1989). Listing, drawing, and gesturing in design: A study of the use of shared workspaces by design teams. PhD thesis, Department of Mechanical Engineering, Stanford University, California, April. Also available as research report SSL-89-3, Xerox Palo Alto Research Center, Palo Alto, California.

(shared workspace, evaluation)   This dissertation is a descriptive study of the shared workspace activity of small groups working on conceptual design tasks, activities that include listing, drawing and gesturing. The paper presents: a methodology for observing and analysing collaborative design activity; a detailed description and analysis of key aspects of shared workspace activity; a set of specific recommendations for the design of tools to support shared workspace activity. This thesis is required reading for the designer of a shared workspace.

TANG, J. C. (1991). Findings from observational studies of collaborative work. *Int J Man Machine Studies*, **34**(2), pp. 143–160, February. In the special edition on CSCW & Groupware. Republished in Greenberg, 1991.

(shared workspace, evaluation)   This paper is an expanded version of Tang and Leifer's 1988 paper. The work activity of small groups of 3 to 4 people was videotaped and analysed in order to understand collaborative work and to guide the development of their listing, drawing, gesturing, and talking around a shared drawing surface. The result is a set of design implications for tools that support shared workspace activity.

TANG, J. C. & LEIFER, L. J. (1988). A framework for understanding the workspace activity of design teams. In *Proceedings of the Conference on Computer-Supported Cooperative Work (CSCW '88)*, pp. 244–249. Portland, Oregon, September 26–28, ACM Press.

(shared workspace, evaluation)   Tang and Leifer used detailed transcripts of design sessions to examine the possible purposes behind activities of a small design team who share a drawing surface. They found that artifacts, when combined with a person's gestures, are just as valuable for representing ideas and for engaging attention. A graphic evolves along with ideas into a final artifact, and gesturing is used for pointing and focusing attention during the collaboration. They conclude that too much attention has been paid to the artifacts left behind from collaborative meetings. In many cases, these are just marks that are inherently meaningless. The process of creating drawings and gesturing to them may be as important to the design process as the drawings themselves.

TANG, J. C. & MINNEMAN, S. L. (1990). Videodraw: A video interface for collaborative drawing. In *ACM SIGCHI Conference on Human Factors in Computing Systems*, pp. 313–320. Seattle, Washington, April 1–5, ACM Press.

(shared workspace, implementation)   This paper describes the empirical foundations and the implementation of VideoDraw, a video-based multi-user sketchpad supporting remote collaboration.

TANG, J. C. & MINNEMAN, S. L. (1991). VideoWhiteboard: video shadows to support remote collaboration. In *ACM SIGCHI Conference on Human Factors in Computing Systems*, New Orleans, April 28–May 2, ACM Press.
(remote meetings, video, implementation) VideoWhiteboard is a prototype tool to support remote shared drawing activity. It provides a whiteboard-sized shared drawing space for collaborators who are located in remote sites. It allows each user to see the drawings and a shadow of the gestures of remote collaborators. VideoWhiteboard enables remote collaborators to work together much as if they were sharing a whiteboard, and in some ways allows them to work together even more closely than if they were in the same room.

TARAZI, M. H. (1989). Object sharing in a multi-user hypertext system. MSc Thesis CCS TR#101, Center for Coordination Science, MIT, Cambridge, Massachusetts, June 1990.
(hypertext, implementation, software design) Object-sharing requirements are described for the Object Lens system, which integrates features of hypertext, object-oriented systems, and rule-based agents. Approaches to object-sharing are evaluated, and a new scheme initiated through email exchange is promoted. Although most of the discussion is specific to Object Lens, the ideas are important for general multi-user interface toolkit construction.

TATAR, D. G., FOSTER, G. & BOBROW, D. G. (1991). Design for conversation: Lessons from Cognoter. *Int J Man Machine Studies*, **34**(2), pp. 185–210, February. In the special edition on CSCW & Groupware. Republished in Greenberg, 1991c.
(idea processors, shared workspace, evaluation) Users encountered unexpected communicative breakdowns when using Cognoter, a multi-user idea organizing tool. Difficulties stemmed from an incorrect model of conversation implicit in the software's design. A more realistic model of the user situation was created, and the tool redesigned.

THIMBLEBY, H., ANDERSON, S. & WITTEN, I. H. (1990). Reflexive CSCW: Supporting long-term personal work. *Interacting with Computers*, **2**(3), pp. 330–336.
(conceptual, data-sharing, social impact) The paper argues that the plight of the individual user can be viewed as a CSCW problem, for the individual frequently acts as multiple persona performing many independent tasks, perhaps in several places. "Reflexive CSCW" is proposed as a CSCW system applicable to personal work.

THOMAS, R. H., FORSDICK, H. C., CROWLEY, T. R., SCHAAF, R. W., TOMLINSON, R. S., TRAVERS, V. M. & ROBERTSON, G. G. (1985). Diamond: A Multimedia Message System Built on a Distributed Architecture. *IEEE Computer*, **18**(12), pp. 65–78. Reprinted in Greif, 1988.
(multimedia, email) Diamond is a multimedia, electronic mail/document system that supports text, graphics, images, speech, and structured documents. The user interface and architecture are described.

TRIGG, R., SUCHMAN, L. & HALASZ, F. (1986). Supporting collaboration in NoteCards. In *Proceedings of the Conference on Computer-Supported Cooperative Work (CSCW '86)*, pp. 153–162. Austin, Texas, December 3–5.
(hypertext, idea processors) This paper focuses on experience with and extensions to NoteCards, a hypertext-based idea structuring system. The forms of collaboration discussed include draft-passing, simultaneous sharing and online presentations. The requirement that mutual intelligibility be maintained between collaborators leads to the need for support of annotative and procedural as well as substantive activities.

TRIGG, R. H. (1988). Guided tours and tabletops: Tools for communicating in a hypertext environment. In *Proceedings of the Conference on Computer-Supported Cooperative Work (CSCW '88)*, pp. 216–226. Portland, Oregon, September 26–28, ACM Press. Reprinted in Greif, 1988.
(hypertext) Trigg, the creator of the Xerox Notecards hypertext system, tackles the "lost in hyperspace" problem—the difficulty of navigating through complex hypertext networks. Unlike sequential documents, the rich inter-connections in hypertext may make it difficult

for the unguided reader to follow paths preferred by the author (eg introductory tours through the document). Trigg introduces two new Notecard techniques to ameliorate this problem: tabletops and guided tours. A tabletop records a specific set of notecards (hypertext fragments) and their layout on a screen. A guided tour is a graphical interface that allows one to navigate between tabletops. Normal notecards can further supplement a tour by pointing to and annotating other cards on the tabletop. In this way, an author can "guide" the reader through the text.

TUENI, M. & LI, J. (1989). Knowledge-based office automation and CSCW. In *Proceedings of the 1st European Conference on Computer-Supported Cooperative Work (EC-CSCW '89)*. Gatwick, UK, September 13–15, Computer Sciences House, Slough, UK.

UNIVERSITY OF GUELPH (1987). *The second Guelph symposium on computer conferencing*. University of Guelph, Guelph, Ontario, Canada, June 1–4.
(collection, remote meetings, asynchronous conferencing, education) The Guelph symposium concentrated mostly on remote and asynchronous conferencing, and people's experiences in using it. Papers were presented in several sections. 1. Distance and adult education; 2. Socio-psychological issues; 3. Computer conferencing applications; 4. General educational issues; 5. Electronic conferencing and beyond; 6. Electronic message interchange; and 7. Research applications of computer conferencing.

UNIVERSITY OF GUELPH (1990). *The third Guelph symposium on computer mediated communication*. University of Guelph, Continuing Education Division, Guelph, Ontario, Canada, May 15–17.
(collection) The Guelph symposium contains several parts and sections. Part 1: Applications for individuals: a) distance and on-site education; b) library and information services. Part 2: Applications for organizations: a) computer supported cooperative work; b) in-house training; c) managerial applications. Part 3: Applications for communities: a) rural and remote; b) gerontology; c) third world development; d) international communities of interest.

VALACICH, J. S., DENNIS, A. R. & NUNAMAKER, Jr, J. F. (1991). Electronic meeting support: The GroupSystems concept. *Int J Man Machine Studies,* **34**(2), pp. 262–282, February. In the special edition on CSCW & Groupware. Republished in Greenberg, 1991c.
(decision support, face-to-face meetings, evaluation)   This paper highlights the theoretical assumptions behind the design of the University of Arizona's 'GroupSystem' face-to-face meeting room and its workings. Of particular importance is that GroupSystems has been well-studied; 15 experimental and field studies are summarized and contrasted here. The authors then provide recommendations for developers of electronic meeting rooms based upon the lessons learnt.

VERSHKOV, A. & ROUSSAKOV, A. (1989). Cooperatives in the USSR. In *Proceedings of the 1st European Conference on Computer-Supported Cooperative Work (EC-CSCW '89)*. Gatwick, UK, September 13–15, Computer Sciences House, Slough, UK.

VERTELNEY, H. (1990). An environment for collaboration. In B. LAUREL, Ed., *The art of human–computer interface design*, pp. 161–170. Reading, Massachusetts: Addison-Wesley.
(overview)   The purpose of collaboration technology is to facilitate and enhance the daily work and interactions of people and machines bound together under the umbrella of a common goal, project, or job. This chapter looks at how work on complex projects gets accomplished, emphasizing the key components of communication, cooperation, and coordination of dispersed people. A working environment is envisioned where database, communications and user-interface technologies are sewn together to support the real activities of people involved in projects.

VICTOR, F. & SOMMER, E. (1989). Supporting the design of office procedures in the DOMINO system. In *Proceedings of the 1st European Conference on Computer*

Supported Cooperative Work (EC-CSCW '89). Gatwick, UK, September 13–15, Computer Sciences House, Slough, UK.

VOGEL, D. R. & NUNAMAKER, J. F. (1990). Design and assessment of a group decision support system. In J. GALEGHER, R. E. KRAUT & C. EGIDO, Eds, *Intellectual Teamwork: Social Foundations of Cooperative Work*, pp. 511–528. Hillsdale, New Jersey: Lawrence Erlbaum Associates.

(decision support, face-to-face meetings)   The design and use of the University of Arizona's Group Decision Support System is described. Included are the behavioural realm in which the system is intended to operate and users' reports about their experiences with the system.

WATABE, K., SAKATA, S., MAENO, K., FUKUOKA, H. & OHMORI, T. (1990). Distributed multiparty desktop conferencing system: Mermaid. In *Proceedings of the Conference on Computer Supported Cooperative Work (CSCW '90)*, pp. 27–38. Los Angeles, California, October 7–10, ACM Press.

(remote meetings, shared workspace, video, evaluation)   Mermaid is an ISDN-based distributed multiparty desktop conferencing system. Participants can interchange information through video, voice and multimedia documents. The environment includes electronic writing pads, image scanners, video cameras, and microphone-installed loudspeakers. The system is evaluated informally for both performance and usability.

WATSON, R. T., DESANCTIS, G. & POOLE, M. S. (1988). Using a GDSS to facilitate group consensus: Some intended and unintended consequences. *MIS Quarterly*, **12**(3), pp. 463–478, September.

(decision support, evaluation)   The study examines the effects of a group decision support system in resolving conflicts of personal preference. The three experimental conditions were: a computer-based support system; a manual, paper and pencil, support system; no support whatsoever. In general, the technology appeared to offer some advantage over no support, but little advantage over the pencil and paper method.

WEEDMAN, J. (1991). Task and non-task functions of a computer conference used in professional education: a measure of flexibility. *Int J Man Machine Studies*, **34**(2), pp. 303–318, March. In the special edition on CSCW & Groupware. Republished in Greenberg, 1991c.

(asynchronous conferencing, evaluation)   What is computer-mediated communication used for? Some systems are based upon the assumption that communication is related to a specific task or action which can be captured and formalized (eg the Coordinator, Winograd, 1988). Weedman noticed that typical asynchronous computer communication also has a large non-task component used for such things as social exchange, expressing frustrations, and so on. She argues that since variety and vigour of communication is important to successful collaboration, the underlying technology should be flexible enough to support informal as well as formal talk.

WHITE, G. M. (1990). A formal method for specifying temporal properties of the multi-user interface. In S. GIBBS & A. A. VERRIGHN-STUART, Eds, *Proceedings of IFIP WG8.4 Conference on Multi-User Interfaces and Applications*, Crete. North Holland.

WHITESIDE, J. & WIXON, D. (1988). Contextualism as a world view for the reformation of meetings. In *Proceedings of the Conference on Computer-Supported Cooperative Work (CSCW '88)*, pp. 369–376. Portland, Oregon, September 26–28, ACM Press.

(conceptual)   Foundations for research and action in the area of group work are examined. Contextualism is discussed in depth.

WHITTAKER, S., BRENNAN, S. E. & CLARK, H. H. (1991). Coordinating activity: An analysis of interaction in computer-supported cooperative work. In *ACM SIGCHI Conference on Human Factors in Computing Systems*. New Orleans, April 28–May 2, ACM Press.

(evaluation, shared workspace) Authors examined mediated remote communication using a shared electronic whiteboard with and without the addition of a speech channel. First, permanent media such as the whiteboard enables users to construct shared data structures around which to organise their activity. Second, this permanence allows users to abandon some (but not all) of the turn-taking commonly used in spoken conversation and to organize their activities in a highly parallel manner. With addition of the speech channel, people still used the whiteboard for the content of the communication, while using speech for coordinating the process of communication.

WINOGRAD, T. (1988a). A language/action perspective on the design of cooperative work. *Human Computer Interaction*, **3**(1), pp. 3–30. Reprinted in Greif, 1988. An earlier version appeared in CSCW '86.
(protocols, semi-structured messages) This paper introduces a perspective based on language as action, and explores its consequences for practical system design. The language/action perspective is contrasted to a number of other currently prominent perspectives, and is illustrated with an extended example based on studies of nursing work in a hospital ward. The author shows how it leads to particular analyses of that work, which reveal potentials for creating new designs that can make the work (and the workers) more effective.

WINOGRAD, T. (1988b). Where the action is. *Byte*, December.
(semi-structured messages, protocols) This paper gives a simple description of speech acts and its basis behind the Coordinator. Sample screens from the Coordinator are shown along with its description.

WINOGRAD, T. & FLORES, F. (1986). *Understanding computers and cognition: A new foundation for design*. Ablex, Norwood, New Jersey.
(conceptual, protocols, semi-structured messages) This book looks at the philosophy and theory of artificial intelligence and human cognition. Amongst other things, it looks at computer systems from the language/action perspective (speech acts).

WITTEN, I. H., THIMBLEBY, H. W., COULOURIS, G. & GREENBERG, S. (1991). Liveware: A new approach to sharing data in social networks. *Int J Man Machine Studies*, **34**(3), pp. 337–348, March. In the special edition on CSCW & Groupware. Republished in Greenberg, 1991c.
(data sharing, implementation) A large part of a group process is information sharing. While networked computers usually allow people within an institution to share information across common data files, networks are rarely available for loosely-coupled social groups. This paper describes Liveware, a socially productive benign virus used to spread information across intermittently connected people and groups. Unlike conventional wired networks, Liveware is cheap, does not require a technical infrastructure, and is intrinsically intertwined with social convention of "casual" information sharing by mobile and flexible work groups.

WOITASS, M. (1990). Coordination of intelligent office agents—applied to meeting scheduling. In S. GIBBS & A. A. VERRIGHN-STUART, Eds, *Proceedings of IFIP WG8.4 Conference on Multi-User Interfaces and Applications*, Crete. North Holland.

WRIGHT, K. (1990). The road to the global village. *Scientific American*, pp. 83–94, March.
(overview, conceptual) This lay article speculates on the "global village" (Marshall MacLuhan's vision of an interconnected worldwide society) and how it may be brought about by the convergence of computing and communications technologies. Various human–computer perspectives are reviewed by interview bites from familiar sources such as PARC, MIT Media Lab, etc. Technologies such as Multimedia, groupware, and Virtual Environments are also raised.

WRYCZA, S. (1989). The impact of CASE tools on teamwork of information systems developers. In *Proceedings of the 1st European Conference on Computer-Supported Cooperative Work (EC-CSCW '89)*. Gatwick, UK, September 13–15, Computer Sciences House, Slough, UK.

WULFF, W., EVENSON, S. & RHEINFRANK, J. (1990). Animating interfaces. In *Proceedings of the Conference on Computer-Supported Cooperative Work (CSCW '90)*. Los Angeles, California, October 7–10, ACM Press.
(software design)   Requirements for prototyping tools in user interface and system design are discussed, and "Animating Interfaces" is introduced as one collaborative, iterative approach to the rapid conceptual prototyping and simulation of interfaces and associated functionalities. The Animating Interface process is described, and illustrated by example.

YAKEMOVIC, K. C. B. & CONKLIN, E. J. (1990). Report on a development project use of an issue-based information system. In *Proceedings of the Conference on Computer-Supported Cooperative Work (CSCW '90)*. Los Angeles, California, October 7–10, ACM Press.
(semi-structured messages, protocols, decision support, hypertext)   It has long been recognized that certain kinds of vital information—usually informal and unstructured, often having to do with why certain actions are taken—are usually lost in large projects. One explanation may be that this kind of information is too unstructured to be readily captured and retrieved. The paper reports a field study in which a simple structuring method called IBIS was used over a long time period to record and retrieve this kind of information, using very simple technology. Implications to hypertext and groupware are provided.

YODER, E., AKSCYN, R. & MCCRACKEN, D. (1989). Collaboration in KMS, a shared hypermedia system. In *Proceedings of the SIGCHI Human Factors in Computing Systems*, pp. 37–42. Austin, Texas, April 20–May 4, ACM Press.
(hypertext, data sharing)   This paper describes how the KMS hypermedia system was used for collaborative work. Six fundamental issues were addressed via the shared-database capabilities of KMS and particular aspects of its data model.

Author Index

All authors cited within the chapters of this book (except the annotated bibliography) are included in this index. Numbers indicate pages where each author is cited. The contributors to this collection of papers are shown in *italic*, with the first page number of their article in **bold** type.

Subject Index